September 10–13, 2013
Florence, Italy

**Association for
Computing Machinery**

Advancing Computing as a Science & Profession

DocEng'13

Proceedings of the 2013 ACM Symposium on
Document Engineering

Sponsored by:
ACM SIGWEB

Supported by:
Adobe, Hewlett Packard, Xerox, & Università Degli Studi Firenze

Association for Computing Machinery

Advancing Computing as a Science & Profession

The Association for Computing Machinery
2 Penn Plaza, Suite 701
New York, New York 10121-0701

Notice to Past Authors of ACM-Published Articles

ISBN: 978-1-4503-1789-4 (Digital)

ISBN: 978-1-4503-2611-7 (Print)

Additional copies may be ordered prepaid from:

ACM Order Department
PO Box 30777
New York, NY 10087-0777, USA

Phone: 1-800-342-6626 (USA and Canada)
+1-212-626-0500 (Global)
Fax: +1-212-944-1318
E-mail: acmhelp@acm.org
Hours of Operation: 8:30 am – 4:30 pm ET

Printed in the USA

Symposium and PC Chairs' Welcome

It is our great pleasure to welcome you to the *2013 ACM Symposium on Document Engineering* (*DocEng 2013*) which is being held September 10-13, 2013 in Florence, Italy. This symposium series remains the premier international forum for presentations and discussions on principles, tools and processes that improve our ability to create, manage and maintain documents. This year continues the focus on the digital humanities from last year's symposium and introduces a new focus: eBooks, their impact and supporting technologies. A highlight will be three keynote speeches in these areas by Floriana Esposito (Università degli Studi "Aldo Moro" Bari), Alastair Dunning (The European Library) and Steve Pettifer (University of Manchester).

We are also proud of three new events in this year's symposium. We have introduced a Doctoral Consortium to provide expert advice to students undertaking a PhD in the field of document engineering, "Birds of a Feather (BoF)" discussion groups as well as a DocEng Best Student Paper Award that complements the existing ACM SIGWEB DocEng Best Paper Award.

As in previous years, the first day of the conference is devoted to workshops. We received 6 workshop and tutorial proposals from which 3 exciting workshops were selected: Document Changes: modeling, detection, storing and visualization (DChanges); Collaborative Annotations in Shared Environments (DH-CASE); and Reimagining Digital Publishing for Technical Documents.

This year's symposium attracted a large number of submissions from all around the world: North and South America, Europe, Asia, Africa and Oceania. We received 50 full paper submissions of which 16 were accepted (32%) and a further 64 short paper, application note and poster submissions of which 31 were accepted (48%), with a further 6 accepted as posters. These covered a wide variety of topics: Digital Humanities, Layout and Presentation Generation, Version Control, Search and Sense Making, Architecture and Processes, Document Recognition and Analysis, Multimedia, and Metadata and Annotation.

We want to thank all of those who contributed papers, ensuring a high-quality technical program and an exciting and interesting conference. We are very grateful to the hard working program committee and the additional reviewers who prepared almost 350 thoughtful and thorough reviews and then participated in the final selection discussions.

We also wish to thank ACM SIGWEB, Adobe, HP, Xerox and the University of Florence for their support and the many people who have helped with organization including the Publicity Chair Tamir Hassan, the Local Arrangements Chair Enrico Francesconi, the Doctoral Consortium Chair Cerstin Mahlow, the BoF Chair Patrick Schmitz and the workshop organizers. Special thanks to Peter King, the Chair of the Steering Committee, for his wise counsel; Ethan Munson for his liaison with SIGWEB and to the other members of the Steering Committee and last year's chairs, Patrick Schmitz and Cyril Concolato, for their helpful advice. We are also grateful to Lisa Tolles for her flexibility with deadlines.

We hope that you find the symposium interesting and thought provoking and that it provides you with the opportunity to share ideas with other researchers and practitioners from around the world.

Simone Marinai
DocEng 2013 Symposium Chair
University of Florence

Kim Marriott
DocEng 2013 Program Chair
Monash University

Table of Contents

Session 4: Architecture & Processes

Session Chair: Ethan Munson *(University of Wisconsin, Milwaukee)*

Session 5: Document Recognition & Analysis I

Session Chair: Charles Nicholas *(University of Maryland, Baltimore County)*

Session 6: Document Layout & Presentation Generation I

Session Chair: Steven Bagley *(University of Nottingham)*

Session 7: Document Recognition & Analysis II

Session Chair: Steven Simske *(Hewlett Packard Laboratories)*

Session 8: Metadata & Annotation

Session Chair: Stefano Ferilli *(University of Bari)*

Session 9: Multimedia I

Session Chair: Dick Bulterman *(Centrum Wiskunde & Informatica)*

Session 10: Posters & Demonstrations

Session Chair: Peter King *(University of Manitoba)*

Session 11: Document Layout & Presentation Generation II

Session Chair: Niranjan Damera-Venkata *(Hewlett Packard Laboratories)*

Session 12: Multimedia II

Session Chair: Cécile Roisin *(Université Pierre Mendes-France and INRIA)*

Workshops

DocEng 2013 Symposium Organization

Symposium Chair: Simone Marinai *(University of Florence, Italy)*

Program Chair: Kim Marriott *(Monash University, Australia)*

Doctoral Consortium Chair: Cerstin Mahlow *(University of Konstanz, Germany)*

BoF Chair: Patrick Schmitz *(University of California, Berkeley, USA)*

Local Arrangements Chair: Enrico Francesconi *(ITTIG CNR, Italy)*

Publicity Chair: Tamir Hassan *(University of Konstanz, Germany)*

Steering Committee Chair: Peter King *(University of Manitoba, Canada)*

Steering Committee: David Brailsford *(University of Nottingham, UK)*
Dick Bulterman *(Centrum Wiskunde & Informatica, The Netherlands)*
Ethan Munson *(University of Wisconsin-Milwaukee, USA)*
Charles Nicholas *(University of Maryland, Baltimore County, USA)*
Maria da Graca C. Pimentel *(Universidade de Sao Paulo, Brazil)*
Cécile Roisin *(Université Pierre Mendes-France and INRIA, France)*
Steven Simske *(Hewlett Packard Laboratories, USA)*
Jean-Yves Vion-Dury *(Xerox Research Center Europe, France)*
Anthony Wiley *(HP Exstream, USA)*

Program Committee: Apostolos Antonacopoulos *(University of Salford, UK)*
Steven Bagley *(University of Nottingham, UK)*
Helen Balinsky *(Hewlett Packard Laboratories, UK)*
Uwe M. Borghoff *(Univ. der Bundeswehr München, Munich, Germany)*
David Brailsford *(University of Nottingham, UK)*
Dick Bulterman *(Centrum Wiskunde & Informatica, The Netherlands)*
Pablo Cesar *(Centrum Wiskunde & Informatica, The Netherlands)*
Boris Chidlovskii *(Xerox Research Center Europe, France)*
Paolo Ciccarese *(Harvard Univ. & Massachusetts General Hospital, USA)*
Michael Collard *(The University of Akron, USA)*
Cyril Concolato *(Telecom ParisTech, France)*
Niranjan Damera-Venkata *(Hewlett Packard Laboratories, USA)*
Stefano Ferilli *(University of Bari, Italy)*
Pierre Geneves *(CNRS, France)*
Gersende Georg *(French National Authority for Health (HAS), France)*
Luiz Fernando Gomes Soares *(PUC-Rio, Brazil)*
Michael Gormish *(Ricoh Innovations, USA)*
Matthew Hardy *(Adobe Systems, USA)*
Nathan Hurst *(Amazon, USA)*

ACM DocEng 2013 Sponsor & Supporters

Sponsor:

Supporters:

Symbolic Machine Learning Methods for Historical Document Processing

Floriana Esposito
Dipartimento di Informatica
Universita' degli Studi "Aldo Moro"
Campus, v. Orabona 4, Bari, Italy
+390805443264
floriana.esposito@uniba.it

ABSTRACT

Numerous valuable historic and cultural sources – a major part of our cultural heritage – are currently imperilled and scattered in various national archives. Arts and Humanities are sciences that are mainly based on the interpretation of cultural objects such as texts, paintings and works of arts, or historical/ethnological remains and monuments. Such objects are often unique, very valuable, fragile, irreplaceable and locally preserved in scientific collections at museums, in archives, or in urban and historic areas. Archives, museums and other cultural institutions do not simply conserve these objects. They also manage a large of documentation on them in the form of photo collections, expertise, records, scientific studies and analyses. Both the objects themselves as well as the supplementary documentation are often accessible only through physical contact with users. Duplicates such as text documents (e.g., critical editions), or image documents (facsimiles, photographs) on paper are extremely expensive in terms of manpower, know-how and printing costs, and often these expenses cannot be justified for a small scientific audience. Electronic formats for object documentation might alleviate this access problem. Numerous initiatives have been started and supported to highlight and investigate a variety of challenges that museums and other culture-historical institutions are facing in an increasingly digital, media saturated landscape.

However, full knowledge and usage of this material are severely impeded by access problems, due to the lack of appropriate content-based search and retrieval aids that help users to find what they really need even when electronically and digitized copies are available. Preserving contents does not consist in simply storing them, but in actively transforming them to adapt them technically and keep them intelligible. Moreover, many informal and non-institutional contacts between cultural archives constitute specific professional communities which today, however, still lack effective and efficient technological support for cooperative and collaborative knowledge working. The creation of digital libraries, enhanced by annotation collaboratory facilities, is the technological response to bundle documents, interpretation knowledge, work processes and an expert network in a very flexible working environment.

Object and document collections in the Arts and Humanities always represent work in progress. The inventory at cultural

DocEng'13, September 10–13, 2013, Florence, Italy.
ACM 978-1-4503-1789-4/13/09.
http://dx.doi.org/10.1145/2494266.2494291

institutions is growing steadily due to donations, acquisitions, and by virtue of their own daily scientific and conservation services. These additions must be incorporated into the existing collections, but often space difficulties, problems of scientific know-how and lack of personnel have to be dealt with. Professionals and experts classify, analyze, assess and expose or edit these objects and documents. Highly qualified external specialists are frequently difficult to locate, if they are not part of a scholarly network. Internal experts are often overburdened with routine work in times of small cultural budgets and can only invest time sporadically and intermittently in integrating new inventories. Many scientific members of cultural institutions have temporary contracts and leave after a few years, taking with them a great part of the accumulated know-how.

The intrinsic nature of the document processing procedures supporting the progressive work on historic material, as outlined in this introduction, poses several constraints that require solutions specifically tailored to the tasks mentioned above. Over the years, Intelligent Systems are becoming valuable working instruments for researchers involved in humanistic sciences. The new challenge is now to provide these people with tools that are able to facilitate the fruition and investigation of the cultural heritage, so that even non-experts or communities of researchers may use up-to-date tools for both their personal work and for collaborative purposes. Technologically, the World Wide Web can serve both as a standard communication platform for such communities and as a gateway for document-centered digital library applications. Yet, while the Web may solve the problem of the diffusion and access of this material in its digital form, new automated tools are needed to allow a more intelligent processing and a personalized utilization of this knowledge. According to the situation previously described, besides the effectiveness and the efficiency of such solutions, such automatic tools must be able to cope with situations in which the continuous growth of the available material and knowledge is a fundamental and unavoidable issue. Hence, there is the need for a system component that is able to build incrementally upon previously acquired knowledge through diverse reasoning mechanisms. Specifically, the availability of systems that can automatically identify and separate document classes and meaningful parts inside them would alleviate experts from the need to accomplish low-level tasks, thus allowing them to focus on more intellectual interpretation-intensive tasks. For such systems to be successful in a real operating environment, however, their behavior and results must be comprehensible to human experts, which can happen only when symbolic representations are used. The choice of these symbolic mechanisms, which resemble closely the human way of reasoning, also allows a more direct comprehension and control of the knowledge synthesized at every step of the process.

In the talk, different experiences and projects in the cultural heritage application domain are briefly presented and the symbolic Machine Learning approaches, developed by the LACAM Lab. of the Department of Computer Science of the University of Bari, are presented. Since the 90's Document Engineering has been one of the elective application domains for the research group working in the field of Conceptual Learning, Inductive Logic Programming and Statistical Relational Learning. The research projects ([1], [2], [3], [4]) financed by the UE and by the Italian Ministry of Research have allowed the development and the vast experimentation in the domain of Cultural Heritage preservation with different general purpose ML methods and tools. The proprietary systems WISDOM++ [5], ATRE [6], INTHELEX [7], DOMINUS [8] are characterized by the intensive exploitation of intelligent techniques in each step of the document processing, from the acquisition to the layout analysis, from classification to interpretation, from text categorization to semantic indexing for information retrieval purposes.

For example, in the project Collate (Collaboratory for Annotation, Indexing and Retrieval of Digitized Historical Archive Material), which aimed to provide a support for archives, researchers and endusers, worked with digitized historic/cultural material. A large corpus of multi-format documents concerning rare historic film censorship forms from the 20's and 30's, fig.1 (a), but also including newspaper articles, photos, stills, posters and film fragments, provided by three major European Film archives, had to be processed. The application of different symbolic learning methods in the diverse phases of the automatic document processing, from the image document acquisition to the layout correction and analysis, from document classification to understanding, allowed to keep contents accessible in their integrity and intelligible according to their meaning. The possibility of understanding the content of a part of a document, basing on the layout, is reported In fig. 1, where an example of a censorship card is shown, with the automatically acquired rule for the recognition of the logic block of the film title, expressed in terms of position and relationships with other logical layout blocks. The application of symbolic ML methods allows to organize and classify documents, to cope with the incrementality and the need for continuous updating and refining classification theories and concepts, in order to improve accuracy according to new available documents.

Techniques for text categorization and information extraction can be applied to selected blocks and provide information that can be added to the documents as metadata, in order to improve the effectiveness and efficiency of the retrieval procedure. In document image understanding, the possibility of associating relevant text to underlying informative content allows to search documents at a semantic level rather than just at a syntactic one, in the perspective of the *Semantic Web*.

Categories and Subject Descriptors
I.7.5 [**Document and Text Processing**]: Document Capture; I.2.6 [**Artificial Intelligence**]: Learning

Keywords
Concept learning methods; Inductive Logic Programming; Incremental Learning, Semantic Processing

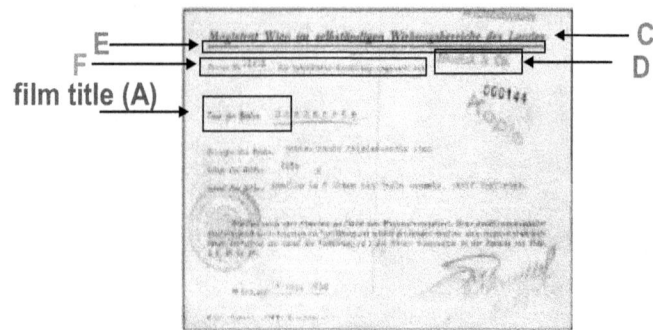

a)   An example of FAA censorship card

```
logic_type_film_title(A):-
page_first(B), part_of(B,A), part_of(B,D), type_of_text(A),
pos_upper(A), type_of_text(D), pos_upper(D), part_of(B,C),
height_very_small(C),type_of_text(C),pos_center(C),pos_upper(
C), width_very_large(E), height_smallest(E),
type_of_hor_line(E), pos_center(E),pos_upper(E),
height_very_very_small(F),pos_left(F),pos_upper(F),
on_top(E,D),on_top(E,F),alignment_left_col(F,A).
```

b)   The rule automatically induced for interpretation

Fig.1

REFERENCES
[1] ESPRIT project 5203 **INTREPID** (**IN**novative **T**echniques for **RE**cognition and **P**rocess**I**ng of **D**ocuments).
[2] ESPRIT project 29159 **CONCERTO** (**CONCE**ptual indexing, querying and **ReT**rieval of digital d**O**cuments).
[3] IST project **COLLATE** 20882 (**COLLA**boratory for Annotation, Indexing and Retrieval of Digitized Historical Archive Materials).
[4] FAR Miur **CHAT** - "Cultural **H**eritage fruition & e-learning applications of new **A**dvanced (multimodal) **T**echnologies". (2006-2009)
[5] Altamura O., Esposito F. Malerba D. (2001). Transforming Paper Documents into XML format with WISDOM++. *Int. Journal on Digital Libraries*, vol.4, 2-17, ISSN: 1432-5012
[6] Esposito F., Malerba D., Lisi, F.A. (2000). Machine Learning for Intelligent Processing of Printed Documents. *Journal of Intelligent Information Systems*, Vol. 14, 175-198, ISSN: 0925-9902
[7] Esposito F., Ferilli S., Fanizzi N. , Basile T.M.A., Di Mauro N. (2003). Incremental Multistrategy Learning for Document Processing. *Applied Artificial Intelligence*, Vol. 17, 859-883, ISSN: 0883-9514
[8] Esposito F., Ferilli S., Basile T.M.A., Di Mauro N.(2008) Machine Learning for digital Document Processing: from layout analysis to metadata extraction. In *Machine Learning in Document Processing and Recognition*, Marinai, S., Fujisawa, H. (eds.). Studies in Computational Intelligence, vol. 90, 105-138. Springer, Berlin.

2

Revisiting a Summer Vacation:
Digital Restoration and Typesetter Forensics

Steven R. Bagley
School of Computer Science
University of Nottingham
Nottingham NG8 1BB, UK

srb@cs.nott.ac.uk

David F. Brailsford
School of Computer Science
University of Nottingham
Nottingham NG8 1BB, UK

dfb@cs.nott.ac.uk

Brian W. Kernighan
Department of Computer Science
Princeton University
Princeton, NJ 08540, USA

bwk@cs.princeton.edu

ABSTRACT

In 1979 the Computing Science Research Center ('Center 127') at Bell Laboratories bought a Linotron 202 typesetter from the Mergenthaler company. This was a 'third generation' digital machine that used a CRT to image characters onto photographic paper.

The intent was to use existing Linotype fonts and also to develop new ones to exploit the 202's line-drawing capabilities. Use of the 202 was hindered by Mergenthaler's refusal to reveal the inner structure and encoding mechanisms of the font files. The particular 202 was further dogged by extreme hardware and software unreliability.

A memorandum describing the experience was written in early 1980 but was deemed to be too "sensitive" to release. The original *troff* input for the memorandum exists and now, more than 30 years later, the memorandum *can* be released. However, the only available record of its visual appearance was a poor-quality scanned photocopy of the original printed version.

This paper details our efforts in rebuilding a faithful retypeset replica of the original memorandum, given that the Linotron 202 disappeared long ago, and that this episode at Bell Labs occurred 5 years before the dawn of PostScript (and later PDF) as *de facto* standards for digital document preservation.

The paper concludes with some lessons for digital archiving policy drawn from this rebuilding exercise.

Categories and Subject Descriptors

D.2.3 [**Software Engineering**]: Coding Tools and Techniques; I.7.2 [Document and Text Processing]: Document Preparation–*Markup languages; Photocomposition / typesetting*

Keywords

Digital restoration, reverse engineering, archiving, *troff*, PostScript fonts, chess fonts, Linotron 202

1. INTRODUCTION

In the 1970s, the Computing Science Research group at Bell Labs, where C and Unix were created, was very active in document preparation research — tools for creating and printing technical documents such as scientific papers and books. That research led to a number of interesting and innovative software tools.

The central component was a program called *troff*, originally written by Joe Ossanna around 1972. *Troff* preprocessors were written for mathematical expressions (*eqn*, by Brian Kernighan and Lorinda Cherry), tables (*tbl*, by Michael Lesk), bibliographic citations (*refer*, again by Lesk), figures and diagrams (*pic*, by Kernighan) and graphs (*grap*, by Jon Bentley and Kernighan).

Troff flourished until the advent of TeX, and is still used for Unix manual pages (the man command uses *nroff*, the typewriter version of *troff*). The suite of *troff* tools is still in use, most often through the modern and polished implementations of *groff*, originally by James Clark; *geqn*, *gtbl*, *gpic* and *grap* are also available.

During the 1970s, the typesetting tools were complementary to some of the other research activities at Bell Labs. For example, in 1974 *eqn* was the first program to use the then-new compiler-compiler *yacc* to implement an unconventional language; *pic* and *grap* also used *yacc* and the *lex* lexical analyzer generator. They were also used to produce high-quality printed documentation like the Unix Programmer's Manual. Perhaps most important, they were used to typeset technical books, where they helped authors to ensure that complex material was free of errors introduced by copy-editors and printers. Some of those books are still in print, for instance "The C Programming Language", exactly as they were first created by these tools.

The original typesetting equipment used at Bell Labs was a slow and literally klunky typesetter, the Graphic Systems model C/A/T, or "CAT". This typesetter, which was intended for small newspapers, produced output on a roll of photographic paper that was advanced a line at a time after being exposed to character images. It had only four simultaneous fonts and 15 sizes. This slow and limited machine served the community well — indeed, its existence spurred the development of *eqn* and *tbl* — but by the late 1970s, it was nearing the end of its useful life. Fortunately better things were on the horizon, with typesetters that created character images digitally on a CRT, not by shining light through a stencil.

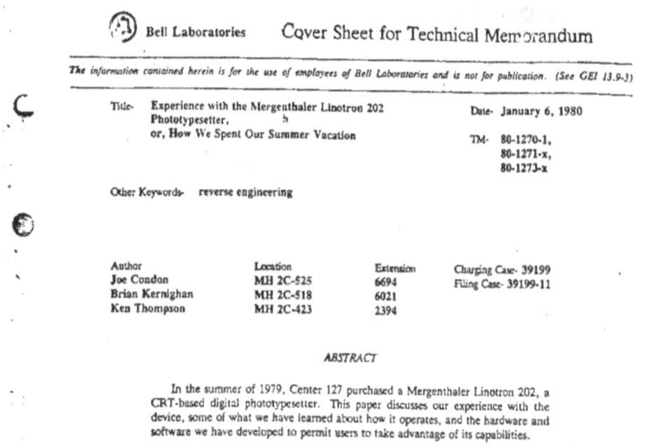

Bell Laboratories Cover Sheet for Technical Memorandum

The information contained herein is for the use of employees of Bell Laboratories and is not for publication. (See GEI 13.9-3)

Title- **Experience with the Mergenthaler Linotron 202 Phototypesetter, or, How We Spent Our Summer Vacation**

Date- **January 6, 1980**

TM- **80-1270-1, 80-1271-x, 80-1273-x**

Other Keywords- **reverse engineering**

Author	Location	Extension	
Joe Condon	MH 2C-525	6694	Charging Case- 39199
Brian Kernighan	MH 2C-518	6021	Filing Case- 39199-11
Ken Thompson	MH 2C-423	2394	

ABSTRACT

In the summer of 1979, Center 127 purchased a Mergenthaler Linotron 202, a CRT-based digital phototypesetter. This paper discusses our experience with the device, some of what we have learned about how it operates, and the hardware and software we have developed to permit users to take advantage of its capabilities.

Figure 1a: Original page-scan of cover sheet

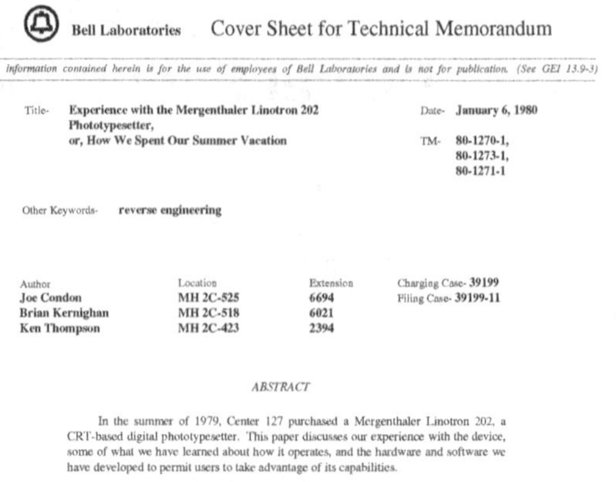

Bell Laboratories Cover Sheet for Technical Memorandum

The information contained herein is for the use of employees of Bell Laboratories and is not for publication. (See GEI 13.9-3)

Title- **Experience with the Mergenthaler Linotron 202 Phototypesetter, or, How We Spent Our Summer Vacation**

Date- **January 6, 1980**

TM- **80-1270-1, 80-1273-1, 80-1271-1**

Other Keywords- **reverse engineering**

Author	Location	Extension	
Joe Condon	MH 2C-525	6694	Charging Case- 39199
Brian Kernighan	MH 2C-518	6021	Filing Case- 39199-11
Ken Thompson	MH 2C-423	2394	

ABSTRACT

In the summer of 1979, Center 127 purchased a Mergenthaler Linotron 202, a CRT-based digital phototypesetter. This paper discusses our experience with the device, some of what we have learned about how it operates, and the hardware and software we have developed to permit users to take advantage of its capabilities.

Figure 1b: Re-typeset version of cover sheet

The group, primarily Brian Kernighan (BWK), spent a lot of time in 1978 exploring new typesetting equipment. The hope was that for a modest price it could get a faster machine that had fewer limits on fonts and sizes, and (a gleam in the eye) might have sufficiently high resolution that it could be used for drawing figures and even for half-tone images.

After much study, an apparently suitable typesetter was found: the newly announced Linotron 202, produced by Mergenthaler, one of the oldest companies in the business. Its likely cost would be about $50,000, where competing machines were at least twice as expensive, and its specifications implied that it would be much faster than the CAT, far more flexible, and have much higher resolution. Yielding to a modest amount of lobbying, management agreed to the purchase, and the new machine was ordered.

While awaiting delivery, a fair amount of spadework was done, largely by BWK. Ossanna's *troff* was inextricably tied to the idiosyncrasies of the CAT; the number of fonts, the specific character sizes, and many other properties were all wired into the syntax of *troff*, as was detailed knowledge of the intricate device commands to send to the CAT to make it operate.

Clearly this had to be fixed. Unfortunately, Joe Ossanna had died late in 1977, leaving a very powerful but complex and inscrutable program. Accordingly BWK spent a considerable amount of time figuring out (at least approximately) how *troff* worked, and converted it into what came to be known as *ditroff*, for "device independent" *troff*. Many internal limitations were removed, dependencies on the CAT were replaced by parameters, and the output language was converted into a generic format that could be interpreted by drivers for specific devices [1].

Thus when the Linotron 202 was delivered at the beginning of July, 1979, BWK was ready to write a driver for it and move forward. Unfortunately, the 202 turned out to be an operational nightmare. The hardware was flaky and temperamental, Mergenthaler's software was riddled with bugs, the documentation was incomplete and often flat wrong, and even when those problems were temporarily overcome, the machine couldn't be forced into doing what the group wanted it to do.

Eventually all of this was resolved, though only after heroic efforts by Ken Thompson (the creator of Unix) and Joe Condon (creator of the hardware for the Belle chess machine). The 202 went on to be highly successful for the Bell Labs group, and was used for many years until the advent of high-resolution laser printers and PostScript.

Late in 1979, BWK wrote a description of the work, performed largely by Thompson and Condon, entitled "Experience with the Mergenthaler Linotron 202 Phototypesetter, or, How We Spent Our Summer Vacation." This memo included a long description of all of the hardware and software troubles as reported to Mergenthaler, described superficially how Mergenthaler's proprietary, and deeply secret, character encoding scheme had been reverse-engineered, and explained the new software that had been written.

As might have been anticipated, Bell Labs management at the time was distinctly uneasy about releasing this information, and the memo was suppressed; it was never published externally, and had only limited circulation within Bell Labs.

In a parallel universe in Nottingham, David Brailsford (DFB) was also doing research on document preparation using a Linotron 202, some of which is described in the next section. Since BWK and DFB were well acquainted through their shared interests, various kinds of information flowed back and forth across the Atlantic, including at some point a private copy of the 'vacation memo'. And there matters rested until fairly recently, when DFB decided that it would be of technical interest to re-create the memo with modern technology, in as close to identical form as possible: original fonts, layout, etc., but produced ultimately as PDF. We were further encouraged by a professional typographer and mutual friend, Chuck Bigelow, who, from a history of typography standpoint, also wanted the 'vacation memo' to see the light of day.

This paper describes the re-creation process, and what has been learned along the way. It is suggested that the reader first study the restored original document before reading the following sections, which explain how it was produced. The rebuilt memo is now on the web at [2] and the original scanned version, created from a photocopy of 202 output, is at [3].

As an aside, multiple versions of the original vacation memo existed in early 1980, but because it was suppressed, no decision was made on which version to release. At this point we have settled on the version for which we have a hard-copy record of its actual appearance; it also has the official Bell Labs 'cover sheet' for technical memoranda, and it presents, inline, the original (and we hope entertaining) letter of complaint to Mergenthaler. Inevitably, BWK's *troff* source text corresponded closely, but not quite identically, to the version we have decided to replicate. There are half a dozen small differences that either correct layout problems and typos or which clarify the exposition.

Figure 1a shows the top half of the cover sheet (page 0) of the vacation memo in the form of a bitmap scan from the photocopied source document. Figure 1b shows the same page area but fully re-typeset using the *tmac.scover* macros, where we hope the improvement in quality is evident, even at the reduced size.

2. THE TRANSITION YEARS 1980–1985

Bell Laboratories' success with the Linotron 202, and the existence of the vacation memo, soon circulated widely in the UNIX community, not least to the parallel universe of the Computer Science Group (CSG) at the University of Nottingham. In the early 1980s CSG was part of a Department of Mathematics but was equipped with its own PDP 11/70 running the UNIX operating system. A mathematics colleague who was in charge of departmental examinations was appalled by the £18,000 annual cost of sending a large number of end-of-year mathematics examination papers for external typesetting. He asked the CSG if a new PDP11 computer, equipped with *troff* and *eqn* software, and driving a suitable external typesetter such as the Linotron 202, might be able to typeset the papers 'in house,' thereby reducing costs in the medium term.

To the amazement of all concerned, the University itself agreed to front-up the cost of a LSI 11/23 running UNIX, plus whatever typesetting machine Linotype deemed suitable, and after a period of commissioning in the Department of Mathematics, to move the entire system to the University's Examinations Unit. One of us (DFB) was appointed as project manager for the first stages of this effort. The University's longer-term aim was to progress from typesetting mere mathematics towards producing *all* of the University's examination papers in house.

To their great credit, when approached about this project in late 1982, Linotype UK were quick to admit to the problems that Bell Labs had encountered with the 202. As foreseen in the final paragraph of the vacation memo the Omnitech 2100, although slower than the 202, was seen to be 'the way forward,' being both cheaper than the 202 and having the virtue of using laser technology to image directly onto special paper, at a claimed 723 dpi.

The Nottingham team's trials and tribulations were certainly different from those encountered at Bell Labs, while being every bit as frustrating. Essentially the Omnitech was an early high-resolution laser printer, trying to compete with third-generation film-based typesetters by offering high resolution but without the need for photographic post-processing.

Indeed, by the early 1980s, laser printer technology operating in the region of 300 dpi was found to work very well,

but the push by Mergenthaler to get above 700 dpi required expensive specially-coated paper and very finely divided toner.

The details of the Nottingham team's adventures are chronicled in [4], where it will soon be seen that if the Bell Labs team had to be armed with screwdrivers to cope with paper jams on the (UK-designed) Linotron 202, then the Nottingham team needed galoshes to wade through seas of toner-ink, caused by leaks in the toner delivery system to the (US-designed) Omnitech 2100's drum. An alternative version of the Omnitech, using photographic paper or film, was somewhat more satisfactory, though still painfully slow. Eventually, in 1984, the Omnitech 2100 was withdrawn from the market and replaced by the much more reliable Linotron 101.

In a strange twist of fate Nottingham, in late 1983, replaced its trial system of an Omnitech 2100, driven from an LSI 11/23, with a new system consisting of a Linotron 202 (yes !), driven from a PDP 11/44. but still using UNIX and *troff*, Although based on older technology, the 202 positively romped through the work and was a model of sturdiness and reliability. Clearly the four years of extra development on the 202, after the Bell Labs purchase, had done wonders for its robustness.

In the years 1984–87 Nottingham used the 202 for in-house typesetting of all its examination papers. Fortunately this was enough time to recoup the hardware investment because, in 1985, the world of digital documents changed for ever with the advent of the Apple Laserwriter running the Adobe PostScript language. PostScript was designed as a graphics language with a high degree of device-, and resolution-, independence. It implemented the entire range of vector graphics constructs — lines, arcs, splines, etc. — and was able to apply these constructs to the shapes of character glyphs within fonts. Rendering speed was helped by having optimised subroutines for character glyphs within the so-called Type 1 font format, coupled with ingenious 'hinting' techniques for preventing pixel rounding problems at low resolution. Indeed, PostScript on the Apple Laserwriter showed that, even at 300 dpi, there was a market for quality typesetting. Soon afterwards the language migrated to the Linotron 100 and 300 series machines and spread rapidly thereafter. A 'display' version of PostScript was also developed for on-screen preview of PostScript documents and, by 1989, the victory of PostScript, in the print and publishing industries, was total.

All that was now needed, to complete the PostScript saga, was an 'interchange' form of it, optimised for fast rendering, device independence and document exchange. This appeared in 1992 as Portable Document Format (PDF) and it first came with an interpreter called Adobe Acrobat, available initially on Macintosh and PC. In the ensuing 20 years PDF became first a *de facto* standard, and later a full ISO standard, for the interchange of high-quality, print-ready documents of arbitrary complexity.

So, we are now able to make clear the aim of this project, which was simply to rebuild the vacation memo, not just as concatenated low-quality page-scans, but as a typeset-quality PDF file. In this way it could join the various existing PDF archives of Bell Labs memoranda.

Given that the Linotron 202 is long obsolete we needed to consider what combination of software and fonts might best rebuild the vacation memo with good enough quality for readers to get a clear feeling for the 202's capabilities.

3. TOOLS FOR THE REBUILD

In any restoration project there needs to be a degree of continuity between the tools, techniques and materials available at the time the original work was created and those now available at the time of restoration. For example, in a previous restoration project, involving UK Parish Registers [5], the aim was to recreate hard-copy volumes of Derbyshire marriage registers that had gone out of print in the early 20th century. Page scans of these original volumes were available from genealogy web sites, capable of giving reasonable character recognition when fed into OCR software. Recreating the simple tabular layout for the registers was not a problem. The real challenge was to find out whether the fonts used in the original printed registers were still available. The body-text font was readily identified as Caslon (with Old Style figures). The other two fonts used in various headings were accurately identified by *WhatTheFont* as Romana Bold, together with a font in the Gothic style called Fordor Incised. Both of these were initially created in the days of 'hot metal' typesetting but were now available from two different vendors as PostScript fonts. Indeed it is a testament to the availability of tens of thousands of fonts in the digital typesetting era that every bit as much effort seems to have been spent in 'rescuing' old typefaces as in creating new ones.

In the present project things were a little different, because *troff* source code for the memo still existed. But yet again fonts featured large in the restoration effort. The vacation memo needed eight different fonts whose identity was known from the outset. Five of these were readily available but, as we shall see, three fonts had to be recreated from scratch.

The few surviving hard-copies of the vacation memo are simply photocopies of a typeset original, with an appearance very similar to that shown in Figure 1a. On the other hand, because BWK had at least preserved a reasonable approximation to the *troff* source code of what we were trying to replicate, there was no need to resort to OCR for text acquisition. However, the very subject matter of the memo was the exact 'look and feel' achievable on a Linotron 202, an obsolete typesetting machine. Moreover this look and feel had to be replicated as closely as possible in PDF—a format which did not become available until 12 years after the vacation memo was written.

Despite trying hard for an accurate match to the metrics and appearance of the original memo, it was inevitable that small differences in character widths would accumulate. This in turn might cause *troff* to make different line-breaking decisions in the rebuilt version compared to the original. For this reason it was decided that different line breaks could be tolerated in the rebuild, but page breaks would be kept as near identical as possible. This would ensure that the rebuilt memo, like the original, would occupy 14 pages (including the cover sheet), with the main body of the paper ending on page 11. This being said, we took the opportunity of adjusting one or two page breaks to achieve better formatting. A particularly clear example is the 'widow' at the top of page 8 in the page-scan version of the original memo, which has now been taken back onto page 7 in the rebuilt version.

3.1. Software availability

The vacation memo makes clear that the imminent arrival of the Linotron 202 was the spur for BWK to develop *ditroff*. The 202's line drawing capability (nothing more than printing large numbers of dots very close together) also prompted the development of the *pic* language for creating line diagrams [7]. Thus the first step in recreating the vacation memo was to find a version of *ditroff* and its accompanying macros that was ancient enough to cope with 1979-vintage *troff* source code. Fortunately DFB has resolutely used, and maintained, a version of *ditroff* that is of mid-1980s vintage. It still has traditional two-letter names for *troff* fonts, plus the original hyphenation algorithm that pre-dates the introduction of TEX hyphenation in the 1990 version of *ditroff*.

But this still left the problem of locating a corresponding version of the standard *troff ms* macros and, in particular, the original Bell Labs version of the ancillary macros called *tmac.scover*, which control the appearance of cover sheets for Bell Labs internal memoranda.

As part of the release of UNIX System V in the mid-1980s an extra-cost package called Documenters' Workbench (DWB) became available, gathering together *ditroff* and a host of other post-processors and pre-processors.

In a wonderful demonstration of the web as a 'crowd-sourcing' repository, a download of Version 3.3 of DWB (dated 1992 and now free of charge) from the Bell Labs web site revealed that, in addition to DWB's own *mm* macros, there was also a carefully preserved version of the original *ms* macros, including the all-important Bell Labs internal version of *tmac.scover*.

An early triumph was the processing of the *troff* source text for the cover sheet, which after a few minor adjustments gave the output seen in Fig 1(b).

The processing pipeline for the remainder of the vacation memo, under Open SuSe Linux, soon settled down as:

```
pic 202paper.trf | psroff -ms -t | distill6 > 202paper.pdf
```

Here `psroff` is a shell script that invokes *ditroff* and then feeds its output into a PostScript back-end provided by Adobe TranScript 4.0. The PostScript output from this back-end is then converted into PDF by being piped into a Linux-compatible version of Adobe's Distiller 6.0 software. Note that the `-ms` flag, in this case, denotes access to a mid-1980s version of the macro set, together with all the subsidiary macros for cover sheets, etc.

Just as when the vacation memo was first created, the only *troff* preprocessor needed is *pic*. Its first challenge was to handle the code for a line diagram on page 7 of the vacation memo. This drawing shows the component vectors of the Helvetica letter 'e' in the Linotron 202 font representation; it is shown again here in Figure 2.

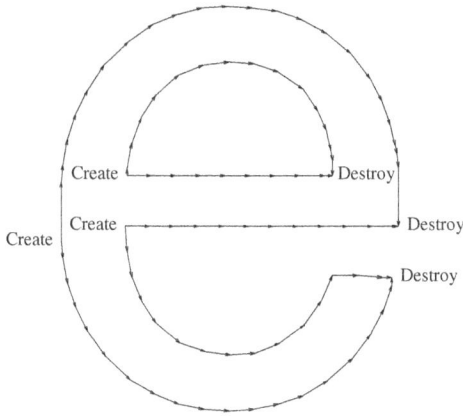

Figure 2: The Linotron 202 line vectors for Helvetica 'e'.

3.2. Font availability

In this section we look at the eight fonts needed for the reconstruction effort. Ideally, for total authenticity, the font recreation should have started from the original, line-segment, font outlines used by the 202 itself (see Figure 2) and using all the knowledge from the 1979 'vacation project' of exactly how these outlines were represented. With some effort the line-segment data could have been converted into Adobe Type 3 (unhinted) PostScript fonts. Two factors ruled out this approach: firstly much of the original Linotron 202 font data appears not to have been archived, either at Bell Labs or at Mergenthaler-Linotype, and secondly the emergence of PostScript Type 1 versions, for six of the eight fonts needed, from Linotype and Adobe, gave a readily available set of PostScript successor fonts.

Once the PostScript revolution got under way in 1985, it was just a matter of time before this language migrated from laser-printers onto higher resolution typesetters. The first such high-resolution typesetting machines to offer PostScript were the Linotron 100 and 300 series. A cross-licensing deal was signed for Adobe's PostScript and Linotype's fonts in that same era. It followed naturally therefore, that a large number of typefaces in the Linotype font catalogue were eventually re-implemented as PostScript Type 1 fonts, created and distributed by Adobe.

For this reason the Adobe Times typeface family was some sort of clear successor to the Linotype Times family used originally on the 202. Moreover the other fonts mentioned on page 8 of the vacation memo (in a table illustrating average number of bytes per character in the 202 encoding scheme) were also readily available for the rebuild project. For reference this table was:

Helvetica	91
Memphis Medium	104
Times Roman	113
Old English	168

Here, Times and Helvetica are standard fonts, supplied with just about any PostScript-based typesetter. Memphis was also readily available as an Adobe font while Old English, despite being supplied by Linotype for use on the 202, is actually a Monotype font, and hence was not

PostScript-converted by Adobe. Nevertheless, it proved to be readily available as a PostScript font from the same FontShop (in Cheltenham UK) that used to supply fonts for the entire Linotron range.

Of the three fonts that had to be reconstructed from scratch, two of them — Print Out and ChessKLT — were sufficiently problematic as to merit entire sections to themselves, later on in this paper. All that remains, for the moment, is to devote brief sub-sections to the questions of the Courier font and the Bell Labs logo and its variants.

3.2.1. The Courier typeface

The monospaced Courier typeface was commissioned by IBM and designed by Howard Kettler in 1955. IBM's decision not to copyright or trademark it has led, over the years, to numerous variants being available. The font aims to replicate the effect of a typewriter striking through a ribbon onto a sheet of paper and Adobe's PostScript Type 1 Courier is proportioned to set 10 characters per inch at a 12-point body size. It remains a mystery as to why Linotype did not make Courier available for its typesetting machines (though many other proportionally-spaced typewriter faces *were* available).

Despite the availability, on the 202, of a fixed-pitch font called Print Out, which was given the *troff* name of PO (see later section), the programmers at Bell Labs still felt the need for the Courier font. Page 8 of the vacation memo relates how artwork for Courier was taken from the second-generation CAT typesetter and was then scanned and converted for use on the 202 and given the 'traditional' *troff* constant-width font name of CW. A sample of this font is shown near the top of page 11 of the memo, where it will also be noticed that several non-ASCII symbols (e.g., arrows, open box and cent) were present. In deciding how to replicate this font for the present rebuild project, some other considerations needed to be addressed.

From the earliest days of PostScript typesetting, Adobe realised that the Courier family needed to be a component of the 'Adobe 13' standard fonts, available with all PostScript typesetters, since it had achieved a status of a *de facto* standard for tasks such as program printouts.

Unfortunately, it has been a considerable source of frustration, to many users over the years, that Adobe's Type 1 version of Courier, and variants such as Courier New, are now rather too 'light' in colour to harmonise readily with typeface families such as Times Roman.

For this reason it was decided to use an online, publicly available, Courier Dark from Hewlett-Packard to emulate the appearance of the CAT constant-width font on the 202. The download was initially available as a TrueType font for PC use, but after format conversion in FontForge it was exported as an Adobe encoded Type 1 font.

Figure 3 shows a bitmap scan of the CW font, extracted from page scans of the vacation memo, alongside the typeset reconstructed version based on Courier Dark.

3.2.2. The Bell Logo font

From the earliest years of the second-generation CAT typesetter, Bell Labs always made sure that the Bell

```
a b c d e f g h i j k l m n o p q r s t u v w x y z
A B C D E F G H I J K L M N O P Q R S T U V W X Y Z
0 1 2 3 4 5 6 7 8 9 &¨. , : ; ? ! ( ) - ' ` – $ ¢ % ⌐
/ ' [ ] * " # ~ @ + ¬ ¦ \ > < = ^ _ { } | ↓ → ← ↑ ↘ ⌐
```

Figure 3a: Bitmap scan of GSI-CAT CW font

```
a b c d e f g h i j k l m n o p q r s t u v w x y z
A B C D E F G H I J K L M N O P Q R S T U V W X Y Z
0 1 2 3 4 5 6 7 8 9 & . , : ; ? ! ( ) - ' ` – $ ¢ % ⌐
/ ' [ ] * " # ~ @ + ¬ ¦ \ > < = ^ _ { } | ↓ → ← ↑ ↘
```

Figure 3b: Re-typeset version using Courier Dark

System logo was present within its Special Font, which consisted of mathematical and other symbols. UNIX users outside of Bell Labs just had to accept that any callout of the Bell logo, via \(bs, would absolutely *not* deliver the Bell logo but, in all probability, something like ♥.

In order to recreate the Bell logo as a font character, the first requirement was high-quality artwork. Once again the web in general, and Google Images in particular, came up with the goods. A 27 Kbyte drawing was found of sufficiently high resolution (well in excess of the 1000 × 1000 units resolution of a Type 1 font glyph) that the Adobe Streamline program was able to fit it with a very accurate outline. Once the outline was imported into Adobe Illustrator it was easy to export it as an Encapsulated PostScript .eps file.

The Bell logo ⊕ is required (at various point sizes) for the top of the vacation memo cover sheet, the top right of page 1 of the memorandum and also as an in-line insert near the foot of page 1. Initial tests were performed with the *psfig* program [8] for effecting inserts of PostScript material into *ditroff* source code. Once this was working correctly Adobe Illustrator was used, once again, to create the 'sideways' version ⊗ which appears just over half way down page 9 of the vacation memo. The visual effect was achieved by selecting just the inner 'bell' element within the outer circle of the logo, and rotating it clockwise by 45 degrees. After further testing with *psfig* the two versions of the logo were imported into a special two-character font called BL, created under Fontographer.

4. REBUILDING THE Print Out (PO) FONT

For reasons we have been unable to ascertain, Linotype did not make Courier available as its fixed-pitch typeface family for the Linotron typesetters. Instead, they bundled in a fixed-pitch font called Print Out which had upright and bold versions. Print Out can be seen in action near the foot of page 9 of the vacation memo, where a sample of it is displayed. It is also appears as the chosen font for BWK's letter of complaint to Mergenthaler which stretches from page 3 to page 6 of the memo.

Extensive enquiries in England, Germany and the US failed to find a copy of it and the news, from what remains of the Linotype organisation [†], is that Print Out was never converted for PostScript use. It's not too difficult to discern the reason: Print Out is not exactly an elegant thoroughbred. This font would have to be completely re-drawn if a PostScript version could not be found,

---

[†] Since 2007 Linotype has become a subsidiary of Monotype. This may well reflect the harsh new realities of the digital fonts era, but it still feels akin to Ford being taken over by General Motors.

Even so, recreating this font, while not difficult, took several tens of hours of painstaking effort. Fortunately DFB had been given a Linotype Font Shop catalogue in 1983. This catalogue had a high-quality sample of Print Out, very clearly the product from a professional printing press and imaged onto good-quality glossy paper. This sample was certainly a little larger in point size than the examples available in the memo but how much larger?

We already know that standard PostScript Type 1 Courier is proportioned to set 10 characters per inch at a 12 point body size. This equates to 1/10 of an inch in character width or 7.2 points (assuming we adopt the 'Adobe point' which has 72 points per inch). Now, 7.2/12 = 0.6 which means that the width of Adobe Courier is 600 units on the standard 1000-unit em square used in Type 1 fonts.

However, many typewriter-derived typefaces are proportioned so as to mimic pica-sized (12 point) type. Here the basic proportions of the glyphs will be 1.2 times wider than the 600 em-units that define the 10 point designs. Given that 600 × 1.2 = 720, it follows that fixed-width designs for such typefaces will set only 10 × 600 / 720 = 8.33 characters per inch at 12 point. Finally, the above calculations imply that if the 26 upper-case alphabetic characters of a fixed-pitch font are typeset in sequence, with no spacing between them, then the total width will be 26 / 8.33 = 3.12 inches.

The first three lines of the Printout sample in the font catalogue were as shown in Figure 4a. Moreover, the width, in the catalogue, of the upper-case letters on the second line of Figure 4a was 3.1 inches: the sample was indeed indicative of a typeface with a native body sizing of 12 point and a set width of 720 units.

The font-catalogue sample for the PO font was scanned at 600 dpi and Photoshop was then used to separate out each glyph and export it as a .tif file. These glyphs were then read in to Adobe Streamline to fit curves around them. The resulting outlines were exported as .eps outlines.

At this stage it became urgent to identify the provenance of the Print Out font. Chuck Bigelow pointed out that it had close similarities to proportionally-spaced typefaces, such as Corona and Century Schoolbook. A small clue led to the final identification — the 'ear' at the upper right of Print Out Roman's lower-case g looked identical to that on the same character in Excelsior Roman. Excelsior is a precursor of Corona and both of these typefaces had been PostScript-converted by Adobe in the mid-1980s.

4.1. Creating the basic shapes for Print Out

The way ahead was now daunting, but very clear. Each of the fitted outlines for the scanned Print Out glyphs was imported into Fontographer, as a template background layer for a new Print Out font.

abcdefghijklmnopqrstuvwxyz
ABCDEFGHIJKLMNOPQRSTUVWXYZ
1234567890

Figure 4a: Sample of scanned PO font at 600 dpi

abcdefghijklmnopqrstuvwxyz
ABCDEFGHIJKLMNOPQRSTUVWXYZ
1234567890

Figure 4b: Re-typeset sample from the new PO font

Then one by one, the corresponding glyph outlines were copied over from Excelsior to act as a starting point for the foreground layer. The character widths of the alphabetic glyphs, in Excelsior, range from 333 for 'i' to 1000 for 'W'. But now all of these shapes have to be coerced into a fixed-pitch 720-unit width and re-moulded to match the scanned-in outline in the template layer. For some glyphs (such as W, M, w, m and n) major surgery was necessary to reduce or remove prominent serifs, followed by compression of the stem spacings. By contrast, narrow letters such as i and l needed serifs to be extended and the crowning dots of i and j needed lowering and enlarging. Varying degrees of stretching, shrinking and minor surgery were also necessary on the bowls, loops, tails, crossbars and counters for characters such as b, d, f, g, j, p, q, t, and y.

Since the Excelsior digits 0-9 were already designed at a fixed pitch of 556 units, relatively little stretching and adjustment was needed to adapt them for a 720-unit set width. Adjustments to the various bracket and punctuation glyphs were easy and relatively minor, usually amounting to little more than stretching of stems and minor adjustments to stem weights.

In all of these adjustments a close watch needs to be kept on x-heights of lower-case letters; the PostScript Type 1 version of Lucida Typewriter, from Bigelow and Holmes, was used as a guide. This font is also a fixed-pitch, pica-size, 12 pt design with an x-height set at 530 em-units. This x-height seemed to correspond well with the 12 pt x-heights for PO seen in Figure 4a. However, the non-linear nature of human vision means that this is only the start of the story; a host of small height adjustments has to be made to lower-case letters to make them 'look right.'

4.2. Sidebearings for Print Out glyphs

The final task in creating the PO font was to adjust the left and right sidebearings for each character. To illustrate, let us consider the letter o in the PO font. Within the set width of 720 em units the glyph itself occupies 594 units. This leaves 126 units for the sidebearings, i.e., the space before and after the glyph itself. Other things being equal the spacing of a fixed-pitch font is never going to look as elegant as a proportionally-spaced one. However, the worst of the visual effects can be mitigated a little by moving glyphs very slightly left or right within the fixed-width character cell.

So, as a first approximation to getting things right, the spare space for sidebearings, in each Print Out character, was allocated, left and right, in the same ratio as in Lucida Typewriter. Thereafter multiple further sidebearing adjustments have to be done, firstly to harmonise the way that single-stem and multi-stem characters appear in conjunction with the letter o. Having tried strings such as

nonono and uououo one then progresses to doing all the lower-case characters, against o, in turn. Once this has been completed one can move on to harmonising strings of the most frequently occuring digraphs in the English language such as thththth, hehehehe, anananan, inininin, and so on.

As can readily be imagined, the whole effort is a time-consuming compromise. A tweak of sidebearings that makes one digraph look pleasing will almost certainly make some other digraph look awkward.

Examples of original and rebuilt Print Out can be seen in Figure 4 and also, at greater length, in the original and rebuilt versions of the vacation memo.

5. APPENDIX DIAGRAMS

The Appendix to the vacation memo was written by Joe Condon. In it he presents diagrams showing the detailed nature of the parallel interface between the PDP11 and the 202. These interconnection and logic diagrams were created in UNIX *plot* format. A converter called *pltroff* had been written by BWK to map *plot* codings into *pic*, but initially we could find no trace of the C source code for it.

Thus we decided to recreate the *pic* for figures A1–A3 from scratch, since DFB already had an extensive library of *pic* shapes suitable for the logic gates in these figures. We also recreated the 'ff1' box in Figure A2 (missing from page A-2 of the page-scan original). The smaller body size of the Courier (CW) font made the numberings on the diagrams much more legible than they were on the original page scans, where PO had been used.

We later found source code for *pltroff* in FreakNet's Media Lab [9], but decided to retain the hand-optimised *pic* diagrams in the rebuilt Appendix.

6. RE-CREATING THE CHESS FONT

As more and more of the rebuilt memo attained the typeset quality we were seeking, the one object that increasingly cried out for attention was the diagram on page 9 of the memo, showing Ken Thompson's chess font in action.

Thompson himself (KLT) was contacted to find out if he could help. His reply [10] initially held out hope that he might be able to locate the original 202 chess font in his archives. Sadly this has not materialised, but he revealed that the artwork for his chess pieces came from *Chess Life*, where the the pieces were logo headings to the different sections in the magazine. The scanning and font construction was done, in a hurry, to illustrate a series of books by David Levy (an International Chess Master).

The helpful thing about KLT's original font is that, given the need to produce something quickly, the chosen outlines were simple and seemingly based on drawings that were one inch square with a grid resolution of 0.05 inch. This simplicity meant that it was easy to create mock-ups of the piece shapes using *pic* and these approximate shapes were then handed over to Steve Bagley (SRB) for further development. The hope was that a fully functioning PostScript font could be devised that was reasonably faithful to the 202 original.

In terms of actually reproducing the chess board illustration in the vacation memo, a fascinating insight into what went on in 1979 was given by KLT's *troff* typesetting code for that board position, which was as follows

```
.ft CH
zyayiydyiygyiycytez
zikiaqbaibz
zbibijqbbsdz
ziaiaiaiaz
zailiaiaiz
ziaslaijiaz
zjqjjiaqjaqjz
zxixoxixmxixaxixaz
```

Now, there was no reason for us, necessarily, to design the font so as to match this typesetting source code. But we thought an analysis of the above instructions would be instructive — and so it proved.

We note, at the very outset, that neither the black nor the white queen shape appears in Figure 5a — the chessboard position seen in the vacation memo. However, all other pieces do occur in Figure 5a and this enables the detective work to begin.

Each of the eight rows of characters in the typeset input starts and finishes with z, so it is likely that this letter corresponds to vertical segments of the edging that surrounds the board. Corresponding edging pieces for the top (y) and bottom (x) boundaries can be seen in lines 1 and 8, where these letters are interleaved with other letters representing the actual chess pieces on that row. Since there are no backspacing motions, x and y must behave as overstriking, i.e. zero-width, characters. Analysis of line 5 of the *troff* input against the corresponding, unoccupied, row of the board shows that a must be a white square and i a black (shaded) square. After a little more work we discover that the black pieces (pawn to king) occupy character slots b–g. By contrast, the white pieces occupy j–o.

This only leaves the problem that, by default, all of these black (or white) pieces will be typeset on a white background. To achieve a black rook on a shaded background (e.g., at the top right of the board at position h8 in chess notation) the required coding seems to be te, which shows that KLT has cunningly superposed a black rook, e, shape on top of what must be a shaded background with a rook shape cut out of it, and this has been assigned to the letter t of the CH font. A little more analysis then shows that these 'cutout shapes' for the various pieces must occupy positions q–v and, like the edging pieces already discussed, must be treated by *troff* as being of zero width. A confirmation of much of the above analysis came, yet again, from the Freaknet repository [9], which yielded the *ditroff* width metrics for the CH font. These metrics confirmed that all of the characters in the ASCII range

a–z were in use and all of the shapes assigned to these positions did indeed have constant width, with the zero-width characters being exactly those we had predicted.

6.1. Shapes of the king and queen pieces

At first sight the white and black kings (at squares b1 and e8, respectively, on the vacation memo chessboard — see Figure 5a) might seem to be completely different designs. In particular the white king seems to be adorned with an inverted black diamond at the very top. However, closer inspection shows that the 'black diamond' effect on the original diagram results from the scaling down of a white cross, accompanied by a generous helping of ink bleed at the various stages of photocopying.

Artwork for the missing queen shape in KLT's chess font — a three-pointed crown — was eventually obtained from the cover, and the interior, of one of the aforementioned books by David Levy [11]. Improved artwork for the other shapes was also obtained from that same source.

6.2. From *pic* shapes to PostScript fonts

The creation of a Type 3, unhinted, replica of the CH font proceeded as follows. The piece shapes created by DFB in *pic* were first exported via *ditroff* and Adobe Distiller to PDF, one to a page, and at a size of 8 inches wide. The programmatic nature of *pic* allowed us to create the shapes easily, but it did throw up some problems of its own. Firstly, *pic* creates outlines, not filled shapes. Secondly, *pic* creates each line, arc, or spline individually, in the order specified by the *pic* programmer. It makes no attempt to create a connected path but such a path is essential for 'fillable' shapes like the black pieces.

An Objective-C program was written that parses the PDF definitions for the pieces, and builds paths from the individual lines produced by *pic*. Each piece is parsed into an array of lines and a set of points is built up containing the start and end points for each line. The algorithm then picks a point from the set and finds all lines that either start or end at that point. Ideally, this enables pairs of lines to be joined together and replaced by a single line, which is then put back into the array. The algorithm continues until no more lines can be joined together. The result is a series of joined lines that all start and end at the same point, which represent the distinct segments of the original shape

For instance, the rook decomposes into two segments: the pedestal and the battlements, while the king has three components. These segments can then be exported as normal PostScript paths (with any curves flattened into straight lines to echo the way that the 202 approximated a curve) and then filled to form the black pieces in the font.

6.3. Black and white pieces

The approach described above gives paths that can be used to form the black pieces. Inspection of KLT's chess characters, see Figure 5a, shows that, almost certainly, he created the white pieces out of the black ones by drawing an exterior outline and then throwing away the black interior. Exactly the same procedure was followed in recreating the CH font: further software was written that took the path for the black pieces and produced a new outline, which was

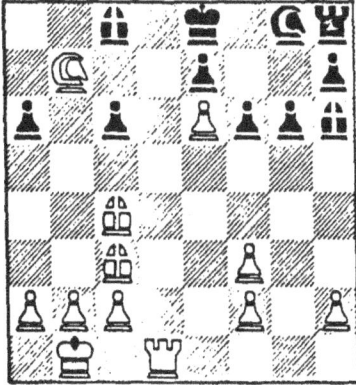

Figure 5a, Original chess diagram from the vacation memo

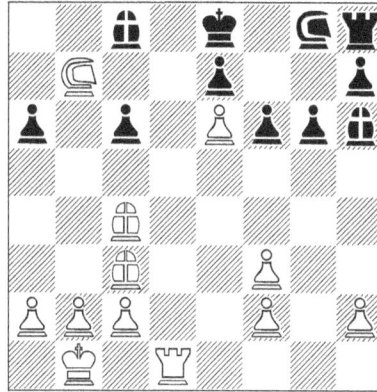

Figure 5b: Same chess position typeset in the CH font.

Figure 5c: Starting board, typeset in the CH font.

equivalent to a stroke around the outer edge of the path. This was produced by taking each segment of the path and calculating the position of a new line segment that was parallel, and to the left of, this piece by the desired width of the line. This results in a series of new, but disconnected, line segments. The lines were reconnected by shrinking or extending them until they intersected with the immediately preceding line segment. For this process to work correctly all the paths must be drawn in a clockwise direction and so the paths were pre-processed to impose this condition.

6.4. Creating the cutouts

The final process was to create the "shaded square with piece hole" glyphs described above. This again was performed programmatically by considering the intersections between the piece path and the path representing the hatching lines for the black square. It was realised that the calculations could be simplified if everything was transformed such that the hatch line was running horizontally along the x-axis from the origin. This approach highlighted a number of interesting optical side effects that needed to be mitigated. Firstly, cutting the lines based on the black-piece path data still produced visible collisions since the actual imaged line is wider than the mathematical one. This required the cutter software to use an enlarged path (similar to the mechanism used to create the outline) and also to consider the width of the hatch line.

In essence the process consists of calculating the intersection coordinates of each diagonal shading line with the various segments of the chess piece that is to be superimposed upon them. Once they are calculated the chopped line lengths are shrunk by about 5%, to give a fit that is tight, but not too tight. Problems arise with diagonal lines that very nearly intersect the chess shapes. These near-tangential lines are precisely the 'optical side effects' referred to in the previous paragraph.

6.5. Results

Figure 5b shows that a close approximation to KLT's typeset chessboard diagram can be rebuilt and with a visual quality far better than that available from the page-scanned

version in Figure 5a. As a test of the viability of the rebuilt font, Figure 5c shows a chess-game starting position, typeset from our new font; it also shows the newly discovered shapes for the black and white queens.

7. CONCLUSIONS

The work done on the Linotron 202 in 1979 was influential, though only indirectly. Document preparation was a major area of research for a significant number of computer scientists, and it provided an outlet for innovative work in tools, languages and even mathematics; think of the progression from *tbl* and *eqn* to TeX, and from simple character outlines to Metafont. And the importance of allowing authors to typeset their own work should not be underestimated; though that was once unusual, it is now the norm for most technical authors.

But the work described in the vacation memo was, in some ways, just a little too early. Deducing how the fonts were encoded is a graphic example of how security by obscurity is ultimately doomed; no matter how well a secret seems to be protected, a sufficiently motivated attacker is likely to find a weak spot. Even if Mergenthaler had been more willing to share its expertise, however, few small research operations could afford an expensive machine for experiments; it was only the promise of production use that made the 202 viable at Nottingham, for example.

Once hardware costs dropped by an order of magnitude with the advent of PostScript and the laser printer (Bell Labs got its first laser printer, from Imagen, around 1982), the field opened up to a great wave of creativity: people with new ideas could put them into practice without having to be font designers and without having to buy expensive machines. Of course not everyone was a skilled font designer; quite the contrary, and the new wave also unleashed a tide of poor-quality fonts and rampant font piracy. But, in the end, quality shows; once Adobe and Linotype began distributing high-quality PostScript fonts these standards became the norm. Of course these fonts helped us greatly with the work on the vacation memo; had it been some non-Mergenthaler typesetter, conversion of the fonts we needed into PostScript format, with the same character metrics, might have been less easy.

PostScript is a fusion of typography, computer graphics and programming language design. The typesetter design community, talented though it is, would not have come up with PostScript. Nor would the computer science community have come up with the rich repertoire of fonts that came from typography. Today, tools like Fontographer enable mere computer scientists to work on fonts like PO, but lasting designs will only come from professionals.

It has been almost as much fun to work on reconstruction as it was to work on the original projects at Bell Labs and Nottingham. But computer archaeology has its problems. To paraphrase George Santayana, "Those who do not archive the past are condemned to recreate it." During this reconstruction, we have been frequently surprised and often discouraged by how much information has disappeared in 30 years. Most obvious, the details of the Mergenthaler character representation, a very clever and compact technique that was reverse-engineered only with painstaking detective work, seems to have gone completely. The representation was never written down, except implicitly in the *ad hoc* programs that were written to process fonts, and those programs have long since disappeared. Perhaps someone at Mergenthaler-Linotype has the information, and clearly there are analogous and documented mechanisms used by PostScript, but it is unfortunate that this part of history seems to be gone forever.

The fonts that were laboriously constructed to take advantage of the 202 typesetter have in some cases disappeared as well, notably the chess font that SRB has had to reconstruct, but also the Print Out font that was for many purposes quite a reasonable alternative to Courier. The hardware itself, and the specialized software that ran on it, has also gone completely.

On the other hand we have had cause to bless our own pack-rat mentalities. For example, we found the 1983 Linotype font catalogue and we also had a preserved copy of the *troff* source of the vacation memo, with a version of *ditroff* capable of processing it. There are clearly a large number of other digital pack rats, to whom we are grateful, because we have been repeatedly and pleasantly surprised by how much apparently lost information can be found on the web by diligent search and occasional serendipity.

It seems clear that the world needs more archival sites that record useful information. And this is not too difficult in the modern era of cheap computer storage. The recorded information needs to include data, data formats, and programs for processing them. Almost any modern document is a complex amalgam of components that depend on other components, so gathering the complete set that is necessary to recreate it is exceptionally difficult. The authors of this paper have seen this in books, technical papers and programs, and of course in hardware of all sorts. Perhaps this paper will serve as a kind of reminder of the importance of saving *everything*, in one's best guess about formats that will last.

8. ACKNOWLEDGEMENTS

Profound thanks are due to Chuck Bigelow, who encouraged us to undertake this project and who gave endless tutorial advice to DFB during hours of work on the PO font. Thanks also to Ken Thompson for the information he supplied about his chess font, and to Andy Walker for pointing us to reference [11].

It will be readily apparent just how much a project of this sort is indebted to John Warnock, and his colleagues at Adobe Systems Inc., for developing PostScript and PDF.

Thanks to the invaluable cooperation of Lucie Cohn and Ed Hummel at Alcatel-Lucent (the parent of Bell Labs today), the rebuilt paper can now be seen at [2].

9. REFERENCES

[1] B. W. Kernighan, "A Typesetter Independent TROFF," Computing Science Technical Report No. 97, Bell Laboratories, Murray Hill, New Jersey 07974, March 1982.

[2] Joe Condon, Brian Kernighan, and Ken Thompson, "Experience with the Mergenthaler Linotron 202 Phototypesetter, or How We Spent Our Summer Vacation," Computing Science Technical memorandum, January 6, 1980. Available online (rebuilt version) at: http://www.cs.princeton.edu/~bwk/202

[3] Joe Condon, Brian Kernighan, and Ken Thompson, "Experience with the Mergenthaler Linotron 202 Phototypesetter, or How We Spent Our Summer Vacation," Computing Science Technical memorandum, January 6, 1980. Available online (original page scans) at: http://www.cs.princeton.edu/~bwk/202

[4] D F Brailsford, "In-house production of Examination Papers using *troff*, *eqn* and *tbl*," in *Proceedings PROTEXT I Workshop, Dublin*, pp. 21–28, Boole Press, October 1984. http://eprints.nottingham.ac.uk/363/1/protext.pdf

[5] David F. Brailsford, "Automated Re–typesetting, Indexing and Content Enhancement for Scanned Marriage Registers," in *Proceedings of the ACM Symposium on Document Engineering (DocEng09)*, pp. 29–38, ACM Press, 15–18 September 2009.

[6] Myfonts.com, *WhatTheFont:* font identification software. http://new.myfonts.com/WhatTheFont.

[7] B. W. Kernighan, "PIC — A Language for Typesetting Graphics," *Software — Practice and Experience*, vol. 12, no. 1, pp. 1–21, January, 1982.

[8] N. Batchelder and Trevor Darrell, *Psfig — A Ditroff Preprocessor for PostScript files*, Computer and Information Science Dept., University of Pennsylvania, 1988. Internal Report.

[9] Martin W. Guy, Various 202 font widths and other *ditroff* programs and resources. http://medialab.freaknet.org/martin/tape/stuff/ditroff/

[10] Ken Thompson, Personal Communication, 8th December 2012.

[11] David Levy, Kevin O'Connell, and David Watt, *The Sicilian Defence,* Imprint Editions, 1981. http://www.amazon.co.uk/dp/0907352006

Interacting with Digital Cultural Heritage Collections via Annotations: The CULTURA Approach

Maristella Agosti
Dept. of Information Engineering
University of Padua
Via Gradenigo, 6/a
Padua, Italy
agosti@dei.unipd.it

Owen Conlan
Knowledge and Data
Engineering Group
Trinity College
Dublin, Ireland
Owen.Conlan@scss.tcd.ie

Nicola Ferro
Dept. of Information Engineering
University of Padua
Via Gradenigo, 6/a
Padua, Italy
ferro@dei.unipd.it

Cormac Hampson
Knowledge and Data Engineering Group
Trinity College
Dublin, Ireland
hampsonc@cs.tcd.ie

Gary Munnelly
Knowledge and Data Engineering Group
Trinity College
Dublin, Ireland
munnellg@tcd.ie

ABSTRACT

This paper introduces the main characteristics of the digital cultural collections that constitute the use cases presently in use in the CULTURA environment. A section on related work follows giving an account on efforts on the management of digital annotations that are pertinent and that have been considered. Afterwards the innovative annotation features of the CULTURA portal for digital humanities are described; those features are aimed at improving the interaction of non-specialist users and general public with digital cultural heritage content. The annotation functions consist of two modules: the FAST annotation service as back-end and the CAT Web front-end integrated in the CULTURA portal. The annotation features have been, and are being, tested with different types of users and useful feedback is being collated, with the overall aim of generalising the approach to diverse document collections and not only the area of cultural heritage.

Categories and Subject Descriptors

H.3.7 [**Information Storage and Retrieval**]: Digital Libraries - *collection, dissemination, systems issues, user issues*. H.3.5 [**Information Storage and Retrieval**]: Online Information Services - *data sharing, Web-based services*.

Keywords

Cultural heritage collections, digital cultural heritage collections, digital libraries and archives, digital library system, annotation, hypertext, digital humanities, adaptive environment.

1. INTRODUCTION

The CULTURA project[1] aims to create an innovative information and communications technology (ICT) environment in which users with a range of different backgrounds and expertise can collaboratively explore, interrogate and interpret complex and diverse digital cultural heritage collections. At the conclusion of the project, the resulting environment will be a system which has pushed forward the frontiers of technology in the creation of community and content aware interfaces to digital humanities collections.

The CULTURA environment is service oriented and is composed of a set of services which are integrated to create a rich and engaging experience that supports users of different categories, which range from academic and professional users to the general public. The services are conceived and developed to be applicable to a wide variety of cultural collections. The potential generality of the environment is demonstrated by the fact that CULTURA is supporting different use cases that are represented by the IPSA[2] and 1641[3] collections, which differ in morphology, language, modality and metadata. This means that the environment and the supported services need to consider the peculiarities of different documents and different ways of making use of them by diverse categories of users. One of the supported services which must be designed and made available, taking into specific account the peculiarities of the documents of different collections, is the annotation service.

The paper is structured as follows: Section 2 presents the two use cases that at present are managed by the environment, and Section 3 gives a critical account of the most relevant work and approaches to the design and management of digital annotations. Section 4 illustrates the adopted annotation model together with the main characteristics of the search model. Section 5 introduces the annotation interaction model that has been envisaged and implemented in the environment, and a specific account on the anchoring of annotations is reported. Section 6 details the

---

[1] http://www.cultura-strep.eu/
[2] http://ipsa.dei.unipd.it/en_GB/home
[3] http://1641.tcd.ie/about.php

architecture that manages the interaction with annotations, and section 7 reports on the characteristics of the CULTURA environment and on the efforts that have been put in place for evaluating its annotation features. Section 8 presents some initial results of a user trial that was performed with FAST-CAT. Finally, Section 9 concludes the paper and presents some insights on future developments.

2. USE CASES

The CULTURA environment is supporting different use cases that are represented by the IPSA and 1641 collections, which differ in many characteristics that are presented briefly in this section.

IPSA (*Imaginum Patavinae Scientiae Archivum* - Archive of images to support the study of scientific research at Padua University) is a digital archive of illuminated manuscripts that includes both astrological codices and herbals produced mainly in the Veneto region, in Northern Italy, during the XIV and XV centuries. The digital archive has been conceived starting from the corpus of the historical and very innovative illustrations produced in the centuries under the influence of the Paduan School. The online archive was created specifically for professional researchers in History of Illumination to allow them to compare the illuminated images held in the collection and verify the development of a new realistic way of painting closely associated with the new scientific studies that were flourishing at the University of Padua in the XIV century, particularly thanks to the teaching of Pietro d'Abano. Disclosing new relationships between images is one of the main purposes of research in art history, because it brings further knowledge on a painter or an illuminator, on a work of art, or on a whole specific artistic period. According to this particular user requirement, in IPSA professional researchers are provided with tools that allow them to link and annotate images, so they are able to keep track of their considerations on the illuminations and their relations [5].

Due to involvement in the CULTURA project, it was decided to open the archive to other categories of users, such as non-domain professional researchers, student communities and the general public. Between May and October 2012 relevant data from IPSA was selected to constitute the collection to be imported in the CULTURA environment for use as a case study to test the new environment and its functions.

The 1641 Depositions are a collection of noisy text documents, mainly of a legal nature, dating from the 17th Century. They primarily contain witness testimonies from Protestants, but also some Catholics, from all social backgrounds. The collection, which has been digitized and transcribed, contains over 8,500 depositions or 20,000 pages, in which men and women of all classes and from all over Ireland told of their experiences following the outbreak of rebellion by the Catholic Irish in October 1641. This body of material provides a unique source of information for the causes and events surrounding the 1641 rebellion and for the social, economic, cultural, religious, and political history of seventeenth-century Ireland, England and Scotland. This is typical of the category of digital resource which will benefit most from CULTURA as it is inconsistent in spelling, punctuation, nomenclature and word forms, and reflects a cultural outlook quite different to the modern one.

From a technical perspective, the 1641 Depositions represent a textually rich digital humanities collection. This is in contrast to the IPSA collection, which is highly visual in nature and presents different challenges for digital humanists. The Depositions have

active communities of interest because of their wider social and historical implications that transcend geographical and chronological boundaries and continue to shape opinions and values to this day. The depositions display important similarities to much of the user-generated content found on the World Wide Web today. They are inconsistent in almost every aspect, including spelling, punctuation, case and language. The entire collection of 1641 Depositions have now been processed and integrated into the CULTURA environment. This processing involved the normalisation of text, the extraction of entities (people, places, dates etc.) and their relationships, as well as the use of social network analysis. Once processed and integrated into CULTURA, a range of services to help the exploration and analysis of the 1641 Depositions (and collaboration around the collection) are made available to users.

3. RELATED WORK

Almost everybody is familiar with annotations and has his or her own intuitive idea about what they are. These are drawn from personal experience and the habit of dealing with types of annotation in everyday life, e.g. jottings for the shopping, taking notes during a lecture or adding a commentary to a text. This intuitiveness makes annotations especially appealing for both researchers and users: the former propose annotations as an easy understandable way of performing user tasks, while the latter feel annotations to be a familiar tool for carrying out their own tasks.

Many user studies have been conducted to understand annotation practices and to discover common annotation patterns. Marshall [26] has categorised annotations along several dimensions that reflect the form annotations may take on. Others have focussed on the design and development of document models and systems which support annotations in specific classes of management systems, such as digital libraries, the Web, laboratory systems and working groups, databases, and adaptive environments. This work has led to different viewpoints about what an annotation is; as reported in [7]. We can consider annotations to be metadata, content, a form of context, as hypertext, or as dialog acts. In the context of the CULTURA environment three of those viewpoints are more relevant: metadata, content, and hypertext. Taking this into account we briefly and critically examine what these three points mean, and we make reference to previous work.

Annotations are metadata because they can be considered as additional information which concerns existing content, i.e. they are metadata, as they clarify in some way the properties and the semantics of the annotated content. An example of the use of annotations as metadata is MPEG-7 [27, 28], which is an ISO/IEC standard developed by the MPEG (Moving Picture Experts Group) committee. MPEG-7 serves for annotating and describing multimedia content data, and supports some degree of interpretation of the information meaning, which can be passed onto, or accessed by, a device or a computer code. MPEG-7 is not aimed at any one application in particular; rather, the elements that MPEG-7 standardizes support as broad a range of applications as possible.

Another example, in the context of the database management area, sees annotations as "information about data such as provenance, comments, or other types of metadata" [12], which is a sort of data that is added to an existing database. It could be additional data that for whatever reason cannot be stored in the original database, or it could be some form of metadata such as comments, probabilities, timestamps that are not normally regarded part of the basic database design [24].

It has recently been observed that, in order to determine how annotations should be propagated through database queries, it is necessary to have some structure on them. Although various forms of annotation have been considered in some detail, each form has been considered in isolation; Buneman and Kostylev have proposed a hierarchical model of annotation in which there is no absolute distinction between annotation and data [14], in this case annotations can be considered both as metadata and content as in [29] where annotations are additional content which concern existing content, and they increase existing content by providing an additional layer of content that elucidates and explains the existing one. This viewpoint about annotations entails an intrinsic dualism between annotation as content enrichment and annotation as stand-alone document [2]: 1) annotations as content enrichment are considered as mere additional content regarding an existing document and as a result they are not autonomous entities but in fact they rely on previously existing information resources to justify their existence; 2) annotations as stand-alone documents are considered as real documents and are autonomous entities that maintain some sort of connection with an existing document.

Annotations can allow the creation of new relationships between existing content, by means of links that connect annotations together with existing content. Using this viewpoint we can consider that existing content and annotations constitute a hypertext [4, 6], according to the definition of hypertext provided in [1]. This hypertext can be exploited to provide alternative navigation and browsing capabilities, but also to offer advanced search functionalities. Furthermore, [26] considers annotations as a natural way of creating and increasing hypertexts that connect information resources in a digital library management system by actively engaging users. The hypertext which exists between information resources and annotations enables different annotation configurations that are threads of annotations, i.e., an annotation made in response to another annotation, or sets of annotations, i.e. a bundle of annotations on the same information resource [2, 3].

As has been pointed out, annotations have been adopted in a variety of different contexts, such as content enrichment, data curation, collaborative and learning applications, and social networks, as well as in various information management systems, such as the Web (semantic and not), digital libraries, and databases. The role of annotations in digital humanities is well known and documented [3, 7, 9-11, 18]. The authors of [38] propose a general framework for annotating large archives of historical image manuscripts. The work is similar in spirit to the work that has been done for the IPSA application on the automatic discovery of relationships among images in illuminated manuscripts [8]; however in [38] the authors are focusing on the lower level primitives to support such work using different feature spaces such as shape, colour and texture, and their relevant contribution is in introducing a novel technique for calculating weighting parameters, without having a labelled training data collection.

Subsequently, many different tools which allow for the annotation of digital humanities content have been developed. Unfortunately, tools designed specifically for an individual portal are typically only compatible with that system. More general solutions, which can be easily distributed across various sites, have been developed, but these systems often have limited functionality e.g. only enabling the annotation of a single content type or not having sharing features [31, 34].

Many different web-centric proposals have been envisaged, including the project developed by the World Wide Web Consortium (W3C) activity on Annotea[4] [23]. Starting from the work done on Annotea, other relevant efforts have been developed, in particular the Open Annotation Collaboration[5], that also focussed on humanities [34], and the Annotation Ontology[6]. Those efforts can be considered predecessors of the Open Annotation Community Group[7], which is the active W3C group that has published the Open Annotation Core Data Model[8]. This model specifies an interoperable framework for creating associations between related resources and annotations, using a methodology that conforms to the Architecture of the World Wide Web. This model has the potential to become a standard and to be widely adopted.

The approach that has been chosen in CULTURA is very much that of a service-centric rather than a web-centric environment, but the defined concepts ensure that all of the modelling and architectural requirements are covered similarly to the relevant web-centric efforts that have been mentioned. Before designing the annotation tools for the CULTURA project, the Text-Image Linking Environment (TILE) [35] was assessed. However TILE, was not adopted, because it is a web-based tool for creating and editing image-based electronic editions and digital archives of humanities texts, and the creation of electronic editions is not required in the context of CULTURA.

FAST-CAT (Flexible Annotation Semantic Tool - Content Annotation Tool) is a generic annotation system that is being developed as part of the CULTURA project [21-22] and that directly addresses the challenge of providing a convenient and powerful means of annotating digital content. The remainder of this paper reports on the characteristics of FAST, the backend service providing powerful annotation functionalities, and CAT, the frontend Web annotation tool, and discusses how its features are tackling important challenges within the Digital Humanities field. A key aspect of CULTURA is the development of an online environment that empowers users at various levels of expertise to investigate, comprehend and contribute to digital cultural collections. FAST-CAT is a key component of this environment and is currently being trialled with the help of different user groups.

4. FAST ANNOTATION MODEL
The FAST annotation service adopts and implements the formal model for annotations proposed by [9], which captures both syntactic and semantic aspects of annotations. The adopted model has been also embedded in the reference model for digital libraries developed by DELOS, the European network of excellence on digital libraries [15].

---

[4] http://www.w3.org/2001/Annotea/
[5] http://www.openannotation.org/
[6] http://www.jbiomedsem.com/content/2/S2/S4
[7] http://www.w3.org/community/openannotation/
[8] http://www.openannotation.org/spec/core/

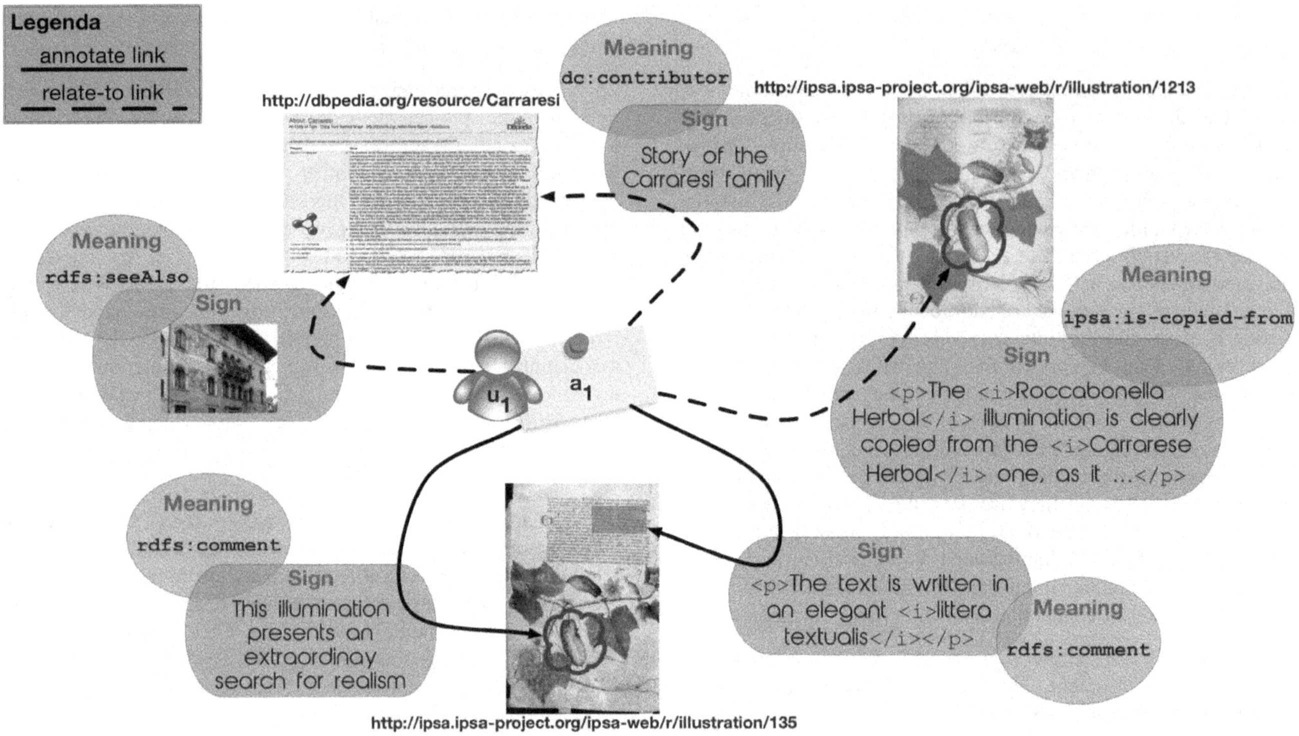

Meaning
dc:contributor

http://dbpedia.org/resource/Carraresi

http://ipsa.ipsa-project.org/ipsa-web/r/illustration/1213

Sign
Story of the Carraresi family

Meaning
rdfs:seeAlso

Sign

Meaning
ipsa:is-copied-from

u₁   a₁

Sign
`<p>`The `<i>`Roccabonella Herbal`</i>` illumination is clearly copied from the `<i>`Carrarese Herbal`</i>` one, as it ...`</p>`

Meaning
rdfs:comment

Sign
This illumination presents an extraordinay search for realism

Sign
`<p>`The text is written in an elegant `<i>`littera textualis`</i>``</p>`

Meaning
rdfs:comment

http://ipsa.ipsa-project.org/ipsa-web/r/illustration/135

Figure 1. Example of annotation.

According to this model, an annotation is a compound multimedia object which is constituted by different signs of annotation. Each sign materializes part of the annotation itself; for example, we can have textual signs, which contain the textual content of the annotation, image signs, if the annotation is made up of images, and so on. In turn, each sign is characterized by one or more meanings of annotation, which specify the semantics of the sign; for example, we can have a sign whose meaning corresponds to the title field in the Dublin Core (DC) metadata schema[9], in the case of a metadata annotation, or we can have a sign carrying a question of the author's about a document whose meaning may be "question" or similar.

An annotation has a scope which defines its visibility (public, shared, or private), and can be shared with different groups of users. Public annotations can be read by everyone and modified only by their owner; shared annotations can be modified by their owner and accessed by the specified list of groups with the given access permissions, e.g. read only or read/write; private annotations can be read and modified only by their owner.

Figure 1 shows an example of annotation which summarizes the discussion so far. The annotation, with identifier a1, is authored by the user ferro. It annotates an illustration from the *Carrarese Herbal*, f. 162v, whose identifier is http://ipsa.ipsa-project.org/ipsa-web/r/illustration/135 and which belongs to the IPSA digital archive. The annotation relates to another illustration from the *Roccabonella Herbal*, f. 42r, whose identifier is http://ipsa.ipsa-project.org/ipsa-web/r/illustration/1213 in the IPSA digital archive; in addition, it relates also to the DBpedia page of the *Carraresi*

⁹ http://dublincore.org/

family, http://dbpedia.org/resource/Carraresi,. which endorsed the production of the *Carrarese Herbal*.

In particular, a1 annotates two distinct parts of the *Carrarese Herbal*. It annotates a region of the illustration representing a cucumber by using a textual sign whose content is "This illumination presents an extraordinary search for realism" and whose meaning is to be a comment in the RDFS namespace, i.e. a comment according to the RDF Schema W3C recommendation [13]. It also annotates a region of the manuscript with a textual sign whose content is "The text is written in an elegant *littera textualis*" and whose meaning is to be a comment in the RDFS namespace. Note how the content of the sign is plain text in the first case and HTML in the second case to allow for richer formatting. In general, the content of a sign is specified by its MIME media type and this allows for great flexibility and for embedding different formats, such as XML, RDF, and so on.

a1 relates the *Carrarese Herbal* to the *Roccabonella Herbal*, in particular to a region of an illustration representing a cucumber as well, with a textual sign whose content is "The *Roccabonella Herbal* illumination is clearly copied from the *Carrarese Herbal* one, as it shows the same disposition of the elements of the plant in the page, the same search for realism and the same attention to the light effects on the surface of the leaves, the fruits and the flowers." and whose meaning is to be copied from another illustration in the IPSA namespace. This annotation thus represents the outcomes of the actual work of an historian of art, who conducted his/her own research on these two herbals, to determine that one was copied from the other.

Moreover, a1 relates the *Carrarese Herbal* to the DPpedia page of the *Carraresi family*, which endorsed the herbal, with two signs: a textual sign whose content is "Story of the Carraresi family" and whose meaning is contributor in the Dublin

Core metadata schema; and, an image sign with a picture of a building of the *Carraresi family*, whose meaning is "see also" in the RDFS namespace.

The flexibility inherent in the annotation model allows us to create a connective structure, which is superimposed to the underlying documents managed by digital libraries. This can span and cross the boundaries of different digital libraries and the Web, allowing the users to create new paths and connections among resources at a global scale.

4.1 Search Model

The presence of both structured and unstructured content within the managed resources calls for different types of search functionalities, since structured content can be dealt with exact match searches while unstructured content can be dealt with best match searches. These two different types searches may need to be merged together in a query if, for example, the user wants to retrieve annotations by a given author about a given topic; this could be expressed by a boolean AND query which specifies both the author (structured part) and the content (unstructured part) of the annotations to be searched. Nevertheless, boolean searches are best suited for dealing with exact match searches and they need to be somewhat extended to also deal with best match searches. Therefore, we need to envision a search strategy able to express complex conditions that involve both exact and best match searches. The "P-norm" extended boolean model proposed by [33] is capable of dealing with and mixing both exact and best match queries, since it is an intermediate between the traditional boolean way of processing queries and the vector space processing model. Indeed, on the one hand, the P-norm model preserves the query structure inherent in the traditional boolean model by distinguishing among different boolean operators (and, or, not); on the other hand, it allows us to retrieve items that would not be retrieved by the traditional boolean model due to its strictness, and to rank them in decreasing order of query-document similarity. Moreover, the P-norm model is able to express queries that range from pure boolean queries to pure vector-space queries, thus offering great flexibility to the user.

The hypertext that connects documents to annotations calls for a search strategy that takes it into consideration and allows us to modify the score of annotations and/or documents according to the paths in the hypertext. For example, we could consider that an annotation, retrieved in response to a user query, is more relevant if it is part of a thread where other annotations have also been retrieved in response to the same query rather than if it is part of a thread where it is the only annotation that matches the query.

The FAST Context Set [17] has been defined in order to provide a uniform query syntax to FAST by using the Contextual Query Language (CQL) [30], developed and maintained by the Library of Congress in the context of the Z39.50 Next Generation (ZING) project[10]. FAST provides conformance to CQL up to Level 2.

For example, a possible query to search information about the Roccabonella herbal and where it is copied from is:

```
    annotation.general = Roccabonella
                and/match==fuzzy
annotation.concept.identifier = is-copied-from
```

---

[10] http://www.loc.gov/standards/sru/

where the first clause is a best match query, the second clause is an exact match query and a relaxed boolean search is performed.

5. CAT ANNOTATION INTERACTION MODEL

CAT is a Web annotation tool developed with the goal of being able to annotate multiple types of documents and assist collaboration in the field of digital humanities. At present, CAT allows for the annotation of both text and images. The current granularity for annotation of text is at the level of the letter. For image annotations, the granularity is at the level of the pixel. This allows for extremely precise document annotation, which is very relevant to the Digital Humanities domain due to the variety of different assets that prevail.

CAT can create two types of annotation, the first of which is a targeted annotation – a comment which is associated with a specific part of a document. This may be a paragraph, a picture or an individual word, but the defining feature is that the text is directly associated with a specific subset of the digital resource.

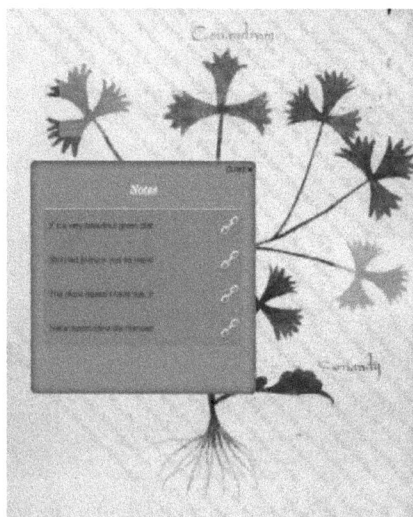

Figure 2. Some notes have been associated to a document.

The second type, a note, is simply attached to the document as shown in Figure 2 where some notes have been associated with a resource. A note is not associated with a specific item. Rather, it serves as a general comment about the document as a whole.

The annotations created using CAT allow an individual to link their comments to other, external sources. This is hugely beneficial for teachers using digital cultural collections and for students from primary to university level as well as experienced researchers. As can be seen in Figure 1, the addition of links to a resource can greatly enrich the amount of information it contains. Each link has comment text associated with it allowing a researcher to explain why this specific link is important or how it supports their point.

While CAT is beneficial for researchers and educators, it is also being used as an important source of user data for the content provider. For a digital humanities site, annotations can provide an insight into which entities are of interest to a user. If a user is frequently annotating a document, it is likely that this document is of interest to them. Furthermore, if the text being annotated is analysed, it may be possible to discern specific entities of interest within the document. This can be used to drive a personalised recommender service, populating it with entities pertaining to an individual user. A digital humanities site which could recommend resources that are relevant to users would be profoundly useful, and would help improve the effectiveness with which researchers interact with their domain.

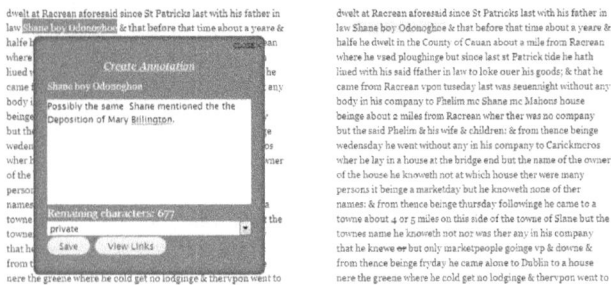

Figure 3. User creates a targeted annotation on a body of text about a person of interest.

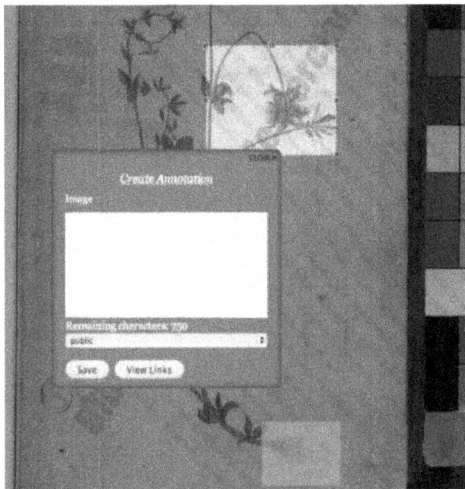

Figure 4. User can create an annotation on an image of interest.

5.1 Annotation Pointers

Here we present the means by which CAT identifies the placement of an annotation within a web document using a serialised pointer to a location.

For text, this serialized representation takes the form:

<PathStart>;<OffsetStart>;<PathEnd>;<OffsetEnd>

Where:

- <PathStart> is the path to the element which contains the start of the user's selection.
- <OffsetStart> is the offset into the start element where the beginning of the selected text may be found.
- <PathEnd> is the path to the element which contains the end of the user's selection.
- <OffsetEnd> is the offset into the end element where the end of the selected text may be found.

For images, the form is:

<Path>;<OffsetX>;<OffsetY>;<AnnotationH>;<AnnotationW>

Where:

- <Path> is the path to the annotated image.
- <OffsetX> and <OffsetY> are the position of the upper left corner of the annotation.
- <AnnotationH> and <AnnotationW> are the height and width of the annotation within the image.

In both cases, the path is computed using a modified version of the open source Okfn annotator [31] range class. In order to improve cross browser compatibility, CAT replaces Okfn's XPath pointers with CSS selectors. There are two reasons for this change. Firstly, different browsers will render pages in different ways, which means that XPath is not always a reliable means of locating a specific element in the markup. Secondly, support for XPath has been removed from current releases of jQuery. CSS selectors, however, are still supported and hence are the more suitable choice.

Additionally, rather than using browser ranges, CAT uses Rangy [32] ranges. Rangy is an open source JavaScript library which creates a virtual representation of a selected range that is independent of the browser being used. Rangy can then map this virtual range to the current page, taking into consideration the browser being used. Pointers are generated with respect to this virtual range so that the result should always evaluate to the same document location regardless of the environment. FAST is flexible enough that it can store this annotation representation without any modification, either to itself or to CAT.

5.2 Expanding Functionality of CAT

Within the context of CULTURA, CAT gives access to targeted sections of a document. Simply by selecting a region of interest (within text or images), a toolbar is presented which provides the user with a button to launch the annotation tool. This toolbar is now exposed to other services within the portal, allowing for live interfacing with a document.

By way of example, CULTURA provides a normalization service which resolves anomalies in the archaic text of the 1641 Depositions [25]. Access to this service is now provided to the user via CAT. A new button (based on a default CAT button class) has been added to the toolbar which launches CAT with the normalisation service (See Figure 5). By using this toolbar, the normalization service can access the robust ranges used in FAST-CAT to perform targeted processing of text. While the primary design and focus of CAT was to provide a reliable means of annotating document text, the way it has been implemented means that site developers can easily access its functionalities, thus providing a powerful method of connecting their services with specific parts of a document.

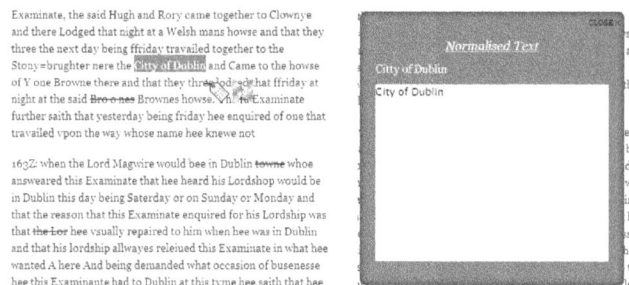

Figure 5. Normalization exposed to user via CAT

6. ARCHITECTURE

6.1 FAST Architecture

The FAST annotation service adopts a three-layer architecture, separating the data and service logic from the application and interface logic. All the resources managed by the system, e.g. annotations, signs, meanings, users, and so on, are exposed via a REST interface at HTTP level [19] which offers basic operations to create, read, update, delete, and link these resources together. The REST interface also supports the search and retrieval of resources according to the search model and query language described in Section 4.1.

All the resources are exposed in two formats: XML, according to the FAST XML Schema[11], to make resources available in an application neutral way and to favour interoperability; and, JSON to facilitate the design and development of rich and interactive Web 2.0 applications that utilise an AJAX-based approach.

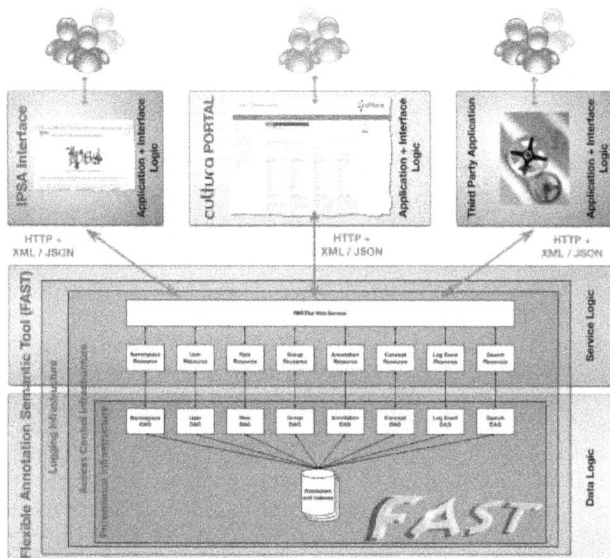

Figure 6. Architecture of the FAST annotation service.

Figure 6 shows the architecture of the FAST annotation service. The Content Annotation Tool (CAT) application and the CULTURA portal represent two possible applications built on top of FAST.

In the data logic layer, a Data Access Object (DAO)[12] takes care of mapping the object oriented representation of the resource to the underlying relational representation of them. The data logic also manages the Provenance Infrastructure, which keeps the history of all the modifications and events related to each resource in order to be able to reconstruct its full history. Each action on a resource originates a provenance event in the form of a statement `<when> <who> <predicate> <what> <why>`, which details when and who performed the given predicate e.g. CREATE, UPDATE etc. on the specified resource (what) for what reason (why) and keeps a dump of the resource itself.

As discussed above, the service logic layer translates from the object oriented representation of the resources to their XML or JSON representations and makes them available via a REST API. So, for example, it is possible to read an annotation performing a HTTP GET to the `/annotation/{id};{ns}` URI, where `id` is the identifier of the annotation, `ns` is its namespace, and in the HTTP header `accept`, you can specify whether XML or JSON has to be returned.

Transferral to the data and service logic layers are the responsibility of the Logging and Access Control infrastructures. The former records all the events happening at the system and database level. Moreover, the interaction at the REST HTTP level is recorded according to the W3C Extended Log File Format [20]. Note that log events are exposed as resources as well, so it is possible to create applications to read, visualise, and search them according to the search model described in Section 4.1. The Access Control Infrastructure takes care of authentication and authorization in a twofold way: user roles define which actions e.g. read annotation or create annotation, a user is allowed to perform; and resource scope and user groups define which resources a user can actually access. For example, a user may be entitled to read annotations by its role but he/she cannot read a specific annotation because of insufficient access permissions.

The FAST annotation service has been developed by using the Java programming language, which ensures good portability of the system across different platforms. We used the PostgreSQL DataBase Management System (DBMS)[13] for the actual persistence of annotations and its full text extension for indexing and searching the full text components of the managed resources. The Apache Tomcat Web container and the Restlet framework have been used for developing the FAST RESTful Web Application.

6.2 CAT Architecture

The architecture of the CAT annotation tool is comprised of two layers; a client-side front end, coded using JavaScript and jQuery, and a Drupal 7 module back end[14], written in PHP, as illustrated in Figure 7.

The front end runs in the user's browser and provides them with a user interface through which they can interact with annotations. When a user has chosen a particular course of action the data is passed into the logic module where their request can be processed. Depending on the nature of the request, certain third party libraries may be used in the procedure. For example, in the process of annotating a text object, the location of the text in the document must be recorded in a cross platform manner. In order to do this, a representation of the highlighted range is generated using rangy. This is a purely virtual range which means it is slightly slower than using the browser's range, but it has the advantage of being cross platform. Using a modified version of the Okfn path finder, the logic then computes a serialized path to the selected location represented by rangy which can be stored as a pointer in FAST. When annotating images, the process is the same except that jCrop [16] provides details of the selected region rather than Rangy. Retrieving an annotated region is simply the reverse of this process.

---

[11] http://ims.dei.unipd.it/data/xml/fast.3.10.xsd

[12] http://www.oracle.com/technetwork/java/dataaccessobject-138824.html

[13] http://www.postgresql.org/

[14] http://drupal.org/

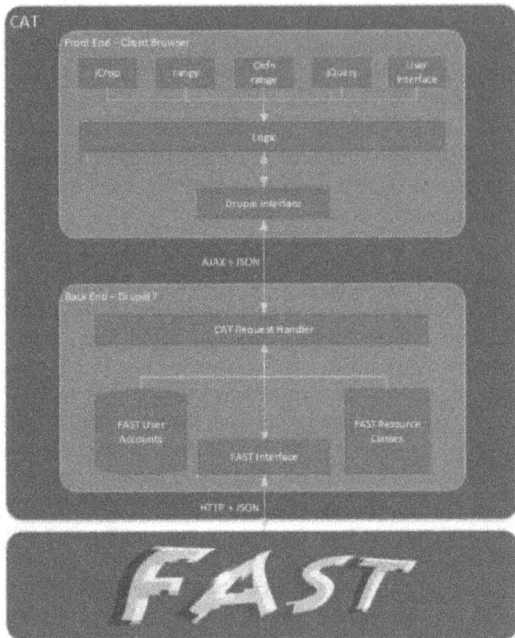

Figure 7. Architecture of the CAT annotation tool.

The representation of an annotation created here is a simplified version of the FAST description of the annotation. This is to minimize the amount of data that a user must send and receive to and from the server. For example, details such as namespaces are added on the back end rather than on the front end (and thus are managed by the site administrator). Furthermore, when managing details such as groups, the user's permissions are derived from the verbose annotation description on the server and then passed as a single value in the simplified representation.

The Drupal 7 module on the back end acts as a relay between FAST and the user. Requests for annotation creation, deletion, download etc. are passed from the front end to a request handler function on the back end. This callback function structures the data sent by the front end so that it conforms to the FAST schema and then generates the HTTP packets to be transferred. There is some logic applied at this point to determine which packets need to be sent and in what order for the request to be fulfilled. Once the system is ready, the packets are sent on to FAST. The Drupal module then waits for a response from the remote service. When one is received, the result is returned to the front end via the same callback function through which the request was initially made.

The choice of a Drupal module as a means of implementation means that adding FAST-CAT to any site using the Drupal CMS should be a very simple process. Additionally, as the Drupal module is only acting as a relay, it should be a relatively simple process to swap out the back end for a more server agnostic implementation, allowing FAST-CAT to be deployed on any website, rather than only those using the Drupal 7 content management system.

Certain requests such as creating and viewing annotations require user authentication by FAST. As FAST is a stand-alone service, it maintains its own record of user accounts and login details. This means that for each user who is registered on the CULTURA site, a separate account must be created for them in FAST. CAT performs this registration automatically.

7. THE CULTURA ENVIRONMENT

CULTURA is a three year, FP7 funded project, scheduled to finish in February 2014. Its main objective is to pioneer the development of personalised information retrieval and presentation, contextual adaptivity and social analysis in a digital humanities context. In its current form, it aims to provide adaptive and personalized access to two historical collections – the 1641 Depositions [36] and IPSA [37].

FAST-CAT has been integrated into the environment in order to provide users with an additional means of interacting with the portal, as well as to provide some feedback for CULTURA's user model regarding a user's interests. At present, CULTURA (and by extension FAST-CAT) is being evaluated by three groups of users. A team of MPhil students and professional researchers from Trinity College Dublin are using FAST-CAT as part of their teaching, collaboration and research into the 1641 Depositions. These users will be testing the annotation tool in a free form manner. How they choose to annotate and what content they label is entirely determined by their own needs.

Providing an alternative insight to FAST-CAT is a group of secondary school students from Lancaster who used the annotations as part of a project they were given during a lesson. Their experience was more guided than that of the MPhil students as they were directed to highlight information or points of interest using FAST-CAT and then deliver a presentation using annotations to help with organization. The focus of this lesson was on the 1641 Depositions.

Masters students in Padua will test the image annotation functionality of FAST-CAT as part of their research into the Imaginum Patavinae Scientiae Archivum (IPSA) [37] collections of illuminated manuscripts. Similarly to the MPhil students, the approach of these Masters students to annotating documents will be determined by their own research methodology. The intention is not to guide the users on how to use FAST-CAT, but rather to make them aware of the functionality provided and observe how they choose to apply it.

The various features offered by FAST-CAT and its user interface will be evaluated in detail and comparisons will be drawn between the manner in which different user groups availed of annotations depending on their level of expertise and the type of documents examined. Furthermore, FAST-CAT will also help to drive CULTURA's comprehensive user model by providing the site with updates on the user's behaviour regarding document annotation.

8. EVALUATION

At present, only the results of the trial with 21 secondary school students from Lancaster, mentioned in Section 7, have been collated and analysed. For this evaluation, the students were divided into three groups and provided with activity sheets describing research questions for the 1641 Depositions which they were to investigate using the CULTURA portal.

The annotation tool was provided to give team members a means by which they could draw their peers' attention to specific areas of the document, share ideas and store personal notes. In this capacity, FAST-CAT excelled, and the tool was used extensively by all parties. When completing a survey at the end of the study, several participants made reference to annotations as a fundamental and valuable tool for this form of collaboration. Indeed 11 of the 21 participants cited the annotation tool as the

Indeed 11 of the 21 participants cited the annotation tool as the most helpful service provided by the CULTURA environment.

Despite the positive feedback received about the annotation tool, a number of issues were raised by the students. For instance, there was a difficulty in distinguishing between different users' annotations. All annotations appeared on the page as a yellow highlight over the text. As the number of annotations on a page increased, it became increasingly difficult to identify the owner of a particular comment. While functionality was provided to hide annotations that didn't belong to the individual user, it was clear that better controls were required to help with this aspect of the tool. In the questionnaire that followed this experiment, a number of students mentioned that access to a palette of colours for their annotations, so that each member of a team could produce different coloured highlights on the text, would be desirable. This suggested functionality will be applied to CAT in the next phase of implementation.

As these students were not professional historians, many struggled with the archaic and non-standard version of English that the 1641 Depositions are written in. As such, it was mentioned frequently that an ability to read a normalised version of the text was desirable. As mentioned in Section 5.2 this feature has now been added to CAT, with the ability for users to highlight any text and have it rendered to them in a normalised fashion.

Overall, FAST-CAT was very well received by the test group and will go through several more iterations in the course of the CULTURA project. Evaluation studies are ongoing, and feedback from the entire spectrum of users (professional historians to members of the general public) will be accounted for in the design of the annotation tool.

9. CONCLUSIONS AND FUTURE WORK

It is the belief of the authors that FAST-CAT has huge potential as an annotation tool within the digital humanities field. However, it is still a young tool with much room for future expansion and enhancement. Some of the required additions are already known and are currently being developed within the timescale of the project. Others will be dependent on user feedback from test groups as they identify issues they experience within their domains. Some project researchers are working closely with the users to evaluate the usefulness of the environment and to guide its further development/refinement. This process is crucial to the effective design of an environment that will be useful for a range of users who come to the resource, and the collections that it makes available.

As was previously mentioned, it is possible to make FAST-CAT more server agnostic by swapping out the Drupal 7 back end for a more general php script. It is expected that this script will be developed and provided with future versions of FAST-CAT so as to increase the range of portals to which it may be applied. Further to this, another part of the future development of FAST-CAT will be focused on improving the user's experience. It is intended that the tool be as intuitive and easy to use as possible. How this will be achieved is to be this based on the feedback given by the user groups during the CULTURA trials.

10. ACKNOWLEDGMENTS

The authors would like to thank Chiara Ponchia for her valuable advice on aspects related to the illuminated manuscripts.

We are most grateful to our referees for their very helpful comments.

The CULTURA (contract no. 269973) and the PROMISE network of excellence (contract n. 258191) projects, as part of the 7th Framework Program of the European Commission, have partially supported the reported work.

11. REFERENCES

[1] Agosti, M. (1996). An overview of hypertext. In Agosti, M. and Smeaton, A., editors, *Information Retrieval and Hypertext*. Kluwer Academic, Norwell, pages 27-47.

[2] Agosti, M., and Ferro N. (2003). Annotations: enriching a digital library. In Koch, T., and Sølvberg, I. T., editors, *Proceedings of the 7th European Conference on Research andAdvanced Technology for Digital Libraries (ECDL 2003),* LNCS 2769. Springer, Heidelberg, pages 88-100.

[3] Agosti, M., Ferro, N., Frommholz, I., and Thiel, U. (2004). Annotations in Digital Libraries and Collaboratories - Facets, Models and Usage. In Heery, R. and Lyon, L., editors, *Proc. 8th European Conference on Research and Advanced Technology for Digital Libraries (ECDL 2004)*, pages 244-255. LNCS 3232, Springer, Heidelberg, Germany.

[4] Agosti, M. and Ferro, N. (2005). Annotations as context for searching documents. In Crestani, F. and Ruthven, I., editors, *Proceedings of the 5th International Conference on Conceptions of Library and Information Science - Context: Nature, Impact and Role*. LNCS 3507. Springer, Heidelberg, pages 155-170.

[5] Agosti, M., Ferro. N., and Orio, N. (2005). Annotating illuminated manuscripts: an effective tool for research and education. In: Marlino, M., Sumner, T. and Shipman III, F.M., editors, *Proc. 5th ACM/IEEE-CS Joint Conference on Digital Libraries (JCDL 2005)*, ACM Press, New York, USA, 2005, pages 121-130.

[6] Agosti, M. and Ferro, N. (2006). Search Strategies for finding annotations and annotated documents: the FAST Service. In Larsen, H. L., Pasi, G., Ortiz-Arroyo, D., Andreasen, T., and Christiansen, H., editors, *Proceedings of the 7th International Conference on Flexible Query Answering Systems (FQAS 2006),* LNAI 4027. Springer, Heidelberg, pp. 270-281.

[7] Agosti, M., Bonfiglio-Dosio, G., and Ferro, N. (2007). A Historical and Contemporary Study on Annotations to Derive Key Features for Systems Design. *International Journal on Digital Libraries*, 8(1):1-19.

[8] Agosti, M., Ferro, N., and Orio, N. (2007). Annotations as a Tool for Disclosing Hidden Relationships Between Illuminated Manuscripts. In Basili, R. and Pazienza, M. T., editors, *Proceedings of AI*IA 2007: Artificial Intelligence and Human-Oriented Computing, 10th Congress of the Italian Association for Artificial Intelligence*, LNCS 4733, Springer, pages 662-673.

[9] Agosti, M. and Ferro, N. (2008). A Formal Model of Annotations of Digital Content. *ACM Transactions on Information Systems (TOIS)*, 26(1):3:1-3:57.

[10] Barbera, N., Meschini, F., Morbidoni, C., and Tomasi, F. (2012). Annotating digital libraries and electronic editions in a collaborative and semantic perspective. In Agosti, M., Esposito, F., Ferilli, S., and Ferro, N., editors, *Digital Libraries and Archives. 8th Italian Research Conference (IRCDL 2012),*. CCIS 354, Springer, Heidelberg, Germany, pages 46-57.

[11] Bélanger, M.-E. (2010, 02 03). Ideals. Retrieved 10 25, 2012, from https://www.ideals.illinois.edu/bitstream/handle/2142/15035/belanger.pdf?sequence=2

[12] Bhagwat, D., Chiticariu, L., Tan, W.-C., and Vijayvargiya, G. (2004) An annotation management system for relational databases. In: Nascimento, M. A., Özsu, M. T., Kossmann, D., Miller, R. J., Blakeley, J. A., and Schiefer, K. B., editors, *Proceedings of the 30th International Conference on Very Large Data Bases (VLDB 2004)*. Morgan Kaufmann, pages 900-911.

[13] Brickley, D. and Guha, R.V. (2004). RDF Vocabulary Description Language 1.0: RDF Schema - W3C Recommendation 10 Feb 2004. http://www.w3.org/TR/rdf-schema/

[14] Buneman, P., Kostylev, E. V., and Vansummeren, S. (2013). Annotations are relative. In Tan, W.-C., Guerrini, G., Catania, B., and Gounaris, A., editors, *Proceedings of the 16th International Conference on Database Theory (ICDT 2013)*. ACM, New York, NY, USA, pages 177-188.

[15] Candela, L., Castelli, D., Ferro, N., Koutrika, G., Meghini, C., Pagano, P., Ross, S., Soergel, D., Agosti, M., Dobreva, M., Katifori, V., and Schuldt, H. (2007). *The DELOS Digital Library Reference Model. Foundations for Digital Libraries*. ISTI-CNR at Gruppo ALI, Pisa, Italy. http://www.delos.info/files/pdf/ReferenceModel/DELOS_DL ReferenceModel_0.98.pdf.

[16] Deep Liquid, jCrop, http://deepliquid.com/content/Jcrop.html

[17] Ferro, N. (2009). Annotation Search: The FAST Way. In Agosti, M., Borbinha, J., Kapidakis, S., Papatheodorou, C., and Tsakonas, G., editors, *Proc. 13th European Conference on Research and Advanced Technology for Digital Libraries (ECDL 2009)*, pages 15-26. LNCS 5714, Springer, Heidelberg, Germany.

[18] Ferro, N. and Silvello, G. (2013). NESTOR: A Formal Model for Digital Archives. *Information Processing & Management*, 49(6):1206-1240..

[19] Fielding, R. T. and Taylor, R. N. (2002). Principled Design of the Modern Web Architecture. *ACM Transactions on Internet Technology (TOIT)*, 2(2):115–150.

[20] Hallam-Baker, P. M. and Behlendorf, B. (1996). Extended Log File Format - W3C Working DraftWD-logfile-960323. http://www.w3.org/TR/WD-logfile.html.

[21] Hampson, C., Agosti, M., Orio, N., Bailey, E., Lawless, S., Conlan, O., and Wade, V. (2012). The CULTURA Project: Supporting Next Generation Interaction with Digital Cultural Heritage Collections. In *Progress in Cultural Heritage Preservation - 4th International Conference (EuroMed 2012)*, pages 668-675. LNCS 7616, Springer, Heidelberg, Germany.

[22] Hampson, C., Lawless, S., Bailey, E., Yogev, S., Zwerdling, N., Carmel, D., Conlan, O., O'Connor, A. and Wade, V. (2012). CULTURA: A Metadata-Rich Environment to Support the Enhanced Interrogation of Cultural Collections. In *Metadata and Semantics Research - 6th Research Conference (MTSR 2012)*, pages 227-238. CCIS 343, Springer, Heidelberg, Germany.

[23] Kahan, J. and Koivunen, M.-R. (2001) Annotea: an open RDF infrastructure for shared Web annotations. In Shen, V. Y., Saito, N., Lyu, M. R., and Zurko, M. E., editors, *Proceedings of the 10th International Conference on World Wide Web (WWW 2001)*, ACM Press, New York, pages 623-632.

[24] Kostylev, E. V. and Buneman, P. (2012). Combining dependent annotations for relational algebra. In Deutsch, A., editor, *Proceedings of the 15th International Conference on Database Theory (ICDT 2012)*. ACM, New York, NY, USA, pages 196-207.

[25] Lawless, S., Hampson, C., Mitankin, P., and Gerdjikov, S. (2013). Normalisation in Historical Text Collections. In *Proceedings of Digital Humanities 2013*, Lincoln, Nebraska, USA [In Press].

[26] Marshall, C. C. (1998). Toward an ecology of hypertext annotation. In Akscyn, R., editor, *Proceedings of the 9th ACM Conference on Hypertext and Hypermedia (HT 1998): links, objects, time and space-structure in hypermedia systems*, pages 40-49. ACM Press, New York.

[27] Martínez, J. M. (editor) (2004). *MPEG-7 Overview*. ISO/IEC JTC1/SC29/WG11N6828. Palma de Mallorca, Spain, pages 74.

[28] MPEG home page, http://www.chiariglione.org/mpeg

[29] Nagao, K. (2003). *Digital content annotation and transcoding*. Artech House Publishers.

[30] OASIS Search Web Services Technical Committee (2012). searchRetrieve: Part 5. CQL: The Contextual Query Language Version 1.0. http://docs.oasis-open.org/search-ws/searchRetrieve/v1.0/searchRetrieve-v1.0-part5-cql.pdf.

[31] Okfn. (n.d.). Okfn Annotator. Retrieved 06 2012, from http://okfnlabs.org/annotator/

[32] Rangy, http://code.google.com/p/rangy/

[33] Salton, G., Fox, E. A., and Wu, H. (1983). Extended Boolean Information Retrieval. *Communications of the ACM (CACM)*, 26(11):1022–1036.

[34] Sanderson, R. and Van de Sompel, H. (2010). Making web annotations persistent over time. In Hunter, J., Lagoze, C., Giles, C. L., and Li, Y.-F., editors, *Proceedings of the 2010 Joint International Conference on Digital Libraries (JCDL 2010)*. ACM, pages 1-10.

[35] TILE. (2011). TILE: text-image linking environment. Retrieved 07 2012, from http://mith.umd.edu/tile/

[36] Trinity College Dublin, 1641 Depositions. http://1641.tcd.ie/

[37] Università degli Studi di Padova, IPSA (*Imaginum Patavinae Scientiae Archivum*). http://ipsa.dei.unipd.it/en_GB/

[38] Wang, X., Ye, L., Keogh, E., and Shelton, C. (2008). Annotating historical archives of images. In Larsen, R. L., Paepcke, A., Borbinha, J. L., and Naaman, M., editors, *Proceedins of the ACM/IEEE Joint Conference on Digital Libraries (JCDL 2008)*, ACM, pages 341-350.

Early Modern OCR Project (eMOP) at Texas A&M University: Using Aletheia to Train Tesseract

Katayoun Torabi
Texas A&M University
Department of English 4227
College Station, Texas, USA 77843
1-979-458-9265
torabik@neo.tamu.edu

Jessica Durgan
Texas A&M University
Department of Biology 3258
College Station, Texas, USA 77843
1-979-845-2791
durganj@tamu.edu

Bryan Tarpley
Texas A&M University
Department of English 4227
College Station, Texas, USA 77843
1-979-862-4368
bptarpley@tamu.edu

ABSTRACT

Great effort is being made to collect and preserve historic manuscripts from the early modern and eighteenth-century periods; unfortunately, searching the Early English Books Online (EEBO) and Eighteenth Century Collections Online (ECCO) collections can be extremely difficult for researchers because current Optical Character Recognition (OCR) engines struggle to read and recognize various historic fonts, especially in manuscripts of declining quality. To address this problem, the Early Modern OCR Project (eMOP) at the Initiative for the Digital Humanities, Media, and Culture (IDHMC) at Texas A&M University seeks to train OCR engines to read historic documents more effectively in order to make the entirety of these collections accessible to searching. The first step in this project involves using Aletheia Desktop Tool, developed by PRImA Research Lab at the University of Salford, to use documents from the EEBO and ECCO collections to create training sets to aid OCR engines, such as Google's Tesseract, in recognizing the special characters such as ligatures, italics, and blackletter found within early modern fonts. In the year that the Aletheia team has been working to create these font training libraries, we have overcome several problems, including learning how to select, extract, and deliver the data that best suits Tesseract training requirements. This work with Aletheia is part of a larger scholarly project that endeavors to not only make the EEBO and ECCO collections more accessible for data mining purposes for researchers, but also seeks to make available to the public the methodologies, workflow, and digital tools developed during the eMOP project to aid libraries, museums, and scholars in other fields in their efforts to preserve and study our combined cultural history.

Categories and Subject Descriptors

C#, SQL, XML, and XSLT

Keywords

Digital Humanities, Early Modern and Eighteenth-Century Texts, Aletheia Desktop Tool, Tesseract, and Optical Character Recognition Engines.

DocEng '13, September 10-13 2013, Florence, Italy
Copyright 2013 ACM 978-1-4503-1789-4/13/09…$15.00.
http://dx.doi.org/10.1145/2494266.2494304.

1. INTRODUCTION

Currently, roughly 307,000 early modern and eighteenth-century manuscripts are being preserved in the Early English Books Online (EEBO) and Eighteenth Century Collections Online (ECCO) databases, which provide page images and metadata records for each manuscript. While these databases have accomplished a monumental task in acquiring and preserving these historical works, much work remains to be done in improving the access and usability of these texts for scholars. Searching these collections is extremely difficult because current Optical Character Recognition (OCR) engines are not trained to read early modern images and are easily confused by irregular baselines, type heights, special characters, noise, and poor image quality. For example, a researcher might have a very difficult time searching for instances of the word "Success" in texts from 1701 to 1705 within the databases because OCR engines cannot distinguish between the long 's' special character of the period that has a half cross-bar and a modern 'f' with a full cross-bar.

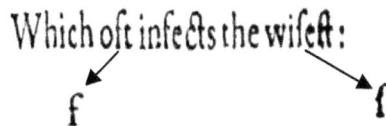

'f' with a full cross-bar   's' with a half cross-bar

Figure 1. The difference between 'f' and long 's'

Certain groups such as Gale Cengage Learning and ProQuest have attempted to correct this problem by manually transcribing these texts and have completed approximately 50,000 of the 307,000 texts in both the ECCO and EEBO collection. This method, however, is extremely time consuming and costly; it also does not provide access to the entire collection, especially in the case of any new acquisitions.

In response to this problem, the Early Modern OCR Project (eMOP) at the Initiative for Digital Humanities, Media, and Culture (IDHMC) at Texas A&M University, funded by a grant from the Andrew W. Mellon Foundation, seeks to create machine readable versions of these texts by training OCR engines to handle the idiosyncrasies of early modern publishing. The IDHMC is headed by Dr. Laura Mandell, and further details of the eMOP project can be accessed at http://idhmc.tamu.edu/emop. Our ultimate goal is to make the entire corpus of the EEBO and ECCO collections, rather than just the metadata, searchable in order to facilitate the data-mining needs of future scholars. The first step of this larger project is the IDHMC's work with Aletheia, a desktop tool developed by the Pattern Recognition and Image Analysis (PRImA) Research Laboratory at the University of

Salford.[1] The Aletheia group, headed by Katayoun Torabi, employs several graduate and undergraduate students in developing a small subset of ground truth files (perfectly corrected texts at the graphemic level) for several early modern and eighteenth-century fonts. These ground truth files will be used to train the Tesseract OCR engine, an open-source tool developed by Google.[2] Compiling ground truth files for use in the training libraries is only the first stage in a complex process which will make texts more searchable and therefore more accessible for scholars in the early modern and eighteenth-century fields in the future.

2. METHODOLOGY

The eMOP project is tasked with an unusually large scope, given that the combined dataset for both EEBO and ECCO contains roughly 45,000,000 TIFF images that must be processed by open-source OCR engines within the timeline provided by the Mellon grant. Despite the significant computing power available to the IDHMC thanks to our partnership with the Brazos Computing Cluster at Texas A&M University, we have found that certain methodologies that may provide higher OCR accuracy rates do not scale well to handle datasets of this size, largely due to the amount of processing time required per page image.

In order to attain the highest OCR accuracy rates possible given the scale of our project, training libraries are created using high quality images of fonts from early modern and eighteenth-century texts provided by Texas A&M's Cushing Memorial Library. Ten to fifteen page images are selected for each font, copied, and saved onto disks as TIFF files. Page images are then assigned to student workers and named according to the first initial and last name of the publisher, the publication year, and the 20-line height. For example, an image from the 1702 *Anno Regni* text, published by Charles Bill would be named cbil1702_116.

Student workers open selected TIFF images with Aletheia, binarize each document (the color image is converted to a black and white image), and remove any noise (blotchiness, bleed-throughs, and other artifacts). The cleaned images are then saved as black and white TIFF documents before running Aletheia's automatic segmentation tool (Aletheia employs Tesseract for this purpose), which attempts to identify the Unicode equivalent for each character, storing the results in a corresponding XML file. Aletheia identifies and defines layout regions, lines, words, and individual glyphs in the text and assigns a set of XY coordinates in the XML file for each defined region. In other words, Aletheia attempts to "read" the text in the page image before assigning each letter, number, and punctuation mark a Unicode value.

---

[1] Apostolos Antonacopoulos, IMPACT Work Package leader for PRImA, University of Salford, has made Aletheia and other tools available at http://www.primaresearch.org/tools.php.

[2] Tesseract was originally developed by Ray Smith and is now being managed at Google. Tesseract is available on Google Code: http://code.google.com/p/tesseract-ocr/. See Ray Smith, "An Overview of the Tesseract OCR Engine," Ninth International Conference on Document Analysis and Recognition, 23-26 September 2007.

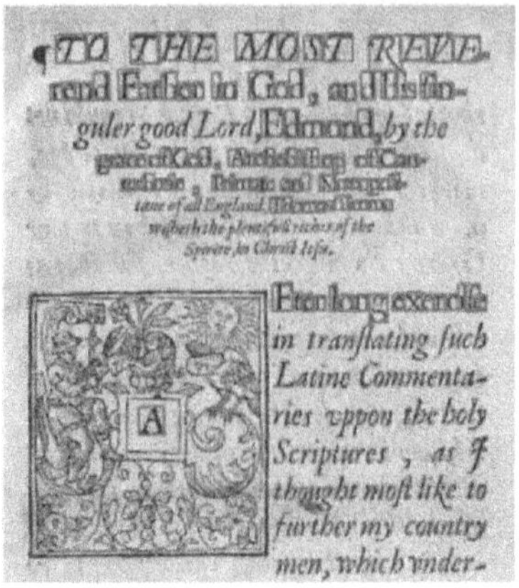

Figure 2. Glyphs defined in Aletheia Desktop

However, because of the difficulties discussed above, Aletheia (or the underlying Tesseract OCR engine) often misreads the text. The tool has difficulty reading letters that are distorted, obscured by noise or ink bleed-through, or especially faint. It also often misidentifies the parameters of each glyph, particularly in the case of special characters, such as long s's, ligatures, italics, rotunda r's, suspension marks, and printer's marks. Compounding this is the fact that the standard Unicode set does not include many of these special characters. In order to address this, the Aletheia team is trained to consistently identify characters not present in the standard Unicode set by using characters designated by the Medieval Unicode Font Initiative (MUFI).

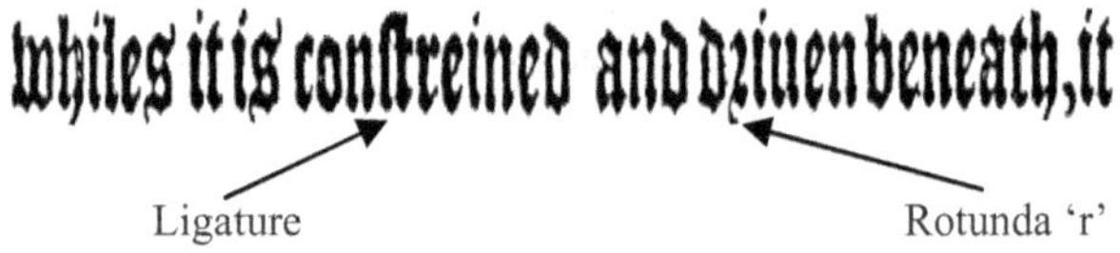

Ligature   Rotunda 'r'

Figure 3. Examples of special characters

Since we are correcting the page image at the graphemic (or glyph) level, we focus our attention on monitoring the coordinates corresponding to each individual letter, punctuation mark, or number. Student workers are responsible for fixing any misreads by: 1) correcting the defined parameters of the glyph and 2) typing in the correct text in the Text Content Box for each corresponding character.

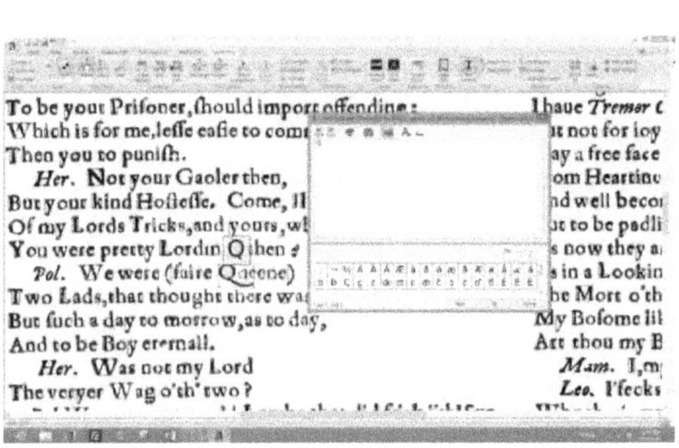

Figure 4: Correcting glyph parameters and text in Aletheia

Ten to fifteen page images are processed in this manner for each font type and comprise a font training set.

3. RESULTS

Altogether, fourteen font training sets have been processed, for a total of 160 completed ground truth XML files.

Font Name	Publisher	Publication Year	Images Processed
JDAY1559_001	John Daye	1559	15
MFLE1633_94_017	Miles Flesher	1633	11
TCOT1632_82_001	Thomas Cotes	1632	11
IJAGG_guyot_83_99	François Guyot	Unknown	13
BRA_2788_002	Pierre Haultin	Unknown	8
cbil1692_110_002	Charles Bill	1692	6
cbil1693_116_001	Charles Bill	1693	10
cbil1702_116_1_001	Charles Bill	1702	14
hhil1686_82_1_001	Henry Hills	1686	15
jbill1628_86_001	John Bill	1628	15
IJAGG_guyot_83_15_B italics	François Guyot	Unknown	12
BRA_2788_004_B italics	Pierre Haultin	Unknown	5
MFLE1633_94_017_B italics	Miles Flesher	1633	11
TCOT1632_82_001_B italics	Thomas Cotes	1632	14

Figure 5. Table of images in the font training library

Each font set contains every available letter in both upper case and lower case. Where possible, each set also includes special font types such as blackletter, Roman type, italics, numbers, drop capitals, as well as any other unique characters and symbols present in the sample manuscripts.

In our initial testing phase, we ran each prepared font set through the Tesseract engine in order to train the OCR engine to read and recognize the characters of those fonts. The font sets prepared through the Aletheia procedure should have provided Tesseract with training that covered a wide range of early modern and eighteenth-century fonts. However, feeding the font sets created in Aletheia directly into Tesseract did not improve its ability to read early modern fonts. In other words, we were unable to train Tesseract with the data output from Aletheia alone. It was necessary, therefore, to add another step to the training process by developing a tool, called Franken+, in order to bridge the gap between Aletheia and Tesseract for historic font training. Franken+, which will be discussed in greater detail in the next section, has drastically improved Tesseract's ability to read and recognize early modern fonts.

4. DISCUSSION

Our initial assumption was that we would be able to import all of the defined and corrected glyphs directly from the Aletheia Desktop tool into Google's Tesseract in order to provide the engine with the largest possible data set from which to train. We posited, for instance, that if we could feed fifty instances of the cbil1702_116 font's letter 'a' into Tesseract, providing samples of both good and poor quality glyphs, then the engine could use this variety to create a flexible definition of the letter 'a.' After sufficient training in this manner, we hoped it would then be able to recognize every subsequent instance of that cbil1702_116 letter—no matter the condition of the manuscript. Thus, our initial approach was to apply an XSLT[3] script to the Aletheia XML output in order to generate a Google box file for each page. The box file would then be used by Tesseract to identify where various letters are located on its corresponding TIFF image during the

Tesseract training process, in which TIFF images and their corresponding box files are ingested by Tesseract in order to produce a language file enabling Tesseract to better read a specific set of identifiers (such as idiosyncratic characters in a historic font).

We found that the problems with this approach were twofold. First, Tesseract does not appear to train using "fuzzy logic." In other words, training with deformed instances of letters seems to confuse Tesseract rather than increase its ability to recognize further instances of that letter as originally hypothesized. Instead, Tesseract prefers what we call a "Platonic ideal," or near perfect examples for each letter, in order to establish how to read a font initially. After we train Tesseract using the ideal forms of the letters, it can more easily recognize letters that are deformed or imperfect.

The second problem that we encountered was that a small number of glyphs had been misidentified, despite our care in assigning glyph values to boxes in Aletheia. Compounding this problem was Tesseract's sensitivity, which led Aletheia to automatically identify several artifacts in the image as glyphs which were actually random pixels. While these pixels are too small for the human eye to catch and correct in Aletheia's interface, Tesseract registered these incorrectly identified pixels as letters, skewing the entire training process.

For those two reasons, Bryan Tarpley developed a program written in C# that we refer to in-house as Franken+. Franken+ (and its predecessor FrankenFile) is named after Mary Shelley's nineteenth-century novel *Frankenstein* because of the way the program stitches together extracted images of each glyph as identified in Aletheia. Franken+ uses a MySQL database to associate each image of a letter with its corresponding Unicode character. The user can then choose any letter in a drop down box and see all of the extracted images that correspond to that letter, allowing him or her to quickly eliminate any misidentified characters or imperfect instances of that letter. In the end, the user is left with the best images for each character in the working alphabet, which can then be used for Tesseract training purposes.

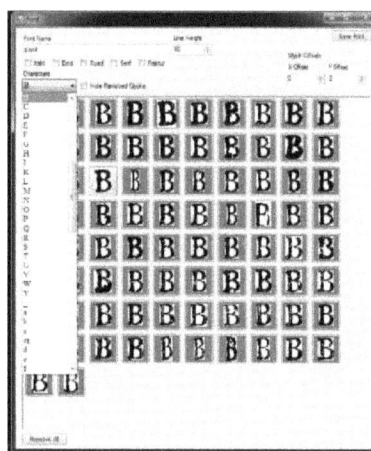

Figure 6. Undesirable glyphs being eliminated using the Franken+ tool.

Once we have eliminated all but the best instances of a letter, the next step is to use Franken+ to stitch together a massive TIFF image comprised of letters and words as found in selected Text Creation Partnership hand-keyed texts (ground truth transcriptions of early modern texts). This creates a synthetic image of the

---

[3] XSL stands for EXtensible Stylesheet Language. A "Transformation" of XML data into other formats using this language is referred to as XSLT.

original early modern text that corresponds at the glyph level, but substitutes the ideal forms of each character for letters of poor quality. We use this synthetic image and its corresponding box file to train Tesseract in lieu of the Aletheia output.

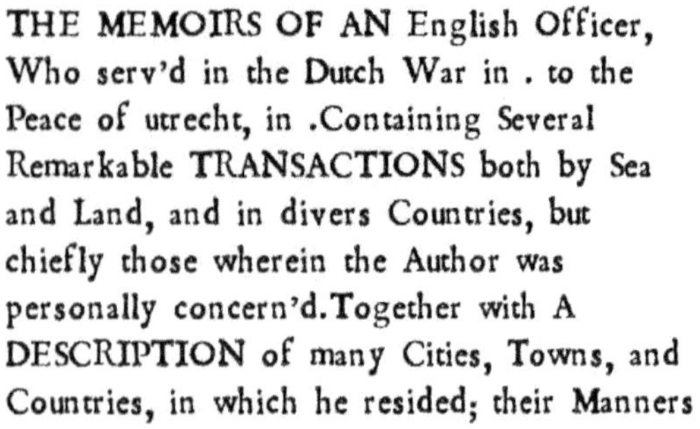

THE MEMOIRS OF AN English Officer, Who serv'd in the Dutch War in . to the Peace of utrecht, in .Containing Several Remarkable TRANSACTIONS both by Sea and Land, and in divers Countries, but chiefly those wherein the Author was personally concern'd.Together with A DESCRIPTION of many Cities, Towns, and Countries, in which he resided; their Manners

Figure 7. Synthetic image created by Franken+

Because Tesseract, like all OCR engines, was designed to recognize modern, machine produced fonts, we learned that we cannot simply train it to recognize earlier fonts in poor condition by providing large amounts of data. Instead, we must provide quality over quantity. By using Franken+ to create a Platonic ideal for each character of each early modern and eighteenth-century font that we process through Aletheia, we bring the character images closer to Tesseract's modern expectations. Preliminary tests results have revealed that this approach is appropriate for the Tesseract training process, as the training data created by the Franken+ tool has drastically increased Tesseract's ability to read and recognize the two early modern fonts tested so far. We are confident that Franken+ will serve as an effective bridge between Aletheia and Tesseract.

At this point in the process, the training libraries have been created using Aletheia Desktop and the tools are in place to begin the next stage of the eMOP project: full-scale testing on Tesseract. Word frequency lists are being generated using hand-keyed ground truth files for inclusion in these training libraries. Once trained, we will OCR the entire EEBO and ECCO corpus of 307,000 manuscripts. At that point, intensive post-processing is performed on each of the resulting texts involving dictionary work and crowd-sourced corrections for particularly difficult texts.[4]

Team eMOP will then return the results to Gale and ProQuest for uploading into their databases, with the end result being a substantial improvement in EEBO and ECCO searching and data mining for researchers. Furthermore, we will also make available our methodologies and digital tools worldwide so that libraries, museums, and scholars in other literary and cultural fields may use them in their own digital preservation processes.

5. REFERENCES

[1] Antonacopoulos, Apostolos, Clausner, Christian, and Pletschacher, Stefan. 2011. Aletheia - An Advanced Document Layout and Text Ground-Truthing System for Production Environments. *Eleventh International Conference on Document Analysis and Recognition* (Beijing, China, September 18-21, 2011). DOI = http://www.icdar2011.org/fileup/PDF/4520a048.pdf.

[2] Mandell, Laura. 2012. Mellon Foundation Grant Proposal: "OCR'ing Early ModerdernTexts". Grant Proposal. DOI= http://idhmc.tamu.edu/emop/.

[3] MUFI (Medieval Unicode Font Initiative). DOI= http://www.mufi.info/

[4] Smith, Ray. 2007. An Overview of the Tesseract OCR Engine. *Ninth International Conference on Document Analysis and Recognition* (Curitiba, Brazil, September 23-26, 2007). DOI= http://www.informatik.uni-trier.de/~ley/db/conf/icdar/.

---

[4] A discussion of the various post-processing procedures falls outside the scope of this article. However, a detailed description of these procedures can be found here: http://emopwiki.tamu.edu

Uncertain Version Control in Open Collaborative Editing of Tree-Structured Documents

M. Lamine Ba
Institut Mines–Télécom;
Télécom ParisTech; LTCI
Paris, France
mouhamadou.ba@
telecom-paristech.fr

Talel Abdessalem
Institut Mines–Télécom;
Télécom ParisTech; LTCI
Paris, France
talel.abdessalem@
telecom-paristech.fr

Pierre Senellart
Télécom ParisTech &
The University of Hong Kong
Paris, France & Hong Kong
pierre.senellart@
telecom-paristech.fr

ABSTRACT

In order to ease content enrichment, exchange, and sharing, web-scale collaborative platforms such as Wikipedia or Google Docs enable unbounded interactions between a large number of contributors, without prior knowledge of their level of expertise and reliability. Version control is then essential for keeping track of the evolution of the shared content and its provenance. In such environments, uncertainty is ubiquitous due to the unreliability of the sources, the incompleteness and imprecision of the contributions, the possibility of malicious editing and vandalism acts, etc. To handle this uncertainty, we use a probabilistic XML model as a basic component of our version control framework. Each version of a shared document is represented by an XML tree and the whole document, together with its different versions, is modeled as a probabilistic XML document. Uncertainty is evaluated using the probabilistic model and the reliability measure associated to each source, each contributor, or each editing event, resulting in an uncertainty measure on each version and each part of the document. We show that standard version control operations can be implemented directly as operations on the probabilistic XML model; efficiency with respect to deterministic version control systems is demonstrated on real-world datasets.

Categories and Subject Descriptors

H.2.1 [**Database Management**]: Logical Design—*Data models*; I.7.1 [**Document and Text Processing**]: Document and Text Editing—*Version control*

Keywords

XML, collaborative work, uncertain data, version control

1. INTRODUCTION

Version Control in Open Environments. In many collaborative editing systems, where several users can provide con-

tent, content management is based on version control. A version control system tracks the versions of the content as well as changes. Such a system enables fixing error made in the revision process, querying past versions, and integration of content from different contributors. As surveyed in [12, 26], much effort related to version control has been carried out both in research and in applications. The prime applications were collaborative document authoring process, computer-aided design, and software development systems. Currently, powerful version control tools, such as Subversion [18] and Git [15], efficiently manage large source code repositories and shared filesystems.

However, existing approaches leave no room for uncertainty handling, for instance, uncertain data resulting from conflicts. Conflicts are common in collaborative editing tasks, in particular in an open environment. They arise whenever concurrent edits attempt to change the same content. As a result, conflicts introduce some ambiguities in content change management. But sources of uncertainties in the version control process are not only due to conflicts. Indeed, there are inherently uncertain applications using version control, such as web-scale collaborative platforms: Platforms such as Wikipedia [6] or Google Docs [2] enable unbounded interactions between a large number of contributors, without prior knowledge of their level of expertise and reliability. In these systems, version control is used for keeping track of the evolution of the shared content and its provenance. In such environments, uncertainty is ubiquitous due to the unreliability of the sources, the incompleteness and imprecision of the contributions, the possibility of malicious editing and vandalism acts, etc. Therefore, a version control technique able to properly manipulate uncertain data may be very helpful in this kind of applications. We detail application scenarios next.

Uncertainty in Wikipedia Versions. Some web-scale collaborative systems such as Wikipedia have no write-access restrictions over documents. As a result, multi-version documents include data from different users. As shown in [38], Wikipedia has known an exponential growth of contributors and editions per articles. The open and free features lead to contributions with variable reliability and consistency depending both on the contributors' expertise (e.g., novice or expert) and the scope of the debated subjects. At the same time, edit wars, malicious contributions like spams, and vandalism acts can happen at any time during document evolution. Therefore, the integrity and the quality of each article may be strongly altered. Suggested solutions to these critical issues are reviewing access policies for articles discussing hot topics, or quality-driven solutions based on the reputations of authors, statistics on frequency of content change, or the trust a given reader has on the information [10, 20, 29]. But restricting editions on Wikipedia articles to a certain group of privileged contributors does not suppress the necessity of representing and assessing uncertainties. Indeed, edits may be incomplete, imprecise or uncertain, showing partial views, misinformations or subjective opinions. The reputation of contributors or the confidence level on sources are useful information towards a quantitative evaluation of the quality of versions and even more of each atomic contribution. However, a prior efficient representation of uncertainty across document versions remains a prerequisite.

User Preference at Visualization Time. Filtering and visualizing content are also important features in collaborative environments. In Wikipedia, users are not only contributors, but also consumers, interested in searching and reading information on multi-version articles. Current systems constrain the users to visualize either the latest revision of a given article, even though it may not be the most relevant, or the version at a specific date. Users, especially in universal knowledge management platforms like Wikipedia, may want to easily access more relevant versions or those of authors whom they trust. Filtering unreliable content is one of the benefits of our approach. It can be achieved easily by hiding the contributions of the offending source, for instance when a vandalism act is detected, or at query time to fit user preferences and trust in the contributors. Alternatively, to deal with misinformation, it seems useful to provide versions to users with information about their amount of uncertainty and the uncertainty of each part of their content. Last but not least, users at visualization time should be able to search for a document representing the outcome of combining parts (e.g., some of them might be incomplete, imprecise, and even uncertain taken apart) from different versions. We demonstrate in [7] an application of these new modes of interaction to Wikipedia revisions: an article is no longer considered as the last valid revision, but as a merge of all possible (uncertain) revisions.

Approach. Since version control is primordial in uncertain web-scale collaborative systems, representing and evaluating uncertainties throughout data version management becomes crucial for enhancing collaboration and for overcoming problems such as conflict resolution and information reliability management. In this paper, we propose an uncertain XML version control model tailored to multi-version tree-structured documents in open collaborative editing contexts. Data, that is, office documents, HTML or XHTML documents, structured Wiki formats, etc., manipulated within the given application scenarios are tree-like or can be easily translated into this form; XML is a natural encoding for tree-structured data. Work related to XML version control has focused on change detection [17, 21, 27, 32, 39]. Only some, for instance [31, 33, 35], have proposed an extensive semi-structured data model aware of version control; see Section 6 for details. Uncertainty management in XML has received a great attention in the probabilistic database community, especially for data integration purposes. A set of elaborate uncertain (probabilistic) XML data models [9, 22, 30, 37] with several distinct semantics of probability distributions over data items, has been proposed. [9] and [22] follow a general probabilistic XML representation system defining the concept of probabilistic documents (abbr. p-documents) which generalizes previously proposed uncertain XML models.

In our model, we handle uncertain data through a probabilistic XML model as a basic component of our version control framework. Each version of a shared document is represented by an XML tree. At the abstract level, we consider a multi-version XML document with uncertain data based on random events, XML edit scripts attached to them and a directed acyclic graph of these events. For a concrete representation the whole document, with its different versions, is modeled as a probabilistic XML document representing an XML tree whose edges are annotated by propositional formulas over random events. Each propositional formula models both the semantics of uncertain editions (insertion and deletion) performed over a given part of the document and its provenance in the version control process. Uncertainty is evaluated using the probabilistic model and the reliability measure associated to each source, each contributor, or each editing event, resulting in an uncertainty measure on each version and each part of the document. The directed acyclic graph of random events maintains the history of document evolution by keeping track of its different states and their derivation relationships. As last major contribution of this paper, we show that standard version control operations, in particular update operation, can be implemented directly as operations on the probabilistic XML model; efficiency with respect to deterministic version control systems like Git and Subversion is demonstrated on real-world datasets.

Outline. After some preliminaries in Section 2, we review the probabilistic XML model we use in Section 3. We detail the proposed probabilistic XML version control model and some strong properties thereof in Section 4. In Section 5, we demonstrate the efficiency of our model with respect to deterministic version control systems through measures on real-world datasets, and we describe some of the content filtering capabilities (Cf. Section 5.2) of our approach. Finally, we review some related work in Section 6. Initial ideas leading to this work were presented as a PhD workshop article in [13]; the description of the model, with translations of version control operations into operations on the probabilistic XML model, proofs of translation correctness, and experimental validation, are fully novel.

2. PRELIMINARIES

In this section, we present some basic version control notions and the semi-structured XML document model underlying our proposal. A *multi-version document* refers to a set of versions of the same document handled within a version control process. Each version of the document represents a given state (instance) of the evolution of this versioned document. A typical version control model is built on the following common notions.

Document version. A version is a conventional term that refers to a document copy in document-oriented version control systems. The different versions of a document are related by derivation operations. A derivation consists of creating a new version by first copying a previously existing one before performing modifications. Some versions, representing variants, are in a derivation relationship with the same origin. The variants (parallel versions) characterize a non-linear editing history with several distinct branches of the same multi-version document. In this history, a branch is a linear sequence of versions. Instead of storing the complete content of each version, most version control approaches only maintains *diffs* between states, together with meta-information on states. These states (or commits in Git world [15]) model different sets of changes that are explicitly validated at distinct stages of the version control process. A state also comes with information about the context (e.g., author, date, comment) in which these modifications are done. As a consequence, each version depends on the complete history leading up to a given state. We will follow here the same approach for modeling the different versions of a document within our framework.

Version Space. Since the content of each version is not fully saved, there must be manner to retrieve it when needed. The version space represents the editing history over a versioned document (e.g., wiki version history as given in [34]). It maintains necessary information related to the versions and their derivations. As mentioned above, a derivation relationship implies at least one input version (several incoming versions for merge operations) and an output version. Based on this, we model similarly to [15] a version space of any multi-version document as a *directed acyclic graph*.

Unordered XML Tree Documents. Our motivating applications handle mostly tree-structured data. As a result, we consider data as unordered XML trees. Note that the proposed model can be extended to ordered trees (this may require restricting the set of valid versions to those complying with a specific order, we leave the details for future work); we choose unordered trees for convenience of exposition given that in many cases order is unimportant. Let us assume a finite set $\mathcal{L}$ of strings (i.e., labels or text data) and a finite set $\mathscr{I}$ of identifiers such that $\mathcal{L} \cap \mathscr{I} = \emptyset$. In addition, let Φ and α be respectively a labeling function and an identifying function. Formally, we define an *XML document* as an *unordered, labeled* tree $\mathscr{T}$ over identifiers in $\mathscr{I}$ with α and Φ mapping each node $x \in \mathscr{T}$ respectively to a unique identifier $\alpha(x) \in \mathscr{I}$ and to a string $\Phi(x) \in \mathcal{L}$. The tree is unranked, i.e., the number of children of each node in $\mathscr{T}$ is not assumed to be fixed. Given an XML tree $\mathscr{T}$, we define $\Phi(\mathscr{T})$ and $\alpha(\mathscr{T})$ as respectively the set of its node strings and the set of its node identifiers. For simplicity, we will assume all trees have the same root node (same label, same identifier).

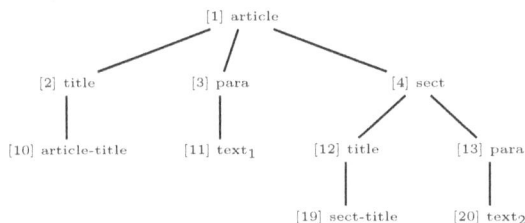

Figure 1: Example XML tree $\mathscr{T}$: Wikipedia article

Example 2.1 *Figure 1 depicts an XML tree $\mathscr{T}$ representing a typical Wikipedia article. The node identifiers are inside square brackets below node strings. The title of this article is given in node 10. The content of the document is structured in sections ("sect") with their titles and paragraphs ("para") containing the text data.*

XML Edit Script. Based on unique identifiers, we consider two basic edit operations over the specified XML document

model: node *insertions* and *deletions*. We denote an insertion by $\text{ins}^{i,\,x}$ whose semantics over any XML tree consists of inserting node x (we suppose x is not already in the tree) as a child of a certain node y satisfying $\alpha(y) = i$. If such a node is not found in the tree, the operation does nothing. Note that an insertion can concern a subtree, and in this case we simply refer with x to the root of this subtree. Similarly, we introduce a deletion as del^i where i is the identifier of the node to suppress. The delete operation removes the targeted node, if it exists, together with its descendants, from the XML tree. We conclude by defining an XML edit script, $\Delta = <u_1, u_2, \ldots, u_i>$, as a sequence of a certain number of elementary edit operations u_j (each u_j, with $1 \leq j \leq i$, being either an insertion or a deletion) to carry out one after the other on an XML document for producing a new one. Given a tree $\mathscr{T}$, we denote the outcome of applying an edit script Δ over $\mathscr{T}$ by $[\mathscr{T}]^\Delta$. Even though in this work we rely on persistent identifiers on tree nodes to define edit operations, the semantics of these operations could be extended to updates expressed by queries, especially useful in distributed collaborative editing environments where identifiers may not be straightforward to share.

3. PROBABILISTIC XML

We briefly introduce in this section the probabilistic XML representation system we use as a basis of our uncertain version control system. For more details, see [9] for the general framework and [22] for the specific PrXML^{fie} model we used. These representation systems are originally intended for XML-based applications such as Web data integration and extraction. For instance, when integrating various semi-structured Web catalogs containing personal data, some problems such as overlapping or contradiction are frequent. Typically, one can find for the same person name two distinct affiliations in different catalogs. A probabilistic XML model is used to automatically integrate such data sources by enumerating all possibilities: (a) the system considers each incoming source; (b) it maps its data items with the existing items in the probabilistic repository to find correspondences and; (c) giving that, it represents the matches as a set of possibilities. The resolution of conflicts is thus postponed to query time, where each query will return a set of possibilities together with their probabilities. The intuition is that resolving semantic issues before an effective integration is unfeasible in this situation. On one hand, it is often a tedious and error-prone resolution process. On the other hand, there might not be any certain knowledge about the reliability of the sources, and data completeness.

p-Documents. A *probabilistic XML representation system* is a compact way of representing probability distributions over possible XML documents; in the case of interest here, the probability distribution is finite. Formally, a probabilistic XML distribution space, or px-space, $\mathscr{S}$ over a collection of uncertain XML documents is a couple (D, p) where D is a nonempty finite set of documents and $p : D \to (0, 1]$ is a probability function that maps each document d in D to a rational number $p(d) \in (0, 1]$ such that $\Sigma_{d \in D}\, p(d) = 1$. A *p-document*, or *probabilistic XML document*, usually denoted $\widehat{\mathscr{P}}$, defines a compact encoding of a px-space $\mathscr{S}$.

PrXML^{fie}: *Syntax and Semantics.* We consider in this paper one specific class of p-documents, PrXML^{fie} [22] (where *fie* stands for *formula of independent events*); restricting to this particular class allows us to give a simplified presentation, see [9, 22] for a more general setting. Assume a set of *independent random Boolean variables*, or *event variables* in short, $b_1, b_2, \ldots, b_m$ and their respective probabilities $Pr(b_1), Pr(b_2) \ldots, Pr(b_m)$ of existence. A PrXML^{fie} p-document is an unordered, unranked, and labeled tree where every node (except for the root) x may be annotated with an arbitrary propositional formula $fie(x)$ over the event variables $b_1, b_2, \ldots, b_m$. Different formulas can share common events, i.e., there may be some correlation between formulas and the number of event variables in the formulas may vary from one node to another.

A valuation ν of the event variables $b_1 \ldots b_m$ induces over $\widehat{\mathscr{P}}$ one particular XML documents $\nu(\widehat{\mathscr{P}})$: the document where only nodes annotated with formulas valuated to true by ν are kept (nodes whose formulas are valuated to false by ν are deleted from the tree, along with their descendants). Given a p-document $\widehat{\mathscr{P}}$, the *possible worlds* of $\widehat{\mathscr{P}}$, denoted as $pwd(\widehat{\mathscr{P}})$ is the set of all such XML documents. The *probability* of a given possible world d of $\widehat{\mathscr{P}}$ is defined as the sum of the probability of the valuations that yield d. The set of possible worlds, together with their probabilities, defines the *semantics* of $\widehat{\mathscr{P}}$, the px-space $[\![\widehat{\mathscr{P}}]\!]$ associated to $\widehat{\mathscr{P}}$.

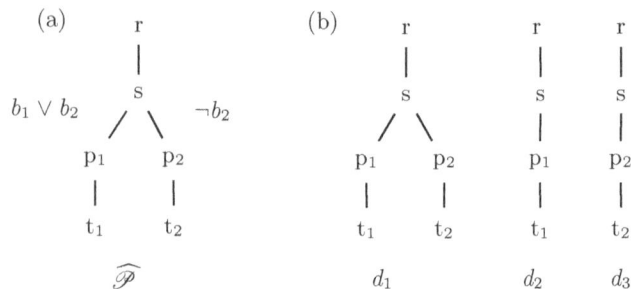

Figure 2: (a) PrXML^{fie} p-document $\widehat{\mathscr{P}}$; (b) Three possible worlds d_1, d_2 and d_3

Example 3.1 *Figure 2 sketches on the left-side a concrete PrXML^{fie} p-document $\widehat{\mathscr{P}}$ and on the right-side three possible worlds d_1, d_2 and d_3. Formulas annotating nodes are shown just above them: $b_1 \vee b_2$ and $\neg b_1$ are bound to nodes p_1 and p_2 respectively. The three possible worlds d_1, d_2 and d_3 are obtained by setting the following valuations of b_1 and b_2: (a) true and false; (b) true and true (or false and true); (c) false and false. At each execution of the random process, the distributional node chooses exactly the nodes whose formulas are evaluated at true given the valuation specified over event variables. Assuming a probability distribution over events, for instance $Pr(b_1) = 0.4$ and $Pr(b_2) = 0.5$, we derive the probability of the possible world d_1 as $Pr(d_1) = Pr(b_1) \times (1 - Pr(b_2)) = 0.4 \times (1 - 0.5) = 0.2$. We can compute similarly the probabilities of all other possible worlds.*

With respect to other probabilistic XML representation systems [9], PrXML^{fie} is very succinct (since arbitrary propositional formulas can be used, involving arbitrary correlations among events), i.e., exponentially more succinct than the models of [30, 37], and offers tractable insertions and deletions [22], one key requirement for our uncertain version control model. However, a non-negligible downside is that all non-trivial (tree-pattern) queries over this model are

#**P**-hard to evaluate [23]. This is not necessarily an issue, here, since we favor in our application efficient updates and retrieval of given possible worlds, over arbitrary queries.

Data Provenance. Uncertain XML management based on the PrXML^{fie} model also takes advantage of the various possible semantics of event variables in terms of information description. Indeed, besides uncertainty management, the model also provide support for keeping information about *data provenance* (or lineage) based on the event variables. Data provenance is information of traceability such as change semantics, responsible party, timestamp, etc., related to uncertain data. To do so, we only need to use the semantics of event variables as representing information about data provenance. As such, it is sometimes useful to use probabilistic XML representation systems even in the absence of reliable probability sources for individual events, in the sense that one can manipulate them as incomplete data models (i.e., we only care about possible worlds, not about their probabilities).

4. UNCERTAIN MULTI-VERSION XML

In this section we elaborate on our uncertain XML version control model for tree-structured documents edited in a collaborative manner. We build our model on three main concepts: version control events, a p-document, and a directed acyclic graph of events. We start by formalizing a multi-version XML document through a formal definition of its graph of version space and its set of versions. Then, we formally introduce the proposed model.

4.1 Multi-Version XML Documents

Consider the infinite set $\mathscr{D}$ of all XML documents with a given root label and identifier. Let $\mathscr{V}$ be a set of *version control events* $e_1, \ldots, e_n$. These events represent the different states of a tree. We associate to events contextual information about revisions (authorship, timestamp, etc.). To each event e_i is further associated an *edit script* Δ_i. Based on this, we formalize the graph of version space and the set of versions of any versioned XML document as follows.

Graph of version space. The *version space* is a rooted directed acyclic graph (DAG) $\mathscr{G} = (\mathscr{V} \cup \{e_0\}, \mathscr{E})$ where: (i) the initial version control event $e_0 \notin \mathscr{V}$, a special event representing the first state of any versioned XML tree, is the root of $\mathscr{G}$; (ii) $\mathscr{E} \subseteq \mathscr{V}^2$, defining the edges of $\mathscr{G}$, consists of a set of ordered couples of version control events. Each edge implicitly describes a directed derivation relationship between two versions. A *branch* of $\mathscr{G}$ is a directed path that implies a start node e_i and an end node e_j. The latter must be reachable from the former by traversing a set of ordered edges in $\mathscr{E}$. We refer to this branch by B_i^j. A *rooted branch* is a branch that starts at the root of the graph.

XML versions. An XML version is the document in $\mathscr{D}$ corresponding to a *set* of version control events, the set of events that made this version happen. In a deterministic version control system, this set always corresponds to a rooted branch in the version space graph. In our uncertain version control system, this set may be arbitrary. Let us consider the set $2^{\mathscr{V}}$ comprising all sub-parts of $\mathscr{V}$. The set of versions of a multi-version XML document is given by a mapping $\Omega : 2^{\mathscr{V}} \to \mathscr{D}$: to each sets of events corresponds a given tree (these trees are typically not all distinct). The function Ω

can be computed from edit scripts associated with events as follows:

- $\Omega(\emptyset)$ maps to the root-only XML tree of $\mathscr{D}$.
- For all i, for all $\mathscr{F} \subseteq 2^{\mathscr{V} \setminus \{e_i\}}$ $\Omega(\{e_i\} \cup \mathscr{F}) = [\Omega(\mathscr{F})]^{\Delta_i}$.

A multi-version XML document, $\mathscr{T}_{mv}$, is now defined as a pair $(\mathscr{G}, \Omega)$ where $\mathscr{G}$ is a DAG of version control events, whereas Ω is a mapping function specifying the set of versions of the document. In the following we propose a more efficient way to compute the version corresponding to a set of events, using a p-document for storage.

4.2 Uncertain Multi-Version XML Documents

A multi-version document will be *uncertain* if the version control events, staged in a version control process, come with *uncertainty* as in open collaborative contexts. By version control events with uncertainty, we mean random events leading to uncertain versions and content. As a consequence, we will rely on a *probability distribution over* $2^{\mathscr{V}}$, that will, together with the Ω mapping, imply a probability distribution over $\mathscr{D}$.

Uncertainty modeling. We model uncertainty in events by further defining a version control event e_i in $\mathscr{V}$ as a conjunction of semantically unrelated random Boolean variables $b_1, \ldots, b_m$ with the following assumptions: (i) a Boolean variable models a given source of uncertainty (e.g., the contributor) in the version control environment; (ii) all Boolean variables in each e_i are independent; (iii) a Boolean variable b_j reused across events correlates different version control events; (iv) one particular Boolean *revision* variable $b^{(i)}$, representing more specifically the uncertainty in the contribution, is not shared across other version control events and appears positively in e_i.

Probability Computation. We assume given a probability distribution over the Boolean random variables b_j's (this typically comes from a trust estimation in a contributor, or in a contribution), which induces a probability distribution over propositional formulas over the b_j's in the usual manner [22]. We now obtain the probability of each (uncertain) version d of as follows: $\mathrm{Pr}(d) = \mathrm{Pr}(\bigvee_{\substack{\mathscr{F} \subseteq \mathscr{V} \\ \Omega(\mathscr{F}) = d}} \mathscr{F})$ with the probability of each set of events $\mathscr{F} \subseteq \mathscr{V}$ given by:

$$\mathrm{Pr}(\mathscr{F}) = \mathrm{Pr}\left(\bigwedge_{e_j \in \mathscr{F}} e_j \wedge \bigwedge_{e_k \in \mathscr{V} \setminus \mathscr{F}} \neg e_k\right). \qquad (1)$$

Example 4.1 *Figure 3 sketches an uncertain multi-version XML document $\mathscr{T}_{mv}$ with four staged version control events. On the left-side, we have the version space $\mathscr{G}$. The right-side shows an example of four possible (uncertain) versions and their associated event set. We suppose that $\mathscr{T}_{mv}$ is initially a root-only document. The three first versions correspond to versions covered by deterministic version control systems, whereas the last one is generated by considering that the changes performed at an intermediate version control event, here e_2, as incorrect. One feature of our model is to provide the possibility for viewing and modifying these kinds of uncertain versions representing virtual versions. Only edits performed at the specified version control events are taken into account in the process of producing a version: in $\mathscr{T}_4$, the node r and the subtrees rooted at s_1, s_3 respectively introduced at e_0, e_1 and e_3 are present, while the subtree p_3 added at e_3 does not appear because its parent node s_2 cannot be*

found. Finally, given probabilities of version control events, we are able to measure the reliability of each uncertain version $\mathscr{T}_i$, for each $1 \leq i \leq 4$, based on its corresponding event set $\mathscr{F}_i$ (and all other event sets that map to the same tree).

We straightforwardly observe, for instance with the simple example in Figure 3, that the amount of possible (uncertain) versions of any uncertain multi-version document may grow rapidly (indeed, exponentially in the number of events). As a result, the enumeration and the handling of all the possibilities with the function Ω may become tedious at a certain point. To address this issue, we propose an efficient method for encoding in a compact manner the possible versions together with their truth values. Intuitively, a PrXML^{fie} p-document compactly models the set of possible versions of an uncertain multi-version XML document. As stressed in Section 3, a probabilistic tree based on propositional formulas provides interesting features for our setting. First, it describes well a distribution of truth values over a set of uncertain XML trees while providing a meaningful process to find back a given version and its probability. Second, it provides an update-efficient representation system, which is crucial in dynamic environments such as version-control–based applications.

4.3 Probabilistic XML Encoding

We introduce a general uncertain XML version control representation framework, denoted by $\widehat{\mathscr{T}_{mv}}$, as a couple $(\mathscr{G}, \widehat{\mathscr{P}})$ where (a) $\mathscr{G}$ is as before a DAG of events, representing the version space; (b) $\widehat{\mathscr{P}}$ is a PrXML^{fie} p-document with random Boolean variables $b_1 \ldots b_m$ representing efficiently all possible (uncertain) XML tree versions and their corresponding truth-values.

We now define the semantics of such an encoding as the uncertain multi-version document $(\mathscr{G}, \Omega)$ where $\mathscr{G}$ is the same and Ω is defined as follows. For all $\mathscr{F} \subseteq \mathscr{V}$, let B^+ be the set of all random variables occurring in one of the events of $\mathscr{F}$ and B^- be the set of all revision variables $b^{(i)}$'s for e_i not in $\mathscr{F}$. Let ν be the valuation of $b_1 \ldots b_m$ that sets variables of B^+ to true, variables of B^- to false, and other variables to an arbitrary value. We set $\Omega(\mathscr{F}) := \nu(\widehat{\mathscr{P}})$.

The following shows that this semantics is compatible with the px-space semantics of p-documents on the one hand, and the probability distribution defined by uncertain multi-version documents on the other hand.

Proposition 4.1 *Let $(\mathscr{G}, \widehat{\mathscr{P}})$ be an uncertain version control representation framework and $(\mathscr{G}, \Omega)$ its semantics as just defined. We further assume that all formulas occurring in $\widehat{\mathscr{P}}$ can be expressed as formulas over the events of $\mathscr{V}$ (i.e., we do not make use of the b_j's independently of version control events). Then the px-space $[\![\widehat{\mathscr{P}}]\!]$ defines the same probability distribution over $\mathscr{D}$ as Ω.*

The proof is straightforward and relies on Equation (1).

4.4 Updating Uncertain Multi-Version XML

We implement the semantics of standard update operations on top of our probabilistic XML representation system. An update over an uncertain multi-version document corresponds to the evaluation of some uncertain edits on a given (uncertain) version. With the help of a triple (Δ, e, e'), we refer to an update operation as $\mathsf{updOP}_{\Delta, e, e'}$ where Δ is an

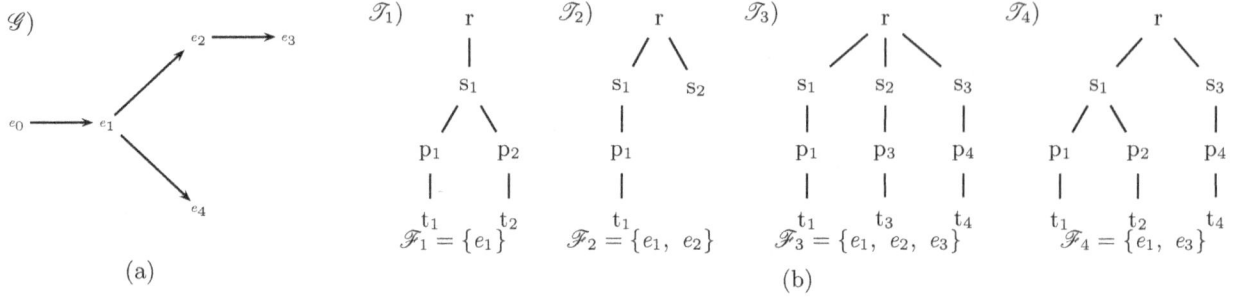

Figure 3: (a) Graph of Version Space; (b) Four versions and their corresponding truth-values

Input: $(\mathcal{G}, \widehat{\mathcal{P}})$, $\text{updOP}_{\Delta,e,e'}$
Output: updating $\mathcal{T}_{mv}$ in $\widehat{\mathcal{T}_{mv}}$
$\mathcal{G} := \mathcal{G} \cup (\{e'\}, \{(e, e')\})$;
foreach *(u in Δ)* **do**
  if $u = \text{ins}^{i,\,x}$ **then**
    $y := \text{findNodeById}\,(\widehat{\mathcal{P}}, i)$;
    if $\text{matchIsFound}(\mathcal{T}_y, x)$ **then**
      $fie_o(x) := \text{getFieOfNode}(x)$;
      $\text{setFieOfNode}\,(x, fie_o(x) \vee e')$;
    else
      $\text{updContent}(\widehat{\mathcal{P}}, \text{ins}^{i,\,x})$;
      $\text{setFieOfNode}(x, e')$;
  else if $u = \text{del}^i$ **then**
    $x := \text{findNodeById}\,(\widehat{\mathcal{P}}, i)$;
    $fie_o(x) := \text{getFieOfNode}(x)$;
    $\text{setFieOfNode}(x, fie_o(x) \wedge \neg e')$;
return $(\mathcal{G}, \widehat{\mathcal{P}})$;

Algorithm 1: Update algorithm

edit script, e is an existing version control event pointing to the edited version and e' is an incoming version control event evaluating the amount of uncertainty in this update. We formalize $\text{updOP}_{\Delta,\,e,\,e'}$ over $\mathcal{T}_{mv}$ as below.

$$\text{updOP}_{\Delta,\,e,\,e'}(\mathcal{T}_{mv}) := (\mathcal{G} \cup (\{e'\}, \{(e, e')\}),\ \Omega').$$

An update operation thus results in the insertion of a new node and a new edge in $\mathcal{G}$, and an extension of Ω with Ω' that we now define. For any subset $\mathcal{F} \subseteq \mathcal{V}'$ ($\mathcal{V}'$ is the set of nodes in $\mathcal{G}$ after the update), we have:

- if $e' \notin \mathcal{F}$: $\Omega'(\mathcal{F}) = \Omega(\mathcal{F})$;

- otherwise: $\Omega'(\mathcal{F}) = [\Omega(\mathcal{F} \setminus \{e'\})]^\Delta$.

What precedes gives a semantics to updates on uncertain multi-version documents; however, the semantics is not practical as it requires considering every subset $\mathcal{F} \subseteq \mathcal{V}'$. For a more usable solution, we perform updates directly on the p-document representation of the multi-version document. Algorithm 1 describes how such an update operation $\text{updOP}_{\Delta,e,e'}$ is performed on top of an uncertain representation $(\mathcal{G}, \widehat{\mathcal{P}})$. First, the graph is updated as before. Then, for each operation u in Δ, the algorithm retrieves the targeted node in $\widehat{\mathcal{P}}$ using findNodeById (typically this is a constant-time operation). According to the type of operation, there are two possibilities.

1. If u is an insertion of a node x, the algorithm checks if x does not already occur in $\widehat{\mathcal{P}}$, for instance by looking for a node with the same label (the function matchIs- Found searches a matching for x in the subtree $\mathcal{T}_y$ rooted

at y). If such a matching exists, getFieOfNode returns its current formula $fie_o(x)$ and the algorithm updates it to $fie_n(x) := fie_o(x) \vee e'$, specifying that x appears when this update is valid. Otherwise, updContent and setFieOfNode respectively inserts the node x in $\widehat{\mathcal{P}}$ and sets its associated formula as $fie_n(x) = e'$.

2. If u is a deletion of a node x, the algorithm gets its current formula $fie_o(x)$ and sets it to $fie_n(x) := fie_o(x) \wedge \neg e'$, specifying that x must be removed from possible worlds where this update is valid.

The rest of this section shows the correctness and efficiency of our approach: First, we establish that Algorithm 1 respects the semantics of updates. Second, we show that the behavior of deterministic version control systems can be simulated by considering only a specific kind of event set. Third, we characterize the complexity of the algorithm.

Proposition 4.2 *Algorithm 1, when ran on a probabilistic XML encoding* $\widehat{\mathcal{T}_{mv}} = (\mathcal{G}, \widehat{\mathcal{P}})$ *of a multi-version document* $\mathcal{T}_{mv} = (\mathcal{G}, \Omega)$, *together with an update operation* $\text{updOP}_{\Delta,e,e'}$, *computes a representation* $\text{updOP}_{\Delta,e,e'}(\widehat{\mathcal{T}_{mv}})$ *of the multi-version document* $\text{updOP}_{\Delta,e,e'}(\mathcal{T}_{mv})$.

PROOF. Let:
$\begin{cases} \text{updOP}_{\Delta,e,e'}(\widehat{\mathcal{T}_{mv}}) = (\mathcal{G}', \widehat{\mathcal{P}'}) \\ \text{updOP}_{\Delta,e,e'}(\mathcal{T}_{mv}) = (\mathcal{G}', \Omega') \end{cases}$ (it is clear that
the version space DAG is the same in both cases). We need to show that Ω' corresponds to the semantics of $\widehat{\mathcal{P}'}$; that is, if we note the semantics of $(\mathcal{G}', \widehat{\mathcal{P}'})$ as $(\mathcal{G}', \Omega'')$, we need to show that $\Omega' = \Omega''$. By definition, for $\mathcal{F} \subseteq \mathcal{V}'$, $\Omega'(\mathcal{F}) = \Omega(\mathcal{F})$ if $e' \notin \mathcal{F}$, and $\Omega'(\mathcal{F}) = [\Omega(\mathcal{F} \setminus \{e'\})]^\Delta$ otherwise. Let us distinguish these two cases.

In the first scenario implying subsets $\mathcal{F}$ which do not contain e', we have $\Omega'(\mathcal{F}) = \Omega(\mathcal{F})$. Since $\mathcal{T}_{mv}$ is the semantics of $\widehat{\mathcal{T}_{mv}}$, we know that $\Omega(\mathcal{F}) = \nu(\mathcal{F})$ for a valuation ν that sets the special revision variable b' corresponding to e' to false. Now, let us look at the document $\nu(\widehat{\mathcal{P}'})$. By construction the update algorithm does not delete any node from $\widehat{\mathcal{P}}$ but just inserts new nodes and modifies some formulas. Suppose that there exists a node $x \in \nu(\widehat{\mathcal{P}})$ such that $x \notin \nu(\widehat{\mathcal{P}'})$. Since $x \in \nu(\widehat{\mathcal{P}})$, x cannot be a new node in $\widehat{\mathcal{P}'}$. Thereby, its new formula $fie_n(x)$ after the update is either $fie_o(x) \vee e'$ or $fie_o(x) \wedge \neg e'$. In both cases, $fie_n(x)$ satisfies ν, because $fie_o(x)$ satisfies ν and ν sets b' (and therefore e') to false. This leads to a contradiction and we can conclude that for all node $x \in \nu(\widehat{\mathcal{P}})$, we have $x \in \nu(\widehat{\mathcal{P}'})$. Similarly, if a node x is in $\mathcal{F}(\widehat{\mathcal{P}'})$, because ν sets e' to false, x will also be in $\nu(\widehat{\mathcal{P}})$. Combining the two, $\Omega''(\mathcal{F}) = \nu(\widehat{\mathcal{P}'}) = \nu(\widehat{\mathcal{P}}) = \Omega(\mathcal{F})$.

The second scenario concerns subsets $\mathscr{F}'$ in which e' appears. We obtain a version $\Omega'(\mathscr{F}')$ by updating $\Omega(\mathscr{F}'\backslash\{e'\})$ with Δ. Let us set $\mathscr{F} = \mathscr{F}'\backslash\{e'\}$. There exists a valuation ν such that $\nu(\widehat{\mathscr{P}}) = \Omega$ (and thus, $\Omega'(\mathscr{F}') = [\nu(\widehat{\mathscr{P}})]^\Delta$) with ν setting all variables of events in $\mathscr{F}$ to true, and making sure that all other events are set to false. Let ν' be the extension of ν where all variables of e' are set to true. It suffices to prove that $[\nu(\widehat{\mathscr{P}})]^\Delta = \nu'(\widehat{\mathscr{P}'})$. First, it is clear that the nodes in $\nu(\widehat{\mathscr{P}})$ which are not modified by Δ are also in $\nu'(\widehat{\mathscr{P}'})$. Indeed, their associated formulas do not change in $\widehat{\mathscr{P}'}$, and hence the fact these satisfy ν are sufficient for selecting them in $\widehat{\mathscr{P}'}$ with the valuation ν'. Suppose now an operation u in Δ involving a node x: u either adds x as a child of a certain node y or deletes x. In the former case, if y exists in $\nu(\widehat{\mathscr{P}})$, then its formula satisfies ν and x is added in the document when it does not already exist. With Algorithm 1, u is interpreted in $\widehat{\mathscr{P}'}$ by the existence of x under y with an attached formula being either $fie_n(x) = e'$ (newly added) or $fie_n(x) = fie_o(x) \vee e'$ (reverted node). As a consequence, $\nu'(\widehat{\mathscr{P}'})$ selects x as in both possible expressions of $fie_n(x)$. Let us analyze the case where u is a deletion of x. If x is not present in $\nu(\widehat{\mathscr{P}})$, i.e., u changes nothing in this document. Through Algorithm 1, u results in a new associated formula set to $fie_n(x) = fie_o(x) \wedge \neg e$ for the node x in $\widehat{\mathscr{P}'}$. Obviously, we can see that x will not be in $\nu'(\widehat{\mathscr{P}'})$ because the satisfiability of $fie_n(x)$ requires the falseness of e' whose condition does not hold in $\mathscr{F}$. Now, if x is found in $\nu(\widehat{\mathscr{P}})$, u deletes the node, as well as its children, from the document. As a result, the outcome does not contain x, which is conform to the fact that $x \notin \nu'(\widehat{\mathscr{P}'})$. We have proved that for all node x in $[\nu(\widehat{\mathscr{P}})]^\Delta$, x is also in $\nu'(\widehat{\mathscr{P}'})$. By similar arguments, we can show that the converse is verified, i.e., for all node x in $\nu'(\widehat{\mathscr{P}'})$, x belongs to $[\nu(\widehat{\mathscr{P}})]^\Delta$. $\square$

The semantics of update is therefore the same, whether stated on uncertain multi-version documents, or implemented as in Algorithm 1. We now show that this semantics is compatible with the classical update operation of version control systems.

Proposition 4.3 *The formal definition of updating in uncertain multi-version documents implements the semantics of the standard update operation in deterministic version control systems when sets of events are restricted to rooted branches.*

PROOF. (Sketch) The update in our model changes the version space $\mathscr{G}$ similarly to a deterministic version control setting. As for its evaluation over the set of versions, we only need to show that the operation also produces a new version by updating the version mapping B_0^i (with e the ith version control event in $\mathscr{G}$) with Δ as in a deterministic formalism. For building the resulting version set, the operation as given above is defined such that for all subset $\mathscr{F} \subseteq \mathscr{V}$ with $e \in \mathscr{F}$, we carry out Δ on $\Omega(\mathscr{F})$ for producing a new version $\Omega'(\mathscr{F} \cup \{e'\})$. Amongst all the subsets satisfying this condition, obviously there is at least one which maps to B_0^i. $\square$

We conclude by showing our algorithm is fully scalable:

Proposition 4.4 *Algorithm 1 performs the update process over the representation of any uncertain multi-version XML*

document with a constant time complexity with respect to the size of the input document. The size of the output probabilistic tree grows linearly in the size of the update script.

PROOF. The first part of the algorithm consists in updating $\mathscr{G}$. This is clearly a constant-time operation, which results in a single new node and a single new edge in $\mathscr{G}$ for every edit script. As for the second part of the algorithm, i.e., the evaluation of the update script over the probabilistic tree, let $|\widehat{\mathscr{P}}|$ and $|\Delta|$ be respectively the size of the input probabilistic document $\widehat{\mathscr{P}}$ and the length of Δ. By implementing $\widehat{\mathscr{P}}$ as an amortized hash table, we execute a lookup of nodes in $\widehat{\mathscr{P}}$ based on `findNodeById` or `matchIsFound` in constant time. (`matchIsFound` requires storing hashes of all subtrees of the tree, but this data structure can be maintained efficiently – we omit the details here.) The upper bound of Algorithm 1 occurs when Δ consists only of insertions. Since the functions `getFieOfNode`, `updContent` and `setFieOfNode` also have constant execution costs, we can state that the overall running time of Algorithm 1 is only a function of the number of operations in Δ. As a result, we can conclude that the update algorithm performs in $O(1)$ with respect to the number of nodes in $\widehat{\mathscr{P}}$ and $\mathscr{G}$.

At each execution, Algorithm 1 will increase the input probabilistic tree by a size bounded by a constant for each update operation, together with the size of all inserts. To sum up, the size increase is linear in the size of the original edit script. $\square$

5. EVALUATION OF THE MODEL

This section describes the experimental evaluation of the proposed model, based on real-world applications. We first present a comparative study of our model with two popular version control systems Git and Subversion, in order to prove its efficiency. Then we describe the advances in terms of content filtering offered by our model.

All times shown are CPU time, obtained by running in-memory tests, avoiding disk I/O costs by putting all accessed file systems in a RAM disk. Measures have been carried out using the same settings for all three systems.

5.1 Performance analysis

We measured the time needed for the execution of two main operations: the commit and checkout of a version. The tests were conducted on Git, Subversion, and the implementation of our model (PrXML). The goal is to show the feasibility of our model rather then to prove that it is more efficient than the mentioned version control systems. We stress that, though for comparison purposes our system was tested in a deterministic setting, its main interest relies in the fact that it is able to represent uncertain multi-version documents, as we illustrate further in Section 5.2.

Datasets and Implementation. As datasets, we used the history of the master branches of the *Linux kernel development* [4] and the *Apache Cassandra project* [1] for the tests. These data represent two large file systems and constitute two examples of tree-structured data shared in an open and collaborative environment. The Linux kernel development natively uses Git. We obtained a local copy of its history by cloning the master development branch. We maintained up-to-date our local copy by pulling every day the latest changes from the original source. We followed a similar process with the Cassandra dataset (a Subversion repository).

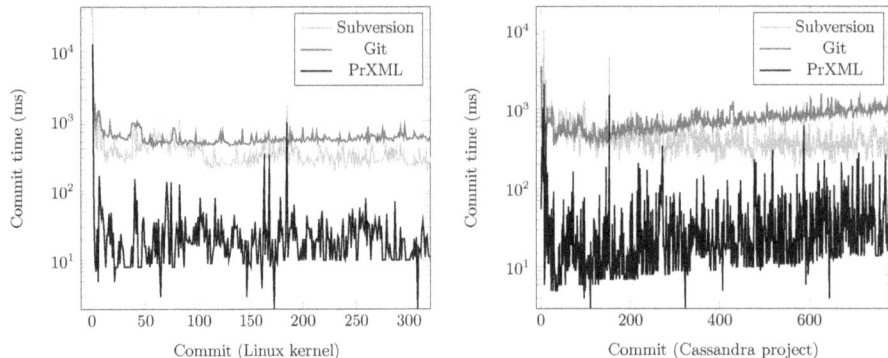

Figure 4: Measures of commit time over real-world datasets (logarithmic y-axis)

In total, each local branch has more than ten thousand commits (or revisions). Each commit materializes a set of changes, to the content of files or to their hierarchy (the file system tree). In our experiments, we focused on the commits applied to the file system tree and ignored content change. We determined the commits and the derivation relationships from Git and Subversion logs. We represented the file system in an XML document and we transposed the atomic changes to the file system into edit operations on the XML tree. To each insertion, respectively deletion, of a file or a directory in the file system corresponds an insertion, respectively a deletion, of a node in the XML tree.

We implemented our version control model (PrXML) in Java. We used the Java APIs SVNKit [5] and JGit [3] to set up the standard operations of Subversion and Git. The purpose was to perform all the evaluations in the same conditions. Subversion uses a set of log files to track the changes applied to the file system at the different commits. Each log file contains a set of paths and the change operations associated to each path. As for Git, it handles several versions of a file system as a set of related Git tree objects represented by the hashes of their content. A Git tree object represents a snapshot of the file system at a given commit.

Cost analysis. Figures 4 and 6 compare the cost of the *commit* and the *checkout* operations in Subversion, Git, and PrXML. The commit time indicates the time needed by the system to create a version (commit), whereas the checkout time corresponds to the time necessary to compute and retrieve the sought version. The obtained results show clearly that PrXML have good performance with respect to Git and Subversion systems. The experiments were done using the datasets obtained from the Linux Kernel and Cassandra projects, as indicated above. For both datasets, we observe in Figure 4 that our model has in general a low commit cost[1] (note that the y-axes are logarithmic on Figure 4).

An in-depth analysis of the results show that the commit costs depend in our model on the number of edit operations associated to the commits (see Figure 5), as implied by Proposition 4.4. However, PrXML remains efficient compared to the other systems, except for some few commits characterized by a large number of edits (at least one hundred edit operations). This can be explained by the fact that our model performs the edit operations over XML trees, whereas Git stores the hashes of the files indexed by the

---

[1]Our measures of the commit time in PrXML include the computation cost of the edit scripts Δ.

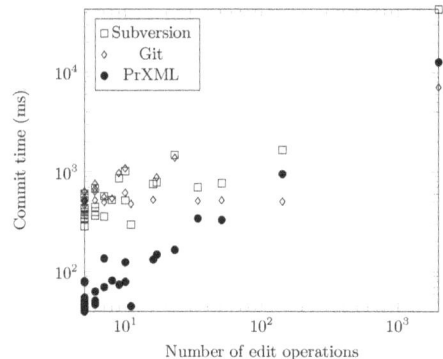

Figure 5: Commit time vs number of edit operations (for edit scripts of length ≥ 5)

directory names, and Subversion logs the changes together with the targeted paths in flat files. An insertion of a subtree (a hierarchy of files and directories) in the file system can be treated as a simple operation in Git and Subversion, whereas it requires a series of node insertions in our model.

Our model is able to generate linear versions (corresponding to event sets that are rooted branches) as well as arbitrary ones. However, traditional version control systems are only able to produce linear versions. As a consequence, in this paper we focused our experiments on retrieving linear versions for comparison purposes. Figure 6 shows the measures obtained for the checkout of successive versions in PrXML, Git and Subversion. The x-axis represents version numbers. Retrieving a version number n requires the reconstruction of all previous versions (1 to $n-1$). The results obtained show that our model is significantly more efficient than Subversion for both datasets (Linux Kernel and Cassandra projects). Compared to Git, PrXML has a lower checkout cost for initial versions, while it becomes less efficient in retrieving recent versions for the Cassandra dataset. Note that, traditional version control models mostly use reversible diffs [33] in order to speed up the process of reconstructing the recent versions in a linear history.

5.2 Filtering capabilities

Efficient evaluation of the uncertainty and automatic filtering of unreliable contents are two key issues for large scale collaborative editing systems. Evaluation of uncertainty is needed because a shared document can result from contri-

34

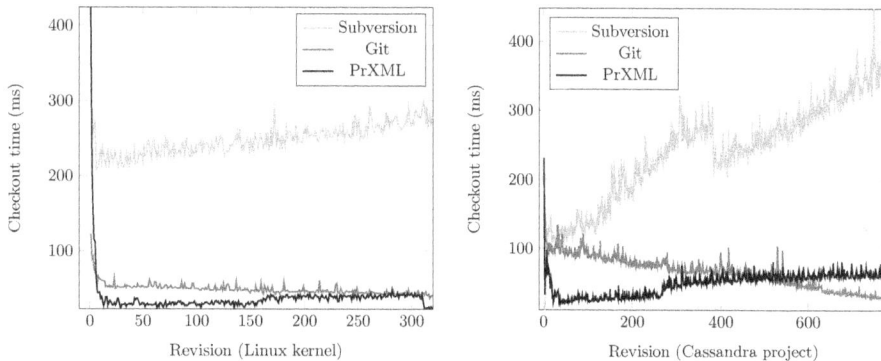

Figure 6: Measures of checkout time over real-world datasets (linear axes)

butions of different persons, who may have different levels of reliability. This reliability can be estimated in various ways, such as an indicator of the overall reputation of an author (possibly automatically derived from the content of contributions, cf. [10]) or the subjective trust a given reader has in the contributor. For popular collaborative platforms, like Wikipedia, an automatic management of conflicts is also necessary because the number of contributors is often very large. This is especially true for documents related to hot topics, where the number of conflicts and vandalism acts can evolve rapidly and compromise document integrity.

In our model, filtering unreliable contents can be done easily by setting to false the Boolean variables modeling the corresponding sources. This can be done automatically, for instance when a vandalism act is detected, or at query time to fit user preferences and opinion about the contributors. A shared document can also be regarded as the merge of all possible worlds modeled by the generated revisions. We demonstrate in [7] an application of these new filtering and interaction capabilities to Wikipedia revisions: an article is no longer considered as the last valid revision, but as a merge of all possible (uncertain) revisions. The overall uncertainty on a given part of the article is derived from the uncertainty of the revisions having affected it. Moreover, the user can view the state of a document at a given revision, removing the effect of a given revision or a given contributor, or focusing only on the effect of some chosen revisions or some reliable contributors.

We also tested the possibility for the users to handle more advanced operations over critical versions of articles such as vandalized versions. We chose the most vandalized Wikipedia articles (Cf. *Wikipedia:Most vandalized pages*), and we used our model to study the impact of considering as reliable some versions affected by vandalism. We succeeded in reconstructing the chosen articles as if the vandalism had never been removed; obtaining this special version of the article is very efficient, since it consists in applying a given valuation to the probabilistic document, which is a checkout operation whose timing is comparable to what is shown in Figure 6. Note that in the current version of Wikipedia, the content of vandalized versions is systematically removed from the presented version of an article, even if some users may want to visualize them for various reasons. Our experiments have shown that we can detect the vandalism as well as Wikipedia robots do, and automatically manage it in PrXML, keeping all uncertain versions available for checkout.

6. RELATED WORK

Our previous work. We present in [7,13] initial studies towards the design of an uncertain XML version control system: [7] is a demonstration system focusing on Wikipedia revisions and showing the benefits of integrating an uncertain XML version control approach in web-scale collaborative platforms; [13] is a PhD workshop paper with early ideas behind modeling XML uncertain version control.

Version Control Systems. While a lot of work was carried out on version control in object-oriented systems (e.g., [8, 11, 14, 19]), recent research and tools are focusing on document-oriented models. Many products, seen as *general-purpose systems*, are used for version control over different kind of documents. *Subversion, ClearCase, Git, BitKeeper,* and *Bazaar* are some examples of them. In general, the considered approaches do not take into account the semantics of the changes represented by the successive versions. The concern is the reconstruction of the committed versions, rather then the understanding of the evolution of the modeled world. In Subversion [18] and similar systems, version control is based on edit distance algorithms designed for flat text, whereas the Git family [15] of tools uses cryptographic approaches. For XML and structured documents, both techniques are inadequate because the semantics of the changes is crucial in this case. A lot of work was done on change detection on XML documents, and different *XML diff* tools have been developed [17,27,32]. An in-depth analysis of the proposed approaches can be founnd in [16]. Besides that, XML version control models such as [33] and [35] store all versions in the same XML document, and extend the XML schema of the latter with some elements used for the identification of each version. However, the drawback of these approaches is the redundancy of the content shared between different versions and the cost of the updates operations.

Probabilistic XML. Uncertainty handling in XML was originally associated to the problem of automatic Web data extraction and integration. In this context, uncertainty may have different origins: the extraction process, the unreliability of the data sources, the incompleteness of the data, etc. Several efforts have been made and some probabilistic approaches have been proposed (see [28] for a survey), especially the work of van Keulen et al. [36,37]. Then a representation system that generalizes all the existing models was proposed in [9] and [22]; we refer to [25] for a survey of the probabilistic XML literature.

7. CONCLUSION

We presented in this paper an uncertain XML version control model tailored to multi-version tree-structured documents, in open collaborative editing contexts. This is one of the first actual work focusing on concrete applications of the existing literature on probabilistic XML [9,22–25,30,37]. The comparison of our model to the most popular version control systems, done on real-world data, shows its efficiency. Moreover, our model offers new filtering and interaction capabilities which are crucial in open collaborative environments, where the data sources, the contributors and the shared content are inherently uncertain. The main direction for future developments is the support of more complex version control operations, notably *merging*. Similarly to insertions and deletions, it is possible to implement merging by directly modifying the p-document, leading to an efficient management of uncertain versions. At last, the model could be extended to also support other kinds of edit operations like *moves* of intermediate nodes in XML.

8. ACKNOWLEDGEMENTS

This work was partially supported by the Île-de-France regional DROD project, and the French government under the STIC-Asia program, CCIPX project. We would like to thank the anonymous reviewers for their valuable suggestions on improving this paper.

9. REFERENCES

[1] Cassandra Project. http://cassandra.apache.org/.
[2] Google Drive. https://drive.google.com/.
[3] Java Git. http://www.eclipse.org/jgit/.
[4] Linux Kernel. https://www.kernel.org/.
[5] [Sub]Versioning for Java. http://svnkit.com/.
[6] Wikipedia Platform. http://www.wikipedia.org/.
[7] T. Abdessalem, M. L. Ba, and P. Senellart. A probabilistic XML merging tool. In *EDBT*, 2011. Demonstration.
[8] T. Abdessalem and G. Jomier. VQL: A query language for multiversion databases. In *DBPL*, 1997.
[9] S. Abiteboul, B. Kimelfeld, Y. Sagiv, and P. Senellart. On the expressiveness of probabilistic XML models. *VLDB Journal*, 18(5), 2009.
[10] B. T. Adler and L. de Alfaro. A content-driven reputation system for the Wikipedia. In *WWW*, 2007.
[11] A. Al-Khudair, W. A. Gray, and J. C. Miles. Dynamic evolution and consistency of collaborative configurations in object-oriented databases. In *Proc. TOOLS*, 2001.
[12] K. Altmanninger, M. Seidl, and M. Wimmer. A survey on model versioning approaches. *IJWIS*, 5, 2009.
[13] M. L. Ba, T. Abdessalem, and P. Senellart. Towards a version control model with uncertain data. In *PIKM*, 2011.
[14] W. Cellary and G. Jomier. Consistency of versions in object-oriented databases. In *VLDB*, 1990.
[15] S. Chacon. Git Book. http://book.git-scm.com/.
[16] G. Cobéna and T. Abdessalem. A comparative study of XML change detection algorithms. In *Services and Business Computing Solutions with XML: Applications for Quality Management and Best Processes*. IGI Global, 2009.
[17] G. Cobéna, S. Abiteboul, and A. Marian. Detecting Changes in XML Documents. In *ICDE*, 2002.
[18] B. Collins-Sussman, B. W. Fitzpatrick, and C. M. Pilato. *Version Control with Subversion*. O'Reilly Media, 2008.
[19] R. Conradi and B. Westfechtel. Towards a uniform version model for software configuration management. In *System Configuration Management*, 1997.
[20] G. de la Calzada and A. Dekhtyar. On measuring the quality of Wikipedia articles. In *WICOW*, 2010.
[21] L. Khan, L. Wang, and Y. Rao. Change detection of XML documents using signatures. In *Real World RDF and Semantic Web Applications*, 2002.
[22] E. Kharlamov, W. Nutt, and P. Senellart. Updating Probabilistic XML. In *Updates in XML*, 2010.
[23] B. Kimelfeld, Y. Kosharovsky, and Y. Sagiv. Query evaluation over probabilistic XML. *VLDB Journal*, 18(5), 2009.
[24] B. Kimelfeld and Y. Sagiv. Modeling and querying probabilistic XML data. *SIGMOD Rec.*, 37(4), 2009.
[25] B. Kimelfeld and P. Senellart. Probabilistic XML: Models and complexity. In Z. Ma and L. Yan, editors, *Advances in Probabilistic Databases for Uncertain Information Management*. Springer-Verlag, 2013.
[26] A. Koc and A. U. Tansel. A survey of version control systems. In *ICEME*, 2011.
[27] T. Lindholm, J. Kangasharju, and S. Tarkoma. Fast and simple XML tree differencing by sequence alignment. In *DocEng*, 2006.
[28] M. Magnani and D. Montesi. A survey on uncertainty management in data integration. *J. Data and Information Quality*, 2, 2010.
[29] S. Maniu, B. Cautis, and T. Abdessalem. Building a signed network from interactions in Wikipedia. In *DBSocial*, 2011.
[30] A. Nierman and H. V. Jagadish. ProTDB: probabilistic data in XML. In *VLDB*, 2002.
[31] S. Rönnau and U. Borghoff. Versioning XML-based office documents. *Multimedia Tools and Applications*, 43, 2009.
[32] S. Rönnau and U. Borghoff. XCC: change control of XML documents. *CSRD*, 2010.
[33] L. I. Rusu, W. Rahayu, and D. Taniar. Maintaining versions of dynamic XML documents. In *WISE*, 2005.
[34] M. Sabel. Structuring wiki revision history. In *WikiSym*, 2007.
[35] C. Thao and E. V. Munson. Version-aware XML documents. In *DocEng*, 2011.
[36] M. van Keulen and A. de Keijzer. Qualitative effects of knowledge rules and user feedback in probabilistic data integration. *VLDB Journal*, 18, 2009.
[37] M. Van Keulen, A. de Keijzer, and W. Alink. A Probabilistic XML Approach to Data Integration. In *ICDE*, 2005.
[38] J. Voss. Measuring Wikipedia. In *ISSI*, 2005.
[39] Y. Wang, D. J. DeWitt, and J.-Y. Cai. X-Diff: An Effective Change Detection Algorithm for XML Documents. In *ICDE*, 2003.

LSEQ: an Adaptive Structure for Sequences in Distributed Collaborative Editing

Brice Nedelec, Pascal Molli, Achour Mostefaoui, Emmanuel Desmontils
LINA, 2 rue de la Houssinière
BP92208, 44322 Nantes Cedex 03
first.last@univ-nantes.fr

ABSTRACT

Distributed collaborative editing systems allow users to work distributed in time, space and across organizations. Trending distributed collaborative editors such as Google Docs, Etherpad or Git have grown in popularity over the years. A new kind of distributed editors based on a family of distributed data structure replicated on several sites called Conflict-free Replicated Data Type (CRDT for short) appeared recently. This paper considers a CRDT that represents a distributed sequence of basic elements that can be lines, words or characters (sequence CRDT). The possible operations on this sequence are the insertion and the deletion of elements. Compared to the state of the art, this approach is more decentralized and better scales in terms of the number of participants. However, its space complexity is linear with respect to the total number of inserts and the insertion points in the document. This makes the overall performance of such editors dependent on the editing behaviour of users. This paper proposes and models LSEQ, an adaptive allocation strategy for a sequence CRDT. LSEQ achieves in the average a sub-linear spatial-complexity whatever is the editing behaviour. A series of experiments validates LSEQ showing that it outperforms existing approaches.

Categories and Subject Descriptors

I.7.1 [**Document and Text Processing**]: Document and Text Editing—*Document management*; C.2.4 [**Computer-Communication Networks**]: Distributed Systems—*Distributed applications*; D.2.8 [**Software Engineering**]: Metrics—*Complexity measures*

Keywords

Distributed Documents; Document Authoring Tools and Systems; Distributed Collaborative Editing; Real-time Editing; Conflict-free Replicated Data Types

1. INTRODUCTION

Distributed collaborative editing systems [4, 5, 6] such as Google Docs, Etherpad or Git are now widely used and allow users to work distributed in time, space, and across organizations. A new kind of distributed editors [12, 20] appeared based on Conflict-Free Replicated Data Types (CRDTs) [11, 21, 16]. A CRDT is a distributed data type replicated over several sites [15, 14]. A CRDT cannot implement any centralized data structure but for instance can implement a counter, a set, a tree, etc. In this paper we consider a special family or CRDTs that implement a sequence of basic elements such as lines, words or characters that we call *sequence CRDT*. For our purpose and as a first step, we only consider two basic operations on a sequence, the insert and the delete operations. Compared to the state of the art, editors based on sequence CRDTs are more decentralized and scale better. However, they have a linear space-complexity with respect to the number of insertions. Consequently, they heavily depend on the editing behaviour. Some editing scenarios lead to a permanent loss in performance.

In order to preserve the total order on the elements of the sequence, a unique and immutable identifier is associated with each basic element of the structure (character, line or paragraph according to the chosen granularity). This allows distinguishing two classes of sequence CRDTs: (i) Fixed size identifier (also called the tombstones class). This class includes WOOT [11], WOOTO [20], WOOTH [1], CT [7], RGA [13], [23]. In this class, a tombstone replaces each suppressed element. Although it enjoys a fixed length for identifiers and it has a space complexity which depends on the number of operations. For example, a document with an history of a million operations and finally containing a single line can have as much as 499999 tombstones. Garbaging tombstones requires costly protocols in decentralized distributed systems. (ii) Variable-size identifiers. This class includes for example Logoot [21]. It does not require tombstones, but its identifiers can grow unbounded. Consequently, although it does not require garbage protocols, its space complexity remains till now linear with the number of insert operations. Thus, it is possible to have only a single element in the sequence having an identifier of length 499999. Treedoc [12] uses both tombstones and variable size identifiers but relies on a complex garbage protocol when identifiers grow too much.

In this paper, we propose a new approach, called LSEQ, that belongs to the variable-size identifiers class of sequence CRDTs. Compared to the state of the art, LSEQ is an adaptive allocation strategy with a sub-linear upper-bound in its spatial complexity. We experimented LSEQ on synthetic sequences and real documents. In both cases, LSEQ outperforms existing approaches.

The remainder of the paper is organized as follows. Section 2 delineates the background on variable-size identifiers class of sequence CRDTs and motivates this work. Then, Section 3 details LSEQ and the three parameters that control the growth and the selection of the identifiers. It describes each parameter with its aim and its defect. Also, how their composition overcomes their respective weaknesses. Section 4 validates the approach by showing the effect of each one of the three parameters of LSEQ and also by comparing the proposed approach to Logoot. Finally, Section 5 reviews related works.

2. PRELIMINARIES

Distributed collaborative editing systems consider a sequence of characters replicated on n sites. Each site manages a local copy of the sequence called local replica. At some moments, the local replica can differ from some other sites' local replica. Each site can *insert* and *delete* characters in the sequence without any locking mechanism. Then, all sites exchange and deliver the operations. When any site delivers an insert operation, the state of the local replica may be different from the state of another replica.

The system is correct if: (i) It converges i.e. all local replicas of the sequence are equal when the system is idle. It corresponds to the eventual consistency property [8]. (ii) It preserves all partial order relations $\prec$ between characters. If a site inserts the character x between the characters a and b ($a \prec x \prec b$), this relation is preserved on each sites' replica. It corresponds to the property of intention preservation in Operational Transformation algorithms [19] used by Google Docs.

Let us illustrate this with an example. Assume that all the replicas of a sequence of characters are equal and that the sequence looks like ...*abcd*.... Consider that a site inserts the character e between b and c and also consider that at the same moment, another site inserts a character f between b and c. It results in two relations $b \prec e \prec c$ and $b \prec f \prec c$. Once every site has delivered all the changes on their local replica, the union of these two relations merges into a partial relation without any precedence between e and f. Consequently, two final states are possible *abefcd* and *abfecd*. The role of the sequence CRDTs is to build a linear extension of the partial order formed by the intentions of all users to obtain a unique total order.

Variable-size sequence CRDTs encode order relations into identifiers. For example, the operation $insert(a = 10 \prec x \prec b = 15)$ can be sent as $insert(x, 12)$. This strategy does not require keeping tombstones, however it is easy to see that identifiers can grow quickly and significantly degrade the overall performance of the system. In the worst case, the system requires to re-balance identifiers implying the use of a consensus algorithm.

In this paper, we focus on keeping the identifiers as small as possible hence avoiding any costly protocol to re-balance them. Definition 1 states a document as a set of pairs (elt, id) where elt can be a character or a line and id are unique immutable identifiers defined on the set of all possible identifiers $\mathcal{I}$. $\mathcal{I}$ has an order relation $<$ which is dense and strictly totally ordered i.e. if $x, y \in \mathcal{I}$ and $x < y$ then $\exists z \in \mathcal{I}, z \neq x, z \neq y, x < z < y$. $alloc(p, q)$ is the allocation strategy function that generates $id \in \mathcal{I}$. In Definition 2, we state that an id is a sequence of numbers, $id_1 < id_2$ if id_1 precedes id_2 in lexicographic order. This sequence is an efficient way to represent a dense order.

DEFINITION 1 (MODEL OF A DOCUMENT).
A document is a set $\mathcal{D} = \{(elt, id)\}$ *with two operations:*
- *insert(p $\in \mathcal{I}$, elt, q $\in \mathcal{I}$):- $\mathcal{D} \cup \{(elt, id_{elt})\}$*
  where $id_{elt} = alloc(p, q)$ with $p < id_{elt} < q$
- *delete(id $\in \mathcal{I}$):- $\mathcal{D}/\{(elt, id)\}$*

DEFINITION 2 (VARIABLE-SIZE IDENTIFIER). *A variable-size identifier id is a sequence of numbers* $id = [p_1.p_2 \ldots p_n]$ *which can designate a path in a tree*[1].

In Figure 1, we represent a document as a tree where each identifier is a path from the root to a leaf. In this example, each level has a maximum capacity (arity of the tree node) set to 100. A leaf is an element of the sequence. For instance, [10.13] is an identifier referencing the element b. Assume a user wants to insert an element z between two existing elements identified by p and q:
- if $p = [11]$ and $q = [14]$, there is room for insertion. Both identifiers [12] and [13] are valid choices for the new element.
- if $p = [14]$ and $q = [15]$, there is no room at this level. Since the model does not have further levels, the allocation function *alloc* initiates a new level. Then, it chooses among this bunch of newly available identifiers: between [14.0] and [14.99].

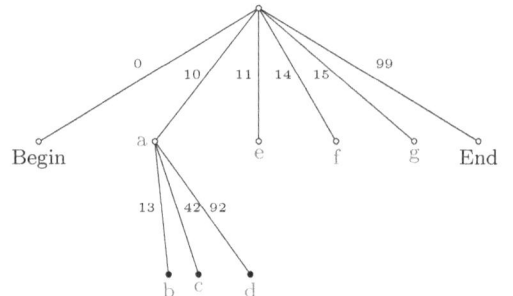

Figure 1: Underlying tree model of a variable-size identifiers sequence CRDT. Depth-1 contains four identifiers [10], [11], [14] and [15] labeling the elements a, e, f and g respectively. Also, depth-1 contains the bounds of the sequence $\langle[0], Begin\rangle$ and $\langle[99], End\rangle$. Depth-2 contains three identifiers [10.13], [10.42], and [10.92] labelling b, c and d respectively.

2.1 Allocation strategies

The Logoot paper [21] already highlighted the importance of allocation strategies (*alloc*). Indeed, experiments concerned two strategies. (1) *Random*: randomly choosing between the identifiers of the two neighbours. It delivers poor performance because the identifiers quickly saturate

---

1. Identifiers should include site ID to ensure the uniqueness property. However, for clarity purposes and in order to focus on allocation strategy, we did not include any site ID in this definition.

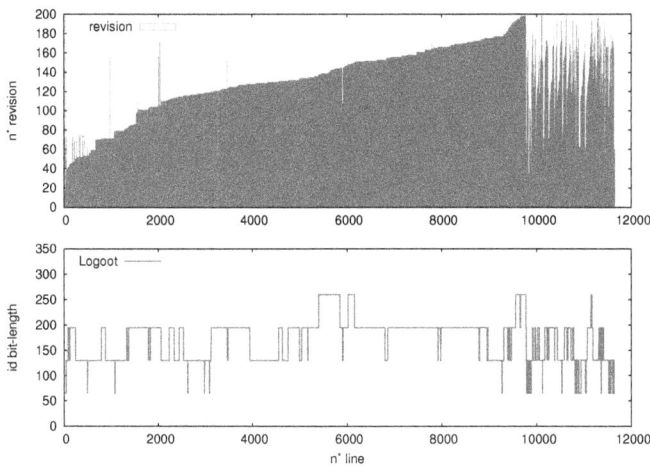

(a) A page of 12k lines mostly edited at the end.   (b) A page of 170 lines mostly edited at the beginning.

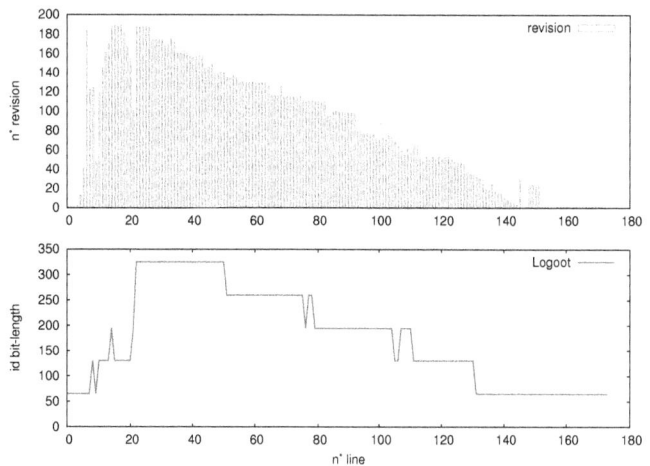

Figure 2: Experiments made on a Wikipedia pages. The top figure shows the spectrum of the page (revision number of each line). The bottom figure shows the bit-length of the identifier assigned to each line. The allocation strategy is *boundary* from the Logoot approach.

the space, resulting in the creation of new levels. As consequence, the size of identifiers grows quickly. (2) *Boundary*: randomly choosing between the identifiers of the two neighbours bounded by a *boundary* maximum value. The strategy allocates the new identifiers closer to their preceding identifier. Of course, it works well when the editions are performed right-to-left.

Figures 2a and 2b show the editing behaviour and the bit-length of allocated identifiers on two Wikipedia pages. The top part shows the spectrum associated with the pages. A spectrum gives an overview of the editing behaviour associated with a page. It gives the revision number of each line of a document, i.e., the relative date of their insert operation. As the left spectrum suggests, most of the insert operations situate the new elements at the end of the document, i.e., the last lines of the page are more recent. On the opposite, the second spectrum shows that most of the insert operations situates the newest elements at the beginning of the document. The bottom figures associate the bit-length of the identifier of each line of the document using the *boundary* strategy. In the first figure, we consider a page of 12k lines. Identifiers do not exceed 256 bits and they are well spread between levels $[1-4]$. It leads to a satisfying average of 169.7 bits/id. On the contrary, the editing behaviour on the second document (see figure 2b) that has only 170 lines does not fulfills the right-to-left editing behaviour assumed by the *boundary* strategy. In this case, we observe, on an existing document, the worst-case of linear growth of the size of identifiers. The average bit-length is 172.25 bits/id over 5 levels.

2.2 Issues and motivations

Most of existing CRDTs' allocation strategies make the assumption of right-to-left and top-to-bottom editing behaviour. This strong hypothesis allows better space management but other behaviours may lead to a quick decrease in performance. Therefore, it makes the distributed collaborative editor unsafe.

In order to build an efficient distributed collaborative editor based on a sequence CRDT, we need an adaptive allocation function *alloc*, i.e., an allocation strategy independent of an editing behaviour. *The unpredictability of the editing behaviour makes the allocation of identifiers challenging. At any time, the CRDT knows what happened in the past and the current operations. Still, inferring the upcoming operations is complex if not impossible.*

DEFINITION 3 (PROBLEM STATEMENT).
Let $\mathcal{D}$ be a document on which n insert operations have been performed. Let $\mathcal{I}(\mathcal{D}) = \{id | (\_, id) \in \mathcal{D}\}$. The function $alloc(id_p, id_q)$ should provide identifiers such as:

$$\sum_{id \in \mathcal{I}} \frac{log_2(id)}{n} < O(n)$$

The problem statement concerns the allocation function *alloc* which should have a sub-linear upper-bound in its space complexity. Such function would greatly improve the current state of art since the document does not require any additional costly protocol: the average size of identifiers being under an acceptable bound.

3. LSEQ ALLOCATION FUNCTION

LSEQ applies a very simple strategy: each time it creates a new level in the tree between two identifiers p and q, it doubles the base of this depth and it randomly chooses a strategy among *boundary+* and *boundary-*. *boundary+* allocates from p plus a fixed boundary, *boundary-* allocates from q minus a fixed boundary. The boundary never changes whatever the depth of the tree.

The following idea is the foundation of this approach: as it is complex to predict the editing behaviour, the principle is to sacrifice some depths of the tree with the certainty that the reward will compensate the loss. In other words, if LSEQ chooses the wrong strategy at a given depth, it will eventually choose the right one in the next depths. Since it doubles the base at each new depth, when the right strategy is found, it will overwhelm the cost of the lost depths.

3.1 Base Doubling

Logoot's [21] underlying allocation strategy always uses the same base to allocate its identifiers. With regard to the tree representation, it means that the arity is set to *base*. A high base value is not profitable if the number of insert operations in this part of the sequence is low. On the contrary, keeping a constant base value when the number of insert operations starts to be very high does not allow to fully benefit of the *boundary* strategy. For instance, Figure 2a presents experimental results from a Wikipedia page that has 12k lines which justifies the usage of a large base unlike Figure 2b with only 170 lines. Knowing the dilemma, the objective is to adapt the base according to the number of insertions in order to make a better reflection of the actual size of the document. Since it is impossible to know *a priori* the size of the document, the idea is to start with a small base due to the empty sequence, and then to double it when and where necessary, i.e. when the depth of identifiers increases.

Doubling the base at each depth implies an exponential growth of the number of available identifiers. Thus, the model corresponds to the exponential trees [3, 17, 2] and consequently it benefits of their complexities. An exponential tree of depth k can store up to $N_k = N_{k-1} + k * k!$ identifiers where $N_1 = base$. In other words, the arity of a node depends of its depth: a node has twice more children than its parent node, and the root has *base* children.

Knowing this exponential tree model, the binary representation of the identifier is $\Sigma_{i=1}^{id.size} b * 2^i$ where b is the initial base (conveniently a power of 2). Practically, if the initial base is 2^4 then, there are 2^{4+1} possibilities to choose an identifier at depth 1, 2^{4+2} at depth 2, etc.

The base doubling relies on the following assumption: the lack of space triggers the growth of identifiers. Therefore, an inefficient allocation strategy will entail an excessive growth of the identifier size as the system doubles the base frequently and the additional depths are more and more costly.

3.2 Allocation Strategies

[21] introduced two allocation strategies: *boundary* and *random*. In the experiments, the former outperforms the latter. However, the *boundary* strategy is heavily application dependent. If a user mainly performs insert operations at the end of the document the allocation will perform well. However, front editing will cause a quick linear growth of the size of identifiers.

With LSEQ, we introduce the allocation strategy named *boundary–*. Basically, this strategy is the opposite of the original *boundary* strategy. In this paper, we rename *boundary* to *boundary+*. Let us consider an insert operation between two elements with the identifiers p and q. While the *boundary+* strategy preferably allocates a position near the preceding identifier p, the *boundary–* strategy allocates a position near the succeeding identifier q. Indeed, *boundary–* starts from position q and subtracts a boundary value instead of starting from position p and adding a boundary value. The arithmetic operation explains the names given to these strategies. Figure 3 shows the results obtained by these two strategies with the same neighbours and random value. The left figure shows the *boundary+* strategy which ends up with [50.11] while the right figure shows the *boundary–* strategy which ends up with [50.89]. They leave free space

for future insertions of 88 identifiers at the end and at the beginning respectively.

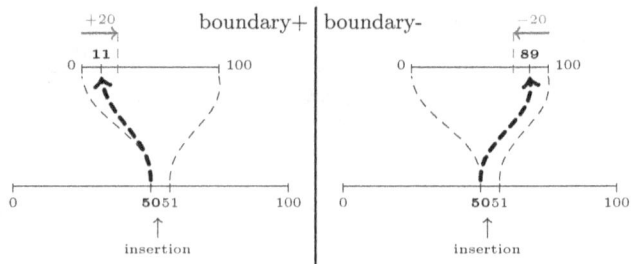

Figure 3: Choice of the digit part of identifiers in *boundary+* (left) and *boundary–* (right). In both cases: constant base is set to 100, boundary value is set to 20 and the random number is 11. The results are [50.11] (*boundary+*) and [50.89] (*boundary–*).

As expected, while the *boundary+* algorithm handles the end editing, the *boundary–* algorithm aims the front editing. They both have an antagonist weakness. Thus, *boundary–* cannot be used alone safely, just like *boundary+*.

3.3 Strategy choice

Current variable-size sequence CRDTs rely on a unique strategy that is not versatile in the sense that it does not adapt to all editing behaviour. As it is impossible to know *a priori* the editing behaviour and then, obtain the best strategy for every sequence, LSEQ randomly alternates between *boundary+* and *boundary–*. Thus, when LSEQ increases the identifier size, it has $\frac{1}{2}$ chance to choose either *boundary+* or *boundary–*. This kind of choice implies lost depths but the main idea is: some depths are lost indeed, nevertheless it is acceptable if the reward compensates the losses.

Algorithm 1 details the allocation function LSEQ. The departure base is set to 2^4 (depth-0) and the *boundary* to 10. The collection S stores the strategy choices. It starts empty. Three parts compose the algorithm. (1) The first part processes the interval between the two identifiers p and q at each depth until one identifier at least can be inserted. The step limits the interval where *alloc* will allocate the new identifier. (2) The second part determines the allocation strategy. If the function did not allocate any identifiers at this depth yet, it randomly chooses among *boundary+* and *boundary–*. Then it saves this choice for future decisions in S. (3) The final part of the algorithm constructs the new identifier. Depending on the strategy, it draws a random value using the *step* previously processed, and adds/subtracts this value to the *prefix* of p/q at the wanted depth. The *prefix* function takes an identifier *id* as argument, and copies it until it reaches *depth*. If the identifier size is smaller than the requested depth, the function appends a zero to the copy for each missing depth. Each number in the sequence that composes the identifier must be carefully encoded in the base depending on the depth. Line 35 refers to *base(cpt)*. It is a very simple function that computes the base value at a given depth (*cpt*). Thus, $0_{base(cpt)}$ means that the binary representation of 0 uses $log_2(base(cpt))$ bits. Consequently, the add and the subtract operations do not require additional computation compared to regular arithmetic operations.

Figure 4 illustrates the allocation strategy LSEQ by showing its underlying tree model. First the empty sequence

Algorithm 1 LSEQ allocation function

```
 1: let boundary := 10;          ▷ Any constant
 2: let S := {};                 ▷ map<depth,boolean>
 3:       ▷ true: boundary+
 4:       ▷ false: boundary−
 5:
 6: function ALLOC(p, q ∈ I)
 7:     let depth := 0;
 8:     let interval := 0;
 9:     while (interval < 1) do     ▷ Not enough for 1 insert
10:         depth + +;
11:         interval := prefix(q, depth) − prefix(p, depth) − 1;
12:     end while
13:     let step := min(boundary, interval);    ▷ Process the
    maximum step to stay between p and q
14:
15:     if not(S.exist(depth)) then     ▷ add the new entry
16:         let rand := RandBool();
17:         S.set(depth, rand);
18:     end if
19:     if S.get(depth) then     ▷ boundary+
20:         let addVal := RandInt(0, step) + 1;
21:         let id := prefix(p, depth) + addVal;
22:     else                     ▷ boundary−
23:         let subVal := RandInt(0, step) + 1;
24:         let id := prefix(q, depth) − subVal;
25:     end if
26:     return id;
27: end function
28:
29: function PREFIX(id ∈ I, depth ∈ ℕ*)
30:     let idCopy := [ ];
31:     for (cpt := 1 to depth) do
32:         if (cpt < id.size) then     ▷ Copy the value
33:             idCopy = idCopy.append(id.at(cpt));
34:         else        ▷ Add 0 encoded in the right base
35:             idCopy = idCopy.append(0_{base(cpt)});
36:         end if
37:     end for
38:     return idCopy;
39: end function
```

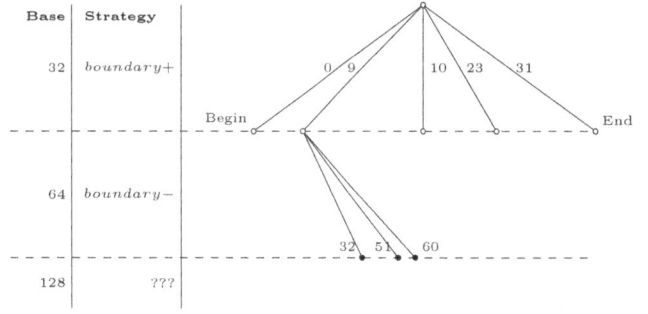

Figure 4: Underlying tree model of LSEQ containing three identifiers at depth-1. The randomness makes the first and second elements very close regarding their identifiers ([9] and [10]). The sequence requests three other elements between these two. The chosen strategy is *boundary−* and since LSEQ doubles the base at each depth, it allocates the fresh identifiers closer of [10.64].

4. EXPERIMENTATION

This experimentation section is comprised of two parts. The first part focuses on highlighting the behaviour of LSEQ on extreme cases. The measurements capture the effect of a large number of insert operations on the identifier sizes. We synthesized different editing behaviours. Analyses are made step by step to bring out the contribution of each component to LSEQ. Previous experiments [1, 12, 21] focused on average setups and did not consider such extreme setups.

The second part of experiments aims to validate if LSEQ also performs well on average setups. In order to do so, we compare Logoot identifiers to LSEQ identifiers on representative Wikipedia pages with antagonist editing behaviours. We choose Logoot as it delivers overall best performances for variable-size sequence CRDTs according to [1].

The experiments focus on the digit part of identifiers. Indeed, the source and clock part of identifiers are common to all the variable-size identifiers approaches. They do not impact on the complexity and can be drastically compressed. Consequently, it is the digit part that reflects the significant improvements.

In order to evaluate LSEQ performance, we developed a Java framework called LSEQ and released the source on GitHub platform under the terms of the GPL licence [2].

4.1 Synthetic Documents Experiments

We designed three experimental setups of synthetic sequences, namely monotone editing behaviour in one position (first and last position), and totally random insertions. The monotonic insertions algorithms choose a particular element and continuously insert new elements before/after this element. For the front editing, it targets the beginning of the document and inserts continuously after it. The end editing, it targets the end of the document and inserts continuously before it. The random behaviour randomly inserts elements in the range $[0 − doc.size[$. The insertions algorithms perform a large number of insert operations on the sequence (up to 10^6). Furthermore, each operation only concerns one element at a time.

In these experiments, we measure the average bit-length of the digit part of identifiers on four different configurations.

---

contains only two identifiers: the beginning ([0]) and the end ([31]). The sequence needs three additional identifiers between [0] and [31]. First, LSEQ randomly assigns *boundary+* as allocation strategy to the depth-1. Then, it employs this strategy to allocate the three new identifiers ([9], [10], [23]). The randomness makes the first and second elements very close in terms of identifier distance. Unfortunately, the sequence requests three other identifiers between these two. Consequently, the depth has to grow to contain these new elements. Since LSEQ have not used any strategy at this depth yet, it must randomly choose one. Here, the choice is *boundary−*. Therefore, this strategy allocates the three new identifiers. Furthermore, the underlying exponential tree model extends the number of possible identifiers to 64. In this example, the resulting fresh identifiers are [9.32], [9.51] and [9.60].

This example highlights the principle of LSEQ. Figure 4 depicts an exponential tree model that clearly grows in arity over depths. It means more and more available identifiers when the tree grows. This design aims to adjust the depth of the tree to the number of insert operations. The next section aims to demonstrate experimentally that LSEQ achieves sub-linear space complexity in extreme setups and also outperforms state-of-the-art CRDTs on real documents.

2. https://github.com/Chat-Wane/LSEQ

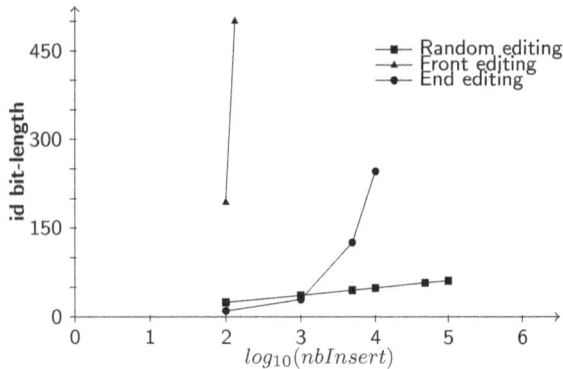

Figure 5: Simple *boundary+* setup (**B**) with *base* = 2^{10} and *boundary* = 10

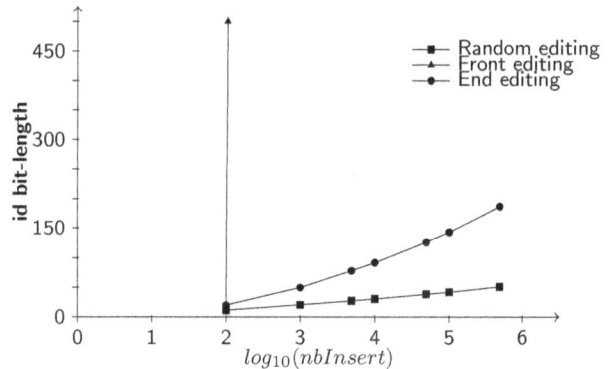

Figure 6: Base doubling setup (**D**) (*base* = $2^{4+id.size}$, *boundary* = 10)

In order of appearance: a simple *boundary+* strategy (**B**), a base doubling (**D**) at each new depth, a Round-Robin strategy choice (**RR**) and a random strategy choice with base doubling (**LSEQ**).

Boundary **B** Experiment.

OBJECTIVE: to show that *boundary+* does not adapt itself neither to any monotonic editing behaviour nor to the number of insert operations. The expected space complexity is linear compared to the number of inserts in any monotonic editing behaviour. The random editing should lead to a logarithmic size of identifiers.

DESCRIPTION: the measurements concern the average bit-length of the digit part of identifiers. The checkpoints are 100, 1000, 5000, 10000, 50000, 100000 insert operations. The experimental setup is **B** with the following parameter values: a *boundary+* strategy with *boundary* = 10 and a constant *base* = 2^{10}. It corresponds to the Logoot approach with lower values.

RESULTS: Figure 5 shows on the x-axis the number of insertions with a logarithmic scale and on y-axis the average bit-length of identifiers. As expected the identifiers size grows when the number of insertions increases. **B** handles the random editing behaviour with a logarithmic average growth of its identifiers. However, with both front and end editing behaviour, the curve is linear compared to the number of insertions. The end editing remains acceptable in comparison of front editing, but the linear growth would eventually lead to the need of a costly re-balance protocol.

REASONS: The front and end editing behaviours tend to unbalance the underlying tree model of **B**. The *boundary+* allocation strategy has been designed to handle edition at the end. It reserves more space for identifiers at the end, predicting future insertions. The obverse is less space for identifiers at front, therefore the front editing behaviour unbalances the tree even more quickly (leading to a worst-case space complexity of the total identifier size of $O(nb\_insert^2)$). For the same reason, the random editing behaviour leads to logarithmic space complexity: the tree model is balanced.

Base doubling **D** experiment.

OBJECTIVE: to show that **D** is not suitable in any case because it does not adapt on the editing behaviour. However, it constitutes an improvement over **B** due to its scalability

in terms of insertions number. Indeed, it has a sub-linear upper-bound when the editing behaviour is the expected one. Since **D** uses a *boundary+* allocation strategy, the sub-linear upper-bound is on the end editing. On the other hand, the expectation on the front editing is even worse than the first experiment (with **B**). The random editing should stay with its logarithmic shape unchanged.

DESCRIPTION: like the previous experiment, this experimentation concerns the average bit-length of identifiers. The **D** setup provides the new identifiers. *boundary+* and base doubling compose this setup. The variables are *boundary* = 10 and a base starting from *base* = $2^{4+depth}$. The measures are taken at 100, 1000, 5000, 10000, 50000, 100000, 500000 insertions.

RESULTS: Figure 6 shows on the x-axis the number of insertions on a logarithmic scale, and on the y-axis the average id bit-length. Like **B**, **D** provides constantly growing identifiers. When the editing behaviour is the expected one, the growth is sub-linear compared to the number of insertions. Otherwise, the growth is quadratic. Given this, **D** alone is better than **B** when the current editing behaviour is known. In our context where we have no prior knowledge of the editing behaviour, **D** alone is unsafe.

REASONS: the base doubling assumes that a high number of insertions triggered the creation of previous levels in the tree. Thus, it enlarges the number of available identifiers in the new level. If the insertions saturated the previous levels, then it verifies this hypothesis, resulting in an efficient allocation. Of course, if the base doubling hypothesis is false, in the worst case, each new level will contain only one identifier. Each one of these identifiers will have a space complexity equal to $\sum_{i=1}^{n} (log_2(b) + i)$ where n is the number of insertions and b is the departure base.

Round-Robin alternation **RR** experiment.

OBJECTIVE: to show that a Round-Robin alternation between *boundary+* and *boundary−* provides identifiers with a linear upper-bound and consequently does not scale as regards the number of insertions. However, it is an improvement over **B** and **D**: with no *a priori* knowledge **RR** avoids the trivial worst case.

DESCRIPTION: the experiment focuses on the average bit-length of the digit part of identifiers. The configuration is

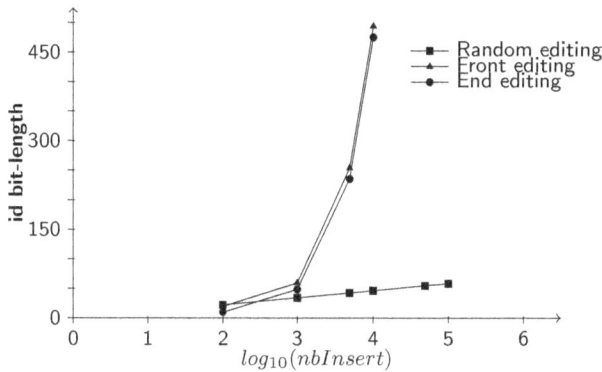

Figure 7: Round-Robin (**RR**) alternation of strategies *boundary+* and *boundary-* ($base = 2^{10}$; $boundary = 10$)

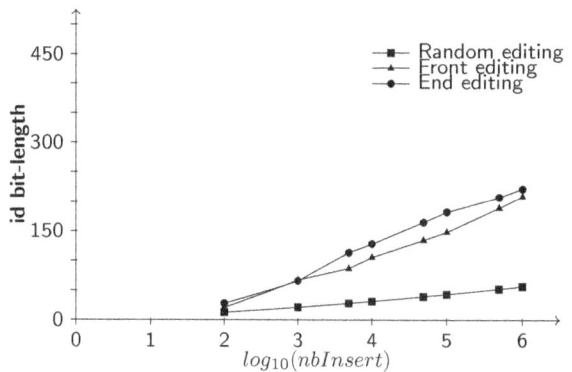

Figure 8: Random alternation (**LSEQ**) of strategies *boundary+* and *boundary-* ($base = 2^{4+id.size}$; $boundary = 10$)

a **RR** setup with two allocation strategies *boundary+* and *boundary-*. The parameters value are *boundary* = 10, and a constant $base = 2^{10}$. The measures are taken at 100, 1000, 5000, 10000, 50000, 100000 insertions.

RESULTS: Figure 7 shows on the x-axis on a logarithmic scale the number of insertions performed on the sequence. The y-axis presents the average bit-length of the digit part of identifiers. While on the random editing behaviour, the identifiers size curve stays in a logarithmic shape, front and end editing are both in linear shape. These observations mean that like **B**, **RR** does not adapt to the number of insertions, and, on the opposite of **B** and **D** it avoids the trivial worst case of front edition. Since every collaborative editing behaviour is a composition of front, end and/or random edition, **RR** is more predictable. However, **RR** remains unsafe because it does not take into account the large number of monotonic insertions.

REASONS: compared to **B**, the average bit-length of identifiers grows two times faster in the case of the end editing behaviour. Indeed, the **RR** alternation of strategies avoids the trivial worst case with the inappropriate editing behaviour (in front). This improvement comes at a cost: half the time **RR** does not employ the well suited strategy, justifying the multiplicative factor of two. The linear space complexity of **RR** stays unchanged compared to **B**. Consequently, **RR** cannot adapt to high number of insertions. **RR** does not overwhelm the loss of one level by the gain obtained in succeeding levels.

LSEQ *experiment.*

OBJECTIVE: to show that LSEQ remedies both problems of (i) editing behaviour dependence and (ii) the non-adaptive behaviour as regards the number of insert operations. The expected space complexity of the identifiers is sub-linear compared to the number of insertions, both in front and end editing. The random editing stays with the logarithmic behaviour.

DESCRIPTION: we measure the bit-length of the digit part of identifiers. The LSEQ approach provides the identifiers. It lazily and randomly assigns either *boundary+* or *boundary-* to each depth. The *boundary* parameter is set to 10 and the base is doubled over depths. Its departure value is $base = 2^4$. The checkpoints of measurement are 100, 1000, 5000, 10000, 50000, 100000, 500000, 1000000 insertions.

RESULTS: Figure 8 shows the average bit-length of **LSEQ** identifiers on the y-axis. The x-axis represents the number of insertions on a logarithmic scale. Both front and end editing are now sub-linear compared to the number of inserts. On this setup, the curves are poly-logarithmic. The average values are close of the **D** setup. It means that LSEQ loses some depths, but future insertions quickly amortize them. More precisely, it means that the base doubling is profitable enough to compensate the previous lost depths. These two changes make LSEQ a suitable safe allocation strategy for sequences.

REASONS: base doubling **B** performs well if its hypothesis is true, i.e., a high number of insertion triggered the creation of levels. The random choices of strategy among *boundary+* and *boundary-* makes the base doubling hypothesis true with a probability of $\frac{1}{2}$. So eventually, **LSEQ** will obtain the expected gain of base doubling. This gain is high enough to overwhelm the loss of previous levels. It results in a sub-linear upper-bound on the space complexity of **LSEQ**.

4.2   Real Documents Experiments

In previous section, we demonstrate experimentally a sub-linear upper-bound for LSEQ. Next, we aim to confirm the LSEQ properties on real documents. As Logoot delivers best overall performances according to [1], we compare LSEQ with Logoot on Wikipedia documents as previously done in [22].

We select Wikipedia documents with a large amount of lines, with front editing and end editing spectrum. We compare the following two setups: (1) Logoot (**L**) as [21] originally described it, (2) a composition of base doubling and Round-Robin strategy choice (i.e. equivalent to LSEQ) (**LSEQ**$^{\approx}$).

End Editing in Wikipedia.

OBJECTIVE: to confirm that **LSEQ**$^{\approx}$ (and consequently LSEQ) brings an improvement on the allocation of identifiers, even in cases where previous approaches are known to be good.

DESCRIPTION: the Wikipedia page chosen [3] to run experiments contains a high amount of lines, mainly added at

---

3. `http://fr.wikipedia.org/wiki/Liste_des_bureaux_de_poste_français_classés_par_oblitération_Petits_Chiffres`

the end. The nature of stored data explains the editing behaviour: a list of postal marking ids applied to letters. Experiments concern two configurations. (1) **L** with a single *boundary+* strategy, and parameters set to $base = 2^{64}$ and $boundary = 1M$, (2) $\mathbf{LSEQ}^{\approx}$ that alternates the two allocation strategies *boundary+* and *boundary−*, and parameters set to $base = 2^{4+depth}$, $boundary = 10$.

RESULTS: Figure 9a shows that, on this document, the bit-length of $\mathbf{LSEQ}^{\approx}$ identifiers is lower than the ones of **L** in the whole document. Table 1 reflects these results: the average bit-length of $\mathbf{LSEQ}^{\approx}$ identifiers is 2.7 times lower than **L** identifiers in spite of the fact that the average size of $\mathbf{LSEQ}^{\approx}$ identifiers (i.e. number of depths) is 2.36 times higher. Therefore, $\mathbf{LSEQ}^{\approx}$ seems to be better suited than Logoot on documents with end editing. It corroborates the observations made in section 4.1.

REASONS: when **L** has to increase the depth of its identifiers, it allocates a large additional space. Each new depth costs 64 bits. It supposedly handles 2^64 more elements. However, the adding of depth happens very quickly when the editing behaviour is not exactly as expected. In particular, the spectrum of the document shows very erratic insertions at the end (in the references and external links part). On the other hand, $\mathbf{LSEQ}^{\approx}$ tries to allocate "when it is needed". It explains why minor editing behaviour changes do not affect a lot the identifiers size. Furthermore, the base doubling of $\mathbf{LSEQ}^{\approx}$ adapts progressively the allocations to the high number of insertions.

		L	LSEQ$^{\approx}$
id-length	avg	2.65	6.25
	max	4	12
id-bit-length	avg	169.7	61.24
	max	256	150

Table 1: Numerical values of experiments on the Wikipedia page edited at the end (corresponding to Figure 9a).

Front Editing in Wikipedia.

OBJECTIVE: to highlight the importance of alternating the allocation strategies in $\mathbf{LSEQ}^{\approx}$. In other words, the *boundary+* strategy of **L** is not sufficient to provide a safe allocation system. Finally, to show that $\mathbf{LSEQ}^{\approx}$ outperforms **L** on documents edited at the beginning.

DESCRIPTION: we choose the Wikipedia page [4]. Since it is a "talk" page, it provides a discussion space. The users mostly inserted elements at the beginning of the document. Once again, we make the measurements on two configurations. (1) **L** with a single *boundary+* strategy, and parameters set to $base = 2^{64}$ and $boundary = 1M$, (2) $\mathbf{LSEQ}^{\approx}$ with the two allocation strategies *boundary+* and *boundary−*, and $base = 2^{4+depth}$, $boundary = 10$.

RESULT: unsurprisingly, the figure 9b shows that using **L**, the identifiers bit-length increases very fast in the beginning of the document while it quickly stabilizes when $\mathbf{LSEQ}^{\approx}$ is used. In Table 2, we observe that the average identifiers bit-length of $\mathbf{LSEQ}^{\approx}$ is 3.31 times lower than the one of **L**. The alternation of strategies allows $\mathbf{LSEQ}^{\approx}$ to quickly find a depth where allocation of identifiers will be efficient, and thereby to amortize previous depths where some spaces

4. http://en.wikipedia.org/wiki/Template_talk:Did_you_know

could have been wasted. These observations confirm the results of section 4.1.

REASONS: $\mathbf{LSEQ}^{\approx}$ does not favour any editing behaviour thanks to its allocation strategies. On the opposite, **L** uses an allocation strategy designed to support end editing, thus, when the antagonist behaviour arises, the identifiers size grow very fast.

		L	LSEQ$^{\approx}$
id-length	avg	2.69	5.29
	max	5	8
id-bit-length	avg	172.25	51.99
	max	320	84

Table 2: Numerical values of experiments on the Wikipedia page edited at the beginning (corresponding to Figure 9b).

4.3 Synthesis

Experiments evaluated the contribution of each part of LSEQ allocation function. They demonstrated that each isolated component cannot achieve sub-linear space complexity. However, their composition with random choice among *boundary+* and *boundary−* and a base doubling can achieve sub-linear space complexity in extreme setups. We also observe this gain on real documents. Consequently, LSEQ is suitable for building distributed collaborative editors that deliver better performance and in a larger scope of usage than state of art.

5. RELATED WORK

Popular distributed collaborative editors such as Google Docs [10] rely on Operational Transformation approach (OT) [18, 19]. OT-based and CRDT-based distributed editors follow the same global scheme of optimistic replication, i.e., generate operations without locking, broadcast to others replicates and re-execute. OT and CRDT mainly differ in their complexities: (i) OT-based editors have constant-time complexity at generation time and a complexity of $O(|H^2|)$ at re-execution time where H is the log of operations. Performance of OT closely depends on the number of concurrent operations present in the system. (ii) LSEQ sequence CRDT has a complexity of $O(k)$ for generation time and $O(k * log(n))$ for re-execution time where n is the number of elements presents in the document and k is proportional to size of identifiers. Unlike OT, the state of the document mainly determines the CRDT performance. LSEQ significantly improves the performance of the sequence CRDTs by keeping k small.

The tombstone class of sequence CRDT includes WOOT [11], WOOTO [20], WOOTH [1], Treedoc [12], CT [7], RGA [13], [23]. In these approach, tombstones (or "death certificates") mark the deleted elements. They provide a simple solution to solve problems of concurrent delete. A clear advantage is to only require fixed-length identifiers, nonetheless the space complexity of tombstone-based sequence CRDTs is linear compared to the number of insert operations performed on the document.

Safely garbaging tombstones in a distributed system is costly because it requires obtaining a consensus for this decision among all participants. In [13, 9], they proposed some solutions related to the garbage collecting mechanism in order to rebalance and/or purge the model of the CRDT. The

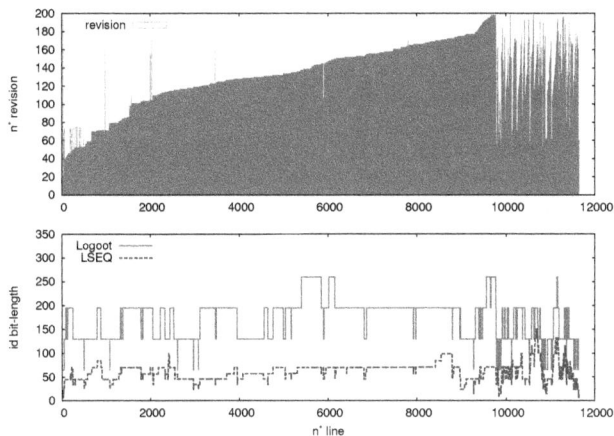

(a) The Wikipedia page has 12k lines and is mostly edited at the end. The average bit-lengths of identifiers are 168.7 and 61.24 for **L** and **LSEQ**$^{\approx}$ respectively.

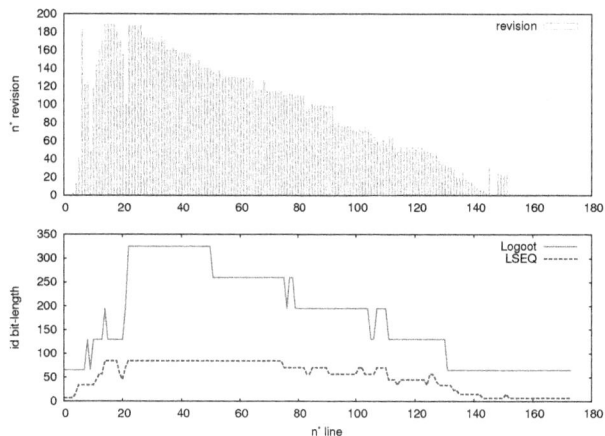

(b) The Wikipedia page has 170 lines and is mostly edited at the beginning. The average bit-lengths of identifiers are 172.25 and 51.99 bit/id for **L** and **LSEQ**$^{\approx}$ respectively.

Figure 9: The top spectrums reflect the editing behaviour performed on Wikipedia pages. The bottom figures shows the identifier bit-length assigned to each line. Two configurations: Logoot (**L**) and Round-Robin with base doubling (**LSEQ**$^{\approx}$).

purge [13] of tombstones requires a full vector clock to keep track of updates on other replicas and to be able to safely remove the tombstones. The *core nebula* [9] approach intends to make the consensus reachable, but constrains the topology of the network and uses an expensive *catch up* algorithm.

The variable-size identifiers class of CRDT includes Logoot [21] and Treedoc [12]. These CRDTs use growing identifiers to encode the total order among elements of the sequence. In the worst case, the size of identifiers is linear in the total number of insert operations done on the document [1]. Logoot and Treedoc [12] have different allocation strategies. Treedoc has two allocation strategies: (i) the first strategy allocates an identifier by directly appending a bit on one of its neighbour identifier. (ii) The second strategy increases the depth of this new identifier by $\lceil log_2(h) \rceil + 1$ (where h is the highest depth of the identifiers already allocated) and allocates the lowest value possible with this growth, in prevision of future insertions.

Logoot's *boundary* strategy and Treedoc's second strategy are very similar, both in their goals and their weaknesses. They assume an editing behaviour in the end, and therefore they become application dependent. Compared to Logoot and Treedoc, LSEQ is adaptive and significantly enlarges the applicability of sequence CRDTs.

In [1], they compared most sequence CRDTs and one OT in an experimental setup. RGA and Logoot obtained best overall performances. In this paper, we completed experiments with more extreme cases and demonstrated that LSEQ outperforms Logoot.

6. CONCLUSION

In this paper, we presented an original allocation strategy for sequence CRDTs called LSEQ. Compared to state of art, LSEQ is adaptive, i.e., it handles unpredictable different editing behaviour and achieves sub-linear space complexity. Consequently LSEQ does not require a costly protocol to garbage or re-balance identifiers, and is suitable for building better distributed collaborative editors based on sequence CRDTs.

Three components compose LSEQ: (1) a base doubling, (2) two allocation strategies *boundary+* and *boundary−*, (3) a random strategy choice.

Although each component cannot achieve sub-linear complexity, the conjunction of three components provides the expected behaviour. Experiments show that even if LSEQ makes a bad strategy choice for one level in the tree, this choice will be overwhelmed by the gain obtained at next levels.

The LSEQ approach is generic enough to be included in other variable-size sequence CRDTs. Current experiments were done with a Logoot basis because it does not require tombstones and therefore is less dependent of the editing behaviour. But we believe that Treedoc's heuristic could be improved with this allocation strategy.

Future works include a formal demonstration of the empiric poly-logarithmic upper-bound in space complexity of LSEQ which implies a probabilistic study of its worst-case. The idea is to prove that its probability of happening is negligible. We also plan to study if concurrency affects LSEQ results, i.e., if each site makes different allocation choices concurrently, does it impact LSEQ performances? Finally, we aim to study if using documents spectrum knowledge and machine-learning approaches can outperform random strategy choice.

7. ACKNOWLEDGEMENTS

We would like to thank the anonymous reviewers for their comments and suggestions which not only strenghten this work but also led to answer some thorny issues about future work.

References

[1] M. Ahmed-Nacer, C.-L. Ignat, G. Oster, H.-G. Roh, and P. Urso. Evaluating CRDTs for Real-time Document Editing. In ACM, editor, *11th ACM Symposium on Document Engineering*, pages 103–112, Mountain View, California, États-Unis, Sept. 2011.

[2] A. Andersson. Faster deterministic sorting and searching in linear space. In *Foundations of Computer Science, 1996. Proceedings., 37th Annual Symposium on*, pages 135–141. IEEE, 1996.

[3] A. Andersson and M. Thorup. Dynamic ordered sets with exponential search trees. *J. ACM*, 54(3), June 2007.

[4] C. A. Ellis and S. J. Gibbs. Concurrency control in groupware systems. In *Proceedings of the 1989 ACM SIGMOD international conference on Management of data*, SIGMOD '89, pages 399–407, New York, NY, USA, 1989. ACM.

[5] C. A. Ellis, S. J. Gibbs, and G. Rein. Groupware: some issues and experiences. *Communications of the ACM*, 34(1):39–58, 1991.

[6] S. Greenberg and D. Marwood. Real time groupware as a distributed system: concurrency control and its effect on the interface. In *Proceedings of the 1994 ACM conference on Computer supported cooperative work*, pages 207–217, 1994.

[7] V. Grishchenko. Deep hypertext with embedded revision control implemented in regular expressions. In *Proceedings of the 6th International Symposium on Wikis and Open Collaboration*, WikiSym '10, pages 3:1–3:10, New York, NY, USA, 2010. ACM.

[8] P. R. Johnson and R. H. Thomas. Maintenance of duplicate databases. RFC 677, Jan. 1975.

[9] M. Letia, N. Preguiça, and M. Shapiro. Crdts: Consistency without concurrency control. *Arxiv preprint arXiv:0907.0929*, 2009.

[10] D. A. Nichols, P. Curtis, M. Dixon, and J. Lamping. High-latency, low-bandwidth windowing in the jupiter collaboration system. In *Proceedings of the 8th annual ACM symposium on User interface and software technology*, pages 111–120. ACM, 1995.

[11] G. Oster, P. Urso, P. Molli, and A. Imine. Data consistency for p2p collaborative editing. In *Proceedings of the 2006 20th anniversary conference on Computer supported cooperative work*, pages 259–268. ACM, 2006.

[12] N. Preguiça, J. M. Marquès, M. Shapiro, and M. Letia. A commutative replicated data type for cooperative editing. In *Distributed Computing Systems, 2009. ICDCS'09. 29th IEEE International Conference on*, pages 395–403. Ieee, 2009.

[13] H.-G. Roh, M. Jeon, J.-S. Kim, and J. Lee. Replicated abstract data types: Building blocks for collaborative applications. *Journal of Parallel and Distributed Computing*, 71(3):354–368, 2011.

[14] Y. Saito and M. Shapiro. Replication: Optimistic Approaches. technical report, 2002.

[15] Y. Saito and M. Shapiro. Optimistic replication. *ACM Comput. Surv.*, 37(1):42–81, Mar. 2005.

[16] M. Shapiro, N. Preguiça, C. Baquero, and M. Zawirski. Conflict-free replicated data types. *Stabilization, Safety, and Security of Distributed Systems*, pages 386–400, 2011.

[17] A. Singh and D. Garg. Implementation and performance analysis of exponential tree sorting. *International Journal of Computer Applications ISBN*, pages 978–93, 2011.

[18] C. Sun and C. Ellis. Operational transformation in real-time group editors: issues, algorithms, and achievements. In *Proceedings of the 1998 ACM conference on Computer supported cooperative work*, CSCW '98, pages 59–68, New York, NY, USA, 1998. ACM.

[19] C. Sun, X. Jia, Y. Zhang, Y. Yang, and D. Chen. Achieving convergence, causality preservation, and intention preservation in real-time cooperative editing systems. *ACM Transactions on Computer-Human Interaction (TOCHI)*, 5(1):63–108, 1998.

[20] S. Weiss, P. Urso, and P. Molli. Wooki: A p2p wiki-based collaborative writing tool. In B. Benatallah, F. Casati, D. Georgakopoulos, C. Bartolini, W. Sadiq, and C. Godart, editors, *Web Information Systems Engineering – WISE 2007*, volume 4831 of *Lecture Notes in Computer Science*, pages 503–512. Springer Berlin Heidelberg, 2007.

[21] S. Weiss, P. Urso, and P. Molli. Logoot: a scalable optimistic replication algorithm for collaborative editing on p2p networks. In *Distributed Computing Systems, 2009. ICDCS'09. 29th IEEE International Conference on*, pages 404–412. IEEE, 2009.

[22] S. Weiss, P. Urso, and P. Molli. Logoot-undo: Distributed collaborative editing system on p2p networks. *IEEE Trans. Parallel Distrib. Syst.*, 21(8):1162–1174, 2010.

[23] W. Yu. A string-wise crdt for group editing. In *Proceedings of the 17th ACM international conference on Supporting group work*, GROUP '12, pages 141–144, New York, NY, USA, 2012. ACM.

Introduction to the Universal Delta Model

Gioele Barabucci
Università di Bologna
Department of Computer Science
and Engineering
barabucc@cs.unibo.it

ABSTRACT

There are currently no shared formalization of the output of diff algorithms, the so called *deltas*. From a theoretical point of view, without such a formalization it is difficult to compare the output of different algorithms. In more practical terms, the lack of a shared formalization makes it hard to create tools that support more than one diff algorithm.

This paper introduces the universal delta model: a formal definition of changes (the pieces of information that records that something has changed), operations (the definitions of the kind of change that happened) and deltas (coherent summaries of what has changed between two documents). The fundamental mechanism that makes the changes as defined in the universal delta model a very expressive tool, is the use of encapsulation relations between changes: changes are not only simple records of what has changed, they can also be combined into more complex changes to express the fact that the algorithm has detected more nuanced kinds of changes. The universal delta model has been applied successfully in various projects that served as an evaluation for the model. In addition to the model itself, this paper briefly describes one of these projects: the measurement of objective qualities of deltas as produced by various diff algorithms.

Categories and Subject Descriptors

I.7.1 [**Document and Text Editing**]: Version control

General Terms

Design

Keywords

Delta model; diff; patch; edit script; versioning.

DocEng'13, September 10–13, 2013, Florence, Italy.
Copyright is held by the owner/author(s). Publication rights licensed to ACM.
ACM 978-1-4503-1770-2/13/09 ...$15.00.
http://dx.doi.org/10.1145/2494266.2494284.

1. INTRODUCTION: INCOMPATIBLE DELTA MODELS

Deltas can be produced for various reasons: they may be used as a record of what has changed (in versioning systems), to show what has changed in a human-readable way (in visualization tools), to propose changes to other collaborators (in code review tools), to update a document to a newer version (using patching tools).

Regardless of their purpose, any tool that wants to use a delta must first understand it, i.e. understand its underlying model. The tool must be able to understand what are the documents referenced by the delta, what are the changes that have been found, on what elements of the document the changes are to be applied and what are the effects of the application of a change to the source document.

There is however no single shared conceptual model used to define changes and deltas: almost every algorithm uses its own model and the existing standalone models are specific to a single domain. The lack of a single widespread model has both theoretical and practical drawbacks. From a theoretical point of view it makes it hard to compare the existing diff algorithms: are the sets of changes detected by the two algorithms the same? are the deltas produced by an algorithms more expressive than those produced by another? From a practical point of view the fact that different algorithms employ different models means that the APIs they export are different (and sometimes deeply incompatible) and this makes the development of tools that support more than one algorithm cumbersome.

An analysis of the existing models shows that, although they are almost all different and incompatible with each other, they all share a sizable core of common constructs and mechanisms.

The proposed universal delta model UniDM provides a shared conceptual model for deltas; its universality lies in the fact that it can be used by any diff algorithm, regardless of the kind of documents they deal with and of the set of operations they are able to detect. The core of the model defines in formal terms what deltas, changes and operations are. In addition to this, the model describes what documents are and what it means to compare them, especially when they are seen not only as simple streams of bits but also as container of more abstract information modeled upon a certain stack of models (e.g. literary documents that are stored in DocBook document, that, in turn, are XML trees, that, in turn, are serialized as streams of Unicode characters and, last, as bits).

The rest of this paper is structured as follows. First, a cursory review of existing models and their shortcomings is presented in section 2. Section 3 describes the main contribution of this paper, the universal delta model. Section 4 discusses how the presented model has helped in the extraction and analysis of qualities of deltas. Finally, section 5 summarizes the main points of this research and suggests future works.

2. EXISTING DELTA MODELS

The need for a shared delta model arises in different contexts and has already been discussed in various fields [16, 14]. However, regardless of the importance of having a single shared model, most of the current algorithms do not use one such model, relying instead on their own ad-hoc models, often undocumented and embedded in the code of the reference implementation. Standalone models have been proposed in literature, but these models are meant for use in a single particular field (e.g. to describe changes to ontologies) or only with a particular document format (e.g. XML).

The most frequently seen delta models are embedded delta models: models that have been developed for use in a specific algorithm. Most of the time, these models are only an abstract representation of the data structures used by the algorithm to keep track of the differences it finds.

The most common embedded models are those modeled after the model used by the Hunt-McIlroy algorithm [10], where the documents are seen as sequences of lines, each line is represented by its hash and the changes are stored as scripts of the qed editor, i.e. addition, deletion and modification of a line. It is interesting to note that in this first and basic model one can already find the distinction between changes that are detected directly by the algorithm and changes that are found in later, when a refinement stage merges together the changes that have already been detected. Subsequent algorithms for line-based diff have all used similar models, although each model has its own distinctive features that differentiate it from the others. For example a slightly different model is used in the Burns-Long algorithm [6] where removal are implicit and additions are codified as copies. Algorithms for non-linear documents (i.e., trees as in the case of XML documents or graphs in the case of RDF datasets) all use similar models tuned for the peculiarities of their target document format.

Standalone delta models, differently from embedded delta models, are models that have been designed to be independent of the algorithm that uses them. These models are often inspired by existing embedded models or APIs (e.g. the model described by Rönnau et al. [16] is a refinement of the underlying model originally used in a versioning API for office documents [19]). Standalone models aim at providing a representation of changes that can be used by more than a single algorithm. To do so, they describe changes and deltas in more abstract terms, separating the important part of the concepts from the implementation details. Examples of standalone models are the model proposed by Rönnau et al. [16] for XML documents, the Delta ontology [5] for RDF datasets and the Klein's model [11] for OWL ontologies.

The flaws of the existing models can be classified broadly in the following categories. Each of these models:

- focuses on a single kind of document or

- is specific to a single algorithm or

- does not address the fact that the same document can be seen at different abstraction levels.

The main limitation of all the existing models is that they are defined only for a particular kind of documents, i.e. they only work with line-based text files or only with XML files or with OWL ontologies, etc. While this is understandable from the point of view of simplicity and ease of implementation, it also forces the restatement of the very same concepts (addition, deletion, update, move, etc.) for each kind of document.

The fact that many models are strictly coupled with a specific algorithm is also a concern. This fact leads to two problems. First, these models are not explicitly defined and documented, thus they must be extracted from the steps of the algorithm or from the code of the implementation. Second, they only model the parts of the delta that are strictly needed by the algorithm in which they are found.

Another problem with most of the existing models is that they ignore the fact that, in many cases, documents are composed of parts with different "behaviors" and that a document can be seen at different abstraction levels, some of which are compatible and comparable, other which are not. Take for example the case of literary XML documents. They are normal XML documents in which the main content is the text contained in the elements. Diff algorithms for XML documents that want to address the text nodes in a particular way should be able to reflect the fact that the operations on text nodes are different from the operations on content of the text nodes are different from those that can be made on the tree structure formed by the other nodes, mainly element nodes. It is necessary, then that the delta model has the ability to describe text changes along with tree operations.

The conclusion that arises from the analysis of the state of the art is that there is a big overlap of concepts and "view of the world" between all the existing models. However, these similarities are rarely recognized, and, in fact, have not yet been exploited to create a universal delta model.

3. UNIDM: THE UNIVERSAL DELTA MODEL

The main contribution presented in this paper is a universal model of document and deltas: UniDM. This model is able to express deltas produced by different algorithms on different kinds of documents and based on arbitrary sets of recognized operations. What is shown in this section is just an extract of the complete model. A detailed, formal description of the universal delta model can be found in the PhD thesis "A universal delta model" [2].

The core of the universal delta model is the description of deltas, how they aggregate changes, how changes can be used to expose the detection of sophisticated, domain-specific modifications and how basic and format-specific operations can be defined. In addition to this, the model provides also a simple formalization of what documents are and what are they composed of. The formalization of documents allows the changes to refer with precision and without ambiguities to the different parts of the documents they are modifying.

3.1 Documents

Documents are the mean through which knowledge is stored, transmitted and processed. Although the pure knowledge is the subject of interest to be stored, such knowledge must be transformed into a finite, representable set of symbols in order to be processed by automated tools.

The set of choices one makes about how to structure the pure knowledge in a document forms the so called *model of the document*. The model describes, for instance, if the information is organized in a linear or in a hierarchical fashion, or what are the possible fields to use to store the information (e.g., the given name of a person goes in the field called "FirstName", not "Name" or "GivenName", while the last name goes in the field called "SName", not "Surname"). The content of the document, shaped according to the chosen model is transformed into a sequence of bits using a *document format*, i.e. a set of rules that states how to map a certain aspect of the model (e.g., a certain field or a value) into a string of bits.

In contemporary documents, format rules do not usually translate models directly into strings of bits. Instead, formats translate from high-level models into lower-level models. XML is an example of a model that is widely used as a lower level on top of which other models are defined. Many document formats are now XML-based, this means that the specifications of the document format indicate how to translate their constructs into XML trees, not strings of bits. The translation of these XML trees into characters is delegated to the grammar of XML, not embedded directly in the document format. The generated characters are, in turn, formatted according to some encoding, for example UTF-8 or ASCII. This situation leads to the vision of a document as a "cake" of stratified abstraction level, each with its own model.

At each abstraction level different there are different kinds of elements that can be used to store the document knowledge. At the textual level there are characters, that can be binary octets, as is the case in ASCII, or longer strings of variable length, as is the case in UTF-8; at the XML level there are nodes, comments, processing instruction, etc. The whole content of a document at a certain abstraction level is fully described by the set of its elements and the set of relations between them. The elements carry the data of the document; the elements' relations store additional information about the elements, for example their order in the document or the way they are nested in each other.

What follows is a simple formalization of documents a stratified collection of abstraction levels.

Definition (**Document**) *A document (D) is a finite unit of stored knowledge, whose content is available at various levels of abstraction (D_{L_n}).*

$$D = (D_{L_0}, D_{L_1}, \dots, D_{L_n})$$

Definition (**Level of abstraction**) *A level of abstraction (D_{L_n}) is a view on a document where the stored information is seen as a group of elements (E_n) and relations between elements (R_n) created according to a certain model (M).*

$$D_{L_n} \equiv (E_n, R_n, M)$$

Definition (**Model**) *A* model *is a specification that indicates how the pieces of information are to be thought of and how they relate to each other.*

Definition (**Format**) *A* format *is a set of rules that specify how a document (D_1) modeled according to a model (M_1) can be transformed into a document (D_2) based on another model (M_2), usually a simpler lower-level model.*

$$F_{M_1, M_2}(D_1) = D_2$$

It must be noted that diff algorithms rarely work at the topmost abstraction level; most of the times documents are compared at their bitstream level (e.g., binary diff), at the textual level (e.g., in UNIX grep) or at the first non-textual abstraction level (e.g., XML diff tools). While all these comparisons are equally valid and correct, the lower the compared abstraction level is, the less meaningful the produced deltas are bound to be.

3.1.1 Document structure

While all the documents are linear at the bitstream level, at more abstract levels the information is often modeled in non-linear ways. For example XML documents are seen as particular hierarchical documents and RDF knowledge bases as graphs of linked resources. There are various special cases of document structure that can be identified.

The most general kind of document structure is the graph structure, as it does not impose any limit on the kind of relations that exist between the elements of the document. The hierarchical structure, instead, requires that only containment and sequence relations are used, thus limiting the ability to create arbitrary links between elements. Last, the linear structure impose that not even containment relations be used, only sequence relations are allowed and they also need to form a total order over the elements.

Definition (**Graphical document**) *A graphical document is a documents whose elements are linked by relations of any kind.*

Definition (**Hierarchical document**) *A hierarchical document (or tree document) is a document where elements are linked using only containment and sequence relations.*

$$IsDocHierarchical(D) \equiv D.R = D.R_{order} \cup D.R_{containment}$$

Definition (**Linear document**) *A linear document is a document whose elements are linked using only sequence relations and the sequence relations define a total order over the elements of the document.*

$$IsDocLinear(D) \equiv D.R = D.R_{order} \wedge$$
$$AllElementOrdered(D.E, D.R)$$

3.1.2 Comparability

The point of using difference algorithms is finding parts of documents that differs, i.e. that are not the "same". The concept of difference relies thus on that of equivalence: without an equivalence relation between documents or parts of document it would not be possible to highlight what is different.

The simplest equivalence relation one can think of is the bitstream-level equivalence, it is also universal because all the electronic documents must have a bitstream representation. However, comparisons at the bitstream level (the so called binary comparisons) produce low quality deltas in almost all cases. Knowledge of the used format allows the production of deltas that are both smaller and more readable. In fact, many comparisons are higher text comparisons or format specific comparison. This means that more equivalence relations are needed, one for each model.

Another aspect that must be taken into account when comparing documents is that some of their abstraction levels may not be comparable, i.e. there is no equivalence relation defined between the models used at the same abstraction layer. Take, for example, the abstraction levels of two XML Schema documents as illustrated in figure 1. The first document has been saved using the canonical serialization, the second using the XDTD serialization [4].

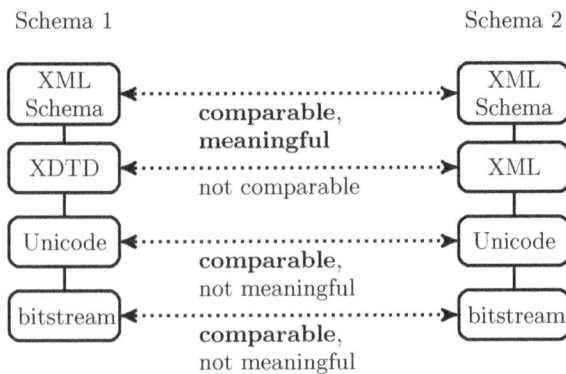

Schema 1   Schema 2

comparable, meaningful

not comparable

comparable, not meaningful

comparable, not meaningful

Figure 1: Abstraction levels for two XML schemas in different serialization

In this case there are levels at which it is sensible to compare, levels where it is not possible to compare and levels where a comparison is possible but with poor results. In the case depicted in figure 1, at the topmost abstraction level both files are seen as collections of XML Schema declarations. These declarations are hard to compare because finding equivalent declarations is not a computationally trivial task; on the other hand, a comparison between these two levels would probably produce an high quality result. A comparison at the second level, instead, between an XML document and an XDTD document is not possible as there is no equality relation defined for this combination of models. Comparison at the lowest levels is possible as both models are based on Unicode and produce a bitstream in the end. However, these comparisons will hardly produce anything useful: the most probable delta that can be produced at these levels is a trivial delta in which all the content of the source document is removed and replaced with all the content of the second document. This phenomenon appears also when the compared files are two different serializations of the exact same schema.

3.2 Deltas

A delta is a collection of changes and change relations. The changes stored in the delta are the changes detected by the algorithm and modeled as described in the following section. The change relations are objects used to describe

various relations that may exist between changes; for example, an application order relation between the changes c_1 and c_2 states that, for the delta to be correct, the c_1 must be applied before c_2.

*Definition (**Delta**) A delta $\Delta_{S,T}$ is a tuple of changes (C) and change relations (R) that describes how to transform the source document (S) into the target document (T).*

$$\Delta_{S,T} \equiv (C, R)$$

Deltas are used to group together the changes found by an algorithm during or after the comparison of two documents. As such, they may be regarded as the main output of a diff algorithm but also as the working object used by an algorithm during its computations.

The changes by themselves are not enough to constitute a working delta. There are various other pieces of information about the changes that must be recorded for the delta to be useful. The most basic additional information that is needed is the order in which the changes must be applied, or the lack of such an order (i.e., when changes do not depend on each other). Another useful information about the changes is whether they have been assembled starting from other changes or if they have been natively detected. All these pieces of information are recorded in the delta using change relations (the set R).

In general terms, change relations are objects used to record that a certain relation exists between certain changes. The meaning and the intended effects of a change relation are described by the kind of that relation.

*Definition (**Change relation**) A change relation is a tuple describing the fact that there exist a relation of type K between the changes C_1 and the set of changes C_2.*

$$r = (K, C_1, C_2)$$
where K is the relation kind, $C_1, C_2 \subset C$

The two most common kinds of change relations are application order relations and encapsulation relations. Application order relations describe the (partial or total) order in which changes should be applied, for example "the changes c_3, c_7, c_{89} must all be applied before the changes c_4, c_{12}, c_{72}". Encapsulation relations records the fact that a change has been detected as the consequence of the detection of other smaller changes, for example "the change c_{34} encapsulates changes c_{12}, c_{31}, c_{21}".

3.3 Changes

The differences found by a diff algorithm are expressed as a set of changes in the delta, C. Each of these changes describes an operation that must be done on the source document to make it reconcile one of the found difference, in other words to make the source document more similar to the target document.

Some of these changes are considered *atomic changes* because they are found and generated by the algorithm looking only at the content of the source and target documents. Other changes, instead, have been generated by analyzing some of the changes that have already found. This happens for instance in the Hunt-McIllroy algorithm [10] where pairs of additions and deletions changes are aggregated into update changes or in Papavassiliou et. al [14] where similar pairs of basic changes on ontologies such as DOMAIN-REMOVED(prop, d_1) and DOMAIN-ADDED(prop, d_2) are aggregated into DOMAIN-CHANGED(prop, d_1, d_2). Changes of the latter kind, generated taking into account also other changes, are called *complex changes* and the link between the generated changes and the changes used to generate it are recorded through *encapsulation relations* (the R set in $\Delta_{S,T}$), a kind of change relation.

Changes and changes relations can be described more formally using the following definitions.

Definition (**Change**) *A change is a record of the fact that part of the source document S must be changed using operation op with parameters p in order to produce a patched document S'.*

$$c = (op, p) \mid S' = \varphi(S, c)$$

Definition (**Encapsulation relation**) *An encapsulation relation is a kind of change relation that links a container change to its encapsulated changes.*

$$R_{encapsulation} \equiv \{r \mid r \in R, r.K = encapsulation\}$$

Definition (**Atomic change**) *An atomic change is a change that does not encapsulate any other change.*

$$C_{atomic} \equiv \dot{C} \equiv \{c \mid c \in C, \forall r : r \in R_{encapsulation},$$
$$r = (k, c_1, c_2), c_1 \notin c\}$$

Definition (**Complex change**) *A complex change is a change that encapsulates at least one other change.*

$$C_{complex} \equiv \bar{C} \equiv \{c \mid c \in C, \forall r : r \in R_{encapsulation},$$
$$r = (k, c_1, c_2), c_1 = \{c\}, c_2 \neq \emptyset\}$$

Definition (**Top level change**) *A top level change is a change that has not been encapsulated in any other change.*

$$C_{TopLevel} \equiv \hat{C} \equiv \{c \mid c \in C, \forall r : r \in R_{encapsulation},$$
$$r = (k, c_1, c_2), c \notin c_2\}$$

3.3.1 Encapsulation justification

The generation of complex changes follows rules dictated by the algorithm and by the semantics of its operation. For example, an update may require the presence of an addition change and of a deletion change on the same element. A complex change can be generated only if all the necessary other changes that contribute to its meaning are available. Changes like this, used to justify the generation of a complex change are the *main encapsulated changes* of the container change. For example, in an ontology, an OWL-CLASS-ADDED(Person) change cannot be generated without the presence of a OWL-CLASS-DECLARED(Person) change. There are however other changes that could be encapsulated by a OWL-CLASS-ADDED(Person) change, but that, by themselves

are not enough to justify the generation of that change. These changes are called *additional encapsulated changes*. For example, a OWL-DOCUMENTATION-ADDED(Person) change could be encapsulated by a OWL-CLASS-ADDED(Person) change, but, on the contrary, the simple presence of a OWL-DOCUMENTATION-ADDED(Person) change is not enough to justify the generation of an OWL-CLASS-ADDED(Person) change.

Definition (**Main encapsulated changes**) *The main encapsulated changes is the subset of encapsulated changes without which the generation of the encapsulating complex change could not be justified.*

Definition (**Additional encapsulated changes**) *The additional encapsulated changes is the subset of encapsulated changes that are not needed to justify the generation of the encapsulating complex change.*

3.3.2 Classification of changes

Not all the complex changes are generated for the same reason. Complex changes that have been generated to group together a sequence of similar operations done to adjacent elements are called *range changes*. An example of range change is REMOVE-LINES(8,12) that groups together the changes REMOVE-LINE(8), REMOVE-LINE(9), ..., REMOVE-LINE(12). Another kind of complex changes are *structural changes*, generated when a certain structure is recognized in a group of changes, for instance REMOVE-SUBTREE encapsulates various REMOVE-ELEMENT changes on elements that, together, form a proper subtree. Last, *meaningful changes* are changes generated to convey a certain meaning to a group of changes when taken together, for example HTML4-REMOVE-CHAPTER groups changes such as a HTML4-REMOVE-H2 and various HTML4-REMOVE-PARAGRAPH.

The aim of an algorithm influences heavily the kind of complex changes it generates: algorithms that want to create concise deltas will support and detect range changes as they allow the generation of deltas with fewer top-level changes. Differently, algorithms that make an effort to find more advanced changes (e.g. NDiff [8]) or to generate domain-specific changes (e.g. PROMPTDiff [13] or OnEX [9]), will try to generate as many structural and meaningful changes as possible, using their knowledge of the domain to find meaning in the already generated changes.

Definition (**Range change**) *A range change is a change that encapsulates similar changes made to a range of elements.*

Definition (**Structural change**) *A structural change is a change that encapsulates changes into a structure that resembles the structure of the elements in the document or the way the users made their modifications.*

Definition (**Meaningful change**) *A meaningful change is a change that encapsulates different changes with the purpose of providing a meaning to that group of changes.*

3.4 Operations

Once an algorithm has detected a difference, it records it as a change. The kind of the change is called its operation. For example, the change ADD("Hello","32") has operation ADD. This means that the diff algorithm has detected a change that fits the description and the semantics of the ADD operation and that the data on which it has detected this change, i.e., the parameters of the operation, are the string "Hello" and the position index "32".

In order for these operations to be understood by the tools that read the deltas, each operation must have an associated semantics. The semantics of the operations operates on two objects: the arguments of the operation and the content of the source document. Using this information, the semantics of an operation describe how to transform a part of the source document into a part of the target document, reconciling one of the differences found by the algorithm.

Not all algorithms detect the same set of operations. It is the task of the designers of an algorithm to decide which operations it should or should not detect; it is quite common for algorithms to waive the ability to recognize many different operations to achieve a lower computational complexity.

Definition (**Operation**) *An operation is a function that takes a document (D_1) and a list of parameters (P) and returns a new document (D_2).*

$$op : D_1 \times P \to D_2$$

The parameters of an operation are used by the semantics of the operation itself to understand on which parts of the document the operation must operate and to supply data that is not present in the source document, for example elements that have been added and are present only in the target document. There are two types of parameters: pointer parameters (that are used to refer to a single element of a document, e.g. "the third byte" or "the first child of the forth child of the root node") and data parameters (that carry immediate data elements, e.g. a string of bytes or an XML node).

There two main kinds of pointer parameters: position pointers (for linear structures) and ID pointers (for graphs). Pointers to linear structures are simple 0-based integers that point to the position between two element, i.e. the pointer n points at the position between element n and $n + 1$. These pointers can be used only on linear documents (or linear portions of documents) for which the order of the elements is defined via sequence relations. For document where an order is not defined or for portions of documents for which an order is not defined (e.g. the attributes of XML documents) ID pointers must be used. An ID pointer id points to the element e for which the relation $e.ID = id$ holds. The use of pointers instead of tree or graphs paths has been chosen by various authors [17, 20] to simplify the application of deltas with pointer-based merge algorithms.

Definition (**List of parameters**) *The* list of parameters *of an operation defines which pieces of data must be supplied for its application.*

$$P = (p_1, p_2, \ldots, p_n)$$

Definition (**Pointer parameter**) *A pointer parameter is an operation parameter that refers to a document element through a pointer.*

Definition (**Data pointer**) *A data parameter is an operation parameter that is composed of the actual data used to perform the operation.*

3.4.1 *Operation composition and extensible catalogs*

The composition of operations is the mechanism through which it is possible to define complex operations in terms of simpler operations. This mechanism reflects the way atomic and complex changes work: a complex change aggregates atomic changes or other complex changes; the operation used by the aggregating complex change is a composition of the operations of the aggregated changes.

In practical terms, the composition of operations is obtained requiring the application of other operations as part of the semantics of the operation itself. These applications are done via the `apply` function.

The composition mechanism allows for the definition of extensible catalogs of operations. These catalogs start defining a base of atomic changes (usually ADD and REMOVE on graph elements) and build staked layers of more meaningful complex changes on top of each other. First structural changes are defined (e.g. TREE-REMOVE, for hierarchical documents), on top of these, format-specific changes are defined (e.g. XML-TREE-REMOVE, for XML documents), then domain-specific operations (e.g. DOCBOOK-SECTION-REMOVE, for DocBook documents), sub-domain-specific operations (e.g. DOCBOOK-INTRODUCTION-REMOVE, for Doc-Book documents written using a particular set of guidelines) and so on.

An example of operation is TREE-CHILD-ADD, shown in figure 2, used to add an element to the ordered set of children of an element in a tree document. An example of complex operation created composing other operation is TREE-NODE-UNWRAP, shown in figure 3, used to remove an element and move its children to the parent of the remove element.

Definition of TREE-CHILD-ADD

Parameters
e (element) child to add
e_{parent} (element) parent element
p (position) position of added child

Conditions
$length\,(childrenOf\,(e_{parent})) \leq p$

Effects

$$E' = E \cup \{e\}$$
$$R' = R \cup \{(:contains, e_{parent}, e)\}$$
$$\cup \{(:sequence, e_{p-1}, e)\,, (:sequence, e, e_p)\}$$
$$\setminus \{(:sequence, e_{p-1}, e_p)\}$$

Figure 2: Semantics of tree-child-app

4. ANALYSIS OF DELTAS USING UNIDM

To evaluate the soundness and effectiveness of the universal delta model, it has been applied in various scenarios. In particular, UniDM has been used, first, as the pivot model for the analysis of the quality (and qualities) of the deltas produced by different algorithms, and second, as the native

Definition of TREE-NODE-UNWRAP

Parameters

e_w (element) wrapper element
$B = \{b_1, b_2, \ldots, b_n\}$ (set of elements) wrapped elements

Conditions

$\forall b \in B : b \in E$
$AllElementOrdered\,(B, R)$

Effects

$E' = E \cup \{e_w\}$
$R' = R \setminus \{r \in R_{containment} : (r.A = e_w, r.B = b)\}$
$\qquad \setminus \{r \in R_{order} : (r.A \notin B \vee r.B \notin B)\}$
$\qquad \cup \{\forall b \in B : (\text{:contains}, e_w, b)\}$

Figure 3: Semantics of tree-node-unwrap

model of OntoEv [1], a tool that uses deltas to identify the various phases occurred during the development of an OWL ontology. This section will briefly report on how UniDM made possible the analysis of the deltas produced by various diff algorithms. An in-depth discussion of this topic will appear in an separate article.

Historically, designers of diff tools were mainly concerned about the computational complexity of their diff algorithms and the length of the produced edit scripts. Recently, instead, users started giving more relevance to the quality of deltas, designing tools that could produce *better* results: more readable, more usable, more natural [8, 18]. There are, however, no definitions of what does it mean for a delta to be *more readable* that another, or when a delta is *more natural* than another. Getting these definitions right is hard because they are task- and user-dependent: the same delta may be fit for use for a certain task (e.g., very compact binary diff are good for the storage of previous versions of a source code file) but unfit for others (e.g., the same compact binary diff is hard to use in a code review process). It is possible to rephrase the last sentence as: the set of interesting features a delta should have changes in relation to the task it is meant to be used for.

A possible but inconvenient solution to the problem of evaluating the fitness of a certain algorithm, is to have an expert of the task evaluate a sample of deltas generated by various algorithms on the same set of documents. The main problems with this approach is that it is tedious and cumbersome for the expert to analyze all these deltas and that this evaluation is bound to be subjective.

A better solution would be to have a tool perform an evaluation similar to that of the expert. Such a tool should first extract from the deltas some objective measurements and then use these measurements to calculate some fitness metrics. At this point, the role of the expert is limited to stating what is the weight that a certain metric should have in the evaluation of the diff algorithms for their domain.

4.1 Objective features

The are various objective features that can be extracted from a delta. The most basic feature is the number of changes produced by an algorithm; for algorithms that are able to recognize more advanced changes, one can also ex-

tract the number of such complex changes and rate their complexity. In this evaluation, instead of writing a separate feature extractors for each delta produced by a different algorithm, all the deltas have been converted, without loss of information, into deltas that follow the universal delta model; the feature extraction tool, thus, focuses only on UniDM deltas. The universal delta model is rich in information and exposes many different properties of the deltas, properties that are usually present in the other models but hidden or strongly coupled with other pieces of information. Examples of the features that can be extracted from changes expressed in a UniDM delta are:

population the total number of changes of which a change is composed of, including itself and the recursive closure of the encapsulated changes;

depth the maximum number of encapsulation layers that must be crossed to reach an atomic change;

width the number of distinct changes encapsulated directly inside the change;

num touched elements the number of distinct pieces of information that are included as part of the change or of the encapsulated changes;

num modified elements the minimum number of elements that must be modified by the change to fulfill its purpose.

There are also features that can be calculated on the whole delta, with a direct count or by combining measures of individual changes:

num top-level the number of changes that are not encapsulated in any other change;

population the sum of the population property of all changes;

num touched elements the sum of the touched elements of all changes;

num modified elements the minimum number of distinct pieces of information that must be modified in order to turn the original document into the modified one.

4.2 Qualities and metrics

The objective features extracted from the delta forms the basis on top of which more complex metrics are built. These metrics are used to describe qualities of the delta that go beyond the usual count of produced changes or the computational complexity of the algorithm. Each quality is, thus, described by a metric, as summarized in by Cobena et al. [7]: "quality is described by some minimality criteria [...] Minimality is important because it captures to some extent the semantics that a human would give when presented with the two versions".

There are currently six metrics defined for UniDM deltas: precision (how many non-modified elements have been included in the delta), conciseness (how much the changes found in the delta have been grouped into bigger changes), meaningfulness (how much of the delta conciseness is due to the use of high-level complex changes), aggregation (how much of the inner parts of the delta, not only of its topmost level, is expressed using complex changes instead of atomic changes), economy (how changes have been produced) and separability degree (how dependent on each other are the changes in the delta).

4.2.1 Precision

Precision indicates how many non-modified elements have been included in the delta. Values of precision near 1 indicate that the delta contains almost only information about the occurred modifications; values near 0 indicate that almost all the information carried in the delta is redundant.

$$Precision(\delta) = \frac{\text{modified-elements}(\delta)}{\text{touched-elements}(\delta)}$$

There are cases where extreme precision is required, for example when transmission bandwidth or storage space is scarce. In these cases every repeated byte is a wasted byte. Some algorithms go to great lengths to produce very precise deltas, especially binary diff algorithms [15]. On the other hand, deltas that are too precise are very hard to read and interpret by a human, For this reason most algorithms give away a bit of precision to include some contextual information around the real modification, so that the user can understand better what is being changed and where.

4.2.2 Conciseness

Conciseness indicates how much the changes found in the delta have been grouped into bigger changes. A very concise delta is a delta whose number of top-level changes has been reduced through the use of the various encapsulation mechanisms.

$$Conciseness(\delta) = 1 - \frac{\text{number-of-top-level}(\delta)}{\text{population}(\delta)}$$

Algorithms can reduce the number of changes needed to express the modifications by grouping small changes into bigger changes, sometimes at the expenses of clarity or redundancy.

4.2.3 Meaningfulness

Meaningfulness indicates how much of the delta conciseness is due to the use of complex changes. An high meaningfulness score indicates that the algorithm has been able to express much of what has been changed using meaningful changes, going beyond the simple detection of atomic changes.

$$Meaningfulness(\delta) = \frac{\text{number-top-level}_{complex}(\delta)}{\text{number-top-level}(\delta)}$$

A delta that is composed only of atomic changes has a meaningfulness value of 0. On the contrary, a delta where all the atomic changes have been grouped into complex changes has a meaningfulness values of 1.

4.2.4 Aggregation

Aggregation indicates how much of the inner parts of the delta, not only of its topmost level, is expressed using complex changes instead of atomic changes. The better suited a conceptual diff schema is, the more likely an algorithm is to aggregate atomic changes into complex changes; an algorithm that know HTML operations will be able to detect more complex changes than an algorithm limited to XML operations or, even, to pure text.

$$Aggregation(\delta) = \frac{\text{number-atomic-in-complex}(\delta)}{\text{population}_{atomic}(\delta)}$$
$$= 1 - \frac{\text{number-top-level}_{atomic}(\delta)}{\text{population}_{atomic}(\delta)}$$

While this metric is positively correlated to abstraction, it focus on measuring *how much* has been aggregated in complex changes rather than *whether* complex changes have been used to express the most superficial level of the delta.

4.2.5 Separability degree

The separability degree of a delta measures how much a delta can be split in smaller independent deltas. It is calculated as the number of maximally connected graphs (using changes as vertex and references to other changes as edges) that can be found in a delta.

$$Separability(\delta) = |\{\mathcal{I}_i\}|$$

$$\text{where} \quad \mathcal{I}_i = \{c | c \in Changes, \\ \forall rc \in c.\, \text{referenced-changes}(\delta), \\ rc \in \mathcal{I}_i, rc \notin \mathcal{I}_{n \neq i}\}$$

Deltas with a low separability degree value, and thus with changes whose application that depend on each other, tend to be hard to apply without creating conflicts, something that should be taken in consideration if the deltas are used in collaborative efforts where simultaneous and possibly conflicting modifications to the same document happen often.

4.3 Experimental results

The experiments that have been carried out, i.e. the application of these metrics to real-world XML document, show two results. First, the metrics are able to show that different algorithms produce deltas with significantly different qualities. Second, that UniDM is a viable exchange format for delta produced by different algorithms.

The analysis tool has been run on four diff algorithms with very different design goals: JNDiff [8], Faxma [12] and XyDiff [7] and the trivial diff algorithm (i.e. the algorithm that produces a delta that removes all the content of the source document and adds all the content of the target algorithm). The set of documents already used in this experiment is the same that has been used in the evaluation of JNDiff.

The results of the analysis, one of which is graphically illustrated in figure 4, highlight how the different algorithms focus on different qualities of the deltas. The document illustrated in that figure is an XML representation of a bill debated in Italian senate, marked up using the Akoma Ntoso document format [3]. It is clear from the graph that JNDiff has a much better support for finding and producing more precise deltas. On the contrary, XyDiff produces much more verbose and redundant deltas, a side-effect of the fact that the speed of the XyDiff algorithm comes from its greedy comparison process.

Aside from the analysis itself, that is outside scope of this paper, it must be noted that the use of UniDM in this analysis has had three positive effect. First, it made it possible to define in precise terms the needed features and metrics. Second, it made it easy to extract these features and to calculate the metrics for deltas created by very different algorithms, this is an effect of the fact that UniDM makes explicit relations between changes that are only implicit in other delta models. Last, it simplified the development of the tool that performed the analysis, as the core of it (the feature extraction mechanism and the calculation of the metrics) had to be written only once and not for each algorithm that has been

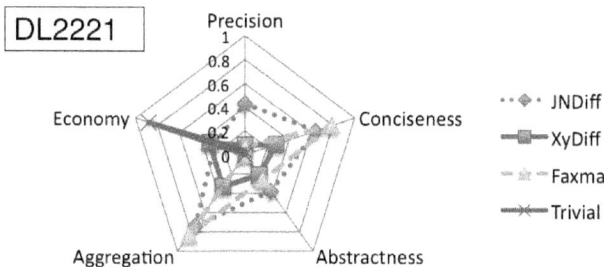

Figure 4: Metrics for DL2221

analyzed. It should be noted that, thanks to the universality of the model, it is possible now to compare not only how XML-based diff algorithms perform on a certain set of documents, but also how other, more generic algorithms perform, for example line-based textual diff or binary diff algorithms.

5. CONCLUSIONS

This paper introduced the universal delta model: UniDM. UniDM is a model for deltas that is able to express deltas generated by any diff algorithm. This model defines how changes record information about something has been modified in the document, what are the operations of these changes, how operations can be combined together to define more meaningful, domain-specific operations and how deltas are used to group together all the changes that have been found between two documents.

In comparison with other existing models, the universal delta model is not limited to deltas created for certain kind of documents, it can be used in any algorithm and is able to indicate the abstraction level at which the comparison has been performed.

6. REFERENCES

[1] BARABUCCI, G. OntoEv: See how an ontology has evolved through its development. http://barabucc.web.cs.unibo.it/ontoev.

[2] BARABUCCI, G. A universal delta model. PhD thesis, Università di Bologna, Apr. 2013.

[3] BARABUCCI, G., CERVONE, L., PALMIRANI, M., PERONI, S., AND VITALI, F. Multi-layer markup and ontological structures in Akoma Ntoso. In AI Approaches to the Complexity of Legal Systems. Complex Systems, the Semantic Web, Ontologies, Argumentation, and Dialogue - International Workshops AICOL-I/IVR-XXIV Beijing, China, September 19, 2009 and AICOL-II/JURIX 2009, Rotterdam, The Netherlands, December 16, 2009 Revised Selected Papers (2010), P. Casanovas, U. Pagallo, G. Sartor, and G. Ajani, Eds., vol. 6237 of Lecture Notes in Computer Science, Springer, pp. 133–149.

[4] BARABUCCI, G., AND VITALI, F. XDTD as a simple validation language for XML-based legal documents. In Legal Knowledge and Information Systems - JURIX 2009: The Twenty-Second Annual Conference on Legal Knowledge and Information Systems, Rotterdam, The Netherlands, 16-18 December 2009 (2009), G. Governatori, Ed., vol. 205 of Frontiers in Artificial Intelligence and Applications, IOS Press, pp. 1–10.

[5] BERNERS-LEE, T., AND CONNOLLY, D. Delta: an ontology for the distribution of differences between RDF graphs. http://www.w3.org/DesignIssues/Diff, 2009. accessed Nov 26, 2012.

[6] BURNS, R., BURNS, A. C., AND LONG, D. D. E. A linear time, constant space differencing algorithm. In Performance, Computing, and Communications Conference, 1997 (feb 1997), IEEE International, pp. 429–436.

[7] CÓBENA, G., ABITEBOUL, S., AND MARIAN, A. Detecting changes in XML documents. In Proceedings of the 18th International Conference on Data Engineering, San Jose, CA, USA, February 26 - March 1, 2002 (2002), R. Agrawal and K. R. Dittrich, Eds., IEEE Computer Society, pp. 41–52.

[8] DI IORIO, A., SCHIRINZI, M., VITALI, F., AND MARCHETTI, C. A natural and multi-layered approach to detect changes in tree-based textual documents. In Enterprise Information Systems, 11th International Conference, ICEIS 2009, Milan, Italy, May 6-10, 2009. Proceedings (2009), J. Filipe and J. Cordeiro, Eds., vol. 24 of Lecture Notes in Business Information Processing, Springer, pp. 90–101.

[9] HARTUNG, M., KIRSTEN, T., GROSS, A., AND RAHM, E. Onex: Exploring changes in life science ontologies. BMC Bioinformatics 10 (2009).

[10] HUNT, J. W., AND MCILLROY, M. An algorithm for differential file comparison. Tech. Rep. 41, AT&T Bell Laboratories Inc., 1976.

[11] KLEIN, M. Change Management for Distributed Ontologies. PhD thesis, Vrije Universiteit Amsterdam, Aug. 2004.

[12] LINDHOLM, T., KANGASHARJU, J., AND TARKOMA, S. Fast and simple XML tree differencing by sequence alignment. In Proceedings of the 2006 ACM Symposium on Document Engineering, Amsterdam, The Netherlands, October 10-13, 2006 (2006), D. C. A. Bulterman and D. F. Brailsford, Eds., ACM, pp. 75–84.

[13] NOY, N. F., AND MUSEN, M. A. PROMPTDIFF: a fixed-point algorithm for comparing ontology versions. In Proceedings of the Eighteenth National Conference on Artificial Intelligence and Fourteenth Conference on Innovative Applications of Artificial Intelligence, July 28 - August 1, 2002, Edmonton, Alberta, Canada (2002), R. Dechter and R. S. Sutton, Eds., AAAI Press / The MIT Press, pp. 744–750.

[14] PAPAVASSILIOU, V., FLOURIS, G., FUNDULAKI, I., KOTZINOS, D., AND CHRISTOPHIDES, V. On detecting high-level changes in RDF/S KBs. In The Semantic Web - ISWC 2009, 8th International Semantic Web Conference, ISWC 2009, Chantilly, VA, USA, October 25-29, 2009. Proceedings (2009), A. Bernstein, D. R. Karger, T. Heath, L. Feigenbaum, D. Maynard, E. Motta, and K. Thirunarayan, Eds., vol. 5823 of Lecture Notes in Computer Science, Springer, pp. 473–488.

[15] PERCIVAL, C. Naive differences of executable code. http://www.daemonology.net/bsdiff/, accessed Nov 26, 2012, 2003.

[16] RÖNNAU, S., AND BORGHOFF, U. M. Versioning XML-based office documents. *Multimedia Tools and Applications 43*, 3 (2009), 253–274.

[17] RÖNNAU, S., PAULI, C., AND BORGHOFF, U. M. Merging changes in XML documents using reliable context fingerprints. In *Proceedings of the 2008 ACM Symposium on Document Engineering, Sao Paulo, Brazil, September 16-19, 2008* (2008), M. da Graça Campos Pimentel, D. C. A. Bulterman, and L. F. G. Soares, Eds., pp. 52–61.

[18] RÖNNAU, S., PHILIPP, G., AND BORGHOFF, U. M. Efficient change control of XML documents. In *Proceedings of the 2009 ACM Symposium on Document Engineering, Munich, Germany, September 16-18, 2009* (2009), U. M. Borghoff and B. Chidlovskii, Eds., ACM, pp. 3–12.

[19] RÖNNAU, S., SCHEFFCZYK, J., AND BORGHOFF, U. M. Towards XML version control of office documents. In *Proceedings of the 2005 ACM Symposium on Document Engineering, Bristol, UK, November 2-4, 2005* (2005), A. Wiley and P. R. King, Eds., pp. 10–19.

[20] THAO, C., AND MUNSON, E. V. Using versioned tree data structure, change detection and node identity for three-way XML merging. In *Proceedings of the 2010 ACM Symposium on Document Engineering, Manchester, United Kingdom, September 21-24, 2010* (2010), A. Antonacopoulos, M. J. Gormish, and R. Ingold, Eds., pp. 77–86.

Version Aware LibreOffice Documents

Meenu Pandey
Department of EECS
University Of Wisconsin-Milwaukee
Milwaukee, WI 53201-0784, USA
mpandey@uwm.edu

Ethan V. Munson
Department of EECS
University Of Wisconsin-Milwaukee
Milwaukee, WI 53201-0784, USA
munson@uwm.edu

ABSTRACT

Version control systems provide a methodology for maintaining changes to a document over its lifetime and provide better management and control of evolving document collections, such as source code for large software systems. However, no version control system supports similar functionalities for office documents.

Version Aware XML documents integrate full versioning functionality into an XML document type, using XML namespaces to avoid document type errors. Version aware XML documents contain a preamble with versions stored in reverse delta format, plus unique ID attributes attached to the nodes of the documents. They support the full branching and merging functionalities familiar to software engineers, in contrast to the constrained versioning models typical of Office applications.

LibreOffice is an open source office document suite which is widely used for document creation. Each document is represented in the Open Office Document Format, which is a collection of XML files. The current project is an endeavor to show the practicality of the version aware XML documents approach by modifying the LibreOffice document suite to support version awareness. We are modifying LibreOffice to accept and preserve both the preamble and the IDs of the version aware framework. Initially, other functionality will be provided by wrapper applications and independent tools, but full integration into the LibreOffice user interface is envisioned.

Categories and Subject Descriptors

I.7.1 [**Document and Text Processing**]: Document and Text Editing—*document management*; D.2.7 [**Software Engineering**]: Distribution, Maintenance, and Enhancement—*version control*

Keywords

user collaboration, XML, version aware

DocEng'13, September 10–13, 2013, Florence, Italy.
ACM 978-1-4503-1789-4/13/09.
http://dx.doi.org/10.1145/2494266.2494269

1. INTRODUCTION

Version control systems provide a methodology for maintaining changes to a document over its lifetime as a collaborative team develops it. Typical version control systems, like Subversion [6], Mercurial [5] , and Git [1], provide the functionality for version repository creation, storage and retrieval of versions from a repository and creation of a graph of versions via branch and merge operations. These tools often require access to a central repository or a shared file system to store the versioned data. Experience has shown that it is a useful service for a large technical user base.

However, for office documents, the user base is typically non-technical. Also, while the documents often go through many revisions, they are often standalone objects or are part of small collections. Thus, the overhead of creating and managing a repository is hard to justify.

One approach to track different revisions of a document is to save them by different names that suggest the evolution of the document. In this approach, collaboration can be achieved by manual branching and merging, but this can be a cumbersome and confusing task. Branch and merge functions for office documents can aid users by keeping track of multiple revisions of a document within the document itself, maintaining branch information for the document when multiple authors work on it simultaneously, and later by merging those parallel changes into a unified version when needed. The ability to track changes of a document is important for many official (user manuals, regulatory documents, technical design documents, etc.) as well as for personal documents.

Office document software does provide simple version control, in the form of current version/past-version (Microsoft Office) or linear document histories (LibreOffice). While this support for versions is helpful, it is insufficient for collaboration in large teams because parallel editing is not supported. This can force users to perform manual merges to integrate changes from multiple sources. Some cloud storage systems offer versioning and collaboration support for stored documents but they do not provide the systematic support for collaboration that a version control system does.

We aim to show that the addition of branch and merge functionality to LibreOffice [3] will facilitate collaboration with less manual effort. The first step towards this goal is to convert LibreOffice ODF files into version aware documents and provide the basics of version control support.

In the rest of the paper we introduce version aware approach for xml documents and how it can be implemented for LibreOffice documents. In subsequent sections, we explain the load and save process of LibreOffice document and how necessary changes for version awareness can be made persistent throughout the LibreOffice document lifecycle.

2. BACKGROUND AND RELATED WORK

Conventional office document programs already support simple forms of version control. Microsoft Word has a "Track Changes " feature that can be viewed as a two version system. When changes are being tracked, there is a notion of the current version and of a single previous version. Differences between these versions are tracked and a user can decide whether or not to accept the changes. LibreOffice also stores textual documents in a compressed archive that holds a series of files that represent a linear document history. Each document is represented in the Open Office Document Format, based on XML [9]. Users can choose different versions if this is needed. Changes can be recorded and authors can accept or reject the changes between versions but it does not provide three-way merge functionality and does not support simultaneous editing by multiple authors. Thus, neither system supports true collaboration because neither one provides any services for merging parallel edits of the same base document. Whether existing LibreOffice version control functions can be used for better change detection is left for future work.

Conventional source code version systems support branch and merge operations with tools like diff3 [2] which assumes that the source material is raw text and that line breaks represent frequent and meaningful delimiters within files. In fact, modern office document systems often store all their content in XML files with exactly two lines: one for the XML declaration and the second for the rest of the content. In this context, meaningful merging of XML content is challenging, because it is difficult to be certain how to match XML element content between two versions. Some systems use approximate signatures [4], while Thao and Munson showed that using unique IDs allows for an efficient merging algorithm [7]. Based on this work, Thao [8] proposed a new Version Aware document framework using the following elements:

1. a special namespace (called "molhado") to separate the versioning information from the application's normal content;

2. a revision history element in a preamble location that holds the version history information in reverse delta format.

3. XML signature elements to prevent users from altering the version data without detection; and

4. a unique identifier attribute for every element of the document content so that changes between different versions can be identified easily.

In a version-aware document, the latest version contains the complete document content, while previous versions can be retrieved by applying a chain of deltas to the latest version. Each sub-element of the revision history element stores information about the edit operations performed in previous versions. The main edit operations are: attribute value update within any element, changes in node sequences, node deletion, node addition, and node name update. This versioning framework also includes an efficient 3-way merge algorithm that requires each XML node to have a unique ID.

Unique IDs are important for efficient matching of nodes between versions. If correctly maintained by an editing system, they allow the versioning system to match nodes between versions even when some nodes have undergone substantial transformations. Unique IDs also help to identify conflicts between two versions, which are currently expected to be resolved manually by the authors.

As a version-aware document contains the entire document history, users do not need to interact with any version repository. Thus users will gain the ability to access past versions, especially gaining the ability to recover contents that were deleted in multiple revisions in the past. Also, the system will provide support for authors to work simultaneously on the same sections of the document by creating separate version branches and to later merge their changes. Non-conflicting changes can be merged automatically while conflicting changes will need manual effort.

A first application of this framework was made using the Inkscape SVG editor, via addition of a wrapper application that manages the maintenance of versioning information in Inkscape saved files. This worked well because SVG editors are designed with the expectation that other applications might add namespace-protected content that should be preserved. In contrast, our first attempts to use the version-aware framework with LibreOffice failed because the versioning information was tolerated by the application, but not preserved during a load-edit-save interaction cycle. This problem has forced us to make deeper changes to the implementation of the LibreOffice software so that it can support the version aware preamble and element unique identifiers.

3. APPROACH AND IMPLEMENTATION

It will not be surprising to learn that a production quality office document system uses a complex file representation. A LibreOffice ODF document is a zip compressed archive that contains four XML files: meta.xml, settings.xml, content.xml, styles.xml. The "meta.xml" and "settings.xml" files do not affect the content of the document. The "styles.xml" contains information about the styles used within the document. The "content.xml" file stores the main content of the document including text, pictures etc. Thus, if the content.xml and styles.xml files can accept the four changes described above, then a LibreOffice document will be version aware. Currently, our main focus is applying the four modifications changes to the content file. We are leaving the changes to the style file for future work. The problem, of course, is that LibreOffice was not designed with version awareness in mind. Furthermore, it did not begin its life as an open source project, so documentation is limited.

In LibreOffice, the document is saved as a set of files on disk but is represented by a rather different document model in memory. During the document load operation, an import filter converts the XML files into this document model. Similarly during a save operation, an export filter converts the document model into XML format. Every element and attribute of the content file has a corresponding data structure in the document model. So, any changes made to the content file that are not part of the LibreOffice document model are not saved during the save operation.

Our approach is to write a wrapper application that will read the content file and will add the "molhado" namespace, the unique identifiers, the revision preamble and the authentication signature for every version of the document,

```
❶  <?xml version="1.0" encoding="UTF-8" standalone="no"?>
    <office:document-content xmlns:office="urn:oasis:names:tc:opendocument:xmlns:office:1.0"
    xmlns:chart="urn:oasis:names:tc:opendocument:xmlns:chart:1.0"
                                                .
                                                .
❷  xmlns:molhado="http://www.cs.uwm.edu/molhado"
    xmlns:xsi="http://www.w3.org/2001/XMLSchema-instance" molhado:id="0" office:version="1.2">
❸  <molhado:revision-history cur-rev-id="54836a0a-e9ef-11e2-ba57-1803732ba9aa" cur-user="meenu" id="revision-history"
    max-id="160">
❹    <molhado:revision id="5483b82b-e9ef-11e2-ba57-1803732ba9aa" name="1" parents="">
       <molhado:attr-del attr="xmlns:molhado" nodeid="0" value="http://www.cs.uwm.edu/molhado"/>
     </molhado:revision>
❺  <Signature xmlns="http://www.w3.org/2000/09/xmldsig#">
     <SignedInfo>
      <CanonicalizationMethod Algorithm="http://www.w3.org/TR/2001/REC-xml-c14n-20010315"/>
      <SignatureMethod Algorithm="http://www.w3.org/2000/09/xmldsig#rsa-sha1"/>
      <Reference URI="#revision-history">
       <Transforams>
        <Transform Algorithm="http://www.w3.org/2000/09/xmldsig#enveloped-signature"/>
       </Transforms>
       <DigestMethod Algorithm==="http://www.w3.org/2000/09/xmldsig#sha1"/>
       <DigestValue>cqJ+PvU3WJ6SLYgLv6Xklol2Fx8=</DigestValue>
      </Reference>
     </SignedInfo>
     <SignatureValue>GejGlBWqBZniMLAmRqePH6/xfRtnG2addGSQqphlC+qmvmYxxFh7yDHo+PnkoCClt8NfUUnbqugosgGTHePTIA==
     </SignatureValue>
     <KeyInfo>
      <KeyValue>
       <RSAKeyValue>
        <Modulus>ltgInCRrK7k2OIX6ZnXoe6RZ9A2kIJooGb/zRYD18tb3I/AFlk0OkSO43aiQXz/MTmQtCb4IJVOK5/5uUWl0Hw==</Modulus>
        <Exponent>AQAB</Exponent>
       </RSAKeyValue>
      </KeyValue>
     </KeyInfo>
    </Signature>

    </molhado:revision-history>
❻  <office:scripts molhado:id="1"/>
    <office:font-face-decls molhado:id="2">
      <style:font-face molhado:id="3" style:name="Lohit Hindi1" svg:font-family="'Lohit Hindi'"/>
      <style:font-face molhado:id="4" style:font-family-generic="roman" style:font-pitch="variable"
       style:name="Liberation Serif" svg:font-family="'Liberation Serif'"/>
                              .
                              .
                              .
    </office:document-content>
```

Figure 1: Content.xml file after applying required changes for version awareness. Namespace *molhado* is defined first. New elements of *revision-history* and *signature* are added. Rest of the elements in xml are assigned a *unique ID*.

as needed. Document size increases once all the needed changes are applied to document by the wrapper application. In addition, the core LibreOffice source code has had to be modified to persist this information through a complete load-edit-save cycle. This task is not straightforward because of the particulars of the LibreOffice implementation, which does not exploit inheritance as much as one might hope, especially in the area of element attributes.

When LibreOffice writer loads an existing ODF file, an xmlreader object reads all the XML files and instantiates objects for every element type. These classes are called Import Context classes and have data members that correspond to the attributes of the respective XML element. First, those data members are assigned the corresponding attribute values. Second, based on the context of the XML element type, the corresponding universal network object (UNO) services are called such as - Paragraph, PageCount, TextCursor etc. Each UNO service has properties which are set by the import contexts created earlier. Then all the UNO service objects are stored in memory as a pool of items, which defines the document model. The document saving operation is straightforward. It creates export context classes for all

the items in the item pool and then saves them into XML format.

To accommodate the proposed changes we have made the following changes to the LibreOffice code base:

1. All namespaces are stored in a namespace map in LibreOffice. So the molhado namespace has been added to that namespace map.

2. New elements like signature and revision history are preserved during load and save by making new classes for these elements that save their attributes over the lifecycle of the document.

3. Every XML node needs a unique ID that should not change over the lifetime of the document versions. The unique IDs are essential for identifying nodes that have undergone substantial transformations and can still be matched with their original version. Preservation of the unique IDs for every element requires changes to be made at multiple entry points of the XML elements. The main high level elements in the content.xml are fonts, styles, text, table and number where the functionality can be added to store the unique ids of those elements and their children elements. As every XML

element has a corresponding UNO service, the addition of the new ID attribute in each XML element should be accompanied by the addition of a UNO service property as well.

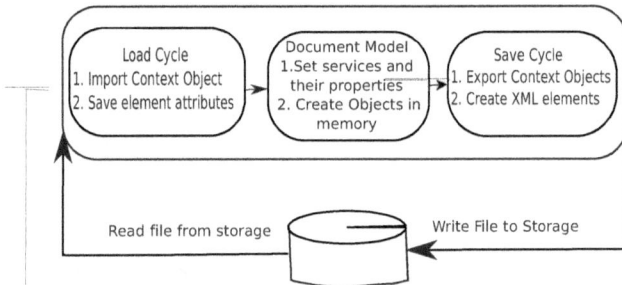

Figure 2: LibreOffice document lifecycle.

As unique IDs should be accomodated for every XML element type, we need to modify the implementation of LibreOffice to support three key operations:

1. Load and save ID attribute in import context classes during XML load operation.

2. Add the ID property to the corresponding UNO services and save IDs of every node in memory.

3. Extract ID property and save it in XML format' during export operation.

Once the changes in content.xml are preserved by the LibreOffice application, our wrapper applications will be able to perform three-way XML merging in order combine changes made in parallel by multiple authors.

4. RESULTS

LibreOffice is a long-lived and complex system and determining how to modify it has been a challenging task. We have successfully added our additional namespace and the preamble containing the version history and signature so that they persist through load-edit-save cycles. The key challenge has been to determine the life-cycle of document content elements and to find a good point at which to insert our IDs. At the time of writing, we have been able to make the IDs persist for paragraph elements and for text fields used in forms. But our solution for paragraphs will be quite cumbersome to reproduce for other related elements and we are looking for a more general control point to support the IDs.

The document size increases as additional information is stored in content.xml. File size change for a LibreOffice document with 150 nodes in content.xml is approximately 1.5KB for a first revision when namespace, revision history, ID and signature information is added. It is expected to increase with every revision as incremental revision history will be added. Currently the exact file size change information is not determined because LibreOffice strips off the unique IDs for many xml elements. Thus, versioning framework does not work correctly to calculate change history between versions.

5. CONCLUSION

This application note describes the implementation of the version aware framework for LibreOffice "writer" documents. It also suggests modifications required for the LibreOffice code base so that our changes can persist throughout the document's lifecycle. A version aware LibreOffice document will contain a complete change history and will be able to undergo three-way XML merging and conflict resolution so that document collaboration and management will be possible without the use of a conventional version control repository.

This work shows that it is possible to provide many of the sophisticated features of modern software version control systems in a context designed for less sophisticated users. Branching and merging tasks are already being performed by office document authors, but without adequate automated support. The version aware document approach integrates easily with office document systems because it is designed to work with the XML representation that those systems have already accepted. Thus, full-blown branching and merging can be accessible to non-technical users working on everyday documents.

6. REFERENCES

[1] Git - fast version control system. http://git-scm.com.
[2] GNU diff3. http://www.gnu.org/software/diffutils/.
[3] LIbreOffice. http://docs.libreoffice.org/.
[4] T. Lindholm. A three-way merge for XML documents. In *Proceedings of the 4th ACM Symposium on Document Engineering*, pages 1–10. ACM Press, 2004.
[5] Mercurial SCM. http://mercurial.selenic.com.
[6] Subversion. http://subversion.tigris.org.
[7] C. Thao and E. V. Munson. Using versioned tree data structure, change detection and node identity for three-way XML merging. In *Proceedings of the 10th ACM Symposium on Document engineering*, DocEng '10, pages 77–86, New York, NY, USA, 2010. ACM.
[8] C. Thao and E. V. Munson. Version-aware XML documents. In *Proceedings of the 11th ACM Symposium on Document engineering*, DocEng '11, pages 97–100, New York, NY, USA, 2011. ACM.
[9] Extensible Markup Language (XML). http://www.w3.org/XML/.

Interactive Text Document Clustering using Feature Labeling

S. N. Nourashrafeddin
Faculty of Computer Science
Dalhousie University
Halifax, Nova Scotia
Canada B3H 4R2
nourashr@cs.dal.ca

Evangelos Milios
Faculty of Computer Science
Dalhousie University
Halifax, Nova Scotia
Canada B3H 4R2
eem@cs.dal.ca

Dirk Arnold
Faculty of Computer Science
Dalhousie University
Halifax, Nova Scotia
Canada B3H 4R2
dirk@cs.dal.ca

ABSTRACT

We propose an interactive text document method, which is based on term labeling. The algorithm asks the user to cluster the top keyterms associated with document clusters iteratively. The keyterm clusters are used to guide the clustering method. Rather than using standard clustering algorithms, we propose a new text clusterer using term clusters. Terms that exist in a document corpus are clustered. Using a greedy approach, the term clusters are distilled in order to remove non-discriminative general terms. We then present a heuristic approach to extract seed documents associated with each distilled term cluster. These seeds are finally used to cluster all documents. We compared our interactive term labeling to a baseline interactive term selection algorithm on some real standard text datasets. The experiments show that with a comparable amount of user effort, our term labeling is more effective than the baseline term selection method.

Categories and Subject Descriptors

I.5.3 [**Clustering**]: Algorithms

Keywords

Active feature supervision, term clouds, term clustering

1. INTRODUCTION

Clustering plays an important role for browsing in document collections. Grouping similar documents provides invaluable information about the text topics. The problem of clustering is widely studied in the data mining literature and numerous algorithms have been proposed for text document clustering [1]. However, the output of the existing algorithms might be different from what users intend. Each user likes to cluster documents according to her point of view [2, 13]. In addition, there is no ground truth for many

DocEng '13, September 10–13 2013, Florence, Italy
Copyright © 2013 ACM 978-1-4503-1789-4/13/09...$15.00
http://dx.doi.org/10.1145/2494266.2494279

datasets in practice and it is the user who evaluates the quality of clusterings. These issues require the involvement of the users' expectations in the clustering process.

Document and term supervision are two kinds of interaction used in text clustering. Labeling documents [3], or specifying *"must-link"* or *"cannot-link"* pairwise constraints among them [4, 6, 7, 9, 14, 23, 24] have been proposed in the traditional semi-supervised algorithms as document supervision. On the other hand, specifying discriminative terms to form a feature set has been proposed in [12, 13] as a term supervision approach.

Traditional semi-supervised algorithms usually involve user preferences as prior knowledge to the clustering process. The supervision is usually in the form of document supervision. The knowledge is incorporated in the clustering process to generate clusters matching the user preferences. This approach of collecting users' preferences raises the following questions:

1. What is the best way to collect a set of documents in order to elicit user preferences? Is random selection a reliable approach for this purpose?

2. Most existing semi-supervised algorithms consider user supervision as a noise-free and consistent input [3, 4, 6, 7, 9, 14, 23, 24]. However, users may make mistakes in supervising documents with similar topics. The accuracy of the input knowledge is dependent on the user expertness and also on the selection method used to collect documents for supervision. How much do noisy inputs affect the quality of clusterings?

3. Feature (term) labeling is used in the classification problem to incorporate users' expectations [10, 20]. The users are asked to label important terms for classes. It has been demonstrated that feature labeling is effective in document classification. Is feature labeling a good approach in text document clustering? We propose an interactive feature-labeling text clusterer in this work. Our experiments show that our proposed feature labeling improves the quality of clusterings significantly.

Feature supervision is used in [12, 13] to actively form a feature set for text document clustering. The user is asked to specify discriminative terms during the phase of document supervision. A feature set is then formed using the terms specified as discriminative.

We ask the label of terms instead of asking about discriminative terms in this work. After generating document clusters, their corresponding top keyterms are extracted to form term clouds. The user then performs term labeling in the form of reorganizing the keyterms among term clouds. The keyterms in the supervised term clouds are subsequently used to generate new document clusters. We perform term supervision for a few iterations until the user chooses to terminate.

Compared to the active feature selection proposed in [12, 13], our feature labeling has the following advantages:

1. We promote better insight into document clusters by generating term cloud containing top keyterms associated with a document cluster, which provide an intuitive description of the topic of the cluster.

2. Rather than using standard clustering techniques such as k-means, which do not typically work well for text data [1], we propose a new document clustering algorithm using term clusters.

3. The user can adjust the number of document clusters in our proposed algorithm through merging, splitting, or even removing term clouds.

The remainder of this paper is organized as follows. Section 2 reviews some interactive text clustering algorithms. Section 3 reviews some unsupervised feature selection methods for text data. Section 4 explains the proposed text clustering algorithm in detail. Our feature-supervised text clustering is explained in Section 5. Experimental results on some real text datasets are reported in Section 6. Section 7 includes conclusions and future work.

2. RELATED WORK

In this section, we review some feature-supervised algorithms proposed for text document clustering. The users of these algorithms can guide the clustering process in the form of term supervision.

An interactive feature selection framework for document clustering is proposed in [12]. Initial document clusters are obtained using k-means with the top m terms selected by the mean-*TFIDF* method, which is an unsupervised feature selection method for text data [22]. The quality of a term in this method is proportional to the average of its *tf-idf* values over all documents. Treating current document clusters as classes, the χ^2 statistic [11] is then used to create a ranked list of terms. The top terms of this list are then presented to the user for supervision. The user gives one of two answers regarding each term presented. She either accepts the term as a discriminative one or she does not know. The feature set of the next round of clustering consists of those terms accepted by the user as discriminative.

A feature selection method is proposed in [13] to enhance semi-supervised document clustering algorithms. The user is asked to identify discriminative terms during the phase of document supervision. The supervised documents with the feature set, formed by the discriminative terms, are used to guide the clustering algorithm. Similar to most semi-supervision algorithms [3, 4, 6, 7, 9, 14, 23, 24], the feature selection of this algorithm is just performed once in the beginning of the clustering process and the users do not have any chance to interact with the process ever after.

We ask for the cluster label of terms instead of just asking about discriminative terms in this work. Our experiments show that with a comparable amount of user effort, the clustering algorithm based on feature labeling outperforms the ones based on feature selection mentioned above.

A text document clustering algorithm is proposed in [8], which is capable of producing multiple clusterings of the same data based on different point of views. Following a spectral clustering algorithm [21], a Laplacian matrix is generated using the cosine similarity among documents. Eigenvectors corresponding to the smallest second to $(m + 1)$-th eigenvalues are then computed. The k-means algorithm with $k = 2$ is applied on each of m eigenvectors to produce m clusterings. For each clustering, the top terms associated with each of two clusters are then extracted to display to the user. The user then inspects these terms to determine the eigenvectors that result in meaningful clusterings. The combination of the accepted eigenvectors are subsequently used to generate document clusterings. In this algorithm, the user has no chance to change the clustering process. She either accepts or rejects the clusterings generated from the eigenvectors. Our proposed algorithm lets the user reorganize the keyterms of clusters instead of just accepting or rejecting them. She can even change the cluster of keyterms thoroughly. The keyterms are then used to re-cluster documents in our work.

An active text document clustering based on frequent itemsets is proposed in [18]. An initial set of frequent itemsets is first obtained. A frequent itemset consists of those terms, which co-occur in documents more than a threshold value called minimum support. The k-means algorithm is then used to cluster the frequent itemsets. For each cluster, a list of top itemsets is extracted and the user is asked to select the best itemset from the list. The clusters are then adjusted based on the selected itemsets. After adjusting clusters by the user for a few iterations, each document is assigned to the nearest cluster using cosine similarity. A noiseless oracle is presented in the algorithm to simulate user interactions. From the top itemsets of each cluster, the oracle returns the best itemset based on the true label of documents. The simulated users are assumed to never make any mistake and it is not clear how sensitive this algorithm is to noisy user feedback.

3. FEATURE SELECTION

In this section, we review four unsupervised feature selection methods that are widely used for text clustering. These methods assign a score to each feature. The features with higher scores can be selected to form a new feature space.

3.1 Mean-tfidf

Similar to the document vectors, each term can be represented as a vector of documents. Each entry of this vector indicates the degree of importance of the term in the respective document. For each term, the mean of its *tfidf* values over all documents is measured in this method [22]:

$$\text{Mean-TFIDF}_j = \frac{1}{N} \sum_{i=1}^{N} tfidf_{ij} \qquad (1)$$

where N is the number of documents in the corpus. The higher the mean-*tfidf* (MT) score, the better suited the term to be included in the new feature space. The computation complexity of this technique is $O(N)$ for each term.

3.2 Var-tfidf

Instead of using the mean value, the variance of *tfidf* values over all documents is computed in this method [15]. Using Eq. 1, the var-*tfidf* (VT) score is computed using the following formula:

$$\text{Var-tfidf}_j = \frac{1}{N-1} \sum_{i=1}^{N} (tfidf_{ij} - \text{Mean-TFIDF}_j)^2 \quad (2)$$

Discriminating terms have higher var-*tfidf* scores. The computation complexity of this technique is $O(N)$ for each term.

3.3 Entropy Rank

In this method, the quality of each term is measured by the entropy reduction when the term is removed [16]. Terms are removed in turn and then the entropy is measured. If removing a term results in the maximum entropy, the term is the most important one. The entropy of term t is measured using the following formula:

$$\text{Entropy}(t) = -\sum_{i=1}^{N} \sum_{i=1}^{N} S_{ij} \cdot \log(S_{ij}) + (1 - S_{ij}) \cdot \log(1 - S_{ij}) \quad (3)$$

where S_{ij} is the similarity between the document d_i and d_j when term t is removed and is computed by the following formula:

$$S_{ij} = e^{-\alpha \cdot dist_{ij}}, \alpha = -\frac{\ln(0.5)}{\overline{dist}} \quad (4)$$

where $dist_{ij}$ is the distance between the document d_i and d_j when term t is removed and $\overline{dist}$ is the average distance among the documents after the term t is removed. The time complexity of computing *Entropy Rank* (ER) score is $O(N^2M)$ for each term, where M is the number of terms.

3.4 Term Contribution

In this method, the quality of each term is computed as its overall contribution to the document similarities [16]. The *Term Contribution* (TC) score is defined as:

$$TC(t) = \sum_{i,j \cap i \neq j} f(t, d_i) \cdot f(t, d_j) \quad (5)$$

where $f(t, d_i)$ is the feature value of the term t in the document d_i, which is *tfidf* in this work. The time complexity of this method is $O(N^2)$ for each term.

4. METHODOLOGY

We represent a text corpus as a document-term matrix in the bag of words model [1]. Documents and terms are represented as row and column vectors in this matrix. Each entry of the matrix is term frequency–inverse document frequency (*tf-idf*) that indicates the importance of a term in the respective document.

Since the number of terms in a text dataset is often multiple times larger than the number of documents, it has been proposed to first focus on term clusters [19]. Following the same approach, the proposed algorithm is based on the idea that before finding document clusters, it is better to focus on term clustering and the keyterms that represent topics. Our proposed algorithm consists of three phases:

1. Term clustering

2. Topic keyterm selection

3. Document clustering

The structure of our algorithm is depicted in Fig. 1. In Phase 1, fuzzy c-means is used to cluster terms (columns of the document-term matrix). Fuzzy c-means groups the terms into k term clusters. We designed our algorithm assuming that the number of term clusters is equal to the number of document clusters, k. The initial number of document clusters is user-defined. We will explain in Section 5 how users can identify a value for k using our interactive feature-supervised algorithm.

We also assume that each term cluster includes some keyterms representing a topic. Some general terms are also included, which are not useful in the clustering process. Using the term clusters without any prior analysis causes the quality of document clusters to deteriorate [19]. The goal of Phase 2 (Topic keyterm selection) is to distill these general terms and keep only the topic keyterms in term clusters. From topic keyterms, we extract some documents called representative documents, which are used as seeds to cluster all documents.

A document centroid is generated for the representative documents associated with each term cluster. The distances between documents and the centroids are then used in Phase 3 for document clustering. The main steps of our proposed algorithm are shown in Algorithm 1.

4.1 Term Clustering

The presence of similar topics is a common case in text clustering. Similar topics share common terms and each term usually belongs to multiple topics with different degrees of relevance. This is a key issue in term clustering.

The integration of the fuzzy paradigm with the simplicity and efficiency of k-means, make fuzzy c-means a good candidate for term clustering. Given a document-term matrix, we apply fuzzy c-means on the term vectors to generate k term clusters. For a matrix with M term vectors $\{t_1, t_2, ..., t_M\}$, fuzzy c-means generates k term clusters $\{TC_p\}_{p=1}^{k}$ such that the following objective function is locally minimized [5]:

$$F_z = \sum_{i=1}^{M} \sum_{p=1}^{k} u_{ip}^z dist^2(t_i, \mu_p) \quad (6)$$

where z is a real number larger than 1, u_{ip} is the degree of membership of t_i in the term cluster TC_p, and μ_p is the centroid of TC_p.

We use the maximum method to defuzzify the final membership matrix [5]. Each term is assigned to the term cluster with the largest membership value.

4.2 Topic Keyterm Selection

The input of this phase consists of k term clusters each including a set of terms. We assume that only high-score terms represent topics and the other terms are non-discriminative [15]. We present a greedy approach to extract these discriminative terms. Our greedy approach consists of the following steps:

1. For each term, we first compute its score using one of the methods described in Section 3.

2. We then compute an average score for each term cluster. The average score is the mean of scores of all terms included in the term cluster.

3. In each term cluster, those terms whose scores are smaller than the cluster average score are removed. The remaining high-score terms are used in Phase 3 (Document clustering).

4.3 Document Clustering

The input of this phase consists of k distilled term clusters, each including a set of discriminative keyterms. Each set characterizes a set of documents called representative. Representative documents are those documents that are close to each other in the subspace spanned by discriminative keyterms. We extract these representative documents using the following steps:

1. We first compute a term-centroid for each term cluster. A term-centroid is the column average of the term vectors corresponding to the terms included in the term cluster. It is a vector with dimensionality equal to the number of documents.

2. We then apply k-means with $k = 2$ on the term-centroid (in a one dimensional space) to partition its elements into two clusters. One cluster includes elements with near-zero values and the other cluster includes elements with values larger than zero. Only elements with large values correspond to the representative documents.

Algorithm 1 Our proposed text document clustering algorithm

Input: *a document-term matrix, k*
Output: *k document clusters*
1: *use fuzzy c-means to generate k term clusters*
2: *remove non-discriminative terms from the term clusters*
3: **for** *each distilled term cluster* **do**
4:   *extract representative documents*
5:   *compute a document centroid for the representative documents*
6: **end for**
7: **for** *each document in the dataset* **do**
8:   *measure its distances to the document centroids*
9:   *compute its memberships in document clusters as the inverse of the distances*
10: **end for**

A sample of four term-centroids for four classes of the 20-Newsgroups dataset is shown in Fig. 2. Each column of this $N \times k$ gray scale image corresponds to a term-centroid and each row is a document. Black areas contain near-zero *tf-idf* values while light areas contain larger *tf-idf*. The representative documents of each term-centroid have larger values compared to the non-representative documents as shown in Fig. 2. It is noteworthy to mention that a representative document can be linked with more than one term cluster in this phase.

The extracted representative documents are finally used to cluster all documents using the following steps:

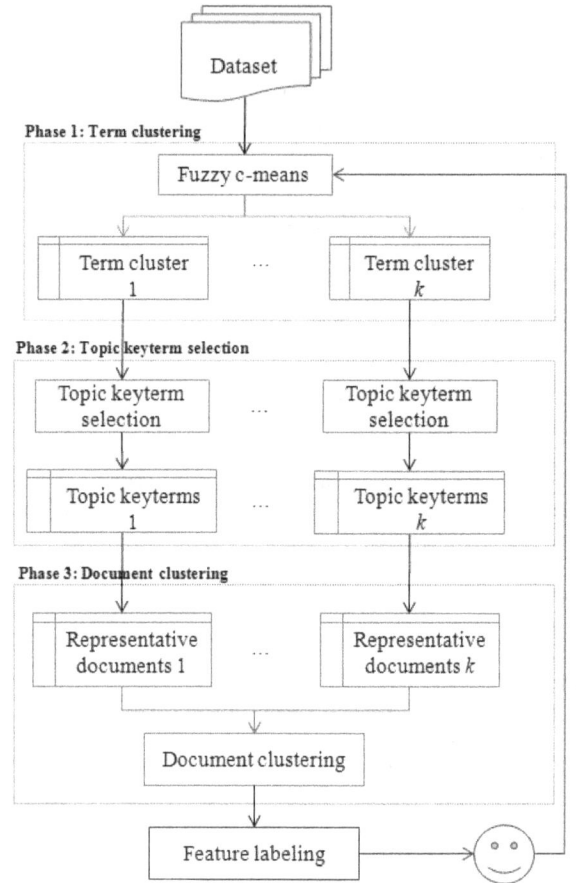

Figure 1: The structure of our feature-supervised text clustering algorithm. Fuzzy c-means is used for term clustering. A greedy approach distills the term clusters in order to remove non-discriminative terms. Representative documents associated with each term cluster are then extracted and used as seeds to cluster all documents. The top keyterms of the current document clusters are then extracted and displayed to the user in the form of term clouds. The user performs term labeling on the term clouds. The supervised term clouds are subsequently used to re-cluster terms.

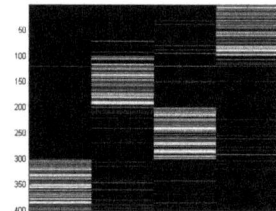

Figure 2: A sample of four term-centroids generated from four classes of the 20-Newsgroups dataset. The block structure of the representative documents (light areas) is clear in this image.

1. For each term cluster, we compute a document centroid over its representative documents. A document centroid is the row average of the document vectors corresponding to the representative documents.

2. The distances of each document to the document centroids are then computed. The memberships of documents in document clusters are then measured as the inverse of these distances. In this way, each document has a membership value in each document cluster.

5. FEATURE-SUPERVISED CLUSTERING

In this section we explain how feature supervision can be added to our algorithm. The top keyterms of document clusters are extracted for this purpose. The keyterms are then exposed to the users so as to let them guide the algorithm.

The supervision starts after document clustering is done as shown in Fig. 1. A hard partitioning of documents is first produced such that each document is assigned to the cluster with the largest membership value. Treating document clusters as true classes, the χ^2 statistic is then used to extract top keyterms. For each document cluster, we sort the χ^2 values in descending order. The first f terms form the top keyterms of each document cluster.

A term cloud is subsequently created for each document cluster using its respective top keyterms. The term clouds are displayed to the user and she can modify them using the following options:

1. Remove a term from a term cloud.

2. Assign a term to another term cloud.

3. Assign a term to multiple term clouds.

It is also possible to merge two or more term clouds, split or even remove them. In this way, the user can specify the number of document clusters she prefers to generate.

After term supervision, we use the term clouds to initialize a membership matrix for fuzzy c-means to re-cluster terms. The membership matrix has k columns corresponding to the k clouds of keyterms, and M rows corresponding to the M terms of the dataset.

The matrix is randomly initialized except for those keyterms that exist in the supervised term clouds. For those keyterms, only their corresponding entries of the term clouds are set to one. The initialized membership matrix is then fed into fuzzy c-means to generate new term clusters. Given the new term clusters, we re-cluster documents. We perform these interactions for a few iterations until the term clouds of document clusters satisfy users.

We used a feature oracle to simulate user interactions and evaluate our feature labeling. The oracle of this study knows the label of terms. Given the true labels of documents, the χ^2 statistic is computed for this purpose. Each term is then assigned to the class with the largest χ^2 value.

Since users may make mistakes in supervision, our feature oracle has a parameter P_{exp} that indicates the degree of user expertness. $P_{exp} = 1$ corresponds to the perfect user, and $P_{exp} = 0$ means no supervision is performed. Based on this parameter the simulated user either assigns a term to a term cloud correctly or she does not know. In the latter case, she might remove the term from a cloud or assign it to a random cloud. The probability of removal is set to 0.5 and the probability of random assignment is set to $0.5/k$ in this case. The main steps of the simulated feature labeling are shown in Algorithm 2. The structure of our feature supervised clustering is also shown in Fig. 1.

Algorithm 2 Our feature labeling oracle

Input: k term clouds
Output: k supervised term clouds
1: **for** each term cloud **do**
2:    **for** each term in the term cloud **do**
3:       **if** rand[0,1] < P_{exp} **then**
4:          assign the term to the true cloud
5:       **else if** rand[0,1] < 0.5 **then**
6:          remove the term from the term cloud
7:       **else**
8:          generate a random number between 1 and k
9:          assign the term to the random term cloud
10:       **end if**
11:    **end for**
12: **end for**

The amount of user effort of our feature labeling can be measured using the following formula:

$$\text{user-effort} = \frac{k * f}{M} * \text{number\_of\_iterations} \qquad (7)$$

where f is the number of terms in each term cloud before supervision, k is the number of term clouds, which is the number of term clusters in our experiments.

6. EXPERIMENTAL RESULTS

In this section, we first evaluate the feature selection methods explained in Section 3 using our proposed text document clusterer. We then show the benefits of our feature labeling clusterer as compared to a baseline feature selection clusterer, which is inspired by the algorithms proposed in [12, 13].

6.1 Datasets and Implementation

In our experiments, we used six standard datasets whose characteristics are summarized in Table 1. The last column of the table shows the percentage of zero values that exists in the document-term matrices of the datasets. *LA Times* consists of documents about six topics including *Financial*, *Foreign*, *National*, *Metro*, *Sports*, and *Entertainment*. This dataset is created from the TREC-9 collection[1]. *Classic4* is one of the well-known benchmark datasets used in text clustering. It is created from the *SMART* data repository[2] containing abstracts of papers about medical, information retrieval, aerodynamics, and computing algorithms. The last four datasets are derived from the *20-Newsgroups* dataset [13]. This dataset consists of approximately 20000 news articles grouped into 20 different topics[3].

Stop-word removal, stemming, and removing low-variance terms [19] are applied to the datasets in a pre-processing step. Each dataset is then represented as a document-term matrix in the bag of words model. The effect of document length is reduced by using the $L2$ norm to normalize the length of document vectors to one.

---

[1]http://trec.nist.gov/data/qa/t9_qadata.html
[2]ftp://ftp.cs.cornell.edu/pub/smart/
[3]http://qwone.com/ jason/20Newsgroups/

Table 1: Summary of the text datasets used in our experiments

Dataset Name	No. of Docs	No. of Terms	k	Sparsity
Classic4	7094	5099	4	99.53%
LA Times	6279	6845	6	98.23%
News-sim3	2924	4697	3	99.01%
News-rel3	2624	4947	3	98.20%
News-multi7	6632	7006	7	99.09%
News-multi10	9586	8827	10	99.30%

Table 2: Average and standard deviation of the quality of clusterings generated by Algorithm 1 in 50 runs with different term scorings

	MT	VT	ER	TC
Classic4	0.93±0.07	0.94±0.04	0.93±0.08	0.93±0.06
	0.81±0.08	0.82±0.04	0.81±0.08	0.80±0.07
LA Times	0.65±0.04	0.66±0.03	0.66±0.02	0.65±0.02
	0.48±0.04	0.49±0.03	0.50±0.03	0.48±0.03
News-sim3	0.70±0.07	0.72±0.06	0.70±0.08	0.70±0.07
	0.31±0.07	0.32±0.06	0.30±0.08	0.30±0.06
News-rel3	0.65±0.05	0.66±0.05	0.66±0.06	0.64±0.07
	0.37±0.07	0.40±0.06	0.38±0.08	0.35±0.09
News-multi7	0.75±0.04	0.76±0.04	0.78±0.03	0.75±0.04
	0.68±0.03	0.69±0.02	0.72±0.02	0.67±0.02
News-multi10	0.74±0.03	0.76±0.03	0.77±0.03	0.73±0.03
	0.66±0.01	0.67±0.01	0.70±0.02	0.65±0.01

We used Euclidean distance to cluster document vectors since their length is normalized to one and cosine distance to cluster term vectors.

6.2 Evaluation Measures

We used the true labels of documents to evaluate clusters. We consider the hard partitioning of documents in our experiments since our benchmark datasets are single-labeled.

A confusion matrix is formed after each clustering. Each element of this matrix indicates the number of common documents between the corresponding cluster and class. The dimensionality of this matrix is k by k. This confusion matrix is subsequently used to compute *Fmeasure* and *Normalized Mutual Information* (*NMI*) [17].

6.3 Term Scoring

In the first round of experiments, we evaluate the feature selection methods explained in Section 3. Our proposed text document clusterer, Algorithm 1, is used for this purpose. We ran the clusterer 50 times for different term scoring methods, which are used in Phase 2 of our proposed algorithm to remove general terms. The average and standard deviation of the quality of clusterings obtained are reported in Table 2. The first value in each cell corresponds to the average of *Fmeasures* and the second one corresponds to the average of *NMIs*.

ER and VT have produced the best results in these experiments. However, the time complexity of ER is $O(N^2M^2)$ while VT has $O(NM)$ time complexity. The conclusion of these experiments is that either method can be used for term

scoring if the running time is not a big concern. Otherwise, VT is the better method in case of large datasets.

6.4 Feature Labeling vs. Feature Selection

In the second round of experiments, we show the benefits of our feature labeling clusterer as compared to a baseline active feature selection clusterer, which is inspired by the algorithms proposed in [12, 13]. The main steps of our active feature labeling and the active feature selection algorithm are shown in Algorithm 3 and Algorithm 6 respectively.

Our feature-labeling clustering algorithm, Algorithm 3, calls the feature labeling oracle, Algorithm 2, in order to simulate user interactions. This oracle knows the true cloud of each term in advance.

Algorithm 3 Our active feature-labeling clusterer

Input: *a document-term matrix, k, m*
Output: *k document clusters*
1: *obtain initial k document clusters using Algorithm 1 with m best terms based on mean-TFIDF*
2: **repeat**
3:     *compute χ^2 values for all terms using the current document clusters*
4:     *sort all terms according to their average χ^2 values in document clusters and obtain the ordered list T*
5:     **for** *each document cluster* **do**
6:       *generate a term cloud using its f top terms based on the χ^2 values*
7:     **end for**
8:     *perform feature labeling by using Algorithm 2*
9:     *use the term clouds to re-initialize Algorithm 1 and obtain k document clusters with the terms included in the term clouds and (m - number_of_terms (term clouds)) best terms of T*
10: **until** *the maximum number of iterations is reached or the user chooses to terminate*

The baseline feature-selection clustering algorithm, Algorithm 6, calls the feature selection oracle, Algorithm 4, in order to simulate user interactions. In this oracle, the simulated user accepts a term as discriminative if the term was among the top m terms of the dataset. Using the true labels of documents, the χ^2 statistic is used to form a reference set of the top m terms. The average of χ^2 values of each term in all document classes is computed for this purpose. The top m terms corresponding to the top average values form the reference set. The value of m is user-defined.

The user may make mistakes in specifying discriminative terms. She may accept a term while the term is not discriminative and vice versa. To simulate these mistakes in Algorithm 4, the feature selection oracle randomly picks a term from the bottom half of T, which is considered as a noisy term, and adds it to the current *FeatureSet*.

It is worth mentioning that the number of queries submitted to both feature labeling and selection oracles are the same in our simulations. The definition of all variables used in the simulations are shown in Table 3.

In our proposed feature-supervised algorithm, Fig. 1, all the terms are used for document clustering. However, only the best m terms are used in Algorithm 3. We considered this change only to make our proposed algorithm comparable to the Algorithm 6.

Algorithm 4 Feature selection oracle

Input: *an ordered list T*
Output: *FeatureSet*
1: *FeatureSet = []*
2: **for** *each term in T* **do**
3:    *present the term to the user and get reply*
4:    **if** *rand[0,1] < P_{exp}* **then**
5:      **if** *the user accepts the term* **then**
6:        *add the term to the current FeatureSet*
7:      **end if**
8:    **else if** *rand[0,1] < 0.5* **then**
9:      *randomly pick a term from the bottom half of T and add it to the current FeatureSet*
10:    **end if**
11: **end for**

Algorithm 5 Feature re-weighting

Input: *a document-term matrix, FeatureSet, g*
Output: *a re-weighted document-term matrix*
1: **for** *each term in the FeatureSet* **do**
2:    *multiply its corresponding term vector by g*
3: **end for**
4: *normalize all the document vectors using L2 norm*

Algorithm 6 Active feature-selection clusterer

Input: *a document-term matrix, k, m*
Output: *k document clusters*
1: *obtain initial k document clusters using k-means with m best terms based on mean-TFIDF*
2: **repeat**
3:    *compute χ^2 values for all terms using the current document clusters*
4:    *sort all terms according to their average χ^2 values in document clusters and obtain the ordered list T*
5:    *perform feature selection using Algorithm 4 and the ordered list $T(1:B)$*
6:    *perform feature re-weighting using Algorithm 5*
7:    *obtain k document clusters using k-means with the terms of the FeatureSet and (m - size_of(FeatureSet) best terms of T)*
8: **until** *the maximum number of iterations is reached or the user chooses to terminate*

Table 3: Definition of the variables used in the simulated feature-supervised algorithms

Variable	Definition
k	the number of document clusters
	the number of term clusters
	the number of term clouds
f	the number of keyterms in
	each term cloud before user supervision
m	the size of feature set used for
	document clustering
g	the coefficient used for re-weighting
	terms in FeatureSet
P_{exp}	the degree of user expertness
B	oracle budget $(k*f)$

6.5 Results and Discussion

We evaluated the performance of two active feature-supervised clusterers on six datasets using two evaluation measures. For each dataset, we ran the experiments in the following way:

- Each feature-supervised algorithm is run 50 times for each degree of expertness $P_{exp} = \{0, 0.1, 0.2, ..., 1.0\}$ and each size of feature set $m = \{500, 1000, 1500, 2000\}$.

- The average *Fmeasures* and *NMIs* of these 50 runs are then computed, which are depicted in Fig. 3 to Fig. 8. Since the standard deviations of *NMIs* and *Fmeasures* are much smaller than the averages, we have not shown them in the plots.

- The number of terms, f, in each term cloud before supervision is 20. Only two iterations of feature supervision are considered in our experiments. The feature re-weighting coefficient, g, in Algorithm 5 is 10.

The experimental results show that our feature labeling outperformed feature selection in most cases. This is more evident when the topics of document clusters are similar, specifically in *News-sim3* and *News-rel3*.

Except for *Classic4* where neither feature supervision method could improve the quality of clusters significantly, our feature labeling method generates much better clusters as the user expertness increases.

The experiments also reveal that our proposed document clustering outperformed *k*-means in all cases. This fact can be observed in Fig. 3 to Fig. 8 when no user supervision is involved ($P_{exp} = 0$).

As the size of feature set, m, increases from 500 to 2000, the quality of clusters mostly increases for both methods, regardless of the degree of user expertness. This observation indicates that it is more useful to focus on feature labeling than feature selection and use all the terms that exist in a dataset in our experiments.

7. CONCLUSION AND FUTURE WORK

We proposed a new text document clustering algorithm using term clusters and their discriminative topic keyterms. In our algorithm a new heuristic approach is proposed to find seed documents called representative documents.

We then proposed an active feature labeling approach for our document clusterer. The top keyterms of document clusters can be used to form term clouds so as to display to the users. Not only users can reorganize the terms in the term clouds in order to determine the topics of document clusters preferred, they can also increase or decrease the number of clouds. In this way, users can adjust the number of document clusters interactively in practice. We did not examine this option since the true number of document classes in benchmark datasets is used for evaluation in this work. As future work, we will provide an interactive visualization to support our feature-labeling document clusterer and evaluate this option.

This work also demonstrated that with a comparable amount of simulated user interactions, our feature labeling is more effective than the feature selection method used in this work as a baseline. This observation suggests that feature labeling is a better way to incorporate users in text document clustering. Besides, term clouds promote a better

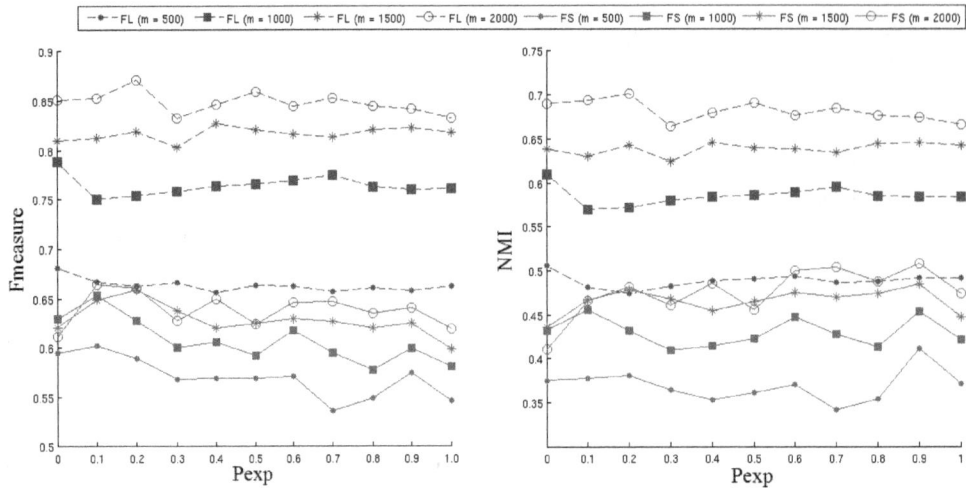

Figure 3: The quality of clusters based on active feature labeling (FL) and active feature selection (FS) on *Classic4*. Neither feature labeling nor feature selection could improve the quality of clusters significantly. This might be because the terms recommended by the χ^2 statistic are not good features for clustering this dataset.

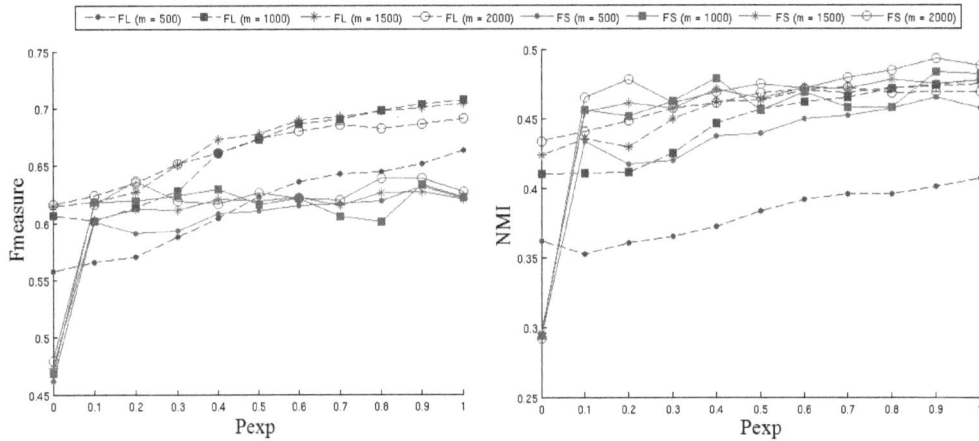

Figure 4: The quality of clusters based on active feature labeling (FL) and active feature selection (FS) on *LA Times*. Both feature labeling and feature selection methods improved the quality of clusters. The quality of the clusterings of the algorithms is similar based on *NMI*.

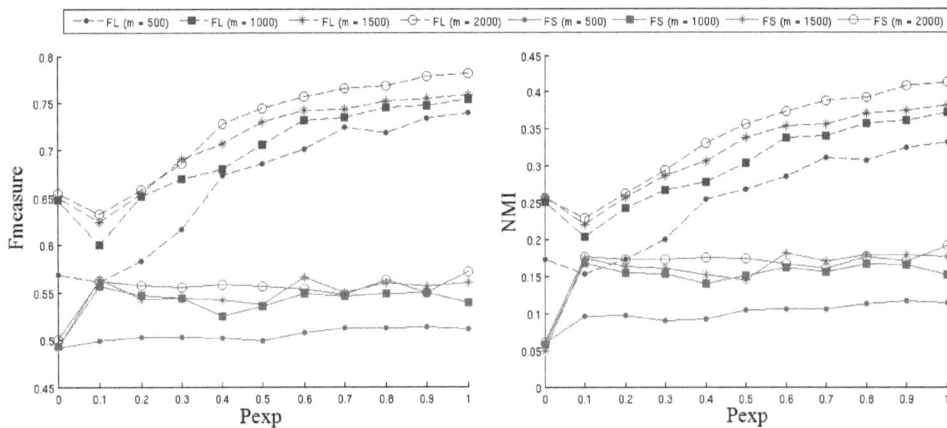

Figure 5: The quality of clusters based on active feature labeling (FL) and active feature selection (FS) on *News-sim3*. Our feature labeling algorithm significantly outperformed the feature selection algorithm. As the degree of expertness increases, the quality of our feature labeling clusterings improves more.

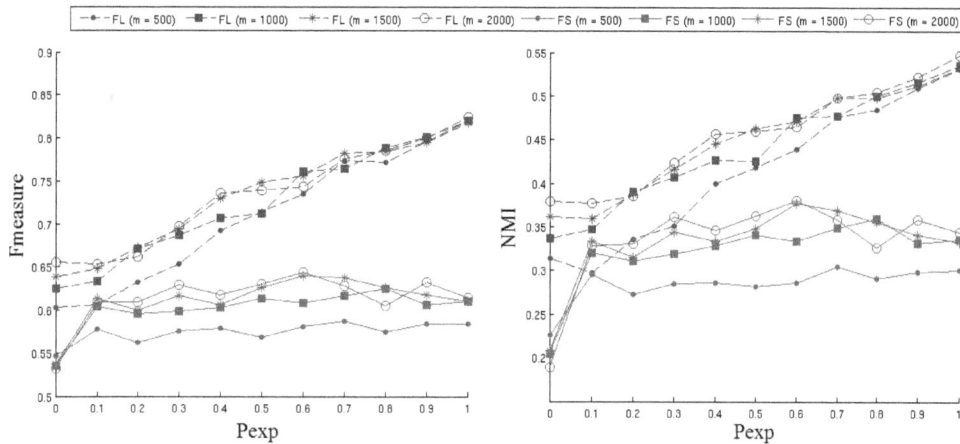

Figure 6: The quality of clusters based on active feature labeling (FL) and active feature selection (FS) on *News-rel3*. Our feature labeling is much more effective than the feature selection method. Unlike our feature labeling, there is not much improvement in the feature selection results.

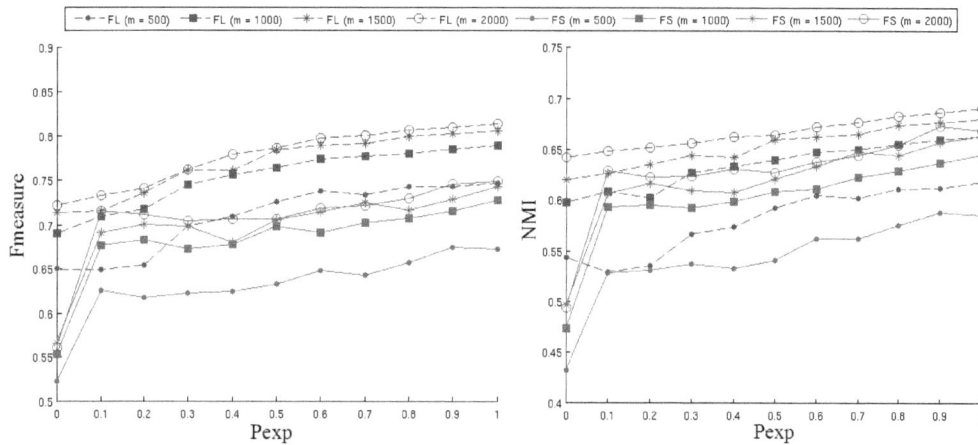

Figure 7: The quality of clusters based on active feature labeling (FL) and active feature selection (FS) on *News-multi7*. Both feature labeling and feature selection methods improved the quality of clusters. Active feature labeling generates better results compared to the active feature selection.

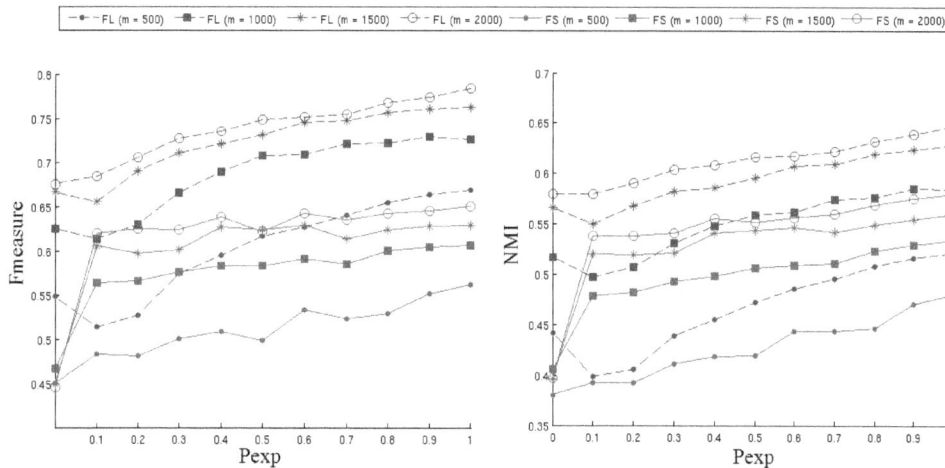

Figure 8: The quality of clusters based on active feature labeling (FL) and active feature selection (FS) on *News-multi10*. Both feature labeling and feature selection methods improved the quality of clusters. Active feature labeling outperformed the active feature selection.

insight into text topics than exposing single terms to the users in practice.

Acknowledgment

This research was supported by the NSERC (Natural Sciences and Engineering Research Council of Canada) Business Intelligence Network.

8. REFERENCES

[1] C. Aggarwal and C. Zhai. A survey of text clustering algorithms. In C. C. Aggarwal and C. Zhai, editors, *Mining Text Data*, pages 77–128. Springer US, 2012.

[2] J. Attenberg, P. Melville, and F. Provost. A unified approach to active dual supervision for labeling features and examples. In *Proceedings of the 2010 European Conference on Machine Learning and Knowledge Discovery in Databases: Part I*, number Part I, pages 40–55. Springer-Verlag, Berlin, Heidelberg, 2010.

[3] S. Basu, A. Banerjee, and R. J. Mooney. Semi-supervised clustering by seeding. In *Proceedings of the Nineteenth International Conference on Machine Learning*, ICML '02, pages 27–34, San Francisco, CA, USA, 2002. Morgan Kaufmann Publishers Inc.

[4] S. Basu, A. Banerjee, and R. J. Mooney. Active semi-supervision for pairwise constrained clustering. In *Proceedings of the SIAM International Conference on Data Mining*, pages 333–344, 2004.

[5] J. C. Bezdek. *Pattern Recognition with Fuzzy Objective Function Algorithms*. Kluwer Academic Publishers, Norwell, MA, USA, 1981.

[6] M. Bilenko, S. Basu, and R. J. Mooney. Integrating constraints and metric learning in semi-supervised clustering. In *Proceedings of the twenty-first International Conference on Machine Learning*, ICML '04, pages 11–, New York, NY, USA, 2004. ACM.

[7] D. Cohn, R. Caruana, and A. McCallum. Semi-supervised clustering with user feedback. *Constrained Clustering: Advances in Algorithms, Theory, and Applications*, 4(1):17–25, 2003.

[8] S. Dasgupta and V. Ng. Towards subjectifying text clustering. In *Proceedings of the 33rd international ACM SIGIR Conference on Research and Development in Information Retrieval*, SIGIR '10, pages 483–490, New York, NY, USA, 2010. ACM.

[9] I. Davidson and S. S. Ravi. Clustering with constraints: Feasibility issues and the fc-means algorithm. In *Proceedings of the fifth SIAM International Conference on Data Mining*, pages 138–149, 2005.

[10] G. Druck, G. Mann, and A. McCallum. Learning from labeled features using generalized expectation criteria. In *Proceedings of the 31st annual International ACM SIGIR Conference on Research and Development in Information Retrieval*, SIGIR '08, pages 595–602, New York, NY, USA, 2008. ACM.

[11] L. Galavotti, F. Sebastiani, and M. Simi. Experiments on the use of feature selection and negative evidence in automated text categorization. *Research and Advanced Technology for Digital Libraries*, pages 59–68, 2000.

[12] Y. Hu, E. E. Milios, and J. Blustein. Interactive feature selection for document clustering. In *Proceedings of the 2011 ACM Symposium on Applied Computing*, pages 1143–1150, New York, NY, USA, 2011. ACM.

[13] Y. Hu, E. E. Milios, and J. Blustein. Enhancing semi-supervised document clustering with feature supervision. In *Proceedings of the 27th Annual ACM Symposium on Applied Computing*, SAC '12, pages 929–936, New York, NY, USA, 2012. ACM.

[14] D. Klein, S. D. Kamvar, and C. D. Manning. From instance-level constraints to space-level constraints: Making the most of prior knowledge in data clustering. In *Proceedings of the Nineteenth International Conference on Machine Learning*, ICML '02, pages 307–314, San Francisco, CA, USA, 2002. Morgan Kaufmann Publishers Inc.

[15] J. Kogan, C. Nicholas, and V. Volkovich. Text mining with information-theoretic clustering. *Computing in Science and Engineering*, 5(6):52–59, Nov. 2003.

[16] T. Liu, S. Liu, Z. Chen, and W. Ma. An evaluation on feature selection for text clustering. In *Proceedings of the 20th International Conference on Machine Learning (ICML'03)*, pages 488–495, 2003.

[17] C. D. Manning, P. Raghavan, and H. Schütze. *Introduction to Information Retrieval*. Cambridge University Press, New York, NY, USA, 2008.

[18] R. Marcacini, G. Correa, and S. Rezende. An active learning approach to frequent itemset-based text clustering. In *21st International Conference on Pattern Recognition (ICPR)*, pages 3529–3532, 2012.

[19] S. N. Nourashrafeddin, E. Milios, and D. V. Arnold. An evolutionary algorithm for feature selective double clustering of text documents. In *Proceedings of IEEE Congress on Evolutionary Computation (CEC'13)*, pages 446–453, Cancun, Mexico, June 20-23 2013.

[20] H. Raghavan, O. Madani, and R. Jones. Interactive feature selection. In *Proceedings of the 19th International Joint Conference on Artificial Intelligence*, IJCAI'05, pages 841–846, San Francisco, CA, USA, 2005. Morgan Kaufmann Publishers Inc.

[21] J. Shi and J. Malik. Normalized cuts and image segmentation. *IEEE Transactions on Pattern Analysis and Machine Intelligence*, 22(8):888–905, 2000.

[22] B. Tang, M. Shepherd, E. Milios, and M. I. Heywood. Comparing and combining dimension reduction techniques for efficient text clustering. In *Proceedings of the Workshop on Feature Selection for Data Mining, in conjunction with SIAM International Conference on Data Mining*, pages 17–26, 2005.

[23] W. Tang, H. Xiong, S. Zhong, and J. Wu. Enhancing semi-supervised clustering: a feature projection perspective. In *Proceedings of the 13th ACM SIGKDD International Conference on Knowledge Discovery and Data Mining*, KDD '07, pages 707–716, New York, NY, USA, 2007. ACM.

[24] K. Wagstaff, C. Cardie, S. Rogers, and S. Schrödl. Constrained k-means clustering with background knowledge. In *Proceedings of the Eighteenth International Conference on Machine Learning*, ICML '01, pages 577–584, San Francisco, CA, USA, 2001. Morgan Kaufmann Publishers Inc.

A Graph-based Topic Extraction Method Enabling Simple Interactive Customization

Ajitesh Srivastava
Birla Institute of Technology
and Science, Pilani
India
ajitesh.srivastava@live.in

Axel J. Soto
Dalhousie University
Halifax, Canada
soto@cs.dal.ca

Evangelos E. Milios
Dalhousie University
Halifax, Canada
eem@cs.dal.ca

ABSTRACT

It is often desirable to identify the concepts that are present in a corpus. A popular way to deal with this objective is to discover clusters of words or topics, for which many algorithms exist in the literature. Yet most of these methods lack the interpretability that would enable interaction with a user not familiar with their inner workings. The paper proposes a graph-based topic extraction algorithm, which can also be viewed as a soft-clustering of words present in a given corpus. Each topic, in the form of a set of words, represents an underlying concept in the corpus. The method allows easy interpretation of the clustering process, and hence enables the scope of user involvement at various steps. For a quantitative evaluation of the topics extracted, we use them as features to get a compact representation of documents for classification tasks. We compare the classification accuracy achieved by a reduced feature set obtained with our method versus other topic extraction techniques, namely Latent Dirichlet Allocation and Non-negative Matrix Factorization. While the results from all the three algorithms are comparable, the speed and easy interpretability of our algorithm makes it more appropriate to be used interactively by lay users.

Categories and Subject Descriptors

I.2.7 [**Natural Language Processing**]: Text analysis; H.5.2 [**User interface**]: Natural Language

General Terms

Algorithms, Theory

Keywords

Topic extraction, soft clustering, visual text mining

1. INTRODUCTION

Information seeking on large collections of documents is not something that only "Big Data" analysts have to deal with. Exploring and browsing large corpora have become common activities for users of modern digital libraries. While information retrieval and search engines have brought important computational aids to users by searching and accessing documents within a short time, in many cases search engines are not sufficient. For example, users also need to find documents similar to the ones they already found, while also understanding what pieces of information make a given document be similar to others. This type of analysis is possible by using the notion of *topics* that are underlying a document and that may be shared by other documents in a corpus.

Topics can also help to overcome problems associated with the calculation of similarity in the traditional bag-of-words model [19]. The assumption of the bag-of-words models is that documents are similar to each other based on the words they share. Clearly, this model does not account for synonyms, as it will treat synonyms as completely different words. On the other hand, words that are related to each other can be aggregated under a same topic. In addition, topics can be seen as a soft-clustering of words, i.e. possibly overlapping sets of words, which allows assigning one word to more than one topic. This repetition of the same word in different topics allows modeling word polysemy.

Some corpora are hand-labeled with topic information. However, given the large scale of modern document collections and their rapid growth, human annotation of every document is hard to achieve. Therefore, several automatic methods for topic extraction have been proposed for large scale corpora [5, 14, 23] in different topic extraction paradigms.

One problem that most fully automatic topic extraction methods face is that their results may not be relevant to the user's understanding of the topics. For instance, topics can be too broadly or too specifically generated. While these methods allow some sort of customization, this is usually done by tuning of parameters, which may not be intuitive for most lay users. A different aspect of this problem is that sometimes the customization of the method requires re-running the method several times until a desired behavior is obtained. In very large corpora, having to run the same topic extraction method several times involves sometimes an unaffordable waste of time. In addition, even for a same user, optimal parameter setting is usually corpus-dependent, and hence this process has to be applied for any new collection of documents the user wants to explore.

In this paper we present a novel topic extraction method *WoSeT-n*, that uses a graph-based technique to come up

DocEng'13, September 10–13, 2013, Florence, Italy.
Copyright 2013 ACM 978-1-4503-1789-4/13/09 ...$15.00.
http://dx.doi.org/10.1145/2494266.2494280.

with sets of words, or *word-sets*, that tend to co-occur in the corpus. These word-sets are then merged to generate topics, where the more these word-sets are merged, the more general topics get. The reciprocal also applies: the less the word-sets are merged, the more specific topics get. This degree of specificity of topics in our method is controlled by an overlap parameter. As opposed to letting the user choose this parameter with an exact value, it is set by the presentation of representative word-set examples, where the user indicates whether a given word-set pair should be merged or not. Also, all generated topics are shown to the user listed in a decreasing order of importance, and a suggested upper bound for the number of topics to retain is proposed. The user can just accept the suggestion, or explore the topics and change the number of topics without any additional computation.

The interactive customization of the method that was described in the previous paragraph is done through the use of a visual interface allowing non-expert users to internally define parameters of the method. This approach follows the premise proclaimed by visual analytics methods [12, 26], that brings together automated computations with users' input through an interactive interface. In addition to the proposal of this interactive topic extraction method, we show results comparing our method (using different parameterizations) in a quantitative manner aiming at comparing our approach with other state-of-the-art automatic approaches regarding the usefulness of the topics generated. In this case we consider the topic extraction methods as dimensionality reduction methods, where the calculated topics are used as features to represent the documents, and then the reduced representation is evaluated in the context of document classification.

This paper is organized as follows. The next section discusses works related to this paper. Section 3 presents our novel approach for extraction of topics, while Section 4 describes how this method allows incorporating the user for intuitively customizing it. In Section 5 we present quantitative results that aim at comparing our approach with other state-of-the-art approaches regarding the usefulness of the topics generated. Finally, Section 6 discusses the results and summarizes the major contributions of this paper.

2. RELATED WORK

One of the first methods for topic extraction within the text mining literature was Latent Semantic Analysis (LSA) [14]. This method is based on a singular value decomposition of the document-term matrix. This decomposition allows representing documents using a new set of features, latent variables, or topics, which are linear combinations of the original features. Non-negative matrix factorization (NMF) [23] is another type of linear algebra algorithm that decomposes the document-term matrix into a document-topic and a topic-term matrix, with the important constraint that the decomposed matrices should be non-negative. While NMF has been used in many domains it is well suited for text as the non-negative constrain allows obtaining more interpretable topics than in LSA [29]. Therefore, several works have applied NMF for obtaining topics from large collections of documents [2, 16, 31].

Another important class of topic extraction methods is topic models which are based on the idea that documents are generated using words drawn from different topics (i.e.

documents are a mixture of topics), where a topic is a probability distribution over words [4, 25]. There are different types of these probabilistic generative topic models [10, 13, 15], out of which Latent Dirichlet Allocation [5] stands out as one of the most popular.

Topic extraction methods have been applied to many different kinds of document collections, such as emails [2], scientific abstracts [5, 8], news [30] and social media [32]. Thereby, topic extraction methods represent valuable tools for the exploration of document collections and the discovery of an underlying structure of the documents [4]. However, one limiting factor for embracing these types of approaches is the difficulty in their proper application by non-expert users or in influencing the results. For instance, while there are methods for incorporating constraints and penalty functions in NMF [7], or for setting the hyper-parameters in LDA [9] (which considerably affect the topics obtained by the methods), it also imposes a significant burden on the user's side, requiring a good understanding of the inner workings of the method.

Another example is the selection of the total number of topics extracted from a corpus. This is considered one of the most problematic issues in topic models [28]. The reason is that the number of topics has to be defined at the beginning of the algorithm, and its choice has an important impact on the results. Coming up with such a value tends to be a rather arbitrary choice. If it needs to be changed, the LDA algorithm should be recomputed from the beginning.

The method proposed in this paper allows the user to influence the resulting topics by simple interactions. The method starts with a graph-based soft-clustering method that resembles a two-way k-nearest neighbour method [27]. Using the result of the soft-clustering method, the user provides feedback on the degree of overlap the soft clusters should have. This type of interaction where an algorithm learns from the user is usually referred in the machine learning literature as *active learning* [22].

There are some related works in the area of user-supervised clustering [1, 11], where users identify a set of constrains for the objects or features (words) to be clustered. In our method, user feedback is requested on the final results (clusters of words) rather than on the individual instances to be clustered (documents or words), we also keep to a minimum the load imposed on the user by pre-computing as much as we can before interacting with the user. This also enables a prompt visualization of the results after the provision of the feedback. To the best of the authors' knowledge, no other work has focused on involving the user in the task of topic extraction [20]. We facilitate this involvement by providing a visual interface that allows the user to provide feedback without requiring any knowledge of the topic extraction algorithm. Other works have focused on the task of visualizing topic models to be consumable by lay users [6]. However, this approach does not allow any refinement of the topic results.

Finally, we compare our method to other topic extraction methods by using the topics as new features to represent document content. The evaluation of these new features is done via measuring performance on automatic classification of the documents into a set of predefined classes. This type of evaluation for extracted features is typically used for comparing dimensionality reduction approaches [16, 24].

3. METHODOLOGY

Our topic extraction method WoSeT-n starts with a graphical representation of the vocabulary, where the vertices are the words and edges between pairs of words carry a weight representing relatedness of the words, which is based on their co-occurrence in the corpus. From this graph small sets of words are identified, such that in each word-set the words have high similarity with each other. These word-sets are overlapping as a word can be a part of several word-sets. A topic is formed by merging of those word-sets that have pair-wise overlap greater than a threshold. The method is detailed is the following subsections.

3.1 The WoSeT-n method

Let $\mathbf{A}$ be the document-term matrix where the rows represent documents and columns represent words. The element $\mathbf{A}(i,j)$ represents the tf-idf scores [18]. Based on these scores we form a graph $G_\mathbf{V}$ where each word in the vocabulary $\mathbf{V}$ is represented as a node and the weights of the edges between the nodes are calculated as

$$e(w_i, w_j) = \sum_k \mathbf{A}(k,i)\mathbf{A}(k,j). \qquad (1)$$

These weights represent the similarity between the words that are connected by the edge. We note from Equation 1 that the edges incident on words with low tf-idf scores for many documents will carry low weights.

We form another graph G_n^d, where nodes are the words in $\mathbf{V}$ and edges are defined in the following way. For each node (word) w_j in $G_\mathbf{V}$, we look for its top-n neighbouring nodes, i.e. those that are linked with maximum weights to w_j, and establish a directed edge from w_j to each of these n nodes. From this directed graph we find all the pairs of nodes $\{w_i, w_j\}$ that are connected in both directions, i.e. from w_i to w_j and from w_j to w_i as well. Each of these bidirectional edges are replaced by an undirected edge and all other directed edges are removed from G_n^d. We call this new undirected graph thus obtained G_n^u. If $adj(G)$ denotes the adjacency matrix of a graph G, then we can define this new graph from the following matrix element-wise *and* operation:

$$adj(G_n^u) = adj(G_n^d) \odot adj(G_n^d)^T. \qquad (2)$$

DEFINITION 3.1. *We define a word-set W_i as a set constituted by word i and all its neighbours in G_n^u.*

Note that there are as many word-sets as words and these word-sets may overlap. Since the number of neighbours of a node in G_n^d is n, it follows from Equation 2 that the degree of a node in G_n^u is at most n, and hence the size of a word-set can not exceed $n+1$. Also there may be some word-sets which have only one word (singletons). This happens because these words (nodes) were not among the top-n of any other node. Figure 1 shows an example of the word-set generation process from a graph using $n=5$.

Next, we form our clusters of words or topics by merging these word-sets based on a criterion of overlap between them. We merge the word-sets which have overlaps above a predefined threshold δ. The overlap between word-sets W_i and W_j is calculated simply as

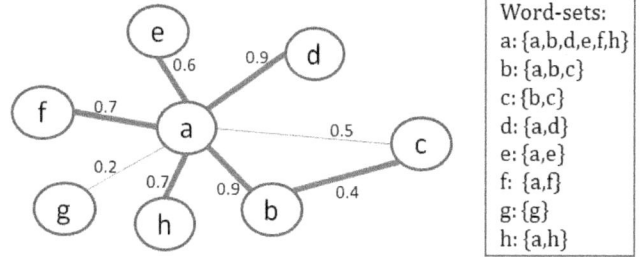

Figure 1: Word-sets generated using $n = 5$ ($\mathbf{W_5}$). Edges in bold reflect the connections of the graph G_n^u.

$$O_W(W_i, W_j) = \frac{|W_i \cap W_j|}{\min\{|W_i|, |W_j|\}}. \qquad (3)$$

The generation of topics from word-sets is done following Algorithm 1. Henceforth we refer to this algorithm applied to word-sets $\mathbf{W_n}$ as 'WoSeT-n'. The algorithm takes as input the set of all word-sets $\mathbf{W_n}$, the overlap matrix O_W, a threshold δ and the number of topics t to be produced (δ and t are user-defined parameters). If the overlap between any two word-sets is greater than the threshold δ, they are considered to belong to the same topic. First, the *SortOnSize* function sorts the word-sets into a list *Ordered_W* in descending order of their sizes. Within the main loop, to create the ith topic T_i the first element of this ordered list is removed from the list and added to T_i. Inductively all those word-sets in *Ordered_W*, which have overlap greater than δ with any of the existing word-sets in T_i, are removed from *Ordered_W* and added to T_i. Note that this 'addition' of a word-set to a topic is done using the multiset union operation ($\uplus$), which keeps track of the number of times a word w_j is added to T_i. This number indicates a membership score of word w_j in topic T_i. After all the topics have been formed, they are rearranged based on their sizes by the *SortOnSize* function. Finally, the first t topics are returned from the ordered set of all topics $\mathbf{T}$.

3.2 Choice of δ

The choice of δ decides whether two word-sets should be considered to be parts of a same topic or not. If δ is chosen to be 1, two word-sets will be merged only if one is contained in the other, i.e. one is a subset of the other. On the other hand if δ is 0, two word-sets will be merged if they have at least one word in common. In that case, the maximum number of topics that can be formed is equal to the number of connected components in G_n^u. It is easy to see that the choice of δ puts an upper bound on the maximum number of topics that can be formed. Figure 2 demonstrates the effect of δ on the fraction of words from the vocabulary, that is included after forming t topics. Note from the figure that the fraction remains much less than one even after including all the topics. This is due to an implicit filtering of unimportant words as explained in the next subsection.

3.3 Sorting on size

The algorithm assumes that the edge weight between the words in $G_\mathbf{V}$ is a good measure of relatedness, and thus a

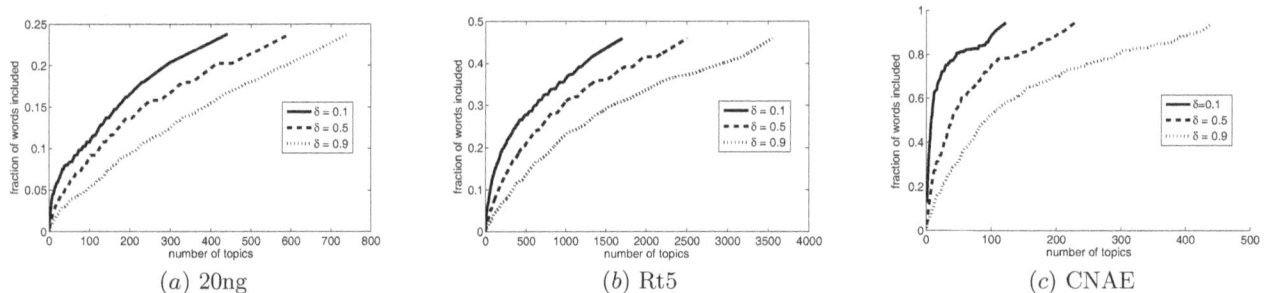

(a) 20ng $\qquad\qquad$ (b) Rt5 $\qquad\qquad$ (c) CNAE

Figure 2: Fraction of words from the vocabulary included in terms of the number of topics considered. Each line represents different overlap threshold values (δ). The topics for all the three datasets were generated from $\mathbf{W_{10}}$

Algorithm 1 WordSets_to_Topics

```
function WORDSETS_TO_TOPICS(Wₙ, O_W, δ, t)
    Ordered_W ← SortOnSize(Wₙ)
    T ← ∅
    i ← 0
    while Ordered_W ≠ ∅ do
        W₀ ← RemoveFirst(Ordered_W)
        Tᵢ ← W₀
        for all Wⱼ ∈ Ordered_W do
            for all Wₖ ∈ Tᵢ do
                if O_W(Wₖ, Wᵢ) > δ then
                    Tᵢ ← Tᵢ ⊎ Wᵢ
                    i ← i + 1
                    RemoveFromList(Ordered_W, Wᵢ)
                end if
            end for
        end for
        T ← [T, Tᵢ]
    end while
    T ← SortOnSize(T)
    return First_topics(T, t)
end function
```

---

word which is not among the top-n neighbors of any other nodes (or is among the top-n neighbours of few other nodes), does not convey sufficient co-occurrence information to be considered for inclusion in a topic. Therefore, word-sets that are small and do not overlap much with the larger ones can be excluded from forming topics. This leads to the first hypothesis of WoSeT-n:

Hypothesis 1. *The words contained in larger word-sets are more 'important' than those contained in smaller ones.*

Therefore, the algorithm first arranges the word-sets in decreasing order of size, so that one may choose to terminate the algorithm when small word-sets are encountered. In our experiments, we stopped the algorithm when we started encountering singletons, i.e, word-sets of size 1.

Similarly, formation of a large topic implies that its words were highly connected to each other, and so we also rearrange the topics in decreasing order of size and select the first t topics (last two steps of Algorithm 1). This is based on the second hypothesis of WoSeT-n:

Hypothesis 2. *The words that are included in the first t topics of $\mathbf{T}$ are more 'important' than those included later (or not included at all).*

One sensible way of measuring word importance is using information gain [19] (IG) of the word w_j.

$$IG(w_j) = \sum_{i=1}^{|\mathbf{L}|} P(L_i, w_j) \log \frac{P(L_i, w_j)}{P(L_i)P(w_j)}$$
$$+ \sum_{i=1}^{|\mathbf{L}|} P(L_i, \bar{w}_j) \log \frac{P(L_i, \bar{w}_j)}{P(L_i)P(\bar{w}_j)} \quad (4)$$

where $|\mathbf{L}| = \{L_1, L_2, \ldots, L_l\}$ is the set of all document labels in the corpus. From an information-theoretic point of view, the higher the information gain of a word, the higher its importance is. In a later section we demonstrate that the hypotheses of the algorithm hold true for the datasets used in the experiments.

3.4 Complexity

The complexity of the major steps in WoSeT-n are as follows:

- Finding the top-n words for each word involves sorting the neighbors of each word in $G_\mathbf{V}$. Since this graph is usually dense, it takes $O(|\mathbf{V}| \log |\mathbf{V}|)$ time for each word and $O(|\mathbf{V}|^2 \log |\mathbf{V}|)$ for the whole vocabulary. Once the sorting is done, top-n for each word can be fetched in $O(n|\mathbf{V}|)$.

- Overlap calculation can be done by counting the edges between pairs of words in G_n^u and adding the count to the appropriate word-set pair. This step has a complexity of $O(|\mathbf{V}|^2)$.

- The merging of word-sets has a complexity of $O(\sum_i(|W_i|))$ $= O(|E(G_n^d)|+|\mathbf{V}|)$, where W_i is a word-set and $|E(G_n^d)|$ is the number of edges in G_n^d. Since G_n^d is highly sparse, the complexity reduces to $O(|\mathbf{V}|)$.

- The complexity of sorting of topics based on their size is $O(|\mathbf{T}| \log |\mathbf{T}|)$.

The most expensive steps are the first two, which are the formation of G_n^u (or equivalently $\mathbf{W_n}$) and O_W respectively. Once these two are computed and passed to Algorithm 1, it takes $O(|\mathbf{V}| + |\mathbf{T}| \log |\mathbf{T}|)$. Also, for practical purposes the algorithm is stopped when small word-sets are encountered so the merging takes much less than $O(|\mathbf{V}|)$. This is an important advantage of our algorithm that changing the value of threshold parameter δ requires reiteration of only the last two steps which take $O(|\mathbf{V}|)$ time. The change in number of topics t does not require any re-computation at all.

4. USER INTERVENTION

In this section we present how our topic extraction method can be parameterized based on user's feedback. The interaction with the user is done in two steps, where the user first determines the specificity of the topics (controlled by threshold parameter δ) and then the user decides upon the number of topics (named t in Algorithm 1) he or she wants to describe the collection of documents by. The design of 'WoSeT-n' allows users to get the results based on their input after a short time lapse of computationally inexpensive operations (see Section 3.4). This prompt interactivity encourages users to 'explore' with different feedback alternatives. User's interaction with the system is provided through a visual interface[1], which was implemented in Javascript and using the d3.js library[2].

4.1 Setting the Threshold Parameter

The threshold parameter δ determines whether two word-sets should be merged based on their overlap. This parameter impacts the specificity of the topics by needing more or less topics to make use of the same number of words, as we have shown in Figure 2. Rather than letting the user to set a value for this parameter, we aim at learning it by monitoring the feedback from the user upon the presentation of pairs of word-sets. Learning a parameter from users' behavior is more convenient than asking the user to set it. This is because, first, it does not require the user to understand the function of the parameter in the method, and second, a parameter choice is dataset dependent (as it happens in most text mining methods).

The feedback process works as follows. The user is shown a pair of word-sets and is asked whether the word-sets should be merged or not. Figure 3 shows the interface that is provided to serve this purpose, which consists of a bipartite graph for each word-set pair with links showing words in common.

In order to set a value for δ from user's feedback, we take the sequence of steps described in Algorithm 2. The algorithm takes as input the set of word-sets $\mathbf{W_n}$, overlap matrix O_W and the depth of search n_d. The idea of the algorithm is to employ a binary search over the user's implicitly desired δ value. We start the search assuming a value of $\delta = 0.5$ (represented by the variable mid), and we present the user two word-sets whose overlap between them is approximately equal to mid (this is done by the function $Pick\_WordSet\_Pair$). Based on the response of the user the search interval is reduced as indicated in the algorithm. At the end of n_d iterations we append the value of mid to the list Δ. The whole process is repeated until the user chooses to discontinue. The final estimation of δ is given by the average of all the values in Δ.

The precision of the binary search is determined by n_d. Let us assume that $\hat{\delta}$ is the user's implicitly desired value for δ, then after the jth iteration of the binary search, we get

$$|\hat{\delta} - mid| \leq 2^{-(1+j)}. \qquad (5)$$

Algorithm 2 Estimate_Threshold

  function ESTIMATE_THRESHOLD($\mathbf{W_n}, O_W, n_d$)
    $\Delta \leftarrow \emptyset$
    repeat
      first $\leftarrow 0$
      last $\leftarrow 1$
      mid $\leftarrow 0.5$
      for $j = 1 \rightarrow n_d$ **do**
        $W_1, W_2 \leftarrow$ Pick_WordSet_Pair($\mathbf{W_n}, O_W$, mid)
        Display(W_1, W_2)
        $r \leftarrow$ getResponse()
                  ▷ (User responds as 'yes'/'no')
        if $r = $ 'yes' **then**
          last $\leftarrow$ mid
        else
          first $\leftarrow$ mid
        end if
        mid $\leftarrow$ (first + last)/2
      end for
      $\Delta \leftarrow \Delta \cup \{mid\}$
      Display('Continue')
              ▷ (Ask if user wants to provide more feedback)
      $c \leftarrow$ getResponse()
    until $c = $ 'no'
    $\hat{\delta} \leftarrow$ Avg(Δ)
    return $\hat{\delta}$
  end function

Therefore, in our implementation we have set $n_d = 3$ (i.e. the user needs to provide feedback in series of three consecutive merge questions), which allows us to get a precision of ± 0.0625 to the user's desired value of the threshold parameter.

4.2 Setting the Number of Topics

Following our second hypothesis, if we sort our topics by size, the topics that occur towards the beginning tend to convey more valuable information than those towards the end, and up to a certain point there is little information gain in including small topics. In order to assist the user in the choice of the number of topics t to use for the collection of documents, the system first suggests a value for this parameter. Empirically, we found that an appropriate number of topics can be set by choosing the top topics for which the sum of the number of words contained in them is 50% of the sum of the number of words contained in all the topics[3]. Nevertheless, the user can change the suggestion for the number of topics by, for example, exploring the content of topics ranked close to the cut-off value and decide whether other topics should be included or excluded.

Figure 4 shows a screenshot of our system of this second part of the feedback process. At the top of the screen we have all the topics sorted by size, with a vertical green line indicating the selection for the number of topics to be selected. At the bottom the user can modify the selection and also inspect the content of the different topics.

The words contained in each topic are visualized by using word clouds. Our system provides to the user the option of

---

[1] http://demeter.research.cs.dal.ca/~soto/
IntuitiveTopicModel_20/topicSelection.html
[2] http://d3js.org/

[3] Another way of looking at this cutoff is by considering the point in the horizontal axis of the histogram in Figure 4 that captures 50% of the area under the curve.

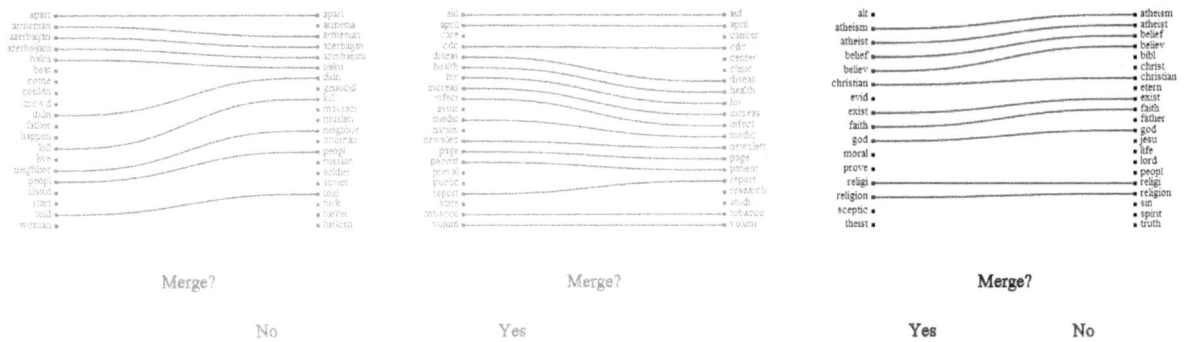

Figure 3: Users can affect the generality/specificity of the topics by indicating whether pairs of word-sets should be merged or not.

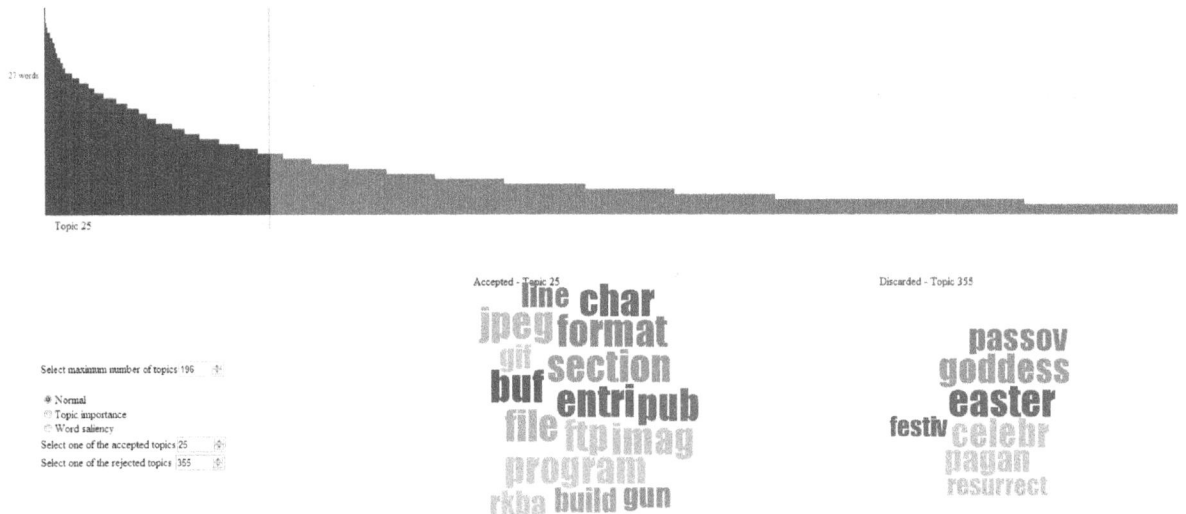

Figure 4: Exploration of the topics and selection of the number of topics interactively. The system also suggests a cut-off value for the number of topics to be considered.

quantifying the font size for a word within a topic in three different ways. In the first one, which we name *Normal*, the word font size is given by the probability of that word in the topic. In the second option (*topic importance*) the font size is scaled according to how many times a given word is part of a topic. The name comes from the fact that words in larger topics will tend to be visualized with bigger fonts. The third option (*word saliency*) scales the font size by considering the uniqueness of each word. For example, if a word is contained in a single topic only, then this word will have a higher relative importance within this topic, and hence will be visualized with a larger font. This last option is also related to the *distinctiveness* criterion used in [6], although in our case we used a measure inspired from tf-idf weighting [19].

5. EXPERIMENTS

5.1 Datasets

The experiments were performed on the following three datasets:

- **20ng:** This is a subset of the 20 newsgroup dataset[4], which consists of randomly selected 11293 documents with the words stemmed and stop words removed. The vocabulary consists of 8163 words. There are 20 labels distributed almost uniformly over the 11293 documents. Some of the 20 labels are related to each other and can be grouped to get 6 labels[5].

- **Rt5:** This is a pre-processed subset of Reuters-21578[6]. The top 5 most frequent categories were selected to get 6632 documents with a vocabulary size of 17296 words.

- **CNAE:** This dataset, containing 1080 documents, has descriptions of Brazilian companies categorized into 9 labels. The vocabulary consists of 856 words obtained after pre-processing[7].

[4]https://sites.google.com/site/renatocorrea02/ng2011293x8165itrn.mat
[5]http://qwone.com/~jason/20Newsgroups/
[6]http://www.cad.zju.edu.cn/home/dengcai/Data/Reuters21578/Reuters21578.mat
[7]http://archive.ics.uci.edu/ml/datasets/CNAE-9

5.2 Feature Reduction using Topics

By considering the topics as new features, the documents can be represented in a much lower dimensional feature space. We compared the feature reduction obtained by WoSeT-n with those obtained by LDA and NMF. For LDA the hyperparameters were set to $\alpha = 50/t$ and $\beta = 200/|\mathbf{V}|$. Gibbs Sampling was used for inference in LDA which has a complexity of $O(tNI)$ [17], where t is the number of topics, N is the number of occurrences of all the words in the corpus and I is the number of iterations. In our experiments, I was set to 400. For NMF we used the Matlab implementation, which is based on an alternating least-squares algorithm that runs in $O(t|D||\mathbf{V}|I)$ [3], where $|D|$ is the number of documents, and I is the number of iterations. We used the default value of $I = 100$. Table 1 shows the computation requirement of updating parameters in the algorithms used.

Table 1: Comparison of amount of computation required after a parameter change in LDA, NMF and WoSeT-n

Algorithm	Parameter	Complexity
LDA	α, β, t	$O(tNI)$
NMF	t	$O(t|D||\mathbf{V}|I)$
WoSeT-n	n	$O(n|\mathbf{V}|)$
	δ	$O(|\mathbf{V}|)$
	t	$O(1)$

The evaluation of this feature reduction was done by measuring the accuracy of two classifiers in the task of classifying the documents in the reduced feature space. The feature reduction was done by a linear combination of features expressed mathematically as

$$\mathbf{A}' = \mathbf{AT}, \qquad (6)$$

where $\mathbf{A}$ is the matrix of tf-idf scores as defined in Equation 1, $\mathbf{T}$ is the matrix representing assignment of words to topics such that $T(i,j)$ is the membership score of w_j in topic T_i, and $\mathbf{A}'$ is the representation of the documents in reduced feature space.

Table 2: Classification accuracies for 20ng using topics to represent documents

	t	Naive Bayes	Decision Tree
LDA	20	0.73 ± 0.012	0.58 ± 0.014
	40	0.74 ± 0.011	0.56 ± 0.021
	80	0.74 ± 0.007	0.57 ± 0.009
NMF	20	0.62 ± 0.007	0.45 ± 0.006
	40	0.62 ± 0.013	0.45 ± 0.005
	80	0.62 ± 0.016	0.45 ± 0.012
WoSeT-n	20	0.64 ± 0.007	0.47 ± 0.005
	40	0.68 ± 0.010	0.51 ± 0.009
	80	0.72 ± 0.007	0.54 ± 0.008

Tables 2, 3 and 4 show the results of 5-fold cross-validation accuracies on 20ng, Rt5 and CNAE respectively. We applied two classification algorithms, Multinomial Naive Bayes [21] and Decision Tree [21], varying number of topics (features) $t = 20, 40$ and 80. We experimented with several value of n for top-n and concluded that for a large vocabulary (like that of 20ng and Rt5) top-20 should be used, and top-10 should be used for a small one (like the vocabulary of CNAE). Therefore, we have presented the results for 20ng and Rt5 using WoSeT-20, while WoSeT-10 was used for CNAE. In all the results reported for WoSeT-n, δ was set to 0.1.

Table 3: Classification accuracies for Rt5 using topics to represent documents

	t	Naive Bayes	Decision Tree
LDA	20	0.86 ± 0.004	0.87 ± 0.016
	40	0.85 ± 0.010	0.87 ± 0.008
	80	0.87 ± 0.009	0.87 ± 0.010
NMF	20	0.88 ± 0.011	0.88 ± 0.007
	40	0.88 ± 0.013	0.88 ± 0.008
	80	0.88 ± 0.009	0.88 ± 0.008
WoSeT-n	20	0.88 ± 0.007	0.82 ± 0.012
	40	0.89 ± 0.005	0.83 ± 0.011
	80	0.89 ± 0.012	0.85 ± 0.007

The results indicate that LDA performed the best on 20ng, but considerably worse than NMF and WoSeT-n on CNAE. NMF seems to be the least sensitive to the variation in the number of topics. WoSeT-n performed the best on CNAE (with the exception of $t = 20$). On Rt5, WoSeT-n had the best performance using Naive Bayes, while NMF outperformed other methods using Decision Tree. Overall, the results suggest that the accuracies obtained with WoSeT-n are comparable to those obtained with LDA and NMF.

Table 4: Classification accuracies for CNAE using topics to represent documents

	t	Naive Bayes	Decision Tree
LDA	20	0.68 ± 0.014	0.57 ± 0.035
	40	0.73 ± 0.035	0.67 ± 0.061
	80	0.74 ± 0.029	0.67 ± 0.028
NMF	20	0.83 ± 0.028	0.65 ± 0.038
	40	0.83 ± 0.035	0.68 ± 0.075
	80	0.83 ± 0.031	0.67 ± 0.036
WoSeT-n	20	0.80 ± 0.032	0.62 ± 0.035
	40	0.87 ± 0.016	0.70 ± 0.027
	80	0.91 ± 0.028	0.75 ± 0.055

5.3 Evidence to Support WoSet-n Hypotheses.

To support the first hypothesis of WoSeT-n, that larger word-sets have more important words, we studied the pattern of the mean information gain of the words included for a given size of word-set. From Figure 5, it can be concluded that although the curves are not always strictly increasing, the mean information gain of words included in large word-sets is much greater than those in the small ones.

For the second hypothesis of WoSeT-n, which states that the words included in the larger topics (also generated earlier in Algorithm 1) are more important, we studied the variation of the mean information gain of the words included when t topics have been formed. It can be observed from Figure 6 that for all the datasets, the information gain drops with inclusion of more topics. This implies that the smaller topics contain words of lower information gain, and hence, words included in the earlier and larger topics are more important.

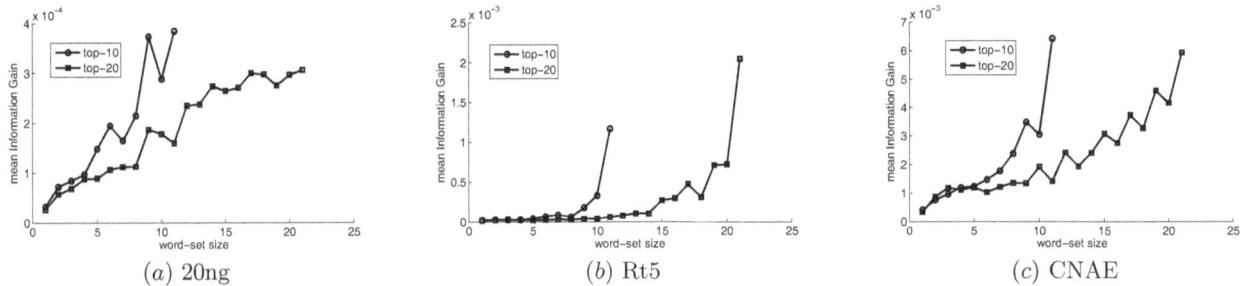

(a) 20ng (b) Rt5 (c) CNAE

Figure 5: Mean information gain of the words included in a word-set of given size.

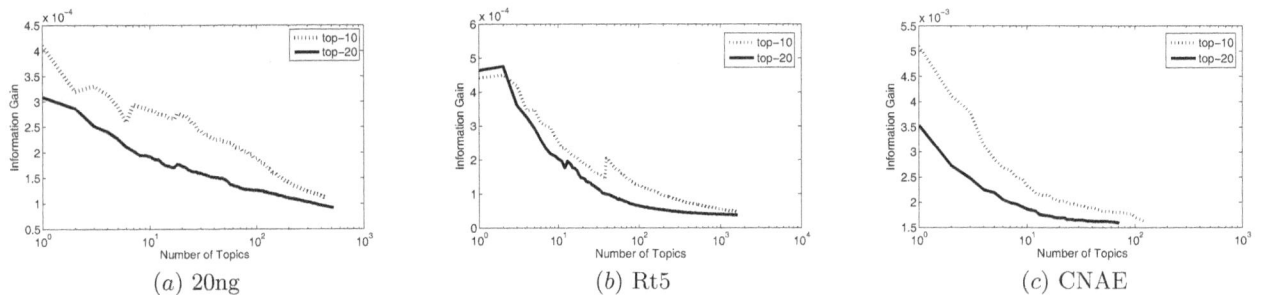

(a) 20ng (b) Rt5 (c) CNAE

Figure 6: Mean information gain of the words included in the first t topics.

6. CONCLUSIONS

In this work we have presented a method for extraction of topics from a collection of documents. The method allows its parameterization, and hence the customization of the extracted topics by users who do not need to know the mathematical details of the method. This customization is done through a visual interface, where the user first defines how specific or general the topics should be, and then how many topics should be extracted from the collection. The algorithm is designed in such a way that the final list of topics can be obtained almost immediately after the user's feedback is provided. The speed of our approach makes the method very appealing in case the user wants to interact and see the result of different feedback inputs.

We have also compared our method in the absence of any user interaction to other popular topic extraction approaches, namely Latent Dirichlet Analysis (LDA) and Non-negative Matrix Factorization (NMF). We assessed the performance of the different methods by using the topics for representing documents more compactly and then by using this representation as input of text classifiers. We trained two different classifiers using three text datasets and we found that all methods are on par with subtle differences arising from dataset complexities and sizes.

Future work in this area can focus on the support of the user during the exploration of documents within a digital library. In this way, our method can be coupled with other visual text mining approaches in such a way that the topics can be used to summarize documents, or to find documents related to a given topic. In this regard, there are several challenges in human-computer interaction on how a user should effectively interact with a large collection of documents and understand what each topic is about.

Acknowledgments

The authors thank MITACS, The Boeing Company and NSERC for funding of this work.

7. REFERENCES

[1] S. Basu, A. Banerjee, and R. J. Mooney. Active semi-supervision for pairwise constrained clustering. In *Proceedings of the SIAM International Conference on Data Mining*, pages 333–344, 2004.

[2] M. W. Berry and M. Browne. Email surveillance using non-negative matrix factorization. *Computational & Mathematical Organization Theory*, 11(3):249–264, 2005.

[3] M. W. Berry, M. Browne, A. N. Langville, V. P. Pauca, and R. J. Plemmons. Algorithms and applications for approximate nonnegative matrix factorization. *Computational Statistics & Data Analysis*, 52(1):155–173, 2007.

[4] D. M. Blei and J. Lafferty. Topic models. *Text mining: Classification, Clustering, and Applications*, 10:71, 2009.

[5] D. M. Blei, A. Y. Ng, and M. I. Jordan. Latent Dirichlet allocation. *The Journal of Machine Learning Research*, 3:993–1022, 2003.

[6] J. Chuang, C. D. Manning, and J. Heer. Termite: Visualization techniques for assessing textual topic models. In *Proceedings of the International Working Conference on Advanced Visual Interfaces*, pages 74–77. ACM, 2012.

[7] I. S. Dhillon and S. Sra. Generalized nonnegative matrix approximations with bregman divergences. In *Neural Information Processing Systems*, pages 283–290, 2005.

[8] T. L. Griffiths and M. Steyvers. Finding scientific topics. *Proceedings of the National Academy of*

Sciences of the United States of America, 101(Suppl 1):5228–5235, 2004.

[9] G. Heinrich. Parameter estimation for text analysis. Technical report, University of Leipzig, Germany, 2005.

[10] T. Hofmann. Probabilistic latent semantic indexing. In *Proceedings of the 22nd Annual International ACM SIGIR Conference on Research and Development in Information Retrieval*, pages 50–57. ACM, 1999.

[11] Y. Hu, E. E. Milios, J. Blustein, and S. Liu. Personalized document clustering with dual supervision. In *Proceedings of the 2012 ACM Symposium on Document Engineering*, pages 161–170. ACM, 2012.

[12] D. A. Keim, J. Kohlhammer, G. Ellis, and F. Mansmann. *Mastering the information age - Solving problems with visual analytics*. Eurographics Association, 2010.

[13] J. Lafferty and M. Blei. Correlated topic models. In *Advances in Neural Information Processing Systems*, pages 147–155. Citeseer, 2006.

[14] T. K. Landauer, P. W. Foltz, and D. Laham. An introduction to latent semantic analysis. *Discourse Processes*, 25(2-3):259–284, 1998.

[15] W. Li and A. McCallum. Pachinko allocation: Dag-structured mixture models of topic correlations. In *Proceedings of the 23rd International Conference on Machine Learning*, pages 577–584. ACM, 2006.

[16] Y. Liu, R. Jin, and L. Yang. Semi-supervised multi-label learning by constrained non-negative matrix factorization. In *Proceedings of the National Conference on Artificial Intelligence*, volume 21, page 421. Menlo Park, CA; Cambridge, MA; London; AAAI Press; MIT Press; 1999, 2006.

[17] Z. Liu, Y. Zhang, E. Y. Chang, and M. Sun. PLDA+: Parallel latent dirichlet allocation with data placement and pipeline processing. *ACM Transactions on Intelligent Systems and Technology (TIST)*, 2(3):26, 2011.

[18] C. D. Manning, P. Raghavan, and H. Schütze. *Introduction to information retrieval*, volume 1. Cambridge University Press Cambridge, 2008.

[19] C. D. Manning and H. Schütze. *Foundations of Statistical Natural Language Processing*. MIT Press.

[20] F. Olsson. A literature survey of active machine learning in the context of natural language processing. Technical report, Swedish Institute of Computer Science, 2009.

[21] F. Sebastiani. Machine learning in automated text categorization. *ACM Computing Surveys (CSUR)*, 34(1):1–47, 2002.

[22] B. Settles. Active learning literature survey. Technical report, University of Wisconsin, Madison, 2010.

[23] D. Seung and L. Lee. Algorithms for non-negative matrix factorization. *Advances in Neural Information Processing Systems*, 13:556–562, 2001.

[24] A. J. Soto, M. Strickert, G. E. Vazquez, and E. Milios. Subspace mapping of noisy text documents. In *Advances in Artificial Intelligence*, pages 377–383. Springer, 2011.

[25] M. Steyvers and T. Griffiths. Probabilistic topic models. In *Handbook of Latent Semantic Analysis*, volume 427, pages 424–440, 2007.

[26] J. J. Thomas and K. A. Cook. A visual analytics agenda. *Computer Graphics and Applications, IEEE*, 26(1):10–13, 2006.

[27] S. Vadapalli, S. R. Valluri, and K. Karlapalem. A simple yet effective data clustering algorithm. In *Data Mining, 2006. ICDM'06. Sixth International Conference on*, pages 1108–1112. IEEE, 2006.

[28] H. Wallach, D. Mimno, and A. McCallum. Rethinking LDA: Why priors matter. *Advances in Neural Information Processing Systems*, 22:1973–1981, 2009.

[29] Y.-X. Wang and Y.-J. Zhang. Non-negative matrix factorization: a comprehensive review. *IEEE Transactions on Knowledge and Data Engineering*, 25(6):1336–1353, 2011.

[30] X. Wei and W. B. Croft. LDA-based document models for ad-hoc retrieval. In *Proceedings of the 29th Annual International ACM SIGIR Conference on Research and Development in Information Retrieval*, pages 178–185. ACM, 2006.

[31] W. Xu, X. Liu, and Y. Gong. Document clustering based on non-negative matrix factorization. In *Proceedings of the 26th Annual International ACM SIGIR Conference on Research and Development in Information Retrieval*, pages 267–273. ACM, 2003.

[32] W. Zhao, J. Jiang, J. Weng, J. He, E. Lim, H. Yan, and X. Li. Comparing twitter and traditional media using topic models. *Advances in Information Retrieval*, pages 338–349, 2011.

Searching Online Book Documents and Analyzing Book Citations

Zhaohui Wu†, Sujatha Das†, Zhenhui Li‡, Prasenjit Mitra‡†, C. Lee Giles‡†
†Computer Science and Engineering, ‡Information Sciences and Technology
Pennsylvania State University, University Park, PA 16802, USA
{zzw109, gsdas}@psu.edu, {jessieli, pmitra, giles}@ist.psu.edu

ABSTRACT

Academic search engines and digital libraries provide convenient online search and access facilities for scientific publications. However, most existing systems do not include books in their collections although several books are freely available online. Academic books are different from papers in terms of their length, contents and structure. We argue that accounting for academic books is important in understanding and assessing scientific impact. We introduce an open-book search engine that extracts and indexes metadata, contents, and bibliography from online PDF book documents. To the best of our knowledge, no previous work gives a systematical study on building a search engine for books.

We propose a hybrid approach for extracting title and authors from a book that combines results from CiteSeer, a rule based extractor, and a SVM based extractor, leveraging web knowledge. For "table of contents" recognition, we propose rules based on multiple regularities based on numbering and ordering. In addition, we study bibliography extraction and citation parsing for a large dataset of books. Finally, we use the multiple fields available in books to rank books in response to search queries. Our system can effectively extract metadata and contents from large collections of online books and provides efficient book search and retrieval facilities.

Categories and Subject Descriptors

H.3.7 [**Information Storage and Retrieval**]: Digital Libraries; I.7.5 [**Document and Text Processing**]: Document Capture—*Document analysis*

General Terms

Measurement, Experimentation, Algorithms

Keywords

Book Search, Book Structure Extraction, Book Citation Analysis

1. INTRODUCTION

Many challenges arise from electronic publishing. Not only is more publishable content being released digitally and made available online, but several printed books are being digitized. *Thus, what is the best way to organize and access information from online books.* Google Books[1] has become the leading project for this. In 2010, Google estimated that since the invention of printing, approximately 130 million unique titles had been published[2]. In addition, we've seen recent initiatives such as the Gutenberg[3], OCA (Open Content Alliance)[4], and Million Book Project[5]. Although these projects have made progress in indexing the increasing number of online books, there are several challenges yet to be addressed.

Techniques for accurately extracting metadata from books enable better search. Machine learning approaches have been shown to be effective for extracting metadata from scientific papers and office documents [11, 13]. However, the metadata in books is in diverse formats and is different and typically richer than that in scientific papers. Therefore, novel features and techniques are required to address metadata extraction from books.

Another interesting difference between scientific papers and books is the table of contents or ToC. The ToC of a book concisely captures the logical structure of a book. Accurate extraction of the table of content is a challenging task for book retrieval systems. ToC recognition was previously studied to enable inside book search and navigation [7, 21]. However, they assume entries at the same level in a ToC share consistent features and each entry can be matched to the related title in the body part. We found those assumptions do not always hold in large diverse book datasets, while more common properties are regularities of the numbering, ordering and indentation.

In addition to the above differences, books and scientific papers differ with respect to their bibliographic references. The bibliographic formats and layouts are more varied in books than those in scientific papers. In addition, unlike papers where references typically are found at the end, a bibliography for a book could appear in various locations such as the end of each chapter, the end of the book, or

---

[1] http://books.google.com/
[2] "Books of the world, stand up and be counted! All 129,864,880 of you." Google Books Search. August 5, 2010.
[3] http://www.gutenberg.org/
[4] http://www.opencontentalliance.org/
[5] http://archive.org/details/millionbooks

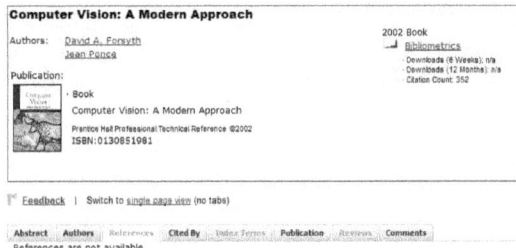

Figure 1: The absence of book references

before a back-of-the-book index. Furthermore, there is no standard citation format.

Book citations [18, 19] have been studied but not on a large scale dataset. Google Scholar recently integrated Google Books data to provide a more complete citation graph that now includes books. Thus, it is now possible to find the references of a book during a book search. In addition, Thomson Reuters has released their Book Citation Index, giving researchers access to the citation network between books and the wider world of scholarly and scientific research and full bibliographies from books and book chapters [6]. However, to the best of our knowledge, there are no academic search engines or digital libraries that provide a citation list of a book that enables navigation to the sources cited in a book, even though this facility is typically available for papers (for example, in CiteSeer [9]). As an example of what happens with prominent publishers, the ACM Digital Library does not include references for books, as shown in Figure 1.

This paper introduces a search engine for online books. These books are taken from PDF files crawled from open resources on the web that our crawler believes to be books. We create rules based on ISBN, table of contents and number of pages to identify books among other crawled PDF documents. Next, we design extraction techniques to harvest metadata such as title, authors, ISBN, etc., as well as table of contents and bibliography. To effectively extract title and authors, we devise a novel hybrid approach based on an ensemble method which entails voting from multiple sources, including CiteSeer metadata, a rule based extractor derived from sampled books, and a SVM based extractor. The ground truth of the SVM based extractor is queried from a Web knowledge base (Google Books). We also propose techniques for extracting the table of contents and bibliography in order to gain a better understanding of a book's structure and bibliographical roles. These table of contents and chapter titles are indexed for use in inside book search. Using these indexed fields, we design an efficient ranking model for better ranking results for book search.

We demonstrate experimentally that our system can effectively extract metadata and table of contents at a large scale. Using our techniques, we were able to construct a book citation dataset containing the bibliography of 28,714 books with more than 2 million citations mentions [7]. Our citation analysis using this bibliographic data indicates that book citations are valuable and should be considered in research and scholarly assessment.

---

[6]http://wokinfo.com/products_tools/multidisciplinary/bookcitationindex/

[7]The book citation dataset is online and will be provided upon request

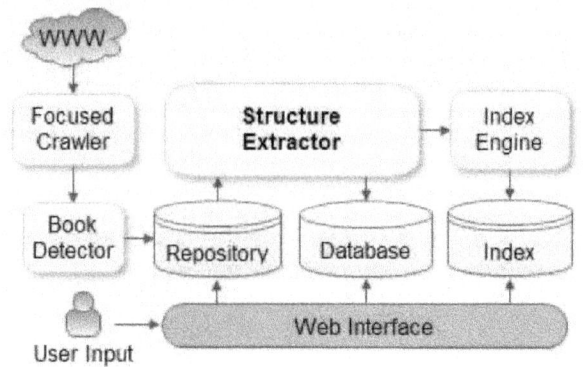

Figure 2: Architecture of the search engine demo

The rest of the paper is organized as follows. Section 2 introduces the architecture of the system, consisting of four major components: crawler and book detector, structure extractor, index engine, and web interface. Section 3 discusses technical details of each component. Section 4 describes experimental evaluations and analysis. Section 5 studies the related work. Finally, we present conclusions and future work in section 6.

2. ARCHITECTURE

We first briefly introduce the system architecture in this section, shown in Figure 2. The focused crawler, namely the CiteSeerX crawler [8], has crawled nearly 3 million PDF documents for CiteSeerX [9]. It crawls online documents based on black and white URL lists [28]. The book detector filters potential books from crawled PDF documents and then copies those book PDF documents to our system's repository. The structure extractor extracts the metadata, ToC and bibliography information, stores important metadata information such as title, authors and ISBNs in database. and sends the books' indexed fields (including title, authors, chapter titles, table of contents, etc.) to an ndex engine. The index engine manages the index by providing add, update, delete functions. The web interface is provided for user input and shows ranked retrieved results (SERP).

The popular open source enterprise search platform Apache Solr [10] is used as the index engine and apache tomcat [11] as the web server. A working system can be visited online [12], running on a Red hat Enterprise Linux Server.

3. IMPLEMENTATION

3.1 Crawler and Book Filter

The crawler focuses on online PDF, PS, and compressed files found from a white list containing over 700,000 URL seeds, covering many academic and research institutes all over the world [28]. Quality of seeds is evaluated by multiple factors such as number of online documents, rate of generating new documents, and the academical reputation or rank

---

[8]http://csxstatic.ist.psu.edu/about/crawler

[9]http://citeseerx.ist.psu.edu/

[10]http://lucene.apache.org/solr/

[11]http://tomcat.apache.org/

[12]http://sundance.ist.psu.edu:8080/solr1/index.html

of a URL's institute. The crawler periodically updates its white list based on historical evaluations. It also contains a black list of less than 1000 URLs. Since the crawler maintains a huge white list, it limits its crawling depth to 2 to avoid unnecessary crawling of other sites. Currently, it has crawled nearly 3 million unique online PDF documents.

The book detector filters books from the crawled documents. There is no exact definition of a book. An ISBN number certainly can be regarded as a valid indicator. We thus informally define a book as any document satisfying the following three rules: 1) there exists table of contents in its first 20 pages; 2) there is a valid ISBN number in some page before the table of contents; 3) the number of its total pages is larger than 100. Unfortunately, the strong ISBN based rule found only 4905 books. However, several online books are unofficial copies provided by their authors without ISBNs. To cover those books, we weaken our constraints to only 1) and 3). Using rule 3) can retrieve 196,425 documents while adding rule 1) makes the number decrease to 73,982. These 73,982 documents are then stored in the repository as book candidates for further processing.

3.2 Extractor

We note that a common structure for a digital book includes three parts: front material, body and back material. The front material usually consists of frontispiece, title page, copyright page, table of contents, list of figures, list of tables, dedication, acknowledgments, foreword, preface and introduction. The body refers to the text or contents and is often divided into chapters. The back material contains appendix, glossary, index, notes, bibliography and colophon[13]. Our structure extractor is responsible for extracting metadata information and hierarchical structure. The metadata includes title, authors, ISBN, publish date and copyright. Since ISBN, date, copyright can be detected using strong rules, our main focus is on title and authors extraction. We extract table of contents to represent the hierarchical logical structure of a book. We also extract references either at the end of a book or the end of each chapter for book citation analysis.

3.2.1 Metadata Extraction

ISBNs can be readily detected by just searching for the string "ISBN". A sequence of digits following "ISBN" can be interpreted as the ISBN number. However, this might be incorrect if "ISBN" is not in the right page. For example, we found ISBNs of other books appear in the body of a book. To make sure the matched ISBN is valid for the book, we only search for ISBN patterns in the first 8 pages. The ISBN patterns include two types, one for a 10-digit ISBN and another for 13. As regular expressions, it appears as:
$'i\s?s\s?b\s?n(10|[\s-]10)?[:-]?[\s]\{0,5\}([\dx-]\{13\})'$
$'i\s?s\s?b\s?n(13|[\s-]13)?[:-]?[\s]\{0,5\}([\dx-]\{17\})'$
When compiling or searching, we use the ignorecase mode.

Title and authors of books can come from three sources. First, we import the existing title and authors information from CiteSeerX database. However, that accuracy cannot be guaranteed since those are extracted by a metadata parser trained for scholarly papers, whose titles and authors can be quite different from those of books. However, since that metadata is available, it can be used as an initial metadata candidate.

Second, we develop new title and authors extractors based on heuristic rules derived from a small sample of books. We assume that title and authors are always on the same page, i.e. the title page, and the title page is before ToC, foreword or preface. We limit the title page candidates to a range from page 1 to the first page having table of contents, foreword or preface. If no such page is found, we use a page 1 to 10 as the default range. For each title page candidate, we then extract title or authors candidates based on multiple heuristics using font size, layout, length, and number of occurrences. A title or authors candidate is a visual text block containing several continuous lines without a newline break and significant font size change. In each page, the block with the maximum font size will be selected as a title candidate; the previous block and the next 2 blocks of the title candidate will be selected as authors candidates. In addition, the first block and the last block in each page are considered as authors candidate. Finally, we select the title candidate with most occurrences as the title. If there is a tie, then choose the one with larger font size. For all author candidates that start with 'By' or 'Edited by' is considered as an authors block. Otherwise, we choose the candidate which contains most naming words by looking it up in an external name dictionary containing 159,291 names.

Third, we harvest title and authors from Google Books through its API using ISBN search[14], which we believe is the best source of ISBN data. Querying using the 4905 ISBNs other well known sources, including Abebooks[15], Amazon book[16], ISBNSearch[17], and BookFinder4U[18], we retrieved 814, 1275, 1170, 1301 books respectively while Google Books returned 4329 books with valid title and authors and which covered all others. The first four pages of these 4329 books are then extracted line by line and represented by features shown in Table 1. The lines with text content matched to the title and authors are labeled class '1' and class '2' respectively; other lines are labeled class '0'. By ruling out those not being successfully extracted or perfectly matched, we finally have 2496 books we consider as ground truth. We use Libsvm [1] to train a 3-class model on all the lines extracted from the 2496 books and apply it to all other books without title and authors.

Finally, the title and authors information of a book not in ground truth is identified based on "vote" from the above three sources. If more than one of them agree on the title T or author A, then T will be set as the title, or A will be one of the author. However, if all of them disagree, we simple choose the results from the third source.

3.2.2 Table of Contents Extraction

In general, to effectively extract the ToC from a document, three sub-tasks need to be addressed: ToC detection, parsing and linking [14, 23]. ToC detection attempts to locate the boundary of the ToC, usually based on explicit heuristics. ToC parsing extracts the semantics and the hierarchy of the ToC, after which the ToC will be interpreted as a tree

---

[13]http://en.wikipedia.org/wiki/Book#Digital_format

[14]https: //www.googleapis.com/books/v1/volumes?q=isbn: ISBN&key=API Key

[15]www.abebooks.com/servlet/SearchResults?isbn=ISBN

[16]www.amazon.com/gp/search/ref=sr_adv_b/?field-isbn=ISBN

[17]http://www.isbnsearch.org/isbn/ISBN

[18]www.bookfinder4u.com/IsbnSearch.aspx?mode=direct&isbn=ISBN

Table 1: Features used in book metadata extraction (all feature values are rescaled to [0, 1] for training)

Feature	Description	Value type
font size	*Initial Font*: the font size of the starting character	float
	Average Font: the average font size of all the characters	float
	Font Changes: number of changes in font size	int
location	*Start X, End X, Start Y, End Y*: the coordinates of the line block in the page	float
	Line Number: the (order) number of the line within the page, e.g. 2 indicates the second line	int
	Page Number: the (order) number of the page	int
text	*Bag-of-word*: Top 200 words selected by DF rank in the whole dataset; 1 indicates a word is in the line	boolean
others	*Number of Words*: the total number of words in the line	int
	Number of Digits: the total number of digital words in the line	int

where each node represents an entry in the ToC. ToC linking determines the corresponding content in the body text w.r.t each entry in the ToC. We summarize the challenges of ToC recognition as follows by examining our book dataset. First, there are various types of ToC, making it difficult to find universal rules or templates governing all possible ToCs. For example, a ToC could be a full page, multiple pages, or part of a page; some documents may have multiple ToC (one for the whole document and one per chapter). Second, a ToC might contain noisy or inconsistent content. For example, there may exist some decorative content within a ToC page, or some entries of a ToC may be in multiple lines whose styles are inconsistent. Third, text in a ToC does not necessarily contain the exact title of the body sections. However, previous work assumes entries of the same level share consistent features and every entry can always be linked to the related title in the body part [7, 21].

Our ToC recognition is based on the following rules: 1) a ToC is generally in the first few pages of the document; 2) a ToC usually contains some regularities of numbering and indentation; 3) a ToC generally contains ordered references correlated (but not exactly matched) to titles or sections in body pages. The last property can also be broken into 5 sub-properties: 1) contiguity: a ToC consists of a series of contiguous references to some other parts; 2) ordering: the references and the referred parts appear in the same order in the document; 4) no self-reference: all references refer outside the contiguous list of references; 5) distinctness: the link from the references of ToC to the outside parts is injective, or every reference refers to a distinctive part. Our method does not rely on visual features such as font size or layout so that we can do the detection purely based text, which is much more efficient for large scale extraction.

3.2.3 Bibliography Extraction

Bibliography usually has obvious indicators such as "References", "Bibliography" or "Sources". However, unlike papers, books may have a bibliography at the end of each chapter. Thus, we need to search bibliography in the whole body of book rather than in only the last few pages. If we find a line contains only one of the three keywords and the lines followed are ordered reference items, we identify it as a bibliography block. We search the ordered number at the beginning of each reference until there are no continuously increasing number found in the following 30 lines. 30 seems like a large distance for references. But we do find some references contained near 10 lines. Also we believe that the distance between two bibliography blocks in two chapters will be much larger than 30. All the bibliographic files are

Table 2: Rules for generating venue alias

Rule	Examples of Venue Name
None	IEEE Transactions on Pattern Analysis and Machine Intelligence
Transactions->Trans. Journal->J Proceedings->Proc.	IEEE Trans. on Pattern Analysis and Machine Intelligence
Remove "of", "on", "in", "the"	IEEE Trans. Pattern Analysis and Machine Intelligence
Acronymization	IEEE Trans. PAMI
Pure acronymization	PAMI
Manual edit	IEEE Trans. Pattern Anal. Machine Intell.

extracted using the above heuristics from the pre-extracted text files.

We assign each book a unique document ID for our system. Our bibliography extractor successfully extracted bibliographic files from 28,714 PDFs in the whole book document collection containing 73,982 PDFs. The total number of reference mentions is 2,501,497. The other documents include unextracted PDF documents whose bibliography consisted of references without order number. We checked a small sample of these and found all of them not in computer science. The dataset contains all bibliographic files, where the file name responds to a book ID. In a bibliographic file, every two continuous references are separated by a new line.

3.2.4 Citation Analyzer

The citation analyzer has four main functions, including reference parsing, citation normalization, citation counting, and literal errors handling.

Reference parsing

It parses all references using ParsCit [2] and then improves the parsed results using an external name dictionary of authors and a thesaurus of venue names. Author names are collected from CiteSeerX database while thesaurus of venue is constructed based on rules and manual editing. Table 2 shows the rules using "IEEE Transactions on Pattern Analysis and Machine Intelligence" as an example. The acronymization keeps the prefix part such as "IEEE Transactions on", "Journal of", and "Proceedings of", while pure acronymization does not, as shown in the fourth row and fifth row. Manual editing refers to an unusual venue alias found from the data which are added to the thesaurus manually.

Citation Normalization

Citations to the same source may have widely varied formats including various placement and presentation of author names, venues, and dates. Sometimes there are even errors. As such it is necessary to normalize various citations to the same work, especially to count the number of citations to a given work. The normalization is based on matching authors, title and venue, depending primarily on

Table 3: Common literal due to PDF extraction

Literal type	Example
Absence of the initial	heoretical, bject-Oriented, ommunication
Split of one word	Springer- Verlag, L ATEX, MEM- OIRS
Corrupted string	Int\\\\\l Conf., O\\\Reilly

Table 4: Index fields

Name	Type	Stored	MultiValued
id	string	true	false
title	text_general	true	true
chapter_title	text_general	true	true
contents	text_general	true	false
body	text_general	true	false
isbn	text_general	true	false
authors	text_general	true	false
publish_date	string	true	false
links	string	true	true
googleID	string	true	false
text	text_general	false	true

the correctness of title. That is to say, two citations will be marked as the same source if they have exact the same title. Otherwise, if the edit distance of the two titles is less than a threshold, say, 5% of the max length of the two titles, we check the similarity of authors and venues. Citations without titles are not included for now.

Citation counting

The primary statistic we explore is the number of "cited by" books of works, venues, and institutes, which we further employ as a metric to measure their impact. Simply, if there are 100 books citing works from an institute, the number will be 100. The other one is the total number of citations to an institute, a venue and a work. It will always be larger than the former since there can be more than one citations in a book to an institute, a venue and a work. The two statistics are strongly dependent on the quality of reference parsing and citation normalization.

Literal errors handling

A problem cannot be neglected is the unpredictable literal errors generated during the PDF extraction. We list the three most common literal types found in our dataset in Table 3. For a word in "absence of the initial" or "split of one word", we find the closest "clean" reference to the reference it appears in based on edit distance and then correct it to the counterpart word in the "clean" reference. We do the same processing in the case when there is "corrupted string" in only a single word of a reference and choose to ignore it if there are more than two words corrupted.

3.3 Indexing and Ranking

We show the index fields and types in Table 4, which are configured in the Solr schema.xml [19]. The field "id" is defined as the *uniqueKey*; "contents" refers to the table of contents; "body" is the full text except the bibliography; "links" indicates the URL where the document comes from; "googleID" refers to the unique ID of the book in Google Books database, based on which we can get the page of the book in Google Books search. The "text" field is set to be the *defaultSearchField*. The default search field "text", contains "id", "title", "authors", "chapter_title", "contents" and "body". This setting enable us to search insides a book. We use the simple TFIDF based relevance model to rank the returned book list of a given query based on the weighted averaged score on all the *defaultSearchFields*.

$$s(q, f_i) = w(q, f_i) \cdot N(q) \cdot \sum_{t \in q} (tf(t, f_i) \cdot idf(t)^2 \cdot norm(t, f_i))$$

where $tf(t, f_i)$ correlates to the term's frequency, defined as the number of times term t appears in the field f_i; $idf(t)$ stands for Inverse Document Frequency; $w(q, f_i)$ is a score factor based on how many of the query terms are found in the specified field; $N(q)$ is a normalizing factor used to make scores between queries comparable; $norm(t, d)$ encapsulates a few (indexing time) boost and length factors.

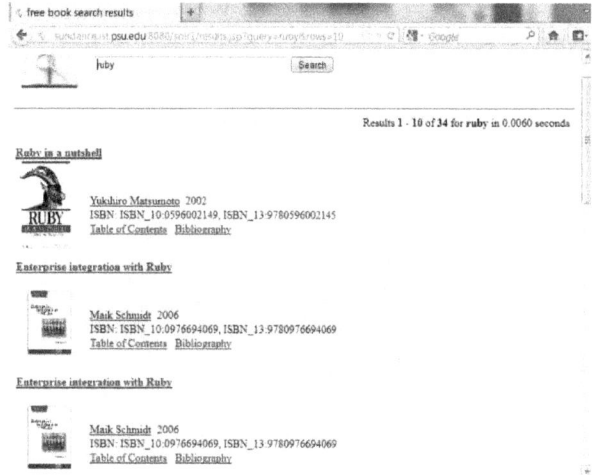

Figure 3: Results of searching "ruby"

3.4 Interface

We provide a simple style search interface. The searching result page is shown in Figure 3, where each block consists of title of the book, the book cover, the most relevant chapter title, authors, ISBN, table of contents, and bibliography. Each page contains 10 blocks, showing the top 10 returned results. The title links to a download page of the book while the book cover links to a html version of the book which can provide navigation using page numbers. The html version of a book is converted using PDFMiner[20]. There are 27,637 books with HTML copies. In Figure 4, there are no chapter titles shown in the top 3 results of searching "ruby", but we can see "3.2 classification by SVM" as the most relevant chapter title. It also shows the table of contents in a dynamic html table, providing a quick glance for the overall content and structure of a book. In the future we will build a link between table of contents and the html pages. Then by clicking an item in the table of contents, one can go directly to the page of a book.

4. EVALUATION

We first evaluate the extractors and the search engine. The extractors were evaluated on small labeled books randomly sampled from the whole book collection. For the later, human evaluation on different queries based on mul-

---

[19]http://wiki.apache.org/solr/SchemaXml

[20]http://www.unixuser.org/ euske/python/pdfminer/ index.html

Figure 4: Example of table of contents

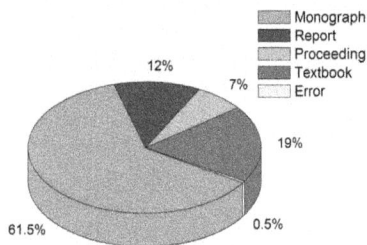

Figure 5: Components of the books

Table 5: Experimental evaluation for the extractors

Extractor Name	dataset size	precision	recall
Title	100	87%	89%
Authors	100	90%	92%
Table of Contents	147	85%	90%
ISBN	300	99%	97%
publish date	300	95%	90%
Copy right	300	92%	94%
Bibliography	200	96%	93%

The rule-based extractor achieves precision of 78% and recall of 81% on the 2496 books. To gain better performance on the whole data collection, we train the SVM model on the whole 2496 books. A small manually labeled set (out of the 2496 books with ground truth) of size 100 is used for testing. For table of contents extraction, it uses another dataset containing 147 books with table of contents manually labeled. The reason we choose different datasets for different extractors is some books do not have all of this information. For example, some books with a valid ISBN do not have a ToC. ISBN, copy right and publish date are easier tasks based on the same dataset. As we can see from the results, rule-based extractors can achieve an acceptable accuracy for most metadata. However, title and authors of more varieties are much more difficult than those with notable patterns. Even our hybrid approach based on the existing rule-based extractor and SVM-based extractor does not achieve comparable performance to other metadata extractors. We check the correctness of bibliographic files extracted from the 28,714 books. Again, we randomly sample 200 bibliographic files and check them manually. We find all the bibliographic files are correctly extracted. However, literal errors generated during PDF extraction are unavoidable. For example, one word might be split into two words and multiple words may be merged into a single one. We find 916 occurrences "he Art of Computer Programming" and 513 occurrences of "raduate Texts in Mathematics", where the first letter of "The" and "Graduate" is missingf. It's difficult to get the exact statistics of all these literal errors and then automatically correct them. These errors are first ignored when parsing references and calculating the statistics for each element such as work titles, venues, and institute. We then investigate the original ranking list of all these elements to find the principal heuristics that can help to rectify the missing numbers. Here, we group all titles using edit distance and then assign the longest one as the representative.

tiple metrics is presented. In addition, citation analysis is studied based on the constructed book citation dataset.

4.1 Components of Books

Ideally, we hope there is a valid ISBN for every book in the dataset. However, ISBN is detected in only less than 5000 books. Note sometimes ISBN appears as a picture bar-code which cannot be detected. We then manually check 200 books randomly sampled from the whole set. We classify them into 5 categories, including monograph, report, proceeding and textbook. A monograph is a detailed scholarly work of a single specialized subject. Usually it is derived from a Phd thesis or multiple research papers. Since an official Phd thesis also has an ISBN, we count a Phd thesis as a monograph. Reports refer to unpublished book-like documents from a university, government, or company. Proceedings are paper collections from a conference, workshop or journal. Since proceedings usually have an ISBN, we do not rule them out. Textbooks here represent the more traditional books including course books, reference books, and manuals. The type of books is shown in Figure 5. Error indicates one corrupted PDF filled with error codes. If we count textbook and monograph as appropriate books, we get at least 80% of those in our book citation dataset.

4.2 Extraction Evaluation

We list our evaluation results for each extractor in Table 5. The 5-fold cross validation in the 2496 books for the SVM based extractor achieves an classification accuracy of 89%.

4.3 Search Evaluation

Basic statistics about the book search engine is listed in Table 6, including the total number of indexed books, the number of books with bibliographic files, the number of books with HTML copies, the number of books with more than 200 pages and the number of books with GoogleID. Metadata including title, authors, publish date of books with googleID is imported from Google Books by its API. We evaluate the relevance using the precision of the top 10 responses by manually checking a set of queries. Results of ten selected queries are shown in Table 7, based on precision, total number of returned results and response time. Since the exact number of relevant books for each query is unknown, the recall is not given. From the table, we can see that the search engine gives relevant results in the first page

Table 6: Book search engine statistics

Indicator	Number
Total indexed books	59,207
Bibliography files	28,714
HTML files	27,637
Books with 200+ pages	25,680
Books with googleID	5,945

Table 7: Searching evaluation

Query	Precision	#Results	Time
ruby	100%	34	0.005 s
python	100%	110	0.003 s
java	90%	1,467	0.004 s
matlab	100%	447	0.009 s
SQL	100%	414	0.004 s
database	100%	3,139	0.004 s
machine learning	100%	6,497	0.006 s
decision tree	50%	5,376	0.011 s
topic model	20%	18,347	0.001 s
latent dirichlet allocation	100%	2095	0.014 s

(top 10 results) for most domain-specific keywords queries. However, when a query is composed of general words, e.g. decision tree, topic model, the precision gets lower because the default operator for query parser is set to be "OR". For query "decision tree", the other 5 irrelevant returned results are about trees in data structure and decision in management. For "topic model", the two words are more general than "decision" and "tree", thus the result is even worse. However, the query operator "AND" can also be specified by set q.op=AND. A comparison to Google Books Search based on 8 different features is summarized in Table 8, including size, ranking, online preview, advance search, speed, open access, table of contents, and bibliography. For the ranking feature, our search only shows the matched results in title and chapter titles, while Google Books can give the exact matches in the pages of a book with priority to title and chapter titles. Although our search engine cannot compare to Google Books on many features, it has certain special features such as complete open access and a more complete table of contents and bibliographic information.

4.4 Overview of Book Citations

Previous work show that the most highly cited works are from books and book chapters [10, 18]. However, the value of book citations has been mostly ignored. We first investigate the number of citations from books. As shown is Figure 6, the distribution is nearly uniform around the average (87)

Table 8: Comparison with Google Books

Features	The Demo	Google Books
Size	59,207	>100,000,000
Ranking	title,ch_title	title,ch_title,full text
Online preview	yes	yes
Advance search	no	yes
Speed	0.01s	0.5s
Open access	All	< 1%
Table of Contents	Yes	Yes
Bibliography	Yes	No

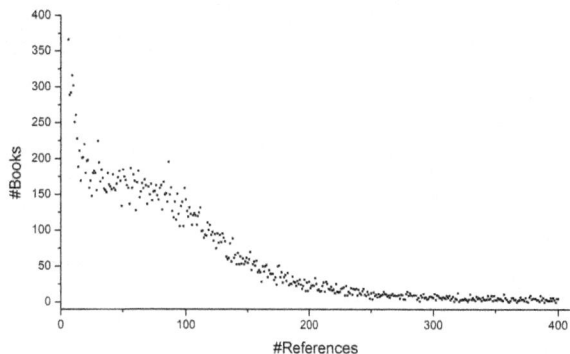

Figure 6: Distribution of number of references in books

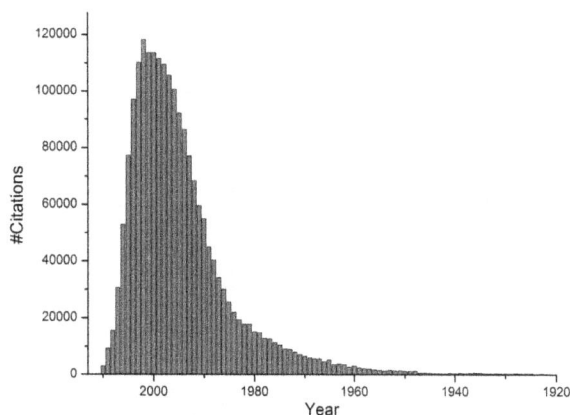

Figure 7: Number of citations each year

but steeper decreasing before 20 and after 100. Number of citations of most books (76%) range in [20, 200] while long tail appears after 200. Furthermore, we found that manual or reference books tend to have few references than academic books. The more abundant citations from books offer a wider research assessment than citation datasets of the same scale from papers. We speculate that while papers tend to cite more topic-similar peer works, books would cover a much broader literature. We believe this would make book citations a valuable source for academic assessment.

The evolving trend of number of citations each year since 1920 is shown in Figure 7. We believe the peak will keep growing in time while the left side will keep a steeper cliff shape at around 10 years. The growing trend from left to right suggests a number of publications produced each year is increasing. The steeper cliff shape implies that books tend to cite older work of several years which at the time would have been the state of art. Figure 7 may also imply the citation preference over time of a single book, considering that the number of references of most books is around the average. We conjecture that when a book is written, most works are cited in some year range. Before this year range, less will be cited as the years decrease. After that, less will be cited as the years increase. To prove or disprove this conjecture would be interesting.

4.5 Most Highly Book Cited Documents

Table 9: Document rank based on book citations

Title	Cited by	#Citations	CiteSeer Rank	Google	ISI Search	ISI Cited
Introduction to Algorithms (B)	982	1080	2	28558	-	72
Computers and Intractability (B)	753	809	1	40578	-	4
Numerical Recipes in C: The Art of Scientific Computing (B)	676	749	127	442	-	58
The Art of Computer Programming (B)	604	1832	74	27270	-	28
Digital Image Processing (B)	566	844	-	7987	-	91
Elements of Information Theory (B)	526	563	5	26485	-	25
Partial Differential Equations (B)	518	1308	-	12404	Y	38
Graduate Texts in Mathematics (B)	513	931	-	3358	-	29
Communicating Sequential Processes (J)	474	609	15	14579	Y	1394
Genetic Algorithms in Search, Optimization and Machine Learning(B)	361	1164	4	50264	-	2
A mathematical theory of communication (J)	356	390	10	49992	Y	9800
Compilers: Principles, Techniques, and Tools (B)	356	368	-	10964	-	2
Communication and Concurrency (B)	344	379	17	8934	-	2
Design Patterns: Elements of Reusable Object-Oriented Software (B)	337	377	8	27325	-	9
Statistical Learning Theory (B)	334	427	3	37675	-	27
The C++ Programming Language (B)	332	358	119	7998	-	1
The Java Language Specification (B)	324	348	88	6430	-	2
Computer Architecture: A Quantitative Approach (B)	304	323	12	9560	-	4
Introduction to Automata Theory, Languages, and Computation (B)	296	969	14	12695	-	1
Ordinary Differential Equations (B)	274	587	-	7182	-	15

The most highly cited documents in our book dataset are listed in Table 9. In the title, "(B)" indicates a book while "(J)" indicates a journal paper. The "CiteSeer rank"[21] represents the rank of most cited computer science citations generated from documents in CiteSeerX database in 2011. "Google" represents the "cited by" number of a document provided by Google Scholar. Since there might be duplicate results in Google Scholar, we choose the one with the highest "cited by" number. The "ISI Search" column shows whether a work is indexed by ISI, "Y" indicating yes otherwise no. If yes, the number of "ISI Cited" is the "Times Cited" number of the document in ISI search results. Otherwise, we use "Cited Reference Search" provided by ISI Web of Science to find the number of cited references[22].

The first evident finding is most highly cited documents of books, as expected, are books. There are only 2 journal papers in the top 20 documents. Since a previous study showed books are favored by papers citations, we may conclude that the most highly cited documents of all research publications are books. However, from the CiteSeer rank and Google "cite by" numbers, we can see the most highly cited documents of books are different from those of papers. There are 5 books (marked by "-") are out of top 200 in CiteSeer rank, suggesting that some books favored by books may not receive high citations from papers. A key finding here is that those highly cited books are absent in ISI, or not indexed by the Book Citation Index of ISI. By checking the "Cited Reference Search", we find there are very few citations to those books in the ISI database. The only exception is "Partial Differential Equations", which is searchable in Web of Science of ISI but being cited only 38 times.

4.6 Venue Rank

An key role of citation analysis is to measure importance of venues using citation based metrics [25, 26]. The impact factor (IF) [8] provided by ISI might be, if not the most satisfactory one, the most popular one for measuring journals. In a given year, the impact factor of a journal is the average number of citations received per paper published in that

journal during the two preceding years[23]. Google Scholar uses *h-index*, or the largest number h such that at least h articles in that venue were cited at least h times each[24]. We rank the venues based on the number of "cited by" books and list the top 20 of them in Table 10, with the IF (2009) and h-index shown in the fourth and fifth column for each venue. The IF value is queried using MedSci[25] relying on ISI and the h-index is from SCIMAGO[26] based on scopus[27].

The results shown in Table 10 offer several interesting observations. First, books prefer to cite more documents from journals rather than from conferences. All the top 30 venues are journals except ACM SIGCOMM. With the exception of LNCS, a book like conference proceedings as the second most highly cited venue by books, suggests that conference proceedings are not good citation sources for books. Second, the most highly cited venues are premier journals, indicating the "cited by" is a potential valuable metric for measure venues. We can see all venues are SCI indexed journals except LNCS and ACM SIGCOMM. Only 5 journals have an IF lower than 1 while half of them have an IF higher than 2. Third, there is no strong correlation between the "cited by" number and IF or h-index. A possible reason is our dataset is independent on ISI data or scopus data. Thus the "cited by" numbers from our book citations are missing in their statistics. For example, if they consider the 13,297 citations from 6,431 books, surely, the IF value and h-index of Communications of ACM will increase.

5. RELATED WORK

5.1 Book Structure Extraction

The book structure extraction attempts to harvest the logical structure of a book (pictured by table of contents) and the metadata including title, authors, ISBNs, publisher, etc. Book table of contents (ToC) recognition has been extensively studied in the document analysis and recognition

---

[21]http://citeseerx.ist.psu.edu/stats/citations
[22]Our queries were conducted on May 9 2012.

[23]http://thomsonreuters.com/products_services/science/academic/impact_factor/
[24]http://scholar.google.com/intl/en/scholar/metrics.html
[25]http://www.medsciediting.com/sciif.asp
[26]http://www.scimagojr.com/journalsearch.php
[27]http://www.scopus.com/home.url

Table 10: Venue rank based on book citations

Venue name	Cited by	#Citations	IF (2009)	h-index
Communications of the ACM	6431	13297	2.35	101
LNCS	3618	34740	-	75
Theoretical Computer Science	2893	10167	0.838	59
Physical Review Letters	2425	32877	7.621	349
Science	2565	6886	31.364	678
IEEE Transactions on Pattern Analysis and Machine Intelligence	2246	10274	5.027	169
IEEE Transactions on Computers	2152	4708	1.604	66
Journal of the ACM	2085	4000	3.375	72
IEEE Transactions on Software Engineering	2070	10020	2.216	88
ACM Computing Surveys	2013	6794	7.806	62
Operations Research	1691	6417	1.995	65
IEEE Transactions on Information Theory	2042	10034	2.725	155
Nature	1500	5365	36.101	698
ACM Transactions on Programming Languages and Systems	1490	2826	1.167	45
IEEE Journal on Selected Areas in Communications	1487	7498	4.232	140
Parallel Computing	1437	3489	1.086	37
Automatica	1426	2815	2.171	114
Annals of Math.	1406	2380	3.179	53
Information Sciences	1376	2220	2.833	61
ACM SIGCOMM	1322	5214	-	-

community [3, 4, 7, 21]. However, those methods based on ad hoc rules only work for a small size and domain-specific book set. It is still a challenging problem to design a ToC recognition algorithm that can be effectively applied to large scale heterogeneous books [14]. Gao et al. studied both ToC and metadata extraction from PDF book documents by modeling them as a matching problem on the bipartite graph [6]. Feng et al. studied how to restructure the OCR output of books using a Hidden Markov Model (HMM) based hierarchical alignment algorithm [5]. Metadata extraction has also been studied as an information extraction problem using classification models such as SVM for scholarly papers [11], or using sequential labeling models for general office documents [13]. While the techniques for training our SVM based extractor is similar to [11], we use a novel hybrid voting approach and our ground truth is harvested from Web.

5.2 Book Search and Retrieval

Book search and retrieval has focused on designing a better indexing to support inside book search. H. Wu et al. reported an experimental book search system that supports both database and IR style index structures. Their findings suggest that fielded retrieval is a suitable strategy to apply to collections of books [27]. W. Magdy et al. examined the effect of indexing different parts of digitized books on retrieval in response to specific information needs. These results indicate that certain portions of books, specifically titles and headers, are more valuable than other parts of books [22]. However, the evaluation of search and retrieval over large book repositories is still a difficult task. G. Kazai et al. used crowdsourcing for book search evaluation and found that well designed crowdsourcing can be an effective tool for the evaluation of book IR systems [15, 16]. A similar problem has also been tested in the social book search task [17].

5.3 Book Citation Analysis

Books and monographs play significant roles in research communication. The absence of citations from most books and monographs from the Thomson Reuters/Institute for Scientific Information databases (ISI) has been criticized, but attempts to include citations from or to books in research evaluation in our opinion has not been that successful. Kousha and Thelwall studied the book citations analysis in science, social science, and humanities disciplines using Google Books and showed it to be a valuable new source of citation data for the social sciences and humanities[18]. They argued that in book-oriented disciplines such as the social sciences, arts, and humanities, online book citations may be sufficiently numerous to support peer review research evaluation [19]. However, to the best of our knowledge, none studied the large scale citations from books from Web. Our effort is similar to automatic citation analysis such as CiteSeer [10, 20], thought their focus is on conference and journal papers. In addition, using citation data to rank scholars or institutes has long been an important area of research [12, 24].

6. CONCLUSIONS AND FUTURE WORK

We present a search engine for online books in PDF format. The search engine explores multiple methods for navigating books and supports searches on metadata, table of contents and bibliography. We discussed techniques for extracting metadata from PDF books. In particular, we devised for extracting the title and authors information a novel hybrid approach based on a voting from multiple sources: CiteSeer metadata, a rule based extractor derived from sampled books, and a SVM based extractor learned from web knowledge. In addition, we also proposed methods for extracting the table of contents and bibliography. Using the extracted bibliography from books, we enhanced citation analysis in recent academic search engines by constructing a book citation dataset. Our initial, statistical analysis using this dataset shows that in computer science and related disciplines, books citations are valuable and should not be neglected in peer review research evaluation.

Future goals would be to further improve the accuracy of metadata and ToC information by designing better extractors and aggregating available metadata from other systems and to provide more navigation functions inside book search. For example, it would be useful to build links between ToC and the body pages and to develop metrics that capture the impact of book citations to institutes, venues and authors. Then the full scholarly document citation graph can be updated using citations to and from books.

7. ACKNOWLEDGEMENTS

We gratefully acknowledge support from the CiteseerX team, the National Science Foundation, and useful comments from referees.

8. REFERENCES

[1] C.-C. Chang and C.-J. Lin. LIBSVM: A library for support vector machines. *ACM Transactions on Intelligent Systems and Technology*, 2:27:1–27:27, 2011.

[2] I. G. Councill, C. L. Giles, and M. yen Kan. Parscit: An open-source crf reference string parsing package. In *Proceedings of the Language Resources and Evaluation Conference*, pages 661–667, 2008.

[3] H. Dejean and J.-L. Meunier. On tables of contents and how to recognize them. *International Journal on Document Analysis and Recognition*, 12(1):1–20, 2009.

[4] H. DÃľjean and J. L. Meunier. Structuring documents according to their table of contents. In *Proceedings of DocEng*, pages 2–9, 2005.

[5] S. Feng and R. Manmatha. A hierarchical hmm-based automatic evaluation of ocr accuracy for a digital library of books. In *Proceedings of JCDL*, pages 109–118, 2006.

[6] L. Gao, Z. Tang, X. Lin, Y. Liu, R. Qiu, and Y. Wang. Structure extraction from pdf-based book documents. In *Proceedings of JCDL*, pages 11–20, 2011.

[7] L. Gao, Z. Tang, X. Lin, X. Tao, and Y. Chu. Analysis of book documents' table of content based on clustering. In *Proceedings of ICDAR*, pages 911–915, 2009.

[8] E. Garfield. Impact factors, and why they won't go away. *Nature*, 411(6837):522–522, 2001.

[9] C. L. Giles, K. D. Bollacker, and S. Lawrence. Citeseer: an automatic citation indexing system. In *Proceedings of the third ACM conference on Digital libraries*, DL '98, 1998.

[10] A. A. Goodrum, K. W. McCain, S. Lawrence, and C. L. Giles. Scholarly publishing in the internet age: a citation analysis of computer science literature. *Information Processing Management*, 37(5):661 – 675, 2001.

[11] H. Han, C. L. Giles, E. Manavoglu, H. Zha, Z. Zhang, and E. A. Fox. Automatic document metadata extraction using support vector machines. In *JCDL*, pages 37–48, 2003.

[12] J. E. Hirsch. Does the h index have predictive power? *Proceedings of the National Academy of Sciences*, 104(49):19193–19198.

[13] Y. Hu, H. Li, Y. Cao, D. Meyerzon, and Q. Zheng. Automatic extraction of titles from general documents using machine learning. In *Proceedings of JCDL*, pages 145–154, 2005.

[14] Y. Jayabal, C. Ramanathan, and M. J. Sheth. Challenges in generating bookmarks from toc entries in e-books. In *Proceedings of DocEng*, pages 37–40, 2012.

[15] G. Kazai, J. Kamps, M. Koolen, and N. Milic-Frayling. Crowdsourcing for book search evaluation: impact of hit design on comparative system ranking. In *Proceedings SIGIR*, pages 205–214, 2011.

[16] G. Kazai, M. Koolen, J. Kamps, A. Doucet, and M. Landoni. Overview of the inex 2010 book track: Scaling up the evaluation using crowdsourcing. In *Comparative Evaluation of Focused Retrieval*, pages 98–117. 2011.

[17] M. Koolen, J. Kamps, and G. Kazai. Social book search: comparing topical relevance judgements and book suggestions for evaluation. In *Proceedings of CIKM*, pages 185–194, 2012.

[18] K. Kousha and M. Thewall. Google book search: Citation analysis for social science and the humanities. *Journal of the American Society for Information Science and Technology*, 60(8):1537–1549, 2009.

[19] K. Kousha, M. Thewall, and S. Rezaie. Assessing the citation impact of books: The role of google books, google scholar, and scopus. *Journal of the American Society for Information Science and Technology*, 62(11):2147–2164, 2011.

[20] S. Lawrence, F. Coetzee, G. Flake, D. Pennock, B. Krovetz, F. Nielsen, A. Kruger, and C. L. Giles. Persistence of information on the web: Analyzing citations contained in research articles. In *Proceedings of CIKM*, pages 235–242, 2000.

[21] X. Lin and Y. Xiong. Detection and analysis of table of contents based on content association. *International Journal on Document Analysis and Recognition*, 8(2):132–143, 2006.

[22] W. Magdy and K. Darwish. Book search: Indexing the valuable parts. In *BooksOnline*, 2008.

[23] S. Marinai, E. Marino, and G. Soda. Table of contents recognition for converting pdf documents in e-book formats. In *Proceedings of DocEng*, pages 73–76, 2010.

[24] J. Ren and R. N. Taylor. Automatic and versatile publications ranking for research institutions and scholars. *Commun. ACM*, 50(6):81–85, June 2007.

[25] X. Shi, J. Leskovec, and D. A. McFarland. Citing for high impact. In *Proceedings of JCDL*, pages 49–58, 2010.

[26] Y. Sun and C. L. Giles. Popularity weighted ranking for academic digital libraries. In *Proceedings of ECIR*, pages 605–612, 2007.

[27] H. Wu, G. Kazai, and M. Taylor. Book search experiments: Investigating ir methods for the indexing and retrieval of books. In *ECIR*, pages 234–245, 2008.

[28] J. Wu, P. Teregowda, J. P. F. Ramírez, P. Mitra, S. Zheng, and C. L. Giles. The evolution of a crawling strategy for an academic document search engine: Whitelists and blacklists. In *Proceedings of ACM WebSci*, 2012.

Near Duplicate Detection in an Academic Digital Library

Kyle Williams[‡], C. Lee Giles[†‡]

[‡]Information Sciences and Technology, [†]Computer Science and Engineering
Pennsylvania State University, University Park, PA 16802, USA
kwilliams@psu.edu, giles@ist.psu.edu

ABSTRACT

The detection and potential removal of duplicates is desirable for a number of reasons, such as to reduce the need for unnecessary storage and computation, and to provide users with uncluttered search results. This paper describes an investigation into the application of scalable *simhash* and *shingle* state of the art duplicate detection algorithms for detecting near duplicate documents in the CiteSeer[X] digital library. We empirically explored the duplicate detection methods and evaluated their performance and application to academic documents and identified good parameters for the algorithms. We also analyzed the types of near duplicates identified by each algorithm. The highest F-scores achieved were 0.91 and 0.99 for the simhash and shingle-based methods respectively. The shingle-based method also identified a larger variety of duplicate types than the simhash-based method.

Categories and Subject Descriptors

I.7.5 [**Document and Text Processing**]: Document Capture—*Document Analysis*

General Terms

Experimentation, Measurement, Performance

Keywords

Near duplicate detection, simhash, shingles

1. INTRODUCTION

Digital documents have literally changed the way in which documents are discovered, shared and managed through easy versioning, copying and dissemination. As a result, there has been an explosion in the amount of digital documents that are available and digital libraries have arisen as a means of managing these vast quantities of information. Some dig-

ital libraries, such as the arXiv[1], allow for users to submit academic papers for inclusion, whereas others, such as CiteSeer[X][2], automatically collect papers through focused crawling. In both cases, it is possible that near duplicate documents are added to the digital library collections. For instance, in the case of the arXiv, users might make minor revisions to a document and submit it as a new document rather than updating their existing submission. Similarly, in the case of CiteSeer[X], similar versions of a paper may exist at multiple locations on the Web and these multiple versions may be automatically added to the collection as a result of the automatic crawling and ingesting.

There has been significant research in near duplicates on the Web; however, there has not been as much research in detecting near duplicates in digital libraries of academic papers and whether methods for duplicate detection on the Web are easily transferable to this domain. Two state of the art duplicate detection algorithms exist: *simhash* [2] and *shingle*-based methods [1]. In this paper, we investigate the use of these two algorithms for finding near duplicates in CiteSeer[X], which is a real-world digital library of academic papers. We measure the precision and the recall of the two algorithms under varying conditions, we experiment to find suitable parameters for the algorithms, and we investigate the types of duplicates detected by each algorithm.

In presenting these contributions, the rest of this paper is laid out as follows. Section 2 discusses related work and Section 3 describes the duplicate detection algorithms used in this study. Section 4 presents the evaluation and, lastly, conclusions are presented in Section 5.

2. RELATED WORK

A state of the art method for detecting duplicate Web pages was proposed by Broder et al. [1]. Broder et al. made use of shingles for duplicate detection in the AltaVista search engine and described efficient algorithms for finding near duplicates in large collections. The simhash algorithm [2] is another state of the art algorithm for duplicate detection that maps a high dimensional feature space to a fixed-size fingerprint [6] and Manku et al. [6] developed an efficient algorithm for finding duplicate documents in a collection. A study comparing the shingle and simhash methods on a dataset containing over 1.6 billion web pages found that both algorithms worked poorly for detecting duplicate web pages from the same site, but worked well for detecting duplicate

---

[1]http://arxiv.org/
[2]http://citeseerx.ist.psu.edu/

web pages from different sites [4]. Furthermore, it was found that combining the approaches improved results [4].

A technique for duplicate document detection, known as I-Match, is based on collection statistics with the idea being that removing terms that occur very frequently or very infrequently in a collection is a good basis for identifying duplicates by calculating the checksum of the most significant terms in a document [3]. To detect near duplicate books, techniques have been developed based on the hashing of the metadata associated with each book [7] as well as identifying unique words that appear in books and finding near duplicates by aligning the longest common sequences of words [8]. Lastly, one of the few studies to focus on academic documents used concept trees to detect similar documents [5].

As this discussion has shown, there have been several different approaches to duplicate detection, with the simhash and shingle-based methods being state of the art. In this study, we test the use of these state of the art methods for detecting near duplicate academic documents, with a specific focus on parameters for near duplicate detection and the type of near duplicates detected by each method.

3. ALGORITHMS

3.1 Simhash

The simhash algorithm maps a high dimensional feature space to a fixed-size fingerprint [6]. The process involves calculating a *hash* that represents each document and then detecting near duplicates by identifying documents that have similar hashes. The calculation of the hash is not described here due to space constraints; however, the method is the same as used by Manku et al. [6] with each document being represented by a 64-bit hash and with each token in a document contributing an equal weight to the final bit-hash. The distance (and thus similarity) between document bit-hashes is calculated using the Hamming distance.

To find near duplicates, the method proposed by Manku et al. [6] is used. In this approach, two documents are considered as being near duplicates if the Hamming distance between their two hashes is at most k. For a pre-determined k, the method partitions each document bit-hash into $k + 1$ sub-hashes and stores each sub-hash and the ids of documents that contain the sub-hash in $k + 1$ tables. For a query document, the hash of the document is calculated and partitioned into $k + 1$ sub-hashes. Each of the sub-hashes are looked up in the $k + 1$ tables and the Hamming distance is calculated between the full hash of the query document and the full hash of each document in the tables that shares a sub-hash with the query document. Using this approach, if two documents differ by k bits then at least one of the $k + 1$ sub-hashes is guaranteed to match.

To find near duplicates, two passes are made through the data. In the first pass, hashes are calculated for all documents and the sub-hashes stored in tables and in the second pass each hash is used as a query while making sure not to match a query document with its entry in the hash tables.

3.2 Shingles

Shingles are sequences of tokens of length w that appear in a document and the similarity of two documents can be calculated based on the number of shingles that they have in common [1]. Since it is computationally infeasible to calculate the similarity of the sets of all of the shingles for every

document, a method based on the *sketch* of a document is used instead. To calculate the sketch of a document, each shingle in a document is hashed using h hash functions and a list is maintained of the minimum hash values found for each hash function. The sketch of a document is then its set of h minimum hash values and the similarity of two documents is estimated based on the overlap of their sketches [4]. In this study, we make use of hash functions in the form of: $h(x) = (Ax + B) \mod p$, where x is the shingle, p is a large prime, which we set to $2^{32} - 1$, and A and B are random integers in the range $[1, p]$.

To find near duplicates based on their sketches, each document is represented by pairs of the h minimum hash values - M_h - and the document ID in the form of $<M_h, doc\_id>$ and a list of all the pairs for all documents is compiled. This list is then used to build a second list of documents that have a M_h in common in the form of $<M_h, doc\_id_1, doc\_id_2>$. This second list can then be scanned and the number of M_h that each pair of documents $<doc\_id_1, doc\_id_2>$ have in common can be counted and then divided by h to calculate the resemblance of the two documents.

4. EVALUATION

To evaluate the algorithms, 100,000 documents were randomly sampled from the CiteSeer^X collection and those that contained a minimum of 15 tokens (after preprocessing) were retained, which was 95,558 documents. Each document was processed using standard information retrieval processing and the calculation of hashes and the extraction of shingles was based on the full text of the documents. No clustering took place when detecting near duplicates, since random pair sampling was used for evaluating precision and recall similar to the approach used in other studies [4, 6]. In deciding whether or not a pair of papers are near duplicates, the following should be true: the papers should have the same (or very similar) titles and authors; there should be significant overlap in the text (maximum of a paragraph different); and there should be significant overlap in the citations.

To evaluate precision for each treatment, which represents a variation in the parameters for duplicate detection, $n = 20$ pairs of documents that were identified as being near duplicates were randomly sampled. The n pairs were then manually checked in order to determine whether or not the documents were near duplicates and precision was calculated. Since no gold standard exists, it is impossible to accurately measure recall. Thus, recall is instead estimated by maintaining a list of all of the true positives identified during the precision calculation for each treatment, which we refer to as the *duplicate list*. The recall of each treatment is then estimated by comparing the documents returned by that treatment to the duplicate list. In total, the true duplicate list contained 360 unique duplicate pairs.

4.1 Detecting Duplicates

Simhash.

Experiments were conducted for different Hamming distance values of k, where $k = \{0, 1, 2, ..., 10\}$. Figure 1 (a) shows the the precision, recall and F-score. As can be seen from the figure, there is perfect precision when $k = 0$, which is to be expected since, in this case, each document has exactly the same hash. Thereafter, the precision decreases as k increases. When a Hamming distance of 5 is allowed, the

Table 1: Cosine similarity for different k

0	1	2	3	4	5	6	7	8	9	10
1	0.97	0.97	0.99	0.89	0.97	0.81	0.75	0.66	0.54	0.49

precision is approximately 0.65; however, precision decreases significantly beyond this point, ultimately ending up at less that 0.2 for $k > 7$. The recall also increases as k increases. This is to be expected since higher values of k allow for documents with larger Hamming distances between their hashes to be considered near duplicates. When $k > 3$, the recall exceeds 0.9. The F-score is highest at 0.91 and occurs when $k = 3$. At this point, the precision is 0.94 and the recall was 0.88. Interestingly, $k = 3$ was also the optimal value found for duplicate Web page detection [6].

Shingles.

The number of hashes that were used to represent a sketch for a document was set to 84 as this has previously been used in other studies [1, 4]. Three different shingle sequence lengths $w = \{5, 8, 10\}$ were experimented with and the minimum required resemblance R for a pair of documents to be considered duplicates was also varied. Figures 1 (b) and (c) show the precision and recall. As can be seen from the figure, the length of the shingles and the minimum resemblance both have little effect on the precision, with each having a minimum precision of 0.95. As the resemblance requirement is relaxed, the recall increases. Furthermore, shorter shingle lengths result in higher recall, which is intuitive since shorter shingle lengths allow for more differences among the sequences of tokens that appear in the documents. The highest recall of 0.98 occurs when $w = 5$ and $R = 50\%$. The maximum F-score of 0.99 occurs when $w = 5$ and $R = 50\%$. At this point the precision is 1 and the recall is 0.98.

Thus, this experiment has shown that both algorithms perform well and, with the right parameters, can successfully be applied to detecting duplicate academic documents.

4.2 Analysis of Duplicates

We analyzed the cosine similarity between the $n = 20$ near duplicates pairs that were randomly sampled for each method and results are shown in Table 1 for different values of k for the simhash method. As can be seen from the table, as k increases the cosine similarity decreases. Interestingly, there is a large difference between the cosine similarity and precision in Figure 1 (a) for some k. For instance, for $k = 6$ the average cosine similarity is 0.81, but the precision is only 0.2. Since many of these papers are based on computer science, one possible reason for this could be due to significant overlap in common mathematical notation among papers, thus leading to similar hashes for different papers. Thus, the simhash method using single word tokens may not be appropriate for near duplicate detection for documents that make use of a large amount of standard notation. For the shingles method, regardless of the shingle size w or the resemblance, the minimum cosine similarity was 0.97 and was 1 in the majority of cases. This corresponds with precision of almost 1 achieved by the shingles method, regardless of the shingle length and resemblance.

We also analyzed the types of duplicates returned by each method for the best performing parameters and labeled each true positive as being *exact*, a *preprint* (missing page num-

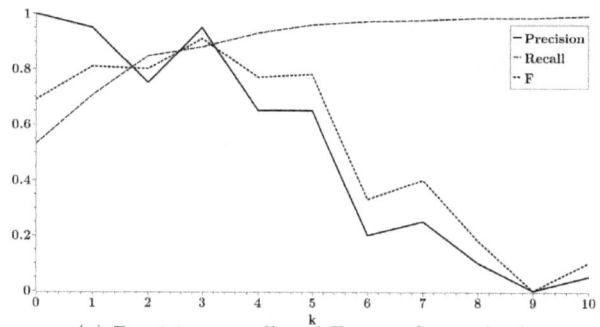

(a) Precision, recall and F-score for simhash

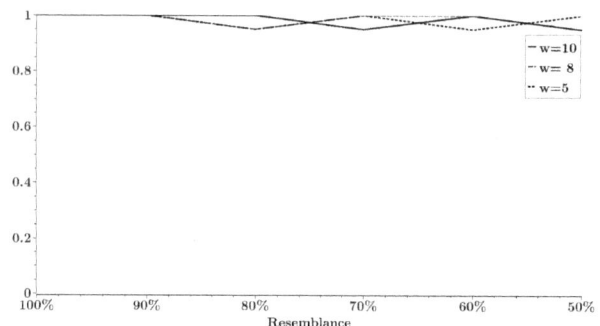

(b) Precision for shingles with different lengths

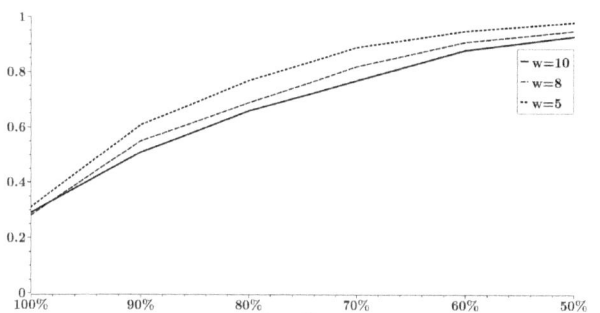

(c) Recall for shingles with different lengths

Figure 1: Performance of algorithms

bers, copyright notice, different formatting, etc), or a *different version/draft* (minor differences in content, dates, and revision numbers). Table 2 summarizes the results of the types of near duplicates detected. As can be seen from the table, most of the duplicates returned by each method are in fact exact duplicates; however, some of them are also preprints and different versions/drafts of the same paper. The shingle-based method appears to return a more even distribution of different types of near duplicates, thereby suggesting that it is better than simhash at detecting different types of near duplicates.

4.3 Number of Duplicates Returned

Figure 2 (a) shows the number of duplicates returned for simhash as k increases. When $k = 0$, 769 pairs of documents are returned. Thereafter, there is an exponential increase in the number of documents returned as k increases and it approaches 120 000 when $k = 10$. Based on the performance of the simhash algorithm, it is likely that the majority of documents returned when $k > 5$ are false positives.

Table 2: Types of near duplicates

Method	Exact	Preprint	Content/Version
Simhash	12	3	4
Shingles	9	5	6

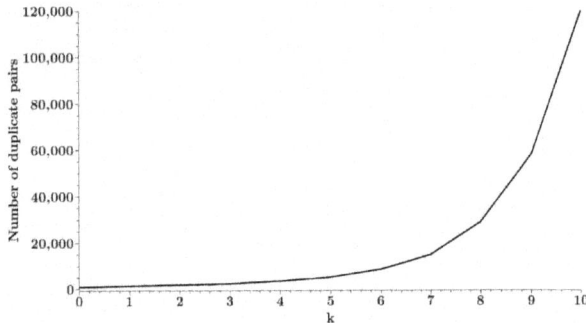

(a) simhash with different values for k

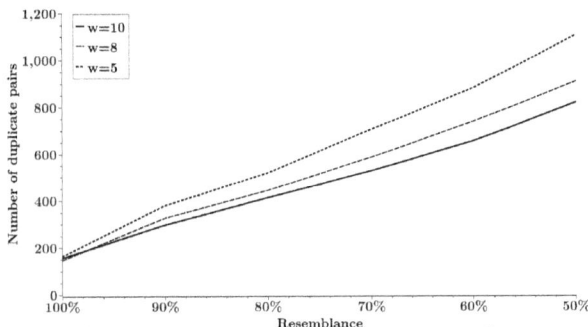

(b) shingle method with different values for w

Figure 2: Number of duplicates returned

For shingles (Figure 2 (b)), lower values of w return more near duplicate pairs. This is in line with intuition, since lower values of w require that documents have shorter sequences of tokens in common and thus are more likely to match. Furthermore, Figure 2 (b) also shows that the number of duplicate pairs returned increases linearly as the similarity threshold is reduced. On average, reducing the required resemblance by 10% leads to 157.35 new document pairs being found. These results reveal something interesting about the shingle-based method, specifically, that near duplicate papers generally have high shingle similarities and reducing the similarity threshold does not lead to a large increase in the number of near duplicates returned. Given the performance of the shingles algorithm, it is likely that most of the near duplicates returned are true positives.

The results discussed above show that the two algorithms perform quite differently when the criteria for detecting duplicates are relaxed. For the simhash algorithm, increasing k leads to an exponential increase in the number of duplicates returned, whereas decreasing the similarity threshold for the shingle-based method leads to a linear increase in the number of duplicates returned. Thus, from the perspective of processing time, tuning these parameters is important so as to minimize the number of false comparisons made. As is shown in Figure 1, for the best parameter values we found, most of the comparisons made were between true positives.

5. CONCLUSIONS

We investigated the application of two state of the art duplicate detection methods to academic documents and identified parameters that could successfully be applied to achieve high precision and recall. We also analyzed the types of duplicates retrieved and, since the papers in the CiteSeer^X collection are collected through automatic crawling, this provides some evidence of the types of freely available academic documents on the Web. One question that arises is what should be done with these different versions of documents once near duplicates have been detected. For instance, they could be merged into a single record or all except a single copy could be deleted. In both cases, the question arises as to which version should be considered *authoritative*? We believe automatic document disposition could be used to address this problem. The goal would be to identify and rank duplicates based on pre-defined criteria and then take action in accordance with a policy that dictates how near duplicates should be treated. We also believe that it would be useful to investigate the use of different features for the detection of duplicates, for instance, different weights could be applied to different parts of a document, such as weighting the authors and titles of papers higher than the main text.

Acknowledgments

We gratefully acknowledge partial support by the National Science Foundation under Grant No. 1143921 and useful suggestions from Madian Khabsa and Sagnik R. Choudhury.

6. REFERENCES

[1] A. Broder, S. Glassman, M. Manasse, and G. Zweig. Syntactic Clustering of the Web. *Computer Networks and ISDN Systems*, 29(8-13):1157–1166, Sept. 1997.

[2] M. Charikar. Similarity Estimation Techniques from Rounding Algorithms. In *Proceedings of the 34th Annual ACM Symposium on Theory of Computing*, pages 380–388, 2002.

[3] A. Chowdhury, O. Frieder, and D. Grossman. Collection Statistics for Fast Duplicate Document Detection. *ACM Transactions on Information Systems*, 20(2):171–191, 2002.

[4] M. Henzinger. Finding Near-Duplicate Web Pages. In *Proceedings of the 29th Annual International ACM SIGIR Conference on Research and Development in Information Retrieval*, pages 284–291, Aug. 2006.

[5] P. Lakkaraju, S. Gauch, and M. Speretta. Document Similarity Based on Concept Tree Distance. *Proceedings of the 19th ACM Conference on Hypertext and Hypermedia*, pages 127–132, 2008.

[6] G. Manku, A. Jain, and A. D. Sarma. Detecting Near-Duplicates for Web Crawling. *Proceedings of the 16th International Conference on World Wide Web*, pages 141–149, 2007.

[7] L. Padmasree, V. Ambati, J. Chandulal, and M. Rao. Signature Based Duplication Detection in Digital Libraries. *Signature*, 2006.

[8] I. Z. Yalniz, E. F. Can, and R. Manmatha. Partial Duplicate Detection for Large Book Collections. *Proceedings of the 20th ACM International Conference on Information and Knowledge Management*, pages 469–474, 2011.

Augmenting Digital Documents with Negotiation Capability

Jerzy Kaczorek
Dept. of Intelligent Interactive Systems
Faculty of ETI
Gdansk University of Technology, Poland
jkaczorek@gmail.com

Bogdan Wiszniewski
Dept. of Intelligent Interactive Systems
Faculty of ETI
Gdansk University of Technology, Poland
bowisz@eti.pg.gda.pl

ABSTRACT

Active digital documents are not only capable of performing various operations using their internal functionality and external services, accessible in the environment in which they operate, but can also migrate on their own over a network of mobile devices that provide dynamically changing execution contexts. They may imply conflicts between preferences of the active document and the device the former wishes to execute on. In the paper we propose a solution for solving such conflicts with automatic negotiations, allowing documents and devices to find contracts satisfying both sides. It is based on a simple bargaining model reinforced with machine learning mechanisms to classify string sequences representing negotiation histories.

Categories and Subject Descriptors

I.7.1 [**Document and Text Processing**]: Document and Text Editing—*Document management*; I.2.11 [**Artificial Intelligence**]: Distributed Artificial Intelligence—*intelligent agents*; H.5.3 [**Group and Organization Interfaces**]: collaborative computing—*computer-supported cooperative work*

Keywords

Active document, automatic bargaining, mobile computing

1. INTRODUCTION

Mobile Interactive Document (MIND) architecture developed in the MENAID project [4] enables proactive digital documents to travel through an open network of geographically separated locations, carry any useful content conforming to the MIME standard, and provide services enabling interaction with collaborators, their respective local devices and third-party external services [1]. Owing to the notion of policies incorporated in their logical structure, MIND documents are *mobile* and *intelligent*. The former involves a document workflow combining *activities* and *transitions*, while

DocEng'13, September 10–13, 2013, Florence, Italy.
Copyright 2013 ACM 978-1-4503-1789-4/13/09
http://dx.doi.org/10.1145/2494266.2494305 ...$15.00.

the latter implies ability to resolve conflicts between preferences of the active document and the characteristics of the device where it is executed. Activities are performed by collaborators interacting with document-agents carrying content to their personal devices, and involve such operations as text editing, merging, splitting, copying, form filling, and so on. Transitions from one collaborator to another are performed automatically by documents between their respective locations. While locations of collaborators are specified firmly with their email addresses, devices they use when performing activities, may change significantly – from a powerful workstation with a trusted company network connection, to a laptop accessing a public (open) WiFi network in a hotel room, to a smartphone or cellphone on a plane in flight, thus without any network access at all.

Clearly, an active document must be able to adjust to such dynamic execution contexts, often in a non-cooperative setting, as the execution devices (or rather their owners) may impose their own policies governing the way document workflow activities may be executed. Conflicts arising between active documents and execution devices must be resolved in a way that satisfies both parties, for otherwise a workflow process could not be completed. Therefore we propose to introduce negotiation as a general technique for adapting active documents to varying client system requirements. By "adapting" we mean reaching agreement on a certain set of attributes of a service the document receives from the device. Negotiation is necessary to cope with an unlimited number of attributes and their combinations, which may occur in various proactive document systems – depending on their particular semantics, classes of problems solved and types of execution devices used. Further in the paper we introduce the use of this technique for the MIND architecture as an example, using a set of service attributes used in our current implementation of the system.

2. NEGOTIATION PROCESS

We model offers with trees, which are based on the logical structure of *Collaboration Protocol Profile* (CPP) documents used by ebXML to declare preferences of collaborating partners [5]. Each path in such a tree constitutes an offer consisting of five items, representing attributes of possible execution contexts of each activity: who shall be its actual *performer*, and what are the current network *availability*, its *performance* characteristics, the current execution device *security* and its possible *reliability* levels.

Values of each component item are of two types: one is a *public* content of each possible offer, and another is *private* preference, used by each respective partner to rank offers. Therefore trees of each partner are internally sorted from the most to the least valued offer. Figures 1 and 2 indicate conflicting preferences of the execution device: a laptop owner preferring not to be using a company network, and an active document willing to do everything on its own, most preferably from inside a company network.

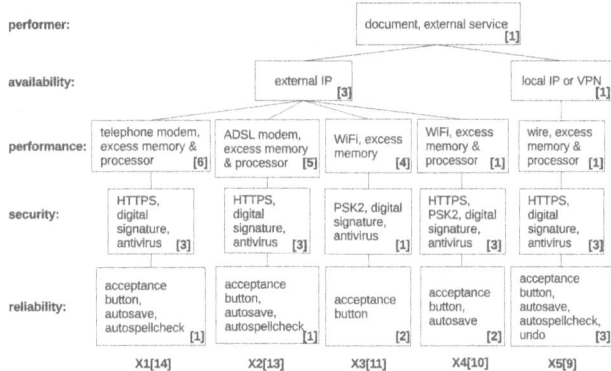

Figure 1: Preferences of an execution device

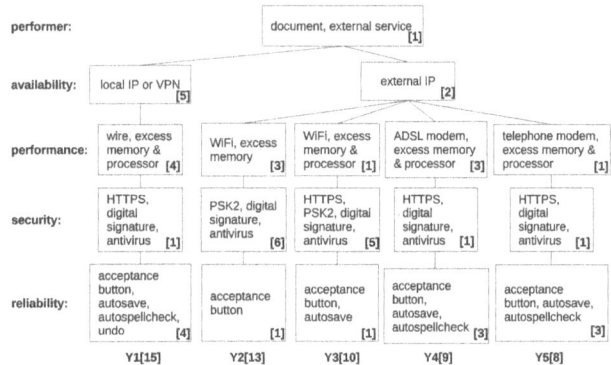

Figure 2: Preferences of a proactive document

2.1 Bargaining model

Negotiation of values of a multi-item contract, as specified by trees above, is a non-zero game, where each side can win some wealth. The question is how to organize the entire process, so that each party may get as much as it can in the current execution context. We have proposed for that a simple bargaining (economic) model [2] with a utility function valuating offers as a sum of element preferences along each respective CPP tree path. Offers are chosen by each partner from its tree, starting from the leftmost (most valuable) one. Bids are exchanged until one negotiating party repeats any offer presented by its opponent before.

Bids with trees in Figures 1 and 2 would be the following:
$1 : Y_1[15] \Rightarrow X_5[9]$, $2 : X_1[14] \Rightarrow Y_5[8]$, $3 : Y_2[13] \Rightarrow X_3[11]$, $4 : X_2[13] \Rightarrow Y_4[9]$, $5 : Y_3[10] \Rightarrow X_4[10]$, $6 : X_3[11] \Rightarrow Y_2[13]$, where labels X and Y denote respectively the negotiating parties, an execution device and the document, indexes of the initiating party 1, 2, 3 denote consecutive rounds (offer, counteroffer), brackets provide values of exchanged bids for each side, and $\Rightarrow$ points alternative valuation of the offer by the receiving opponent. Initial bid Y_1 was made by the document, while X_3 made by the execution device is the fi-

nal one, since it repeats Y_2 offered before by the document. A contract is specified in Figure 3 with a tree similar to a logical structure of the *Collaboration Protocol Agreement* document used by ebXML [5].

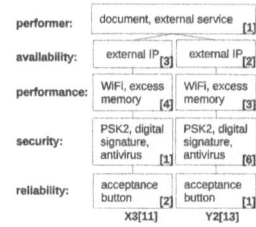

Figure 3: Negotiated collaboration agreement

CPP trees considered in the above example are relatively simple. In a more realistic scenario, however, execution contexts of active documents may be much more diversified – given the variety of personal devices used by collaborators, their preferences, as well as the abundance of workflow cases and classes of active documents that may be designed to resolve them. To avoid combinatorial explosion leading to the excessive number of rounds during the negotiation process more rigid classification of active documents and their execution contexts is necessary.

2.2 Negotiation policies

We started our analysis from the observation that not all offers that can be described with CPP trees make sense (or are worth considering) in each particular execution context. This has lead us to the concept of negotiation policies. The idea is that upon arrival an active document is aware of what kind of device it will be provided with, so what offers will not be considered for sure, and what is their commonly agreed *partial ordering*. Collaborators reserve the right, however, to keep detailed ordering of their CPP trees private, as they wish to satisfy the incoming document at the lowest possible cost. In consequence, bargaining can be performed in a *semi-cooperative* setting, where parties are free to make offers, but some *a priori* agreements concerning the execution circumstances apply. These "circumstances" are described with respective sets of rules for designing CPP trees for each party, which constitute in fact specific negotiation policies.

Before going to a detailed example consider a coding scheme of offer components defined in Table 1. All five previously mentioned execution aspects are classified and coded with symbols, used later in expressions defining the respective policy rules. For example, D denotes a class of active documents that can perform a given activity automatically, e.g., fetch data from an indicated user's repository, as opposed to a document of class W, which requires a user (worker) to do the job, e.g. read and approve its content. The reliability aspect (in the lowest row of Table 1) has just four simple classes, shown already in Figures 1 and 2, i.e. class H includes all such features as acceptance and undo buttons, autosave and auto spell-check, while the remaining symbols L, B and F represent subsets including only some of them.

2.2.1 Execution device context

Execution devices may be one of the following: workstations (WS), laptops (LT), tablets (TB), smartphones (SM), and cellphones (CP). Their technical features vary, what may significantly affect the way a given activity is per-

Table 1: Negotiated items

execution aspect	offer components
performer	document (D), worker (W), both (J)
availability	separated (S), connected from outside (E) or inside (I) organization
performance	network unknown (U), WiFi (R), phone (M) or ADSL (A) modem, wire (N)
security	public (P) or private (K) network, HTTPS (T), secure connection (C)
reliability	low (L), back-up (B), no fail (F), high (H)

formed. For example, workstations and laptops do not differ very much in their computational power, but the latter are mobile, thus more often using alternative network connections, like WiFi, ADSL or telephone modems. Tablets or smartphones in turn do not have regular keyboards, what may limit interaction between active documents and their users, while cellphones add to a limited keyboard also a low speed and costly network connection. Each device of the classes listed above may perform the activity when connected to the network or disconnected. This also determines what an active document could and could not do while on the execution device. Based on that we distinguish ten execution contexts:

$$\{WS, LT, TB, SM, CP\} \times \{connected, disconnected\} \quad (1)$$

In Table 2 we specify rules for building context specific sets of offers as CPP trees for two example execution contexts, a laptop connected to any network, and a smartphone out of reach of any network. The CPP tree root is denoted by ϵ, possible connections between tree levels with $\rightarrow$, and elements at respective levels with symbols from Table 1. Moreover, elements in curly brackets $\{\}$ may be specified in a tree in any order.

Table 2: Example device policy rules

LT connected	SM disconnected
$\epsilon \rightarrow D$	$\epsilon \rightarrow D$
$D \rightarrow \{E, I\},$	$D \rightarrow S$
$E \rightarrow \{R, M, A, N\}, I \rightarrow \{R, N\}$	$S \rightarrow U$
$\{M, A, N\} \rightarrow \{P, T\}, R \rightarrow \{P, K, T, C\}$	$U \rightarrow P$
$\{P, K, T, C\} \rightarrow \{L, B, F, H\}$	$P \rightarrow \{L, B, F, H\}$

2.2.2 Document classes

MIND documents split in three classes, depending on what kind of functionality they bring to the execution device and what level of autonomy a document may get from the current activity performer. Passive (PS) documents make their content accessible for processing with user tools, installed locally on the execution device. Reactive (RA) documents are more autonomous in keeping under control what users can do with their content, but expect users to initiate certain actions. Finally, proactive (PA) documents initiate all necessary actions, call local or external services and take over the interaction with the user. Depending on the actual security policy they may consider their content *protected* or *open*, and the strain imposed on the execution device when executing the activity as *heavy* or *light*. We get 12 classes of documents, each with its own set of policy rules:

$$\{PS, RA, PA\} \times \{protected, open\} \times \{heavy, light\} \quad (2)$$

Table 3 specifies rules for building CPP trees for proactive documents with a protected content and light stress on the execution device in two alternative execution modes: with and without network access.

Table 3: Example document policy rules

network required	network not required
$\epsilon \rightarrow D$	$\epsilon \rightarrow D$
$D \rightarrow \{E, I\},$	$D \rightarrow S$
$E \rightarrow \{R, M, A, N\}, I \rightarrow \{R, N\}$	$S \rightarrow U$
$\{M, A, N\} \rightarrow T, R \rightarrow \{K, C\}$	$U \rightarrow P$
$\{K, T, C\} \rightarrow \{B, H\}$	$P \rightarrow \{B, H\}$

2.3 Reproducibility of contracts

The notion of a semi-cooperative setting based on negotiation policies leads to the significant reduction of the size of CPP trees needed by active documents to bargain over contracts with execution devices. However, it does not provide any mechanism that may help active documents to pass one another any knowledge on what contracts could be won with specific devices in various contexts. A naive approach would be when each document stores its negotiation histories with each encountered device and shares it with other companion documents. With that, reproducibility of contracts could be provided, i.e., instead of negotiating contracts all over again a document could repeat the one known from its past encounters, or encounters of its companions. The problem is, however, that the negotiation histories might be to large to be stored in a mobile document agent memory. We propose to solve this problem by introducing a machine, or rather document, learning approach, used in sequence classification [6].

3. DOCUMENT LEARNING APPROACH

The example contract specified with the tree in Figure 3 has been negotiated by an active document and its execution device in three rounds. Obviously, trees specified in Figures 1 and 2 would have much more paths if execution aspects listed in Table 1 were specified in more detail. This is the case of our prototype implementation of MIND documents, where some CPP trees may reach the size of 80000 or more paths, leading to excessively long negotiation histories. The question to be asked here is whether it is possible to represent negotiation histories as sequences of symbols and train active documents to classify n-symbol sequences by recognizing k-grams, short sequences of up to k consecutive symbols ($k << n$). If trained, a document may be able to guess a contract during the next encounter with the execution device, as well as pass this ability to other documents, in case they may encounter this device context in the future. Because of a semi-cooperative setting – in this case a commonly agreed assumption that offers in CPPs are always sorted in the decreasing order, documents may be trained with sequences containing offers communicated only by the devices.

3.1 Coding of offers

A more detailed analysis of execution contexts indicated by Formula 1 yields a certain number of subclasses of each negotiated item listed before in Table 1. Subclasses of negotiated items are identified with unique labels, used in *context dictionaries* to specify what subclasses may appear at each level of a CPP tree in each particular execution context. For example, context dictionary of a laptop described in Table 2 is shown in Table 4; it details a CPP tree in Figure 1. For example, D_1, D_2 and D_3 denote subclasses of contexts enabling documents to perform their activities solely with the embedded functionality, or with local tools provided by the device, or with services external to both, E_5, E_6 and E_7 denote various types of resources available to documents, and so on. Detailed description of each subclass is beyond the scope of this short paper – we list them just to indicate the size of the space of possible negotiation histories.

Table 4: An example context dictionary

item	item subclass
performer	$D1$, $D2$, $D3$
availability	$E5$, $E6$, $E7$, $I5$, $I6$, $I7$
performance	$A4$, $M4$, $N4$, $R1$, $R2$, $R3$, $R4$
security	$C4$, $K2$, $K3$, $K4$, $T2$, $T3$, $T4$
reliability	$H3$, $H4$, $F1$, $F2$, $F3$, $F4$

3.2 Training sets

Negotiation histories $h_m = \sigma_{m_1}\sigma_{m_2}...\sigma_{m_n}$, $m = 1, 2, .., Q$ are sequences of length $|h_m|$, with offers from set $HS = \{\sigma_1, \sigma_2, ..., \sigma_q\}$. Each offer in HS uses symbols from the related context dictionary, q is the maximum number of offers in one CPP tree, and Q is the number of all paths in all CPP trees, possible in a given context. Special coding function $PREC : HS \times HS \to \{0, 1\}$, such that $PREC(\sigma_i, \sigma_j) = \{0 : i > j, 1 : i < j\}$, defines conversion of a set of negotiation histories into a training set:

$$LE = (map\ PREC) \circ (filter\ i \neq j) \qquad (3)$$

Negotiation history h for the contract in Figure 3 consists of $|h| = 3$ offers: $\sigma_1 = D_3 E_7 M_4 T_4 H_4$, $\sigma_2 = D_3 E_7 A_4 T_4 H_4$, $\sigma_3 = D_3 E_7 R_2 K_4 F_1$. Note that the upper bound for the maximum size of a single CPP tree with symbols from a given context dictionary is a product of the numbers of symbols provided for each item, i.e. $||HS|| \leq 5292$, while the upper bound for the number of possible negotiation histories is a product of their respective permutations, i.e. $m \leq 79 \cdot 10^{12}$. In order to convert a set of negotiation histories into a training set each h_m is coded as sequence $seq(h_m)$ of unique natural numbers. For h considered before we get $seq(h) = 3, 2, 1$, and generate $<(4,3,1),(4,2,1),(3,2,1),(3,4,0),(2,4,0),(2,3,0)>$ with LE. Such vectors of pairs of offers derived from negotiation histories is put to a neural network along with the negotiated contracts to train it. Note that the training set describes relative orderings of each possible pair of offers in recorded histories, rather then define ordering of entire sequences. A trained network can later guess contracts based on the initial k offers returned by the execution device.

3.3 Testing

Document learning based on the presented model of negotiation histories has been implemented with a neural network simulated in MATLAB. It has ten neurons in one hidden layer and two neurons in the output layer. Our initial test results are promising – after training the network with a vector derived with LE from a set of $Q = 12$ k-grams (with $k = 4$) of sequences related to the context specified in Table 4, it was able to precisely guess over 50% of contracts, and further 40% close to the optimal ones.

It was possible to improve the above results by retraining the network, but a better solution was increasing the number of histories to have more pairs of offers in the training set.

4. CONCLUSIONS

A question may be asked what happens when an undertrained active document makes an imprecise guess of the contract during its encounter with an execution device. For the bargaining model used in our approach it does not pose any problem, as an imprecisely guessed contract may just delay reaching an agreement – it will be rejected by the execution device and negotiations continued for a few more rounds. To speed that up and make parties more willing to compromise a discount factor $\delta \in (0, 1)$ may be used to diminish valuation of the next round offer compared to the presently considered one [2].

When adapting proactive documents to their execution contexts a technique based on the media queries may be considered [3], as an alternative to negotiation and machine learning proposed here. However, the problem with media queries is that their sets of *media types* and *media features* have to be defined beforehand, as a commonly agreed standard to all documents and devices. In real life, proactive documents may not know the type of a device they would execute on, so queries might not resolve to true. Negotiation can cope with that, as only the set of service attributes in a negotiated contract has to be agreed beforehand, regardless of the actual classes of available devices. Classes of these devices may be implicitly learned by documents with each successfully negotiated contract.

Our plans for future work include experiments to determine the optimal size of training sets and k-grams for contract prediction – using neural networks and the naive Bayes classifier first, and next adopting reinforcement learning mechanisms to enable active documents to discover new execution contexts in a truly open environment.

5. ACKNOWLEDGMENTS

This work was supported by the National Science Center grant no. DEC1-2011/01/B/ST6/06500.

6. REFERENCES

[1] M. Godlewska and B. Wiszniewski. Distributed MIND - a new processing model based on mobile interactive documents. In *Proc. PPAM 2009*, volume 6068 of *LNCS*, pages 244–249. Springer, 2010.

[2] J. Kaczorek and B. Wiszniewski. A simple model for automated negotiations over collaboration agreements in ebXML. In *Proc. 13th Conf. on Commerce and Enterprise Computing (CEC)*, pages 167–172. IEEE, 2011.

[3] Media Queries. W3C Recommendation. http://www.w3.org/TR/2012/REC-css3-mediaqueries-20120619/, June 2012.

[4] MeNaID project home page. Methods and tools of next generation document engineering. http://www.menaid.org.pl.

[5] OASIS. *Collaboration Protocol Profile and Agreement Specification Version 2.0*, September 2002.

[6] Z. Xing, J. Pei, and E. J. Keogh. A brief survey on sequence classification. *SIGKDD Explorations*, 12(1):40–48, 2010.

A Framework for Usage-based Document Reengineering

Madjid Sadallah
DTISI - CERIST
Alger, Algérie
msadallah@cerist.dz

Benoît Encelle
Université de Lyon
CNRS Université Lyon 1
LIRIS, UMR5205,
F-69622, France
bencelle@liris.cnrs.fr

Azze-Eddine Maredj
DTISI - CERIST
Alger, Algérie
amaredj@cerist.dz

Yannick Prié
Université de Nantes
LINA - UMR 6241
CNRS, France
yannick.prie@univ-nantes.fr

ABSTRACT

This ongoing work investigates usage-based document reengineering as a means to support authors in modifying their documents. Document usages (i.e. usage feedbacks) cover readers' explicit annotations and their reading traces. We first describe a conceptual framework with various levels of assistance for document reengineering: indications on reading, problem detection, reconception suggestions and automatic reconception propositions, taking our example in e-learning document management. We then present a technical framework for usage-based document reengineering and its associated models for documents, annotations and traces representation.

Categories and Subject Descriptors

H.5.2 [**Information Interfaces and Presentation**]: User Interfaces; I.7.4 [**Document and Text Processing**]: Electronic Publishing

Keywords

Digital reading, Reading usages, Annotations, Traces, Document reengineering, Document reconception

1. INTRODUCTION

A paramount concern of document authors, be these documents paper or digital, is to best convey knowledge by sustaining document reading, understanding and appropriation. However, designing documents that are received the way the author wishes has always been difficult, partly because of the intrinsic difficulty of structuring ideas and writing, partly because the readership and its reactions are not known at the time of writing. The digital world increases this difficulty by multiplying the possibilities related to mixed medias and interactivity, hence increasing the complexity of documents with the use of multimedia content, more and more interactivity, etc. While such documents promote innovative uses, their usages are neither

DocEng'13, September 10–13, 2013, Florence, Italy.
Copyright 2013 ACM 978-1-4503-1789-4/13/09 ...$15.00.
http://dx.doi.org/10.1145/2494266.2494309.

totally known nor easily predictable. Digital documents are also easily editable/alterable and can be updated on a regular basis, be it for their conception (e.g. a scientific article) or their reconception (e.g. a course that evolves). Moreover, appropriate authoring/reading tools can allow the establishment of a persistent, two-ways communication concerning documents between authors and readers. As a result, it becomes possible for authors to consider reader usages and feedbacks as a *knowledge source* when reconceiving their documents in order to enhance their appropriation for instance.

This article presents our ongoing work to explore some issues related to usage-based document reengineering. Being the content creators, authors are in best position to update their documents by considering readers' document usage traces (records of their interactions on the reading tool, representing the history of their actions and readers' annotations). We claim that authors should be provided with assistance during this reconception task; hence, we propose a conceptual framework to give them various levels of assistance: indications on reading, problem detection, reconception suggestions and automatic reconception propositions. This serves us then to elaborate a more technical framework that included models for documents, annotations and traces representation.

The remainder of this paper starts by a short review of relevant background. Section 3 introduces some key concepts and briefly describes our general conceptual framework. Section 4 outlines the technical framework proposal. We finally conclude and highlight some future work.

2. RELATED WORK

Based upon *Adaptive systems* like AH (Adaptive Hypermedia) [2], many tools tailor contents to individual users [11]. Some of these tools have been implemented to monitor users' activities and to analyze their interactions and annotations. For instance, comments (i.e. explicit document annotations) left by readers on Web documents can be analyzed and used to help summarizing these documents [6]. Other tools use trace-based analysis. For instance, many *Technology-Enhanced Learning* systems use traces for tracking learners' activity in order to personalize the learning experience and environment [4, 10, 7, 5]. Another kind of trace-based tools concerns digital reading systems supported by content providers like *Google Books*[1] and *Amazon Kindle*[2]. These tools have the ability to collect and

[1] http://books.google.com/
[2] https://kindle.amazon.com/

retain very detailed information about readers, their usages and their habits.

To reduce the amount of data resulted from interaction tracing, storage and processing, and in order to enable aggregating this data into more human and machine meaningful units, many authors use semantic modeling of activity traces. The theory of *Modeled Trace* (noted *M-Trace*) permits to establish such a modeling [10]. According to this theory, a trace is a set of timestamped observed elements (i.e. *obsels*) representing the interaction between the user and the system. A trace model defines constraints on contained obsels (i.e their structures, types and possible interrelations). A modeled trace (M-Trace) is a trace together with its trace model. A *Trace-Based Management System* (*TBMS*) is used to store and manage M-Traces. Within a TBMS, two types of M-Traces can exist: *primary traces* (i.e. *initial traces*) and *transformed traces* (i.e. *higher level traces*). A *primary trace* is collected from external sources and stored as an M-Trace while M-Traces created after performing transformation operations on existing traces are called *transformed traces*.

3. USAGE-BASED DOCUMENT REENGI- NEERING

3.1 Document reengineering

Document engineering is concerned with principles, tools and processes that improve our ability to create, manage, and maintain documents in any forms an in all media. Modern digital documents are nowadays no longer single-version with static content, they are *"live"*: multimedia, multi-user, dynamic and thus multi-version [1]. Consequently, these documents are never in a final state of absolute stability: *reengineering* can be applied on them. According to [3], *"reengineering, also known as both renovation and reclamation, is the examination and alteration of a subject system to reconstitute it in a new form and the subsequent implementation of the new form"*. Regarding documents and from our point of view, the main goal of what we call "document reengineering" is to improve document structures and document content in order to facilitate their appropriations by readers. These documents are usually described along different structures which drive different possible representations. Being multimedia, these documents combine objects of different nature like text, sound, image and video; hence, they are usually modeled following four dimensions not totally independent [9]: 1/ logical (document organization into for instance chapters, shots, etc.), 2/ spatial (graphic layout), 3/ temporal (temporal ordering of the multimedia objects) and 4/ hypermedia or links (relations between documents and document fragments).

3.2 Using usages for reengineering documents

In the digital publishing and reading context, we define *usage-based document reconception* as a kind of reengineering that alters document content and structures in response to readers' explicit feedback (i.e. annotations), or implicit ones (i.e. reading traces). In this paper, we define a trace as *a temporal sequence of observed elements recorded from interactions between a reader and a document, through a reading tool*. Considering usage feedbacks for reengineering purposes assumes that the reading tool has firstly the ability

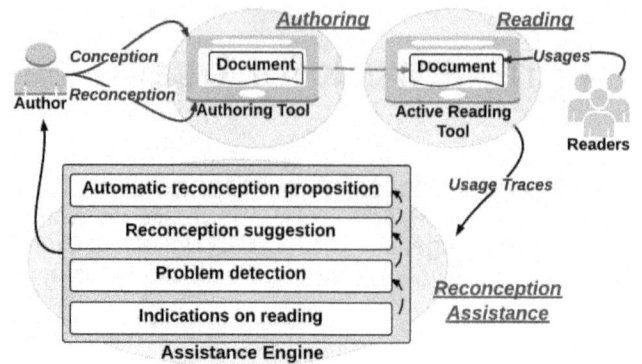

Figure 1: Overview of the reconception model

to monitor readers, intercepting and eventually interpreting their interactions. The relevance of such feedbacks in regards to document reengineering will greatly depend with readers' involvement in content appropriation. Active reading can foster readers' involvement, as stated in [8]: document *active reading* provides a chance to best engage readers towards contents and enhance appropriation and understanding. Hence, the reading tool has secondly to provide active reading functionalities in order to improve the potential usefulness of such usage feedbacks.

3.3 Conceptual model for usage-based document reengineering

While our approach can be applied to any document, we instantiate it within the technical context of the Learning Content Management System **Claire**[3]. Claire aims to offer a simple, yet robust tool for authoring, improving and disseminating educational content. Our usage-based document reengineering proposal is based on the general model of figure 1. Instrumenting an active reading tool, data about usages (i.e. reader interactions: reading trace and annotations) is analyzed by an *assistance engine* which may then assess possible and appropriate document reconceptions. We identify four main levels of author assistance, each level exploiting data from the previous one. All of these levels are illustrated in the following using Claire use cases, where an author presents his course to a group of students and performs course assisted-reconception.

- *Level 0:* **Indications on reading.** The assistance engine can compute and present the author with indications on how the document has been read. *Example:* giving the author the percent of readers that have followed a given link may help him to understand the relevance of that link.

- *Level 1:* **Problem detection.** Based on the previous level, the assistance engine may detect problems in the reading process but not give any suggestion on how to fix them. *Example:* if a video component has never been watched longer than its first seconds, the engine reports to the author this fact as an unexpected behavior.

---

[3] *Community Learning through Adaptive and Interactive multichannel Resources for Education.*
`http://www.projet-claire.fr/`

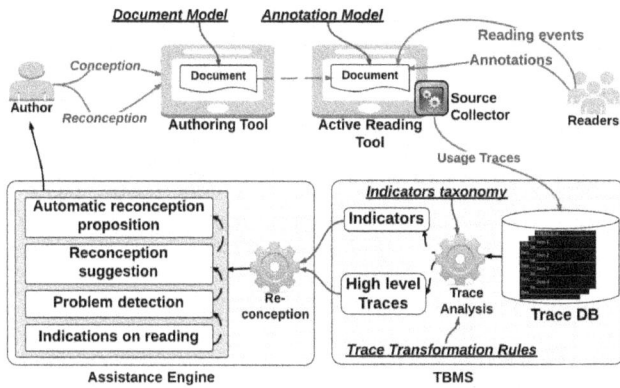

Figure 2: Overview of the technical framework

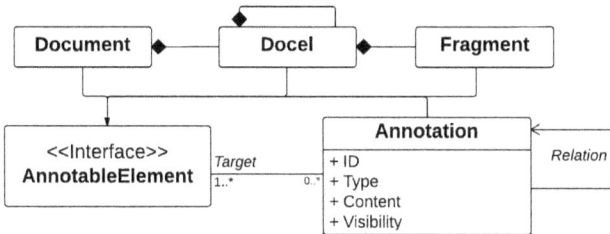

Figure 3: Document and annotation generic model

- *Level 2:* **Reconception suggestion.** At this level, not only the system detects problems but in addition, it may supply suggestion. However, the system is unable by itself to achieve these suggestions. *Example:* if many readers of a course document usually go back to a previous chapter, the engine may suggest ways of getting rid off them, for instance to include a recall of the main concepts already seen in a previous lesson unit.

- *Level 3:* **Automatic reconception proposition.** At this level, the engine may detect problems and resolve them automatically. Consequently, a reconception can be presented to the author for review and validation. *Example:* if many zooms are performed on a part of the document, the system can automatically readjust and increase its size or fonts for a text.

4. TECHNICAL FRAMEWORK

Based on the general usage-based document reengineering conceptual model, an illustration of our framework proposal is presented on figure 2. Once a new document is conceived by an author, it is published. The active reading of the document produces a set of obsels (*primary traces*) collected by a *Source Collector* installed on the reading tool. This data is then sent into the *Trace-Based Management System TBMS* to be stored and processed. Once indicators and high level traces are computed, these can be used by the assistance engine to perform reconception and to ensure different levels of assistance. As shown on the figure, a set of data models are introduced to describe many related features. In the following, we introduce some of these for documents, annotations and traces description.

4.1 Documents

Document reconception may target and affect both document content and its structures (spatial adjustment, temporal synchronization, etc.). This motivates document modeling in order to well describe the document features and structures that may be directly or indirectly involved in an interaction or a reconception. Figure 3 introduces a generic logical model to describe digital documents. A *document* is considered as the nesting and composition, at different levels of granularity, of *docels* (document elements) which are the building blocks to represent formal elements and composition units. Each element is associated with a list of attributes that describe its composition, placement, synchronization and behavior. A *fragment* is a logical part of a document element. It can be defined using spatio-temporal coordinates.

We have instantiated this generic model for representing *Claire* data structures. Three levels were defined. The lower one is called *assets*, typically describing a title, paragraph, graphics, etc. A *granule* is composed of a set of assets and generally represents a course chapter. A pedagogical *module* — a *document*— is a coherent assembly of granules that typically forms a course.

4.2 Annotations

We define a document annotation as any information provided by a user that is associated with a whole document or a part of it. Since explicit annotation structuring and typifying allows automatic processing and analysis, we propose a generic model contained within figure 3. An annotation target can be one or more document elements and/or fragments and/or annotations, all of these referred as "annotable element". Each annotation has one and only one type. The available annotation types depend on the nature of the "annotable element". Among the types we have defined within the Claire project are: *Question*, *Form error* (formal mistake like spelling, grammar, etc.), *Content error* (mistake in the content, for instance in a source code), *Comment*, *I understood* (to point out that an item has been useful for understanding), *I did not understand* (to report a lack of understanding), *Lecture notes* (personal notes) and *Other* (a custom annotation). We also have *Highlighting* to emphasize some document parts (such annotations do not have content) and *Linked annotation* to associate an annotation to another one (to annotate an annotation). Another aspect of annotations is their visibility to control their availability to different types of users. In Claire project, an annotation can be *private* (only available to the author of the annotation), *to author/reviewer* (only available to the annotator and to the author and reviewers), *group* (only available to a specific group of users) or *public*.

4.3 Initial traces

We consider traces as *modeled Traces* [10], their model is presented on figure 4. Each observed element (*obsel*) is associated to a user and connects a specific action with a document element *docel*. We have identified some generic actions (*obsel types*) that are commonly used by digital readers and divided them into four main classes:

- **Navigation**. This class covers common navigation actions like *following links*, *visiting specific URLS*, *scrolling* (spatially and/or shifting in time) and moving *back* and *forward* in navigation history.

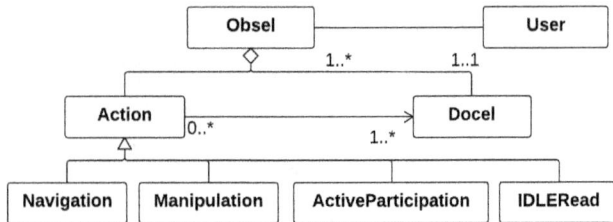

Figure 4: Trace model

- **Manipulation.** This class refers to readers manipulation actions on the document content (e.g. *select*, *find*, *print*, *zoom*, *copy* and *bookmark*) and context (e.g. activating system interface to *open/close/download* the document). Particular media related actions cover the very common ones (*play/pause/stop*, *seek*, etc.).

- **Active participation.** User explicit participation is mainly expressed in terms of annotation actions. These actions include: *adding/altering/deleting* one's annotations, *annotating/opening/closing* an annotation, *highlighting*, etc.

- **Idle Read.** This class describes a reading that mostly appears passive (without significant interaction). It can also characterize the user inactivity (or absence).

4.4 High-level traces and indicators

The assistance engine is responsible of traces analysis and interpretation. Two kinds of results can be produced: a/ **high level traces** generation: a *transformation process* performs transformations on the primary trace to interpret and abstract it. Such transformations include filtering, rewriting and aggregating obsels; b/ various *reading indicators* computation: these are variables computed to characterize readers' interaction against a specific monitored feature or event (e.g.: unread sections, visited/unvisited links, interaction level, spent time on specific parts). To this end, a meaningful taxonomy of these indicators has first to be established. Using these two kinds of analysis results, authors can be assisted during the reengineering tasks following the four levels already presented in the conceptual framework. The author can choose to consider an arbitrary set of feedbacks originated from a single reader, a given group of readers or the entire readership. The end result is a new version of the document which can in turn be subject to further revisions.

5. CONCLUSION AND FUTURE WORK

The ongoing work presented in this paper focuses on some issues related to usage-based document reengineering. Ideas presented are twofold: how to reconceive documents by exploiting readers' feedbacks and how to assist authors to achieve such reconceptions. As a result, a conceptual framework for document reengineering is presented that uses readers' usage feedbacks (reading traces and annotations) and offers authors various levels of assistance. A technical framework and associated data models are then developed according to this conceptual framework.

Future work will focus on the conception of suitable means and tools to assess reconceptions, using the primary traces and going through the suitable trace transformations and indicators computation. Proper reconception being tightly related to the technical context, we rely on Claire project to conduct interviews with some course authors in order to identify the actual reconception needs and therefore to precise/specialize the different associated models. This will serve us then to elaborate a meaningful set of transformations and indicators for enhancing documents that are provided to learners. The ongoing implementation of the technical framework and its future integration within Claire will be our first proof of concept. Thereafter, we can consider expanding our proposals to other application areas.

6. REFERENCES

[1] H. Balinsky and S. J. Simske. Secure document engineering. In *Proceedings of the 11th ACM symposium on Document engineering*, pages 269–272. ACM, 2011.

[2] P. Brusilovsky. Adaptive hypermedia. *User modeling and user-adapted interaction*, 11(1-2):87–110, 2001.

[3] E. J. Chikofsky, J. H. Cross, et al. Reverse engineering and design recovery: A taxonomy. *Software, IEEE*, 7(1):13–17, 1990.

[4] C. Choquet and A. Corbière. Reengineering framework for systems in education. *Journal Of Educational Technology and Society*, 9(4):228, 2006.

[5] S. D'mello and A. Graesser. Autotutor and affective autotutor: Learning by talking with cognitively and emotionally intelligent computers that talk back. *ACM Transactions on Interactive Intelligent Systems*, 2(4):23:1–23:39, 2012.

[6] M. Hu, A. Sun, and E.-P. Lim. Comments-oriented document summarization: understanding documents with readers' feedback. In *Proceedings of the 31st annual international ACM SIGIR conference on Research and development in information retrieval*, SIGIR '08, pages 291–298. ACM, 2008.

[7] J.-C. Marty, T. Carron, and P. Pernelle. Observe and react: interactive indicators for monitoring pedagogical sessions. *International Journal of Learning Technology*, 7(3):277–296, 2012.

[8] M. McLaughlin. Reading comprehension: What every teacher needs to know. *The Reading Teacher*, 65(7):432–440, 2012.

[9] C. Roisin. Authoring structured multimedia documents. In *Proceedings of the 25th Conference on Current Trends in Theory and Practice of Informatics: Theory and Practice of Informatics*, SOFSEM '98, pages 222–239, London, UK, UK, 1998. Springer-Verlag.

[10] L. S. Settouti, Y. Prié, J.-C. Marty, and A. Mille. A trace-based system for technology-enhanced learning systems personalisation. In *Proceedings of the 2009 Ninth IEEE International Conference on Advanced Learning Technologies*, ICALT'09, pages 93–97. IEEE Computer Society, 2009.

[11] D. Smits and P. De Bra. Gale: a highly extensible adaptive hypermedia engine. In *Proceedings of the 22nd ACM conference on Hypertext and hypermedia*, HT'11, pages 63–72, New York, NY, USA, 2011. ACM.

Visual Saliency and Terminology Extraction for Document Annotation

Benjamin Duthil, Mickael Coustaty,Vincent Courboulay, Jean Marc Ogier

L3i Lab - University of La Rochelle - Av Michel Crepeau

17042 La Rochelle, France

bduthil, mcoustat, vcourbou, jmogier @univ-lr.fr

ABSTRACT

The document digitization process becomes a crucial economical issue in our society. Then, it becomes necessary to be able to organize this huge amount of documents. The work proposed in this paper tends to propose a new method to automatically classify document using a saliency-based segmentation process on one hand, and a terminology extraction and annotation on the other hand. The saliency-based segmentation is used to extract salient regions and by the way logo, while the terminology approach is used to annotate them and to automatically classify the document. The approach does not require human expertise, and use *Google Images* as a knowledge database. The results obtained on a real database of 1766 documents show the relevance of the approach.

Categories and Subject Descriptors

J.0 [**Computer Applications**]: GENERAL

Keywords

Visual Saliency, Terminology Extraction, Document Annotation

1. INTRODUCTION

According to the Oxford Dictionary, a logo is a *symbol or other small design adopted by an organization to identify its products, uniform, vehicles, etc.* By the way, they correspond to an important information to retrieve, classify and analyze documents. Facing to the dramatic explosion of number of documents to process, logo spotting and recognition have evolved as a practical and reliable supplement to the OCR. Indeed, without understanding a foreign language, we can easily classify documents by using their logos. It is also possible to cluster birth-certificate or marriage contract by recognizing the logo of the city. For instance, imagine Mr Washington that got married with Ms Paris in London, it could be difficult to disambiguate these names by only

DocEng'13, September 10–13, 2013, Florence, Italy.

Copyright 2013 ACM 978-1-4503-1789-4/13/09 ...$15.00.

http://dx.doi.org/10.1145/2494266.2494299.

using an OCR approach. Then, we assume that a logo conveys enough information to understand the main purpose of the emitting company (line of business, company name, etc.). Thus, in the context of content based image retrieval (CBIR), the logo spotting techniques provides an important cues to allow document recognition. But generally, most of the techniques for document classification or retrieval have been applied to binary documents.

In this paper, we propose an original administrative documents annotation process based on the cooperation between a visual saliency approach and a terminology extraction. The paper is organized as follows: Section 1.1 presents the related works, and section 2 describes the global scheme of the proposed approach. The next section presents the experimental results while section 4 draws a conclusions and some perspectives.

1.1 Related works

Numerous approaches on logo localization and detection have been reported in the literature over the last decades. If the first trials done on binary documents [2, 9], more and more approaches tend to apply these techniques to color documents [1, 6]. One of the first approach, initiated by Pham [9] in 2003, was developed for logos detection in grayscale document images. Detection is based on the hypothesis that the spatial density of the foreground pixels within a given windowed image that contains a logo is greater than those of non-logo regions. Alajlan introduced an approach for retrieving the envelope of logo [2]. Motivated by studies in Gestalt theory, he used a hierarchical clustering and a fusion stage on a set of 110 black and white logos. Two majors drawbacks can be mentionned: the first one is the absence of color cues, and the second one is the particular family of tested logo. Only logos that can be grouped with a same particular spatial proximity, area, shape features and orientation were used, which is quite restrictive. In 2007, Zhu and Doermann [14] proposed an approach for logo detection and extraction that classifies and localizes logos using a boosting strategy across multiple image scales. In 2008, Zeggari [1] developed a logo extraction algorithm based on two properties of logos: spatial compactness and colorimetric uniformity. First, the image content is reduced and transformed using mathematical morphology operators to decrease the distance between the identical logo parts. Afterwards the logo regions of spatial and chromatic densities are detected. Rusinol and Llados proposed in [11] to use a bag of words approach to categorize document. More recently, in 2011, [6] proposed a method for logo detection in color documents. The proposed rotation and scale invariant

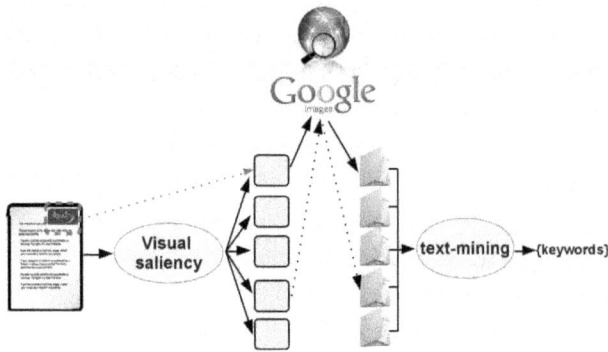

Figure 1: Global diagram

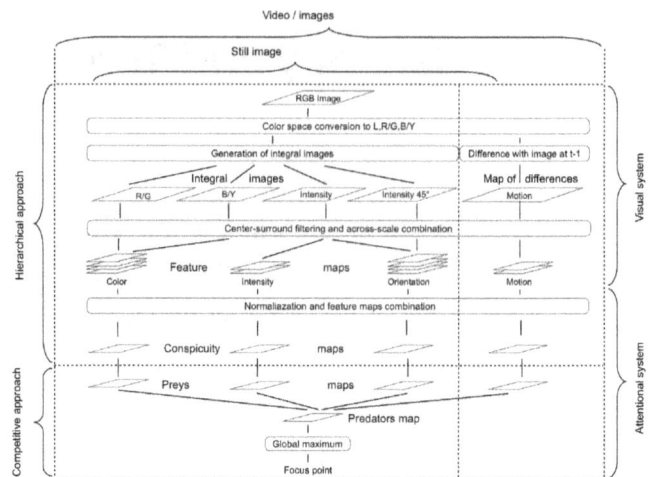

Figure 2: Architecture of the computational model of attention

method is based on the Gaussian Mixture Markov Random Field which labels the pixels in the documents as foreground or background with respect to the query logo. Then a shape descriptor is applied to the foreground regions to verify the presence of the logo. As a conclusion authors mentioned the advantage of color for detecting logos for document classification without any heuristic information. In 2012, Sahbi et al [12] design a novel variational framework able to match and recognize multiple instances of multiple reference logos in image archives. Authors considered logos as constellations of local features and matched by minimizing an energy function. Most of the mentioned methods are quite restrictive in the hypothesis they used and are time consuming, besides they only used low levels features. Our target is to propose a method that performs either on black and white but also on color document, correctly scanned or degraded image, and that performs with unknown logo. Besides all, we want to propose a method that combine image and text mining techniques, two communities rarely and hardly combined.

2. PROPOSED APPROACH

Our approach relies on a three steps process summarized in Figure 1. First, we analyze the document saliency to extract the most salient areas (called thumbnails hereafter). In this work, we assume that a logo is a salient part of a document, and it can be extracted using a saliency-based segmentation process (see section 2.1). Secondly, we learn the vocabulary (terminology) associated to each thumbnail of the document. For this, we use *Google Images API* to get some information associated to each thumbnail from web pages. Thus, some keywords and a set of documents are associated to each thumbnail. Finally, based on the documents returned, we extract the terminology associated to each thumbnail of original document using text-mining techniques. One of our main motivations is actually to reduce the semantic gap by proposing an original cooperation between low level image processing and text mining techniques.

2.1 Visual saliency approach

Recenlty, Perreira Da Silva et al. [8] proposes a new hybrid model which allows modeling the temporal evolution of the visual focus of attention and its validation. As shown in figure 2, it is based on the classical algorithm proposed by Itti in ([4]), in which the first part of its architecture relies on the extraction of three conspicuity maps based on low level characteristics computation. These three conspicuity maps are representative of the three main human perceptual

channels: color, intensity and orientation. In [7] Perreira Da Silva et al. propose to substitute the second part of Itti's model by an optimal competitive approach: a preys / predators system. They have demonstrated that it is an optimal way of extracting information. Besides, this optimal criteria, preys / predators equations are particularly well adapted for such a task. Preys / predators systems are dynamic, they include intrinsically time evolution of their activities. Thus, the visual focus of attention, seen as a predator, can evolve dynamically. Besides, without any objective (top-down information or pregnancy), choosing a method for conspicuity maps fusion is hard. A solution consists in developing a competition between conspicuity maps and waiting for a natural balance in the preys / predators system, reflecting the competition between emergence and inhibition of elements that engage or not our attention; Finally, discrete dynamic systems can have a chaotic behavior. Despite the fact that this property is not often interesting, it is an important one in this case. Actually, it allows the emergence of original paths and exploration of visual scene, even in non salient areas, reflecting something like curiosity. [8] shows that despite the non deterministic behavior of preys / predators equations, the system exhibits interesting properties of stability, reproducibility and reactiveness while allowing a fast and efficient exploration of the scene. We applied the same optimal parameters used by Perreira Da Silva to evaluate our approach. The attention model is computationally efficient and plausible [7]. It provides many tuning possibilities (adjustment of curiosity, central preferences, etc.) that can be exploited in order to adapt the behavior of the system to a particular context. In order to illustrate the results obtained with this saliency-based segmentation process, the figure 3 propose an example of administrative document treated during our process, and the most salient thumbnails proposed (surrounded in red).

Figure 3: Example of thumbnails extracted using the proposed saliency-based segmentation process

2.2 Corpus constitution

The objective of this step is to built a corpus of web documents for each thumbnail identified by our visual saliency approach. We use the *Google Images* [1] web search engine in order to link some web pages to each thumbnail extracted. If the input image is recognized, *Google Images* provides the name N of the logo (generally, the company name). This information is used during the learning phase to set up the learning words close to N. The direct identification or recognition by Google of a logo or a thumbnail is not mandatory. This can happen where either the document definition is too low, or if this image is not a logo (the logo in that case could correspond to an area with a fewer saliency), or if *Google Images* doesn't know this logo. However, *Google Images* also offers a list of links related to web pages containing similar images. From these links, we build a corpus $C = \{c_1, \ldots, c_k\}$ of web documents associated to each thumbnail. Let s_q be the different thumbnails extracted from an image. Then, each thumbnail will be associated to a corpus c_q composed of k documents (with $\{q = 1 \ldots k\}$ for an image where k equals to the number of links returned by *Google Images*).

2.3 Annotation

The objective of this step is to extract from the corpus, the terminology related to the original document (see 2.2). All the thumbnails identified in step 1 have not the same degree of importance in the document. Indeed, each thumbnail have a weight P_q that corresponds to the saliency level sensed by our saliency segmentation process (between 0 and 100%). That is why it is necessary to take this weight into account during the learning step. The final score assigned to a word is then weighted by this value.

Moreover, in order to ensure the learning of the descriptors related to the logo, we use a window [3, 10] to guarantee the semantic proximity between the name of the logo and the keywords associated. More formally, the words in the immediate neighborhood of the name N_q of the logo are first selected inside a window $\mathcal{F}$ of size sz in a document doc:

$$\mathcal{F}(N, sz, doc) = \{w \in doc/d_{noun}(N, w) \leq sz\} \quad (1)$$

with $d_{noun}(r, w)$ being the distance corresponding to the number of nouns (considered as meaningful terms [5]) separating a word w from N in the document doc [3] and sz the number of noun at right of N and the number of noun at left of N.

[1]Google Images : http://images.google.fr/

The use of a window $\mathcal{F}$ allows filtering and limiting the scope of the semantic distance between the name of the logo and the other terms in the window. To consider the name returned by *Google Images* as a "germ" [3, 10] implies that the web search engine was able to identify the logo. The thumbnails where no logo are identified by *Google Images* are ignored at this time.

The representativity $X(W, sz)$ of a word is computed using tf-idf measure [13], saliency weight and considering only the words (nouns) include in $\mathcal{F}$. For each thumbnail s_q where *Google Images* has identified a logo with his associate name N_q, representativity (tf-idf) of a each word (noun) W is weighted using the saliency weight related to the considered thumbnail. So, the more a thumbnail is prominent and characteristic for the original document, the more important the words related to this thumbnail will be. For all thumbnails, the calculated frequencies of each word W are added and a lexicon of word is created. This lexicon is sorted and allows identifying the most representative words for a logo. Some example of automatically extracted keywords from thumbnails is presented in table 1.

Logo	associated words	Logo	associated words
	ACM computing ACM Association Machinery Symposium		**Banque Postale** bank client services financing management

Table 1: Example of words automatically learned

3. EXPERIMENTAL RESULTS

In this section we evaluate the method on a corpus composed of 1766 administrative documents distributed in 4 classes of documents (marriage act (M-A), birth certificate (B-C), insurance certificate (I-C), bank account details (B-A-D)). This database was provided by one of a world-class Document Capture solution vendor. Each document contains one of the 196 logos identified in the corpus. Documents are scanned in 200 dpi black and white. We used classical indicators to evaluate classification such as *Precision* and *Recall*. *Precision* is computed by considering the error in the identification of a logo: the system identifies a logo that is not the real logo. *Recall* is computed using the number of logos correctly identified by the system. Our results are presented in table 2.

	I-C	M-A	B-C	B-A-D	All classes
Recall	95.5	22.5	60.4	**71.7**	*80.6*
Precision	100	100	100	100	*100*

Table 2: Classification results for each class of the 1766 documents: marriage act (M-A), birth certificate (B-C), insurance certificate (I-C), bank account details (B-A-D)

The results show the relevance of the approach. The differences between each class is explained by the document quality. For example, the quality of "marriage act" documents is very poor which explains the low *recall*. In addition, the number of different logos to identify is different in each class and increases the difficulty. However, the results are remarkable, we obtain an average *recall* of **80.6** and a *precision* of **100**. The *precision* (100) highlights the robustness of the approach.

4. CONCLUSION AND PERSPECTIVES

To conclude, we have presented a new automatic document annotation method based on logo recognition. It relies on a salient area segmentation process on one hand, and on a terminology extraction and annotation on the other hand. The saliency-based segmentation is used to extract the logo and some salient regions, while the terminology approach is used to annotate them and to automatically classify the document. The approach does not require human expertise. The use of *Google Images* avoids the construction of a local database. In addition, when a new logo is found, the system is able to provide a classification, which is impossible even if the local database is updated. In perspectives, we planned to extend it to natural scene images, in order to automatically annotate them and to propose a conceptual synopsis of the scene. Figure 3 illustrates an example of this, in which a picture of a desktop has been shooted with a mobile phone. Started from our works, we planned to automatically extract the most salient regions, and to automatically associate some keywords (in this example, some examples of keywords are proposed in the table near from the figure 4).

Associated keywords
Senseo
Vittel
Black-Berry

Figure 4: Example of natural scene picture, the most-salient thumbnails associated and the automatically extracted keywords

5. REFERENCES

[1] Zeggari Ahmed. Logos extraction on picture documents using shape and color density. In *IEEE International Symposium on Industrial Electronics, ISIE*, pages 2492–2496, 2008.

[2] Naif Alajlan. Retrieval of Hand-Sketched Envelopes. In *International Conference Image Analysis and Recognition, ICIAR*, pages 436–446. Springer-Verlag, 2007.

[3] Benjamin Duthil, François Trousset, Mathieu Roche, Gérard Dray, Michel Plantié, Jacky Montmain, and Pascal Poncelet. Towards an automatic characterization of criteria, DEXA '11. In *Proceedings of the 22nd International Conference on Database and Expert Systems Applications DEXA 2011*, page 457, 2011.

[4] Laurent Itti, Christof Koch, E. Niebur, and Others. A model of saliency-based visual attention for rapid scene analysis. *IEEE Transactions on pattern analysis and machine intelligence*, 20(11):1254–1259, 1998.

[5] Georges Kleiber. Noms propres et noms communs : un problÃÍme de dÃÍ'nomination. *Meta*, pages 567–589, 1996.

[6] Farshad Nourbakhsh, Dimosthenis Karatzas, Ernest Valveny, and Josep Llados. Color Logo Detection and Retrieval in Document Collections. In *Ninth IAPR International Workshop on Graphics RECognition - GREC*, 2011.

[7] Matthieu Perreira Da Silva, V Courboulay, A Prigent, and P Estraillier. Evaluation of preys / predators systems for visual attention simulation. In *VISAPP 2010 - International Conference on Computer Vision Theory and Applications*, pages 275–282, Angers, 2010. INSTICC.

[8] Matthieu Perreira Da Silva and Vincent Courboulay. Implementation and evaluation of a computational model of attention for computer vision. In *Developing and Applying Biologically-Inspired Vision Systems: Interdisciplinary Concepts*, pages 273–306. Hershey, Pennsylvania: IGI Global., August 2012.

[9] Tuan D. Pham. Unconstrained logo detection in document images. *Pattern Recognition*, 36(12):3023–3025, December 2003.

[10] Sylvie Ranwez, Benjamin Duthil, Mohameth-François Sy, Jacky Montmain, and Vincent Ranwez. *How ontology based information retrieval systems may benefit from lexical text analysis*. Springer, 2012.

[11] Marçal Rusinol and Josep Llados. Logo Spotting by a Bag-of-words Approach for Document Categorization. *2009 10th International Conference on Document Analysis and Recognition*, pages 111–115, 2009.

[12] Hichem Sahbi, Lamberto Ballan, Giuseppe Serra, and Alberto Del Bimbo. Context-dependent logo matching and recognition. *IEEE transactions on image processing : a publication of the IEEE Signal Processing Society*, 22(3):1018–31, March 2012.

[13] G. Salton and C. S. Yang. On the specification of term values in automatic indexing. *Journal of Documentation.*, 29(4):351–372, 1973.

[14] Guangyu Zhu, Stefan Jaeger, and David Doermann. A robust stamp detection framework on degraded documents. In Kazem Taghva and Xiaofan Lin, editors, *SPIE 6067, Document Recognition and Retrieval XIII*, pages 60670B–60670B–9, January 2006.

An Adaptive Thresholding Algorithm Based on Edge Detection and Morphological Operations for Document Images

Renata F.P. Neves
Universidade Federal de Pernambuco
Centro de Informática
Recife, Pernambuco, Brazil
+55-81- 2126-8430
rfpn@cin.ufpe.br

Cleber Zanchettin
Universidade Federal de Pernambuco
Centro de Informática
Recife, Pernambuco, Brazil
+55-81- 2126-8430
cz@cin.ufpe.br

Carlos A.B Mello (IEEE Member)
Universidade Federal de Pernambuco
Centro de Informática
Recife, Pernambuco, Brazil
+55-81- 2126-8430
cabm@cin.ufpe.br

ABSTRACT

This paper presents a new algorithm to threshold document images. The proposed algorithm deal with complex background images, illumination and aspect variants, back-to-front interference, variation of brightness and different positioned shadows. The algorithm have two phases. The first one uses edge detection and morphological operations to identify the text on the image. The second phase uses the positions of the text to define the threshold value in an adaptive process. Our approach presents promising results in images with complex background released from the Document Image Binarization Contest (DIBCO) when compared with other literature and competition thresholding algorithms.

Categories and Subject Descriptors

I.4.6 [**Image Processing and Computer Vision**]: Segmentation – *pixel classification*

Keywords

Thresholding, handwritten document, segmentation, binarization

1. INTRODUCTION

Originally, the binarization was a study to find the best way to archive important documents, like historical or bank documents, because memory was scarce. After this phase, as the binarization is an important step to recognize the text in the documents, the study pass to be done in specific situations, like historical documents (newspaper, letters, books), bank checks, postal code, and others. In all of these cases, the scanned images were in the best possible way and with high technical quality.

The binarization/thresholding process is the first part of OCR recognition [1]. The binarization phase identifies which pixel belongs to the foreground image (the text you wish to recognize) and which belong to the background (pixels that represent the document paper). A misclassification of these pixels can impair in subsequent stages of processing.

The main difficulty of thresholding algorithms is to find the optimal threshold value for images with a complex background. The images with complex background (e.g. historical documents) have several factors that make difficult the search for this optimal value. Problems as focus of the image; variation of brightness; document wears by time, which degrade the paper creating stains; back-to-front interference: when the text/image written on the back of the paper appears in the front; the presence of shadows; variant illuminations and other situations.

This paper proposes a new method to threshold images with complex background considering the above-mentioned problems. We compare the proposed approach in the DIBCO databases with literature and competition thresholding algorithms.

In the next section, we present some important thresholding algorithms devoted for this challenging task. Section 3 describes the proposed algorithm and the experiments and results in Section 4. To conclude, the Section 5 presents the analysis of the new approach.

2. RELATED WORKS

Sezgin and Sankur presented in [2] an extensive study of binarization algorithms that contains a brief description of 40 different algorithms. In this study, the authors subdivided the algorithms into 6 categories: (i) algorithms based on the histogram; (ii) algorithms based on the relationship between the pixels of the object and background; (iii) algorithms based on attributes of the object as the similarity between images binarized and grayscale; (iv) spatial algorithms; (v) local algorithms; and (vi) entropy-based algorithms.

The methods based on the histogram of an image (i) works analyzing peaks, valleys and curvatures of the pixels distribution to find the ideal threshold. An example is the algorithm two peaks [3]. This technique searches for two highest peaks in the histogram. The threshold value is the mean value between these peaks.

The Otsu [4] algorithm is an example of algorithms based on the relationship between the pixels of the object and background (ii). In this approach, the histogram is divided into two class (C0 and C1) representing the object and the background. The color responsible for its division is the threshold value and calculated by function minimization.

The technique proposed by Huang and Wang [5] is an example of algorithms based on attributes objects like the similarity between threshold images and grayscale images (iii). It works based on a fuzzy index. For each possible threshold value, it is calculated the fuzzy index that minimize the distance between the grayscale image and the threshold image. The threshold value is the one that has the lower index because it indicates that the images are more similar.

The spatial methods (iv) use statistic information among the pixels to define the threshold. The Katz and Brink [6] algorithm uses the correlation between pairs of colors in the gray scale. The pair ($t1$, $t2$) with the major correlation will be chosen to split the histogram into three parts. Colors below $t1$ will be turned into black; colors above $t2$ will be turned into white; while colors between $t1$ and $t2$ will have their neighbor analyzed. If one neighbor has the pixel value larger than $t2$, it will be turned into white.

The local and adaptive binarization techniques (v) may use more than one threshold based on the colors in a region to binarize an image. Niblack [7], for example, analyses the neighborhood defined by a window n x n to define the threshold based on the average color of the region added to the standard deviation multiplied by a bias.

Entropy-based algorithms (vi) calculate the threshold analyzing the entropy of the image. Pun [8] proposes an algorithm that split the entropy into two parts: object entropy and background entropy. The approach tries to find the value t that maximizes the entropy function.

However, the classical algorithms described in [2] not have good results in all kind of documents. Usually, an algorithm works well for a specific kind of document but not for others. For example, they work in images with back-to-front interference, but do not work well for a document with faded ink. Because of this, the scientific community has been holding thresholding competitions [9][10][11][12][13] for the binarization of document images with the purpose of finding algorithms with good performances on a wide variety of images.

Among the algorithms developed specifically to deal with binarization of documents and do not compared in these competitions, we can mention the algorithm proposed by Estrada and Tomasi [14] . This algorithm focuses on eliminating of the back-to-front interference using histogram hysteresis. In this technique, they assume that there is a threshold tH, indicating that all colors below this value belong only to the ink (foreground). There is also a threshold value tL to which all colors above this value belong only to the paper (background). The main idea is to recover in H (image resultant by the use of tH as threshold) the ink classified in L (image resultant by the use of tL as threshold) and that are connected with the pixels classified as ink in H.

Yang and Yan [15] presented an algorithm for binarization of documents to works with high luminance variation in the image and / or large stains or dark watermarks. The algorithm performs an analysis on the stroke width and the background of the binarized images, identifying possible variations in luminance and stains or watermarks.

Bolan Su, Shijian Lu and Chew Lim Tan [16] proposed a binarization algorithm based on the maximum and the minimum colors for the detection of high contrast in the image and use it to identify the border of the main objects and to define the optimal threshold value. The algorithm was initially created for the competition of binarization of documents held in 2009 (DIBCO 2009) [10] but was not published until 2010.

Chen and Leedham [17] presented a binarization technique to work with complex backgrounds of historical documents,

especially documents with back-to-front interference. The algorithm decomposes the image using quad-tree decomposition algorithm [1] and it analyses all sub-images based on gray level co-occurrence matrix (GLCM) [1] based on word direction to define a local threshold.

Neves and Mello [18] proposed an algorithm to binarize documents with complex background. The algorithm was divided in three phases. In the first one the text is located from the image. In the next phase, the objects identified as text are separated in windows and in the last phase, these windows are thresholded using statistical information's.

3. THE PROPOSED ALGORITHM

The proposed algorithm extends the Neves and Mello [18] method. The new method has two main phases: the first one is responsible to identify the main objects in the document using edge detection and morphological operations. The second phase analyses each identified object to define a local threshold value for its region. The rest of the document is classified as background.

3.1 Object Identification

The first phase tries to find the object by its edge. It is an important step to eliminate variation in the brightness. Our experiments showed that the best way to detect edge in documents with complex background is using the canny method [1] followed by morphological operations. The proposed algorithm applies a histogram expansion in the original image I followed by the canny edge detector to find the image edge I_{edge} (Figure 1.b). After this phase, we use two morphological operations to connect the border of the identified objects: dilation (Figure 1.c) and closing (Figure 1.d).

These operations result in the dilated image and we use a closing operation to fill holes in the identified objects - $I_{objects}$ (Figure 1.d). If the structuring element used in morphological operations is a n x n window, where n is the average stroke-run of the text, the object is filled out. Otherwise, only the edge is identified, as presented in Figure 1(d), where the headline has just a border detected because the stroke run is large and the main text is completely identified

a   b

c   d

Figure 1. a)Original image; b)Edges detected by canny; c) Dilated image; d) I_object: final image with the main objects identified.

In previous experiments the value $n = 5$ presented promising results in the images from DIBCO dataset.

3.2 Binarization

To binarize the image we find the threshold for each object in $I_{objects}$. The connected objects are labeled in the image I_{label}. For each label is evaluated the average of the pixels in the same position on grayscale image I.

It is expected in the label area, the most of the pixels belonging to the ink and only a few groups belonging to the background. This average should be a good value to threshold the label L. As the label, L can represent the complete object or just an edge of the text image, a more accurate analysis need to be performed: the image is binarized in two ways and the resultant images combined. The first resultant image I_1 is defined by the coordinates that limits the label as show in Figure 2. The image is binarized according the following equation (1):

$$I_1(x,y) = \begin{cases} white, & if \ I(x,y) > T[L] \\ black, & if \ I(x,y) \leq T[L] \end{cases} \qquad (1)$$

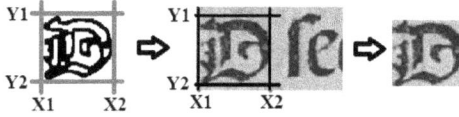

Figure 2. The image is bounded by the coordinates of the label.

The second image I_2 is binarized according to the pixels in the label positions. Positions with the value less than T[L] are classified as black (ink) and the others as white (background).

$$I_2(x,y) = \begin{cases} white, & if \ I_{label}(x,y) == L \ and \ I(x,y) > T(L) \\ black, & otherwise \end{cases} \qquad (2)$$

The rest of the not labeled image is classified as background (white). If there are holes in objects in the image, we use a morphological operation to fill them to obtain the final I_2.

After this, both images are compared. Pixels with the same value are maintained, while pixels with divergent values are converted to white (background).

$$I_{final}(x,y) = \begin{cases} black, & if \ I_1(x,y) = I_2(x,y) \\ white, & otherwise \end{cases} \qquad (3)$$

4. EXPERIMENTS AND RESULTS

To perform the experiments with the new method we used the same databases used in the Document Image Binarization Contest 2009 (DIBCO 2009) [10], in Handwritten Document Image Binarization Competition 2010 (H-DIBCO 2010) [11] and in DIBCO 2011 [13]. In these images, we can find the major complexities on background of handwritten and printed documents. All of these images have the ground truth image that help us to compare the algorithms.

To verify the algorithms performance we use F-measure (FM), Peak Signal to Noise Ratio (PSNR), Negative Rate Metric (NRM), Misclassification penalty metric (MPM), Geometric mean accuracy (GA). The same measures proposed in DIBCO 2009 [9] and proposed in ICFHR 2010 Contest: Quantitative Evaluation of Binarization Algorithms [11] are used. For each measure, the algorithms were ordered from the best to worst and then receive a value for their positions. Next, we add the position values obtained in each measure for each algorithm. They are then placed in ascending order that represents the best algorithm down to the worst.

The new method is compared to eleven algorithms described in Section 2. Thus, we can compare our algorithm to classical algorithms and with algorithms created specifically to work with complex background documents (the measure results are presented in Table 1). The proposed method is compared yet to the two best algorithms listed by the H-DIBCO 2012 [13]. The Table 2 presents the measure results.

According to the experiments presented in Table 1, the proposed approach achieved the highest F-measure, PSNR and GA, and the lowest MPM and the third lowest NRM. With these values, the algorithm placed the first position in the ranking. Comparing the algorithm with the two best algorithms from H-DIBCO 2012 [13] (Nicholas R. Howe in first position and Thibault Lelore and Frédéric Bouchara in second position), the algorithm obtained the second place (see Table 2).

Despite the great performance, statistically the results are similar to the Neves and Mello [21] proposal. The main difference is that this new proposal works well in headlines and some degraded ink, and is faster as its complexity was reduced. To prove this point, in the Figure 3 the same image is binarized with both algorithms. In left column is presented the result with the proposed approach and in the right side the images generated by Neves and Mello [21] proposal.

Figure 3. Resultant images. Left images of new algorithm; Right images of the Neves and Mello [18] proposal.

5. CONCLUSION

In this paper, we proposed a new algorithm to threshold document images. The main objective of binarization is to obtain a high quality bi-level image for document recognition. The challenge is to identify the color that separates correctly the main objects of the document from the complex background. Local algorithms are more appropriate for these cases as they can deal with specific regions of the document. However, the most algorithms can deal with just one kind of background complexity. In documents with back-to-front interference, for example, local algorithms tend to emphasize the interference, making the process of recognition very difficult, or when they work well on this situation it erase cases of weak ink. This tradeoff is a challenging task.

Table 2. Results from the two best algorithms from H-DIBCO 2012.

Approach	Results				
	FM	PSNR	NRM	MPM	GA
Proposed	$\mu = 90.72$ $\sigma = 2.28$	$\mu = 19.32$ $\sigma = 1.41$	$\mu = 0.037$ $\sigma = 0.017$	$\mu = 0.42$ $\sigma = 0.41$	$\mu = 0.93$ $\sigma = 0.01$
Howe [13]	$\mu = 84.54$ $\sigma = 19.2$	$\mu = 19.17$ $\sigma = 3.92$	$\mu = 0.062$ $\sigma = 0.079$	$\mu = 1.82$ $\sigma = 6.57$	$\mu = 0.89$ $\sigma = 0.18$
Lelore/ Bouchara [13]	$\mu = 92.68$ $\sigma = 4.03$	$\mu = 20.57$ $\sigma = 2.19$	$\mu = 0.038$ $\sigma = 0.017$	$\mu = 1.18$ $\sigma = 2.45$	$\mu = 0.96$ $\sigma = 0.04$

The proposed algorithm deal with complex background images. It is based on two main phases trying to segment the image according to its objects and dealing with each region separately. The algorithm was tested in the database used in DIBCO 2009 [10], in H-DIBCO 2010 [11], in DIBCO 2011 [13] and H-DIBCO

2012 [13]. We analyzed the performance of the algorithm by the same metrics used in the contest DIBCO 2009 and in ICFHR 2010 [12] and it placed first among the other algorithms used in the experiments (classical and specific algorithms for document images) and the second place considering just H-DIBCO 2012 and the best algorithm from the contest.

Table 1. Results from the eleven algorithms described in related work applied in DIBCO 2009, H-DIBCO 2010 and DIBCO 2011 database.

Approach	Results				
	FM	*PSNR*	*NRM*	*MPM*	*GA*
Proposed	$\mu = 88.90$ $\sigma = 4.65$	$\mu = 18.22$ $\sigma = 1.97$	$\mu = 0.055$ $\sigma = 0.028$	$\mu = 0.63$ $\sigma = 0.71$	$\mu = 0.93$ $\sigma = 0.02$
Neves and Mello [18]	$\mu = 88.30$ $\sigma = 3.88$	$\mu = 17.85$ $\sigma = 2.70$	$\mu = 0.058$ $\sigma = 0.021$	$\mu = 1.68$ $\sigma = 2.37$	$\mu = 0.93$ $\sigma = 0.03$
Otsu [4]	$\mu = 80.69$ $\sigma = 16.41$	$\mu = 16.08$ $\sigma = 4.03$	$\mu = 0.104$ $\sigma = 0.111$	$\mu = 7.52$ $\sigma = 18.20$	$\mu = 0.91$ $\sigma = 0.04$
Estrada, Tomasi [14]	$\mu = 76.07$ $\sigma = 16.03$	$\mu = 14.84$ $\sigma = 3.84$	$\mu = 0.124$ $\sigma = 0.118$	$\mu = 7.93$ $\sigma = 18.21$	$\mu = 0.89$ $\sigma = 0.06$
Chen, Leedham [17]	$\mu = 66.31$ $\sigma = 21.65$	$\mu = 14.84$ $\sigma = 2.46$	$\mu = 0.043$ $\sigma = 0.036$	$\mu = 4.22$ $\sigma = 9.48$	$\mu = 0.71$ $\sigma = 0.19$
Brink [6]	$\mu = 75.49$ $\sigma = 22.37$	$\mu = 14.83$ $\sigma = 5.70$	$\mu = 0.135$ $\sigma = 0.140$	$\mu = 8.63$ $\sigma = 20.37$	$\mu = 0.84$ $\sigma = 0.24$
Su, Lu, Tan [16]	$\mu = 68.72$ $\sigma = 16.82$	$\mu = 13.57$ $\sigma = 2.67$	$\mu = 0.185$ $\sigma = 0.078$	$\mu = 4.09$ $\sigma = 10.05$	$\mu = 0.82$ $\sigma = 0.19$
Huang [5]	$\mu = 65.31$ $\sigma = 28.48$	$\mu = 12.42$ $\sigma = 5.85$	$\mu = 0.209$ $\sigma = 0.166$	$\mu = 54.88$ $\sigma = 101.16$	$\mu = 0.90$ $\sigma = 0.06$
Yang and Yan [15]	$\mu = 65.53$ $\sigma = 13.16$	$\mu = 12.52$ $\sigma = 2.76$	$\mu = 0.198$ $\sigma = 0.093$	$\mu = 4.81$ $\sigma = 7.79$	$\mu = 0.84$ $\sigma = 0.06$
Niblack [7]	$\mu = 41.76$ $\sigma = 15.10$	$\mu = 6.84$ $\sigma = 1.09$	$\mu = 0.362$ $\sigma = 0.063$	$\mu = 23.40$ $\sigma = 15.94$	$\mu = 0.86$ $\sigma = 0.03$
Pun [8]	$\mu = 28.81$ $\sigma = 11.79$	$\mu = 4.05$ $\sigma = 0.70$	$\mu = 0.413$ $\sigma = 0.042$	$\mu = 397.1$ $\sigma = 389.9$	$\mu = 0.75$ $\sigma = 0.03$
Two Peaks [3]	$\mu = 20.00$ $\sigma = 8.81$	$\mu = 1.84$ $\sigma = 0.57$	$\mu = 0.443$ $\sigma = 0.028$	$\mu = 13,267$ $\sigma = 42,493$	$\mu = 0.52$ $\sigma = 0.09$

6. ACKNOWLEDGMENTS

The authors would like to thank CAPES and FBV to partially sponsored this research.

7. REFERENCES

[1] Gonzalez, R., Woods, C., Richard, E. 1992. *Digital Image Processing*, Addison-Wesley, 1992.

[2] Sezgin, M., Sankur, B. 2004. *Survey over image thresholding techniques and quantitative performance evaluation.* Journal of Electronic Imaging, vol. 1, no. 13, pp. 146-165.

[3] Parker, J. R. 1997. *Algorithms for Image Processing and Computer Vision*, John Wiley and Sons.

[4] Otsu, N. 1978. *A threshold selection method from grayscale histogram*, IEEE Transaction on Systems, Man and Cybernetics, vol. 8, pp. 62-66.

[5] Huang, L. K., Wang, M. J. 1995. *Image thresholding by minimizing the measures of fuzziness.* Pattern Recognition, vol. 28, no. 1, pp. 41-51.

[6] Katz, S. W., Brink, A. D. 1993. *Segmentation of Chromosome Images.* Communications and Signal processing, pp.85-90.

[7] Niblack, W. 1986. *An Introduction to Image Processing.* Prentice-Hall.

[8] Pun, T. 1981. *Entropic thresholding, the new approach.* Computer Graphics and Image Processing, vol. 16, pp. 210-239.

[9] Gatos, B., Ntirogiannis, K., Pratikakis, I. 2009. *DIBCO 2009: document image binarization contest.* International Conference on Document Analysis and Recognition, pp. 1375-1382.

[10] Pratikakis, I., Gatos, B., Ntirogiannis, K. 2010. *H-DIBCO2010 – Handwritten Document Image Binarization Competition.* 12th International Conference on Frontiers in Handwriting Recognition, pp. 727-732.

[11] Paredes, R., Kavallieratou, E., Lins, R. D. 2010. *ICFHR 2010 Contest: Quantitative Evaluation of Binarization Algorithms.* 12th International Conference on Frontiers in Handwriting Recognition, pp.733-736.

[12] Pratikakis, I., Gatos, B., Ntirogiannis, K. 2011. *ICDAR 2011 Document Image Binarization Contest (DIBCO 2011).* International Conference on Document Analysis and Recognition, pp. 1506-1510.

[13] Pratikakis, I., Gatos, B., Ntirogiannis, K. 2012. *ICFHR 2012 Competition on Handwritten Document Image Binarization (H-DIBCO 2012)*, 13th International Conference on Frontiers in Handwriting Recognition, pp. 813-818.

[14] Estrada R., Tomasi C. 2009. *Manuscript bleed-through removal via hysteresis thresholding*, International Conf. on Document Analysis and Recognition, pp. 753 - 757.

[15] Yang, Y., Yan, H. 2000. *An adaptive logical method for binarization of degraded document images*, Pattern Recognition, vol. 33, pp 787-807.

[16] Su,B., Lu, S., Tan, C. L. 2010. *Binarization of historical document images using the local maximum and minimum.* ACM International Conference Proceeding Series. Proceedings of the 9th IAPR International Workshop on Document Analysis Systems. pp. 159-166.

[17] Chen, Y., Leedham, G. 2005. *Decompose algorithm for thresholding degraded historical document images.* IEEE Proceedings - Vision, Image and Signal Processing, vol. 152, no. 6, pp. 702-714.

[18] Neves, R. F. P., Mello, C. A. B. 2011. *A Local Thresholding Algorithm for Images of Handwritten Historical Documents*, 2011 IEEE International Conference on Systems, Man, and Cybernetics, vol. 1. pp. 2934-2939.

Information Extraction Efficiency of Business Documents Captured with Smartphones and Tablets

Daniel Esser, Klemens Muthmann, Daniel Schuster
Computer Networks Group
Dresden University of Technology
01062 Dresden, Germany
{daniel.esser,klemens.muthmann,daniel.schuster}@tu-dresden.de

ABSTRACT

Businesses and large organizations currently prefer scanners to incorporate paper documents into their electronic document archives. While cameras integrated into mobile devices such as smartphones and tablets are commonly available, it is still unclear how using a mobile device for document capture influences document content recognition. This is especially important for information extraction carried out on documents captured in a mobile scenario. Therefore this paper presents a set of experiments to compare automatic index data extraction from business documents in a static and in a mobile case. The paper shows which decline in extraction one can expect, explains the reasons and gives a short overview over possible solutions.

Categories and Subject Descriptors

I.7.5 [**DOCUMENT AND TEXT PROCESSING**]: Document Capture—*Document analysis, Optical character recognition (OCR)*

General Terms

EXPERIMENTATION

Keywords

Mobile tagging; Information extraction; Evaluation

1. INTRODUCTION

Capturing and processing paper documents is still of high importance for all kinds of business as well as non-profit organizations. Organizations need a fast and accessible way to add such documents to their electronic document archives and annotate them with metadata for easy retrieval if required. The metadata is usually provided in the form of index entries, simple key value pairs identifying the document's content and role within the company. An invoice document for example might have entries such as sender, receiver, amount or invoice items.

DocEng'13, September 10–13, 2013, Florence, Italy.
Copyright 2013 ACM 978-1-4503-1770-2/13/09 ...$15.00.
http://dx.doi.org/10.1145/2494266.2494302.

High accessibility is only possible if the workflow from paper to the organization's electronic archives is as short as possible. In many cases this consists of a clerk using a scanner and a desktop application. Today however most people own smartphones and tablets that are equipped with high-quality cameras. Using these devices for document capture is quite appealing as they enable to capture documents anytime, anywhere and to immediately upload them to the document archive.

There already exist systems for indexing and archiving scanned documents like SmartFix [5] or the OpenText Capture Center [7]. Other systems provide mobile document capture capabilities such as the work by Patel [6] or Receipts2Go [4]. However there is yet no efficiency evaluation available on what it means to introduce mobile document images to an indexing system which used to work on scanned documents.

Especially considering the decrease of document capture quality, we want to know how much this influences the quality of extracted metadata index entries. Therefore this work presents an overview of the differences in quality we encountered using the same system for automatic document indexing in a mobile case compared to a static case. We present results for different mobile scenarios and discuss encountered errors as well as proposals for future solutions.

The remainder of this paper is organized as follows. At first we discuss different variables influencing mobile document capture. Then a short overview of the intelligent indexing approach is explained, together with some details on how mobile capturing might influence the results. Afterwards the main part of this paper gives an overview of our experimental setup and results. The results are discussed in detail in Section 4.3 after which the paper closes with conclusions and an overview of future work.

2. CAPTURE QUALITY

There is a multitude of variables which influences the quality of mobile document capturing. We used lighting, type of paper and tilt of the mobile device for the analysis in this paper.

Lighting is the amount of light a document receives while being captured. In the static case, a bright lamp integrated into a scanning device is used to achieve the best lighting possible. In the mobile case lighting depends on the time of day or the artificial light available. For our experiments we recorded documents within three common lighting scenarios, we expect to be near to real-world capturing. Table 1 shows an overview of those levels (with light measured in Lux).

Table 1: Lighting quality levels

Class	Lux	Scenario
L1	780–1097	Bright daylight
L2	116–430	Artificial direct lighting
L3	26–29	Artificial indirect lighting

The type of paper influences the contrast between the document's background and text. We expect darker recycling paper to cause more errors than high quality white paper.

Table 2: Paper quality levels

Class	Paper type	Scenario
P1	White	External documents
P2	Recycling	In-house documents

Lastly we also evaluated the influence of the tilt of the device. To measure bad device position we placed our capture device at an angle of 45° compared to the document plane and contrast those results to positioning the device flat and directly above the document.

Table 3: Tilt quality levels

Class	Position	Scenario
T1	Flat	Standing in front of document
T2	45°	Sitting in front of document

3. TEST SETUP

Our experiments are based on Intellix, a commercial quality extraction system which identifies similar looking documents out of the training set on a kNN basis. On this set of similar looking documents, three types of extraction steps are executed. First, it tries to identify fields with similar value across the set of similar looking documents which often applies for document type and sender. Second, it tries to identify index fields with values at nearly the same position (using bounding boxes of user-tagged values in training documents). Third, it uses context words in the surrounding of tagged fields in the training documents. Details about the extraction workflow can be found in [3, 8]. A similar workflow was first described by Cesarini et al. [1] and is likely to be found in other document processing systems as well.

The extraction workflow works on structured OCR output produced by a commercial OCR engine which we consider as a black box. We believe this is a common approach in document indexing as commercial OCR engines offer the best OCR quality available. We will discuss later on which part of the errors are due to a decrease in OCR accuracy and could possibly be diminished by tuning OCR parameters.

To access the Intellix indexing service a static and a mobile client were provided. The static client is a simple Java-based command line tool capable of sending a whole corpus of documents to the Intellix service and evaluating the results. The mobile client is an application written for Apple iOS. The client is able to take pictures from documents and detects the document's border using the well known Hough transform. In addition a homography matrix rectifies the image. The mobile client is also able to present the results and provide user corrections for the extracted values via the same Web service. Figure 1 shows our client at work.

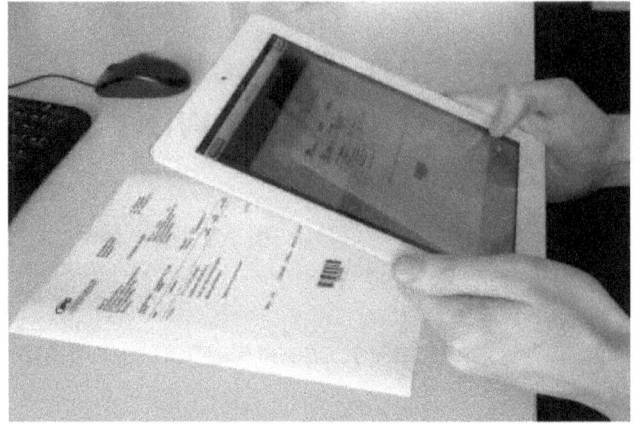

Figure 1: Capturing a business document with our iOS application. The current view shows the Intellix edge detection algorithm.

Our initial document corpus consists of 12,500 documents, captured with a customary scanner and tagged and corrected according to commonly used fields in document archiving. Beside a minimal set of fields to enable structured archiving (*document type, recipient, sender, date*), we added further popular fields like *amount, document number*, and *subject* based on a survey carried out by our project partner DocuWare. Out of this initial set, we randomly generated a subset of 1,000 static documents (C_1) and captured them using the internal camera of an iPad 3 (5-megapixel with autofocus) in combination with our Intellix iOS application (C_2). Therefore we established perfect circumstances to ensure a high recording quality.

To evaluate the influence of different quality levels, we randomly selected another subset of 200 documents. These documents were captured by our iPad 3 multiple times using different lighting, paper, and orientation scenarios. Altogether we created five scenarios resulting in five corpora (C_A-C_E), whose configurations can be seen in Table 4.

Table 4: Configurations

Category	Lighting	Paper	Tilt
A	L1 (good)	P1 (white)	T1 (flat)
B	L2 (medium)	P1 (white)	T1 (flat)
C	L3 (bad)	P1 (white)	T1 (flat)
D	L1 (good)	P2 (recycling)	T1 (flat)
E	L1 (good)	P1 (white)	T2 (45°)

For evaluation, we used the common metrics precision, recall, and F1-measure adopted by Chinchor and Sundheim [2] to the domain of information extraction for MUC-5. As the system user expects only correct results, we ignored error class "partial" and tackled this kind of extractions as wrong. Overall values were calculated using a micro-averaging approach by averaging single results across all recognized labels. To ensure significant evaluation results, each test was repeated ten times with changing document order.

4. EXPERIMENTS AND RESULTS

The following experiments mainly try to answer two research questions. First, how do documents captured on a

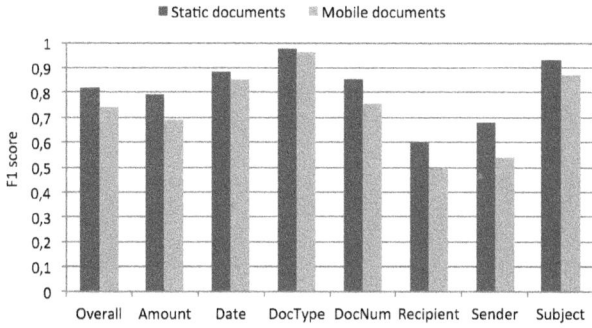

■ Static documents   ■ Mobile documents

Figure 2: Comparison of overall and field-by-field results using static and mobile captured documents.

mobile device compare to documents captured by a scanner regarding the efficiency of the information extraction? Second, how big is the expected further decrease in information extraction efficiency, if the mobile capturing was done under bad environmental conditions as described in Section 2?

4.1 Capture Mode Comparison

To be able to compare the two capture modes, namely scanner vs. mobile device, we pre-trained our system with 4,000 static documents. Afterwards we evaluated the system twice using the same set of 1,000 documents captured by a scanner (C_1) as well as captured by the iPad client (C_2). Figure 2 shows the system behavior.

Altogether we reach a F1 score of 81% for documents captured by a scanner and 73% for the same documents captured by a mobile device. As expected, the results of mobile captured documents are below the ones of static documents. The differences range between 1 and 14 percentage points, depending on the type of index field. Especially the differences for the document type are typically small due to the fact that this index field is detected by a classification, which is less prone to OCR errors. Sender and recipient contain the largest spread (12 and 14 percentage points). The values of such index fields are typically much longer than others, which increases the probability of OCR errors.

4.2 Mobile Capture with Bad Quality

To prove our expectations according to the extraction of documents with different quality levels, we pre-trained our system using 1000 mobile documents (C_2) captured with perfect circumstances. For each quality category, we evaluated the performance on a fresh system using 200 test documents (C_A-C_E). Figure 3 shows the results of this test.

As expected, documents from category A perform best. Guaranteeing ideal lighting and orientation conditions and using white paper for documents results in extraction rates around 75% F1-measure. While the kind of paper, a document is printed on, does only marginally effect the rating (D - L1/P2/T1 - 72%), changes in lighting circumstances significantly reduce the overall results. Documents captured with medium lighting (B - L2/P1/T1) reach F1-measure around 70%, while documents recorded with bad lighting (C - L3/P1/T1) can be extracted with 67%. The location of the camera according to the document has the biggest influence on the extraction results. Capturing at an angle of 45° while sitting, even after optimizing the picture by our

mobile application, results in a F1-measure 17 percentage points lower (E - L1/P1/T2 - 58%) than the results of our best category A.

If we look at the field-by-field results in Figure 3, we can see nearly constant values for index fields document type and sender. As already mentioned, for both fields we provide algorithms, which rather classify than extract these values. OCR errors do not effect the results as much as the results of other fields.

Within the results for category E (L1/P1/T2), we can see an interesting characteristic. While outcome for "amount" is quite comparable to the other categories, other index fields, especially the ones that occur in the top half of the documents perform much lower. We expect this behavior because of the limitation of mobile device cameras to use only one region as focal point. While the bottom of the captured document is sharp enough to produce good OCR results, the top of the document gets more and more diffuse.

4.3 Error Analysis

To get an overview of errors that occur by using mobile captured documents, we analyzed the results from our comparative test between static and mobile versions. Therefore we manually tagged each erroneous extraction that has occurred in a mobile document but was correctly identified in the appropriate static document. Altogether we could identify six error classes (ordered by occurrence):

1. *Wrong extraction (30%):* The extracted value is completely wrong. There is no similarity between extracted and valid value (i.e. "02/21/2013" vs. "invoice").

2. *OCR - Character (25%):* Extracted and valid value differ only by OCR character errors (i.e. "invoice" vs. "invuice").

3. *Partial extraction (19%):* The extracted and valid value overlap. Either too many or too few characters for valid value were extracted (i.e. "ACME Ltd." vs. "ACME").

4. *Missing extraction (15%):* No value was extracted, although a valid one exists (i.e. "02/21/2013" vs. "-").

5. *OCR - Tokenization (9%):* Extracted and valid value differ only by wrong detected word tokenization (i.e. "ACME Ltd." vs. "AC MELtd.").

6. *Spurious extraction (2%):* A value was extracted, although there is no value for this field (i.e. "-" vs. "02/21/2013").

Two-third of failures while processing mobile documents are partly based on our algorithms. While we use kNN search and layout-based extraction algorithms that mainly focus on the position of fields within the document, movements while capturing are hard to handle for them. Wrong, missing and spurious extractions (47%) tend to be constituted by the detection of similar looking documents.

Partial extractions, which are responsible for 19% of all errors, are based on movements while capturing. Although our iPad application tries to normalize recorded documents, our algorithms produce this kind of error due to small movements and deformations.

Only one-third of analyzed extraction errors are based on OCR. 9% of all failures lead to a wrong tokenization of words. Missing or extended spaces are typically seen in sender and recipient names.

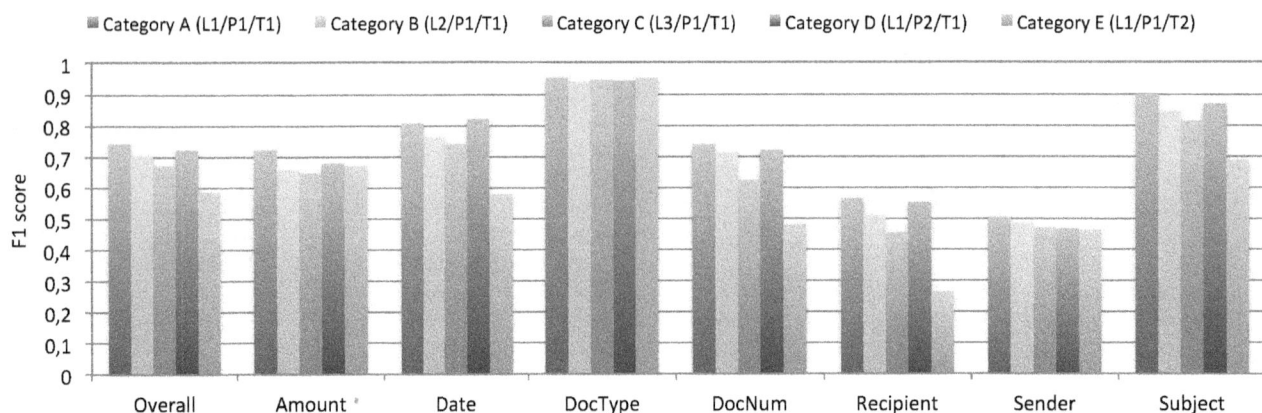

Figure 3: Comparison of overall and field-by-field extraction results for each quality category.

4.4 Discussion

The best way to overcome bad extraction results for mobile recorded documents is quite easy. Ensuring perfect circumstances according to lighting, paper and position of the mobile device guarantee high extraction rates. In practice perfect conditions are mostly rare. To minimize the trade-off we propose different solutions.

The limitations of mobile device cameras to focus only single regions leads to bad OCR results, when captured with an angle of 45°. Automatically capturing a document multiple times with different focuses and adding it afterwards to a completely sharp version can be a solution.

Altogether mobile applications have to get smarter. Right before hitting the shutter, the user has to be informed how the quality of the capture can be increased. Possible solutions are measurements of lighting level or identification of depth information to avoid partly blurred documents.

5. CONCLUSION

This paper presents a comparison of the efficiency of index data extraction on business documents captured either by a scanner or by a mobile device using the commercial quality extraction system Intellix. It shows that quality drops around 8% points F1 score, when capturing with mobile device cameras in an optimal way. The quality decrease will raise up to 20% and more if bad lighting or tilt compared to the paper plane occur during capturing. The problems for this loss in quality are an increase in OCR errors, movements, and distortions.

While the concrete numbers may vary from system to system, our error analysis shows the different types of errors and thus offers clues to tackle at least part of the quality decrease by improving OCR and extraction algorithms. We plan to work in this direction to improve the capturing experience for mobile users. Furthermore, improved user interfaces telling the user how to get the best extraction results on capturing would be of great help.

Nevertheless, the results described in this paper already show the feasibility of capturing business documents with mobile devices. With expected ongoing improvements in OCR quality, extraction algorithms and quality of camera hardware, we believe mobile capturing to be soon the preferred way for archiving paper documents.

6. ACKNOWLEDGMENTS

This research was funded by the German Federal Ministry of Education and Research (BMBF) within the research program "KMU Innovativ" (fund number 01/S12017). We thank our project partners from DocuWare for insightful discussions and providing us with the document corpus used for evaluation.

7. REFERENCES

[1] F. Cesarini, S. Marinai, and G. Soda. Retrieval by layout similarity of documents represented with mxy trees. In *Document Analysis Systems*, 2002.

[2] N. Chinchor and B. Sundheim. Muc-5 evaluation metrics. In *Proceedings of the 5th conference on Message understanding*, MUC5 '93, pages 69–78, 1993.

[3] D. Esser, D. Schuster, K. Muthmann, M. Berger, and A. Schill. Automatic indexing of scanned documents - a layout-based approach. In *Document Recognition and Retrieval XIX (DRR)*, San Francisco, CA, USA, 2012.

[4] B. Janssen, E. Saund, E. Bier, P. Wall, and M. A. Sprague. Receipts2go: the big world of small documents. In *Proceedings of the 2012 ACM symposium on Document engineering (DocEng '12)*, 2012.

[5] B. Klein, A. Dengel, and A. Fordan. smartfix: An adaptive system for document analysis and understanding. *Reading and Learning*, pages 166–186, 2004.

[6] X. Liu and D. Doermann. Mobile retriever: access to digital documents from their physical source. *International Journal of Document Analysis and Recognition (IJDAR)*, 11(1):19–27, 2008.

[7] Opentext. Opentext capture center. http://www.opentext.com/2/global/ products/products-capture-and-imaging/products-opentext-capture-center.htm, 2012.

[8] D. Schuster, K. Muthmann, D. Esser, A. Schill, M. Berger, C. Weidling, K. Aliyev, and A. Hofmeier. Intellix - end-user trained information extraction for document archiving. In *Document Analysis and Recognition (ICDAR)*, Washington, DC, USA, 2013. (accepted for publication).

Dominant Color Segmentation of Administrative Document Images by Hierarchical Clustering

Elodie Carel, Vincent Courboulay, Jean-Christophe Burie, Jean-Marc Ogier

L3i, University of La Rochelle
Avenue Michel Crépeau
La Rochelle, France
{elodie.carel, vincent.courboulay, jean-christophe.burie, jean-marc.ogier}@univ-lr.fr

ABSTRACT

This paper addresses the problem of color documents images segmentation in an industrial context. Automated Document Recognition (ADR) systems highly reduce time and resource costs of companies by managing their huge amount of administrative documents, and by optimizing their workflow. Most of the time, a binarization is performed due to their historical industrial process. Therefore, colorimetric information can improve the process. In this paper, we propose a hierarchical clustering based approach to extract dominant color masks of documents. Indeed, our dataset comprises different kind of scanned administrative document images such as invoices, forms, letters, and so on. We do not know *a priori* the number of dominant colors on our documents. These masks will further feed the inputs to an OCR in order to bring extra-information about the colorimetric context. This approach requires neither user interaction nor setting steps. Experiments on several types of documents show the relevance of the proposed approach

Categories and Subject Descriptors

H.4 [**Information Systems Applications**]: Miscellaneous; I.5 [**Pattern Recognition**]: Clustering

Keywords

Document analysis, dominant colors, clustering

1. INTRODUCTION

Nowadays, companies have to deal with huge volumes of administrative documents such as invoices, forms, letters and so on. Automated Document Recognition (ADR) systems highly reduce time and resource costs. To do this, the document is input to an Optical Character Recognition (OCR). Most of the time, a binarization is performed in order to simplify the image. Indeed, color processing is complex and requires a lot of computational resources. But what

was necessary some years ago is becoming less and less important now that hardware and processing are improving. So, it is interesting to investigate what color could bring to the dematerialization chain. Two problems appear with the binarization strategy. First, it requires this extra step. And then, the performance decreases when the segmentation fails. It can happen when elements overlap. For example, Fig. 1 shows some issues companies can have to deal with: highlighting regions, corrective red overload on black text, or text/graphics overlapping. A color-based segmentation could improve the process. Then, the color information is meaningful. And it provides semantic information to describe elements which could be used for creating new color descriptors.

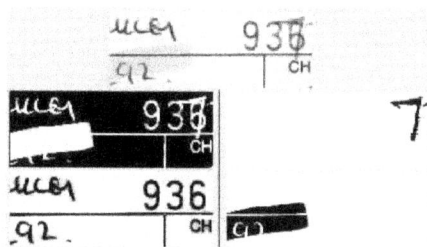

Figure 1: Issues: example of colors mask to be extracted

Here, we will focus on the extraction of dominant color masks. Fig. 1 shows some samples of what we would like to obtain. We stand at the beginning of the dematerialization chain. This work aims at using the color to bring extra-information to the OCR and to improve the segmentation process. The main idea is to make the color layers appear on different masks. These masks will be black and white images with elements belonging to one color appearing in black. So, they can feed the traditional process. But they will also have metadata about their color. Another interest will be to separate elements with different colors and thus avoid post-processing. The paper is organized as follows. Section 2 presents the state-of-the-art. Then, our approach is described in section 3. Results are discussed in section 4. Finally, we conclude in section 5.

2. STATE-OF-THE-ART

As far as the authors know, there are only few works about the use of the color for document analysis. That is why we studied approaches for both document images and real world images. This literature review has been conducted under the theme of the description of the color in the image processing field. The second part has been devoted to the segmentation of dominant colors. Finally, we have investigated clustering approaches in a more important way.

First, we have to define what a color is, and how many dominant colors we might expect for a document. In the literature, van den Broek et al. (2008) experimentally confirm that humans categorize colors into a limited number of eleven basic colors: black, white, red, green, yellow, blue, brown, purple, pink, orange, and gray. Then, these colors can be divided into two groups: the chromatic colors, for which a specific hue is defined (i.e. red, green, blue ...), and achromatic categories (i.e., black, gray, and white).

For some applications, it can be relevant to handle these categories with different operations since achromatic pixels bring no information about the hue. The common approach to separate pixels is a thresholding of the saturation channel (Kim et al. 2009). Indeed, chromatic pixels have a high value of saturation. Ouji et al. (2011) introduce a new pseudo-saturation measure which is valid for both dark and light pixels. Aït Younes et al. (2005) describe the color thanks to fuzzy sets in order to classify images based on dominant colors. On the one hand, they use nine fundamental colors determined by the hue attribute of the HLS space. On the other hand, they also consider the lightness and saturation attributes to associate qualifiers (i.e. somber, dark, luminous, ...) to the description of the color.

About the segmentation, Aït Younes et al. limit the value of color ranges according to linguistic names of colors. A hue can be associated to two colors with a membership degree. Karatzas (2008) extends the Hough Transform to a combined spatial-lightness space. He aims at extracting color gradients considering them as planes in this space. The author proposes to modify the parameters to be able to deal with homogeneous areas. Ramella and Sanniti di Baja (2011), for example, use histogram thresholding which is a common approach where colors are defined by peaks of the histogram. But histograms consider only the color and not the spatial information of pixels. That is why the resulting image can be over segmented and that a merging step can be necessary.

Some other approaches consider clustering techniques. Clustering is the operation of grouping together pixels sharing similar properties in order to get homogeneous regions. A color is then described by a cluster. The idea is to search for compact and well separated clusters. A review of data clustering has been written by Jain (2010). K-means is widely used because of its simplicity. Therefore, the number of class has to be defined in a first step and the results depend on the initialization of the clusters centroids. The fuzzy c-means extends the k-means with fuzzy logic. Each point can belong to several clusters with a degree of membership. These last two methods belong to the *flat clusterings* by opposition to the *hierarchical clusterings* which build a tree of clusters. A hierarchical clustering follows either an agglomerative way (considering each point as a cluster and then recursively gathering the closest together), or a divisive approach (putting all the points in one cluster and recursively splitting it into smaller clusters).

We aim at extracting only dominant colors on the image. That means that pixels having close colorimetric properties have to be group together into regions. Histograms consider only the colorimetric information of pixels. Younes et al. (2005) limits the number of colors. They also fix the boundaries between different hues. Dealing with a fixed number of colors is not optimized for documents which contain just a few colors. On the other hand, clustering allow the combination of data of different nature. Macaire et al. (2006) propose a spatial-color compactness degree to consider both spatial arrangement of pixels in the image plane, and the dispersion of the color points in the color space. That is why clustering approaches seem the most interesting in our case.

3. PROPOSED APPROACH

In this section, we will describe the main approach. Then, we will go into details by describing the cluster splitting and the stopping criteria.

3.1 Main Approach

Because of the industrial context, user interaction is not allowed. So, process has to be automatically performed. We do not know *a priori* the number of colors (i.e. our classes or clusters) on our documents. That is why, we can not use a flat clustering which requires to specify how many clusters will be handled. A hierarchical clustering based approach seems relevant because the number of clusters will be adapted to the document. We assume that an administrative document contain only few dominant colors (less than 10 in most of the cases). Results will be computed faster with one cluster which will be split rather than considering each point as a cluster and merging them. So, we have preferred a divisive clustering to the agglomerative approach due to the nature of the documents and to our aim which is to get only the dominant color masks (Fig.1).

Many colorimetric spaces exist. But it is commonly known that there is not an optimal space which works for all images. Preliminary tests have been realized with the RGB colorimetric space. Indeed, the image of our dataset are coded with this space. It will avoid a conversion step. In this space, color of pixels is defined by their Red, Green, and Blue channels. We assume that dominant colors are identified as clusters into the 3D space. Clusters have to be compact and well separated. They are described by their cluster center.

Fig.2 resumes the process. The first step puts all points into one cluster. Then, this cluster is split. Two new centers are initialized. The points belonging to the former cluster are distributed among the two new ones thanks to a flat clustering. Here, a k-means is applied.

Once, the new centers have converged, some features are measured and compared to threshold values. These are stopping rules which decide if the cluster can still be split or not. Features give information about clusters homogeneity, connectedness and so on. They will be described later. The process is then iterated until there is no cluster to be split anymore regards the tested features, or until a fixed number of iterations is reached. Dominant colors are leaves of the dendogram.

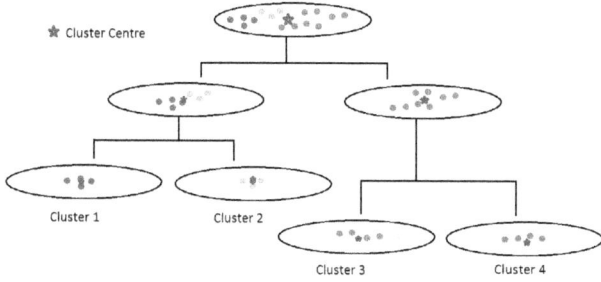

Figure 2: Example of colors mask to be extracted

3.2 Splitting clusters

In this section, the approach to split clusters will be explained. The first step starts with one cluster Z into which we put all the points of the image. Then, this cluster is split in two. The two new values, Z_1 and Z_2, are computed as followed (Ray and Turi, 2000):

$$Z_1 = (C_1 - a_1, C_2 - a_2, C_3 - a_3) \ (1.a)$$

$$Z_2 = (C_1 + a_1, C_2 + a_2, C_3 - a_3) \ (1.b)$$

where C_i is the i-th component and, a_i, a constant which is half of the smaller of (C_i - min_i) and (max_i - C_i). To be sure, to stay inside the cluster, we choose to keep the value of a_i for i, the color component which have the biggest variance. Else, a_i equals 0.

Once we have initialized the new two centers, we have to make them converged using a flat clustering. Here, we have chosen a k-means clustering which is a fast and a common approach. It aims at minimizing the sum of squared distances from all the points to their centers. The points belonging to the former cluster are distributed among the two new ones. The euclidean distance is used.

3.3 Measures used as stopping rules

During the process, we measure some features for each cluster. These features are compared to threshold values. Stopping rules decide if the cluster can still be split or not. We used the spatial-color compactness degree proposed by Macaire et al. (2006). First, they define a region as color subset S of strongly connected pixels with homogeneous colors. Let P be a pixel of a color image I. $N_S(P)$ is the subset of the 8 neighboring pixels of P which belong to S. The connectedness between P and S is defined as:

$$\gamma_S = \frac{Card\{N_S(P)\}}{8} \ (2)$$

The connectedness degree of S is:

$$CD(S) = \frac{\sum_{P \in S} \gamma_S(P)}{Card\{S\}} \ (3)$$

Then, Macaire et al. (2006) combine this degree with a homogeneity degree in order to discriminate real regions.

First, they define a measure of the dispersion of the color points $\sigma(S)$. It is estimated as the square root of the trace of the covariance matrix of the color points representing the pixels of the color-subset S (here our clusters). Then, they computed a local dispersion measure as the mean of the dispersion measures computed for the 8 neighboring pixels of all points belonging to the cluster:

$$\sigma_{local}(S) = \frac{1}{Card\{S\}} \cdot \sum_{P \in S} \sigma(N_S(P)) \ (4)$$

The homogeneity degree $HD(S)$ is defined as:

$$\begin{cases} HD(S) = \frac{\sigma_{local}(S)}{\sigma(S)} \ if \sigma(S) \neq 0 \\ HD(S) = 1 \ otherwise \end{cases} \ (5)$$

To finish, they compute the spatial-color compactness degree of a color-subset S as:

$$SCD(S) = CD(S).HD(S) \ (6)$$

A high value (i.e. close to 1) of this degree means that the pixels belonging to the cluster are both strongly connected and homogeneous in terms of colors. Therefore, documents contain big regions such as background for which this value will stay high because of the number of pixels strongly connected. Those regions will be split and the image will be over-segmented. To reduce this effect, we choose to add a criterion to compare the difference between the max and the min of color components inside the cluster. If the max of these values is under a threshold, we assume that the splitting will produce two clusters with too close centers. That is why, we stop the process for this cluster.

4. RESULTS AND DISCUSSION

We have carried out tests on a dataset of a dozen of documents with a visual evaluation. This is a relatively small base. But it has allowed us to check if this method was relevant. We have also build a tool to create synthetic images. This tool allows to choose the maximum number of color wanted. Then, it draw a random number of big regions (i.e. rectangles and ellipses)to create a complex background. In the same way, smaller regions are displayed, then lines, and finally random text. Fig.3 shows some samples. Thus, the number of colors and the size of regions are known precisely for each document at a pixel level. So, we are able to measure the performance of our process in a more accurate way.

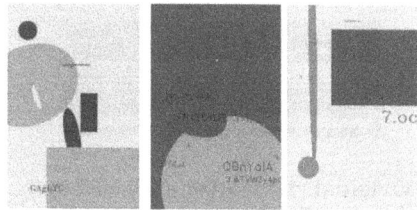

Figure 3: Synthetic images generated by the ground-truth tool

To evaluate the performance, the ground-truth has been used to create 417 synthetic images. The maximum number of iterations has been initialized at 10. So, a maximum of

2^{10} clusters could be found. We measured the number of output color layers under the number of color layers of the ground-truth. The average of layers found is 0.63. This result is not really good. It can be explained this approach is based on threshold values, and so, it fails to divide too close colors. However, it gives a first approximation of the performance. Moreover, we assume that color on documents will be contrasted because there are made to be readable by humans. Then, we have added gaussian noise on the same images. Here, a different problem appears because the noise creates new colors. Thus, we obtained too much masks.

These results are due to the noise because we work at a pixel-level. We have also noticed this problem by a visual examination of the results on real document images. Indeed, most of our images are compressed by JPEG format, and scanning process adds noise on the image. Even if a region looks homogeneous, at a pixel level, there are not crisp edges but areas of transitions. It is particularly obvious for textual area which can appear incomplete on our masks. This problem could be solved by using spatial information, and by improving the image with some pre-processing (e.g. smoothing, region-based rather than pixel-based segmentation).

Nevertheless, our results on documents show that we are able to find the main regions. These regions can be used to extract information about the layout of the document. A black and white mask is associated to its cluster center in order to describe the color. So, it can both feed the inputs to an OCR, as it is done nowadays, and bring extra colorimetric information. The hierarchical clustering takes into account the manifold of our dataset. The number of clusters is dynamically computed. Some stopping criteria allow us to stop the clustering once we have reached compact ant well separated clusters. We have fixed the threshold values of measures previously described. Results seem interesting in the case of overlapping elements with different colors (Fig.4). Indeed, a classical binarization process makes them appear with the same color. So, it makes it more difficult to extract relevant information. However, our approach separates dominant colors. Thus, it can avoid some post-processing steps.

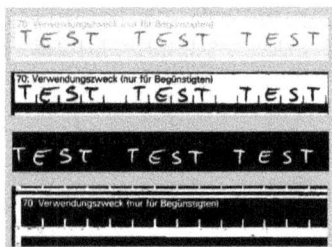

Figure 4: Original (1st), after a classical binarization (2nd), cluster mask 1 from the original (3rd), cluster mask 2 from the original (4th)

5. CONCLUSIONS

In this paper, we have described a hierarchical clustering based approach to extract dominant color masks of administrative documents. Colors are defined by cluster centers. Our stopping rule use a spatial-color compactness degree in order to decide if a cluster contains several dominant colors or not. This approach requires to set up threshold parameters to decide what is a dominant color or not for a specific category of images (e.g. Here, document images). But obviously, the definition of what is a dominant color will depend on the application and on the images. It will also depend on the quality of the desired segmentation (i.e. coarse or finer). Once these thresholds have been set up, the process does not require any extra-interaction with the user.

Experiments on several types of documents show the relevance of this approach as a first step to get a coarse segmentation for an incremental framework. Indeed, big regions appear on our masks. Due to the noise on the images, transition parts still appear on separate masks. That is why the addition of spatial information into the process has been identified as a future work. Dominant color masks can be used in future works to extract the main layout of documents in order to classify them.

6. REFERENCES

[1] E. L. van den Broek, Th.E. Schouten and P. M. F. Kisters, *Modeling human color categorization*, Pattern Recogn. Lett.,29 (8).pp.1136-1144. ISSN 0167-8655, 2008.

[2] A. K. Jain, *Data clustering: 50 years beyond k-means*, Pattern Recogn. Lett., 31(8) 651-666, 2010.

[3] D. Karatzas, *Detecting Gradients in Text Images Using the Hough Transform*, in Proceedings of the 8th International Workshop on Document Analysis Systems, pp. 245–252, 2008.

[4] J.H. Kim, D.K. Shin, and Y.S. Moon, *Color transfer in images based on separation of chromatic and achromatic colors*, in MIRAGE '09, Berlin, Heidelberg: Springer-Verlag, pp. 285-296, 2009

[5] A. Ouji, Y. Leydier, and F. Lebourgeois, *Chromatic / achromatic separation in noisy document images*, IEEE International Conference on Document Analysis and Recognition (ICDAR 2011), 2011.

[6] L. Macaire, N. Vandenbroucke, J. Postaire, *Color image segmentation by analysis of subset connectedness and color homogeneity properties*, Journal Computer Vision and Image Understanding, Volume 102 Issue 1, Pages 105-116, 2006.

[7] G. Ramella and G. Sanniti di Baja, *Color histogram-based image segmentation*, in Proceeding CAIP'11 Proceedings of the 14th international conference on Computer analysis of images and patterns - Volume Part I Pages 76-83, 2011.

[8] S. Ray and RH. Turi, *Determination of number of clusters in K-means clustering and application in colour image segmentation*, (invited paper) in N R Pal, A K De and J Das (eds), Proceedings of the 4th International Conference on Advances in Pattern Recognition and Digital Techniques (ICAPRDT'99), ISBN: 81-7319-347-9, pp 137-143, 1999.

[9] A. Aït Younes, I. Truck and H. Akdag, *Color Image Profiling Using Fuzzy Sets*, Turkish Journal of Electric Engineering & Computer Sciences, 13(3):343-369, 2005.

Optical Font Recognition using Conditional Random Field [*]

Aziza Satkhozhina
Purdue University
School of Electrical and
Computer Engineering
West Lafayette, IN 47907,
U.S.A.
asatkhoz@purdue.edu

Ildus Ahmadullin
Hewlett-Packard Laboratories
Palo Alto, CA, 94304, U.S.A.
ildus.ahmadullin@hp.com

Jan P. Allebach
Purdue University
School of Electrical and
Computer Engineering
West Lafayette, IN 47907,
U.S.A.
allebach@purdue.edu

ABSTRACT

Automated publishing systems require large databases containing document page layout templates. Most of these layout templates are created manually. A lower cost alternative is to extract document page layouts from existing documents. In order to extract the layout from a scanned document image, it is necessary to perform Optical Font Recognition (OFR) since the font is an important element in layout design. In this paper, we use the Conditional Random Field (CRF) model to perform OFR. First, we extract typographical features of the text. Then, we train the probabilistic model using a log-linear parameterization of CRF. The advantage of using CRF is that it does not assume that the typographical features are independent of each other. We demonstrate the effectiveness of this approach on a set of 616 fonts.

Categories and Subject Descriptors

J.7 [**Computers in other systems**]: Publishing

Keywords

document design, page layout, conditional random fields, optical font recognition

1. INTRODUCTION

Automated publishing provides a fully or partially automated document generation capability at low cost. Most automated publishing systems use large databases containing page-layout templates, most of which are created manually. Moreover, the number of layout templates that need to be created and stored grows exponentially with the complexity of the layouts. Instead of creating and storing such a database, a lower cost alternative can be to extract and reuse the layouts of existing documents. The ultimate goal of this research is to develop an automated system that extracts the layout information from a scanned document page, and then reuses the extracted information to generate a new visually similar document with new content [7]. To preserve the style and design of the original document, the system also needs to have a capability of recognizing text fonts from scanned document images. Because our system is intended for non-designer users such as small businesses or individuals, high font recognition accuracy is desirable, but not essential for this application.

While a lot of research has been done on Optical Character Recognition (OCR), not much attention has been given to OFR. OFR consists of identifying the typeface, weight, slope and size of a font without knowing the context of the text. Two major approaches for font recognition may be characterized as (1) using global texture analysis, and (2) using local typographical features. Zhu, Tan et al. [10] proposed an algorithm based on the global texture of document images. They used multidimensional Gabor filters to extract the features from uniform blocks of text, and then identified the fonts using a weighted Euclidean distance classifier. Khoubyari and Hull [2] presented an algorithm that finds frequent function words (such as *the, of, and*, and *to*). They then compared the identified words with a database of function words to identify the dominant font of the text.

Zramdini and Ingold [11] described eight global typographical features that are the most important in discriminating between different fonts. They assumed that the features are independent of each other and used a multivariate Bayesian classifier to identify the font. Results from Zramdini et al. [11] show that the font recognition rate is very sensitive to the length of the test text, relative to that of the training text. For example, if the length of the test text is 4 times shorter than the length of the training text, the recognition rate decreases from 99.02% to 64.15%. In this work, we use typographical features which were identified in [11] augmented by new features of our own design. However, we then use these features within the Conditional Random Field approach to achieve our font classification. This approach does not make the assumption that the features are independent of each other. In Sec. 2, we describe the features that we used. Section 3 describes the CRF model. In Sec. 4, experimental results are discussed.

---

[*]This work was partially supported by the Hewlett-Packard Company.

Figure 1: Illustration of key parameters for typographical features. Width and height are computed from the bounding box of the letter.

2. TYPOGRAPHICAL FEATURES

The inputs to the system were computer-generated or scanned images that contain text with a uniform font. Then, the images were binarized, and lines were found using vertical projection of black pixels. We used connected component analysis to find each letter. Small connected components corresponding to punctuation marks were ignored.

Thirteen typographical features were extracted from connected components to discriminate between the fonts. Eight features were chosen in [11]; and we added five additional features. The features were extracted from each connected component and then averaged over all connected components on each line. This averaging step smoothed the data and signifcantly decreased the amount of training data. The following are the features that were proposed in [11]: (1) density of the horizontal projection, (2) density of the squared values of the derivative of horizontal projection, (3) density of the difference between consecutive scanlines, (4) average height of vertical black-runs, (5) average width of horizontal black-runs, (6) average normalized height, (7) average normalized width, and (8) average space between characters.

It is important to note that these features are calculated only for specific characters. For example, the average normalized width is estimated only from short connected components with nearly square bounding boxes, which correspond to letters such as **a, c, e,** and **n**. However, it may happen that a test case does not contain short and squared letters. A good example for such test case is a header text that sometimes contains only one word. Then, there is no guarantee that some of these features can be estimated from the text. We expect that an automated publishing system may take as its input document images with small amounts of text such as brochures and advertisements. For this reason, we included an additional five features: unnormalized height and width (computed from all connected components), xheight (described in [11]), xratio (ratio of xheight to height), and ratio of width to height. There are dependence relationships between most of these features. For example, the greater the size of the letter is, the greater are the values of the width and height.

3. CONDITIONAL RANDOM FIELD

Conditional Random Field proposed by Lafferty et al [3] is a probabilistic graphical model, which is widely used in pattern recognition and machine learning. It is represented by a graphical structure that describes the conditional independence relationships between random variables. The model is described by probability distributions and these are used to compute the likelihood of a particular font configuration. The advantage of using CRF is that it allows features that depend on each other. In CRF, the nodes are divided into two disjoint sets X and Y, where Y is the set of target variables and X is the set of observed variables. The

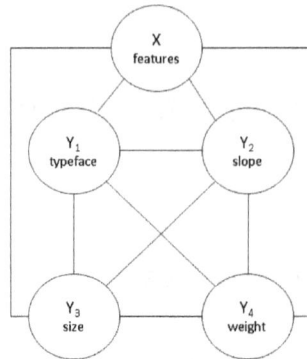

Figure 2: Graphical model for CRF

goal is to predict Y given observed variables X by maximizing $P(Y|X)$.

In our case, set X contains the nodes that represent typographical features; and set Y represents the font. Figure 2 illustrates this model: nodes Y_1, Y_2, Y_3, and Y_4 represent typeface, slope, size, and the weight of the font, respectively. Node X denotes observed variables. Previously, we defined 13 typographical features that can describe the font. We added an additional 14th feature to the set X. It will play the role of a bias, since there should be some probability that the font does not depend on the typographical features. The bias feature value will be always set to 1. The weight of the font can be either regular or bold. Therefore, Y_4 can take one of two possible states. Slope, size, and typeface also can take one of 2, 14, and 11 possible states, respectively. So for a given sample of text, we want to automatically predict the states of the four nodes (typeface, slope, weight, and size). We assume that there are pairwise dependencies between the target variables. These dependencies are represented by edges between all pairs of nodes in set Y. It is important to note that typographical features depend on the font. Consequently, every node in X is connected to every node in Y. Fortunately, the dependencies between the features do not affect our prediction. We are only interested in the probability of text having a particular font given the observation. Therefore, we omit modeling complicated dependencies between typographical features.

There is also a potential function for each node and for each edge. The potential function is a non-negative function that defines the energy of a certain configuration. States with higher potentials are more probable. We assume that all edges belong to an exponential family of distributions. This comes from an assumption that the probability $P(Y|X)$ of nodes being in a particular state is a linear function of the features. We define the potential of node Y_j being in a state y_j given features x as

$$\phi(y_j|x; w^j) = \exp\left\{ w_0^j + \sum_{i=1}^{13} w_i^j x_i \right\}. \qquad (1)$$

Here, x_i is i-th typographical feature function, w_i^j is the weight parameter which describes the influence of i-th feature on label y_j, and w_0^j is a bias weight. We assume that the potential of each edge depends on a single feature only. This is a bias feature; and its value will always be set to 1 for all edges. Then, the potential of an edge that contains nodes Y_i and Y_j is given by

$$\phi(y_i, y_j|\mu^{ij}) = \exp\left\{ \mu^{ij} \cdot 1 \right\}, \qquad (2)$$

where μ^{ij} is a bias weight that describes the relationship between labels y_i and y_j. Now, the total probability of observing a particular font configuration, given typographical features x and the weights is

$$P(Y = y|x; w; \mu) = \frac{1}{Z} \prod_{j \in Y} \phi(y_j|X; w^j) \prod_{\{m,n\} \in E} \phi(y_m, y_n|\mu^{mn}),$$

(3)

where y_m and y_n are the values of the nodes which are connected by an edge belonging to the set of all edges E. Z is the normalization constant, which is equal to the sum over all possible values that each random variable can take:

$$Z = \sum_y \prod_{j \in Y} \phi(y_j|X; w^j) \prod_{\{m,n\} \in E} \phi(y_m, y_n|\mu^{mn}).$$

The task of training CRF is to estimate the parameters w and μ that maximize the log-likelihood of the training data. Once we learn the weights, it becomes easy to predict states of the nodes. The cost function that needs to be maximized is

$$C = \sum_{j \in Y} log\phi(y_j|X; w^j) + \sum_{\{m,n\} \in E} log\phi(y_m, y_n|\mu^{mn}) - logZ.$$

(4)

Assuming that all distributions are exponential guarantees that the cost function is convex [9]. Thus, the minimum can be found using a quasi-Newton optimization method. The minimization of the cost function was done using a deterministic Limited-memory Broyden–Fletcher–Goldfarb-Shanno (L-BFGS) method [4]. L-BFGS has a very low computational cost, and is well suited for optimization problems with a large number of variables.

One of the most difficult problems in training CRF is estimating the normalization function Z, which is called inference. We chose exact inference that works by generating the joint distribution and exhaustively summing it out to get the necessary marginal probabilities. Because our graph contains only unary and pairwise potentials, complete enumeration of all possible font configurations is tractable. We used a Matlab toolbox to build the CRF model [8].

4. EXPERIMENTAL RESULTS

For our experiments, we used two different sets of training and testing text images. One of the sets was created by printing text pages at 300 dpi, and scanning them at 300 dpi. This set contained 168 font models containing 3 typefaces (*Arial, Calibri,* and *Times New Roman*), 2 weights (*regular* and *bold*), 2 slopes (*regular* and *italic*) and 14 font sizes (*8, 9, 10, 12, 14, 16, 18, 20, 22, 24, 28, 36, 48,* and *72* points). A sample English text containing 1337 words was used to generate training images for each font model. During the scanning process, some of the pages were scanned with a noticeable skew and distortion. Therefore, skew correction was applied to all scanned images. A total of 168 test images was prepared, where each image corresponded to exactly one font model. Each test image contained a different number of words, since pages with a larger font could only fit a small number of words, while pages with smaller fonts fit more words on one page. The second set of text images was generated by a computer, and saved as 300 dpi noise-free tiff images. We had 616 different font models containing 11 well-known and popular typefaces (*Garamond, Futura, Franklin Gothic, Helvetica, Rockwell, Cambria, Calibri, Courier New, Gill Sans MT, Tahoma,* and *Times New Roman*), 2 weights (*regular, bold*), 2 slopes (*regular, italic*), and 14 font sizes (*8, 9, 10, 12, 14, 16, 18, 20, 22, 24, 28,*

36, 48, and *72* points). The training text was identical in both test sets.

To evaluate the performance of CRF, we compared its performance with the performance of three other classifiers: Linear Discriminant Analysis (LDA), Mahalanobis, and Naïve Bayes classifiers. All four classifiers used the same feature set and the same training and test page sets. LDA finds linear combinations of the features which cause the largest mean differences between different classes [6]. There are two important measures that need to be defined for LDA. Within-class and between-class measures are given by (5) and (6).

$$S_w = \sum_{j=1}^c \sum_{i=1}^{N_j} (x_i^j - \mu_j)(x_i^j - \mu_j)^T.$$

(5)

Here, c is the number of classes, x_i^j is the ith sample of class j, N_j is the number of samples in class j.

$$S_b = \sum_{j=1}^c (\mu_j - \mu)(\mu_j - \mu)^T.$$

(6)

Here, μ is the mean of all classes. The goal of LDA is to find weights that maximize the between-class measure and minimize the within-class measure.

The Mahalanobis classifier takes into account the correlation in the data and removes several limitations of the Euclidean distance metric. The Mahalanobis distance is defined by

$$MD^2 = (x - \mu)\Sigma^{-1}(x - \mu)^T,$$

(7)

where μ is the mean vector and Σ is the covariance matrix of the features in the class [5]. The classifier calculates the Mahalanobis distance from the target feature vector to every class, and then assigns the feature vector to the class for which the distance is minimum.

The third classifier is a Naïve Bayes classifier which assumes that typographical features do not depend on each other. The classifier works by finding the class which maximizes the posterior probability of the features belonging to that class.

$$\hat{c} = \underset{c}{argmax} \ P(C = c) \prod_{i=1}^n p(F_i = f_i|C = c),$$

(8)

where F represents the feature vector and c is a class.

As can be seen from Tables 1 and 2, CRF was very successful in recognizing the weight and slope of the font for both scanned and computer-generated test sets. In fact, for these two tasks CRF performed the best of the four classifiers. However, the recognition rates for typeface and size were not as high as the rates for weight and slope. For the scanned test pages, CRF did not perform typeface recognition as well as Mahalanobis or LDA. For the computer-generated test pages, CRF did not perform typeface recognition as well as Mahalanobis, but performed better than LDA. With regard to size recognition with scanned text, CRF performed 4th best. However, for size recognition with computer-generated text, CRF was the best.

It is important to note that in the cases where the size was misclassified, the differences between the recognized and the actual sizes were small. Font size misclassification often happened with font sizes from 8 to 16 points. Our results also confirmed the results from [11] where it was observed that size and typeface misclassifications are often related. Since size misclassification often occurred in the range be-

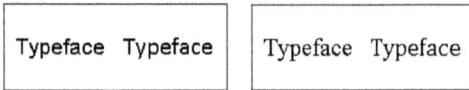

Figure 3: Similar typefaces (from left to right): (a) Arial 16 points; Calibri 18 points (b) Cambria 18 points; Times New Roman 18 points. All fonts have regular weights and slopes.

Table 1: Font recognition rate for scanned test pages

Method	Typeface	Weight	Slope	Size
LDA	0.774	0.774	0.929	0.625
Mahalanobis	0.720	0.863	0.833	0.667
Naïve Bayes	0.369	0.488	0.946	0.518
CRF	0.637	0.827	1.000	0.417

tween 8 to 16 points, typeface misclassification also happened more frequently for fonts with small font sizes. The typeface confusion matrix in Table 3 shows that most typefaces were often identified correctly. However, some of the fonts look very similar and are even hard for a human observer to classify. For example, Futura was identified as Gill Sans MT 37.5% of the time. People can discriminate this typeface pair correctly only 70.4% of the time [1].

5. CONCLUSION

Using CRF as a classifier yielded promising results. The results showed that CRF performed the best in recognition of weight and slope of the text font. Typeface and size recognition rates were not as high as the rates for weight and slope. However, most misclassifcations happened when actual and recognized typefaces were visually similar and the font size was small. We think that this performance is acceptable for an automated publishing system which aims to generate a new document that looks visually similar to the original document.

6. ACKNOWLEDGMENTS

Author AS wishes to express her gratitude to Prof. Sergey Kirshner for the technical discussions on the CRF model and providing help with building the model.

7. REFERENCES

[1] http://typewar.com/stats/typeface_pair/Futura/Gill_Sans.

[2] S. Khoubyari and J. J. Hull. Font and function word identification in document recognition. *Computer Vision and Image Understanding*, 63(1):66–74, January 1996.

[3] J. D. Lafferty, A. McCallum, and F. C. Pereira. Conditional random fields: Probabilistic models for segmenting and labeling sequence data. In *Proceedings of the 18th International Conference on Machine Learning*, San Francisco, California, USA, 282-289 2001.

[4] D. C. Liu and J. Nocedal. On the limited memory BFGS method for large scale optimization. *Mathematical Programming*, 45:503–528, 1989.

[5] R. D. Maesschalck and D. L. M. Delphine Jouan-Rimbaud. The Mahalanobis distance. *Chemometrics and Intelligent Laboratory Systems 50*, pages 1–18, 2000.

[6] A. M. Martinez and A. C. Kak. PCA versus LDA. *IEEE Transactions on Pattern Analysis and Machine Intelligence*, 23(2):228–233, February 2001.

[7] A. Satkhozhina, I. Ahmadullin, J. P. Allebach, Q. Lin, J. Liu, D. Tretter, E. O'Brien-Strain, and A. Hunter. Non-manhattan layout extraction algorithm. In *Proceedings of SPIE 8664, Imaging and Printing in a Web 2.0 World IV*, Burlingame, California, USA, 2013.

[8] M. Schmidt. UGM matlab code for undirected graphical models. http://www.di.ens.fr/ mschmidt/software/ugm.html. 2011.

[9] C. Sutton and A. McCallum. An introduction to conditional random fields. arxiv:1011.4088v1 [stat.ml]. November 2010.

[10] Y. Zhu, T. Tan, and Y. Wang. Font recognition based on global texture analysis. *IEEE Transactions on Pattern Analysis and Machine Intelligence*, 23(10):1192 – 1200, October 2001.

[11] A. W. Zramdini and R. Ingold. Optical font recognition using typographical features. *IEEE Transactions on Pattern Analysis and Machine Intelligence*, 20(8):877–882, August 1998.

Table 2: Font recognition rate for computer-generated test pages

Method	Typeface	Weight	Slope	Size
LDA	0.586	0.819	0.819	0.635
Mahalanobis	0.708	0.819	0.805	0.687
Naïve Bayes	0.344	0.690	0.725	0.583
CRF	0.640	0.904	0.919	0.736

Table 3: Typeface confusion matrix for computer-generated test pages using CRF. Each unit in the table represents one test page. Rows denote ground truth, columns denote recognized typefaces.

Typeface	Garamond	Futura	Franklin Gothic	Helvetica	Rockwell	Cambria	Calibri	Courier New	Times New Roman	Tahoma	Gill Sans MT
Garamond	30	0	4	0	13	3	0	1	4	1	0
Futura	0	30	0	0	0	0	3	0	0	2	21
Franklin Gothic	0	0	46	0	3	5	0	0	0	2	0
Helvetica	0	0	11	16	0	6	1	0	2	18	1
Rockwell	2	0	0	0	44	3	0	5	1	0	0
Cambria	0	0	2	0	6	39	0	0	4	4	1
Calibri	0	0	9	0	0	7	22	0	0	3	15
Courier New	1	0	0	0	0	0	0	55	0	0	0
Times New Roman	7	0	0	0	9	5	0	2	30	3	0
Tahoma	2	0	4	3	10	1	0	1	0	34	1
Gill Sans MT	0	3	1	0	0	0	0	0	0	5	47

A Shape-Based Layout Descriptor for Classifying Spatial Relationships in Handwritten Math

Francisco Álvaro
Instituto Tecnológico de Informática
Universitat Politècnica de València
Valencia, Spain
falvaro@dsic.upv.es

Richard Zanibbi
Department of Computer Science
Rochester Institute of Technology
Rochester, USA
rlaz@cs.rit.edu

ABSTRACT

We consider the difficult problem of classifying spatial relationships between symbols and subexpressions in handwritten mathematical expressions. We first improve existing geometric features based on bounding boxes and center points, normalizing them using the distance between the centers of the two symbols or subexpressions in question. We then propose a novel feature set for layout classification, using polar histograms computed over points in handwritten strokes. A series of experiments are presented in which a Support Vector Machine is used with these new features to classify spatial relationships of five types in the MathBrush corpus (horizontal, superscript, subscript, below, and inside (e.g. in a square root)). The normalized geometric features provide an improvement over previously published results, while the shape-based features provide a natural representation with results comparable to those for the geometric features. Combining the features produced a very small improvement in accuracy.

Categories and Subject Descriptors

I.7.5 [**Document and text processing**]: Document Capture—*Graphics recognition and interpretation*; I.5.4 [**Pattern Recognition**]: Applications—*Computer vision*

General Terms

Design, Experimentation

Keywords

math recognition, spatial relationship classification, shape descriptors

1. INTRODUCTION

Mathematical expression recognition has three primary subproblems [4, 13]: symbol segmentation, symbol recognition and structural analysis. In this paper we focus on classi-

fying spatial relationships between symbols and subexpressions in handwritten expressions, a critical task for structural analysis where the layout of symbols is determined.

For two sets of handwritten strokes representing a pair of subexpressions A and B, our task is to determine their spatial relationship. A or B may be comprised of one or more symbols. We consider five spatial relationships: *horizontal* (AB), *subscript* (A_B), *superscript* (A^B), *below* ($\frac{A}{B}$) and *inside* ($\sqrt{B}$, where A is $\sqrt{\ }$).

Commonly layout in math expressions is classified using bounding box geometry [13]. Simistira *et al.* [11] classify six relationships in handwritten expressions, distinguishing *above* from *below*. We use five relationships, as vertical structures are represented top-down in the MathBrush corpus [8]. They use bounding box geometry for handwritten symbols, normalizing by symbol heights and widths. Vertical centroids for symbols are shifted based on typographic categories (*ascender, descender* or *centered*). Their experiments use a much smaller data set. For typeset math, Aly *et al.* [2] distinguish just horizontal, subscript and superscript relationships using bounding box geometry normalized by virtual ascenders and descenders, with high accuracy.

In this work, we introduce a new normalization for the geometric features of Álvaro *et al.* [1]. We then propose a novel set of shape-based features. Similar shape-based features have been use to detect typographic/layout classes for symbols [10], symbol retrieval [9], symbol segmentation [7], and expression matching [6]. We are not aware of shape-based features that have been applied to spatial relation classification for math expressions.

Experimental results show that the proposed normalization and the novel shape-based descriptor provide competitive results. The combination of both sets of features resulted in a 2.7% mean classification error (10-fold cross-validation) for isolated subexpression pairs.

2. FEATURE DESCRIPTIONS

In this section, we describe geometric features based on the bounding boxes of subexpressions, and a second representation based on the actual shapes of handwritten strokes.

2.1 Geometric Features: Bounding Boxes

Álvaro *et al.* [1] define nine geometric features for spatial relationship classification using a normalization factor F, shown in Figure 1. Originally F was the height of the parent (usually, the leftmost) region A. It is particularly difficult to distinguish horizontal, subscript and superscript relationships, and the difference between the vertical centers

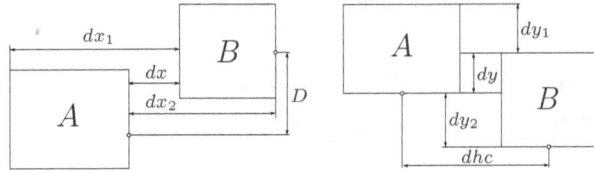

$$H = \frac{\text{height}(B)}{F}; \quad D = \frac{\text{cen}_\text{v}(A) - \text{cen}_\text{v}(B)}{F}; \quad dhc = \frac{\text{cen}_\text{h}(A) - \text{cen}_\text{h}(B)}{F}$$

$$\text{features} = [H, D, dhc, \tfrac{dx}{F}, \tfrac{dx_1}{F}, \tfrac{dx_2}{F}, \tfrac{dy}{F}, \tfrac{dy_1}{F}, \tfrac{dy_2}{F}]$$

Figure 1: Geometric features from bounding boxes of subexpressions A and B using normalization F

of A and B (feature D in Figure 1) has an important role in discriminating these layout classes.

To improve the placement of vertical centroids, symbols are divided into four typographic categories: ascendant (d, λ), descendant (p, μ), normal $(x, +)$ and middle $(7, \Pi)$. For *normal* symbols the centroid is set to the vertical centroid. For *ascendant* symbols the centroid is shifted downward to $(centroid + bottom)/2$. Likewise, for *descendant* symbols the centroid is shifted upward to $(centroid + top)/2$. Finally, for *middle* symbols, the vertical centroid is defined as $(top + bottom)/2$.

In the case of short symbols (e.g. fraction bars), using the height of A for normalization F leads to poor results. We propose a new normalization factor, the distance between the centers of the bounding boxes of the subexpressions. This is more robust against size variations in handwritten symbols.

2.2 Shape Features: Polar Histograms

Many shape descriptors have been defined for image retrieval and object recognition in images [12]. In this section we define a new shape-based feature that is similar to shape contexts [3, 12]. We modify the polar shape matrix [5], which provides a powerful descriptor that is invariant under translation, rotation and scaling. However, we wish to apply this descriptor to determine the relationship between two stroke sets whose their relative position is important. As a result, we do not want rotation invariance.

Given two sets of strokes A and B, let G_A and G_B be the center of mass of their corresponding shapes (i.e. stroke sample points). Using $G = (G_A + G_B)/2$ as a center, we draw n circles with radii equally spaced up to the maximum radius containing A and B. Moving counterclockwise, draw radii dividing each circle into m equal arcs. This descriptor is encoded as a matrix $\mathcal{M}$ such that each row represents a circle and each column represent the angle starting from 0 degrees. Each cell $\mathcal{M}(i, j)$ has one of three values obtained by majority vote of the points located in each bin:

$$\mathcal{M}(i,j) = \begin{cases} -1 & \text{more points from set } A \text{ than } B \\ 0 & \text{empty bin} \\ +1 & \textbf{tie}, \text{ or more points from set } B \text{ than } A \end{cases}$$

Figure 2 illustrates the effect of grid resolution on the polar histogram feature. We see that as the grid size is increased, the representation is more detailed, producing a warped image of the strokes.

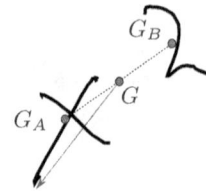

Symbol pair (centers for x, 2 and midpoint shown)

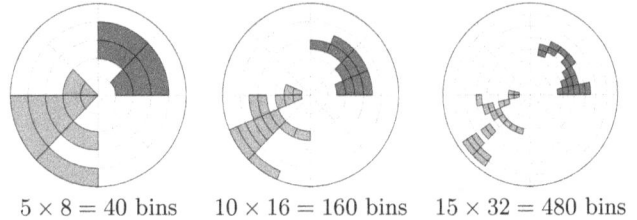

$5 \times 8 = 40$ bins $\qquad$ $10 \times 16 = 160$ bins $\qquad$ $15 \times 32 = 480$ bins

Figure 2: Varying distance (n) $\times$ angle (m) resolution in a polar histogram layout descriptor. Values shown using green (-1), red (+1), and white (0)

The $n \times m$ features are reduced using Principal Component Analysis (PCA). Figure 3 illustrates the proposed descriptor for the five spatial relations considered.

3. EXPERIMENTS

In this section we evaluate our proposed features for spatial relationship classification. The MathBrush database [8] is a public dataset containing $4,654$ online handwritten mathematical expressions. Each expression has several spatial relations between symbols and subexpressions. There were $21,238$ spatial relationships in the data set, classified according to the classes shown in Figure 3.

We use cross validation, splitting the dataset randomly into 10 partitions while keeping the distribution of spatial relations roughly uniform over the partitions. The training set contained 80% of the samples for each class, and the remaining 20% comprised the test set. We used a Support Vector Machine (SVM) classifier with a Gaussian kernel in our experiments. In order to tune the parameters for train-

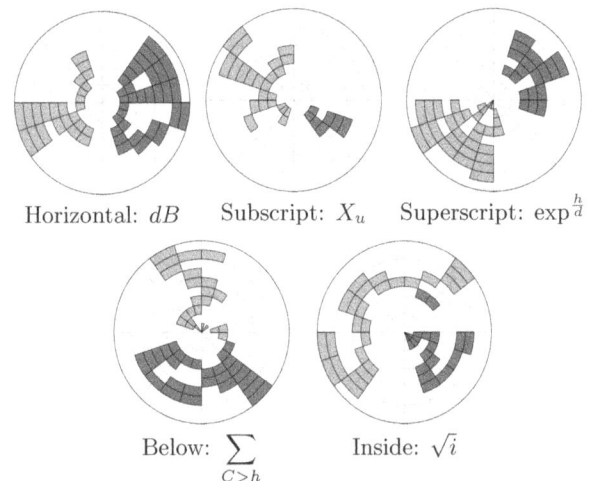

Horizontal: dB $\qquad$ Subscript: X_u $\qquad$ Superscript: $\exp^{\frac{h}{d}}$

Below: $\sum_{C > h}$ $\qquad$ Inside: $\sqrt{i}$

Figure 3: Polar histogram layout descriptors

ing the SVM classifier or to select the parameters of the shape-based features, we also divided the training set (80%) into 70% for training and 10% for a validation set. That split also kept the distribution of the classes, and the best parameters in the validation set were used to finally train the complete training set and compute the error using the test set for each one of the cross-validation partitions.

3.1 Geometric Feature Results

We performed several experiments to test the geometric features described in Section 2.1. First, we computed the classification error using the baseline normalization described in [1] such that F is equal to the height of the parent region A (GEO$_1$). Then, we classified the spatial relations using the new normalization factor, the distance between the center of the bounding boxes (GEO$_2$). Finally, we also extracted the geometric features GEO$_2$ without using the information about symbol categories (ascendant, descendant, normal, middle) in order to measure the influence of this decision (GEO$_3$).

The results in Table 1 show the new normalization by center point distance decreasing the mean classification error rate from 3.62% to 2.84%. The results also show a slight decrease in error when computing a vertical centroid based on symbol typographic categories, with the error decreasing from 3.48% to 2.84%.

3.2 Shape-Based Feature Results

The polar histogram-based descriptor presented in Section 2.2 has parameters that need tuning, specifically the number of circles n and angles m, and the number of principal components d to select. We performed a grid search for several sizes of the descriptor ($n = \{3, 5, 10, 15, 20\}$ and $m = \{8, 12, 16, 20, 24, 28, 32\}$), and for each size, different numbers of principal components were also tested (variance explained from 10% to 90% in increments of 10%). We used one of the 10 partitions extracted from the cross-validation experimentation to tune these parameters (see Figure 4).

We chose $n = 15$, $m = 20$ and $d = 35$ (50% of total variance) as the parameters to perform the cross validation experiments for the shape-based geometric features (SHP). For small grid sizes, results were best when high percentage of variance were accounted for in the PCA dimensions (70%-90%). However, as the grid size increased the variance in bin counts also increased, with the best results being obtained when keeping components covering roughly 50% of the variance.

Table 1: MathBrush symbol relationship classification results (10-fold cross validation). For each feature the number of features (#) and whether typographic symbol classes are used (Cat.) are shown

Feature	#	Cat.	% Error ($\mu \pm \sigma$)
GEO$_3$: $F = \text{dist(centers)}$	9	No	3.48 ± 0.39
GEO$_2$: $F = \text{dist(centers)}$	9	Yes	2.84 ± 0.16
GEO$_1$: $F = \text{height(A)}$	9	Yes	3.62 ± 0.34
SHP: $n = 15, m = 20$	35	No	3.34 ± 0.21
GEO$_2$ + SHP	44	Yes	2.70 ± 0.29

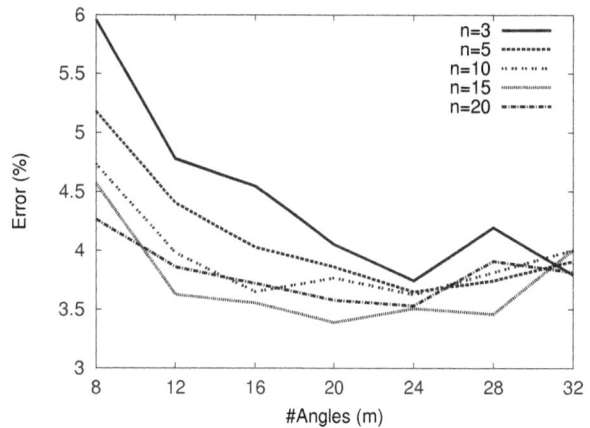

Figure 4: Fitting polar histogram parameters. Error for the best PCA dimension set for each m (angles) $\times$ n (circles) histogram is shown

The polar histogram features obtained a mean classification error of 3.34% (Table 1), without including symbol typographic classes; this is comparable to the accuracy obtained using the geometric features without symbol typographic classes, where error was 3.48%. Interestingly, the standard deviation in error was half as large as that for the bounding box-based features in this case, but within a narrow range (0.21% vs 0.39%).

Table 2 shows the confusion matrix for the GEO$_2$ cross validation experiments. As expected, most errors are produced in the classification of Horizontal, Subscript and Superscript relationships, whereas Below and Inside relationships have few errors.

The SVM classifier is influenced by the prior probabilities of the classes in the training data (Horizontal: 68.9%, Subscript: 5.9%, Superscript: 9.0%, Below: 12.1%, Inside: 4.1%). The Horizontal relationship represents about 69% of the samples, and its recognition error was very low. The Superscript relation had a 6.3% error, but it is the Subscript relation that is most challenging, with more than 20% error: the Horizontal/Subscript confusion is by far the most frequent.

Table 2 also shows the confusion matrix for the shape-based features. The classification errors follow a very similar distribution. Errors in Subscript and Superscript relations are slightly higher, as well as for Inside. The error rate for Below relationships in ground truth is lower, but the classifier has more false positives for the Below relationship.

We tried adding to the shape-based descriptor the information about symbols categories in the relation by displacing the centroids G_A or G_B following the methodology described in Section 2.1. However, this led to weaker results.

Given the good results for both feature types, which use quite different representations, a natural next step was to merge them. This combination led to small improvements in mean classification error to 2.7% (see Table 1). This is unlikely to be significantly different from the GEO$_2$ result, due to the larger standard deviation (0.29% vs. 0.16%).

3.3 Discussion

The polar histogram descriptor obtained results comparable to the geometric features when no symbol information is

Table 2: Confusion matrices for GEO$_2$ (geometric) and SHP (shape) descriptors (10-fold cross validation). Ground truth labels are shown along the rows (FN: false negative rate, FP: false positive rate)

GT	GEO$_2$ Output						SHP Output					
	Hor	Sub	Sup	Below	Inside	FN	Hor	Sub	Sup	Below	Inside	FN
Hor	28888	196	149	7	8	1.2%	28863	251	130	4		1.3%
Sub	498	1993		25	2	20.8%	581	1912		25		24.1%
Sup	239		3597	2		6.3%	322		3514	2		8.4%
Below	18	42	4	5083	9	1.4%	17	23	2	5114		0.8%
Inside	9				1707	0.5%	37	4		22	1653	3.7%
FP	2.6%	10.6%	4.1%	0.7%	1.1%		3.2%	12.7%	3.8%	1.0%	0%	

used, but was outperformed by the geometric features when typographic classes are used to move vertical centroids. One possible direction for future work is to try and incorporate this information into the shape descriptor.

From the results, the proposed descriptors are not sufficient on their own for spatial relationship classification. Language models may be needed to distinguish cases where the geometric conditions represent different relations depending on the symbols involved (e.g. the horizontal relation 'Px' vs. the subscript relation 'p_x').

However, there are opportunities to improve our descriptors, for example using continuous values for the bins in our polar histograms. For both feature types presented, it would be good to find better ways to identify the writing line, middle line (e.g. top of a lower-case 'x'), or a point between these in order to better handle the most common confusions (Horizontal vs. Subscript or Superscript).

4. CONCLUSIONS AND FUTURE WORK

In this paper we dealt with the classification of spatial relations between handwritten mathematical symbols and subexpressions. We presented a new normalization for a set of geometric features and a novel set of shape-based features, which improve upon previously published results. Our new polar histogram-based shape feature provides comparable results to geometric features when no information about symbol typographic categories (e.g. ascender) is used. The combination of both sets of features led to a small improvement in accuracy. In future work, we will consider including symbol typographic classes into the shape-based feature representation, and adding a rejection class, to detect when two subexpressions are unrelated. Finally, our features could be applied to printed expressions and compared with earlier work [2].

5. ACKNOWLEDGMENTS

This work was partially supported by the Spanish MEC under the STraDA research project (TIN2012-37475-C02-01), an FPU grant (AP2009-4363), and by the National Science Foundation (USA) under Grant No. IIS-1016815. The authors thank Lei Hu for helpful discussions.

6. REFERENCES

[1] F. Álvaro, J.A. Sánchez, and J.M. Benedí. Recognition of on-line handwritten mathematical expressions using 2D stochastic context-free grammars and hidden Markov models. *Pattern Recognition Letters*, 2012.

[2] W. Aly, S. Uchida, and M. Suzuki. Identifying subscripts and superscripts in mathematical documents. *Mathematics in Computer Science*, 2(2):195–209, 2008.

[3] S. Belongie, J. Malik, and J. Puzicha. Shape matching and object recognition using shape contexts. *IEEE Trans. Pattern Analysis and Machine Intelligence*, 24(4):509–522, 2002.

[4] K. Chan and D. Yeung. Mathematical expression recognition: a survey. *Int'l J. Document Analysis and Recognition*, 3(1):3–15, 2000.

[5] A. Goshtasby. Description and discrimination of planar shapes using shape matrices. *IEEE Trans. Pattern Analysis and Machine Intelligence*, 7(6):738–743, 1985.

[6] N. S. T. Hirata and W. Y. Honda. Automatic labeling of handwritten mathematical symbols via expression matching. In *Int'l Conf. Graph-Based Representations in Pattern Recognition*, pp. 295–304, 2011.

[7] L. Hu and R. Zanibbi. Segmenting Handwritten Math Symbols Using AdaBoost and Multi-Scale Shape Context Features. *Int'l Conf. Document Analysis and Recognition*, to appear, 2013.

[8] S. MacLean, G. Labahn, E. Lank, M. Marzouk, and D. Tausky. Grammar-based techniques for creating ground-truthed sketch corpora. *Int'l J. Document Analysis and Recognition*, 14:65–74, 2011.

[9] S. Marinai, B. Miotti, and G. Soda. Using earth mover's distance in the bag-of-visual-words model for mathematical symbol retrieval. In *Int'l Conf. Document Analysis and Recognition*, pp. 1309–1313, 2011.

[10] L. Ouyang and R. Zanibbi. Identifying layout classes for mathematical symbols using layout context. *IEEE Western New York Image Processing Workshop*, 2009.

[11] F. Simistira, V. Papavassiliou, V. Katsouros, and G. Carayannis. Structural analysis of online handwritten mathematical symbols based on support vector machines. In *Document Recognition and Retrieval XX*, 2013.

[12] M. Yang, K. Kpalma, and J. Ronsin. A survey of shape feature extraction techniques. In P.-Y. Yin, editor, *Pattern Recognition Techniques, Technology and Applications*, pp. 43–90, 2008.

[13] R. Zanibbi and D. Blostein. Recognition and retrieval of mathematical expressions. *Int'l J. Document Analysis and Recognition*, 15(4):331–357, 2012.

Evaluating Glyph Binarizations Based on Their Properties

Shira Faigenbaum§, Arie Shaus§, Barak Sober§, Eli Turkel
The Department of Applied Mathematics
Tel Aviv University
Tel Aviv 69978, Israel
+972-3-640-6024
alecsan1@post.tau.ac.il, ashaus@post.tau.ac.il,
baraksov@post.tau.ac.il, turkel@post.tau.ac.il
§ These authors contributed equally to this work.

Eli Piasetzky
The Sackler School of
Physics and Astronomy
Tel Aviv University
Tel Aviv 69978, Israel
+972-3-640-9428
eip@tauphy.tau.ac.il

ABSTRACT

Document binary images, created by different algorithms, are commonly evaluated based on a pre-existing ground truth. Previous research found several pitfalls in this methodology and suggested various approaches addressing the issue. This article proposes an alternative binarization quality evaluation solution for binarized glyphs, circumventing the ground truth. Our method relies on intrinsic properties of binarized glyphs. The features used for quality assessment are stroke width consistency, presence of small connected components (stains), edge noise, and the average edge curvature. Linear and tree-based combinations of these features are also considered. The new methodology is tested and shown to be nearly as sound as human experts' judgments.

Categories and Subject Descriptors

I.7.5 [**Document Capture**]: Document analysis

Keywords

Binarization, glyph, evaluation, quality measure, ground truth.

1. INTRODUCTION

The plethora of available binarization algorithms results in different outputs for the same document image. The ensuing need for comparing binarizations, gives rise to the existing ground truth-based (GT) evaluation methodology [1-3]. The evaluation is based on a manual GT creation, and on various GT-versus-binarization measures (e.g., F-measure, PSNR, Distance Reciprocal Distortion, Misclassification Penalty, etc.). Several recent papers [4-6] performed a detailed analysis of this approach, stressing its inherent weaknesses such as subjectivity and the inherent inconsistency within the GT creation process. Among the alternative solutions suggested, are skeleton-based GT variants (maintaining some degree of human intervention) [7-8], automatic GT creation (via another binarization procedure) [9], creation of synthetic document images out of existing GT (applicable if noise model exists) [10-11] and goal-directed approach, e.g. assessing OCR results (applicable if an OCR engine is available) [12]. Trier and Taxt [13] proposed a method somewhat reminiscent of the one specified herein, yet it was performed manually upon visual inspection of binarizations.

This article provides an approach which eliminates the need for GT. The document binarizations are judged automatically, based on the intrinsic properties of their glyphs. Four estimates are introduced: stroke width consistency, proportion of stains, average edge curvature, and proportion of edge noise. In certain scenarios, these may be utilized on their own right. Alternatively, these measures can be combined in order to provide the relative ranking of the binarizations. Producing such a model may involve a train-test procedure, dependent on the task under consideration (human epigraphic analysis, alphabet reconstruction, OCR, etc.).

The purpose of this study is to provide the best available binary image on a glyph scale. The challenging problem of glyph regions extraction, along with its related topics of concern such as broken strokes and touching characters, is outside the scope of this article (the papers [14-16] deal with some of these issues).

2. SUGGESTED GLYPH MEASURES

2.1 Measures Definitions

We start by defining independent binarization quality measures, correlating to common human perception. Four measures, pertaining to different aspects of binarized images, are proposed and formalized. We will work on small binarized images, each containing a single glyph. This can be an outcome of any segmentation algorithm, such as [14-16]. The foreground (valued at 0) and the background (valued at 255) will be denoted respectively as F and B, with $p = (x, y)$ a pixel coordinate.

2.1.1 Stroke width consistency

The local scale consistency of a character stroke width is closely related to the quality of the binarized character. Indeed, partially erased letters, or the presence of stains may introduce discontinuities in stroke width. The idea is not simply to measure the width of a stroke at every point, but to assess the smoothness of its change between adjacent pixels. The measure is defined by the following algorithm (though devised independently, our first step is reminiscent of [17], while steps 2 and 3 are original).

Step 1 – Evaluate the stroke width $SW(p)$ for each $p \in F$:

- For each angle $\alpha \in \{0°, 45°, 90°, 135°\}$, examine the line segments with inclination α passing through p and restricted to F. Among these, denote the *longest* segment as $seg(p, \alpha)$.

- Define $SW(p) = \min_{\alpha} \|seg(p, \alpha)\|_2$.

Step 2 – Calculate the stroke width gradient magnitude $G(p)$:

- Calculate directional derivatives $G_x(p)$ and $G_y(p)$.

- Define the gradient magnitude with respect to L_∞ norm:

$$G(p) = \max(|G_x(p)|, |G_y(p)|)$$

Step 3 – Apply the measure: $M_{SWC} = \underset{p \in F}{mean}(G(p))$

Note that given a clean binarization with gradually changing stroke widths, $G(p)$ yields low values, resulting in a small M_{SWC}.

2.1.2 Stains proportion

The existence of black spots within a white background, or vice versa, is an indication of either an imperfect binarization or the presence of noise. In what follows, we will consider *the stains relative area in pixels*, denoted below as $\|...\|$. While stains count may be used instead, according to our experiments, this measure performs poorly.

The image is partitioned into a set of Connected Components $CC = \{cc_i\}_{i=1}^{N}$; these belong to either F or B. The set of *Stain CCs* is defined as: $SCC = \{cc_i \in CC \mid \|cc_i\| \le T\}$. Throughout our experiments, the value of T was set to 0.5% of the glyph image size.

The measure definition is: $M_{SP} = \sum_{cc_j \in SCC} \|cc_j\| \Big/ \sum_{cc_i \in CC} \|cc_i\|$

2.1.3 Average edge curvature

The "ideal" letter is expected to possess a smooth edge. This is tightly related to the average edge curvature (herein, we use its absolute value):

$$\kappa = \left|\frac{dT}{ds}\right| = \left|\frac{d\theta}{ds}\right| \cong \left|\frac{\Delta\theta}{\Delta s}\right| \qquad (1)$$

where T is the normalized tangent of the edge curve, θ is the tangent angle, and s is the arclength parameter. The computation of the average edge curvature is as follows:

Step 1 – Find the edge via 4-connectivity erosion of F:

$$E = F \setminus erosion(F) \qquad (2)$$

Step 2 – Calculate local angle:
For each pixel $p \in E$, and for each pair of its neighboring pixels $p_1, p_2 \in E$ (assuming 8-connectivity), define the unit vectors $v_k(p) = (p_k - p)/\|p_k - p\|_2$ for $k = 1, 2$. Next, we find $\psi(p)$, the angle between $v_1(p)$ and $v_2(p)$:

$$\psi(p) = \arccos\langle v_1(p), v_2(p)\rangle \qquad (3)$$

The angle $\Delta\theta(p)$, used for the curvature definition, is:

$$\Delta\theta(p) = \pi - \psi(p) \qquad (4)$$

Due to the definition of arccos, $\psi(p) \in [0, \pi]$ and $\Delta\theta(p) \in [0, \pi]$.

Step 3 – Approximate the local curvature:

$$\kappa(p) \cong \Delta\theta(p)/\Delta s(p) \qquad (5)$$

Step 4 – Apply the measure:

$$M_{AEC} = \underset{p \in E}{mean}(\kappa(p)) = \sum_{p \in E} \Delta s(p)\kappa(p) \Big/ \sum_{p \in E} \Delta s(p) \qquad (6)$$

Note that the following also holds:

$$M_{AEC} = \pi - \underset{p \in E}{mean}\big(\arccos\langle v_1(p), v_2(p)\rangle\big) \qquad (7)$$

It should be stated that in certain cases, $p \in E$ might possess more than two neighboring pixels. In such a case, we account for all possible neighboring pairs in Steps 2-4.

2.1.4 Edge noise proportion

Another suggested property is the presence of typical edge noise, which often correlates with the overall quality of the binarization. The paper [18] suggests a procedure involving 12 different convolution kernels, approximating the amount of such noise. Below, we suggest a simplified method, involving 4-connectivity morphological operations.

Step 1 – Find the edge utilizing dilation and erosion of F:

$$\bar{E} = dilation(F) \setminus erosion(F) \qquad (8)$$

Step 2 – Calculate a noise estimate (cl=closure, op=opening):

$$N = \big(cl(F) \setminus F\big) \cup \big(F \setminus op(F)\big) = cl(F) \setminus op(F) \qquad (9)$$

The closure attaches isolated B pixels to F, while the opening performs a dual operation. N provides a set of all isolated pixels.

Step 3 – Apply the measure: $M_{ENP} = \|N\| \big/ \|\bar{E}\|$

2.1.5 Monochromatic binarizations

In general, undesirable scenarios of an almost completely black or white binarization (e.g. due to illumination conditions) should also be addressed for all four measures. Accordingly, cases where an insufficient number of either F or B pixels exist, were detected and handled in the following fashion. Assuming 4-connectivity, if a double-dilation of F left no B pixels, or if a double-erosion of F left no F pixels, all the measures were set to $Inf = 32768$.

2.2 Measure Combinations

The measures presented above can be applied on their own right, each assessing a different glyph characteristic. In fact, in certain settings, we have seen some of them (in particular M_{ENP}) producing judgments comparable to human appraisals. Conversely, these measures can be combined into a joint score or classifier, depending on the task under consideration. These may vary according to the type of writing in question (printed or handwritten), medium, corpora, noise characteristic, binarizations end goal (epigraphical research, glyph reconstruction, OCR), etc. Subsequently, we do not suggest that the combinations derived below to be the ultimate model in all conceivable cases. We do suggest a procedure to derive models for settings comparable to ours. With certain adjustments, these ideas may also be applicable for training binarization quality control apparatus for other tasks.

The combinations dealt with below are linear and tree models, used due to their simplicity. These models require training and testing phases, based on experts' estimations. Such a procedure is presented in the next section.

3. EXPERIMENTAL SECTION

3.1 Motivation and Data Set

The motivation behind this research was an attempt at ranking binarizations according to their suitability for human and computer-based handwriting analysis. Visually appealing binarizations, faithful to the document images, were preferred.

Our database consisted of segmented glyphs, along with their binarizations. We used glyphs originating from two different First Temple Period Hebrew inscriptions: 50 images (glyphs) were taken from Arad #1 [19], while 47 images (glyphs) were obtained from Lachish #3 [20]. The segmentation into individual characters was performed via algorithm [16]. The state of preservation of these ink-over clay samples was poor, presenting a challenge for our methodology.

The 9 binarizations in use were: Otsu [21], Bernsen [22] with window sizes (in pixels) of $w = 50$ and $w = 200$, Niblack [23] with $w = 50$ and $w = 200$, Sauvola [24] with $w = 50$ and $w = 200$, as well as our own binarization [16] with or without unspeckle stage.

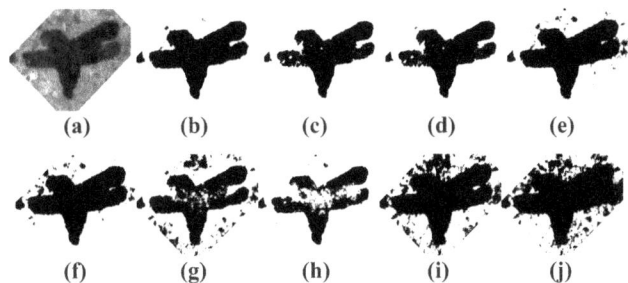

Figure 1. Expert's ranking of one glyph, in decreasing quality order. (a) Original image, (b) Sauvola $w = 200$, (c) Shaus et al. [16] inc. unspeckle stage, (d) Shaus et al., (e) Otsu, (f) Niblack $w = 200$, (g) Niblack $w = 50$, (h) Sauvola $w = 50$, (i) Bernsen $w = 50$, (j) Bernsen $w = 200$.

From the *97 original grayscale images*, a database of *873 (97 x 9) binary images* was constructed. Each set of 9 binarizations, denoted herein as a "binarization block", was judged independently by three different experts. The experts' rankings (from 1=high, up to 9=low) were based on their prior epigraphical knowledge. An example of a single expert's opinion is presented in Fig. 1.

Constructing such a data set with manual ranking information for different binarization procedures is a labor-intensive procedure. This explains the relatively modest size of our database.

3.2 Ranking Prediction

The experiment attempted at creating a model matching the three experts' ranking. The model types under consideration were linear and tree-based regressions [25]. These models used the 4 *rankings* based on the measures M_{SWC}, M_{SP}, M_{AEC} and M_{ENP}. The utilization of rankings, rather than measure values, provides a common scale across different letters. The experiment consisted of model selection and model verification stages. Both necessitate the prerequisites specified in the next sub-section.

3.2.1 Prerequisites

Input data:

As stated previously, each binarization block (containing 9 binarizations) for each of the 97 letters, had 3 expert rankings. Resulting vectors of length 873, containing rankings of binarization blocks in a stacked manner, are denoted as R_1, R_2, R_3 (one for each expert). For training purposes, a combined experts ranking $R_{experts}$ was derived. First, $R_{mean} = mean(R_1, R_2, R_3)$, was calculated (coordinate-wise), possibly containing non-integer values. Then, a re-ranking of R_{mean} enforced scores of $1...9$ within each binarization block, resulting in $R_{experts}$. Such process is denoted below as "re-ranking procedure". In addition, the 4 different measures produced their own rankings for every binarization block, yielding the corresponding vectors R_{SWC}, R_{SP}, R_{AEC} and R_{ENP}.

Model score:

A model m is scored in the following fashion. A prediction produced by the model is re-ranked, resulting in R_m, which is then compared with the experts ranking via standard linear (cor) or Kendall (τ) [26] correlations:

$$c_m = \min_{i=1..3}\left(cor(R_i, R_m)\right), \quad \tau_m = \min_{i=1..3}\left(\tau(R_i, R_m)\right)$$

3.2.2 Model selection stage

Model specifications:

Both linear and tree-based regression models were considered. The independent variables were R_{SWC}, R_{SP}, R_{AEC} and R_{ENP}, while the dependent variable was $R_{experts}$. The linear regression models differed from each other by the presence or absence of independent variables (*15 possible combinations*). The tree regression models differed from each other by the presence or absence of independent variables, as well as by their depths (2 configurations were attempted: default setting of [25], as well as a "forced" tree with 9 leaves). This resulted in a total of *30 tree models* under consideration.

Selection procedure:

The model corresponding to the highest c_m and τ_m scores was selected. As will be seen, in this experiment, both scores resulted in the same selected model.

Success criteria:

Since even human experts differ in their judgments, we do not expect the best model to perform flawlessly, but in a "human-like" fashion. Our golden standards are the *minimal* correlations between pairs of human experts, denoted as c_{expert} and τ_{expert}.

Hence, our optimal model is expected to adhere to:

$$c_m \leq 0.8 \cdot \min_{1 \leq i < j \leq 3}\left(cor(R_i, R_j)\right) = 0.8 \cdot c_{expert} \quad (10)$$

$$\tau_m \leq 0.8 \cdot \min_{1 \leq i < j \leq 3}\left(\tau(R_i, R_j)\right) = 0.8 \cdot \tau_{expert} \quad (11)$$

Selected model:

The selected model, for both c_m and τ_m scores, was a tree with 9 leaves, of depth 6. The tree used rankings from all 4 measures, with the most important one (used for the upper splits) being R_{ENP}, with $c_m = 0.678$ and $\tau_m = 0.543$. Since $c_{expert} = 0.768$ and $\tau_{expert} = 0.634$, the criteria was met.

3.2.3 Model verification stage

The selected *model type* (a tree with 9 leaves and all independent variables) was bootstrapped in order to check its robustness. Each iteration performed a 50-50 test/train separation on the binary blocks level (thus, all the binarizations of a single glyph were assigned either to train or to test data, avoiding possible bias). Subsequently, a *new model* was trained and tested.

The bootstrap included 1000 iterations, resulting in pvalue=0.05 confidence intervals of [0.582, 0.74] for c_m, and [0.454, 0.610] for τ_m. These indicate the robustness of our model.

4. SUMMARY AND FUTURE RESEARCH DIRECTIONS

Following inherent obstacles in GT-based quality evaluation of binary images, we proposed a solution based on several intrinsic properties of binary glyphs. Four binarization quality measures were introduced: stroke width consistency, proportion of stains or edge noise, and average edge curvature. In certain scenarios, these may suffice on their own right. Alternatively, a combination of these scores can be trained for specific purposes, such as paleographical analysis, glyph reconstruction or OCR. For our uses, a tree-based model produced adequate and robust results. Some shortcomings and potential enhancements can be proposed:

- The results of different binarization algorithms, as well as comparison with other methodologies, can be elaborated upon.
- The approach is not limited to the glyph level. If an extraction of words, sentences, or text areas are given, the measures remain applicable. However, this might involve issues such as illumination equalization and text size normalization.
- The size of our training/testing set is limited due to the reasons stated above. A further enlargement of our database is planned in the near future. In particular, testing in different settings (e.g. printed characters) may provide interesting insights related to our methodology. Moreover, if a labeled database is available, an individual combination of measures can be trained for every character, taking into account their different features.
- A potential hazard is an undesired "tailoring" of the binarization algorithms according to the evaluation methodologies employed (e.g. post-processing via median filter). Indeed, any quality measure can result in a binarization algorithm trained (in fact, over-fitted) to target the measure.

5. ACKNOWLEDGMENTS

The research was partially funded by the European Research Council under the European Community's Seventh Framework Programme (FP7/2007-2013)/ERC grant agreement no. 229418. This study was also supported by a generous donation of Mr. Jacques Chahine, made through the French Friends of Tel Aviv University. Arie Shaus is grateful to the Azrieli Foundation for the award of an Azrieli Fellowship.

6. REFERENCES

[1] Gatos, B., Ntirogiannis, K. and Pratikakis, I. 2009. ICDAR 2009 document image binarization contest (DIBCO 2009). In *Proc. of ICDAR '09*, 1375-1382.

[2] Pratikakis, I., Gatos, B. and Ntirogiannis, K. 2010. H-DIBCO 2010 – Handwritten document image binarization competition. In *Proc. of ICFHR '10*, 727-732.

[3] Pratikakis, I., Gatos, B. and Ntirogiannis, K. 2011. ICDAR 2011 document image binarization contest (DIBCO 2011). In *Proc. of ICDAR '11*, 1506-1510.

[4] Barney Smith, E. H. 2010. An analysis of binarization ground truthing. In *Proc. of DAS '10*, 27-33.

[5] Barney Smith, E. H. and An, C. 2012. Effect of "Ground Truth" on image binarization. In *Proc. of DAS '12*, 250-254.

[6] Shaus, A., Turkel, E. and Piasetzky, E. 2012. Quality evaluation of facsimiles of Hebrew First Temple period inscriptions. In *Proc. of DAS '12*, 170-174.

[7] Ntirogiannis, K., Gatos, B., and Pratikakis, 2008. An objective evaluation methodology for document image binarization techniques. In *Proc. of DAS '08*, 217-224.

[8] Ntirogiannis, K., Gatos, B., and Pratikakis, 2013. Performance evaluation methodology for historical document image Binarization. *IEEE Transactions On Image Processing*, Vol. 22(2).

[9] Ben Messaoud, I., El Abed, H., Amiri, H. and Märgner, 2011. A design of a preprocessing framework for large database of historical documents. In *Proc. of HIP '11*, 177-183.

[10] Stathis, P., Kavallieratou, E. and Papamarkos, N. 2009. An evaluation technique for binarization algorithms. *J. of Universal Computer Science 14*, No. 18, pp. 3011-3030.

[11] Paredes, R. and Kavallieratou, E. 2010. ICFHR 2010 contest: Quantitative evaluation of binarization algorithms. In *Proc. of ICFHR 2010*, 733-736.

[12] Trier, Ø. D. and Jain, A. K. 1995. Goal-directed evaluation of binarization methods, *IEEE PAMI 17*, No. 12, 1191-12

[13] Trier, Ø. D. and Taxt, T. 1995. Evaluation of binarization methods for document images. *IEEE PAMI 17, No. 3*. 31-36.

[14] Breuel, T. M., 2001. Segmentation of handprinted letter strings using a dynamic programming algorithm. In *Proc. of DAS 2001*, 821-826.

[15] Casey, R.G. and Lecolinet, E, 1996. A survey of methods and strategies in character segmentation, *IEEE PAMI 18*, No. 7, 690-706

[16] Shaus, A., Turkel, E. and Piasetzky E. 2012. Binarization of First Temple Period inscriptions - performance of existing algorithms and a new registration based scheme. In *Proc. of ICFHR '12*, 641-646.

[17] Epshtein, B., Ofek, E. and Wexler, Y. 2010. Detecting Text in Natural Scenes with Stroke Width Transform. In *Proc. of CVPR '10*.

[18] McGillivary, C., Hale, C. and Barney Smith, E. H. 2009. Edge Noise in Document Images. In *Proc. of AND '09*, 17-24.

[19] Aharoni, Y. 1981. *Arad Inscriptions*. Israel Exploration Society.

[20] Torczyner, H. et al. 1938. *Lachish I: The Lachish Letters*. London.

[21] Otsu, N. 1979. A threshold selection method from gray-level histograms. *IEEE Trans. Systems Man Cybernet. Vol. 9 (1)*. 62-66.

[22] Bernsen, J. 1986. Dynamic thresholding of grey-level images. In *Proc. of ICPR '86*. 1251-1255.

[23] Niblack, W. 1986. *An Introduction to Digital Image Processing*. Prentice-Hall, 115-116.

[24] Sauvola, J. and Pietikainen, M. 2000. Adaptive document image binarization. *Pattern Recognition, Vol. 33*. 225-236.

[25] Tree model, R version 2.12.2. http://www.r-project.org

[26] Kendall, M. 1938. A New Measure of Rank Correlation. Biometrika 30 (1-2), 81-93.

Functional, Extensible, SVG-based Variable Documents

John Lumley

6 Raleigh Rise, Portishead
BRISTOL BS20 6LA, UK
john@johnlumley.net

ABSTRACT

Architectures for documents that vary in response to binding to data, or user interaction, are usually based on limited layout semantics, such as text flows, and simple data variability, such as replacing reserved constructs. By using a generalised XML graphical representation (SVG), decorated with an extensible set of layout intent declarations, and with embedded fragments of XSLT decorated with program retention directives, it is possible to produce self-contained documents that are both highly flexible and extensible and can adapt their presentation to multiple stages of data binding, as well as user interaction. The essentials of the architecture are presented with examples and details of the necessary implementation and support tools, most of which are written in declarative, functional XSLT. Recent developments in XSLT technologies make it possible to consider such documents operating within unmodified browsers - techniques are discussed.

Categories and Subject Descriptors

I.7.2[Computing Methodologies]: Document Preparation — *desktop publishing, format and notation, languages and systems, markup languages, scripting languages*

General Terms: Languages

Keywords: XSLT, SVG, Document construction, Functional programming

1. INTRODUCTION

This paper outlines an architecture for defining variable documents that i) have highly extensible presentational semantics, ii) have few programmatic limitations, iii) can be partially or repeatedly bound to data and adapt content and presentation accordingly, iv) are 'self-contained' and v) require minimal addition to existing standard formats.

DocEng'13, September 10-13 2013, Florence, Italy
Copyright is held by the owner/author(s). Publication rights licensed to ACM.
ACM 978-1-4503-1789-4/13/09...$15.00.
http://dx.doi.org/10.1145/2494266.2494274

Many architectures for variable and customised documents have been developed over the past thirty years both for printing and web-delivered consumption of information. Some involve extensions to desktop publishing and wordprocessing tools (e.g. FrameMaker, MS Word, InDesign), others are generator toolsets (e.g. PHP), and many use intepretation of *markup* within principally textual content (e.g. Troff, LaTeX...) The Web encouraged formats defined in XML syntaxes, with markup organised as propertied trees around the document's textual data and content. Several major (XML-based) formats have been established for the visual presentation of such documents with markup - the HTML family associated with flow-based scrolling reports, XSL-FO for paginated flow documents and SVG for graphical and pictorial content.

A variable document, one that can change 'automatically' in response to data, is often described as a 'template' document which can be processed with a specific data binding to produce an instance. There are two hybrid aspects of markup to be considered:

1. What are the semantics of the presentation? In the HTML family, elements describe logical structures of sections, headers, paragraphs, list, tables etc. within a scrolling-flow context. Detailed styling (colours, fonting, display type...) can be defined by several methods, most notably with CSS pattern-matching rules. XSL-FO has similar logical structures but much more detailed control of placement, decorations and pagination. SVG provides a strict model for placement of overlapping graphical primitives but with no defined model for maintaining relative placement between siblings.

2. How is the data variability described and is it a continual property of the document? Reserved constructs within the template content can define interpolation of an element of a data record ($name) or a limited set of functions ($date('DD-MM-YY'). The effect of even these simple variations have to be projected through the presentation semantics - an excessively long name might for example cause an additional page-break. In general variations may need programmatic constructs such as conditionality, reordering and indirection.

This paper describes an architecture for documents which generalises both of these aspects, whilst making the documents declaratively self-contained. It focusses on document designs whose *logical* structural is mostly that of a tree (i.e. most relationships are between parent-child-sibling and not further removed) and whose *presentational* structure generally follows the same topology as the logical. The types of layout relationship involved in a document can be extended smoothly and monotonically and be resatisfied; the programmatic reponse to data can be declared in a functional manner, which is capable of partial and repeated binding to data. It uses an XML representation interspersing two standard XML dialects (SVG and XSLT) and two declarative XML additions to describe layout intent and retention of programmatic behaviour. Two support tools are required - an executor for the XSLT semantics and a resolver of the layout intent. It is a development from an earlier programme of research in XML-based variable document architectures[8,7].

Figure 1 is a simple graphical document consisting of two nested flow relationships and a set of primitives. As the size of the graphical components (star, circle) is reduced, both the horizontal and the vertical flows shrink, preserving the relationship. Equally well, adding new content (the text block) alters the inner flow, with consequent alterations to the outer flow too.

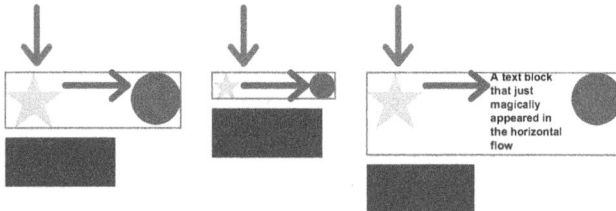

Figure 1. Compound layout responding to alteration in size and content

The remainder of this paper reviews prior art and then presents the basis of the document architecture, with very simple examples. Processing such documents requires two implementation tools, whose design and use is examined. Possibilities of implementing such processing entirely within a browser are discussed. Two substantial document examples are presented, followed by a conclusion and suggestions for further work.

2. PRIOR ART

Most variable document architectures have a fixed layout model with support for limited content variability. We first discuss models for description of layout. At the extreme a special-purpose program can be developed for a given application - the type that is often used for mass-produced individual publications, such as utility statements. In web-based contexts these can often be coded in client- or server-side scripting languages - a typical client-side example is D3[3], an extensive Javascript library that can be used for manipulation of documents, most notably SVG, in response to changes in large-scale datasets.

2.1 HTML & CSS

The semantics of HTML can provide suitable logical structures for documents that are mainly flows of text and tabular arrangements. Decorative styling can be declared through the use of pattern-matching CSS stylesheets, which cover sizing, colouring, fonting, marginal geometry and decoration, in-container alignment and so forth. Absolute positioning can be declared, as can additional (textual) content, such as numbering. Future proposals may target content into different flows or container spaces. But there are limitations: new structure cannot be created (e.g. producing a **sup** element for a footnote number) nor can elements be rearranged or copied, such as would be required for reference citations or footnote/mark pairs. Usually such manipulations require (external) programmatic tools, often as Javascript, sometimes to quite extreme extents (see Beckman & Meijer[2].)

2.2 XSL-FO

XSL-FO was developed to describe, in XML, textual document generation much richer than HTML possibilities at the time. The layout model ('*Formatting Objects*') was a series of content pieces (**fo:block**...) being flowed into a series of containers (**fo:flow**) with a rich set of page definitions, stylings, out-of-line directives

(e.g. footnotes) and so forth. Content interpolation, required for automatically-generated variable documents, used an embedded XML programming language that could both interpolate text and generate FO instructions. This language ('*Transformations*') became a separate entity as XSLT. Whilst the repertoire of layout for text is very rich, XSL-FO layout is not extensible easily.

2.3 SVG-based Layout

SVG defines a visual document as an arbitrary hierarchical collection of primitives. Styling can be modified with CSS sylesheets[1], but SVG provides no inherent geometric constraints between components - several pieces may have been abutted next to each other by a design tool, but if their sizes or positions change, the implied 'flow' relationship is now lost. This section examines cases where SVG-based documents are extended to declare and maintain such layout requirements.

There have been several experiments on active graphics where the SVG has *constant* tree topology. An integrated system of linear inequality constraints was added by Badros *et al*[1]. Numerical properties (attributes) of primitive and group elements can be replaced by named variables and declarative expression constraints (equalities and inequalities) included, relating these variables and some implicit ones (e.g. *rectA.width*). Whilst the solver (which needs to be attached intimately to the SVG renderer) was efficient (using modified Simplex techniques) and capable of handling large networks of constraints, the constraints were strictly linear, which cannot describe the width-height relationship for a text block.

A simpler *acyclic* series of constraint relationships was developed by McCormack *et al*[15] - scalar attributes denoting properties can be replaced by evaluable expressions. These relationships *can* be non-linear, but *must* be acyclic amongst themselves. Precompilers convert these property expressions into a network of dependencies and thence into a JavaScript program, with callbacks attached to 'context-modifying events' such as window resizing or mouse-dragging. Thus only those properties that must be altered as a consequence of the event are actually changed. More general expressions, which include logical, string and vector arguments, mean that properties such as colour could be modified. By altering the 'visibility' of components variable 'topology' in the resulting presentation could be simulated with suitable programming. Macdonald *et al*[14] take a similar approach, using 'component' SVG with JavaScript manipulation.

King *et al*[6] investigated continuous multimedia animation by attaching the application language SMIL (describing event causality over time) to an SVG graphical framework. Links between the two and external events (mouse drags, passage-of-time...) are supported by embedding functional expressions in attributes. Some of these attributes are native to either SMIL or SVG, but others are unique to the combined application. This can then be compiled 'safely' into some appropriate functional framework.

Thompson *et al*[17] extended this idea with more general declarative extensions to XML with functional properties. The primary goal was to support reusable or event-modified behaviour, whose description needed XML fragments and which therefore could not be coded as attributes. They proposed a variant of the static SVG **symbol** and **use** constructs (**template, instance**) with a purely declarative parametrisation model.

These methods define constraints between subcomponents as ex-

---

[1]This is limited - margins have no effect, borders are not drawn.

pressional relationships between parts, usually reducing them to connect sets of graphical atoms or intermediate 'variables'. Lumley *et al*[9,10] takes a more declarative approach: a tree of functional layout combinator nodes and SVG subtrees describes layout intent. A 'flow' relationship between subcomponents would be declared explicitly as an XML element node, whose attribute parameters hold properties of the flow, such as spacing and direction and other group decorative properties (border, margin...). The children of this node are the subparts over which the flow relationship was required. A layout processor resolves the geometry recursively, generating SVG results in a canonical (rectangular) form.

2.4 Continued Variable Data Interpolation

Some documents have a lifecycle that is more extensive than just a single production stage - data is added to them over time and their presentation adapts accordingly - sometimes monotonically, by adding new content, sometimes destructively by removing or modifying existing graphical elements. At any stage they can present useful information visually. Such documents are usually rebuilt totally on demand, from all accumulated data. But with a suitable architecture the document can be the carrier of its own (continual) modification. *TiddlyWiki*(http://tiddlywiki.com) is an example of a browser-borne HTML document that contains its own modifiers, using embedded Javascript.

Consider a variable document $D()$ to be a function. If the result of binding some data x is another variable (yet still 'presentable') document, then it can still considered a function, i.e. $D(x) => D'()$. Binding this to more data y could yield a further variable document $D'(y) => D''()$ and so on.

An earlier paper [11] examined constructing such a continually variable document with the DDF framework[8], using SVG for graphics, XSLT for program and combinatoric layout declarations, all in an XML tree. Continual variability was achieved by copying program into the output presentation and superposing presentation results using XSLT's push mode of processing. None of the operations involved modifying or resatisfying layouts that already existed as presentations within the document.

Subsequent work in [7] introduced two new ideas: a coherent model for propagation of embedded code and declarative description of layout intent by attributive decoration of a presentation. Together these support a more flexible and robust mechanism for actively variable documents, where the variability is defined entirely by structures *buried within the document's presentation*.

3. STANDARD TECHNOLOGIES

The architecture employs two standard technologies - SVG for presentational graphics and XSLT for programmatic modification of an XML tree. Some familiarity with both is needed to understand the later arguments - they are reviewed briefly in this section, as is an important property of necessary tools.

3.1 Scalable Vector Graphics

SVG is an XML-based compliant description of a set of vector graphics primitives, exploiting the tree to group and declare common properties. The primitives include shapes, arbitrary paths and text elements (which do *not* line-wrap), all being defined as vector shapes, and for which various style properties can be defined, such as fill, stroke and opacity. (Images are treated as specialist rectangles.) Affine transformations of geometry are supported, as well as clipping and scaling, definition and interpolations of reusable components and so forth. There are two types of group: `svg:g` provides a node to attach common properties (styling, transformation...) for the descendants of the node, and `svg:svg` defines a translatable group of components. In this architecture the latter is used extensively, with attributes `@x`, `@y`, `@width` and `@height` used to denote position and extent[2].

3.2 XSLT

An XSLT program is normally used to generate an XML result tree as a function of some input XML tree. Often these functions are mild 'transformations' of the input, but they can be anything. The XSLT program itself is described in an XML meta-syntax and is thus *homoiconic* - its representation is one of its principal datatypes - XSLT program can be read (and written) by XSLT, which will become important later. The top-level children of an XSLT program tree are a series of globally-scoped resources - variables, functions, computable attribute sets and pattern-matching templates which can be grouped into 'modes'.

Evaluation of an XSLT program starts with the template that matches the root (`/`) of the incoming XML input - the root become the 'context' focus for subsequent processing. The output is the result of evaluating the children of this template. These can take two principal forms: a concrete result fragment (e.g. `<svg:svg>`...) with a recursive evaluation of its children, or an XSLT instruction. An instruction will either i) generate new content by copying or otherwise processing nodes selected relative to the current context in the input tree, ii) define programmatic action (choice, repetition....) around additional result trees and instructions, or iii) store the result of an evaluation in a single-assignment tree-scoped variable, for subsequent recall. Nodes to compute over are chosen with the use of XPath, with the addition of access to user-defined functions and the values of variables defined in preceding tree scope.

Usually XSLT programs copy and 'modify' the input by recursive matching of templates against the current node. The template will then possibly copy, add new content and process selected children; there is no *delete* action, only *don't copy*. But other models can be used, as in this paper, where the (tree) body of the root-matching template provides the main framework of the result, with sections interpolated and generated beneath dependent on the input data - i.e. the output is more a modification of structures held within the program, than a transformation of the input XML tree. As such there is an important point to be made - no XSLT instruction within that tree can do anything other than (possibly) add extra content to that tree, at the point at which the instruction lies. In particular it cannot delete or replace parts of that tree.

3.3 Good XML Citizens & Tree Isomorphism

A critical property for the model described is that tools (transformers, visualisers) behave as *good XML citizens*. When some software converts an XML tree from one form into another, and the semantics of the transform are such that tree topology is generally preserved (i.e. *tree isomorphic*), then a useful tool will copy unknown information present in the source XML tree *to an equivalent position* in the result XML tree. Attributes in foreign name-

---

[2] `svg:g` can be translated through `@transform` but calculating geometry requires the transform to be parsed, as opposed to statements such as `sum(*/@height)` with `svg:svg`

spaces attached to an element should not only be tolerated, but also be copied across to equivalent elements in the result; foreign elements should be copied into equivalent sibling-relative positions within the result. With these properties robust hybrid systems can be constructed with tree fragments from different syntaxes.

4. ARCHITECTURE

The architecture described has four main components, each of which operates in a separate XML namespace:

1. A visual presentation represented as an SVG tree (`svg:*`), which acts as the top level of the overall document, and is viewable in an SVG-compatible browser, or can be converted to some publishable form, such as PDF.

2. Decorations on the tree describing *geometric layout relationships* between subcomponents. These are defined in a single namespace (prefixed `lay:`) and usually attached as attributes.

3. Embedded sections of XSLT (`xsl:*`) which describe the effect of variable data bindings or other external changes on the document, both in terms of additional content (new graphical pieces) and altered properties (positions, sizes, styling).

4. Decorations on instructions within the XSLT to describe code *retention* or *propagation*, to support continual variable behaviour. These are defined in a single namespace (prefixed `R:`) and attached as attributes.

This use of content in separate namespaces is crucial, as is the requirement that other processing tools (e.g. SVG renderers or converters to PDF) tolerate such foreign content. Figure 2 illustrates the relationship between these four components.

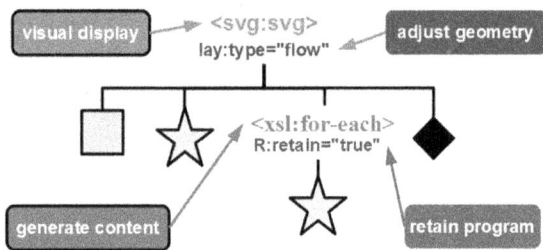

W3C Standards   **Semantic extenders**

Figure 2. Four components of the document architecture

The two standard components (SVG, XSLT) have no knowledge of the semantic extensions but tolerate the existence of directives in their namespaces. SVG ignores XSLT components during display; XSLT treats SVG just like any other result-tree fragment. The layout geometry declarations, when resolved, alter the positions (and sometimes topology) of sections of the SVG. The programmatic retention directives, when processed, modify the XSLT to retain sections of program in the result, to support continual binding. Two tools are required to correctly modify such a document in response to some data binding or other change, such as user interaction. They must:

• Resolve layout requirements in the current state of the document - e.g. move pieces in a flow into correct relative positions and reflect the appropriate size of the group to any parent layout. In effect modify the elements of the document described in `svg:*` to meet the constraints defined in `lay:*`. There are two additional requirements: i) sufficient information is left on the result document that layout can be resolved completely, with a degree of idempotency, and ii)

other embedded information (e.g. an XSLT generator) is both carried forward in *tree-isomorphic* positions in the result and exerts *no* influence on the resulting layout, either through geometry or topology.

• Process the XSLT program embedded within the document over a binding of data, to add, delete or modify sections of the SVG tree according to `xsl:*` instructions. This also propagates code and instructions into the resulting document, under the control of directives (`@R:*`) attached to such elements.

We'll discuss each of these four in turn with simple examples, and then outline the implementation of the processing tools .

4.1 Layout Model

A document with layout is a legal SVG tree, with additional declarations describing required layout relationships between components, most usually over the set of children of a parent node. Most are attributes attached to SVG elements and denote the required relationship to hold over a set of children (`lay:type="flow"`), or a property of that relationship (`lay:spacing="4"`) or a specific role that that element may play in the layout of its parent (e.g. `lay:is.container="true"` declaring a container in a paginated flow). Most relationships follow strict tree-nested scope.

Figure 3 shows a simple set of pieces connected as a flow declared on a parent `svg:svg` element, also shown as a tree[3]. In the first graphic the flow has been established over two components (square and diamond) but is now no longer true when the stars and dragon are added between them in document order. Resolving the flow moves the stars, dragon and diamond and establishes a new overall size for the group.

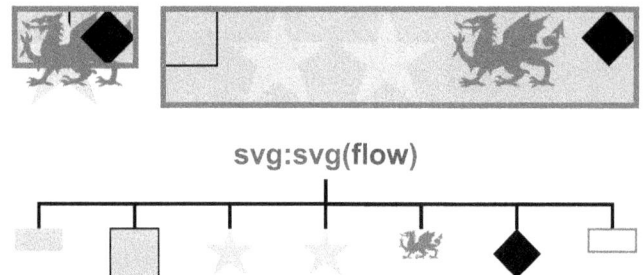

svg:svg(flow)

Figure 3. A simple flow before and after resolution of layout

The extent of the group in this example is displayed by a background and surrounding border, which were declared on the group (`border-color="red"`..) as a decoration. Within SVG such group decorations must be described as first-class graphic objects (often lines) to be visible, and should be contained within the parent at the right point in draw order (and thus will move with the parent). But they are *not* true content, are marked consistently (`lay:type="artifact"`), ignored for purposes of any layout determination within the group and re-calculated whenever layout is resolved, as certainly their positions and size depend upon the true contents of the group.

As each layout produces a canonical `svg:svg` element, with width and height, it can itself be used in a parent layout. Figure 4 adds some depth to the layout, where the stars are arranged in aligned from top-left with an offset.

Many simple tree-scoped, group layouts can be defined in a similar fashion, such as distribution or placement along a path. Their

---

[3]SVG primitives are shown directly in tree diagrams.

resolution usually involves five consistent steps: i) resolve the layout for all the 'true' children (i.e. ignore group artefactual elements), ii) position or otherwise modify (e.g. scale) the envelope geometry (not changing internals) of each child[4], iii) calculate the size of the entire group ensemble, iv) add any necessary artefactual decoration elements and v) form up the group **svg:svg** element with correct size properties.

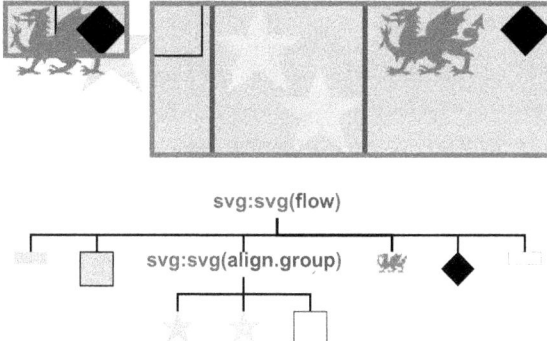

Figure 4. Resolution of a set of nested layouts

A layout must be re-satisfiable *from its result form* after modification to internal properties or content. All necessary information about layout must therefore be retained on the result. If the result is *tree-isomorphic* to its original declaration, internal declarations (e.g. flows buried inside other flows, even if in the same direction) are preserved, as the control attributes (**@lay:type**, ...) have been copied onto the corresponding result nodes.

4.1.1 Complex and one-to-many layouts

For some layouts the parent must interact with the resolution of their children, such as packers, which partition fixed and free space in a container between children, permitting them to adjust to fit. Tree-localisation of layout is not possible and more complex 'negotiation' between parent and child is needed.

Resolution of text-wrapped paragraphs (which SVG does *not* perform) is complex - potentially mixed-font text sections have to be wrapped into a shape defined by the parent (or in some circumstances a higher ancestor) and requires substantial external resources (e.g. font metrics). As seen later, buried and retained **xsl:*** instructions need to be preserved in the correct place in document order, inside the wrapped text.

Sometimes the result of a layout is not a *single* group, but a sequence of them. A sorted relationship (**lay:type="sort"**) requires the document (and hence draw) order of a set of pieces to meet a collation (partial ordering), presumably then to be laid out as children of some immediate ancestor layout. Such a layout only makes sense if it produces a reordered *sequence* of the children. In cases such as pagination there may be no single (container) parent to the sequence of results, but several.

To satisfy the 're-layout' requirement for such one-to-many cases, each member of the sequence of results is identified with the attribute **@lay:functionId**, encoding the type of layout, its parameters and an identity[5] - during re-satisfaction a 'spread group' is collected together and dealt with as a single layout.

4.1.2 Non-localised layout and reuse

Not all layout requirements can be satisfied purely in a local context (i.e. entirely within the purview of the direct parent). As shown in [10] features such as marginal notes and call-outs in text flows usually have *acyclic* layout dependencies and can be most conveniently resolved with *presentational variables*, which also support reuse of graphical content.

SVG has the **svg:use** element which interpolates a graphical component at the given point in drawing order, with possible affine transformation. This isn't totally sufficient for three reasons: i) the definitions have global not local scope which limits use in dynamic situations, ii) they are not parametrisable, as noted in [17] and iii) they cannot be 'searched' with XPath.

Presentation variables are represented as **svg:*** elements, marked with **lay:variable="***name***"** attribute, and with **@display="none"** on the retained layout to suppress display at point of definition, and resolved (interpolated) elements suitable marked as 'indirect' by attributes that reflect their provenance, such as **var:copy-of="***expression***"** or **var:for-each="***expression***"** .

4.2 Content Interpolation with XSLT

We have described how a document declares its internal layout, for satisfaction either *ab initio* or when some change occurs within the document. This section discusses the model for making such changes, principally as a result of binding data.

Fragments of XSLT code are embedded within the document - the results of executing each fragment may generate new content (usually as SVG sub-trees) at the point in the SVG tree at which it is defined. This point is crucial: as with all XSLT, the result of an instruction is placed in the tree directly where the instruction lies - thus an **xsl:copy-of** between **svg:rect** and **svg:circle** will end up with (possibly null) new content replacing the **xsl:copy-of** node exactly *in situ*. Relative document order is preserved - the immediate predecessor to the result will be the rectangle, the immediate follower will be the circle. It is thus possible to control the topological effect of new content accurately, which becomes critical for continually active documents. Such changes can *only* be additive, no XSLT instruction can be placed as a sibling of the rectangle which will remove it. One exception exists, which is key to some of the later semantics: **xsl:attribute** adds an attribute to the parent element of the instruction, which can overwrite the value of an extant attribute (property) of the same name.

Sections of XSLT can appear in two areas of the SVG. Global entities (templates, functions, attribute sets and global variables) are held within an **svg:script** element[6]. Other result-generating instructions (which may of course invoke global resources either through XSLT or XPath) are buried within the main SVG graphical tree: their execution is the only way the SVG tree is modified.

Figure 5 shows graphical and tree views of a very simple example, where for every **star** element child in the input data (in this case 2), a copy of an SVG-valued global variable (a star-shaped **svg:polygon**) is added to the flow, the colour of the first rectangle altered according to the value of any **fill** element and the dragon made visible on the existence of a **dragon** element.

---

[4]Most layouts treat their children by the edges of their bounding boxes (**@x,@width..**), but this is not mandatory - the **tree** layout examines left and right edges as piecewise linear curves

---

[5]Two contiguous layouts of the same type and parameters are not a single layout.

[6]XSLT has no locally-scoped templates or functions.

4.3 Continual Behaviour

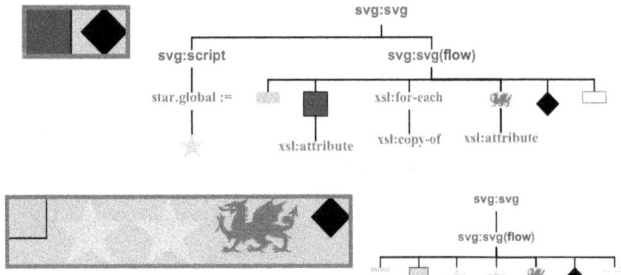

Figure 5. A simple active document, before and after data binding

For a document to be continually active, XSLT generation code needed for processing subsequent document responses must remain within the main SVG tree after previous phases of XSLT evaluation, and in the correct places to generate new content - fragments of code must propagate forward. This requirement is declared adding directives to `xsl:*` elements to control the propagation, such as `R:retain="true"`, which directs that a copy of the instruction should appear in the result of XSLT execution[7].

Suppose that the 'active' elements (square colouring, dragon display and star generator) of Figure 5 were declared to be continuous and thus retained in the document after evaluation. If that were so the tree representation and a possible result, introducing a third star, after a further stage of data binding are shown in Figure 6. How such propagation is performed is discussed later.

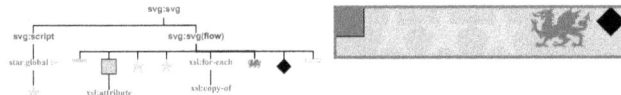

Figure 6. A continual variation of Figure 5

The retained instructions (`xsl:for-each`...) are considered to be a null element as far as layout is concerned, will not be displayed in an SVG viewer, have no influence on geometry and will be copied in place in the resulting resolved flow[8].

There are a small number of possible types of propagation that may be declared in an `@R:retain` attribute:

- `true` - execute the instruction and always retain.

- `while[(expression)]`, `until[(expression)]` - execute the instruction; retain while/until the given XPath expression is true.

For instructions that test or select nodes, the default XPath is the `@test` or `@select` attribute. `xsl:variable` elements have forms of propagation to pass document state to future bindings:

- `evaluated` - evaluate the variable and propagate its *value* indefinitely as the future binding of the variable.

- `accumulate[(init.value)]` - propagate a value that can update from binding to binding, such as `total := sum(charges) + $total`, starting with a possible initial value. The updates are strictly after each complete data binding, and not reassigned during an execution.

---

[7]XSLT tolerates foreign namespace attributes on instructions.

[8]This is not so for topologically-modifying layouts, such as sort-by-size but any eventual (graphical) results from these instructions would be placed correctly on resolving the parent's layout.

- `record` - generate a new variable with a bound value in the result, to record state for processing the next data binding.

4.4 Replacing Content

Thus far XSLT modification of the SVG tree is limited to adding elements and altering attributes. Practical solutions require content to be deleted or replaced. Recall that an XSLT instruction buried in the SVG tree can *only* i) overwrite an attribute property in its parent, or ii) add new elements or text to that point in the tree. It *cannot* alter anything higher in the tree or any of its siblings - to do so we must look to outside a purely XSLT solution.

SVG elements can have a `@display` property controlling whether the construct is ignored by renderers - a value of `none` means the content contributes nothing to the layout, otherwise rendering is conventional. Content might be replaced by switching off old pieces (`display="none"`) and adding new. This has problems: i) it cannot be continued indefinitely, as old content accumulates in the tree, ii) buried and propagated XSLT within old pieces might eventually change the display property, thus resurrecting truly dead material, iii) it would be difficult to distinguish between 'dead' sections and 'zombies' - pieces that are temporarily 'asleep'.

One approach is to place a declaration *above* a piece of content and its possible replacement generator, that will delete the original when replacement occurs. Such a special-purpose 'instruction' can be considered to be a meta-layout (`lay:type="SVG.last"`) which selects only the last of the set of displayable components.

5. IMPLEMENTATION

To evaluate the effects of a variable binding on the document shown in Figure 6 there are two normally separable phases: interpolating the effect of the data on the SVG tree (evaluating the XSLT semantics) and resolving the layout declarative constraints over the resulting SVG. In the examples shown in this paper, these two phases are combined with command-line scripts, but GUI control interfaces are possible.

5.1 XSLT Evaluation

The XSLT semantics of the document can either be interpreted, or, more cleanly, executed by converting the SVG into an XSLT transform that when run on the data produces the correct modified SVG tree. Figure 7 shows the transform generated from the first stage of Figure 5.

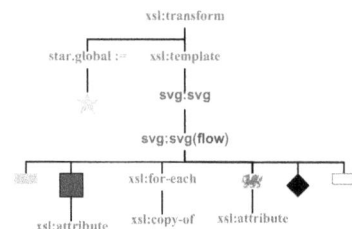

Figure 7. The compiled XSLT for Figure 5

The main SVG tree becomes the result tree (only child) of the 'root-match' template (the one first invoked during XSLT execution) - as a consequence this will be the main output. Recursive processing of `xsl:*` instructions within that tree adds the two stars in the appropriate point in the flow, changes the rectangle fill and overwrites the `@display` property of the dragon image.

Having this simple 'compiler', which builds an XSLT transform from the SVG document, is the key to supporting continual behaviour: instructions that are required to be retained can be recognised and modifications and additions made to the resulting code. For example, we wish to arrange for the instructions (marked **@R:retain="true"**) that alter the square colour, change the dragon visibility and add new stars (**xsl:for-each**), apart from executing, to also appear in the result. We can arrange this if, for each retained instruction, we add another that will generate a (faithful) copy in the output of the execution of the XSLT (Figure 8).

```
<xsl:for-each select="in/star">
        <xsl:copy-of select="$star.global"/>
        </xsl:for-each>
<X:for-each select="in/star" R:retain="true">
        <X:copy-of select="$star.global"/>
        </X:for-each>
```

Figure 8. Modified instructions for code propagation

The output will then contain the *result* of the instruction (which of course might be null) and a *copy* of the instruction, which still declares itself needing indefinite retention. 'Warping forward' the **xsl:** components of the instruction into the **X:** namespace, which aliases back into **xsl:** on execution, achieves the effect. This produces a modified transform shown in Figure 9.

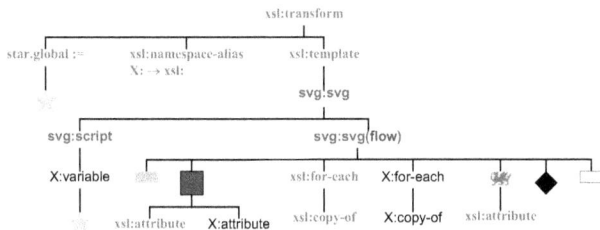

Figure 9. The compiled XSLT for Figure 5 with code retention

With program retention the **svg:script** element, which contains global templates, functions and variables, is added en-block to the result - any such 'continuation' directives contained within trees therein are similarly expanded *once* at the first compilation of the element. Some global code might become redundant later: in the extreme case, when the resulting main SVG contains *no* XSLT fragments, the document has ceased to be further active and all global XSLT sections could be removed. A compiler could arrange that the transform detects such cases in the result and generates minimal necessary output.

5.2 Layout Resolution

The layout resolver (similar to [9]) is an XSLT package containing an expandable set of layout 'agents', coded as **xsl:template** sections, each of which matches a given layout declaration (e.g. **match="svg:svg[@lay:type='flow']"**). As suggested earlier, most have a canonical form which recursively resolves their children (**xsl:apply-templates select="*"**) and then proceeds to position them according to the semantics of that particular layout, before encapsulating the group result. The current suite of supported layouts includes flows, alignment, distribution, grids and tables, pagination, sorting, inequality positional constraints, trees and path placement. Figure 10 shows a typical form of resolution for a flow, coded as a tail-recursive function over the sequence of children with a small number of positional parameters.

The guard **not.layout()** is important - it ensures that buried generators (**xsl:***) or undisplayed SVG (**@display="none"**) do not influence the geometry. For some arrangements, such as columnar (i.e. arrange in rows of *n* items), this guard must also be used for 'counting' purposes.

Agents matching leaf primitives (**svg:rect** ...) return the leaf itself (as they have no **svg:*** children), usually with added declarations of geometric extent (**@lay:x**, **@lay:width**...) computed from the defined properties of the primitive (centre and radii for ellipses, perimeters for paths, an aspect ratio for a referenced image). As the layout resolver is a *good XML citizen*, any children of these primitives (**xsl:***) are preserved. Supporting a new layout involves adding an XSLT template to match the declaring attribute which then takes responsibility for resolving the layout - in many cases this code need only determine the relative placement of a sequence of already resolved children - parent-level actions, such as encapsulation and group decoration are handled by common code.

```
let $spacing := xxx;
flow($children as element()*, $y as xs:double) {
 if(empty($children)) then ()
 else {
  let $h := head($children);
  moveTo.y($h,$y),
  flow(tail($children), $y +
      if(not.layout($h)) then 0 else
         (heightOf($h) + $spacing))
 }
}
```

Figure 10. Resolution of a vertical flow layout

Line-wrapped text is represented as a tree of lines of **svg:text**, containing character sequences, stylistic groupings (**svg:tspan**) and foreign elements (**xsl:***). Flowing such text into a container invokes a Java function with font metric and hyphenation resources to produce a new sequence of **svg:text** lines with text, **svg:tspan** and foreign element sub-trees that are *tree-isomorphic* to the original, in the sense of document order. Such structures contain all information necessary for re-layout.

One-to-many layouts produce a sequence of, rather than a single, result element, with information about their provenance stored on each. A high-priority agent matches the first occurrence of a member of such a group, collects all the following contiguous siblings that are members of the same group and forms a pseudo-group parent with these children. This is then resolved conventionally, generating another result sequence, each labelled with their new provenance, which is then passed up to the resolution of their true parent. (A good example is the 'score-order' sort of section 8.) A companion agent matches each of the following siblings, returning an empty sequence. Note that XSLT instructions can exist comfortably in such a group - the group identifier (**@lay:functionId**), being in a separate namespace, is perfectly legal on an **xsl:*** element.

Resolution of a pagination requires information on containers to be gathered before the sequence of children are processed. Each child is resolved in turn (being passed information on the target container, which for example text block resolution may employ) and packed successively by a tail-recursive algorithm. This produces a sequence of filled containers, constituting a one-to-many result as shown above. For re-satisfaction the container definitions themselves (which may contain background and foreground graphics) must feature in the result - in addition to being marked as members of the group, their role is identified (**@lay:is.container="true"**) and their rendering suppressed (**@display="none"**). A practical paginator needs more complex features, such as diversions for footnotes, floats, breakability etc. This paper is proof that this is possible - *its layout is defined entirely in the architecture described herein.*

Presentational variables (`*[@lay:variable]`) are processed by pre-emptive agents that recognise trees with definitions and interpolations as direct children, add those (resolved) definitions to those in scope, interpolate references and then pass a 'variable-free' definition for normal resolution. Interpolated results which are *elements* are marked with the type of interpolation (e.g. `lay:for-each="expression"`) for subsequent layout resatisfaction. Reuse of static sub-assemblies (`svg:use`) is resolved by decorating the interpolating element with the geometry (`@lay:x`, `@lay:width`...) of the definition which has previously been collected - thereafter it responds similarly to its 'real' siblings.

Some documents may need global adjustment of layout, such as forcing a given page count. Higher-level layouts can be defined that will iterate over the children, adjusting parameters (e.g. altering font size) or content (e.g. removing optional content in overflow situations) until defined goals are (hopefully) reached. Such actions do need some knowledge of the semantics of the layouts beneath them however, and the search space is far from 'smooth'.

6. IMPLEMENTATION IN A BROWSER

Whilst the main focus has been on the production of offline variable documents, recent developments in XSLT implementations [4,5] make it distinctly possible to consider resolving layout (and variable interpolation) within an unmodified browser. An XSLT2.0-compliant complier, coded in JavaScript, can be loaded as a script within a document (HTML or SVG). This will compile a referenced XSLT transform into runtime JavaScript which can then operate on the DOM tree for the document involved. Attachments to events (e.g. `onmouseclick`) are declared as conventional XSLT templates which can examine the tree around the point of action, generating modifications or new content that are applied as 'result documents' to add to or replace sections of the DOM tree.

Using this framework, layout implementations that do not require XSLT extension functions can be executed within the browser displaying the SVG document. Figure 11 shows two stages of a document rendered in the browser: in the first stage the layout declarations are satisfied, in the second mouse interaction has caused the size of several pieces to be altered - the layout has been recomputed to satisfy the directives.

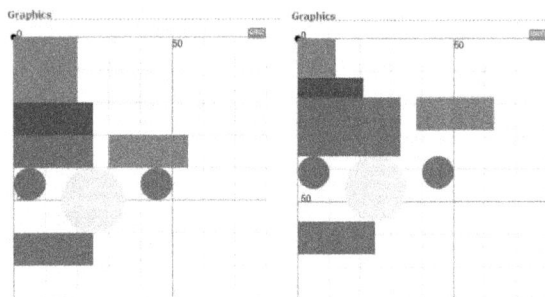

Figure 11. Adaptive layout in a browser

In an interactive context where a single piece is being altered, perhaps by 'rubber-band' resizing, complete recalculation of the entire layout is neither tolerable, nor warranted. For many layouts, the layout of a *child* component (apart from its parent-relative position or size) is independent of both its siblings and the layout context of its parent..

Significant portions of a document tree could thus be invariant to a given alteration of an individual component, though the highest geometry of the document may change. Figure 12 shows the tree

involved in the example. If the size of the yellow circle is altered, we only need re-evaluate the layout of its ancestors: for each in turn we would have i) the declaration of the type of layout involved, as attributes on the node, ii) the old child that has been modified, iii) the replacement component, which has already been laid out and iv) its siblings, which *do not* need re-evaluation.

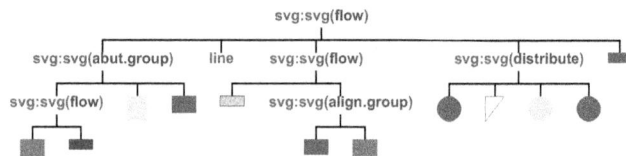

Figure 12. The tree representation of Figure 11

If the replacement can be interpolated in the correct place in document order, a sequence of 'new' children, all individually laid out, can be presented to the parent processing code to arrange. Recursion *toward the root*, (Figure 13) eventually generates a new document, where `resolve($node,$children)` resolves the semantics of a node over the given set of evaluated children.

```
resolve.delta($layout.node as element(),
  $child.old as element()?,
  $child.new as element()*) {
 let $new :=
  resolve($layout.node,
      if(exists($child.old)) then
      ($child.old/preceding-sibling::*,
       $child.new,
       $child.old/following-sibling::*) else
       *)
 if($layout.node/parent::svg:svg[@lay:type]) then
  resolve.delta($layout.node/parent::*,
       $layout.node,
       $new) else
   $new
}
```

Figure 13. Propagating layout changes up the SVG tree

Other approaches to improve re-work are possible. Macdonald[13] and Ollis[16] explore partial (re-)evaluation of layouts and underlying XSLT implementations. Browser-based XSLT also supports in-place addition, modification and removal of attributes on the DOM tree. For layouts which only modify geometry, rather than topology, the effects of some change (e.g. interactive resizing of a component) could be propagated without replacing any section of the DOM. (In effect this automates, completely within the browser, the causal propagation described in McCormack *et al*[15] and King *et al*[6].)

7. EXAMPLE DOCUMENTS

Many 'document applications' are supported by client/server/ database implementations, sometimes sharing processing with client-side Javascript and CSS, either through reference to libraries or embedded in the displayed documents. Document modification usually involves client-server interaction. In this section we show two examples of continually-active self-contained documents using the declarative architecture described in this paper, that consume data progressively and modify presentation at several points and in a non-monotonic fashion.

7.1 Medical Record

Medical records are active 'documents', accumulating data by stages. Figure 14 shows some pages from a medical record document after two successive stages of binding data: patient details, followed by medical notes and readings.

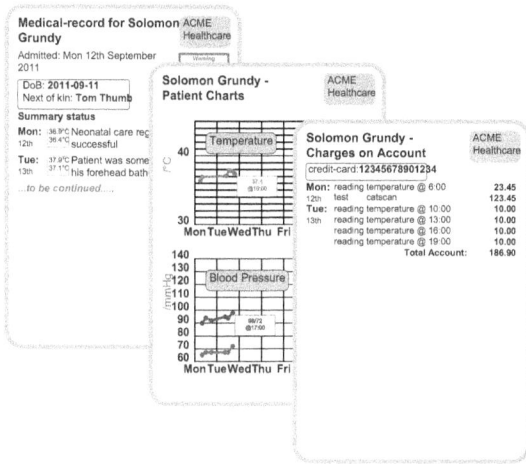

Figure 14. Medical record - patient details & two days

The example has three types of page: i) an initial summary showing patient details, a brief summary for each day and a potential 'warning' display, ii) graphs displaying temperature and blood pressure that chart data progressively and show a label of 'last reading' and iii) a summary of charges, with a running total.

This document is 'active' in several places within its presentation. Each of the graphs, shown at two stages of binding in Figure 15, retains its own generation instructions within the SVG to add new data points and lines (`xsl:for-each select="data-pattern"`). Joining a new set of points to the existing line needs a record of the last point that is accessible from XSLT. By building an `xsl:variable` in the result SVG that holds the last point, and which is preserved through layout resolution, the recorded value can be read by the point-drawing XSLT, to attach a line to the end of the previous graph. This technique - generating bound variables as 'memos', interpolating their previous values and leaving regeneration directives is quite generic, and having tree-scoped locality can themselves be generated on-the-fly.

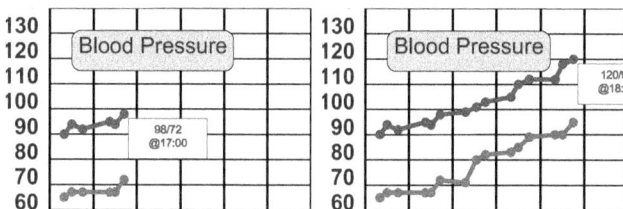

Figure 15. Graphs at two stages of binding

The summary and the accounts pages (shown at conclusion in Figure 16) both add new content to a tabular flow - the SVG structures defining the flows contain code to generate the new content and the flow adapts. Expansion of the accounts flow, due to new charges, moves the 'account total' line, as the flow is re-satisfied. The account running total (`total.account`) is recorded by a 're-generated' variable (`sum(charges) + $total.account`) as discussed for the graphs. As the recorded variable is not accessible until processing for a subsequent binding, the functional nature of the document is not compromised.

The summary page has two other active parts. 'CASE CLOSED' appears when there is known to be no more data: a retained, but unevaluated, generator fires, producing suitable graphics; the generator is now longer retained, so the case cannot now be 'unclosed'. A variable warning section in the top right-hand corner appears when a suitably worrying condition is detected in the *new* data. This uses a hybrid arrangement of XSLT instructions and the

`SVG.last` meta-layout function, to switch visibility and replace content - a macro (`SVG.Reveal`) is expanded by the compiler to suitable code.

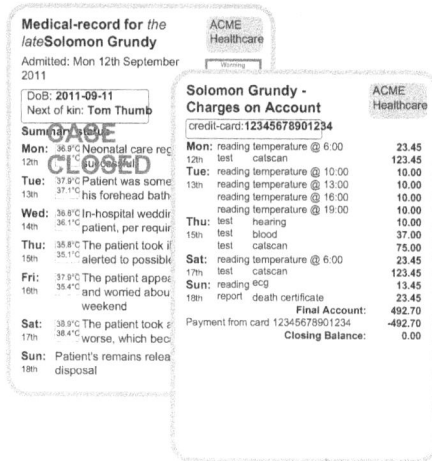

Figure 16. First and last pages after final binding

Figure 17. Modified graphics over four stages of binding

7.2 Paper Reviewing

A self-contained active document can be designed for reviewing conference papers that will i) accumulate and display details of submissions, ii) collect review scores and remarks and marshal them to the correct paper, assessing and displaying an aggregate score and iii) sort the papers into score order.

Figure 18 shows the document at two stages of submission collection - a retained `xsl:for-each` generates a horizontal flow of number/authors/title for each `submission` at the foot of the (vertically flowed) list. This code disappears when `submissions.closed` is encountered in the input and further submissions in any subsequent binding are ignored

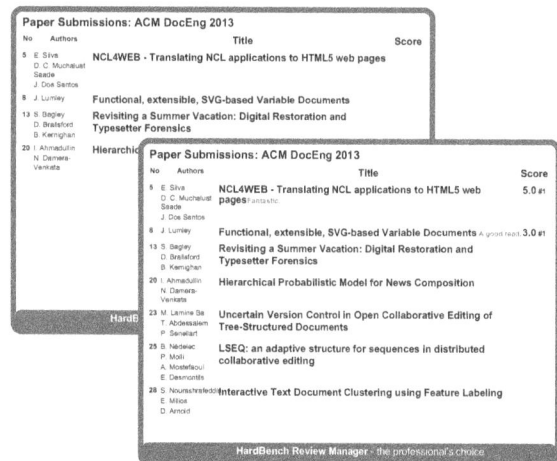

Figure 18. Conference submissions accumulating

The document becomes more interesting as the reviews (`<review no="8" score="5">Fantastic</review>`) begin to arrive. Each paper entry contains, as well as the graphics, a number of embedded XSLT components. An evaluated variable records the number of the paper (`$no`). This is used in later phases to select only reviews destined for this paper (`$my.reviews:= review[@no=$no]`). The title text block has an embedded generator that adds any remark from a review to the text (`<xsl:for-each select="$my.reviews"`...

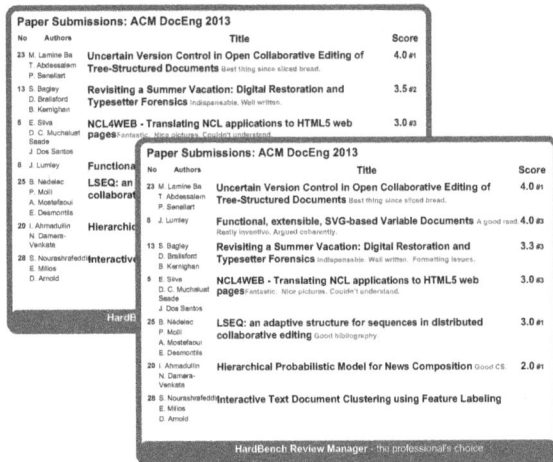

Figure 19. Paper reviews - stages 1 & 3

At the end of the paper's (horizontal flow) entry is a replaceable text block (generator) (`SVG.last`...) displaying the number of reviews and average score. The block is not generated until there is at least one review (`xsl:if test="$count gt 0"`) - then it interpolates values of the average score and the number of reviews received. Two additional 'accumulating' variables placed at the beginning of the entry (`$count += count($my.reviews)` and `$total += sum($my.reviews/@score)` keep track, and a recalculated variable `$average` computes the average score.

Papers are sorted into score order by a `lay:type="sort"` directive which, being one-to-many, is spread across the entire set of papers. The sort collation is determined by an XPath: `lay:sort.by=".//@average"` and `lay:sort.order= "descending"` declares the order. The attribute `@average` has been written onto the 'score' text block by its generator described above.

The documents are small - the empty document has 104 elements and 207 attributes (10kB uncompressed serialisation). After four stages of binding (7 submissions, 18 reviews) these have increased to 394 elements, 1737 attributes and 80kB.

8. CONCLUSION

We have demonstrated a model for self-contained variable documents that mixes SVG and XSLT to provide graphics and programmatic response to data and external events. Two decorative regimes declare requirements for layout relationships and program propagation respectively. Document evaluation requires a resolver to modify SVG geometry and a 'complier/executor' to interpolate the effect of the XSLT and propagate program. That the former works can be seen in this paper itself, whose layout is defined entirely in `svg:*[lay:*]`. The two examples of sections 7 show that continued variable behaviour is possible, with clean and robust (functional) semantics.

Future work will focus on developing further the browser-based implementation, exploring interactive editing of the document variability (building on ideas described in [12]), and exploiting invariances to improve layout performance.

9. REFERENCES

[1] Badros, G., Jojada, T., Marriott, K., Meyer, B., Portnoy, W. and Borning, A. 2001. A constraint extension to scalable vector graphics. In *Proc. 10th World Wide Web Conference, Hong Kong.*

[2] Beckman, B. and Meijer, E. 2013. The story of the teapot in DHTML. *Commun. ACM.* 56, 3(March 2013)50-55.

[3] Bostock, M. 2012. Data-Driven Documents. Retrieved June 24, 2013 from http://d3js.org/

[4] Delpratt, O. and Kay, M. 2013. Multi-user interaction using client-side XSLT. In *XML Prague. February, 2013. Prague, Czech Republic..* 1-22.

[5] Kay, M. 2011. XSLT in the Browser. In *Proceedings of XML Prague 2011.* 125-134.

[6] King, P., Schmitz, P. and Thompson, S. 2004. Behavioral reactivity and real time programming in XML: functional programming meets SMIL animation. In *Proceedings of the 2004 ACM symposium on Document engineering.* 57-66.

[7] Lumley, J. 2012. Documents as Functions. PhD Thesis. University of Nottingham. Retrieved June 24, 2013 from http://etheses.nottingham.ac.uk/2631/

[8] Lumley, J., Gimson, R. and Rees, O. 2005. A Framework for Structure, Layout & Function in Documents. In *Proceedings of the 2005 ACM symposium on Document engineering.* 32-41.

[9] Lumley, J., Gimson, R. and Rees, O. 2006. Extensible Layout in Functional Documents. In *Digital Publishing, Proc. of SPIE-IS&T Electronic Imaging, Vol 6076.*

[10] Lumley, J., Gimson, R. and Rees, O. 2006. Resolving Layout Interdependency with Presentational Variables. In *Proceedings of the 2006 ACM symposium on Document engineering.* 95-97.

[11] Lumley, J., Gimson, R. and Rees, O. 2007. Endless Documents: A Publication as a Continual Function. In *Proceedings of the 2007 ACM symposium on Document engineering.* 174-176.

[12] Lumley, J., Gimson, R. and Rees, O. 2008. Configurable Editing of XML-based Variable-Data Documents. In *Proceedings of the 2008 ACM symposium on Document engineering.* 76-85.

[13] Macdonald, A. 2008. Progressive Document Evaluation. PhD Thesis. University of Nottingham.

[14] Macdonald, A., Brailsford, D. and Bagley, S. 2005. Encapsulating and manipulating component object graphics (COGs) using SVG. In *Proceedings of the 2005 ACM symposium on Document engineering.* 61-63.

[15] McCormack, C., Marriott, K. and Meyer, B. 2004. Adaptive layout using one-way constraints in SVG. Retrieved June 24, 2013 from http://www.svgopen.org/2004/papers/ ConstraintSVG/

[16] Ollis, J. 2011. Optimised Editing of Variable Data Documents via Partial Re-Evaluation. PhD Thesis. University of Nottingham.

[17] Thompson, S., King, P. and Schmitz, P. 2007. Declarative extensions of XML languages. In *Proceedings of the 2007 ACM symposium on Document engineering.* 89-91.

Hierarchical Probabilistic Model for News Composition

Ildus Ahmadullin
Hewlett-Packard Laboratories
1501 Page Mill Road
Palo Alto, CA 94304
ildus.ahmadullin@hp.com

Niranjan Damera-Venkata
Hewlett-Packard Laboratories
1501 Page Mill Road
Palo Alto, CA 94304
niranjan.damera-venkata@hp.com

ABSTRACT

We present a method for the automated composition of personalized newspapers. Traditional newsprint composition is a laborious and expensive manual process. We develop a two level hierarchical page layout model that models aesthetic design choices using local (within article region) and global (page level) prior probability distributions. Given content to be composed, our model can infer the best way to divide a page into layout regions and simultaneously optimize content fit within these regions. We automate decisions on how to paginate articles, flow article text across pages, crop images, adjust whitespace etc. for the best overall newspaper compositions. We also show how content editing which is a very important task in the traditional news workflow can be incorporated in a semi-automated manner within our framework. Our model is a generalization of our prior work on probabilistic modeling of single-flow layouts to enable multiple article flows on a page, while still allowing one or more articles that may break on a page and continue on subsequent pages.

Categories and Subject Descriptors

I.7.4 [**Computing Methodologies**]: Document and Text Processing:Electronic Publishing

Keywords

automated publishing, newsaper layout, probabilistic document model

1. INTRODUCTION

Traditional newspaper composition is an iterative process involving copy editors and professional publication designers who work in concert to make decisions on what content to include and how to format the chosen content for aesthetic presentation. Once a sequence of articles is chosen a publication designer typically looks at a set of pre-formatted layout templates and attempts to make a rough assignment of a sub-sequence of the article content to one or more of the

templates (a.k.a. pagination). The templates and content may then be adjusted to allow a more aesthetic presentation. These often include whitespace adjustment, article title font changes, cropping/scaling of images and breaking longer articles into two for continuation on a subsequent page. Of course the content itself may also be edited to allow a better fit to the chosen design templates. Headlines are often rewritten based on space requirements, and articles may be shortened by clipping at appropriate paragraph boundaries. These design choices may be observed for example by simply observing an expert newspaper designer in action [1].

While professional design works well for traditional news publishing where a single high quality document may be distributed to an audience of millions, it is not economically viable (due to its high marginal cost) for the creation of personalized news that changes per subscriber and by device form factor. In this paper we seek to automate personalized news composition by employing a strategy that seeks to automate several decisions a newspaper publication designer would make manually, such as those described in the previous paragraph. Specifically we leverage our previous work on the probabilistic modeling of design choices in document layout [3] to develop a probabilistic layout model suitable for describing the hierarchical nature (global vs local) of news composition.

Figure 1 shows a diagram of a selection of a global and region templates in the composition of a one page news document. At the global level a typical news page template is composed of different article regions that each accommodate content from a single article. Global page composition may include design choices, including the number of regions on a page, region type (main flow vs. sidebar, continuation region vs. non-continuation), relative arrangement of regions on a page, region height, inter-region whitespace/margins etc. At the local level (within each region) design choices include number of columns to use, selection of a relative configuration of text and images, image selection/omission, image cropping, within-region whitespace adjustment, title font adjustment etc.

In this paper we develop a two level hierarchical probabilistic model that models the local and global design choices of news composition as random variables with associated conditional probability distributions. The model represents the interaction between the local and global design variables for the design of a whole document explicitly using a Bayesian network whose overall probability is a product

---

[1]http://www.layoutexecutive.com/tutorials.html

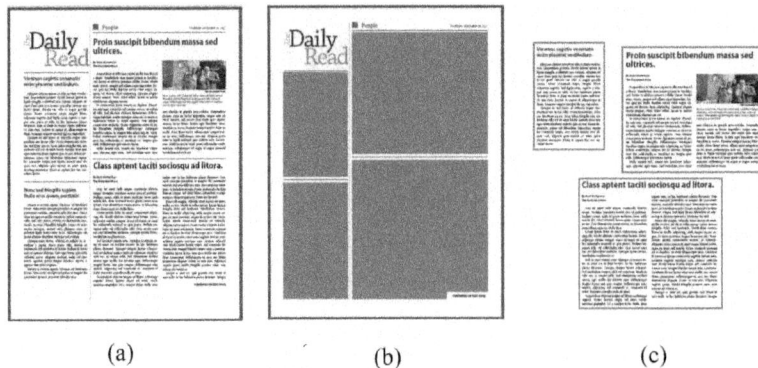

Figure 1: Newspaper style document page and corresponding templates. (a) Original document page, (b) global template, (c) set of local templates with mapped content

of the conditional probabilities of individual design choices at the local and global level.

Given content, a layout may be synthesized that embodies an optimal sequence (over pages) of design choices that maximizes network probability. In this paper we focus on layouts that use a fixed column width for each article since they are most typical of news layouts, but it is straightforward to extend the results to a discrete set of allowed column widths.

Automated Document synthesis/layout literature deals extensively with how given content can be formatted to one or more pages. Page counts are either given or determined by the algorithm. There is however another important free variable that makes a huge impact on layout quality: content selection. Little work has been done in deciding how to edit content along with other layout parameters in order to improve document composition quality. In this work we also discuss a novel content editing framework to improve layout quality.

Section 2 positions this work with respect to other approaches to news composition and our own prior work on the probabilistic modeling of design choices. Section 3 reviews our previous work on probabilistic modeling of document composition. Section 4 describes our hierarchical model for news layout, develops the corresponding layout synthesis algorithm and presents a complexity analysis. Section 5 shows how the framework can be extended to handle content editing. Section 6 presents several examples of the framework in action producing news compositions. Finally, Section 7 concludes the paper by summarizing contributions and indication on future directions.

2. RELATED WORK

Automated document composition has been a topic of much research [10] [8]. A Newspaper is a document characterized by a rectangular tiling of articles to fill available space on the page. Each tile (or article region) is organized into one or more columns of text. Images, if used are allowed to span an integer number of columns. Automated algorithms for newspaper layout use different methods to compute the tilings and assign articles to tiles.

De Oliveira [4] [5] uses dynamic programming to layout a set of articles on a page by splitting the sequence of articles (each with a given desired page coverage percentage)

into a number of rows to be placed from the top of the page to the bottom. The algorithm attempts to create a tiling that tries to approximate the desired article coverage percentages as closely as possible. One issue with this approach is that there may be overflows or underflows (white spaces) when articles are actually rendered into the tiles computed for them (since there is no explicit fitting of article text and images to the page, but only a computation of a space partition that respects pre-assigned coverage percentages). To resolve this the authors simply reduce/increase the font size of each article to ensure a fit. This may not be desirable in many cases.

Strecker and Hennig [12] divide a page into a 4×16. Each article has 8 possible configurations, spanning columns 1-4 and either including an image or not. The articles are assigned to the grid regions using greedy algorithms following a left-right, top-bottom placement strategy. The next empty rectangular region and article to be placed in it are selected based on an objective function evaluation which considers area of item to be placed, whitespace left at bottom and the ratio of region area to remaining space on the page. This is a heuristic local search method and does not globally optimize its objective function.

Another promising class of tilings is generated by a recursive partitioning of the page using a sequence of vertical and horizontal cuts. Such *Guillotine* layouts have been used to position rectangular items having different aspect ratios (such as photos) in a manner that maximizes page coverage [1]. Recently Gange et. al. have [6] provided an elegant dynamic programming solution that *optimally* solves the *fixed-cut Guillotine* layout of text (images are not supported yet). Here articles are assigned to regions that are represented by leaf nodes in a tree representation of a *Guillotine* space partition and the problem is to find the minimum-height layout of the text. Minimum height layouts, while acceptable for many scrolling displays are not well suited for paginated documents with fixed page dimensions, since often whitespace and image sizes may need to be expanded to get a more aesthetic presentation.

In contrast to the prior approaches described above our approach plans to mimic the activities of a publication designer by modeling various design choices with conditional probability distributions as described in the introduction. Our objective function is thus much more complex and is a

142

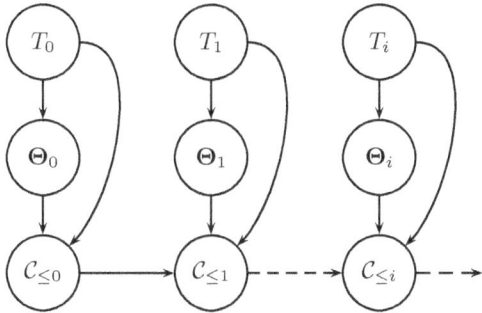

Figure 2: PDM as a graphical model.

product of several conditional probability distributions each representing how well some design choice was made given other design choices. Such modeling of document composition was first introduced in our previous work [3] where we also showed that such structured modeling gave rise to an efficient computational algorithm for layout synthesis. The algorithm globally optimizes our objective function.

This work can be regarded as a generalization (or specialization, depending on your point of view) of the probabilistic model introduced in [3] by decomposing the model for a page into a two level hierarchy enabling article level configuration of the space on a page and region level configuration of space within an article region. Although the model presented in [3] was very general, applicable to arbitrary document composition specific model parameterization was given only for *single-flow* layouts. These are layouts (such as the layout of this DocEng paper) that exhibit a single flow of column-width text that snakes across one or more columns breaking only at the end of the page and continuing at the top of the next column/page. All section/article titles occur in the same text flow. Images however are allowed to span one or more columns and appear at any point after the text referencing it (preferably close of course). Newspapers however, require that text break at the end of each region within a page and possibly even continue on another region on a subsequent page. Images associated with an article must appear in the rectangular region enclosed by that article. Such layouts can be considered *multi-flow* layouts since the text of each article can be considered an independent text flow. Our hierarchical generalization is significant since it now allows such *multi-flow* newspaper layouts to be parameterized and synthesized.

3. PROBABILISTIC DOCUMENT MODEL

In this section we review a structured probabilistic model of designer choice in arbitrary document design [3]. We represent the given set of all the units of content to be composed (ex: images, units of text, sidebars etc.) by a finite ordered set $\mathcal{C}^2$. Text units could be words, sentences, lines of text or whole paragraphs. In the case of a *single-flow* document since there is only one stream of text of width equal to the width of the column, one can break all the text to be laid out into column-width lines (using appropriate defined styles for

---

[2]A more general model which does not include the ordering constraint was presented in [3], but imposing linear order on the content set leads to faster algorithms and will be used in this paper without loss of generality

each text block) in a pre-processing step. A content set may then be represented in terms of lines of column-width text and figures. For example, a content set of 6 lines of text and one figure can be represented by $\mathcal{C} = \{l_1, l_2, l_3, f_1, l_4, l_5, l_6\}$. In this representation of content the lines of text could belong to one or more articles and have different heights based on the fonts used to render them.

In order to compose documents, one must make aesthetic decisions on how to paginate content, how to arrange page elements (text, images, graphics, sidebars etc.) on each page, how much to crop/scale images, how to manage whitespace etc. These decision variables are *not* mutually exclusive, making the aesthetic graphic design of documents a hard problem often requiring an expert design professional. The probabilistic document model (PDM) [3] explicitly models the dependency between key design choices including pagination, choice of relative arrangements for page elements, and page edits (including image re-targeting and whitespace adjustment). The coupling between these design variables is explicitly modeled as a Bayesian network shown in Fig. 2. A probability distribution can be associated with the network by multiplying the conditional probability distributions of each node conditioned only on its parents [11].

$$\mathbb{P}(D, I) = \prod_{i=0}^{I-1} \mathbb{P}(\mathcal{C}_{\leq i} | \mathcal{C}_{\leq i-1}, \Theta_i, T_i) \mathbb{P}(\Theta_i | T_i) \mathbb{P}(T_i) \quad (1)$$

Random set $\mathcal{C}_{\leq i}$ represents choice of a content allocation to the first i pages. Note that content allocation to the ith page (i.e. pagination) is computed as $\mathcal{C}_i = \mathcal{C}_{\leq i} - \mathcal{C}_{\leq i-1}$.

Random variable T_i represents choice of a relative arrangement of page elements for the ith page from a library of page templates representing different possible relative arrangements of content.

Random vector Θ_i encodes template parameters representing possible edits to the chosen template. Possible choices for variable template parameters Θ include figure dimensions, whitespace between page elements, margins etc.

In this paper we treat the page count I as a given constant so $\mathbb{P}(D) = \mathbb{P}(D, I)$. More generally we could treat page count as a random variable also. See [3] for details.

PDM is in fact a *micro* model for document quality that associates a probability (or quality score) with each *conditional* design choice made on each page. The overall probability of a document is the product of these *micro* probability scores. A document $\mathcal{D}$ of I pages is defined by a triplet $\mathcal{D} = \{\{\mathcal{C}_{\leq i}\}_{i=0}^{I-1}, \{\Theta_i\}_{i=0}^{I-1}, \{T_i\}_{i=0}^{I-1}\}$ of random variables representing the various design choices made in the document creation process. The overall quality $\mathbb{P}(D)$ of a document $\mathcal{D}$ is the product of the conditional probabilities of all design choices made. PDM contrasts with *macro* models for document quality [2, 7] that attempt to quantify abstract aesthetic notions such as harmony, balance, regularity etc.

In equation (1) probability distribution $\mathbb{P}(T_i)$ governs relative preference of template T_i from a set Ω of possible templates. The conditional multi-variate probability distribution $\mathbb{P}(\Theta_i | T_i)$ may be regarded as a *prior* probability distribution that determines the *prior* preference (before seeing content) for template parameters. Finally the probability distribution $\mathbb{P}(\mathcal{C}_{\leq i} | \mathcal{C}_{\leq i-1}, \Theta_i, T_i)$ reflects how well the content allocated to the current page fits template T_i when template parameters are set to Θ_i.

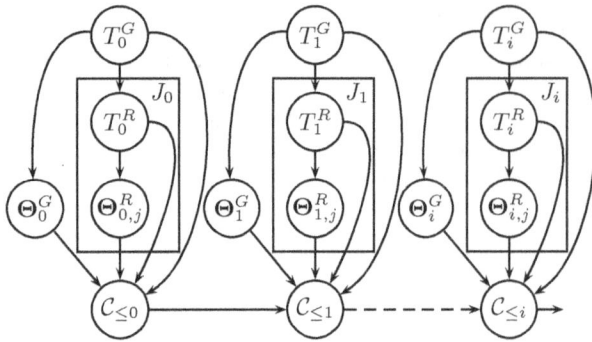

Figure 3: HPDM as a graphical model.

Given a PDM quality model, layout synthesis reduces to the task of computing the optimizing sequences of templates, template parameters, content allocations that maximize overall document probability.

$$\mathcal{D}^* = \underset{\mathcal{D}}{\arg\max}\, \mathbb{P}(\mathcal{D}) \qquad (2)$$

This *inference* task can be performed efficiently using dynamic programming once the probability distributions are defined. See [3] for details.

4. THE HIERARCHICAL MODEL

We generalize the PDM model [3] to a hierachical probabilistic document model (HPDM) to accommodate newspaper-style layouts. We describe the hierarchical nature of newspaper-style documents by introducing two types of templates: global and region. Global templates contain document header and other page static elements along with the document regions assigned to articles. Each region contains content from exactly one article. Region templates describe relative position of document content elements, such as text, figure, captions etc. We also allow some articles be allocated across different pages in the document. In case of a content flow, the initial part of the article content can be allocated on one region and the rest on a region of the succeeding page. Figure 1 shows a diagram of a selection of a global and region templates in composition of a one page news document layout.

4.1 Model development

Let us assume that we have to lay out L news articles. The overall content set $\mathcal{C} = \{\mathcal{C}^1, \mathcal{C}^2, \cdots, \mathcal{C}^L\}$ where C^l is the content set (including lines and figures) for the lth article. For example, a content set for the second article of 6 lines of text and one figure can be represented by $\mathcal{C}^2 = \{l_1, l_2, l_3, f_1, l_4, l_5, l_6\}$. We denote by $\mathcal{C}' = \{\mathcal{C}'^1, \mathcal{C}'^2, \cdots, \mathcal{C}'^L\}$ a set comprising all sets of discrete content allocation possibilities over one or more pages starting with and including the first page. In the preceding example, $\mathcal{C}'^2 = \{\{l_1\}, \{l_1, l_2\}, \{l_1-l_3\}, \{l_1-l_3, f_1\}, \{l_1-l_3, f_1, l_4\}, \{l_1-l_3, f_1, l_4, l_5\}, \{l_1-l_3, f_1, l_4-l_6\}\}$. Note that if the jth article is not allowed to be split and flow across pages, then $\mathcal{C}'^j = \mathcal{C}^j$.

Fig 3 shows a Bayesian network representation of our hierarchical probabilistic model for an I page news composition. As described before, the model is completely characterized by it's equivalent joint probability distribution that can be associated with the network by multiplying the in-

dividual conditional probability distributions of each node conditioned only on its parents [11].

$$
\begin{aligned}
\mathbb{P}(D) &= \prod_{i=0}^{I-1}\prod_{j=0}^{J_i-1}\{\mathbb{P}(\mathcal{C}_{\leq i}|\mathcal{C}_{\leq i-1}, \boldsymbol{\Theta}_i^G, \{\boldsymbol{\Theta}_{i,j}^R\}, T_i^G, \{T_{i,j}^R\})\\
&\quad \times \mathbb{P}(\boldsymbol{\Theta}_i^G|T_i^G)\mathbb{P}(T_i^G)\mathbb{P}(\boldsymbol{\Theta}_{i,j}^R|T_{i,j}^R)\mathbb{P}(T_{i,j}^R|T_i^G)\}
\end{aligned} \qquad (3)
$$

Here $\mathcal{C}_{\leq i} = \{\mathcal{S}^1, \mathcal{S}^2, \cdots, \mathcal{S}^k\}$ is a random set derived by selecting a set of subsets $\{\mathcal{S}^1, \mathcal{S}^2, \cdots, \mathcal{S}^k\}$ from $\mathcal{C}'$ such that $\mathcal{S}^k \subseteq \mathcal{C}'^k$. We denote this relationship by $\mathcal{C}_{\leq i} \lhd \mathcal{C}'$. $\mathcal{C}_{\leq i}$ is simply a possible assignment of article content to the first i pages allowing for partial or split articles. We also denote by $\mathcal{C}_{\leq i-1} \preceq \mathcal{C}_{\leq i}$ the requirement that for any k^{th} element of $\mathcal{C}_{\leq i-1}$, $\mathcal{Q}^k$, $\mathcal{Q}^{\bar{k}} \subseteq \mathcal{S}^k$. This requirement states that content allocated for upto $i-1$ pages must also be included when we consider allocations upto the ith page.

Random variable T_i^G represents a choice of a relative arrangement of article regions for the ith page from a library Ω^G of global page templates representing different possible relative arrangements of articles on a page. Random variable $T_{i,j}^R$ represents choice of a relative arrangement of page elements (text and images) for the jth region of the ith page from a library Ω^R of region templates representing different possible relative arrangements of content in a region.

Random vector $\boldsymbol{\Theta}_i^G$ encodes global template parameters representing possible edits to the chosen global template for the ith page. Possible choices for global template parameters include region dimensions, whitespace between regions elements, page margins etc. Random vector $\boldsymbol{\Theta}_{i,j}^R$ represents region template parameters representing possible edits to the region template for the jth region on the ith page. Possible choices for region template parameters include image dimensions, whitespace within the region, whitespace between lines, region margins etc.

The distribution $\mathbb{P}(T_i^G)$ governs relative prior preferences for global templates. This can be described by a multinomial distribution. However we set this to a uniform distribution over the number of global templates in the library so that there is no prior preference in selecting a particular global template for a page.

The distribution $\mathbb{P}(T_{i,j}^R|T_i^G)$ represents the probability of a particular region template fitting into the jth region of a given global template. Note that there are J_i regions on the ith global template T_i^G. In general, we may try to fit the region template into the region by expanding or contracting its column width. This distribution simply penalizes deviations from a desired column width. If we use a fixed column width for the page and a region template has more columns (is wider) or less columns (is narrower) than the width of the region under consideration, the distribution assigns probability zero to the region template. Otherwise a probability of one is assigned when the number of columns match.

The conditional distribution $\mathbb{P}(\boldsymbol{\Theta}_{i,j}^R|T_{i,j}^R)$ represents the *prior* probability distribution of region template parameters given a specific region template. In general, we model the *prior* distributions of region template parameters of the form $\mathbb{P}(\boldsymbol{\Theta}^R|T^R)$ as multi-variate Normal distributions:

$$\mathbb{P}(\boldsymbol{\Theta}^R|T^R) = \mathrm{N}(\boldsymbol{\Theta}^R|\bar{\boldsymbol{\Theta}}^R, (\boldsymbol{\Lambda}^R)^{-1}) \qquad (4)$$

where $\bar{\boldsymbol{\Theta}}^R$ is the mean of $\boldsymbol{\Theta}^R|T^R$ and $\boldsymbol{\Lambda}^R$ is its precision matrix. If there is more than one choice of region parameters that will fill the page this prior will determine how parameter values are to be adjusted thus affecting the aesthetics of the composition. For this reason we can consider this an *aesthetics* prior that encodes prior knowledge of what makes a region look good. The mean parameter $\bar{\Theta}^R$ is simply the most desired parameter setting for the parameter vector Θ^R and is straightforward to obtain from a designer. In this work we assume that the mean of the parameter prior is given by the designer. Clearly when fitting content to the page, deviation of parameter values from the most preferred region mean values is often required. The precision matrix Λ^R controls which parameters have loose tolerance and may vary more freely and which have tight tolerances and should not deviate much from their means. The precision matrix is typically diagonal and set using specified individual parameter variances. Note that since in typical news layouts, images in a region span integer columns, the image region of a region template has fixed width and need not be parameterized. The image height θ_h however may be varied independently by using auto-cropping or retargeting algorithms, and is thus a region template parameter. We want:

$$\theta_h \approx \frac{I_w}{a} \text{, with precision } \rho \text{, or}$$

$$\theta_h \sim N(\frac{I_w}{a}, \rho^{-1}) \qquad (5)$$

where a is the aspect ratio and I_w is the width of the original image. If we do not want to allow the aspect ratio of an image to change (in the case of pure image scaling) we let $\rho \to \infty$. On the other hand, we may use image re-targeting algorithms to allow the image aspect ratio to change. In this case the value of ρ will determine if we allow small (by setting ρ to a large value) or large (by setting ρ to a small value) changes in aspect ratio. We use the re-targeting algorithm described in [9] in this paper. By estimating retargeting scores for an image at different aspect ratios we can discover which images can be retargeted more aggressively. We can thus set aspect ratio tolerances ρ on an image dependent basis so that some images get cropped/retargeted more than others if needed. Note that if an image is present in a region template the corresponding image height parameter has its mean $\frac{I_w}{a}$ and precision ρ encoded in $\bar{\Theta}^R$ (as an element) and Λ^R (as a diagonal element) respectively.

$\mathbb{P}(\Theta_i^G | T_i^G)$ represents the prior probability of global template parameters and is defined by a multivariate Normal distribution with a mean vector and diagonal precision matrix, similar to the region parameter distributions described above. Thus,

$$\mathbb{P}(\Theta^G | T^G) = N(\Theta^G | \bar{\Theta}^G, (\Lambda^G)^{-1}) \qquad (6)$$

$\mathbb{P}(\mathcal{C}_{\leq i} | \mathcal{C}_{\leq i-1}, \Theta_i^G, \{\Theta_{i,j}^R\}, T_i^G, \{T_{i,j}^R\})$ is the likelihood of a specific content allocation to a page. It reflects how well the content allocated to the current page $(\mathcal{C}_{\leq i} - \mathcal{C}_{\leq i-1})$ fits a specific combination of global template T_i^G and region templates $\{T_{i,j}^R\}$ when global and region template parameters are set to Θ_i^G and $\{\Theta_{i,j}^R\}$ respectively. In general this distribution has the form $\mathbb{P}(\mathcal{A}|\mathcal{B}, \Theta^G, \{\Theta_j^R\}, T^G, \{T_j^R\})$ and is valid for any sets $\mathcal{A}, \mathcal{B} \triangleleft \mathcal{C}'$ with $\mathcal{B} \preceq \mathcal{A}$. Note that the distribution will assign zero probability to cases where the content on a page $\mathcal{A} - \mathcal{B}$ does not match the global template T^G. For example if the content on the current page is for 4 articles and the chosen global template supports only 3 articles this distribution will assign zero probability to that case. Also

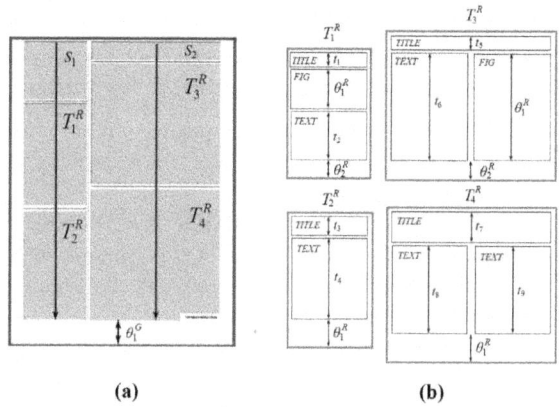

(a)   **(b)**

Figure 4: Template parameterization

the content must also match region templates $\{T_j^R\}$ chosen for that page. For example let us consider that 3 articles are assigned to a page given a global template with 3 articles. If one of the articles has a required image and none of the region templates selected for the 3 global template regions has an image slot again zero probability is assigned. Clearly, for non-zero probability to be assigned by this distribution the content allocation $\mathcal{A} - \mathcal{B}$ to the page should be compatible with global template configuration and region template configurations given for that page. We may further combine these requirements with the distribution $\mathbb{P}(T^R | T^G)$ discussed earlier that checks if the selected region templates fit into the given global template slots. In fact these considerations may be directly incorporated using two lookup tables. The first lookup table takes content on a page as input and outputs a set of matching global templates. For each of these global templates a second lookup table maps each region to a set of matching region templates considering both content configuration and fit.

For a given content allocation and matching global and region templates, there are two considerations that lead to a parameterization of $\mathbb{P}(\mathcal{A}|\mathcal{B}, \Theta^G, \{\Theta_j^R\}, T^G, \{T_j^R\})$. First, how does content allocated to each region fit/fill the region? Second, how do the regions themselves fill the page. Figure 4 shows an illustrative global template (with global template parameters) and corresponding region templates (each with their own set of region template parameters).

Each region template has a desired height h_j^R. If the number of columns in this region template is N_j then the total height available to be filled within the region template is $H_j^R = N_j h_j^R$. Clearly fixed elements like margins and other fixed whitespace take up some of this space. Further, once a content allocation is made to a region, the title and text allocated to the region also occupy some of this space. Therefore, the residual height $\tilde{H}_j^R$ is given by:

$$\tilde{H}_j^R = H_j^R - \sum_{n=1}^{N_j} (f_n + c_n) \qquad (7)$$

where f_n and c_n represent the height of fixed elements/spaces and titles/text respectively along the nth column of the region template[3]. For example, with reference to Figure 4 for region template T_4^R, $\tilde{H}_4 = H_4 - 2\,t_7 - t_8 - t_9$.

To fit the template region, the residual height must be filled by editing the template parameters. This requires:

$$\begin{aligned}
\tilde{H}_j^R &\approx \mathbf{Y}_j^R\,\mathbf{\Theta}_j^R \text{ ,with precision } \alpha \text{ or} \\
\tilde{H}_j^R &\sim N(\mathbf{Y}_j^R\,\mathbf{\Theta}_j^R, \alpha^{-1})
\end{aligned} \tag{8}$$

where the $1 \times dim(\mathbf{\Theta}_j^R)$ matrix $\mathbf{Y}_j^R$ has its kth element equal to the the number of columns in which parameter $\mathbf{\Theta}_j^R(k) = \theta_k^R$ is present. For example, with reference to Figure 4 for region template T_3^R, $\mathbf{Y}_j^R = [1\ 2]$.

Now to consider how regions fill the page we introduce the notion of global paths which play the same role as columns in the previous discussion on fitting content into region templates. Regions may span paths in a global template in much the same manner that an image or title spans columns in a region template. Let the height of the page be h^G. If the global template has P paths, the total height available to be filled for the pth path is $\mathbf{H}^G(p) = M_p\,h^G$ where M_p is the number of columns of the page included in the pth path. The residual path height vector $\tilde{\mathbf{H}}^G$ after content allocation is given by:

$$\tilde{\mathbf{H}}^G(p) = \mathbf{H}^G(p) - \left(f_p + M_p \sum_j \frac{H_j^R - \tilde{H}_j^R}{N_j} I(p,j) \right) \tag{9}$$

where f_p represent the height of fixed elements/spaces (elements S_1 and S_2 in Fig. 4) along the pth path of the global template and $I(p,j)$ is an indicator function that equals one when the jth region is present in the pth path and zero otherwise. These residual path heights must be filled by the global template parameters and the actual region template heights. Therefore, this requires

$$\tilde{\mathbf{H}}^G \approx \mathbf{Y} \underbrace{\left[\begin{array}{c} \mathbf{\Theta}_0^R \\ \mathbf{\Theta}_1^R \\ \vdots \\ \mathbf{\Theta}_{J-1}^R \\ \mathbf{\Theta}^G \end{array} \right]}_{\mathbf{\Theta}} \tag{10}$$

where

$$\mathbf{Y} = \left[\begin{array}{ccccc} \mathbf{Y}_{0,0} & \mathbf{Y}_{0,1} & \cdots & \mathbf{Y}_{0,J-1} & \mathbf{Y}_0^G \\ \mathbf{Y}_{1,0} & \mathbf{Y}_{1,1} & \cdots & \mathbf{Y}_{1,J-1} & \mathbf{Y}_1^G \\ & & \vdots & & \\ \mathbf{Y}_{P-1,0} & \mathbf{Y}_{P-1,1} & \cdots & \mathbf{Y}_{P-1,J-1} & \mathbf{Y}_{P-1}^G \end{array} \right] \tag{11}$$

with sub-matrices $\mathbf{Y}_{p,j}$ given by

$$\mathbf{Y}_{p,j} = \frac{M_p}{N_j}\mathbf{Y}_j^R I(p,j) \tag{12}$$

$\mathbf{Y}_p^G$ is a $1 \times dim(\mathbf{\Theta}^G)$ matrix that has its kth element equal to M_p if $\mathbf{\Theta}^G(k) = \theta_k^G$ is present in the pth path.

For example, assuming a column grid of 3 columns on the page, with reference to Figure 4(b) for the global template $\mathbf{Y}_0^G = [1]$, $\mathbf{Y}_1^G = [2]$ since there is a single global parameter

---

[3]Text and title heights may be calculated for using the font linespacing and the number of allocated lines. Note that text is broken into lines in a preprocessing step as described in Section 3.

appearing in both paths and the second path contains two columns. For this example:

$$\mathbf{Y} = \left[\begin{array}{ccccccc} 1 & 1 & 1 & 0 & 0 & 0 & 1 \\ 0 & 0 & 0 & 1 & 2 & 2 & 2 \end{array} \right]$$

Combining equation (10) and equations (8) we get[4]:

$$\mathbb{P}(\mathcal{A}|\mathcal{B}, \underbrace{\mathbf{\Theta}^G, \{\mathbf{\Theta}_j^R\}}_{\mathbf{\Theta}}, \underbrace{T^G, \{T_j^R\}}_{T}) = \prod_j N(\tilde{H}_j^R|\mathbf{Y}_j^R\,\mathbf{\Theta}_j^R, \alpha^{-1})$$
$$\times N(\tilde{\mathbf{H}}^G|\mathbf{Y}\mathbf{\Theta}, \beta^{-1}\mathbf{I}) \tag{13}$$

where β is the precision associated with equation (10). Note that the above distribution may be rewritten as product of Normal distributions in the template parameters $\mathbf{\Theta}$

$$\begin{aligned}
\mathbb{P}(\mathcal{A}|\mathcal{B}, \mathbf{\Theta}, T) = \ &N\left(\mathbf{\Theta} | \left(\mathbf{Y}^T\mathbf{Y}\right)^{-1}\mathbf{Y}^T\tilde{\mathbf{H}}, \left(\beta\mathbf{Y}^T\mathbf{Y}\right)^{-1} \right) \\
&\times N\left(\mathbf{\Theta} | \left(\mathbf{Z}^T\mathbf{Z}\right)^{-1}\mathbf{Z}^T\tilde{\mathbf{H}}^R, \left(\alpha\mathbf{Z}^T\mathbf{Z}\right)^{-1} \right)
\end{aligned} \tag{14}$$

where $\tilde{\mathbf{H}}^R = [\tilde{H}_0^R\ \tilde{H}_1^R \cdots \tilde{H}_{J-1}^R\ 0]^T$ and

$$\mathbf{Z} = \left[\begin{array}{ccccc} \mathbf{Y}_0^R & & & & \\ & \mathbf{Y}_1^R & & & \\ & & \ddots & & \\ & & & \mathbf{Y}_{J-1}^R & \\ & & & & \mathbf{0}_{1 \times dim(\mathbf{\Theta}^G)} \end{array} \right] \tag{15}$$

The global fit precision β is typically set high to avoid underflows and overflows on a page. The region precision α is typically set to a relatively low value to allow the regions to contract or expand more freely from their nominal desired heights in order to fit content.

4.2 Layout Synthesis

The optimal document (or sequence of design choices) is $\mathcal{D}^* = \{\{\mathcal{C}_{\leq i}^*\}, \{\mathbf{\Theta}_i^{G*}\}, \{T_i^{G*}\}, \{\{T_{i,j}^{R*}\}_{j=0}^{J_i-1}\}, \{\{\mathbf{\Theta}_{i,j}^{R*}\}_{j=0}^{J_i-1}\}\}$. $\mathcal{D}^*$ maximizes equation (3). The maximization (optimal document *inference*) algorithm is very similar to the dynamic programming algorithm derived in some detail in[3] for the maximization of equation (1) and is succinctly summarized in Algorithms 1 and 2.

In the *forward pass* we successively eliminate each variable in (3) by first grouping terms involving the variable and then finding the maxima of these terms with respect to that variable. This gives us functions of the remaining variables. These functions (dynamic programming tables) are then propagated to the next maximization step for further grouping and variable elimination.

In step 1 we group terms involving the global and region parameters and maximize with respect to these parameters. Thus for every valid $\mathcal{A}, \mathcal{B} \lhd \mathcal{C}'$ with $\mathcal{B} \preceq \mathcal{A}$ and all compatible templates $T^G, \{T_j^R\}$ we perform a continuous variable optimization and store the maximum as a table entry in $\Psi(\mathcal{A}, \mathcal{B}, T^G, \{T_j^R\})$. Note that the product $\mathbb{P}(\mathbf{\Theta}^G|T^G) \prod_j \mathbb{P}(\mathbf{\Theta}_j^R|T_j^R)$ may be represented as a Normal distribution in $\mathbf{\Theta}$

$$\mathbb{P}(\mathbf{\Theta}^G|T^G) \prod_j \mathbb{P}(\mathbf{\Theta}_j^R|T_j^R) = N(\mathbf{\Theta}|\bar{\mathbf{\Theta}}, \Lambda^{-1}) \tag{16}$$

---

[4]Clearly, $\mathbf{Y}_j^R, \mathbf{Y}$ are calculated for a specific region template T_j^R and global template T^G respectively while $\tilde{\mathbf{H}}^G, \tilde{H}_j^R$ additionally depend on the content allocation $\mathcal{A} - \mathcal{B}$. These dependencies are left out of the notation to avoid clutter.

Algorithm 1 Computing Document $\mathcal{D}^*$ with HPDM inference: Forward pass

1: $\Psi(\mathcal{A}, \mathcal{B}, T^G, \{T_j^R\}) = \displaystyle\max_{\boldsymbol{\Theta}^G, \{\boldsymbol{\Theta}_j^R\}} \left(\mathbb{P}(\mathcal{A}|\mathcal{B}, \boldsymbol{\Theta}^G, \{\boldsymbol{\Theta}_j^R\}, T^G, \{T_j^R\}) \, \mathbb{P}(\boldsymbol{\Theta}^G|T^G) \prod_j \mathbb{P}(\boldsymbol{\Theta}_j^R|T_j^R) \right)$

2: $\Phi_G(\mathcal{A}, \mathcal{B}, T^G) = \displaystyle\max_{\{T_j^R\} \in \Omega^R} \left(\Psi(\mathcal{A}, \mathcal{B}, T^G, \{T_j^R\}) \prod_j \mathbb{P}(T_j^R|T^G) \right)$

3: $\Phi(\mathcal{A}, \mathcal{B}) = \displaystyle\max_{T^G \in \Omega^G} \left(\Phi_G(\mathcal{A}, \mathcal{B}, T^G) \, \mathbb{P}(T^G) \right)$

4: $\tau_0(\mathcal{A}) \leftarrow \Phi(\mathcal{A}, \emptyset)$

5: $\tau_i(\mathcal{A}) = \displaystyle\max_{\mathcal{B}} \left(\Phi(\mathcal{A}, \mathcal{B}) \, \tau_{i-1}(\mathcal{B}) \right), i \geq 1$

Algorithm 2 Computing Document $\mathcal{D}^*$ with HPDM inference: Backward pass

$i \leftarrow I - 1, \mathcal{A}^* \leftarrow \mathcal{C}$

while $i \geq 0$ **do**

$\quad \mathcal{C}_{\leq i}^* \leftarrow \mathcal{A}^*$

$\quad \mathcal{B}^* = \arg\max_{\mathcal{B}} \left(\Phi(\mathcal{A}^*, \mathcal{B}) \, \tau_{i-1}(\mathcal{B}) \right)$

$\quad T_i^{G*} = \arg\max_{T^G \in \Omega} \left(\Phi_G(\mathcal{A}^*, \mathcal{B}^*, T^G) \, \mathbb{P}(T^G) \right)$

$\quad \{T_{i,j}^{R*}\} = \arg\max_{\{T_j^R\} \in \Omega^R} \left(\Psi(\mathcal{A}^*, \mathcal{B}^*, T_i^{G*}, \{T_j^R\}) \prod_j \mathbb{P}(T_j^R|T_i^{G*}) \right)$

$\quad \boldsymbol{\Theta}_i^{G*}, \{\boldsymbol{\Theta}_{i,j}^{R*}\} = \arg\max_{\boldsymbol{\Theta}^G, \{\boldsymbol{\Theta}_j^R\}} \left(\mathbb{P}(\mathcal{A}^*|\mathcal{B}^*, \boldsymbol{\Theta}^G, \{\boldsymbol{\Theta}_j^R\}, T_i^{G*}, \{T_{i,j}^{R*}\}) \, \mathbb{P}(\boldsymbol{\Theta}^G|T_i^{G*}) \prod_j \mathbb{P}(\boldsymbol{\Theta}_j^R|T_{i,j}^{R*}) \right)$

$\quad \mathcal{A}^* \leftarrow \mathcal{B}^*$

$\quad i \leftarrow i - 1$

end while

---

where $\bar{\boldsymbol{\Theta}} = [\bar{\boldsymbol{\Theta}}^R \ \bar{\boldsymbol{\Theta}}^G]^T$ and

$$\Lambda = \begin{bmatrix} \Lambda^R & \\ & \Lambda^G \end{bmatrix} \tag{17}$$

Also from equation (14) we see that $\mathbb{P}(\mathcal{A}|\mathcal{B}, \boldsymbol{\Theta}, T)$ as also a product of Normal distributions in $\boldsymbol{\Theta}$. Since the parametric forms of each of the distributions in the maximization are all Normal in the template parameters, the product is also a Normal distribution in $\boldsymbol{\Theta}$. The mean of this normal distribution is the desired maximizer we are seeking and can be computed in closed form as $\boldsymbol{\Theta}^* = \mathbf{A}^{-1}\mathbf{b}$, where:

$$\mathbf{A} = \Lambda + \alpha \mathbf{Z}^T \mathbf{Z} + \beta \mathbf{Y}^T \mathbf{Y} \tag{18}$$

$$\mathbf{b} = \Lambda \bar{\boldsymbol{\Theta}} + \alpha \mathbf{Z}^T \tilde{\mathbf{H}}^R + \beta \mathbf{Y}^T \tilde{\mathbf{H}}^G \tag{19}$$

In general, however, there may be bound constraints on some of the components of $\boldsymbol{\Theta}_t$ (ex: figure dimensions cannot be negative). To incorporate these constraints we solve the following bound-constrained least-squares quadratic program.

$$\boldsymbol{\Theta}^* = \arg\max_{\{\boldsymbol{\Theta} : \mathbf{l} \leq \boldsymbol{\Theta} \leq \mathbf{u}\}} (\mathbf{A}\boldsymbol{\Theta} - \mathbf{b})^T (\mathbf{A}\boldsymbol{\Theta} - \mathbf{b}) \tag{20}$$

where $\mathbf{l}$ and $\mathbf{u}$ are lower and upper bound vectors constraining $\boldsymbol{\Theta}$.

The Ψ table essentially stores a score of how well content in the set $\mathcal{A} - \mathcal{B}$ is suited for templates $T^G, \{T_j^R\}$. It is the maximum of a product of three terms. The first term $\mathbb{P}(\mathcal{A}|\mathcal{B}, \boldsymbol{\Theta}^G, \{\boldsymbol{\Theta}_j^R\}, T^G, \{T_j^R\})$ represents how well content fits the page while the second and third terms $\mathbb{P}(\{\boldsymbol{\Theta}_j^R\}|\{T_j^R\})$ and $\mathbb{P}(\boldsymbol{\Theta}^G|T^G)$ assesses how close the parameters of a region and global template are to the designer's *aesthetic* preference. Thus the overall probability (score) is a tradeoff between page fill and a designer's aesthetic intent. When there

are multiple parameters settings that fill the page equally well, the parameters that maximize the prior (and hence are closest to the template designer's desired values) will be favored.

To prune the number of cases for which optimization must be performed in practice, we use the two stage lookup table described in Section 4.1 to get a set of global templates matching the content $\mathcal{A} - \mathcal{B}$ and then for each of these cases, for each region of each global template we lookup a set of region templates that match the content allocation to that region and also fit the space available for each region. Note further, that since $\mathcal{A} - \mathcal{B}$ represents the content allocated to a page, it is bounded by page dimensions. This means that in general, for each $\mathcal{A}$ the valid $\mathcal{B}$'s are in a neighborhood $\mathcal{N}_{\mathbf{f}}(\mathcal{A}) = \{\mathcal{B} : \mathbf{d}(\mathcal{A} - \mathcal{B}) \leq \mathbf{f}\}$. The function $\mathbf{d}(\mathcal{A} - \mathcal{B})$ returns a vector of the counts of the various page elements in the set $\mathcal{A} - \mathcal{B}$. $\mathbf{f}$ is a vector that bounds the numbers of various page elements allowed on a page. For example we may set $\mathbf{f} = [100 \,(\text{lines}), 2 \,(\text{figures})]^T$. This will eliminate an allocation where $\mathbf{d}(\mathcal{A} - \mathcal{B}) = [110 \,(\text{lines}), 2 \,(\text{figures})]^T$.

In step 2 we maximize the table $\Psi(\mathcal{A}, \mathcal{B}, T^G, \{T_j^R\})$ over all valid region templates compatible with the content $\mathcal{A} - \mathcal{B}$ and the global template T^G. This gives us a new table $\Phi_G(\mathcal{A}, \mathcal{B}, T^G)$. Note that since we only compute table entries of Ψ for compatible global and region templates, the term $\prod_j \mathbb{P}(T_j^R|T^G) = 1$. In step 3 we maximize the table $\Phi_G(\mathcal{A}, \mathcal{B}, T^G)$ over all global templates to get the table $\Phi(\mathcal{A}, \mathcal{B})$. The function $\Phi(\mathcal{A}, \mathcal{B})$ scores how well content $\mathcal{A} - \mathcal{B}$ can be composed onto a page, considering all possible relative arrangements of content allowed for that page.

Finally tables $\tau_i(\mathcal{A})$ are computed recursively in step 5. $\tau_i(\mathcal{A})$ is a pure pagination score of the allocation $\mathcal{A}$ to the first i pages. The recursion (5) basically says that the pagination score for an allocation $\mathcal{A}$ to the first i pages, $\tau_i(\mathcal{A})$ is equal to the product of the best pagination score over all possible previous allocations $\mathcal{B}$ to the previous $(i-1)$ pages with the score of the current allocation $\mathcal{A} - \mathcal{B}$ to the current page, $\Phi(\mathcal{A}, \mathcal{B})$.

In the *backward pass* we traverse the tables backward starting from the term $\tau_{I-1}(\mathcal{C})$ that equals the global maximum of equation (3) over all the content. The backward pass successively infers the allocations of content to the previous pages along with templates and template parameters that are on the path to achieving the global maximum.

The dynamic programming approach outlined in this section results in a global optimization of the seemingly complex objective function in equation (3).

4.3 Complexity Analysis

We may analyze asymptotic complexity of this algorithm in a similar manner to the analysis presented in [3]. Algorithm complexity is dominated by table construction in the forward pass. As discussed earlier, the possibilities for set $\mathcal{B}$ may be restricted to a neighborhood $\mathcal{N}_{\mathbf{f}}(\mathcal{A}) = \{\mathcal{B} : \mathbf{d}(\mathcal{A} - \mathcal{B}) \leq \mathbf{f}\}$. Also the template lookup tables provide a finite and bounded number of global templates T^G and region templates , $\{T_j^R\}$ matching content $\mathcal{A} - \mathcal{B}$ (typically the number of configurations does not exceed 100). Thus the construction of table Ψ (which dominates algorithm complexity) grows only with the number of possibilities for the set $\mathcal{A}$.

Let $|\mathcal{C}_{max}|$ be the maximum number of content elements in an article. In the worst case when all articles are allowed to flow, the number of possible allocations of content upto and including a given page (number of possibilities for $\mathcal{A}$) is $|\mathcal{C}^0| + |\mathcal{C}^0||\mathcal{C}^1| + \cdots + |\mathcal{C}^0||\mathcal{C}^1| \cdots |\mathcal{C}^{L-1}|$ which grows as $O(|\mathcal{C}_{max}|^L)$. Thus we have to contend with exponential growth in complexity. At the other extreme if none of the articles are allowed to flow, the number of possibilities for a content allocation is simply L implying linear computational complexity as the number of articles grows. In the general case when there are $L - M$ flow articles and M articles which cannot flow asymptotic complexity is $O(M|\mathcal{C}_{max}|^{L-M})$ for $M > 0$. Thus there are significant computational reasons to bound the number of flow articles in the content set, so that asymptotic complexity would grow linearly with the non-flow articles.

5. CONTENT EDITING

We assume that a fixed page count (or page range) is given and we are allowed to clip content to get the best layout over the desired number of pages. Since clipping of content requires one to understand the meaning of the content we may optionally have a content editor (a human) define clip points for each article at which a content truncation is acceptable. We can automatically define some rules however that facilitate the markup of possible clip points. Clipping must occur only at para boundaries, after at least some percentage or number of paras of an article or at a complete para either before or after an image. Every time we compute a table entry of Ψ (step 1 of algorithm 1) we analyze the allocation $\mathcal{A} - \mathcal{B}$ and explore a finite number of article truncations. We start with the largest allocated article (by text size) and truncate its content at the farthest allowed truncation point. Articles that are to be continued on a subsequent page are not con-

sidered, but continued articles that end on the current page are. We then compute the table entry for Ψ as usual using this allocation. Next, we consider the next largest article (considering truncations) and repeat the process, replacing the table entry if a better score is found. The process terminates after a fixed number of truncations have been explored. This process adds a fixed cost to the computation of a table entry, and hence has no impact on asymptotic complexity. Of course, we have to track which clip points maximized the score, so that we can recreate them when we finally render the page.

Images may be tagged as required or optional. As discussed in Section 4.2 a table entry of Ψ is computed when article content on a page matches a valid combination of global and region templates that can render the content. If an article has required images the article content only matches region templates with at least the same number of image slots. Declaring images as optional allows the algorithm the option of not using the image if the layout can be improved. In this case the article content matches region templates with at least the same number of slots as the required images and at most the same number of slots as the sum of required and optional images. This may result in a matching region template having fewer image slots than the number of optional images. In this case the excess optional images are simply not used.

6. RESULTS

As a practical matter, to use the algorithm one must supply annotated input content and a library of global and region templates.

The input to our news layout engine is an XML file that represents a personalized content structure. This XML may be derived by selecting and filtering content according to a target user profile to create a customized content package (this selection process is outside the scope of this paper). The XML structure is composed of text blocks and figures. We encode content types and logical relationships as XML attributes. We allow three basic elements including text blocks, figures and sidebars (a grouping of figures and/or text blocks that must appear together on a page). Content blocks within the content XML have attributes that denote their type. For example, text blocks may be tagged as head, subhead, list, paragraph, caption or any other publisher defined type. Figures can be optional or required. Further many alternate versions of a figure (ex: different crops from an auto-crop algorithm) may be provided. Explicit page counts or ranges may also be enforced.

Publication designer use a GUI based client authoring tool called the Template Editor to impart a desired "look" to an automatically synthesized document. The Appendix discusses the template library creation process using our authoring tool.

Due to space limitations we validate our algorithms on sample two page news compositions. Our template library has a collection of 82 global templates covering various configurations of two to four articles on a page. These include distinct first and last page global templates. A single article is allowed to start on the first page and continue onto a region of the second page. Our region template collection has 21 region templates allowing different article configurations within a region (1-3 columns, 0-2 figures, and various relative spatial arrangements). Content is generated using a

(a)

(b)

Figure 5: Results from compostions with random content[6]. (a) The layout with the best quality score (b) The layout with the worst quality score.

Lorem Ipsum generator. A randomly chosen image is associated with each article. All images are tagged optional. We want 6 articles on the two pages, including one large article (that continues to the next page), 2 medium size articles and 3 small size articles. An approximate total character budget to fill two pages is taken and divided between the articles. We use this as the mean character count for the articles. In each run of the experiment the order and character count of the articles are randomized. Character counts for each article are varied upto 15% from their nominal budgeted amount using a uniform distribution. This approach simulates significant content variations and may be regarded as a challenging scenario for any automated document composition algorithm. We generate 14 different document compositions from such randomly generated content.

Figure 5(a) shows the highest quality composition acheived by the algorithm while Figure 5(b) shows the layout with the lowest quality score. Overall the layout quality is consistently good due to the many local and global design adjustment options provided by the model. Next, to illustrate the effect of content editing we turn on automated text clipping (with upto 5 para clips allowed per page) as described in Section 5. Figure 6 shows the resulting re-composition of the worst scoring composition. Note that by clipping some paragraphs from the medium sized articles on the first and second pages of the composition in Figure 5(b), an image has been accomodated on the first page, columns are better balanced and extra whitespace has been minimized.

Figure 7 summarizes the quality scores in the experiment with (shown by the circles in the graph) and without (shown by the plus symbol) content clipping. Note how clipping improves the quality of most of the compositions.

7. CONCLUSIONS

This paper presented an approach to automated news composition by probabilistically modeling several hierarchical design choices a publication designer makes in traditional newsprint design. This results in a complex objective func-

Figure 6: Effect of enabling automated text editing on the layout in Fig.5(b)

tion that can be globally optimized. The resulting layouts automate decisions on choice of tilings for each page, configuration of the region within a tile, how to paginate articles, split and flow article text across pages, retarget images within regions, adjust global and region whitespace etc. for the best overall newspaper compositions. We also showed how content editing can be incorporated within our framework. Future work will focus on how to automatically learn the parameters of our model from example layouts.

8. REFERENCES

[1] C. B. Atkins. Blocked recursive image composition. In *MM '08: Proceeding of the 16th ACM international conference on Multimedia*, pages 821–824, New York, NY, USA, 2008. ACM.

[2] H. Y. Balinsky, A. J. Wiley, and M. C. Roberts. Aesthetic measure of alignment and regularity. In *DocEng '09: Proceedings of the 9th ACM symposium on Document engineering*, pages 56–65, New York, NY, USA, 2009. ACM.

[3] N. Damera-Venkata, J. Bento, and E. O'Brien-Strain. Probabilistic document model for automated

---

[6]Default precision parameter settings are $\alpha = 1$, $\beta = 3000$. Whitespace has a *prior* precision of 500 and image heights have *prior* precisions of $\rho = 100$.

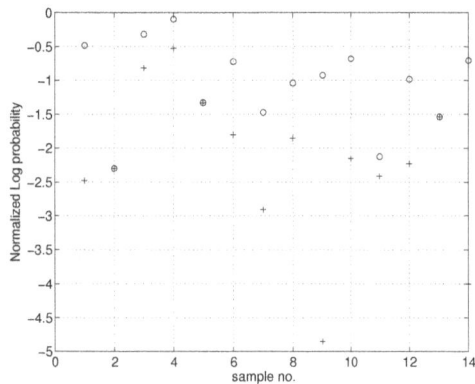

Figure 7: Quality scores from random experiment with (circle) and without (plus) text clipping.

document composition. In *Proceedings of the 11th ACM symposium on Document engineering*, DocEng '11, pages 3–12, New York, NY, USA, 2011. ACM.

[4] J. B. S. de Oliveira. Two algorithms for automatic document page layout. In *DocEng '08: Proceeding of the eighth ACM symposium on Document engineering*, pages 141–149, New York, NY, USA, 2008. ACM.

[5] J. B. S. de Oliveira. Two algorithms for automatic page layout and possible applications. In *Multimedia Tools and Applications*, volume 43, pages 275–301. Springer US, July 2009.

[6] G. Gange, K. Marriott, and P. Stuckey. Optimal guillotine layout. In *Proceedings of the 2012 ACM symposium on Document engineering*, DocEng '12, pages 13–22, New York, NY, USA, 2012. ACM.

[7] S. J. Harrington, J. F. Naveda, R. P. Jones, P. Roetling, and N. Thakkar. Aesthetic measures for automated document layout. In *DocEng '04: Proceedings of the 2004 ACM symposium on Document engineering*, pages 109–111, New York, NY, USA, 2004. ACM.

[8] N. Hurst, W. Li, and K. Marriott. Review of automatic document formatting. In *DocEng '09: Proceedings of the 9th ACM symposium on Document engineering*, pages 99–108, New York, NY, USA, 2009. ACM.

[9] Z. Karni, D. Freedman, and C. Gotsman. Energy-based image deformation. In *Proceedings of the Symposium on Geometry Processing*, SGP '09, pages 1257–1268, Aire-la-Ville, Switzerland, Switzerland, 2009. Eurographics Association.

[10] S. Lok and S. Feiner. A survey of automated layout techniques for information presentations. In *SmartGraphics '01: Proceedings of SmartGraphics Symposium '01*, pages 61–68, New York, NY, USA, 2001. ACM.

[11] J. Pearl. *Probabilistic reasoning in intelligent systems: networks of plausible inference*. Morgan Kaufmann Publishers Inc., San Francisco, CA, USA, 1988.

[12] T. Strecker and L. Hennig. Automatic layouting of personalized newspaper pages. In B. Fleischmann, K.-H. Borgwardt, R. Klein, and A. Tuma, editors, *Operations Research Proceedings*, pages 469–474. Springer Berlin Heidelberg, 2009.

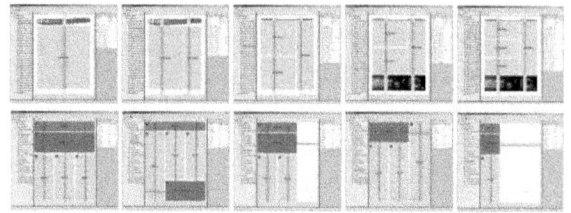

Figure 8: Template Editor screenshots showing a few global (top row) and region (bottom row) templates

APPENDIX

TEMPLATE CREATION PROCESS

1. **Document style sheet creation:** The style sheet has type definitions that are allowed within the content and also the corresponding formatting to be applied to these types. Thus the style sheet may require a heading to use Arial bold font with a specified font size, line spacing etc. The style sheet also defines overall document properties such as, margins, page dimensions etc. Stylesheets can be applied at an article/region specific level. For example an article that is tagged to use a sidebar stylesheet will match only global template regions that also permits the same stylesheet.

2. **Choice of relative arrangements:** The designer creates region and global template configurations. Region templates encode configurations of figures and text that are allowed within a region of the page. Typically the designer is allowed to set the mean, variance min and max range of whitespace and the variance of aspect ratio and min and max heights of images. These settings indicate aesthetic intent since parameters with larger variance will be allowed to vary more than ones with a smaller variance in finding the best document composition. Global templates are constructed in the similar fashion, where instead of figures and textblocks the designer specifies relative position of document regions. We only accept document regions of a rectangular shape. Initially the designer selects number of columns for the page and then the relative position and span of the regions. Similarly he/she sets the mean, variance, min and max values of the heights of each region block and explicitly defines which regions are continuation regions. Figure 8 shows sample region and global templates created using the template editor. Each template is actually auto-created by a wizard that simply requires the number of columns/paths, the number of images/regions and the selection of a position for each (ex: starting column, column span and position-top,middle,bottom). Thus, creating a new template requires only around 30 seconds if the default parameter settings are accepted.

3. **Applying master templates:** Master templates are used to add banners, page decorations, advertisements page numbers, dates, and any other variable content that does not change in number or size when the template is used. A designer may create text or image regions of fixed size on the page and apply them to multiple templates.

150

Balancing Font Sizes for Flexibility in Automated Document Layout

Ricardo Piccoli and João Batista Oliveira

Centro de Pesquisa em Computação Aplicada
Faculdade de Informática — PUC-RS
Porto Alegre, RS, Brazil
ricardo.piccoli@cpca.pucrs.br, oliveira@inf.pucrs.br

ABSTRACT

This paper presents an improved approach for automatically laying out content onto a document page, where the number and size of the items are unknown in advance. Our solution leverages earlier results from Oliveira (2008) wherein layouts are modeled by a guillotine partitioning of the page. The benefit of such method is its efficiency and ability to place as many items on a page as desired. In our model, items have flexible representations and texts may freely change their font sizes to fit a particular area of the page. As a consequence, the optimization goal is to find a layout that produces the least noticeable difference between font sizes, in order to obtain the most aesthetically pleasing layout. Finding the best areas for text requires knowledge of how typesetting engines actually render text for a particular setting. As such, we also model the behavior of the TEX typesetting engine when computing the height to be occupied by a text block as a function of the font size, text length and line width. An analytical approximation for text placement is then presented, refined by using curve fitting over TEX-generated data. As a practical result, the resulting layouts for a newspaper generation application are also presented. Finally, we discuss these results and directions for further research.

Categories and Subject Descriptors

I.7.2 [**Document and Text Processing**]: Document Preparation—*Format and notation, Photocomposition/typesetting*; F.2.2 [**Nonnumerical Algorithms and Problems**]: Geometrical Problems and Computations; G.2.1 [**Combinatorics**]: Combinatorial Algorithms

General Terms

Algorithms, Design

Keywords

automatic document layout, TEX, typography, personalized documents, guillotine layout

1. INTRODUCTION

The rapid growth of the Web and mobile devices as new forms of media targets allowed the emergence of new trends and models for publishing and delivering content to readers. For example, most news agencies today have already both a print and a digital form of their publication available on the Web to their customers. Along with new publication targets, the amount of available information has also grown immensely. This removed the centralized power of traditional publishers to a more distributed and personalized model for delivering information that is relevant to readers. However, traditional publications such as magazines still appeal to customers, mainly because of their aesthetic quality and readability. Digital documents on the other hand, have not been able to make full use of graphic design principles commonly found on printed publications. One reason for this is that digital documents are constantly being changed and updated, both to new content and form factors, whereas traditional publications can be designed in advance, as their content is static.

To overcome such problems, recently there has been a growing interest in research of automated document layout technologies to deal more rapidly with a large volume of information and need for customization. Several methods have been proposed for automating the layout task [16]. Most methods proposed in the recent literature are based on a collection of previously-generated page templates [6, 28, 25], which require expensive graphic design work, and for some scenarios do not offer a reasonable compromise. Other methods attempt to tackle the problem using template-free generative algorithms, often based on constrained optimization techniques, in order to model a space of valid layouts, bound to a set of graphic design guidelines. The approach used largely depends on a trade-off between how often or quickly documents must be produced and design uniqueness. For example, a monthly magazine is usually presented with a high-quality layout that conveys the branding and identity of that magazine. In this case, there will be few, if not at all, variations in a document's content, and a careful design crafted by a professional will be worth the investment. On the other hand, content that should be produced (and consumed) quickly, such as aggregated material from the Web, must be produced quickly and tailored to a large user base.

This is the scenario where automated layout tools are much more relevant.

This work proposes an enhanced guillotine-based [16] layout algorithm that produces unique document layouts tailored to previously-selected content that can be used in different workflows for generating documents. An important benefit of such approach is that each page of a document may hold an unspecified number of items, and is able to generate outputs efficiently for typical instances (up to 40 items on a page). The method defines a set of constraints and finds an optimal solution based on reasonable aesthetic goals. We leverage earlier results from Oliveira [8], but we improve upon the method, in special by optimizing the use of areas by textual elements. Section 2 discusses the previous method in detail.

The main contribution of this paper is an optimization method over the modified layout algorithm that uses the TeX [27] typesetting engine to provide a feedback of the rendering information to the algorithm, in order to optimize requested areas by the items and obtain an optimal distribution of content, thus generating better-quality results. Moreover, to prevent slowdowns caused by repeatedly invoking a typesetting engine, we also present a mathematical model of text area occupation for a specific width, font size and text. Using this model, layouts can be computed more efficiently and compete well with the results obtained when using TeX directly. We present the improved algorithm, the new text optimization method, a model of text area occupation and results for document instances designed for a newspaper appearance.

The rest of this paper is organized as follows. Section 2 discusses the page layout problem in general and recent approaches compared to ours. Section 3 presents the improved layout algorithm. Section 4 presents the new optimization approach to improve the quality of text layout. Section 4.1 presents an analytical model as an alternative to using TeX directly. Experimental results and examples are then presented in Section 4.2. Finally, we provide some final remarks and future research directions for this work in Section 5.

2. RELATED WORKS

Algorithms for automatic page layout have gained more attention from research in recent years [16], in a shift from lower-level typographical concerns such as word spacing and line-breaking [19]. The main problem now consists in distributing large pieces of content such as blocks of text and images into areas of a page, with respect to certain aesthetic criteria or design guidelines [14]. This problem takes many forms, but is almost always formulated as a constrained optimization problem, whose solution is particularly hard as the search space of possible layouts grows quickly with the addition of items and layout possibilities. Previously, layout problems were seen as variations of the Bin Packing problem [22, 12], which has an extensive literature [22, 4] and several variations. However, given aesthetics constraints in the document layout domain, such methods are not straightforward to adapt to this context, and more specialized knowledge on document design is needed to derive better-suited algorithms.

In fact, the page layout problem involves a decision-making process that offers many different possibilities for allocating content to the page [16]. A notion of optimality naturally arises as one would like to produce a design that maximizes some aesthetic or legibility aspects in the layout. Depending on the approach, optimizing layouts can be a computationally challenging task. Indeed, as several authors have pointed out [16, 10, 19], most known document layout problems are in *NP-Hard*. For some current document production workflows however, such as Variable Data Printing [13] – where a large number of customized documents must be produced in a short time –, an expensive algorithm is not well-suited.

Often, layout optimization problems have a high dimensionality in the input domain, due to the number of parameters that play a role in document layout, such as item sizes and positions. To ensure aesthetic quality while still reducing the search space for efficiency, existing methods usually rely on simpler layout models, or use a library of existing layout templates and only enumerate possible adaptations to the existing layouts [6, 17, 25]. When some characteristics regarding the content to be input are known in advance, such as average text length or a fixed number of items, these models tend to work well. Conversely, it is very difficult to apply these same models when content length and input size are unknown beforehand. It is interesting that due to such complexity, several approaches tend to focus on global optimization heuristics [26, 18, 12]. These methods attempt to minimize an objective function that quantifies one or more aesthetic qualities, and usually make use of techniques such as Simulated Annealing [9] or Genetic Algorithms [11] in the hope of finding the best solution(s). However, such techniques are known for requiring long execution times to find approximations that are not guaranteed to be close to an optimum. A common issue is poor convergence to good enough solutions, due to the multiple optimization criteria required for document layout. For this reason, deterministic methods are usually preferred for environments where documents are to be produced quickly and in large volumes (such as in VDP), given their efficiency and predictability of results.

As there are many different approaches and scenarios for automatic layout approaches, we restrict the rest of the discussion in this section to only the more recent works that are similar to our approach and target applications: guillotine-based methods that aim at producing a page from a collection of previously selected items.

Guillotine-based methods [10] are very interesting in contexts such as VDP or Web content aggregation [24], since it can be efficient to generate automatically and is flexible in terms of content placement, as opposed to the use of templates. The guillotine format is commonly used in widespread publications such as newspapers, and thus it is a comfortable and familiar format for readers. In guillotine layout, a page is hierarchically divided in smaller sections by horizontal or vertical lines that run across the extremities of the larger section without crossing any items in the way. The process of producing this type of layout is to recursively split the page into smaller sections until there are enough sections to place each different input item.

Atkins [1, 2] proposed a deterministic algorithm for quickly producing layouts for a photo album application. The layout is constructed as a guillotine tree as in our work, but it is constructed in from the bottom-up by repeatedly joining regions, whereas in our case we build the layout in a top-down procedure, allowing control of the form factor of the page. This approach lacks support for textual items, as texts do not have a single fixed geometry, but rather use area differently under different widths/font size configurations.

Recently, Gange et al. [10] proposed a new guillotine-based algorithm that is able to produce document layouts to be viewed either in a bounded page or in a screen with unbounded vertical or horizontal scrolling support. They study two main variations of the problem: a simpler one where the guillotine structure is already given; and a more difficult one where all layout parameters have to be chosen to minimize the total height of the layout or maximize the number of items allocated to a page. Each text item has a possibly large number of different configurations, given the different results obtained by a line-breaking algorithm for different width configurations. Admittedly, given the large search space of simultaneously generating layouts for several possible configurations of text widths, performance quickly deteriorates for documents containing more than 13 or 18 (for a page divided in columns) items [10].

Oliveira [7] proposed two algorithms for placing items on a page, also based on a guillotine partitioning approach. The first algorithm receives a sequence of fixed-geometry items to be placed in a fixed-size page, while the second allocates regions on a page based on relative areas requested by the input items. The latter algorithm is formulated using dynamic programming and searches for a layout that minimizes the worst placement error of an item on the page. The objective function supports constraints on the aspect ratio of an item to a user-defined allowed range and measures the difference between the requested area by the item and the given area. For flexibility, this method also separates layout and text formatting in two distinct phases. First, text areas are given an area estimate based on their length (e. g. character count). Then a guillotine layout is computed from these estimates and is sent to a typesetting engine (TeX [27] in this case), where the final page is typeset. If some text exceeds its area or leaves white space, the typesetting engine is able to perform adjustments to the font size of each individual item so all areas are fit accordingly, no space is left on the page and no item overlaps another one.

As discussed in Section 1, the algorithm proposed in this work is based on a modification of Oliveira's approach. In our experience, we found that in many cases estimates in font sizes were inaccurate enough for the differences in sizes to be noticeable by readers. (The reasons for this will be more fully discussed in Section 4.) The difference in font sizes in a document is undesirable for many reasons. Although research in typography and aesthetics is still a delicate subject to approach [29, 3], there seems to be a general agreement both from research [21, 29] and graphic design guides [15] that too much variation in type size in a document can be hurtful for aesthetic quality and readability. However, by allowing font sizes to change slightly, an optimization method could quite possibly find better layouts than methods that use fixed sizes if those changes are small enough to pass undetected by the reader's eyes. We are not aware of any research in this regard as of yet.

In Sections 3 and 4 the problem and the main approach of this paper are discussed in more detail.

3. LAYOUT APPROACH

The approach used by the proposed algorithm – henceforth referred to as APL (i. e. Automatic Page Layout) – consists in automatically producing pages in a format that is akin to a newspaper [15], where the page can be recursively decomposed through successive horizontal or vertical bisections. This approach is also called guillotine partitioning [16, 10], and consists in dividing a page area of a specified size into smaller regions through recursive bisections to contain each input element, such that the region areas match each requested area as evenly as possible.

As discussed in Section 1, the algorithm proposed in this section is an enhancement over the second approach proposed in [8]. The main difference between the current and the previous method is that the guillotine layouts produced by the current algorithm are not constrained to a row division scheme (for details see [8]), but now a page can be partitioned freely, thus enabling the algorithm to explore a larger search space for possibly better layouts, as suggested in the previous paper. Moreover, although this algorithm could support the inclusion of images and/or a pagination scheme, we will consider a one-page, text-only version in this paper, for the sake of simplicity of exposing the font balancing method (described in Section 4), which currently does not rely on these features.

To produce a page from an input sequence, the algorithm is divided in different phases, as illustrated in the workflow from Figure 1. These phases will be detailed next in Section 3.1.

3.1 Development

For this problem, we would like to generate guillotine layouts that preserve some of the main aesthetic qualities that define the look & feel of a newspaper, as many readers are comfortable with this format [15]. For instance, newspapers usually divide the page in a vertical grid of equal-width columns, where each story may only take an integer number of columns. This not only helps the reader to perceive structure on the page [15], but also allows the algorithm to generate only layouts that are well aligned. This grid model, as generated by the algorithm, is illustrated in Figure 2.

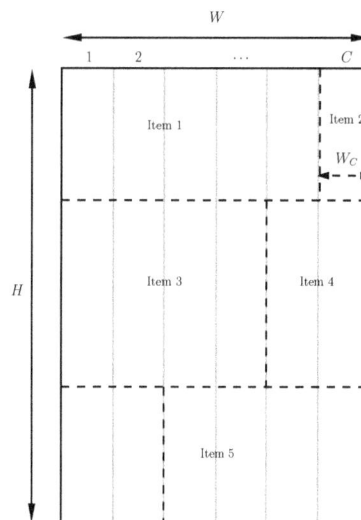

Figure 2: The underlying grid and page model used in APL

We now proceed to describe the layout problem model in detail. Given a page and a sequence of articles to be put on the page, the input data are the following:

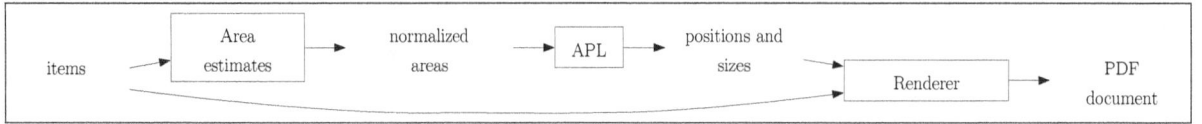

Figure 1: Workflow for generating a document using APL

- a tuple (W, H, C), corresponding to the page width, height and number of vertical columns, respectively;

- a sequence of n areas $A_1, A_2, \ldots, A_n$ corresponding to the lengths of articles $1 \leq i \leq n$.

A solution to the page layout problem thus is to map each item $1 \leq i \leq n$ to a rectangular region $R_i = (c_i, h_i)$ of the page, where c_i is the number of columns that will be taken up by item i and h_i is the height. Note that items always use an integer number of columns, and thus the region width is implicitly computed as $w_i = W c_i / C$. All columns on a page grid have the same width, i. e., $w_c = W/C$.

To further characterize the guillotine layout model, the following requirements and constraints for this problem need to be accounted for:

1. the page must be entirely and homogeneously covered by items, i. e. $\sum_{i=1}^{n} w_i h_i = W H$;

2. the order of the input sequence must be respected in some sense, as items may have a reading order determined by the input order;

3. all items should be placed on the page, i. e. they cannot be deleted;

4. the regions $R_i = (c_i, h_i)$ cannot be rotated and no intersection between any two items is allowed;

5. for legibility and aesthetic reasons, text regions should not be too thin or too wide. Thus, a pair of real values $\Delta_{\min}$ and $\Delta_{\max}$ shall restrict the minimum and maximum tolerated aspect ratios for each region R_i, whose aspect ratios are given by w_i / h_i;

6. any number of items may be placed on a page. For this we need to allow texts to shrink or expand their sizes in order to fit a particular region R_i.

For these requirements, a guillotine partitioning method seems appropriate, as it is fairly easy to translate the guillotine model to a recursive divide-and-conquer strategy that can satisfy the above constraints.

The input order preservation from requirement 2 must be reflected in the document layout. In a guillotine layout, a sequence of items will be split either by a horizontal or a vertical line that runs across the page containing the sequence. Thus, the items in the sequence up to a split index k will be allocated to the left or top side of the guillotine partition (depending on the split orientation), while the items after k will be allocated to the right or bottom side. A western reader usually scans a page in a top-bottom and left-to-right fashion, and thus an item k will always appear higher or to the left of item $k + 1$ [8]. This, however, ensures only a *partial* reading order, and some ambiguities may occur in some layouts when scanning the items sequentially. (i. e. an item

following another one may appear below or to the right of the item being currently read, but never to the left and top simultaneously.) Nevertheless, by disallowing changes in the input order when finding a layout we can obtain a more efficient algorithm, as testing different combinations of input order would require a more computationally expensive approach that would not be capable of producing solutions in a practicable time.

To satisfy requirement 6, items must share the page using relative areas, taking a percentage of the page instead of a fixed value. As such, the sequence $A_1, \ldots, A_n$ must be normalized before being used by the algorithm. In this case, a new sequence of areas $N_1, \ldots, N_n$ is defined such that

$$\sum_{i=1}^{n} N_i = 1 \qquad (1)$$

For simplicity, we define the sum $S(i, j)$ of all areas between A_i and A_j to be

$$S(i, j) = \sum_{k=i}^{j} A_k \qquad (2)$$

The normalized area N_i of an item i is thus defined as

$$N_i = \frac{A_i}{S(1, n)} \qquad (3)$$

3.2 Generating and evaluating alternatives

Given the input description, a layout problem thus consists in distributing a sequence $[i \ldots, j]$ of items $N_i, \ldots, N_j$ to a set of regions $R = R_i, \ldots, R_j$ contained in a larger region (c, h). In a divide-and-conquer [5] approach, we can then successively reduce a problem $\mathsf{L}(i, j, c, h)$ into two smaller sub-problems $\mathsf{L}(i, k, c, h_k)$ and $\mathsf{L}(k + 1, j, c, h - h_k)$ in the case of a horizontal partition, or $\mathsf{L}(i, k, c_k, h)$ and $\mathsf{L}(k + 1, j, c - c_k, h)$ in the case of a vertical partition. Note that each division splits both the current sequence and the region in smaller pieces. The smallest sub-problem will then be the allocation of a single item i into a region $R_i = (c, h)$, which can be trivially evaluated. However, at each problem subdivision step, options of values for k and h_k (or c_k) must be considered. As such, the algorithm must explore different splitting possibilities, searching for a solution that minimizes a certain error measure for item placement.

In the horizontal splitting case, the height of the page can be divided in any real-valued point in the open interval $(0, h)$, for each index k in $i \leq k < j$. To explore horizontal splitting possibilities, our approach is to choose a splitting point based on the sum of areas of the items that will be at each side of the split, and appropriately choose a proportional fraction of h. For vertical splits, since the column grid must be respected, there will be only $c - 1$ possible splitting points in the region, but for each one different partitions of the sequence must also be considered.

The error measure must in some sense measure the quality of the association between an item i and a region $r = (c, h)$. In the case of a single item, the allocation is considered to be as good as is the similarity between the requested area N_i and the relative area offered by $r = (c, h)$:

$$\text{offered} = \frac{c_i\, h}{C\, H}$$

Given the assumption that texts may be resized to fit an area, offered areas that are smaller or larger than the requested area must be penalized accordingly by the error measure. Moreover, regions that have incompatible aspect ratios must be discarded (e. g. by attributing an infinite error $e = \infty$). The complete error function, called as $\text{error}(i, c, h)$, is presented in Algorithm 1.

Algorithm 1: $\text{error}(i, c, h)$ – Placement error function for a single text in a region

---

Input: Item index i, number of columns c in the region and region height h

Output: Placement error for text i

$w \leftarrow W \times c/C$

$ar \leftarrow w/h$

if $ar < \Delta_{\min}$ *or* $ar > \Delta_{\max}$ **then**
| **return** ∞
end

$\text{offered} \leftarrow c \times h / (C \times H)$

Scale difference ratio by the text area

return $w \times h \times (\max(\text{offered}/N_i, N_i/\text{offered}) - 1)$

3.3 Choosing an optimal partitioning

Given the error function from Algorithm 1, we now wish to find a sequence of partitions of the page whose area distribution is equally similar to the relative areas requested by the items. The choice of partitioning must minimize the largest placement error found in one of the two resulting sub-problems from that partition. The algorithm that accomplishes this task is presented in Algorithm 2.

As this problem exhibits the optimal sub-structure property (i. e. an optimal solution to a problem is constructed from optimal solutions to its sub-problems) and overlapping sub-problems (i. e. the same layout sub-problem is reached several times from different partitions), it is possible to solve it more efficiently by turning Algorithm 2 into a dynamic programming method [5] by introducing a look-up table for memoization. The look-up table also enables the reconstruction of the guillotine layout from the optimal solution, and derive other required layout parameters such as the position (x_i, y_i) of item i, as the function in Algorithm 2 only computes the minimal error solution instead of generating the actual layout. A separate algorithm is then needed to reconstruct the layout from the look-up table, but this method is straightforward to obtain given the function in Algorithm 2.

3.4 Rendering

After obtaining the sizes and positions R_i for each item i, the algorithm proceeds to the rendering stage (refer to Figure 1 for a workflow), where a typesetting engine (such as TeX [27] or iText [23]) must be instructed to place each

---

Algorithm 2: $L(i, j, c, h)$ – selects minimal error among candidate layouts

---

Input: Item range [i...j], number of columns c and height h

Output: minimal layout error

if $i = j$ **then**
| **return** $\text{error}(i, c, h)$
end

$\text{minerr} \leftarrow \infty$

Try horizontal splits and select the one with minimal error

for $k \leftarrow i$ **to** $j - 1$ **do**
| $h_k \leftarrow h \times S(i, k) / S(i, j)$
| *The error of this partition attempt is the worse between the two sub-problems*
| $\text{err} \leftarrow \max(L(i, k, c, h_k), L(k + 1, j, c, h - h_k))$
| $\text{minerr} \leftarrow \min(\text{minerr}, \text{err})$
end

Try vertical splits and select the one with minimal error

for $c_k \leftarrow 1$ **to** $c - 1$ **do**
| **for** $k \leftarrow i$ **to** $j - 1$ **do**
| | $\text{err} \leftarrow \max(L(i, k, c_k, h), L(k + 1, j, c - c_k, h))$
| | $\text{minerr} \leftarrow \min(\text{minerr}, \text{err})$
| **end**
end

return minerr

---

region in a page and then insert the corresponding articles. In our work, we decided to use the TeX typesetting engine (along with LaTeX [20]), as TeX is known for fine typographical facilities and programmability. When generating the final document, TeX may be programmed to tailor the final output document for a better look, such as determining better column presentations, changing fonts or adding a top head for a newspaper.

However, given the input constraints and typical instances, there will be seldom a case where region areas will perfectly match an item's requested area. Some reasons for this include the addition of too many or too few items on a page, very large articles or very strict aspect ratio constraints. Since items are allowed by design to change their sizes in order to fit a particular area, the manipulation of the font size can be used to correctly fill a region. By using a simple binary search method and feedback information from the typesetting engine, the exact font size that fills up a region may be determined. Figure 3 shows an example document generated by APL, where the font size differences can be spotted quite easily. Note that the leading (i. e., spacing between baselines) is scaled together with the font size, in order to preserve the same proportional distance between lines for every item.

In general, the difference in font sizes should not be too large, as the optimization goal of APL is exactly to produce a layout whose areas match the items as close as possible. However, since the algorithm only allocates areas based on the lengths of each article, many factors such as white space generated by line-breaking, justification, hyphenation, individual kerning and leading are not taken into account by the algorithm. This is because these parameters are only computed for a text block during the run time of the typesetting engine, and as such they are not considered by the

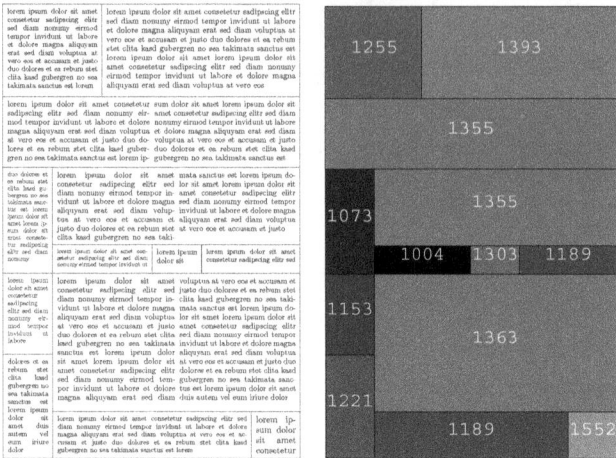

Figure 3: A sample document and a visualization showing font size differences highlighted by gray shades, where lighter shades indicates a larger font and darker shades a small font. The numbers indicate the font size in a scale of $10^{-3} \times$ the font point size (10 points in this case), as it is used in TeX

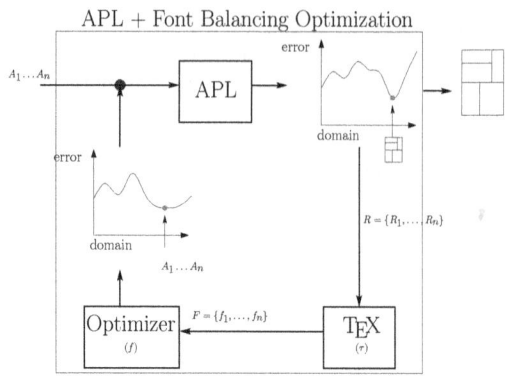

Figure 4: Controlling area estimates in APL with a font optimization method

algorithm. While some changes are small, this is not always the case. For example, if a text containing a single word is to be rendered with a larger font, its area estimate may be computed as simply the length of that word. However, if the text is rendered into a narrow column, that word may be broken by a hyphen into two lines, doubling the amount of required area and forcing a reduction in font size. Given the interplay between these factors, a separate rendering process won't always be able to produce the best results than if it were able to interact with the page layout algorithm. In Section 4 we present an approach that uses TeX to feed back information back into APL for improving area estimation and thus producing better results.

4. OPTIMIZING FONT SIZES

To solve the font size problems with the layout algorithm discussed in Sections 2 and 3.4, a font balancing scheme is proposed in this section. Since the layout algorithm only works on area estimates and has no knowledge of typographical parameters, the proposed method uses font size information obtained from the rendering step in TeX and uses it to improve the initial area estimates from APL. The areas are repeatedly improved until a convergence or stop criteria is met. In fact, this approach is based on the minimization of a new objective function, using the layout algorithm as part of its evaluation. Figure 4 shows how the two functions are connected to minimize the font size difference in layouts.

Essentially, area estimates are initially used as in the original problem. However, the resulting font sizes generated by the typesetting engine area are obtained and fed back to a new optimization process, that explores the domain of areas required by each item. The new objective function can be described by

$$f(A_1, A_2, \ldots, A_n) = \max(F) - \min(F) \quad (4)$$

$$F = \tau(R_1, R_2, \ldots, R_n) \quad (5)$$

where F is the set of resulting font sizes from the typesetting engine for rendered areas $R = (R_1, R_2, \ldots, R_n)$.

Considering that τ is an unknown function that takes a real-valued set R – that can only be described by the algorithms inside the typesetting engine –, any viable optimization strategy must be conservative when evaluating points from domain A, since the evaluation of F is usually an expensive operation. In this sense, we propose two heuristics that attempt to minimize f by making small changes in item areas, and finding the set of areas that produces the least noticeable difference in font sizes. The two proposed heuristics can be described as follows:

1. At each step, all requested areas are changed simultaneously, based on the font sizes informed by F, in the attempt to quickly fix all areas.

2. Increase the requested area of the text with the smallest font. The intuition behind this approach is that always increasing the smallest font will eventually produce uniform fonts across all items.

Figure 5 shows the behavior of both strategies for a simple test case with 6 items.

For the first method, we repeatedly multiply all area estimates from the previous run of the algorithm by the scale factor $\sqrt{1000/f_i}$, where f_i is the generated font size from F for item i. A square root is taken to ensure that items with extreme font sizes won't change too abruptly and steal area from other items, thus difficulting convergence. The value 1000 is chosen as a reference font size, and $1000/f_i$ measures how much every font has to grow or shrink in order to converge to the same size. At each step, the resulting layout may improve or deteriorate in comparison to the previous run. Currently, our control function runs for a specific number of iterations and stores the best result seen during the entire run.

In our tests, we found that when small changes have to be made, the first method converges quickly. However, when areas change significantly, the layout algorithm changes the entire guillotine structure of the page, causing this method to oscillate due to multiple area changes.

To solve this problem, the second heuristic is more conservative. Instead of changing all areas, we repeatedly increase the requested area of the item that produced the smallest font size during the last run. This allows us to control the

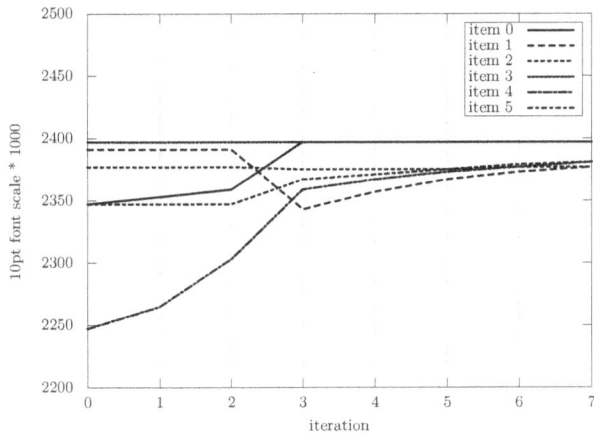

(a) First method: all areas are changed per iteration

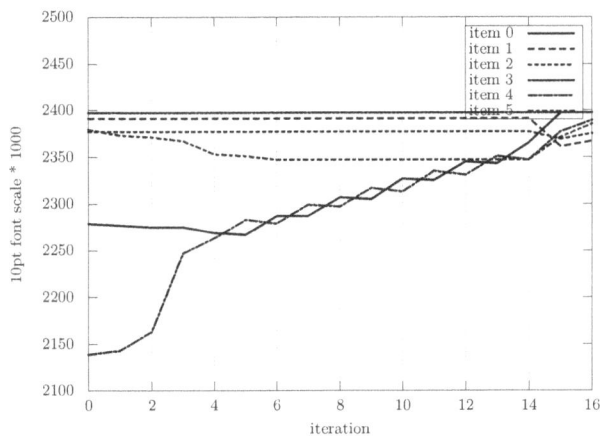

(b) Second method: only the tightest area is changed per iteration

Figure 5: A simple test for 6 items illustrating two heuristics for minimizing the largest font size difference in a document. Each line represents the font size of an item and the x-axis is the current iteration number

precise amount of change to be made in an area, and avoid constant changes in geometry. In fact, a cooling parameter is used that decreases as the font size differences are reduced, ensuring convergence. Figure 6 shows the behavior of both methods when applied to a document with 15 items.

In both methods, a global optimum is never guaranteed, but in our experiments the font size was reduced to acceptable levels in most cases.

4.1 Text typesetting model

In order to prevent slowdowns caused by repeatedly invoking TEX, we attempted to approximate the behavior of paragraph setting using an analytical model. This model attempts to predict the font size that will be used to fill up a region with the input text. In general, when a block of text with length t is set into a box of width w with font point size s, the typesetting engine produces a text block with a height determined by the number of generated lines by the line-breaking mechanism. Assuming that the line-breaking

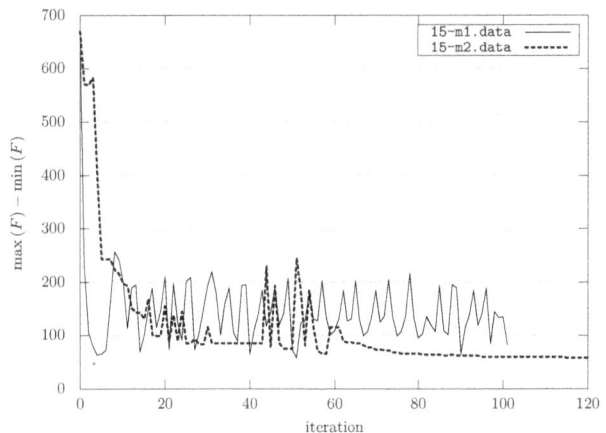

Figure 6: Results for a test document with 15 items (with $\Delta_{\min} = 0.3$ and $\Delta_{\max} = 5$) showing the maximum font size difference encountered for several iterations from each heuristic. Note that the second heuristic converges steadily after a few iterations, as the smaller changes in areas reduce the likelihood of a change in the overall layout structure

algorithm performed well, the text block will have very little white space between words, and the height used by the text block will be determined by the font size and number of lines generated. The number of lines in the text block can thus be roughly estimated by $\left\lceil \frac{s\,t}{w} \right\rceil$. From this we obtain the height taken by the text block as

$$h\,(w,t,s) = \alpha\,s \left\lceil \frac{s\,t}{w} \right\rceil, \qquad (6)$$

where α is a linear coefficient used for curve fitting. Note that the round-up in Equation (6) is necessary as the last line of a text still takes the full height of a line, and thus this number must be an integer. Given a text with length t and a rectangle (w_i, h_i), the font size scaling can be guessed using a binary search procedure that finds the font scaling that produces the closest height value to h_i, using Equation (6).

Using this model, we were able to fit a dataset produced by TEX into the surface defined by this function using `gnuplot`'s non-linear least squares solver.[1] The data was generated by programming TEX to typeset a sample text into a box using several different combinations of widths, number of words (from the same sample text) and font size scalings. Figure 7 shows the surface described by Equation (6) fitting TEX-generated data for a range of different widths, a fixed text length and font sizes for TEX's Computer Modern Roman font (`cmr10` [27]). The actual parameters used for generating this data are shown in Table 1. The input text used was a compilation of several recent newspaper articles written in English. The value for α is shown in Figure 7 as well.

4.2 Experimental results

For comparison purposes, we present a document comprised of 15 text items, generated both with the original algorithm described in Section 3 and with the font balanc-

---
[1] `http://www.gnuplot.info`

Table 1: Parameters for generating TeX data

Width range	Font	Font scaling	Leading	Text lengths	Paragraph setting
10pt...600pt (10pt steps)	cmr10	0.1...10× font size	1.1× font scaling	1...250 words (2...1560 chars.)	justified, no indentation or extra spacing

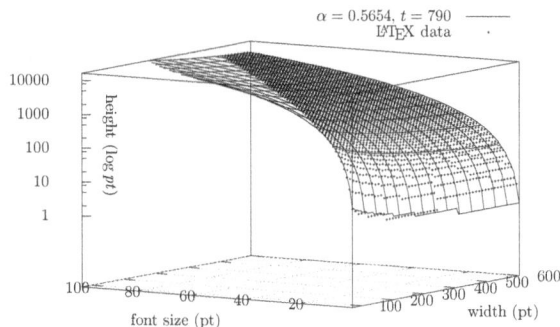

Figure 7: A plot of Equation (6) fitting a set of TeX-generated data. The height is shown in logarithmic scale for convenience

ing mechanism presented in this section. The documents and differences in font sizes are illustrated in Figure 8. For this case, the aspect ratio bounds were $\Delta_{min} = 0.3$ and $\Delta_{max} = 5.0$ and the first method for font balancing was used. The maximum difference in font sizes using the original algorithm is 670/1000 times the 10-point font size, while in the improved method the difference was of 58/1000 times.

Figure 9 shows the results for 2 random test instances using the layout algorithm along with the font balancing scheme proposed in this section. A TeX style file was also configured to use fonts and set columns for a newspaper style.

5. CONCLUSION AND FUTURE WORKS

In this paper we presented an improved method for [7] for automatically producing template-free page layouts. Along with the algorithm, a control scheme was proposed to improve on the difference of font sizes caused by the increased flexibility of this method. This allows the generation of documents in workflows where the number and size of items to be put on a page is not constrained to specific content categories. The font control scheme uses the TeX typesetting engine to interact with the main layout algorithm, which can cause slowdowns in some difficult instances. For this, we also presented an analytical scheme to approximate the font size guessing done by the typesetting engine and thus speed up execution.

In the guillotine-based works discussed in Section 2, the approaches for dealing with text are quite different from one another. Atkins [1, 2] did not consider text placement at all, and instead the work focuses on producing photo album layouts. Gange et al. [10] provide a dynamic programming method that explores a very large search space that considers texts as a collection of different geometries, one for each

possible width. It is also unclear from that paper how the fixed-page version of the problem deals with items that cannot fit, white space at the end of a page or the distribution of items in different pages. Oliveira [7] provides a solution that is optimal only with respect to the distribution of areas, but since paragraph setting only takes place in a separate phase, local adjustments have to be made to the font sizes in order to compensate for poor initial estimates.

Although the proposed method doesn't guarantee optimal solutions, we believe that small differences in font sizes are still a reasonable trade-off for workflows that cannot predict in advance the shape and size of items to be put on a page, such as in Web-to-Print applications [24]. In fact, there are a range of application domains nowadays in which we believe small font size changes are an acceptable trade-off. Examples include the aforementioned Web-to-Print scenario, RSS delivery and social content mash-ups. In general, these are scenarios in which the document life cycle is very short: it has to be produced quickly (with a high degree of personalization, as it is usually targeted at a single individual), and is consumed quickly as well. Although even slight font size changes violate commonly established design principles [15], conveying information effectively in these scenarios should take precedence over visual identity, as long as content legibility is not sacrificed.

Furthermore, while we did not consider semantic relationships between items in the page (e. g. an advertisement that must match the text content) in our approach, a larger workflow could easily prepare proper inputs for the layout engine, and possibly tune the layouts with multiple test runs. Thus, the separation of concerns between content and layout decisions allows the use of the layout engine as a building block in a myriad of different document production workflows, as opposed to a standalone workflow.

For future works, we intend to provide more detailed data regarding the font balancing scheme, and study how much can in fact be improved given a set of test documents. Additionally, we would like to provide a comparison between the approximation model and the original feedback mechanism that uses TeX. Finally, while we have a working version of the algorithm that supports images and automatic pagination, we have yet to study how should the font balancing scheme interact with these features to optimize results further.

6. ACKNOWLEDGMENTS

This paper was achieved in cooperation with Hewlett-Packard Brasil Ltda. using incentives of Brazilian Informatics Law (Law n°. 8.2.48 of 1991).

7. REFERENCES

[1] B. C. Atkins. Adaptive photo collection page layout. In *International Conference on Image Processing*, volume 5, pages 2897–2900, Washington, DC, USA, Oct. 2004. IEEE Computer Society.

[2] B. C. Atkins. Blocked recursive image composition. In *MM '08: Proceeding of the 16th ACM international conference on Multimedia*, pages 821–824, New York, NY, USA, 2008. ACM.

[3] D. Chek, L. Ngo, and J. G. Byrne. Aesthetic measures for screen design. In *OZCHI'98: Proceedings of the Australasian Conference on Computer Human*

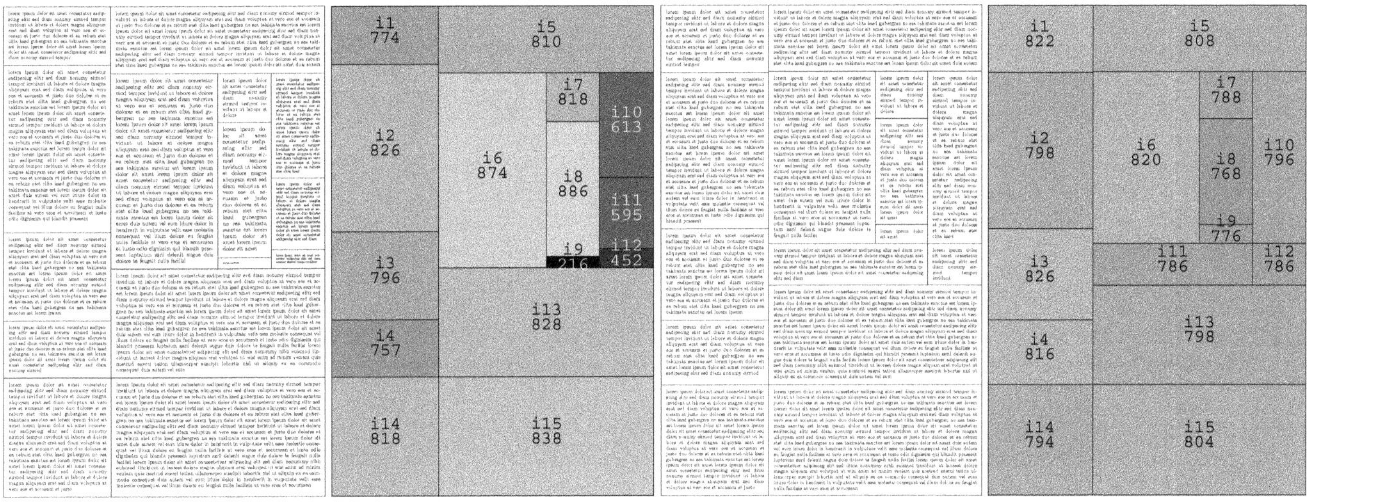

Figure 8: Results for a 15-item document with (right) and without (left) a font balancing scheme. Content ordering is shown by the numbers prefixed by "i"

Figure 9: Examples of documents generated for a newspaper application using APL and the font balancing method

Interaction, page 64, Washington, DC, USA, 1998. IEEE Computer Society.

[4] E. Coffman, G. Galambos, S. Martello, and D. Vigo. Bin packing approximation algorithms: Combinatorial analysis. In D.-Z. Du and P. Pardalos, editors, *Handbook of Combinatorial Optimization*, pages 151–207. Springer US, 1999.

[5] T. H. Cormen, C. E. Leiserson, R. L. Rivest, and C. Stein. *Introduction to Algorithms, Second Edition*. The MIT Press, Cambridge, MA, September 2001.

[6] N. Damera-Venkata, J. Bento, and E. O'Brien-Strain. Probabilistic document model for automated document composition. In *Proceedings of the 11th ACM symposium on Document engineering*, DocEng '11, pages 3–12, New York, NY, USA, 2011. ACM.

[7] J. B. S. de Oliveira. Two algorithms for automatic document page layout. In *Proceedings of the eighth ACM symposium on Document engineering*, pages 141–149, New York, NY, USA, 2008. ACM.

[8] J. B. S. de Oliveira. Two algorithms for automatic page layout and possible applications. *Multimedia Tools and Applications*, 43(3):275–301, 2009.

[9] M. Fleischer. Simulated annealing: past, present, and future. In *WSC '95: Proceedings of the 27th conference on Winter simulation*, pages 155–161, Washington, DC, USA, 1995. IEEE Computer Society.

[10] G. Gange, K. Marriott, and P. Stuckey. Optimal guillotine layout. In *Proceedings of the 2012 ACM symposium on Document engineering*, DocEng '12, pages 13–22, New York, NY, USA, 2012. ACM.

[11] D. E. Goldberg. *Genetic Algorithms in Search, Optimization and Machine Learning*. Addison-Wesley Longman Publishing Co., Inc., Boston, MA, USA, 1989.

[12] E. Goldenberg. Automatic layout of variable-content print data. Master's thesis, School of Cognitive & Computing Sciences, University of Sussex, Brighton, UK, Nov 2002.

[13] A. Gómez, M. C. Penadés, J. H. Canós, M. R. S. Borges, and M. Llavador. DPLfw: a framework for variable content document generation. In *Proceedings of the 16th International Software Product Line Conference – Volume 1*, SPLC '12, pages 96–105, New York, NY, USA, 2012. ACM.

[14] S. J. Harrington, J. F. Naveda, R. P. Jones, P. Roetling, and N. Thakkar. Aesthetic measures for automated document layout. In *DocEng'04: Proceedings of the 2004 ACM symposium on Document engineering*, pages 109–111, New York, NY, USA, 2004. ACM Press.

[15] T. Harrower. *The Newspaper Designer's Handbook*. McGraw-Hill, Boston, MA, USA, 1992.

[16] N. Hurst, W. Li, and K. Marriott. Review of automatic document formatting. In *DocEng'09: Proceedings of the 9th ACM symposium on Document engineering*, pages 99–108, New York, NY, USA, 2009. ACM.

[17] C. Jacobs, W. Li, E. Schrier, D. Bargeron, and D. Salesin. Adaptive grid-based document layout. In *SIGGRAPH '03: ACM SIGGRAPH 2003*, pages 838–847, New York, NY, USA, 2003. ACM Press.

[18] R. Johari, J. Marks, A. Partovi, and S. Shieber. Automatic yellow-pages pagination and layout. *Journal of Heuristics*, 2(4):321–342, 1997.

[19] D. E. Knuth. Breaking Paragraphs Into Lines. In *Digital typography*, CSLI lecture notes, chapter 3, pages 67–155. CSLI Publications, 1999.

[20] L. Lamport. *LaTeX: A Document Preparation System*. Addison-Wesley, Reading, Massachusetts, USA, Boston, MA, USA, 1986.

[21] G. E. Legge and C. A. Bigelow. Does print size matter for reading? a review of findings from vision science and typography. *Journal of Vision*, 11(5), 2011.

[22] A. Lodi, S. Martello, and D. Vigo. Recent advances on two-dimensional bin packing problems. *Discrete Applied Mathematics*, 123(1-3):379–396, 2002.

[23] B. Lowagie. *iText in Action*. Manning Publications Co., Greenwich, CT, USA, 2010.

[24] P. Luo, J. Fan, S. Liu, F. Lin, Y. Xiong, and J. Liu. Web article extraction for web printing: a DOM+visual based approach. In *Proceedings of the 9th ACM symposium on Document engineering*, DocEng '09, pages 66–69, New York, NY, USA, 2009. ACM.

[25] R. Piccoli, J. Oliveira, and I. Manssour. Optimal pagination and content mapping for customized magazines. *Journal of the Brazilian Computer Society*, pages 1–19, 2012. 10.1007/s13173-012-0066-6.

[26] L. Purvis, S. Harrington, B. O'Sullivan, and E. C. Freuder. Creating personalized documents: an optimization approach. In *DocEng '03: Proceedings of the 2003 ACM symposium on Document engineering*, pages 68–77, New York, NY, USA, 2003. ACM.

[27] D. Salomon. *The Advanced TeXbook*. Springer-Verlag, Berlin, 1995.

[28] E. Schrier, M. Dontcheva, C. Jacobs, G. Wade, and D. Salesin. Adaptive layout for dynamically aggregated documents. In *IUI'08: Proceedings of the 13th international conference on Intelligent user interfaces*, pages 99–108, New York, NY, USA, 2008. ACM.

[29] B. Veytsman and L. Akhmadeeva. Towards evidence-based typography: Literature review and experiment design. *TUGboat*, 32(3), 2011.

Document Noise Removal using Sparse Representations over Learned Dictionary

Thanh-Ha Do
Université de Lorraine - LORIA - UMR 7503
Campus scientifique - BP 239
Vandoeuvre-lès-Nancy, France
ha-thanh.do@loria.fr

Salvatore Tabbone
Université de Lorraine - LORIA - UMR 7503
Campus scientifique - BP 239
Vandoeuvre-lès-Nancy, France
tabbone@loria.fr

Oriol Ramos Terrades
Computer Vision Centre
08193 Bellaterra (Cerdanyola)
Barcelona, Espanya
oriolrt@cvc.uab.cat

ABSTRACT

In this paper, we propose an algorithm for denoising document images using sparse representations. Following a training set, this algorithm is able to learn the main document characteristics and also, the kind of noise included into the documents. In this perspective, we propose to model the noise energy based on the normalized cross-correlation between pairs of noisy and non-noisy documents. Experimental results on several datasets demonstrate the robustness of our method compared with the state-of-the-art.

Categories and Subject Descriptors

J.m [**Computer Applications**]: Miscellaneous

Keywords

Sparse Representation, Learned Dictionary, K-SVD, Normalized Cross Correlation, Noise Suppression

1. INTRODUCTION

The performance of many pattern recognition techniques applied on images depends on an accurate control of the noise included into the image. In the case of document image analysis applications, the kind of noise is different compared to the noise found in natural scenes images that are generated by devices like digital cameras or similar.

Therefore, the problem of document denoising has been tackled since the very beginning. There is a vast literature on methods proposing solutions such as median filter [6], morphological filters [16], or curvelets transform [18]. Median filter replaces each pixel in the noisy image by the median of pixels in a neighborhood of that pixel, while morphological filter carries out dilation and erosion operations as denoisy operators. In addition, morphological filtering can discriminate between positive and negative noise spikes, whereas median filter cannot [16]. Both filters, median and

morphological, are appealing because they are easy to implement and perform well with the presence of impulse noise. However, neither of them are efficient for other types of noise like white noise or noise arising from printing, photocopying and scanning processes. This kind of noise not only generally causes undesirable document appearance, but also has a bad influence on document processing performance.

Recent researches obtain good performance in denoising gray-scale images with white noise using Multi Resolution Analysis (MRA) methods [18]. Sparse transforms and MRA methods are applied to a wide range of image processing problems as image compression, image restoration and image denoising [18]. These methods have proven to perform well in terms of Mean Square Error (MSE) measure as well as Peak Signal-to-Noise Ratio (PSNR) measure for essentially white noise (additive and following a Gauss distribution). Moreover, sparse transforms, like curvelets, contourlets, wedgelets, bandelets, or steerable wavelets, have also been successfully applied in document images for removing noisy edges, showing that sparse representation can effectively be used for denoising purposes. Sparse transforms represent images as linear combinations of (atom) functions of a given particular family of functions (dictionary). However, the overall performance of these methods depends on two factors: first of all, a *a priori* knowledge about images which drives the choice of dictionary functions and secondly, the kind of noise found in document images. Recently, curvelets transform has been applied in document denoising with a relative high degree of success [11]. In that approach, the authors take advantage of directional properties of curvelets transform to denoise degraded graphic documents. The results obtained in that work show an improvement in removing noise for document images comparing with other state-of-the-art methods. However, curvelet is one of the pre-defined dictionaries, and therefore can only work well with some kinds of noise and cannot be adapted to arbitrary noise models.

In this paper, we address the task of document denoising by proposing a method which overcomes the difficulties found in denoising methods based on MRA. On the one hand, we apply the K-SVD algorithm to learn a proper set of atom functions adapted to both document characteristics and document noise. On the other hand we propose an energy noise model which allows us to easier set the threshold required for noise removal even if the noise model is unknown.

The remainder of this paper is organized as follows. We introduce the theoretical framework of sparse representations in section 2 and the learning algorithm in section 3. Then, we recall the document degradation models used in experiments (section 4) and we propose the energy noise model in section 5. Next, we discuss the experimental results in section 6 and finally, we give our conclusions in section 7.

2. SPARSE REPRESENTATION

The main idea of the proposed method is to find a dictionary adapted to the properties of the data which will allow us to obtain a denoised version of the original degraded images using sparse representations.

A sparse representation is a linear combination of few atoms (basis functions) of a given dictionary. Mathematically, given a dictionary A and a signal h, we consider the under-determined linear system of equations $h = Ax$, with $A = \{a_1, a_2, \ldots, a_m\} \in R^{n \times m}$, $h \in R^n$, $x \in R^m$, $m \gg n$. If A is a full$-$rank matrix, there will be infinitely many different sets of values for the x_i's that satisfy all equations simultaneously. The set of x can be described using mathematical language. However, from an application point of view, one of the main tasks in dealing with the above system of equations is to find the proper x that can explain h well comparing with others. To gain this well-defined solution, a function $f(x)$ is added to assess the desirability of a would-be solution x, with smaller values being preferred:

$$(P_f) : \min_x f(x) \text{ subject to } Ax = h \qquad (1)$$

If $f(x)$ is the l_0 pseudo-norm $\|x\|_0$ (number nonzero elements in vector x), then the problem (P_f) becomes finding the sparse representation x of h satisfying:

$$(P_0) : \min_x \|x\|_0 \text{ subject to } Ax = h \qquad (2)$$

In general, solving equation (2) is often difficult (NP-hard problem) and one of the choices is to look for an approximate solution using greedy algorithms, such as *Matching Pursuit* (MP) [15], *Orthogonal MP* (OMP) [17], *Weak MP* [19] and Thresholding algorithm [8]. A greedy algorithms is an algorithms that follows the problem solving heuristic of making the locally optimal single term updates with the hope of finding a global optimum. In our case, the set of active columns started from empty is maintained and expanded by one additional column of A at each iteration. The chosen column is a column that maximally reduces the residual l_2 error in approximating h from the currently active columns. The residual l_2 error is evaluated after constructing an approximate including the new column; if it is bounded below a specified threshold, the algorithm terminates.

The other choice is to relax the l_0-norm by replacing it with the l_p-norms for some $p \in (0, 1]$ or by smooth functions such as $\sum_i \log(1 + \alpha x_i^2), \sum_i x_i^2/(\alpha + x_i^2)$, or $\sum_i (1 - exp(-\alpha x_i^2))$. The interesting algorithm of this family is the *FOcal Under-determined System Solver* (FOCUSS) [10]. In this algorithm, the l_p-norm (for some fixed $p \in (0, 1]$) is represented as a weighted l_2-norm by using *Iterative Reweighed Least Squares* (IRLS) method [5].

Another popular strategy is to replace the l_0-norm by the l_1-norm proposed by Donoho *et al* [7]

$$(P_1) : \min_x \|W^{-1}x\|_1 \text{ subject to } Ax = h \qquad (3)$$

The matrix W is a diagonal positive-definite matrix. A natural choice for each entry in W is $w(i, i) = 1/\|a_i\|_2$ [1]. Let $\tilde{x} = W^{-1}x$, then equation (3) is re-formulated as

$$(P_1) : \min_{\tilde{x}} \|\tilde{x}\|_1 \text{ subject to } h = AW\tilde{x} = \tilde{A}\tilde{x} \qquad (4)$$

in which $\tilde{A}$ is the normalized version of A. Equation (4) is the classic basis pursuit format, and the solution x can be found by de-normalizing $\tilde{x}$. Thus, (P_1) is usually used with a normalized matrix. The solution for (P_1) problem can be found by some existing numerical algorithms, such as *Basis Pursuit* by Linear Programming [3] or IRLS (for $p = 1$).

If there exists some appropriate conditions on A and x, like

$$\|x\|_0 \leq \frac{1}{2}\left(1 + \frac{1}{\max_{i \neq j} \frac{|a_i^T a_j|}{\|a_i\|_2 \|a_j\|_2}}\right)$$

then Basic Pursuit as well as OMP give the unique solution of (4) and it is also the unique solution of (P_0).

However, when signals are perturbed by noise it becomes more useful to relax the exact constraint: $h = Ax$ by using instead the quadratic penalty function $Q(x) = \|Ax - h\|_2^2 \leq \epsilon$, with $\epsilon \geq 0$ being the error tolerance. Therefore, an error-tolerant version of (P_0) is defined by:

$$(P_0^\epsilon) : \min_x \|x\|_0 \text{ subject to } \|Ax - h\|_2 \leq \epsilon \qquad (5)$$

In (P_0^ϵ) the l_2-norm is used for evaluation, and the error $Ax - h$ can be replaced by other options, as l_1, l_2, or l_∞.

Observe that problem (P_0^ϵ) as defined above is useful for the given task. Assuming that signal h has noise e with finite energy $\|e\|_2^2 \leq \epsilon^2$, $h = Ax + e$, solving (P_0^ϵ) can help us to find the solution $\hat{x}$. Then, we can recover the unknown denoised signal $\hat{h}$ as $\hat{h} = A\hat{x}$. Similarly, when relaxing l_0-norm to an l_1-norm, we get (P_1^ϵ) known in the literature as *basis pursuit denoising* (BPDN) [7]

$$(P_1^\epsilon) : \min_x \|x\|_1 \text{ subject to } \|Ax - h\|_2 \leq \epsilon \qquad (6)$$

3. LEARNED METHODOLOGY FOR DICTIONARY AND K-SVD ALGORITHM

The optimal solution of the problem (P_1^ϵ) directly depends on the used dictionary A. Our working hypothesis is that if we are able to learn A from a training dataset, then A should be well adapted to the document characteristics and noise. So, in this section, we review learning algorithms, in general, used for constructing a dictionary A and in particular, the learning algorithms we have used: the K-SVD algorithm.

In a general learning methodology, a family l signals $\{h_j\}_{j=1}^l$ is considered as the training database. Our goal is to find a dictionary A in which each signal $h_j \in R^n$ has an optimally sparse approximation $\bar{h}_j \simeq Ax_j$ satisfying $\|\bar{h}_j - h_j\|^2 \leq \epsilon$, or finding:

$$\min_{A, x_j} \sum_{j=1}^l \|x_j\|_1 \text{ subject to } \|h_j - Ax_j\|_2 \leq \epsilon, \text{ for all } j = 1, .., l \qquad (7)$$

This dictionary can be obtained by the learning process that iteratively adjusts A via two main stages: sparse coding stage and update dictionary stage. In the sparse coding

---

[1]$\|x\|_2 \triangleq (\sum_{i=1}^M |x_i|^2)^{1/2}$, with $x \in R^M$

stage, all sparse representations $X = \{x_j\}_{j=1}^l \in R^{m \times l}$ of $H = \{h_j\}_{j=1}^l \in R^{n \times l}$ are found by solving equation (6), on the condition that A is fixed. In the update dictionary stage, an updating rule is used to optimize the sparse representations of the training signals. In general, the way to update the dictionary is different from one learning algorithm to another. There are two well-known dictionary-learning algorithms, named *Method of Optimal Directions* (MOD) by *Engan et al* [9], and K-SVD by *Aharon et al* [1]. These two algorithms behave similarly with a small advantage to the K-SVD [8]. So, we chose the K-SVD algorithm in our paper to construct the learned dictionary.

In K-SVD algorithm [1], the updating rule is to make a modification on dictionary's columns. At this step, we handle to update sequentially each columns a_{j_0} of A such that the residual error (8) is minimized, where X and $\{a_1, ... a_{j_0-1}, a_{j_0+1}, ..., a_m\}$ are fixed,

$$\|H - AX\|_F^2 = \|H - \sum_{j=1}^m a_j x_j^T\|_F^2$$
$$= \|(H - \sum_{j \neq j_0} a_j x_j^T) - a_{j_0} x_{j_0}^T\|_F^2 \quad (8)$$
$$= \|E_{j_0} - a_{j_0} x_{j_0}^T\|_F^2$$

In equation (8), $x_{j_0}^T \in R^l$ is the k-th row in X and the notation $\|.\|_F$ stands for the Frobenius norm. Because X and all the columns of A are fixed excepted the column a_{j_0}, so $E_{j_0} = H - \sum_{j \neq j_0} a_j x_j^T$ is fixed. It means that the minimum error $\|H - AX\|_F^2$ depends only on the optimal a_{j_0} and $x_{j_0}^T$. This is the problem of approximating a matrix E_{j_0} with another matrix which has a rank 1 based on minimizing the *Frobenius* norm. The optimal solutions $\tilde{a}_{j_0}, \tilde{x}_{j_0}^T$ can be given by the *Singular Value Decomposition* (SVD) of E_{j_0} of rank r_1, namely

$$\tilde{a}_{j_0} \tilde{x}_{j_0}^T = Q_1 \tilde{U} Q_2$$

where $Q_1 = \{q_1^1, ..., q_n^1\}$, $U = \text{diag}(\sigma_1, \sigma_2, ..., \sigma_{r_1})$, $Q_2 = \{q_1^2, ..., q_l^2\}$ is the SVD of E_{j_0}: $E_{j_0} = Q_1 U Q_2$; and $\tilde{U}$ is the same matrix as U except that it contains only one singular values σ_1 (the other singular values are replaced by zero). This means $\tilde{a}_{j_0} = q_1^1$ and $\tilde{x}_{j_0}^T = \sigma_1 q_1^2$. However, the new vector $\tilde{x}_{j_0}^T$ is very likely to be filled, implying that we increase the number of non-zeros in the representation of X, or the condition about the sparsity of X can be broken.

This problem can be overcome as follows. Define the group of indexes where $x_{j_0}^T$ is nonzero:

$$\omega_{j_0} = \{i | 1 \leq i \leq l, x_{j_0}^T(i) \neq 0\}.$$

and a matrix $\Omega_{j_0} \in R^{l \times |\omega_{j_0}|}$ is defined $\Omega_{j_0}(\omega_{j_0}(i), i) = 1$ and zeros elsewhere. Let

1. $x_{j_0}^R = x_{j_0}^T \Omega_{j_0}$, $x_{j_0}^R \in R^{|\omega_{j_0}|}$

2. $E_{j_0}^R = E_{j_0} \Omega_{j_0}$, $E_{j_0}^R \in R^{n \times |\omega_{j_0}|}$

and following equation (8), the minimization is equivalent to

$$\|E_{j_0} \Omega_{j_0} - a_{j_0} x_{j_0}^T \Omega_{j_0}\|_F^2 = \|E_{j_0}^R - a_{j_0} x_{j_0}^R\|_F^2 \quad (9)$$

Note that the solution of (9) $\tilde{x}_{j_0}^R$ has the same support as the original $\tilde{x}_{j_0}^T$, and the optimal values $\tilde{x}_{j_0}^R, \tilde{a}_{j_0}$ can be obtained by finding SVD of a subset of the columns of the

error matrix $E_{j_0}^R$ of rank r_2: $E_{j_0}^R = SDV^T$. The solution for $\tilde{a}_{j_0}$ is defined as the first column of S, and the coefficient vector $\tilde{x}_{j_0}^R$ as the first column of V multiplied by d_1, with $D = \text{diag}(d_1, d_2, ..., d_{r_2})$. More details about the K-SVD algorithm can be found in algorithm 1.

Algorithm 1 Learning algorithm K-SVD

INPUT: $A_{(0)} \in R^{n \times m}$; $\{h_i\}_{i=1}^l$; $k = 0$;
1. Initialize: Normalization the columns of matrix $A_{(0)}$;
2. Main Iteration
$k = k + 1$;
while ($\|H - A_{(k)} X_{(k)}\|_F^2$ is not small enough) **do**
  - Solve (P_1^ϵ) to find all sparse representation $\{x_i\}_{i=1}^l$ of $\{h_i\}_{i=1}^l$
  for ($j_0 = 1$ to m) **do**
    - Define: $\omega_{j_0} = \{i | 1 \leq i \leq l, x_{j_0}^T(i) \neq 0\}$
    - Calculate E_{j_0} via equation $E_{j_0} = H - \sum_{j \neq j_0} a_j x_j^T$
    - Let $E_{j_0}^R$ is the sub-matrix of E_{j_0} on the columns corresponding to ω_{j_0}
    - Calculate SVD of $E_{j_0}^R$: $E_{j_0}^R = SDV^T$.
    - Updating: $a_{j_0} = s_1$ and $x_{j_0}^R = d_1 v_1$ with $S = \{s_1, ..., s_n\}$, $V = \{v_1, ..., v_{|\omega_{j_0}|}\}$, $D = \text{diag}(d_1, d_2, ..., d_{r_2})$
  end for
end while
OUTPUT: The result $A_{(k)}$

---

4. DOCUMENT DEGRADATION MODELS

Inspired by several authors like in [12, 11], we have used document noise models for evaluating the proposed method. In 1993, *Kanungo et al* [12] introduced a statistical model for document degradation showing quite realistic results, which gave the following three reasons justifying research on noise models. First of all, noise modeling allows to study recognition algorithms in general, as a function of the perturbation of the input data. Secondly, it permits the evaluation of any algorithm depending on the degradation level. Thirdly, a knowledge of the degradation model can enable us to design algorithms for image restoration. More recently, [2] has proposed the Noise Spread model, inspired on the physics of image acquisition process. According to this model the acquired image is obtained as a result of convolving the source image with the sensor function defined by the Point Spread Function with white noise.

Since the Kanungo noise model [12, 13] is a statistical model, widely used to verify the robustness of document image analysis methods to noise, we use it as noise model in this paper. However, the extension to another model is easy as our method is enabled to denoise documents for which the model of noise is unknown. One of the advantages of degradation models is they permit to generate degraded images controlled by the parameter models. The qualitative results of these images range from quite realistic noisy images to unrealistic, or even highly degraded images in function of the parameters set up. For instance, in Figure (1), symbol images (b) and (d) provide more realistic symbol degradation than (c), (e), (f) and (g).

Bi-level images are represented by white background pixels and black foreground pixels representing the different entities of the document. The Kanungo model needs six pa-

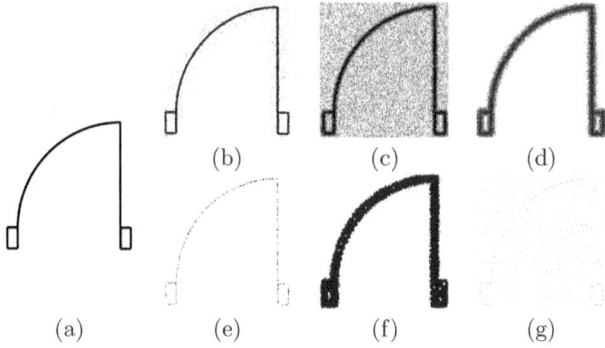

Figure 1: (a): Original binary symbol; from (b) to (g) examples of six levels of Kanungo noise of the GREC 2005 dataset.

rameters α_0, α, β_0, β, η, and k as a function of the pixel distance to the shape boundaries to degrade a binary image. α and α_0 control the probability of flipping a foreground pixel to a background pixel, in other words, these two parameters provide the probability of changing a black pixel to a white one. Similarly, parameters β and β_0 control the probability of changing a background (white) pixel with a foreground (black) pixel. In addition, these two probabilities exponentially decay on the distance of each pixel to the nearest boundary pixel. In contrast, the parameter η is a constant value added to all pixels regardless their relative position to shape boundaries. Finally, the last parameter k is the size of the disk used in the morphological closing operation. The whole process of image degradation can be summarized in the following three steps:

1. Use standard distance transform algorithms to calculate the distance d of each pixel from the nearest boundary pixel.

2. Each foreground pixel and background pixel is flipped with probability $p(0|1, d, \alpha_0, \alpha) = \alpha_0 e^{-\alpha d^2} + \eta$, and $p(1|0, d, \beta_0, \beta) = \beta_0 e^{-\beta d^2} + \eta$

3. Use a disk structuring element of diameter k to perform a morphological closing operation.

5. ENERGY NOISE MODEL

For denoising images using basis pursuit denoising, we need to decide which kind of dictionary A is used along with the best value ϵ in equation (6). From Section 3 we know how to learn a dictionary A adapted to noisy data. In this Section, we explain how to choose the best value ϵ when we apply equation (6) on the image patches with size w.

Denoising in MRA methods assumes that images have been corrupted by an additive white noise. For such noisy images, the energy of noise η is proportional to both the noise variance and size image. For Noise Spread model, authors in [11] empirically supposed that the optimal energy of noise depends on the noise spread relation. However, neither of these two assumptions can be applied to document images where the noise follows a Kanungo noise model instead of white noise. The reason is that in Kanungo model pixels near the shape boundaries have higher probability to

be affected by noise than pixels far from the shape boundaries. On the contrary, white noise model assumes statistical independence between the noise and the image. In fact, the probability that a pixel is perturbed by noise depends only on the variance of the model and does not depend on the position of a pixel in the image. In addition, the parameters used in Noised Spread model are different from the Kanungo's ones, so we cannot use the noise spread relation proposed in [11] to decide the value for ϵ.

Therefore, we propose an energy noise model inspired by [14]. Thus, we evaluate the noise level using the peak values of the normalized cross-correlation between noisy and cleaned documents. Let D being a training dataset including $2t$ documents $(D_i^c, D_i^n), i = 1, ..., t$ where D_i^c is a cleaned document and D_i^n is its noisy version. We define r_i as the peaks of normalized cross-correlation between D_i^n and D_i^c, then the tolerance error value is defined by:

$$\epsilon = cw\bar{r} \qquad (10)$$

where c is a constant value set experimentally, w is the size of patches, $\bar{r}$ is the mean value of the peaks r_i.

We can summarize the procedure for document denoising using sparse representation of a learned dictionary A as follows:

1. *Create a training database* using a sliding window of size $w \times w$ to scan the corrupted image $y \in R^{M \times N}$ with scanning step set to 1 pixel in both directions. All $(M - w + 1)(N - w + 1)$ obtained patches $\{h_j\}_{j=1}^l$, $h_j \in R^{w \times w}$ are considered as the training database.

2. *Create a learned dictionary* using the K-SVD algorithm to create the learned dictionary A from $\{h_j\}_{j=1}^l$.

3. Combine the learned dictionary A with the sparse representation model in the purpose of denoising image, following:

   a. Find the solution of the optimization problem (6) for each patch h_j

   $$\hat{x_j} = \arg\min \|x_j\|_1 \text{ subject to } \|Ax_j - h_j\|_2 \le \epsilon,$$

   b. Compute the denoised version of each patch h_j by $\hat{h_j} = A\hat{x_j}$,

   c. Merge the denoised patches $\hat{h_j}$ to get the denoised image $\hat{y}$.

4. Binarise $\hat{y}$ to get the final result $\tilde{y}$.

6. EXPERIMENTAL RESULTS

We firstly evaluated our algorithm on the GREC 2005 dataset. This dataset has 150 different symbols which have been degraded using the Kanungo's method to simulate the noise introduced by the scanning process. Six sets of parameters are used to obtain six different noise levels as shown in Figure (1).

At each level of noise, a dataset containing 2×50 noisy and cleaned symbols are used to calculate the value of $\bar{r}$ and ϵ (Section 5). We empirically found that the best results in denoising bilevel images are achieved when c in equation (10) belongs to $[0.4, 1]$.

Figure (2) shows one example about the normalized cross-correlation of two images (a) and (b) with its maximum

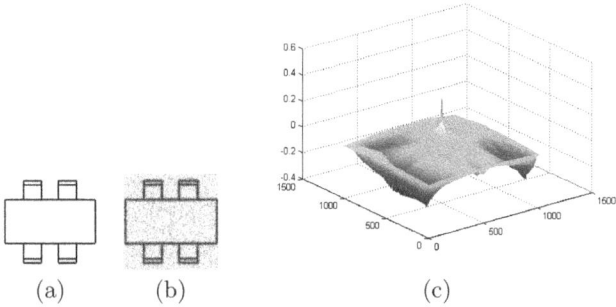

Figure 2: Normalized cross-correlation between two images.

Level	1	2	3	4	5	6
$\bar{r}$	0.9133	0.4412	0.5629	0.3698	0.4413	0.2006

Table 1: The value of $\bar{r}$ at six level of noise.

	Median	OC	Curvelet	Proposed method
Level 1	0.926 (-)	0.937 (-)	0.963 (=)	**0.963**
Level 2	0.630 (-)	0.177 (-)	0.565 (-)	**0.655**
Level 3	0.428 (-)	0.787 (-)	0.389 (-)	**0.826**
Level 4	0.088 (-)	0.001 (-)	**0.459** (+)	0.135
Level 5	0.261 (-)	0.268 (-)	0.263 (-)	**0.284**
Level 6	0.001 (-)	0.000 (-)	0.059 (=)	**0.060**

Table 2: Average value gained by Jaccard's similarity measure.

	Median	OC	Curvelet	Proposed method
Level 1	2.896 (-)	2.454 (-)	**1.403** (=)	1.423
Level 2	21.015 (-)	30.865 (-)	28.421 (-)	**19.687**
Level 3	53.690 (-)	8.899 (-)	57.771 (-)	**8.008**
Level 4	33.599 (-)	36.819 (-)	**19.815** (+)	31.881
Level 5	111.632 (-)	107.358 (-)	110.286 (-)	**98.212**
Level 6	37.863 (-)	37.915 (-)	**35.632** (=)	35.772

Table 3: Average values gained by MSE.

value $r_i = 0.4106$; and table (1) presents the best values of $\bar{r}$ corresponding to each level of degradation.

The learning dictionary was produced using K-SVD algorithm with 50 iterations, and the training dataset includes all 8×8 patches. Those patches were taken from a corrupted image h. The ratio of the dictionary is $1/4$ ($m = 4 \times n$).

To examine the effectiveness of the proposed method, we compare it with three existing methods for denoising binary images: median filtering, morphological operators (opening and closing), and curvelet transform. The median filtering is performed with a window size of 3×3. The morphological operators use a 3×3 structuring element. Curvelets transform has been verified upon the best value of $\eta = c \times \sqrt{MN} \times \sigma^2$, $\sigma \in [0.02, 0.1]$ for each noise level, where M, N is the size of the image. The criterion to choose these best values σ is the average MSE (*Mean Squared Error*).

Moreover, using the traditional MSE to estimate the quality change between the original document and the reconstructed one, all algorithms are evaluated by *Jaccard*'s similarity measure [4]. This measure is computed based on the three values a, b, c as below:

$$S = \frac{a}{a+b+c} \qquad (11)$$

where

$$a = |\{(i,j)|y^0(i,j) = 1, \tilde{y}(i,j) = 1, 1 \le i \le M, 1 \le j \le N\}|$$

$$b = |\{(i,j)|y^0(i,j) = 0, \tilde{y}(i,j) = 1, 1 \le i \le M, 1 \le j \le N\}|$$

$$c = |\{(i,j)|y^0(i,j) = 1, \tilde{y}(i,j) = 0, 1 \le i \le M, 1 \le j \le N\}|$$

a means 'right matches', and b, c mean 'mismatches'; y^0, $\tilde{y} \in R^{M \times N}$ are cleaned and denoised images, respectively. The maximal value of the *Jaccard* measure is one when two images are identical.

Figure (3) shows an exemple of denoised images and table (2) and (3) show the average results obtained by the four methods on 6 levels of noise that are respectively evaluated by MSE and *Jaccard*'s measures. A paired Wilcoxon signed test with a significance level of 5% is used also to check whether the difference between the results obtained by our

method and the ones obtained by the other methods is significant. In these tables, an entry mark by $(-)$ indicates that the corresponding method performs worst than our method. Similarly, an entry marked by $(+)$ indicates that the corresponding method outperforms the proposed method, and an entry marked by $(=)$ indicates that results obtained by the both methods are not significantly different.

Table (2) and (3) also show that at level 5 and level 6, none of the four methods are good enough but other methods are worse than ours. We further examine the set of noisy images at level 4 and we found that the set of noisy patches of the corrupted image cannot provide a good training data since most of patches are trivial (zeros value), making not enough discrimination between $A_{(0)}$ and $A_{(k)}$ (see algorithm 1). This can explain why the curvelets transform method is better than the proposed method at this level of noise. Although at level 1 the Wilcoxon signed test indicates that results obtained by the curvelets and our method are not significantly different, when we zoom the denoised images we found that the intersection of edges are not well restored with curvelet as shown in Figure (4). Since curvelets are smooth functions, they are not well adapted for singularity points.

We also verified our method on real scanned documents created by printing the original documents and scanning printed documents at the different resolutions. By using 15 original documents, we got 12 scanned datasets with different resolutions. Figure (6) shows an example of one of the scanned documents.

The aim is to test our method on real documents with an unknown model of noise twelve scanned images are tested and evaluated using the Structural similarity (SSIM) index. SSIM [20] is also a method for measuring the similarity that is designed to improve MSE, which have proved to be inconsistent with human eye perception. SSIM metric is computed on various windows of images. The distance between two windows s_i and q_i is calculated following the equation (12) where s_i, q_i are taken from the same location of the noisy image and reconstructed image.

$$S(s_i, q_i) = \left(\frac{2\mu_{s_i}\mu_{q_i} + c_1}{\mu_{s_i}^2 + \mu_{q_i}^2 + c_1}\right)\left(\frac{2\sigma_{s_i}\sigma_{q_i} + c_2}{\sigma_{s_i}^2 + \sigma_{q_i}^2 + c_2}\right) \qquad (12)$$

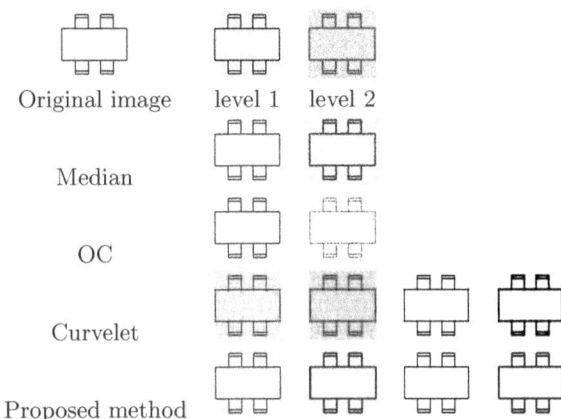

Figure 3: Results of denoising the noisy images with Kanungo model at levels 1 and 2 of degredation. Columns 2 and 3 are the denoised images following each method. Columns 4 and 5 are the binarized denoised images of columns 2 and 3, respectively. For the median and OC, images are already binarized in columns 2 and 3.

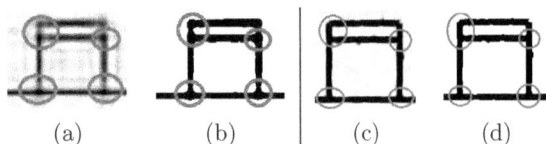

Figure 4: (a), (c): Zoom of denoised images by curvelets and our method, respectively. (b), (d) denoised binary version respectively of (a) and (c).

$\mu_{s_i}, \mu_{q_i}, \sigma_{s_i}, \sigma_{q_i}$ are the average local and the sample standard deviations of s_i and q_i, respectively; $c_1 = (k_1 L)^2, c_2 = (k_2 L)^2$ are two variables to stabilize the division with weak denominator; L is the dynamic range of the pixel-values; and k_1, k_2 are two constants. The resultant SSIM index is a decimal with a value 1 in the case of two identical sets of data. In this paper, SSIM index is calculated on a window size 8×8, and the values of L, k_1, k_2 are respectively $100, 0.01$ and 0.03. Table (4) presents the results in comparison with other methods. We can see that in each case the performance of our approach is good compared to the other.

The last experiment is done on the DIBCO 2009 dataset. This dataset contains images that range from grayscale to color and from real to synthetic. The value of $\bar{r}$ for this experiment equals 0.7321 and is calculated as the same way as described above. Figure (6) presents one learning dictionary build by corrupted patches with size 8×8 on DIBCO images. Figure (7a) gives the documents in DIBCO dataset and its denoised versions got by our approach (Figures (7b) and (7c)).

As the experiment before, the SSIM measure is used with the purpose of comparison. Table (5) presents the results for the 5 handwritten images shown in Figure 7 and we can see that in each case our approach provides a good result. Tables (4) and (5) present the difference results (the last rows) using also a paired Wilcoxon signed test with a significance level of 5%. We can observe that the difference between our approach performance compared to the other methods per-

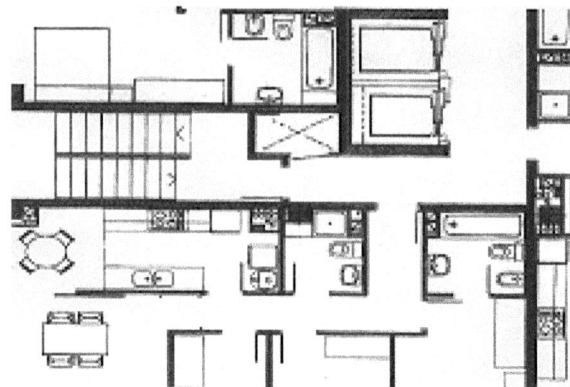

Figure 5: An example of a scanned documents.

Images	Median	OC	Curvelet	Proposed method
1	0.5374	0.4640	0.4693	**0.6834**
2	0.6906	0.5165	0.6184	**0.7534**
3	0.5749	0.5158	0.5057	**0.7421**
4	0.6482	0.4879	0.5666	**0.7454**
5	0.6008	0.5056	0.5186	**0.7458**
6	0.6310	0.4409	0.5320	**0.7145**
7	0.6018	0.5030	0.5244	**0.7580**
8	0.6066	0.4814	0.5199	**0.7381**
9	0.6487	0.4662	0.5638	**0.7456**
10	0.6203	0.4603	0.5377	**0.7317**
11	0.6946	0.4832	0.5987	**0.7685**
12	0.7264	0.4494	0.6274	**0.7733**
Average	0.6320 (-)	0.4812 (-)	0.5485 (-)	**0.7416**

Table 4: The obtained results when comparing proposed method with structural similarity SSIM index.

formance is statistically significant even in the case where the noise model is unknown.

Images	Median	OC	Curvelet	Ours approach
1	0.6420	0.6926	0.7054	**0.9528**
2	0.4628	0.5155	0.5156	**0.9784**
3	0.5115	0.5315	0.5064	**0.8648**
4	0.4595	0.4946	0.4692	**0.8933**
5	0.6953	0.7283	0.7441	**0.9416**
Average	0.5542 (-)	0.5925 (-)	0.5881 (-)	**0.9261**

Table 5: The obtained results with DIBCO 2009 dataset using SSIM measure.

To conclude this section, all evaluation measures have indicated that our method performs better than all of the other methods in most of the cases.

7. CONCLUSIONS

A novel algorithm for denoising document images by using learning dictionary based on sparse representation has been presented in this paper. Learning method starts by building a training database from corrupted images, and constructing an empirically learned dictionary by using sparse represen-

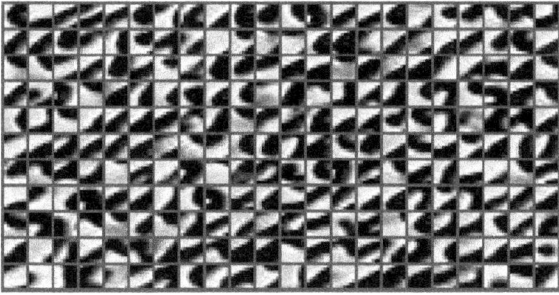

Figure 6: The trained dictionary on DIBCO images with $w = 8$.

tation. This dictionary can be used as a fixed dictionary to find the solution of the basis pursuit denoising problem. In addition, we provide a way to define the best value of the tolerance error (ϵ) based on a measure of fidelity between two images. The efficiency of ϵ has been also approved experimentally on different datasets for different resolutions and different kinds of noise. All experimental results show that our method outperforms existing ones in most of the cases.

8. ACKNOWLEDGEMENTS

Oriol Ramos Terrades, has been partially supported by the Spanish project TIN2012-37475-C02-02.

9. REFERENCES

[1] M. Aharon, M. Elad, and A. Bruckstein. K-svd: An algorithm for designing overcomplete dictionaries for sparse representation. *IEEE Transactions on signal processing*, 54(11):4311–4322, 2006.

[2] E. Barney. Modeling image degradations for improving ocr. In *European Conference on Signal Processing*, pages 1–5, 2008.

[3] S.S. Chen, D.L. Donoho, and M.A. Saunders. Atomic decomposition by basis pursuit. *SIAM Journal on Scientific Computing*, 20(1):33–61, 1998.

[4] S. S. Choi, S. H. Cha, and C. Tappert. A survey of binary similarity and distance measures. *Journal on Systemics, Cybernetics and Informatics*, 8(1):43–48, 2010.

[5] I. Daubechies, R. Devore, M. Fornasier, and C.S Gunturk. Iteratively reweighted least squares minimization for sparse recovery. *Communications on Pure and Applied Mathematics*, 63(1):1–38, october 2009.

[6] E. Davies. *Machine Vision: Theory, Algorithms and Practicalities*. Academic Press, 1990.

[7] D. Donoho and M. Elad. Optimally sparse representation in general (nonorthogonal) dictionaries via l^1 minimization. *Proceeding of the National Academy of Sciences of the United States of America*, 100(5):2197–2202, 2003.

[8] M. Elad. *Sparse and redundant representation: From theory to applications in signal and images processing*. Springer, Reading, Massachusetts, 2010.

[9] K. Engan, S. O. Aase, and J. H. Husoy. Frame based signal compression using method of optimal directions (mod). In *International Conference on Acoustics, Speech and Signal Processing (ICASSP)*, 1999.

[10] I. Gonzalez and B. Rao. Sparse signal reconstruction from limited data using focuss: a re-weighted minimum norm algorithm. *Signal Processing*, 45(3):600–616, March 1997.

[11] V-T. Hoang, E.H. Barney Smith, and S. Tabbone. Edge noise removel in bilevel graphical document images using sparse representation. In *IEEE international conference on Image Processing*, 2011.

[12] T. Kanungo, R. M. Haralick, and I. T. Phillips. Global and local document degradation models. In *Proceedings of the Second International Conference on Document Analysis and Recognition*, pages 730–734, October 1993.

[13] T. Kanungo, R.M. Haralick, H.S. Baird, W. Stuezle, and D. Madigan. A statistical, nonparametric methodology for document degradation model validation. *IEEE Transactions on PAMI*, 22(11):1209–1223, June 2000.

[14] J. P. Lewis. Fast normalized cross-correlation. *Vision Interface*, 1995.

[15] S. G. Mallat and Z. Zhang. Matching pursuits with time-frequency dictionaries. *Signal Processing*, 41(12):3397–3415, 1993.

[16] P. Marrgos and R.W. Schafer. Morphological filters, part 2: Their relations to median, order-statistic, and stack filters. *IEEE Transactions on acoustics, speech, and signal processing*, 35(8):87–134, 1987.

[17] Y. Pati, R. Rezaiifar, and P. Krishnaprasad. Orthogonal matching pursuit: Recursive function approximation with applications to wavelet decomposition. In *Proceedings of the 27th Annual Asilomar Conference on Signals, Systems, and Computers*, pages 40–44, 1993.

[18] J.L. Starck, E.J. Candes, and D.L. Donoho. The curvelet transform for image denoising. *IEEE Transactions on image processing*, 11(6):670–684, 2002.

[19] V. N. Temlyakov. Weak greedy algorithms. *Advances in Computational Mathematics*, 5:173–187, 2000.

[20] Z. Wang, A. C. Bovik, H. R. Sheikh, and E. P. Simoncelli. Image quality assessment: From error visibility to structural similarity. *IEEE Transactions on Image Processing*, 13(4):600–612, 2004.

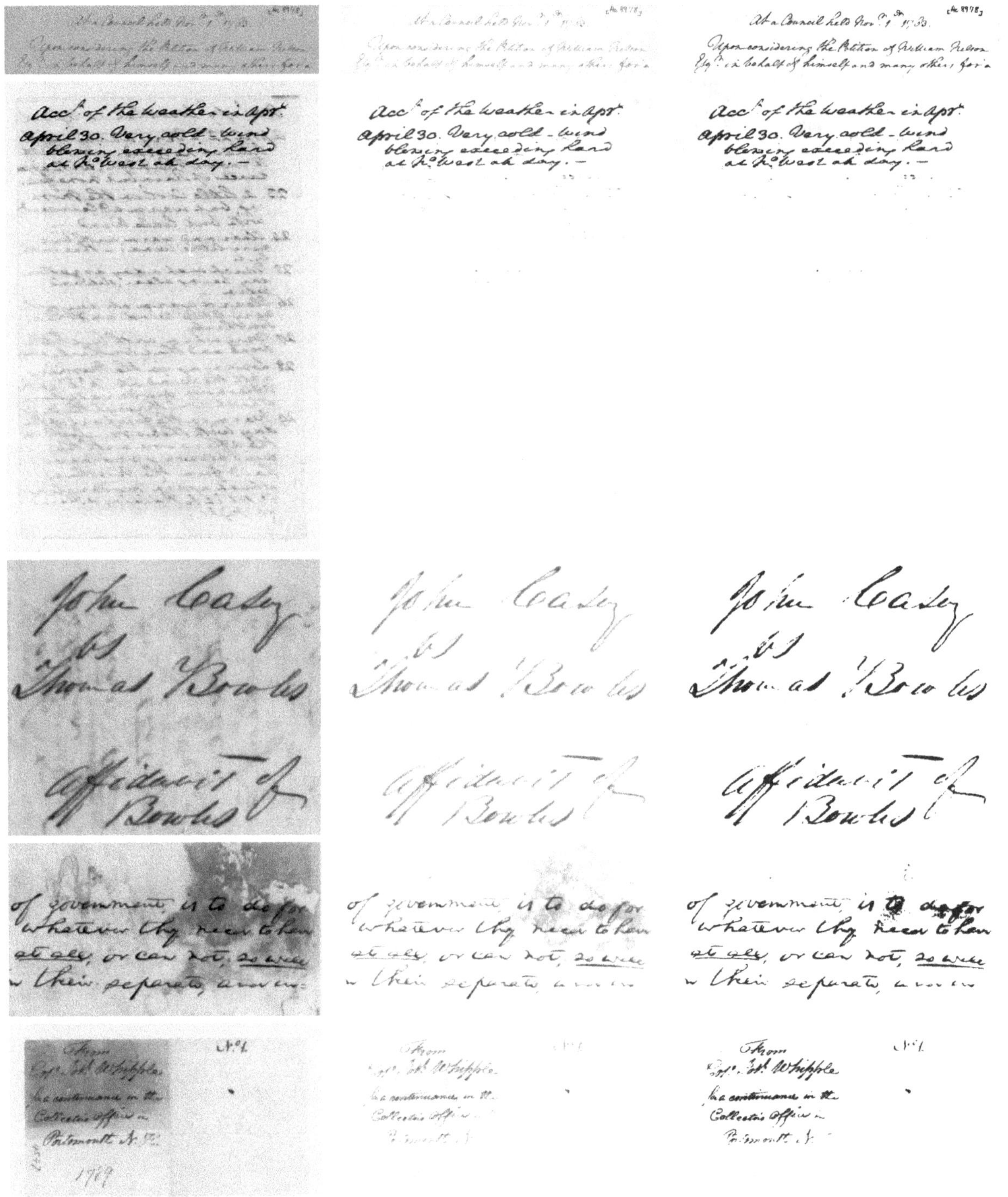

Figure 7: (a) Noisy documents in DIBCO dataset used in Table 5, (b) Denoised documents got by our approach before binarization and (c) After binarization using Otsu's method.

Supervised Polarity Classification of Spanish Tweets based on Linguistic Knowledge

David Vilares
Universidade da Coruña
Campus de Elviña, 15071
A Coruña, Spain
david.vilares@udc.es

Miguel A. Alonso
Universidade da Coruña
Campus de Elviña, 15071
A Coruña, Spain
miguel.alonso@udc.es

Carlos Gómez-Rodríguez
Universidade da Coruña
Campus de Elviña, 15071
A Coruña, Spain
carlos.gomez@udc.es

ABSTRACT

We describe a system that classifies the polarity of Spanish tweets. We adopt a hybrid approach, which combines machine learning and linguistic knowledge acquired by means of NLP. We use part-of-speech tags, syntactic dependencies and semantic knowledge as features for a supervised classifier. Lexical particularities of the language used in Twitter are taken into account in a pre-processing step. Experimental results improve over those of pure machine learning approaches and confirm the practical utility of the proposal.

Categories and Subject Descriptors

H.3.1 [**Information Retrieval and Storage**]: Content Analysis and Indexing—*Linguistic processing*; I.2.7 [**Artificial Intelligence**]: Natural Language Processing—*Text analysis*

Keywords

Document Analysis, Linguistic Analysis, Machine Learning, Opinion Mining, Sentiment Analysis, Twitter

1. INTRODUCTION

Opinion Mining (OM) has become a relevant field of research in the last decade. With the explosion of the Web 2.0, many users employ social media to share their opinions and experiences about products, services or relevant people. In this context, one of the most popular social media is Twitter. In this microblogging network, users express their views in micro documents (tweets) of up to 140 characters, particularly about current topics, which is an important source of information for companies, especially for their business intelligence and marketing departments.

We present a system which classifies the polarity of Spanish tweets taking into account linguistic knowledge. We use as our starting point an external semantic-based OM system, using its output as features for a supervised classifier. We then include POS-tags and syntactic information in the form of syntactic dependencies. Lastly, we provide an automatic

mechanism to enrich and adapt semantic knowledge to a specific domain. We evaluate our proposal with the TASS 2012 corpus, which distinguishes between six different categories. The remainder of this paper is organized as follows. We start by describing our proposal in Section 2. In Section 3 we show the experimental results. Finally, we present conclusions and future work in Section 4.

2. POLARITY CLASSIFICATION HYBRID SYSTEM

The polarity classification task has mainly been tackled from two different perspectives: semantic-based [15] and supervised [9]. Semantic approaches are characterised by the use of semantic orientation (SO) dictionaries or opinion lexicons. They have been applied successfully in many contexts, but their performance drops on Twitter, where there is a high frequency of subjective elements, such as emoticons or Twitter special expressions, which are not included in general opinion lexicons; this results in a low recall [18].

With respect to supervised classifiers, their main drawback is their high domain dependency and the cost of creating new training data. Supervised methods typically represent the text as a bag of words, learning the perception of a word for a specific context. However, their performance drops drastically when the same classifier is used to categorise texts from a different field [13]. In contrast with these approaches, we propose a hybrid system which combines lexical, syntactic and semantic knowledge with machine learning techniques. In particular, linguistic features are used to feed an SMO, an implementation of SVM, presented in [10], and incorporated by default in the WEKA data mining software [5]. Figure 1 shows the general architecture of our proposal, whose components will be described in Section 2.

To train and evaluate our approach we use the TASS 2012 corpus, presented at the Workshop on Sentiment Analysis at SEPLN[1] [17]. It is a collection of Spanish tweets written by public figures that is composed of a training and a test set which contain 7,219 and 60,798 tweets, respectively. Each one is annotated with one of these six categories: *strongly positive* (P+), *positive* (P), *neutral* (NEU), *negative* (N), *strongly negative* (N+) or *without opinion* (NONE). An annotation in four classes was also proposed (P+ and N+ classes are included into P and N, respectively). The gold standard has been generated by a pooling of the submis-

---

[1] Sociedad Española para el Procesamiento del Lenguaje Natural

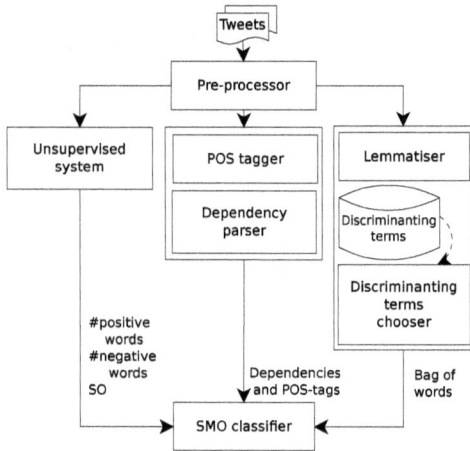

Figure 1: General architecture of the system

sions of the workshop followed by a thorough human review for the thousands of ambiguous cases.

2.1 Pre-processing

As a previous step, all tweets were pre-processed as follows:

- *Emoticon replacement*: We employ the emoticon collection published in [1]. Each emoticon is replaced in the text by one of these five labels: strong positive (ESP), positive (EP), neutral (ENEU), negative (EN) or strong negative (ESN).

- *Most frequent unrecognised abbreviations spell-checking*: We replace some of the most habitual ungrammatical Spanish abbreviations by their grammatical form.

- *URL normalisation*: Web addresses are replaced with the string 'URL'.

- *Laughs normalisation*: Different variants of laughs in Spanish language (*e.g.* 'jjjaja', 'JJEEJJ',...) are normalised as *jxjx* where $x \in \{a, e, i, o, u\}$. For example, 'jjjaja' becomes 'jaja'.

- *Treatment of special Twitter elements ('@'and '#')*: User mentions are modified: we eliminate the '@' symbol and capitalise the first character (*e.g.* '@user' becomes 'User'). Regarding the hashtags, if one appears at the beginning or the end of a tweet, then the complete hashtag is eliminated. Otherwise we only delete the '#'.

2.2 Generic semantic approach (GSA)

We took a purely semantic proposal presented in [16] as a part of our system. This approach carries out segmentation, tokenisation and POS-tagging of texts, to then obtain a dependency tree for each sentence by means of dependency parsing. We then employ the syntactic structure to treat three of the most significant constructions on sentiment analysis: intensification, adversative subordinate clauses and negation. We use dependency types to identify the scope of these constructions and modify the semantic orientation value of the polarity words inside that scope. As a result,

we obtain the SO for each sentence and then aggregate them to calculate the global SO of a text.

We finally include that final SO, and the number of positive and negative words in a tweet, as features for a supervised classifier. We use the Spanish opinion lexicon of Brooke et al. [3] to determine which words are opinionated.

2.3 Morphosyntactic information (MSI)

The employment of POS-tagging information in polarity classification tasks is a widely discussed issue. Pak and Paroubek [8] and Spencer and Uchyigit [12] suggest that certain POS-tags, such as adjectives or personal pronouns, are more frequent in subjective texts. In this respect, we observed a similar tendency in the training set of the TASS 2012 corpus. Table 1 shows a selection of relevant tag frequencies. In the same way, we hypothesise that dependency types are also useful in order to classify the polarity of the tweets.

To test this, we have used the Ancora corpus [14] and the Nivre arc-eager algorithm included in MaltParser [6].

Class	a	n	v	i	f
P+	0.060	0.256	0.111	0.004	0.215
P	0.056	0.266	0.119	0.002	0.198
NEU	0.057	0.254	0.133	0.001	0.163
N	0.050	0.263	0.132	0.001	0.161
N+	0.060	0.266	0.118	0.001	0.154
NONE	0.048	0.299	0.090	0.001	0.220

Table 1: Tag frequencies in the training set: adjectives (a), nouns (n), verbs (v), interjections (i) and punctuation marks (f)

Class	ci	atr	cc	cag
P+	0.008	0.105	0.042	0.004
P	0.010	0.010	0.051	0.000
NEU	0.010	0.141	0.053	0.001
N	0.009	0.000	0.055	0.150
N+	0.007	0.000	0.049	0.145
NONE	0.179	0.008	0.003	0.001

Table 2: Dependency type frequencies in the training set: indirect object (ci), subject complement (atr), adjunct (cc) and agent (cag)

Table 2 shows the frequency of some dependency types[2] on the training set of the TASS 2012 corpus. The frequency distribution of certain dependencies such as the agent is especially relevant, which suggests that Spanish users employ the passive voice more often in negative reviews. To treat both POS-tags and dependency structure, we included the total number of occurrences of each tag and dependency type instance found in each tweet as features for the classifier.

2.4 Domain adaptation (DA)

In Twitter texts, there is a high frequency of some special subjective elements that are not included in generic opinion lexicons. Emoticons, laughs and some Twitter tags, such as *Follow Friday* ('FF') or *Retweet* ('RT'), are some of the

---

[2]We use the Ancora dependency type tags.

clearest examples that, while usually being subjective, do not appear in semantic dictionaries. To improve the performance in a specific domain and in a specific social medium, we have developed an automatic mechanism that enriches and adapts semantic knowledge to a particular field. Our procedure consists of two different and separate tasks: *selection of the most discriminating tokens* and *adaptation of semantic dictionaries*.

2.4.1 Selection of the most discriminating tokens

The goal is to create a ranked list of words to help distinguish between the different categories of the TASS 2012 corpus, and use each word of that list as a feature for the classifier. We use binary occurrence as the weighting factor, because we hypothesise that each word usually appears at most once in a tweet.

Term	Ranking (4 classes)	Ranking (6 classes)
EP (emoticon)	1	1
URL	4	4
FF	30	47
jaja (laugh)	101	11,964

Table 3: Ranking of some of discriminating terms on the training set of the TASS 2012 corpus

We rank the terms by measuring the *information gain* with respect to the class, employing the attribute selection tools provided by WEKA and the training set of the TASS 2012 corpus. To make the selection more robust we used a ten-fold cross-validation. We extracted more than 14,000 discriminating terms. However, only a few hundred of terms provided an information gain greater than zero, so we decide to include only those words. Table 3 shows some effective classifier tokens that are not included in a generic dictionary.

2.4.2 Adaptation of semantic dictionaries

Our generic semantic approach uses a generic opinion lexicon. In order to adapt it to the Twitter domain, we have developed an automatic enrichment mechanism for semantic dictionaries. In the same line as in *Selection of the most discriminating tokens*, we rank the best polarity terms, but in this case, we have only taken into account P+, P, N and N+ classes. We then assign a SO to each ranked term, based on the number of occurrences both in positive and negative tweets, and we add them to the semantic dictionaries. However, the improvement in performance was negligible when this method was used jointly with the *Selection of the most discriminating tokens*.

3. EXPERIMENTAL RESULTS

The TASS 2012 workshop proposed two different tasks about sentiment analysis: classification into six categories (P+, P, NEU, N, N+ and NONE) and classification into four categories (the classes P+ and N+ are included in the classes P and N, respectively). We used the TASS 2012 training and test sets to evaluate our proposal.

Tables 4 and 5 show the results obtained for the two polarity classification tasks: four and six categories. We used the F-measure defined as $F = \frac{2 \times R \times P}{R+P}$, where P is the number of true positives divided by the sum of true and false

Measure	GSA	MSI	DA
F_p	0.631	0.680	0.745
F_{neu}	0.000	0.000	0.054
F_n	0.566	0.603	0.671
F_{none}	0.574	0.564	0.620
Accuracy	0.587	0.615	0.676

Table 4: Results on the test set (4 classes)[2]

Measure	GSA	MSI	DA
F_{p+}	0.609	0.637	0.705
F_p	0.000	0.040	0.307
F_{neu}	0.000	0.009	0.089
F_n	0.452	0.478	0.512
F_{n+}	0.000	0.120	0.441
F_{none}	0.575	0.605	0.648
Accuracy	0.523	0.546	0.600

Table 5: Results on the test set (6 classes)

positives, and R is the number of true positives divided by the sum of the true positives and false negatives. The subscripts in Tables 4 and 5 refer to each category of the TASS 2012 corpus. In both tasks, the GSA approach obtains a good performance. The incorporation of POS-tag and syntactic information improves the classification performance on positive and negative tweets. This reinforces the idea that users employ certain POS-tags and syntactic functions more frequently depending on the polarity of the review. The accuracy obtained by our final approach suggests that, although generic opinion lexicons and the morphosyntactic structure of the tweets are helpful to classify the sentiment of the message we need to incorporate domain semantic knowledge to optimise the performance.

Moreover, in both cases, the performance on neutral tweets is low.[3] We hypothesise that this phenomenon is due to two factors. The first refers to an intrinsic characteristic of neutral tweets: the mixture of favourable and unfavourable opinions complicates the categorisation of these tweets, even more so in Twitter, where users have no space to argue their point of view. The second refers to the ambiguous criteria used in the corpus to distinguish between NEU and NONE tweets, as has been pointed out by some authors [11].

Method	Accuracy (4 classes)	Accuracy (6 classes)
Our proposal (features+SMO)	0.676	0.600
SMO	0.630	0.532
Our features with NaiveBayes	0.582	0.494
Our features with j48	0.574	0.452
j48	0.565	0.482
NaiveBayes	0.523	0.472

Table 6: Performance on the TASS 2012 test set with different methods

Finally, we tested the effectiveness of our features with other classifiers. We selected NaiveBayes and j48 (the WEKA implementation of a C4.5 decision tree). Table 6 shows the per-

---

[3]The small number of the NEU tweets into the TASS 2012 training set (around 2%) makes it difficult for the classifier to learn these tweets satisfactorily.

formance of these classifiers, compared to the corresponding pure machine learning approaches, which use as attributes a vector of words representing the text. In this case, we applied pre-processing of Section 2.1 and lemmatisation steps and we kept the WEKA default configuration. Results suggest that our features are generalizable and outperform the baseline of different classifiers.

4. CONCLUSIONS AND FUTURE WORK

In this paper we describe an approach which uses POS-tag information, dependency structure and semantic knowledge to train a supervised classifier that categorises the sentiment of Spanish tweets. Experimental results show a good performance and suggest that the morphosyntactic structure of the tweets is useful to classify their sentiment.

As future work, there are many aspects that we would like to explore. The current preprocessing of the tweets is quite simple. We would like to determine how an exhaustive normalisation of tweets could help in polarity classification tasks. In this respect, Oliva et al. [7] propose a SMS normalisation system that could enrich our preprocessing module. We would also like to explore how to modify dependency parsing for microtexts. In this line, the approach of Gimpel et al. [4] could be usefully adapted to our proposal. Finally, we believe that the method of Batista and Ribeiro [2] could help to improve the performance of our approach: instead of training a classifier to distinguish between n categories, they train n-1 binary classifiers and combine the final results, exploiting the differences between the different classes.

Acknowledgments

Research reported in this paper has been partially funded by Ministerio de Economía y Competitividad and FEDER (Grant TIN2010-18552-C03-02) and by Xunta de Galicia (Grants CN2012/008, CN2012/319).

5. REFERENCES

[1] A. Agarwal, B. Xie, I. Vovsha, O. Rambow, and R. Passonneau. Sentiment analysis of Twitter data. In *Proceedings of the Workshop on Languages in Social Media*, LSM '11, pages 30–38, Stroudsburg, PA, USA, 2011. ACL.

[2] F. Batista and R. Ribeiro. The L2F Strategy for Sentiment Analysis and Topic Classification. *Procesamiento de Lenguaje Natural*, 50:77–84, 2013.

[3] J. Brooke, M. Tofiloski, and M. Taboada. Cross-Linguistic Sentiment Analysis: From English to Spanish. In *Proceedings of the International Conference RANLP-2009*, pages 50–54, Borovets, Bulgaria, 2009. ACL.

[4] K. Gimpel, N. Schneider, B. O'Connor, D. Das, D. Mills, J. Eisenstein, M. Heilman, D. Yogatama, J. Flanigan, and N. Smith. Part-of-speech tagging for Twitter: annotation, features, and experiments. *HLT '11 Proc. of the 49th Annual Meeting of the Association for Computational Linguistics: Human Language Technologies: short papers*, 2:42–47, 2011.

[5] M. Hall, E. Frank, G. Holmes, B. Pfahringer, P. Reutemann, and I. Witten. The WEKA data mining software: an update. *SIGKDD Explor. Newsl.*, 11(1):10–18, Nov. 2009.

[6] J. Nivre, J. Hall, J. Nilsson, A. Chanev, G. Eryigit, S. Kübler, S. Marinov, and E. Marsi. Maltparser: A language-independent system for data-driven dependency parsing. *Natural Language Engineering*, 13(2):95–135, 2007.

[7] J. Oliva, J. I. Serrano, M. D. Del Castillo, and A. Igesias. A SMS normalization system integrating multiple grammatical resources. *Natural Language Engineering*, 19:121–141, 2013.

[8] A. Pak and P. Paroubek. Twitter as a corpus for sentiment analysis and opinion mining. In *Proceedings of the Seventh International conference on Language Resources and Evaluation (LREC'10)*, Valletta, Malta, May 2010. European Language Resources Association (ELRA).

[9] B. Pang, L. Lee, and S. Vaithyanathan. Thumbs up? sentiment classification using machine learning techniques. In *Proceedings of EMNLP*, pages 79–86, 2002.

[10] J. C. Platt. Advances in kernel methods. chapter Fast training of support vector machines using sequential minimal optimization, pages 185–208. MIT Press, Cambridge, MA, USA, 1999.

[11] X. Saralegi Urizar and I. San Vicente Roncal. Detecting Sentiments in Spanish Tweets. In *TASS 2012 Working Notes*, CastellÃşn, Spain, 2012.

[12] J. Spencer and G. Uchyigit. Sentimentor: Sentiment Analysis on Twitter Data. In *The 1st International Workshop on Sentiment Discovery from Affective Data*, Bristol, United Kingdom, 2012.

[13] M. Taboada, J. Brooke, M. Tofiloski, K. Voll, and M. Stede. Lexicon-based methods for sentiment analysis. *Computational Linguistics*, 37(2):267–307, 2011.

[14] M. Taulé, M. A. Martí, and M. Recasens. AnCora: Multilevel Annotated Corpora for Catalan and Spanish. In N. Calzolari, K. Choukri, B. Maegaard, J. Mariani, J. Odjik, S. Piperidis, and D. Tapias, editors, *Proceedings of the Sixth International Conference on Language Resources and Evaluation (LREC'08)*, Marrakech, Morocco, 2008.

[15] P. D. Turney. Thumbs up or thumbs down?: semantic orientation applied to unsupervised classification of reviews. In *Proceedings of the 40th Annual Meeting on Association for Computational Linguistics*, ACL '02, pages 417–424, Stroudsburg, PA, USA, 2002. ACL.

[16] D. Vilares, M. A. Alonso, and C. Gómez-Rodríguez. Clasificación de polaridad en textos con opiniones en español mediante análisis sintáctico de dependencias. *Procesamiento de Lenguaje Natural*, 50:13–20, 2013.

[17] J. Villena-Román, S. Lana-Serrano, J. C. González Cristóbal, and E. Martínez-Cámara. TASS - Worshop on Sentiment Analysis at SEPLN. *Procesamiento de Lenguaje Natural*, 50:37–44, 2013.

[18] L. Zhang, R. Ghosh, M. Dekhil, M. Hsu, and B. Liu. Combining lexicon-based and learning-based methods for Twitter sentiment analysis. Technical Report HPL-2011-89, HP Laboratories, Palo Alto, CA, 2011.

Hi-Fi HTML Rendering of Multi-format Documents in *DoMInUS*

[Application Note]

Stefano Ferilli
Computer Science
Department - University of
Bari
Bari, Italy
stefano.ferilli@uniba.it

Floriana Esposito
Computer Science
Department - University of
Bari
Bari, Italy
floriana.esposito@uniba.it

Domenico Redavid
Artificial Brain S.r.l.
Bari, Italy
redavid@abrain.it

ABSTRACT

Digital Libraries collect, organize and provide to end users large quantities of selected documents. While these documents come in a variety of formats, it is desirable that they are delivered to final users in a uniform way. Web formats are a suitable choice for this purpose. While Web documents are very flexible as to layout presentation, that is determined at runtime by the interpreter, documents coming from a library should preserve their original layout when displayed to final users. Using raster images would not allow the user to access the actual content of the document's components (text and images). This paper presents a technique to render in an HTML file the original layout of a document, preserving the peculiarity of its components (text, images, formulas, tables, algorithms). It builds on the DoMInUS framework, that can process documents in several source formats.

Categories and Subject Descriptors

H.3.7 [**Information Technology and Systems**]: INFORMATION STORAGE AND RETRIEVAL—*Digital Libraries*; I.7.2 [**Computing Methodologies**]: DOCUMENT AND TEXT PROCESSING—*Document Preparation*

General Terms

ALGORITHMS

Keywords

Layout Analysis; Document Representation; Document Rendering

1. INTRODUCTION

The wide spread of documents in digital formats has caused a significant flourishing of Digital Libraries (DLs), i.e. document repositories aimed at collecting, systematically organizing and providing to interested users large quantities of selected documents, as opposed to the basic retrieval thereof in the Internet through search engines. Documents come to DLs in a variety of formats, ranging from digitized images to born-digital documents, providing different flexibility and adaptivity for displaying purposes. While Web (e.g., HTML or XML) documents are designed to be dynamically organized in the browser's window, presentation-oriented documents (e.g., PS/PDF or raster images) have a rigid organization that ensures they are displayed exactly in the same way independently of the computer and platform. Word processor documents are somehow in the middle, because their appearance is explicitly directed by their source code, but small details may change at rendering time depending on the specific computer, platform and settings.

DLs might want to make (part of all of) their documents available to final users on the Web. Independently of their source format, it would be desirable that all document in a DL are displayed in a uniform way, preserving their original appearance. They might also want to make text, images and other components available separately for copying and pasting. Using raster dumps of the document pages is not a viable solution for these purposes. This introduces the problem of the different level of structural description that is available in the document sources. For instance, PDF explicitly distinguishes basic components in a document (such as text, lines and images), but usually does not include high-level information on the document layout structure. Conversely, PS and raster images are pure graphics, providing no high-level information on the document (physical or logical) content. Thus, the layout structure of the document must be preliminarily identified, and then each frame in this structure must be filled with the actual content, according to its type. Additional problems come for the identification and handling of particular components such as tables, formulas and algorithms.

This paper describes how these problems have been solved in a prototypical document processing and management system called DoMInUS. The next Section introduces DoMInUS and its internal document representation. Then, Section 3 describes the identification and reconstruction of special components. Section 4 reports the overall rendering technique. Finally, Section 5 concludes the paper, discussing the approach and outlining future work issues.

DocEng '13, September 10–13, 2013, Florence, Italy.
ACM 978-1-4503-1789-4/13/09.
http://dx.doi.org/10.1145/2494266.2494272 .

2. DOMINUS

DoMInUS (Document Management Intelligent Universal System) is a framework for document processing and management that embeds several Artificial Intelligence techniques to automatize the whole document lifecycle spanning from its submission to a DL up to its retrieval and fruition by end users [2]. Here we are interested in the *Pre-processing* and *Layout Analysis* steps, that are in charge of identifying the high-level geometrical structure of the document, and specifically to the document representation they are based on. Technical details on how this representation is obtained are not relevant for the purpose of this paper. In fact, being a framework, DoMInUS might exploit interchangeably different combinations of state-of-the-art techniques.

The internal representation of the documents built by DoMInUS is independent of their original format. It includes an XML description of the document organization and content, plus PNG files for its graphical components such as pictures, graphics, formulas, etc.. The main constituent in such a representation is the *XML* file, that is created at the time of document submission and progressively enriched as long as the document processing steps take place. It is organized in a hierarchical structure, expressed by the following tags [3]:

document the whole document

    obstacles the low-level layout information

      page a page in the document

        line a text line in the document

          word a word in the document

            box a fragment of text in the document

        stroke a line segment in the document

        fill a (colored) rectangle in the document

        image a raster image in the document

    layout the high-level layout information

      page a page in the document

        frame a frame in the document page

          block a content block in the document page

As soon as the document is submitted, a PNG raster image for each of its pages is dumped, the XML file is created and the pre-processing phase is started, that fills the *obstacles* section only (so called because it involves elements that represent 'obstacles' for the process of identifying the page background [1]). This section can express the various levels of detail at which the document may be described in its original format. First *box*, *stroke*, *fill* and *image* blocks are created, based on the elementary blocks expressed in PS/PDF documents or on the connected components extracted from raster document images. Then, overlapping or touching *box*es are collected into *word*s. Finally, the *word*s are collected into *line*s, in such a way that multi-column information is preserved, if any. Raster images are just cropped from the PNG dumps and saved, while images that are made up of several graphic elements require a preliminary grouping of these elements, before cropping their overall bounding box. Depending on the source document format, some of these passages may be skipped.

After the above steps are accomplished, the layout analysis phase starts from the *obstacles* section and produces the *layout* one. It works top-down using different techniques [1, 6, 7, 4] depending on the kind of source (PS/PDF, scanned document, etc.) and on the layout style (Manhattan vs. non-Manhattan) [2]. It groups *line*s, *stroke*s, *fill*s and *image*s into rectangular areas of homogeneous content (called *block*s), and then collects semantically related *block*s into *frame*s (rectangular areas of content to which a distinct role can be assigned). While the kind of components is explicit in PS/PDF documents, decision tree models are learned and used in digitized ones to automatically classify the blocks as text, line, graphic or halftone image according to the distribution of foreground and background pixels. Text blocks are filled with the corresponding text, collected from the basic *box* elements in PS/PDF documents, or read using an OCR system in digitized images.

At this point, the content of the original document has been completely translated in the internal XML representation, possibly supported by external files for images. While the high-level layout structure of each page, to be reproduced in the HTML rendering, is drawn from the *layout* section of the XML, the position of specific components (words, images, etc.) is drawn from the *obstacles* section. In fact, all elements in the XML report the bounding box coordinates of the corresponding content in the original document: this allows to know exactly where and how to place them in the HTML rendering of the document.

In case of multi-page documents, all the pages must be included in the final HTML representation. DoMInUS puts all of them in a single file, separated by horizontal rules and endowed with a sequential page numbering (independent from that possibly present in the original pages).

3. COMPONENTS IDENTIFICATION

A crucial point consists in the identification and grouping of special components, such as compound graphics, formulas, tables and algorithms, that are typically not explicitly expressed in the document sources, but are to be handled specifically in subsequent processing steps, among which HTML rendering. We include all these special components as images in the HTML rendering of the document, in order to preserve their original shape and make the rendered document as close as possible to the original. The bounding boxes including these elements in the document are cropped from the document image (or from the raster dump of PS/PDF documents previously obtained), saved as PNG files in a file system folder associated to the document, and referenced by suitable <IMG /> tags in the HTML version. The technique we propose to identify the special components relies on a knowledge-based module, whose parameters must be set according to the specific kind of document at hand. Our future work will include the use of machine learning to automatically set these parameters for each given document.

As said, the text is immediately available in the blocks of the *layout* section, where it was extracted in previous steps. It is reported with no specification of its font attributes. Special characters and symbols are denoted using escape sequences.

While raster images are explicitly represented as single blocks in PS/PDF documents, and usually consist of a single connected component in raster document images, graphics often consist of several geometrical shapes, possibly having some intersection with each other or overlapping bounding boxes. In turn, both images and graphics may overlap to each other and to pieces of text. In these cases, we merge all the components whose bounding boxes overlap, computing the overall bounding box and considering it as a compound graphical element. So, the overall bounding box is cut from the PNG dump of the page and saved as a separate image, to be referenced by the final HTML. Then, the single components are removed from the XML tree: as regards text components in particular, if they were previously included in other frames, after removing them the boundaries of those frames might be no longer valid, and must be resized accordingly.

Concerning tables, we consider *stroke* elements that form some kind of orthogonal grid, and compute their overall bounding box. Then, the strokes and text falling in these areas are removed from the *obstacles* section. To ensure maximum fidelity of the rendering, also tables are cut from the document image, saved and included as images in the HTML output. For tables that are not characterized by an explicit grid structure, their single components (text blocks and lines) are handled as separate elements and placed in the rendered page individually. Work is ongoing to improve the knowledge-based module and make it able to handle these cases as well.

Formulas and algorithms must be determined and restored through progressive aggregation of the low-level components in the *obstacles* section, because the higher-level *block*s of the *layout* section might mix them with normal running text of the document paragraphs. Inspired by [5], we look for peculiar elements in the document and group them into consistent aggregates: *images* of very small size overlapping to text blocks (as potential symbols), *strokes* (e.g., denoting ratios and roots), *box*es whose text suggests the presence of mathematics or code, and so on. More specifically, we define the following classes:

- **mathematical** : escape sequences starting with \ (representing a symbol), standard mathematical or programming operators or separators or names of mathematical functions.

- **numeric** : pure numeric sequences (including no points or commas).

- **variable** : (sequences of) letters in italic typeface.

- **code** : typical programming language keywords, in boldface.

A rule-based module embedding typographic knowledge is used to filter these candidate elements. A sample of such a knowledge, expressed in natural language, is as follows. "Select:

- all **mathematical**s, with their neighbor elements;

- all non-**numeric**s whose size is less than that of their preceding element (useful to select super- and subscripts);

- **variable**s following, or followed by, a **mathematical**;

- **numeric**s placed between two other **numeric**s or preceded by a **mathematical**, a dot, a comma or a **variable** having bigger size;

- **numeric**s followed by a **mathematical**;

- **numeric**s followed by a point or comma which in turn is followed by another **numeric**;

- **code** elements, if including both in the three preceding and in the three subsequent elements at least one **numeric**, **variable**, **mathematical** or other **code** element."

Then, the actual aggregation takes place. Each selected element is merged with all (horizontally or vertically) neighboring elements that fall in an 'extended' area around its bounding box. Horizontally, the extension is bound not to trespass the high-level layout *block* to which the considered element belongs, to avoid merging elements in different blocks (which might spoil column organization).

As regards the identification of formulas, the selected elements are merged first horizontally (to group elements in-line) and then vertically (to group isolated formulas). The elements that are not merged with other mathematical elements in this step are discarded. Vertical merging adopts a different strategy for 'isolated' elements than for 'in-line' elements: having more space around them, the former are expanded more than the latter. Code elements are merged only vertically, iterating the merge in order to include all the code lines in the algorithm. Subsequent merges consider wider expansion areas.

4. RENDERING

Given the initial XML internal representation of DoMInUS and raster dumps of the recognized special components, the final rendering is obtained through the following main steps:

1. load the DOM tree corresponding to the input XML

2. process the DOM tree to identify special components; extract these components from the input page dumps and save them as images

3. remove from the XML tree text elements overlapping the bounding box of special components and reorganize the frames accordingly

4. create an HTML file containing the high-level document structure and a jQuery script

5. create another HTML file, that contains no special components, but correctly places the words in the various frames, suitably aligning the text

6. merge these two files using the `load()` method of the jQuery script placed in the first HTML file

All the XML and HTML handling is carried out using the Document Object Model (DOM) technology[1].

Two HTML files are produced: one deals with the special components, and the other with the exact placement of text components. Within the usual basic structure (`html` —the root of the DOM tree—, `head` and `title` inside of it, and `body` in which the actual document content is to be placed), they both reproduce the different pages of the document, and the various layout components in each of them, using suitably sized and positioned `div` tags whose 'class' attribute specifies their type of content (one of: **page**, **frame**,

---

[1] http://www.w3.org/DOM/

5. CONCLUSION

Digital Libraries aim at collecting, systematically organizing and providing to interested users large quantities of selected documents. While the documents collected in a DL come in a variety of formats, it is desirable that they are delivered to final users in a uniform way, possibly reproducing the original layout and giving the users the opportunity to copy and paste (portion of) their content. Web formats fulfill the first and third requirement, but their layout presentation is determined at runtime by the interpreter. Just displaying documents as raster images would fulfill the first and second requirement, but would not grant the user access to the actual content of the document's components (text and images).

This paper described a technique to render in an HTML file the original layout of a document, preserving the peculiarity of its components (text, images, formulas, tables, algorithms). It builds on the internal document representation format used by the DoMInUS framework, that can process documents in several source formats. Given the encouraging results of its preliminary implementation, future work includes the refinement and improvement of special component recognition step, also by introducing automatic techniques to learn and adapt the parameters used to extract special components to be included in the HTML rendering.

6. ACKNOWLEDGMENTS

The authors would like to thank Claudio Benegiamo for his contribution in implementing the prototype. This work was partially funded by the Italian PON 2007-2013 project PON02_00563_3489339 'Puglia@Service'.

7. REFERENCES

[1] T. Breuel. Two geometric algorithms for layout analysis. In *Proc. 5th Int. Workshop on Document Analysis Systems (DAS)*, volume 2423 of *Lecture Notes in Computer Science*, pages 188–199. Springer, 2002.

[2] F. Esposito, S. Ferilli, T. Basile, and N. Di Mauro. Machine Learning for digital document processing: from layout analysis to metadata extraction. In *Machine Learning in Document Analysis and Recognition*, volume 90 of *Studies in Computational Intelligence*, pages 105–138. Springer, 2008.

[3] S. Ferilli. *Automatic Digital Document Processing and Management*. Springer, 2011.

[4] S. Ferilli, M. Biba, F. Esposito, and T. Basile. A distance-based technique for non-Manhattan layout analysis. In *Proc. 10th Int. Conf. on Document Analysis Recognition (ICDAR)*, pages 231–235, 2009.

[5] X. Lin, L. Gao, Z. Tang, X. Lin, and X. Hu. Mathematical formula identification in pdf documents. In *Int. Conf. on Document Analysis and Recognition (ICDAR), 2011*, pages 1419–1423. IEEE, 2011.

[6] G. Nagy and S. Seth. Hierarchical representation of optically scanned documents. In *Proc. 7th Int. Conf. on Pattern Recognition (ICPR)*, pages 347–349. IEEE Computer Society Press, 1984.

[7] K. Wong, R. Casey, and F. Wahl. Document analysis system. *IBM Journal of Research and Development*, 26:647–656, 1982.

Figure 1: HTML rendering (on the left) of two scientific paper pages (on the right)

stroke, `math`, `code`, `table`). Each `page` partition is also endowed with a `div` reporting its progressive number in the document (starting from 1, independently of the page number in the original document, if any). The former HTML file is the master of the rendered document. Each of its `div` tags links a special component image, except for `page`, that is a container of all the components of a page, and `frame`, that reports the textual content as a stream of characters. It also includes a `script` tag containing a reference to the jQuery library that allows final rendering using the other HTML file. The latter reports only the `frame` structure of the pages, filled with the single *words*, each suitably placed therein using `span` tags. Textual elements are correctly placed at rendering time, using the `load()` method of the jQuery library that inserts in the first HTML the elements of the corresponding frames that are reported in the second HTML.

The technique was qualitatively evaluated on 39 PS/PDF documents (scientific papers, commercial letters) previously processed by DoMInUS, all involving some combination of figures, tables, formulas and algorithms. It revealed satisfying outcomes with marginal problems (mainly concerning text alignment in in-line special components and text overlapping other components), independently of the document type. Figure 1 shows two output HTML pages (on the left) and the corresponding originals (on the right).

PDFX: Fully-automated PDF-to-XML Conversion of Scientific Literature

Alexandru Constantin
aconstantin@cs.man.ac.uk

Steve Pettifer
steve.pettifer@cs.man.ac.uk

Andrei Voronkov
voronkov@cs.man.ac.uk

School of Computer Science
The University of Manchester, United Kingdom
Oxford Road, M13 9PL

ABSTRACT

PDFX is a rule-based system designed to reconstruct the logical structure of scholarly articles in PDF form, regardless of their formatting style. The system's output is an XML document that describes the input article's logical structure in terms of title, sections, tables, references, etc. and also links it to geometrical typesetting markers in the original PDF, such as paragraph and column breaks. The key aspect of the presented approach is that the rule set used relies on relative parameters derived from font and layout specifics of each article, rather than on a template-matching paradigm. The system thus obviates the need for domain- or layout-specific tuning or prior training, exploiting only typographical conventions inherent in scientific literature. Evaluated against a significantly varied corpus of articles from nearly 2000 different journals, PDFX gives a 77.45 F1 measure for top-level heading identification and 74.03 for extracting individual bibliographic items. The service is freely available for use at http://pdfx.cs.man.ac.uk/.

Categories and Subject Descriptors

I.7.5 [**Document and Text Processing**]: Document Capture—*document analysis*; I.2.7 [**Artificial Intelligence**]: Natural Language Processing—*text analysis*

General Terms

Algorithms, Design

Keywords

document structure analysis; PDF conversion; logical structure recovery; PDFX

1. INTRODUCTION

The recent increase in volume of the global research output has given rise to numerous initiatives that focus on automatic document processing. The predominant goal of these approaches has been to reduce the search space for potentially relevant information through means such as intuitive indexing and retrieval, document summarisation or discourse annotation. The added value brought by such services can be quite significant when considering the expeditious publication rate that certain fields of study enjoy, for instance biomedicine and the life sciences. Many such tools, however, work exclusively on plain-text and not camera-ready, typeset publications. This makes their performance dependent on data sources containing noise-free, accurate reconstructions of article narratives. Automating this pre-processing step requires programmatic access to the typographical layout of elements on page as well as to their logical/rhetorical function within the article. For this reason, analysis tools of scientific text often choose to couple themselves to data stores that have human-curated semi-structured representations of articles readily available, such as PMC [3], Scopus [7], DBLP [12] or arXiv [1]. This dependency deters the tools' widespread adoption because much of the information sought by researchers is made available solely within PDF publications with no alternative representation. Without the means to expand their reach to this highly popular format, many promising natural language processing and text mining solutions remain either undiscovered or of little use to potential users.

Notable previous efforts targeting the recovery of structure from the PDF are given in Table 1 along with their capabilities. Except for the machine learning solution SectLabel [13], the tools focus on geometrical analysis and either do not handle or are in their preliminary phases of logical structure recognition. In this paper we present a novel system called PDFX that focuses on logical structure, but handles its geometrical baseline as well. It aims to identify, extract and link these two structures together in order to facilitate an enhanced level of interaction with an article's contents. The method employed is rule-based, iterative and unrestricted with respect to the set of formatting templates that input articles need to adhere to. The only requirement is that they be full-text natively typeset PDF publications, as opposed to PDF images such as scans of paper documents. The 18 logical element types that the system can currently identify (listed in Table 2) cover the principal parts of a typical research article. They are ultimately stored in an XML file with a tag hierarchy that closely follows the JATS standard[1]. The semi-structured nature of the XML serves as a convenient, quick-access route to any of the articles's components.

2. SYSTEM AND METHODS

PDFX carries out a two-stage process in order to address structure recovery. The first stage constructs a geometrical model of the article's contents to determine the spatial organisation of textual and graphical units on page. The second stage draws upon the

DocEng'13, September 10–13, 2013, Florence, Italy.
ACM 978-1-4503-1789-4/13/09.
http://dx.doi.org/10.1145/2494266.2494271.

---

[1]ANSI/NISO Z39.96-2012 standard, JATS: Journal Article Tag Suite - http://jats.niso.org/ - formalised from the NLM Archiving and Interchange Tag Suite

Tool	Output	Geometrical Structure	Logical Structure
pdftotext -bbox [2]	XHTML	pages, words (w/ coordinates)	-
pdftohtml -xml [2]	XML	fontspecs, pages, lines (w/ coordinates, font info), emphasis	-
pdftohtml -c [2]	HTML+CSS	paragraphs; CSS positioning instructions	not explicit
pdf2xml (1) [9, 10]	XML	pages, lines, words (w/ coordinates, font info, rotation, emphasis)	-
pdf2xml (2) [16]	XML	pages, font blocks (size, face, colour), lines (w/ coordinates), images	-
pdftohtmlEX [17]	HTML+CSS	fontspecs, lines, words; CSS positioning instructions	not explicit
pdfextract [11] (work in progress)	XML	pages, columns, lines, regions (w/ coordinates, font info, implicit font face)	title, header, footer, body, reference
LA-PDFText [14]	Text/XML	text blocks (w/ font, line number, height)	title, author, abstract, section, section heading
PDFExtract [6, 5]	XML	fontspecs, pages, paragraphs (w/ coordinates), lines (w/ font info)	title, abstract, section, section heading, body, footnote
SectLabel /ParsCit [13, 8]	XML/HTML	not provided; may be used as input for better logical structure recognition	title, address, affiliation, author, footnote, category, keyword, copyright, body, (sub)section, (sub)section heading, figure, table, caption, construct, equation, list_item, note, reference, email, page
PDFX (this paper)	XML/HTML	logical elements with page and column attributes and block, column and page break markers	title, author, abstract, author footnote, body, (sub)section, (sub)section heading, figure, table, caption, figure/table reference, citation, reference, URI, email, side note, header/footer, page

Table 1: Tools for structure recovery from PDF documents and their capabilities

Front Matter	Body Matter	Back Matter / Others
title	body text	bibliographic item
author	(sub)section	(reference)
abstract	(sub)section heading	URI
author footnote	image	email
	table	side note
	caption	header/footer
	figure/table reference	page number
	bibliographic reference	
	(citation)	

Table 2: Logical elements that PDFX can extract

first to identify different logical units of discourse based on their discriminative features.

The geometrical model baseline is constructed using a library from the Utopia Documents PDF reader [4]. Three core elements of the PDF are identified: pages, words and bitmap images. Each element is modelled as a separate object with its specific features, such as bounding box, orientation, textual content or font information. Document- and page-wise statistics are then gathered to guide the selection of constituent blocks for different logical elements further down the pipeline. Font frequency maps suggest common versus rare features (such as those of the core body text vs. those of a possible title), whilst a font difference between two neighbouring words marks a first level of separation between two distinct logical units. Adjacent words of similar font characteristics are then merged together to form a set of contiguous rectangular blocks with which logical structure inference will commence. An important aspect is that the merging parameters used are defined relative to the font size and font face of each word as well as to the spacing between consecutive words and lines. This approach facilitates tailoring for any logical element type and any article layout, being significantly more flexible than approximating hard-coded numerical parameters.

With the geometrical model and statistics in place, the second stage attempts to determine the semantic roles of the newly created blocks, possibly merging them into logical *regions* in the process.

A sequence of steps aims to identify one logical element type at a time, across the whole article, by tagging regions with certain characteristics.

The first and most important step in the sequence is to identify the core body text along with the reading order of the article. Out of the set of merged blocks, those containing primarily words in the most frequent font of the article are tagged as *body regions*. The dominant body region shape is used to determine the column layout and the intended reading order. Tagging of the rest of the regions is afterwards carried out in a prioritised manner. The priority is dictated by an empirically determined level of difficulty in identifying each logical element type. The elements considered easiest to tag confidently are searched for first. The rest of the identification sequence is as follows: (1) images, (2) DOI, (3) authors, (4) title, (5) outsiders: headers, footers, side notes, page numbers, (6) top-level headings, (7) abstract, (8) captions, (9) lower-level headings, (10) author footnotes, (11) remaining regions, (12) bibliography and bibliographic items, (13) other body regions, (14) tables, (15) in-text references to figures, tables and bibliographic items; URIs and emails.

A trade-off between precision and processing time was made in the system design in that the above sequence does not reiterate. Instead of employing multiple passes until no more new useful information is gained at the end of a pass, we have opted confer each tag assigned to a region an associated binary confidence level. This level can be either 'confident', to mean that the region adheres to concrete rules of a specific element type or 'possible', to signify a partial conformation with these rules. Then, as region identification progresses and new (tag, confidence) information becomes available, two types of events may occur: (A) certain regions may have their tags and/or confidence levels changed to reflect their most likely function in the current context; (B) increasingly more difficult element types become identifiable because of new structural and semantic cues.

The XML output is constructed with the most likely tags of the different regions at the end of the processing sequence. The initially identified contiguous blocks, now encapsulated in logical regions,

```
<region class="TextChunk" page="2" column="2">
   [...] encapsulated in logical regions,
   <marker type="page" number="3"/>
   <marker type="column" number="1"/>
   <marker type="block"/>
   jointly reconstruct the rhetorical [...]
</region>
```

Figure 1: XML example of a PDFX region spanning two columns.

jointly reconstruct the rhetorical structure of the article. Information about the different regions and their organisation is represented using an XML format very close in schema to the JATS standard. The logical *section* elements are implied by the heading hierarchy, being added in and populated during the XML construction. As regions can span multiple blocks, columns or pages, their respective XML elements may contain tags that act as physical position markers in the original text. An excerpt from the processing output of this paper illustrates a region spanning two pages (Figure 1). The intruding figure itself was identified and skipped over when reconstructing the text stream. The *class* attribute of the region, set in accordance with DoCO[2], was added in order to facilitate interoperability with other services. DoCO is an ontology of both physical and logical components of bibliographic documents, well-suited for linking PDFX output to other text processing pipelines.

3. PERFORMANCE

We report the performance of PDFX over 3 datasets of articles readily available both in published PDF form and as ground-truth, manually constructed XML representations.

The first dataset was chosen for comparison purposes against the state-of-the-art. It comprises 39 articles[3] from the field of Computer Science taken from Luong et. al. [13]. The authors have also attempted logical recovery on this collection by means of machine learning techniques. Their tool, SectLabel, was employed on geometrical analysis outputs of the articles (in the form of XML files) provided by third-party OCR software. The second dataset was compiled to ensure a hands-down evaluation on a very wide range of document styles, in effect providing a lower-bound on PDFX's performance. It consisted of the latest publication of every distinct journal from a 2011 snapshot of the PMC Open Access Subset[4]. After filtering out what was considered outside the scope of the study, such as OCR documents, prefaces and supplementary data files, the set comprised 1943 articles in total, spanning an equal number of journals. We consider this collection to be highly relevant for the task of logical structure recovery and have made it available to download at `http://pdfx.cs.man.ac.uk/serve/PMC_sample_1943.zip` for future reference. The archive contains the PDFs, the gold standard XMLs and PDFX's corresponding output (1.5GB in size). Finally, the third dataset was chosen from a practical point of view, for being representative of yearly published research around the world. It was taken from all of Elsevier's publications from the year 2008, kindly provided under a research license by the publishers. We have filtered the collection in the same manner as the PMC dataset and randomly chose 50,000 articles for testing. In contrast to the PMC dataset, style change was not as common here (being the output of a single publisher, albeit

covering many journals), but the topic coverage was significantly wider.

Our standard evaluation procedure was to obtain precision (P), recall (R) and F1 measures for the XML conversions, using the Ratcliff/Obershelp string comparison method [15] to count as a correct match any extracted element found to be at least 95% similar to its ground-truth counterpart. The results for the comparative evaluation are given in Table 3 and also illustrated in Figure 2. Results for the other two datasets are given in Table 4.

Table 3: Performance evaluation for the Luong et. al. dataset. Comparison of F1 scores obtained by SectLabel, reported in [13], and those of PDFX. Scores of elements at which PDFX outperformed SectLabel are in bold.

Category	SectLabel	PDFX
author	97.94	87.02
body	96.97	88.62
email	97.64	**100**
figure	79.93	54.50
figure caption	76.91	**80.05**
page	97.84	92.30
reference (bibliography)	99.50	98.00
top-level heading	93.51	**95.3**
second-level heading	91.39	**93.0**
third-level heading	81.69	42.96
table	79.59	57.00
table caption	80.69	77.92
title	100	100

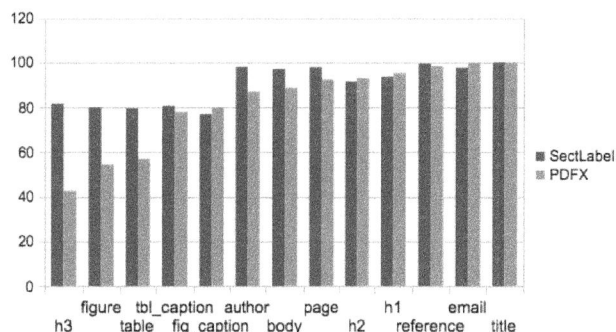

Figure 2: Bar graph view of the results in Table 3 - performance evaluation on the Luong et. al. dataset. Comparison of SectLabel [13] and PDFX.

The comparative evaluation yielded very promising results. Despite it being conducted on a dataset for which SectLabel had been trained, PDFX managed to keep up with the performance of its learned model counterpart and even outperform it at identifying four elements. At title identification, both systems performed flawlessly. PDFX was behind the SectLabel system for the other elements, particularly so for tables, figures and third-level headings. These elements mark the areas in which the visual analysis provided by an OCR system and prior learning of the layout specifics of articles prove valuable.

The automatic evaluation of the PMC dataset (Table 4), while satisfactory at times, was generally unforgiving. This is partly due to the dataset's substantial variety in terms of document styles but also to the ground-truth XMLs not necessarily matching the content of their respective PDF versions. Either because of character encoding issues, human error or intent (such as purposely leaving

---

[2]DoCO - `http:www.purl.org/spar/doco`

[3]The original set had 40 articles, but we were unable to retrieve one of them in natively typeset form and hence removed from the evaluation.

[4]The PubMed Central Open Access Article Subset - `http://www.ncbi.nlm.nih.gov/pmc/tools/openftlist/`

Dataset	Size	h3	table	h2	fig_tbl_ref	abstract	caption	author	citation	bib_item	h1	email	title
Elsevier	50000	83.35	28.78	82.03	89.1	62.01	82.86	94.63	75.46	86.08	90.5	97.61	96.7
PMC_sample	1943	6.05	13.27	27.19	27.52	32.41	54.53	61.65	63.10	74.03	77.45	79.67	85.42

Table 4: Performance results for the PMC and Elsevier datasets for a 0.95 similarity threshold. Precision and recall were computed for each individual article and averaged across each dataset.

out the Author Contribution section from the camera-ready PDF), the two variants differed at times. We ran the evaluation again at a 0.8 similarity threshold in addition to the 0.95 one in order to gain insight into the elements PDFX might still have identified correctly. We saw an average performance increase of 4 F1 points, with strong emphasis on elements with more textual content, abstracts and tables, hence more chances for discrepancies. These two elements saw a 9 and 13 F1 point increase respectively.

The highest results for the automated evaluation were obtained for the Elsevier dataset. This comes to confirm that the typesetting used across the collection is likely less varied on average, but also suggest that the curation level of Elsevier publications is stricter and their content, stylistically rich.

4. APPLICATIONS AND AVAILABILITY

The prime beneficiary of structure analysis of articles is likely to be the field of Text Mining, where knowledge relevant to a specific domain or task is typically searched for in vast document collections. Still, there are also notable use cases for a structure recovery system, when functioning as a personal tool. The following are real-world applications reported by PDFX users:

- *Accessibility support* - relieving the content of formatting additions such as headers or footers to help screen readers maintain fluency of discourse
- *Reading on a small screen* - easier consumption of content on mobile devices, facilitated through reading flow reconstruction
- *Document indexing* - improved through extraction of front-matter metadata
- *Literature recommendation* - improved through identification of bibliographic references
- *Ontology term recognition* - applied to manuscripts available only in PDF form
- *Support for tabular data extraction* - for populating specialised biomedical databases

PDFX is available at http://pdfx.cs.man.ac.uk/ as an interactive web page and free-to-use programmatic web service. Submitted PDF articles are processed on-the-fly. The user is given three options of interacting with the output:

- Access/retrieve the generated XML version.
- View a reconstruction of the article in HTML form, using the generated XML. The core content of the original article is presented as a single-column stream of text, free from elements such as headers, footers or side notes, with figures and tables placed to the side.
- Download an archive containing the entire output, including rendered images, for offline viewing.

An example of this functionality is available at http://pdfx.cs.man.ac.uk/example. Input and output files for each processing job are stored for 24 hours since the time of submission, under randomly-generated URLs.

Acknowledgements. We are indebted to the Utopia Documents team, Stephen Wan, Alex Garnett, the ScienceWISE team, the NLP group at the National University of Singapore, the 2012 Biohackathon attendees as well as all the regular users of PDFX for all their support, valuable feedback and feature suggestions. We also thank Elsevier for providing the article collection for evaluation.

5. REFERENCES

[1] The arxiv e-print database - http://arxiv.org.

[2] The poppler pdf library http://poppler.freedesktop.org/.

[3] The pubmed central archive - http://www.ncbi.nlm.nih.gov/pmc/.

[4] Teresa K Attwood, Douglas B Kell, Philip McDermott, James Marsh, Steve Pettifer, and David Thorne. Utopia documents: linking scholarly literature with research data. *Bioinformatics*, 26(18):i568–i574, 2010.

[5] Øyvind Raddum Berg. High precision text extraction from pdf documents. *MSc - The University of Oslo*, 2011.

[6] Øyvind Raddum Berg, Stephan Oepen, and Jonathon Read. Towards high-quality text stream extraction from pdf: technical background to the acl 2012 contributed task. In *Proceedings of the ACL-2012 Special Workshop on Rediscovering 50 Years of Discoveries*, pages 98–103. Assoc. for Computational Linguistics, 2012.

[7] Judy F Burnham. Scopus database: a review. *Biomedical digital libraries*, 3(1):1, 2006.

[8] Isaac G Councill, C Lee Giles, and Min-Yen Kan. Parscit: An open-source crf reference string parsing package. In *Proceedings of LREC*, volume 2008, pages 661–667. European Language Resources Association (ELRA), 2008.

[9] Hervé Déjean. The pdf2xml project - http://sourceforge.net/projects/pdf2xml/.

[10] Hervé Déjean and Jean-Luc Meunier. A system for converting pdf documents into structured xml format. In *Document Analysis Systems VII*, pages 129–140. Springer, 2006.

[11] CrossRef Labs. The pdfextract project - https://github.com/CrossRef/pdfextract.

[12] Michael Ley. Dblp: some lessons learned. *Proceedings of the VLDB Endowment*, 2(2):1493–1500, 2009.

[13] Minh-Thang Luong, Thuy Dung Nguyen, and Min-Yen Kan. Logical structure recovery in scholarly articles with rich document features. *J. of Digital Library Systems. Forthcoming*, 2011.

[14] C. Ramakrishnan, A. Patnia, E. Hovy, et al. Layout-aware text extraction from full-text pdf of scientific articles. *Source code for biology and medicine*, 7(1):1–10, 2012.

[15] John W. Ratcliff and David Metzener. Pattern matching: The gestalt approach. *Dr. Dobb's Journal*, page 46, 1988.

[16] Matthew Talbert. Mobipocket.com pdf2xml - https://launchpad.net/pdf2xml.

[17] Lu Wang. The pdf2htmlex project - http://coolwanglu.github.io/pdf2htmlEX/.

Recognising Document Components in XML-based Academic Articles

Angelo Di Iorio, Silvio Peroni,
Francesco Poggi, Fabio Vitali
Department of Computer Science
and Engineering
University of Bologna (Italy)
{diiorio,essepuntato,fpoggi,fabio}@cs.unibo.it

David Shotton
Oxford e-Research Centre
University of Oxford (UK)
david.shotton@oerc.ox.ac.uk

ABSTRACT

Recognising textual structures (paragraphs, sections, etc.) provides abstract and more general mechanisms for describing documents independent of the particular semantics of specific markup schemas, tools and presentation stylesheets. In this paper we propose an algorithm that allows us to identify the structural role of each element in a set of homogeneous scientific articles stored as XML files.

Categories and Subject Descriptors

I.7.2 [**Document And Text Processing**]: Document Preparation—*Markup languages*; I.7.5 [**Document And Text Processing**]: Document Capture—*Document analysis*

Keywords

DoCO, XML, document components

1. INTRODUCTION

In most disciplines, academic texts have established models of organisation and structure which are followed, more or less strictly, by all scholars and contributors. Some structures are shared across disciplines and capture very common objects of a text (such as tables, lists, references, front matter, etc.), others are specialised for specific disciplines (such as program listings in computer science works, epigraphs in humanities, medical histories in medicine, and so on).

Markup languages, and in particular XML vocabularies, provide authors with constructs to linearise these structural components. They often express the same components with different elements. For instance, the element *para* in Doc-Book (a semantic markup language for technical documentation [12]), the element *p* of HTML [7], the element *block* of the legislative XML vocabulary called Akoma Ntoso [2], refer all to the same concept of one of a set of vertically-organised containers of text often called a paragraph.

DocEng'13, September 10–13, 2013, Florence, Italy.
Copyright 2013 ACM 978-1-4503-1789-4/13/09 ...$15.00.
http://dx.doi.org/10.1145/2494266.2494319 .

The idea of this work is to shift the analysis of scholarly documents to a higher level of abstraction, dealing with their structural components - such as paragraphs, lists, bibliographic references, etc. - independently of the elements and the format of the markup language they are written in. Our solution is to use a general, strong and shared conceptual model for the description of components, and to match the elements of each XML languages to it according to the best interpretation of their structural semantic roles.

The correct identification of logical components could be used to generate lists and summaries (including tables of content, list of figures, etc.) automatically, to render the content in a Web browser window, and to provide full-scale converters (or, in the worst case, robust stumps open to further development). The interesting aspect is that the same tools work for both *well-known* and *unknown XML vocabularies*. The abstract representation of a document and its components can also be exploited to improve the comprehension of its content, as remarked by [4], and to build *Semantic Publishing* [11] [10] applications. Verifying semi-automatically some structural requirements of scientific papers, such as those expressed in [3] for the inclusion of XML-based vocabularies in PubMed Central, is a further possible application. Finally, on top of the identification of specific and inter-connected constructs – for instance all those structures related to bibliographic references like lists of references, inline citations, citation contexts – it will also be possible to implement sophisticated (cross-language) services for accessing, querying and manipulating such content.

We propose an algorithm for the automatic identification of the structural roles of textual content of academic articles stored as XML files. Finally, we evaluate experimental results on real academic articles.

The rest of the paper is organised as follows. In Section 2 we give an overview of DoCO, our model for document components. In Section 3 we illustrate our algorithm for the automatic recognition of document components. In Section 4 we present the experiments on our algorithm and we discuss the outcome of these experiments. We conclude in Section 5 presenting some development we plan for the near future.

2. DOCUMENT COMPONENTS

Let us consider as an example a well-known component: the *paragraph*. Although the text it contains has meaning, a paragraph can be considered a pure structural component – i.e. a component that carries only a syntactic function.

This fits current usage: markup languages such as HTML and DocBook define a paragraph as a pure structural component, without any reference to a rhetoric function:

- "a run of phrasing content that forms a block of text with one or more sentences" [7];

- "Paragraphs in DocBook may contain almost all inlines and most block elements" [12].

Here the term "block of text" and the verb "contains" emphasise the structural connotation of the paragraph, which is amplified by our direct experience as readers. Experience that implicitly tells us that a particular textual fragment shown in a book or in an HTML page is a paragraph rather than a chapter or a table.

The document component model we use in this work to define the various components of a document is the *Document Components Ontology (DoCO)*[1], an OWL ontology that has been developed so as to bring together the pure structural components of documents and their rhetorical components such as Introduction and Acknowledgments. *DoCO* imports other ontologies: the *Pattern Ontology* (describing structural patterns)[2] [5] and the *Discourse Element Ontology* (describing rhetorical components)[3]. This work focuses on a subset of DoCO that is enough to capture the most relevant part of the structure of scientific papers, i.e.: *paragraphs, footnotes, tables, figures, lists, bibliographic reference lists, front matter, body matter, sections, references, bibliographc references, bibliographies, article title* and *section titles*. More details about DoCO can be found in [9].

3. RETRIEVING TEXTUAL STRUCTURES

In this section we introduce an algorithm that takes as input a set of XML sources of scientific articles (that use the same vocabulary) and recognises the DoCO components introduced in the previous paragraph. This process is fully automatic and schema-independent, relying on no background information about the vocabulary, its meaning, its intended scheme and the actual textual content of the documents themselves. The DoCO classification has also been used as reference model within Utopia Documents [1].

Our algorithm works on XML documents and exploits structural patterns. It analyses each input document separately, and for each it performs the recognition of low-level structural patterns as presented in [5]. This analysis performed separately on each individual document can assign different patterns to the same element, since the document XML schema often allows authors to use the same element in different structural ways. Thus, the algorithm processes each element that has been assigned to more than one pattern separately and proceeds as follows[4]:

1. if an element were associated to exactly two different kinds of *po:Container*, then it applies the "majority wins" rule, otherwise it is associated to *po:Container*;

2. all the elements that are assigned to both the pattern *po:Container* (or its subclasses) and to the pattern *po:Popup* are always considered as *po:Container*;

3. if element *E* is associated to both pattern *P1* and *P2* and *P1* can be used in place of *P2* without changing the document structure, then *E* has pattern *P1*;

4. finally, a majority wins rule is applied to discriminate the remaining ambiguous scenarios.

Then the algorithm applies some heuristics in order to associate one of the textual structures introduced in Section 2 to each element of the document. These rules are applied in the order in which they are presented in the following.

Paragraph. Associate with *Paragraph* all those markup elements that were recognised as *po:Block* in the previous phase and that are the block element with most occurrences in the document.

Section. Associate with *Section* each markup element that contains at least one paragraph or one section, that was recognised as *po:HeadedContainer*, and that is not the XML document element of the document.

Section title. Associate with *SectionTitle* each markup element that is the header of a section (i.e. *po:isContainedBy-AsHeader*).

Body matter. Associate with *BodyMatter* the first markup element that is not the document element, that was recognised as *po:Container* (or any of its subclasses), that was not recognised as *Section* and is not contained (at any level) by sections, and that has children the largest number of element recognised as *Section* (note: it must always contain at least one section).

Front matter. Associate with *FrontMatter* the first markup element that is not the document element, that was recognised as *po:Container* (or any of its subclasses), that was recognised neither as *Section* nor *BodyMatter*, that is not contained (at any level) by sections and body matters, and that has children the smallest number of element recognised as *Section*. In addition, it must be placed before the body matter (if any).

Article title. Associate with *Title* the first markup element that was annotated with pattern *po:Field* or *po:Block* and that was not annotated with *Paragraph*.

Table. Associate with *Table* each markup element that contains at least two elements, that was not associated with any of the aforementioned structures, that was recognised as *po:Table*, that may have a *po:Container* as table header, and that has all the remaining child elements sharing the same name and pattern, which must be *po:Container* or any of its subclasses. In case of multiple descendant candidates, associate with *Table* only the upper element.

List. Associate with *List* each markup element that contains at least one other element, that was not already associated with *Table*, that was recognised as *po:Table*, and that has all the child elements sharing the same name and pattern, which must be one out of *po:Container, po:HeadedContainer, po:Record, po:Field* and *po:Block*.

Figure. Associate with *Figure* each markup element that was not previously annotated with any DoCO structure, that was associated with *po:Milestone* or *po:Meta*, and that has at least one attribute of which value is a valid URL ending with a image extension format.

Table box. Associate with DoCO *TableBox* each markup element that was not previously associated with any

[1]DoCO, the Document Components Ontology: http://purl.org/spar/doco.
[2]PO, the Pattern Ontology: http://www.essepuntato.it/2008/12/pattern.
[3]DEO, the Discourse Element Ontology: http://purl.org/spar/deo.
[4]In the following text we use the prefixes *po* to refer to entities defined in the Pattern Ontology, *deo* to refer to entities defined in the Discourse Element Ontology. Entities without prefixes are defined in the Document Components Ontology.

DoCO structure, that was recognised as *po:Container* (or any subclasses except *po:Table*), and that contains at most three elements, of which at least one was associated with *Table*. In case of multiple descendant candidates, associate with *TableBox* only the upper element.

Figure box. Associate with DoCO *FigureBox* each markup element that was not previously associated with any DoCO structure, that was recognised as *po:Container* (or any of its subclasses except *po:Table*) and contains at most three elements, of which at least one is either a *Figure*, or a *po:Block* containing only *Figure* and no text, or a *po:Container* containing no textual blocks and an element associated with *Figure*. In case of multiple descendant candidates, associate with *FigureBox* only the upper element.

Reference. Associate with *deo:Reference* each markup element that was associated with *po:Milestone*, that has an attribute x with value v equal or similar (e.g. "#" + v) to another attribute y of another element. The latter element must be also linked by the reference element through the DCTerms property *dcterms:references*.

Bibliographic reference list. Associate with *BibliographicReferenceList* the markup element that was associated with *List*, and that has all the children referenced by some reference. In case multiple elements satisfy the previous rules, consider as the bibliographic reference list that *List* that has at least one child referenced twice in the text.

Bibliography. Associate with *Bibliography* the markup element that was annotated with *Section* and either (a) contains a *BibliographicReferenceList* or (b) in which all the children except the section title are referenced by some reference. In case multiple candidates, consider only those which have at least one descendant referenced twice.

Bibliographic reference. Associate with *deo:BibliographicReference* the markup element that is a child of either a *BibliographicReferenceList* or *Bibliography* (excluding section titles), and that is itself a *deo:Reference*.

Footnote. Associate with *Footnote* each markup element that was not associated with any other class, and that was either a *po:Popup* or *po:Container*. In the former case, its closest ancestor annotated with *po:Block* must be also a paragraph, while in the latter case it must be referenced by an element associated with *deo:Reference*.

4. TESTING THE ALGORITHM

We executed our experiment on a set of real XML documents by performing a process consisting of four steps[5].

Gold standard synthesis. We studied the XML vocabulary originally used to mark up the documents, and associated each of its elements with one or more DoCO structures. This analysis was subjective and solely based on our understanding of the semantics of the element, its definition schema and its documentation.

DoCO mapping. The Java implementation of the algorithm described in Section 3 took as input one set documents and produced a map that associated each element with one or more DoCO structure. The algorithm associates structures to each instance of each element in the documents, but there is no effort to enforce one single assignment that holds for the whole vocabulary, since an element may be used with two or more rhetorical characterisation.

---

[5]All the materials and results of the experiments are available online at http://www.essepuntato.it/2013/doco/test.

Results comparison . The two sets of assignments achieved from the two sets of documents were then automatically compared. We measured their agreement in terms of *true positives* (TP), *false positives* (FP) and *false negatives* (FN), and we derived *precision P*, *recall R* and the *F1-score*. We calculated P as `TP/(TP+FP)`, R as `TP/(TP+FN)`, and the F1-score as `2*P*R/(P+R)`.

Discussion. We tested the algorithm on a set of 117 scientific papers encoded in DocBook format, taken from Balisage Proceedings (`http://www.balisage.net`).

We evaluated the outcome of the algorithm against our previously-prepared DoCO mapping. The table shown in Fig. 1 summarizes our comparison through the values of TP, FP, FN, precision, recall, F1-score. It also shows the names of the elements correctly associated with each DoCO structure (TP), and the names of those elements belonging to the FP and FN sets, useful for the following discussion. A point worth highlighting is that the FP and FN assignments present (13% and 12% of the total, respectively) involved only 10 out of the 16 structures taken into consideration.

The overall results, shown in the last row of the table, were encouraging, since the overall values of precision and recall were quite high (0.887 and 0.890, respectively).

For the 4 DoCO structures *Reference*, *Title*, *SectionTitle* and *FrontMatter* (25% of the total of 16 structures examined), the heuristics worked very well on this dataset, giving a perfect match between the outcome of the algorithm and the assignments in the gold standard.

Another clear situation was that no element was assigned to the 2 DoCO classes *BibliographicReferenceList* and *BodyMatter*. This is what we expected, since no element corresponding to these classes had been identified in the preliminary human analysis. However, the absence of false positives for these assignments confirms that the rules employed in our algorithm for such structures are accurate and reliable.

However, in other cases many more options are available to the users in the DocBook vocabulary, some of which were not covered by the heuristics implemented in our algorithm. Consider, for instance, the results for the elements related to bibliographies: the values of precision, recall and F1-score for *Bibliography* and *BibliographicReference* are considerably lower than for other structures, and there is a strong connection between these values. The *Bibliography* is in fact a special *Section* whose content is exclusively made of references. The presence of blocks that are not recognized as bibliographic references, or that do not contain bibliographic references at all, causes the whole section to be mis-classified.

5. CONCLUSIONS

In this paper we proposed an algorithm for the automatic identification of some textual structures in academic articles stored as XML files. We evaluated the algorithm outcomes of a testing session involving real academic articles. Starting from the encouraging tests results, we plan to refine the heuristics we developed, as discussed in more detail in the online materials. Our goal in this work was to first identify the most common DoCO structures within real documents and the extent to which they could be automatically recognised, and second to discover where the current heuristics were failing, so that we could refine them. In future, having made these refinements, we plan to perform an exhaustive analysis on other datasets and involving other DoCO structures. The comparison with the results of similar tools is also

Type	TP	TP elements	FP	FP elements	FN	FN elements	Prec.	Rec.	F1
bibliographic referencelist	0		0		0		-	-	-
paragraph	11562	para	2363	td bibliomixed	1036	para	0.830	0.917	0.871
figurebox	381	figure mediaobject	175	mediaobject imageobject listitem equation	282	figure	0.685	0.574	0.625
list	624	orderedlist itemizedlist keywordset	176	tr variablelist	107	orderedlist itemizedlist	0.78	0.853	0.815
table	135	informaltable variablelist tbody	62	orderedlist table itemizedlist figure thead	41	informaltable tbody variablelist	0.685	0.767	0.723
bibliography	49	bibliography	1	section	54	bibliography	0.98	0.475	0.640
section	1928	section appendix bibliography	0		117	abstract	1.0	0.942	0.970
reference	3408	xref	0		0		1.0	1.0	1.0
title	117	title	0		0		1.0	1.0	1.0
figure	564	imagedata	0		4	imagedata	1.0	0.992	0.996
bodymatter	0		0		0		-	-	-
sectiontitle	1928	title	0		0		1.0	1.0	1.0
frontmatter	117	info	0		0		1.0	1.0	1.0
footnote	392	footnote	24	listitem	59	footnote	0.942	0.869	0.904
bibliographic reference	1032	bibliomixed	2	section	965	bibliomixed	0.998	0.516	0.680
tablebox	52	table	13	figure	67	table	0.8	0.436	0.565
TOTAL	*22289*		*2816*		*2732*		*0.887*	*0.890*	*0.889*

Figure 1: The outcomes of the evaluation of the Balisage set.

needed. There are very interesting solutions that cannot be discussed here because of space limits – e.g. ParsCit [8], which identifies logical structures through a per-line based aggregation algorithm, and AUTOBIB [6], which extracts bibliographic information and rebuilds bibliographic records through a Hidden Markov Model.

6. REFERENCES

[1] Attwood, T. K., Kell, D. B., McDermott, P., Marsh, J., Pettifer, S. R., Thorne, D. (2010). Utopia Documents: linking scholarly literature with research data. In Bioinformatics, 26 (18): i568-i574. DOI: 10.1093/bioinformatics/btq383

[2] Barabucci, G., Cervone, L., Palmirani, M., Peroni, S., Vitali, F. (2009). Multi-layer markup and ontological structures in Akoma Ntoso. In Proceeding of the International Workshop on AI approaches to the complexity of legal systems II (AICOL-II): 133-149. DOI: 10.1007/978-3-642-16524-5_9

[3] Beck, J. (2010). Report from the Field: PubMed Central, an XML-based Archive of Life Sciences Journal Articles. In Proceedings of the International Symposium on XML for the Long Haul: Issues in the Long-term Preservation of XML. DOI: 10.4242/BalisageVol6.Beck01

[4] De Waard, A. (2010). From Proteins to Fairytales: Directions in Semantic Publishing. In IEEE Intelligent Systems, 25 (2): 83-88. DOI: 10.1109/MIS.2010.49.

[5] Di Iorio, A., Peroni, S., Poggi, F., Vitali, F. (2012). A first approach to the automatic recognition of structural patterns in XML documents. In Proceedings of the 2012 ACM symposium on Document Engineering (DocEng 2012): 85-94. DOI: 10.1145/2361354.2361374

[6] Geng, J., Yang, J. (2004). AUTOBIB: Automatic Extraction of Bibliographic Information on the Web. In Proceedings of the 2004 International Database Engineering and Applications Symposium (IDEAS04): 193-204. DOI: 10.1109/IDEAS.2004.1319792

[7] Hickson, I. (2011). HTML5: A vocabulary and associated APIs for HTML and XHTML. W3C Working Draft 25 May 2011. World Wide Web Consortium. http://www.w3.org/TR/html5/ (last visited May 26, 2013).

[8] Luong, M., Nguyen, T. D., Kan, M. (forthcoming) Logical Structure Recovery in Scholarly Articles with Rich Document Features. In International Journal of Digital Library Systems, 1 (4): 1-23. DOI: 10.4018/jdls.2010100101

[9] Peroni, S. (2012). Semantic Publishing: issues, solutions and new trends in scholarly publishing within the Semantic Web era. Ph. D. Thesis. Department of Computer Science, University of Bologna, Italy. http://speroni.web.cs.unibo.it/publications/peroni-2012-semantic-publishing-issues.pdf

[10] Shotton, D. (2009). Semantic Publishing: the coming revolution in scientific journal publishing. Learned Publishing, 22 (2): 85-94. DOI: 10.1087/2009202.

[11] Shotton, D., Portwin, K., Klyne, G., Miles, A. (2009). Adventures in Semantic Publishing: Exemplar Semantic Enhancements of a Research Article. PLoS Computational Biology, 5 (4): e1000361. DOI: 10.1371/journal.pcbi.1000361.

[12] Walsh, N. (2010). DocBook 5: The Definitive Guide. Sebastopol, CA, USA: O'Really Media. Version 1.0.3. ISBN: 0596805029.

Improving Term Extraction by Utilizing User Annotations

Jozef Harinek
Institute of Informatics and Software Engineering
Slovak University of Technology in Bratislava
Ilkovičova, 842 16 Bratislava
xharinek@stuba.sk

Marián Šimko
Institute of Informatics and Software Engineering
Slovak University of Technology in Bratislava
Ilkovičova, 842 16 Bratislava
marian.simko@stuba.sk

ABSTRACT

Automated acquisition of relevant domain terms from educational documents available in social educational systems can benefit from processing a growing number of user-created annotations assigned to the content. Annotations provide us potentially useful information about documents and can improve the results of base Automatic Term Recognition (ATR) algorithms. We propose a method for relevant domain terms extraction based on user-created annotations processing. We consider three basic annotation types: tags, comments and highlights. The final term weight is computed by combining relevant domain terms weights obtained from the individual annotation types and those obtained from the text. The method was evaluated using data from Principles of Software Engineering course in adaptive educational system ALEF and showed that enhancements based on annotation processing yield significant improvement of results.

Categories and Subject Descriptors

I.2.4 [Artificial Intelligence]: Knowledge Representation Formalisms and Methods; I.7.5 [Document and text processing]: Document analysis

Keywords

document analysis, metadata creation, lightweight semantics, ATR, relevant domain term extraction, social annotation, learning

1. INTRODUCTION

The great increase in numbers of documents available in open information spaces calls for advanced processing enabling to access documents effectively and prevent information overload. Advanced processing of documents necessitates having them described in a way they are machine-readable. The elemental way of such description are relevant domain terms (RDT) assigned to documents, which describe the content of the document and represent *conceptual metadata* of document sets. RDTs as lexical references to domain concepts are essential for tasks in ontology learning. They either form a basis of lightweight ontologies [13] or constitute a first step towards heavyweight ontological descriptions [2]. Although relevant domain terms alone as conceptual representation are usually suitable for basic reasoning only, we believe they suffice for tasks related to elemental document recommendation and information filtering.

Methods for RDT acquisition, referred to as methods for automatic term recognition (ATR) [4], vary in level of precision of RDT extraction. It often depends on the domain we extract the RDTs from. Although the results of ATR are not perfect we often cannot afford to have the RDTs extracted by humans. It would be too expensive both in terms of human resources and time. There are usually too many documents to be processed manually and number of RDTs to be assigned is counted in hundreds.

In our work we consider a web-based educational system in which users (students) interact with the educational content. They create annotations to help themselves work with (access, organize, navigate in) the educational content effectively. We view this as a big advantage for educational document processing. We believe we are able to extract potentially useful information from user-created annotations that can help improve RDT extraction from educational resources in both closed educational systems as well as open corpora of educational linked data.

We are motivated by approaches where user-created annotations have been successfully used in various domains, e.g., annotations from tweets were extracted to detect earthquake events [8], or user-created tags were also used for song recommendation [1].

The aim of our research is to explore and evaluate possibilities of enhancing RDT extraction with processing user-created content. We particularly focus on educational documents, which are often rich in user-created annotations as a result of autonomous learning [3]. In this paper we propose a method enhancing traditional ATR algorithms with user-created annotation processing and research how different types of annotations contribute to term extraction.

2. RELATED WORK

In socially oriented web-based systems, user annotations have attracted much attention. Annotation creation is a beneficial activity for users as it helps them work with the documents more effectively (faster navigation, search). This particularly applies for documents that are a part of user's private collection and often represent source of knowledge, such as research papers and learning objects. It has been already shown how a global semantic model can be inferred from some user-created annotation types to semantically annotate web documents [14].

ATR algorithms are used to extract RDTs. They are typically divided in two groups: termhood-based or unithood-based [4]. Termhood algorithms consider the degree of domain specificity and are based on frequency of occurrence of the term (e.g., TF-IDF, Weirdness), unithood algorithms measure the strength of collocation in terms (e.g., Log-likelihood) [4]. There is much research on how to improve the extraction of terms from documents when using various ATR methods. Different approaches to term extraction have different results: one method does outperform others in one domain and does not in another [15].

Several works aim to improve term extraction methods by taking into account various features of the document given. For example, they consider the visual information which is available in HTML documents. In [5], the proposed method processes HTML tags and CSS style sheets in order to capture the visual information of website. Another approach was presented in [12] where tweets were exploited as user-created annotations of web documents referenced in those tweets. The authors showed that tweets can be utilized for relevant terms extraction from web documents (those with poor textual content gave particularly good results).

There are also approaches in the domain of adaptive learning, which aim to automate domain model creation for adaptive course [10]. However, we are not aware of works, which study user-created content for utilization in relevant domain term extraction. There is also lack of works exploiting various annotation types.

3. METHOD FOR RELEVANT DOMAIN TERMS EXTRACTION

When considering educational content in the context of e-learning 2.0 [3], it often has user-created annotations assigned. The annotations are created with intention to help a student who creates them and also his peers when using the educational content. We believe we can improve RDTs extraction from educational content by utilizing such user-created annotations and information extracted from them.

Our method consists of the following steps:

1. Document and annotation pre-processing
2. RDT extraction from document and annotations
3. Combining the results from both sources

For each document in a set we extract RDTs from plain text of a document. We merge all the annotations attached to the document and evaluate user-added value. We extract RDTs from the merged annotation representation and then update the weights of RDTs extracted from the document content.

3.1 Document and annotation pre-processing

First, we need to pre-process the document we obtained. We remove the stop words from the document, lemmatize the text and identify multiword terms.

We assume that the document has some user-created annotations attached. Annotation pre-processing in our method consists of creating an "extended document" E_d of annotations. We create this extended document by merging together all the annotations the document has. We also take into account the author of the annotation. We compute author's *reputation level* and based on this value we later adapt the weight of the annotations he added.

After creating the extended document, we pre-process it similarly to the main text. We remove stop words, lemmatize text and identify multiword terms.

We can employ arbitrary type of annotation in our method. In this paper, we particularly focus on the three types of annotations often used in interactive educational systems: tags, highlights and comments. We believe that we can extract helpful information from these annotations due to their characteristics.

Tag. Tag is an annotation, which has a lot of semantic potential. Users add tags typically to improve navigation in the documents. Tags refer to the documents' content and describe it. They are very likely to represent domain concepts, and they are very "close" to relevant domain terms. However, users can also assign tags irrelevant for domain description (e.g., "read later").

Highlight. Users add highlights only to parts of the text that are important in the document. The highlighted text should show the important words from the text. In this case we know that the text they contain is taken only from the document itself and therefore it does not contain words that are not from the domain at all.

User Comment. Very interesting annotation type from the semantics extraction point of view. Comments may possibly have greater influence on RDT extraction than tags or highlights. In the considered scenario, to add a comment a user selects a part of text and assigns some thoughts to it. It might mean both that it is an important or "bad" part of text. If we are able to filter out comments which are negative we would find the more relevant terms. The challenge is to properly process provided comments and select only those with potential semantic information.

3.2 Relevant domain term extraction

We designed our method to employ an arbitrary existing ATR algorithm for RDTs extraction (e.g., TF-IDF). The only restriction on ATR algorithm is that it yields weighted RDT set for an input document. Depending on the algorithm used, the extraction results may vary and we can achieve smaller or greater improvement in extracted results. We apply an ATR algorithm on both the main text and also the extended document of annotations. As a result, we get two sets of relevant domain terms.

When extracting terms from a *document*, we simply apply selected ATR algorithm, which yields weighted RDT set for the document.

When extracting terms from *annotations*, we deal with several kinds of annotations. If a term is found in all of them, we need to somehow determine the weight of that type of annotation for that particular term. So we combine the individual types of annotations according to the following formula:

$$w_{annot}(t, d) = \sum_{a \in A} \sigma_a * \sum_{u \in U_t} UR(u) * w_{ATR}(t, E_d) \quad (1)$$

where σ_a is relevancy coefficient of the annotation type a, A is set of all annotation types. It applies that $\sum \sigma = 1$. U_t is set of all users who annotated term t, UR refers to reputation level of user, $w_{ATR}(t, E_d)$ is weight of term t in extended document of annotations E_d.

To be able to distinguish quality of annotations we have to know the *reputation level* (user ranking) of users who added them. In the proposed method we can employ various user ranking approaches. They can either utilize known graph algorithms (such as PageRank or HITS adapted to estimate user's proficiency level) or selected statistical measures resulting from user activity. A more detailed description is beyond the scope of this paper. We present the basic example of user ranking later in Evaluation.

3.3 Combining the results

After we extract the relevant domain terms from the document and the annotations, we need to combine them. The weight of annotations can differ in various domains and there might be a change in the parameter setting needed for different document and annotation corpora. The final weight is computed as follows:

$$w_{final}(t,d) = (1-p) * w_{ATR}(t,d) + p * w_{annot}(t,d) \quad (2)$$

where t is term, d is document, p is annotation weight, w_{ATR} is weight obtained by extracting RDTs from text, w_{annot} is weight obtained by extracting RDTs from annotations.

4. EVALUATION

Our primary aim was to verify if utilization of user annotations will indeed improve the results of RDT extraction and what is the contribution of respective document annotation types.

We performed the evaluation by conducting an experiment utilizing the Software engineering course contained within our interactive adaptive educational system ALEF [11]. It consists of 180 documents (learning objects) covering multiple topics from this area. The learning objects have 21,491 (5,348 tags, 15,707 highlights, 436 comments) annotations assigned by 329 students who utilized course materials for learning during 2 years.

Each learning object in ALEF already has weighted term descriptions provided by teachers (domain experts) as a part of semantic layer successfully utilized for learning object recommendation and personalized navigation and summarization [7][6]. We took the provided term descriptions as a gold standard. We evaluated our results against this gold standard. It is not "perfect" (even a teacher is human and it is not possible to describe such amounts of the learning objects completely and flawlessly). However, we believe it is sufficient for this evaluation, where there are too many method configurations to be evaluated manually by experts.

To properly evaluate the proposed method, we divided the dataset (Software engineering course's learning objects) into two sets – training and test set. We performed several simulations to estimate best-performing parameter configuration of the method. Using the obtained configuration, we evaluated our method on test set of documents. We employed 5-fold cross-validation to get data-independent results.

We employed a simple user ranking method in the experiment. It is based on a simplified assumption that the more annotations user adds, the more involved in the course he is, and, as a result, the more he understands the topic. We compute the user proficiency level value reflecting his annotations count in the corpus. The more annotations user adds, the higher rating he gets (we divide users in four groups based on number of annotations they provide) and the more it affects annotation weights (see (1)).

Our goal was to compare performance of a base ATR algorithm with our method and find the right set-up of method parameters in order to achieve the best results in utilizing user-created annotation processing. For the evaluation we selected TF-IDF algorithm. It is easy to employ and it actually shows satisfactory results for basic RDT extraction [4].

First, we extracted plain text from learning documents represented as XML (DocBook) files. After that, we extracted terms from this text using TF-IDF. We took top 15 % of extracted terms as *relevant* domain terms. We also extracted terms from annotations using TF-IDF and also took top 15 % of terms as RDTs. The last step was combining the results together. In our method we have several parameters to be adjusted. Each annotation type has a relevancy level σ_a which falls into interval <0, 1>.

We evaluated the results using Normalized Discounted Cumulative Gain (NDCG) measure. We used this measure since we needed to take into account also the weight-based ordering of the retrieved results and we needed to reflect this in the evaluation of the obtained results (in contrast with traditional set-based precision and recall measures). We computed improvement in relevant domain terms extraction by comparing RDTs obtained by our method with the gold standard obtained from the dataset.

When base ATR algorithm (TF-IDF) was used, the results yielded quite small numbers (NDCG ~ 0.6). We believe it is due to the fact that ATR algorithms do not perform well when applied to small corpora or relatively short documents (some learning objects meet this condition). This only underlines the potential of user-created annotations to improve the results of ATR algorithms in such setting.

When evaluating annotation-based RDTs extracted by the method, we first assessed the particular annotation types. We took each annotation type alone, extracted necessary information and enhanced the relevant domain terms obtained from text using our method. We compared these results with the gold standard. The annotations improved the results up to 29.4 % according to NDCG (29.4 % for tags, 15.1 % for highlights and 11 % for comments) when compared with extraction from text only (see Figure 1). The most influential annotation type was tag. Tags had growing or stable level of improvement with increasing annotation weight p. On the other hand, highlights and comments had growing tendency first and then they fell down when p increased beyond ~ 0.2-0.3. For some p values there was even decrease in NDCG when compared to RDTs extracted from text only. We believe that comments yielded such results because of their rather small frequency in the dataset. In addition, as mentioned above, we performed only basic processing. Some of the comments were not relevant for the document because they were wrongly used as the system issue reporting tool by student users.

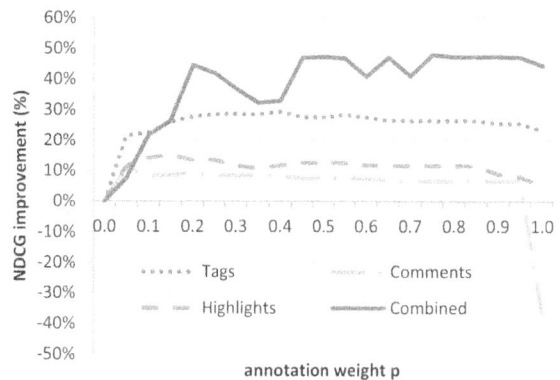

Figure 1. NDCG improvement (in %).

Based on the results obtained by particular annotation type processing we derived relevancy coefficients for the annotation types. We set the parameters $\sigma_{comments} = 0.20$, $\sigma_{highlights} = 0.31$ and $\sigma_{tags} = 0.49$ to reflect the improvement of the particular annotation type when combined with results obtained by processing document content only.

We used the σ parameters to get final weights for RDTs extracted from both document and user-created annotations assigned to the document. We observed the overall performance of our method in relation to parameter p (see Figure 1, *Combined*). The combination of RDTs from annotations with RDTs from text yielded maximal improvement of 47.3 % in RDT extraction at $p = 0.75$ (NDCG = 0.86). The results show that user-created annotation processing indeed has positive effect on final results of RDT extraction. They also show that it is important to consider all three annotation types as they all contribute (though at different level of significance) to the overall improvement. We can see from the results, that RDT extraction results have been improved for relatively small corpora with relatively short documents, where traditional ATR algorithms do not perform well (when applied alone).

The obtained results led to integration of the method into our educational content management system [10] to facilitate teachers (content and metadata authors) educational content authoring.

5. CONCLUSIONS

We presented the method for extracting relevant domain terms from documents having assigned various types of user-created annotations. The novelty of our approach lies in exploring the contribution of various annotation types to term extraction.

The results show that the idea of extending RDT extraction with user annotations processing is very reasonable. We found out that the most promising annotation type for ATR results improvement is tag, which increased the accuracy of RDT extraction as much as 29.4 %. In addition, the other annotation types yield improvement as well – highlights 15.1 % and comments 11 %. This shows that annotation processing indeed helps the RDT extraction.

The very important result is that annotation types' combination outperformed individual annotation types. We showed the aggregated improvement of RDTs extraction is 47.3 % (when using the configuration of the annotation relevancy coefficients obtained from experiments with individual annotation types). These results are very promising and show that power of user crowd (even the student crowd) can be utilized in tasks related with basic stages of ontology engineering/learning. This is in line with the results reported in related works from other domains [9].

We believe in further improvement if we extend the processing of the employed annotation types or involve new types typically present within educational systems. Educational systems are rich in annotation types today as they take advantage of Web 2.0 concepts and provide students interactive learning materials with enhanced user experience.

In this paper we focused on educational content because it is a source of annotation-rich documents. However, our method is applicable on any other domain, where user-created annotations are present (e.g., digital libraries, enterprise knowledge bases).

We showed in the experiments that our assumption about comments (that they might be even more important than highlights) was wrong. We believe it is due to the fact that users did not select the whole important part of the text they added comment to but just a first word of a paragraph or so. It might be also caused by the fact that some of the comments were not only comments to be used as help for the user but comments referring that something is not good in the document text. We believe that better processing of comment's text would help in identifying the irrelevant parts of text. Advanced processing of user annotations remains to be our future work. We will also research substituting TF-IDF with other ATR methods that would help to better adjust the annotation weights. We believe it can improve the RDT extraction results even more.

Acknowledgement. This work was partially supported by the Scientific Grant Agency of Slovak Republic, grant No. VG1/0675/11 and the Slovak Research and Development Agency under the contract No. APVV-0208-10.

6. REFERENCES

[1] Bischoff, K., Firan, C. S., Nejdl, W., Pair, R. 2009. How do you feel about "dancing queen"?: deriving mood & theme annotations from user tags. In *Proc. of the 9th ACM/IEEE-CS joint conf. on Digital libraries*, pp. 285–294.

[2] Cimiano, P. 2006. Ontology learning and population from text, Springer, 347p.

[3] Downes, S. 2005. E-learning 2.0. *eLearn magazine*. Issue 10. ACM, p. 1.

[4] Knoth, P., Schmidt, M., Smrž, P., Zdráhal, Z. 2009. Towards a Framework for Comparing Automatic Term Recognition Methods, In: *Znalosti (Knowledge)* 2009, pp. 83–94.

[5] Lučanský, M., Šimko, M. 2013. Improving Relevance of Keyword Extraction from the Web Utilizing Visual Style Information, In *SOFSEM 2013: Theory and Practice of Computer Science*, Vol. 7741, Springer, pp. 445–456.

[6] Michlík, P., Bieliková, M. 2010. Exercises Recommending for Limited Time Learning. *Procedia Computer Science*. Vol. 1, Issue 2, Elsevier, ISSN 1877-0509, pp. 2821–2828.

[7] Móro, R. Bieliková, M. 2012. Personalized Text Summarization Based on Important Terms Identification. In Proc. of DEXA 2012 Workshops, 23rd Int. Workshop on Database and Expert Systems Applications, IEEE CS, pp. 131–135 .

[8] Sakaki, T., Okazaki, M., Matsuo,Y. 2010. Earthquake shakes Twitter users: real-time event detection by social sensors, In Proc. of the 19th Int. Conf. on WWW, pp. 851–860.

[9] Šimko, J., Tvarožek, M., & Bieliková, M. 2011. Little search game: term network acquisition via a human computation game. In Proc. of the 22nd ACM Conf. on Hypertext and hypermedia, ACM, pp. 57–62.

[10] Šimko, M. Bieliková, M. 2009. Automated Educational Course Metadata Generation Based on Semantics Discovery. In LNCS 5794, *Proc. of European Conf. on Technology Enhanced Learning*, ECTEL 2009, Springer, pp. 99–105.

[11] Šimko,M., Barla, M., Bieliková, M. 2010. ALEF: A Framework for Adaptive Web Web-based Learning 2.0. In KCKS 2010, *IFIP Advances in Information and Communication Technology*, Vol. 324. Springer, pp. 367–378.

[12] Uherčík, T., Šimko, M., Bieliková, M. 2013. Utilizing Microblogs for Web Page Relevant Term Acquisition. In *SOFSEM 2013: Theory and Practice of Computer Science*. LNCS, Vol.7741, Springer, pp. 457–468.

[13] Wong, W., Liu, W., Bennamoun, M. 2012. Ontology learning from text: A look back and into the future. *ACM Computing Surveys (CSUR)*, 44(4), 20.

[14] Wu, X. et al. 2006. Exploring social annotations for the semantic web. In *Proc. of the 15th int. conf. on World Wide Web* (WWW '06). ACM, New York, NY, USA, 417–426.

[15] Zhang, Z., Iria, J., Brewster, Ch., Ciravegna, F. 2008. A Comparative Evaluation of Term Recognition Algorithms. In *Proc. of the 6th Int.Conf. on Language Resources and Eval.*

Using RDFS/OWL to Ease Semantic Integration of Structured Documents

Jean-Yves Vion-Dury
Xerox Research Centre Europe
6 chemin de Maupertuis
38240 Meylan, France
viondury@xeroxlabs.com

ABSTRACT

This paper defines i/ an RDFS/OWL schema to capture the syntactic structure of marked-up documents and ii/ the (reversible) transposition of any XML/SGML/HTML document into a set of conformant RDF triples that convey the relevant tree information, be it meta-information (structure of the tree, attributes, XML comments…) or basic information (textual content).

The translation we propose reuses predefined semantics of RDFS and OWL W3C standards, thus making tree manipulation and transformations homogeneous to common RDF semantic models; once translated, operations on XML/SGML/HTML trees can be much easily integrated into Semantic Web applications (and this applies particularly well to emerging HTML notational systems such as RDFa or micro-formats).

Where this makes sense for application areas, specific document schemas can be totally or partially translated into supplemental RDFS/OWL constraints manageable by inference engines complying with the W3C standards.

Categories and Subject Descriptors

D.2.12 [**Interoperability**]: Data mapping. E.1 [**Data Structures**]: Trees. E.2 [**Data storage representation**]: Linked representations. I.7.2 [**Document Preparation**]: Markup languages, Format and Notations.

General Terms

Documentation, Design, Languages, Standardization.

Keywords

XML representation, RDFS, OWL, Document Models.

1. INTRODUCTION

To access, change, and more generally exploit the information contained in tag based documents (XML, HTML, SGML), the software algorithms rely on some memory model and related Application Programming Interface or API. This presents a great advantage: reusable libraries are organized around well-designed data structures and primitives, and offer standardized way to (re)use the most common functionalities; moreover, libraries, to a

certain extent, may exploit the particularities of various programming languages. Today, the dominant data model for handling XML document is DOM [1], as long as documents can be entirely stored in the memory of the computer hosting the processing algorithms. In other cases, the document syntax is transposed into a temporal model via parsing events, and the management of the memory is left up to the application (that's the dominant SAX [2] standard).

If XML/HTML is a pervasive technology, bringing data and document under a common and universal view, the RDF data model [3] issued from the Semantic Web activities is also called to a great future, pursuing different goals, and, in some sense, going further in capturing and in using more efficiently the inherent semantics of data. Focusing on inference and being greatly generic, RDF can be considered as of lower level and even more universal than XML; based on the so-called triples, graphs (i.e. sets of triples) capture knowledge through generic semantic networks. Both standards will live together with different usage, and are called to collaborate tightly in solving the many interoperability challenges the software industry has to face. Alas, to do so, application engineers today have to use ad-hoc software and must develop extra code to interconnect the two data models inside a common application, because in-memory tree models and RDF stores are so different in practice that no standard (nor de facto practices) provide natural and efficient solutions and methods to address this problem.

2. The Modeling Approach

We define an RDFS/OWL schema to capture the syntactic structure of marked-up documents and a (reversible) transposition of any XML/HTML document into a set of RDF triples that convey the relevant tree information, be it meta-information (structure of the tree, attributes, XML comments …) or "direct" information (textual content of the document).

Where this makes sense for application areas, specific document schemas can be totally or partially translated into supplemental RDFS/OWL constraints manageable by inference engines complying with the W3C standards.

As the translation we propose is based on RDFS and OWL standards (see [3],[4]), it makes tree manipulation and transformations homogeneous to common RDF semantic models; in other words, once translated, operations on XML trees, are easier to integrate to Semantic Web applications through standard or specific inference engines (and this applies particularly well to emerging HTML notational systems such as RDFa or the so-called micro-formats).

2.1 A generic document model

We outline first a general document model that may capture XML standard, but also HTML and SGML as well. A well-formed document can be converted into a tree through a syntactic analysis. Nodes of this tree can have mainly four different types: root, element, text and attribute. To theses main categories, we have auxiliary types: comment and processing-instruction. The table below summarizes the node typology, together with their basic properties in terms of naming, topology and namespace configuration.

Type of node	Standard	Meta information	Upward connection	Downward connection
Root	All	Original URL/Namespace	None	0..N children
Element	All	Name	1 root or Element	0..N children
	XML	Namespace		
Text	all	None	1 root or Element	no
Attribute	all	Name, Value	1 Element	no
	XML	Namespace		no
Comment	All	String	1 Element	no
Processing Instruction	XML,HTML	Name, String	1 Element	no

A more formal way to present all these constraints together is to use an attributed tree grammar (Non-terminals are in italic, URL and URN represent web addresses conformant with Web standard):

Tree ::= **root** (x:URL) [*Node**] |
              root (x:URL, ns:URN) [*Node**]

Node ::= *Element* | *Text* | *Attribute* | *Comment* | *PI*

Element ::= **element** (n:Name) [*Node**] |
              element (n:Name, ns:URN) [*Node**]

Text ::= **text** (s:String)

Attribute ::= **attribute** (n:Name, v:String) |
              attribute (n:Name, v:String, ns:URN)

Comment ::= **comment** (s:String)

PI ::= **pi** (n:Name, v:String)

Note first that the existence of the trees described by this grammar assumes that a lexical/parsing analysis operation can be performed on the linear version of the document, solving lexical and syntactical issues such as space verification, entity resolution, implicit tag substitution (for HTML, SGML), well-formedness checking, and possibly, validity checking according to some relevant schema (XML,SGML). Such trees can be mapped to RDF according to some dedicated RDF triples captured into two

RDF schemas: the first one describes subclass relationships, and the second table defines the properties associated with the node instances.

2.2 RDF classes and OWL constraints
This first schema defines the ontology of nodes, establishing a topological distinction between containing nodes (triple numbered 2 in the table) and terminal nodes (triple #3), and refining them into elements, attributes, text and comments (# 7, 8a, 10).

xxl:XNode rdf:type *owl:Class*   (1)
xxl:CNode rdfs:subClassOf xxl:XNode   (2)
xxl:VNode rdfs:subClassOf xxl:XNode   (3)
xxl:NSNode rdfs:subClassOf xxl:XNode   (4)
xxl:CNode owl:disjointWith xxl:VNode   (5)
xxl:Document rdfs:subClassOf xxl:CNode, xxl:NSNode   (6)
xxl:Element rdfs:subClassOf xxl:CNode, xxl:NSNode   (7)
xxl:Attribute rdfs:subClassOf xxl:VNode, xxl:NSNode   (8a)
xxl:Attribute owl:disjointWith xxl:Comment, xxl:Text   (8b)
xxl:Comment rdfs:subClassOf xxl:VNode   (10)
xxl:Text rdfs:subClassOf xxl:VNode   (11)
xxl:NS rdfs:subClassOf xxl:NSNode   (12a)
xxl:NS owl:disjointWith xxl:CNode, xxl:NSNode, xxl:VNode   (12b)

Definitions #5 and #8b express some fundamental incompatibilities: instances of the CNode class ("Containing Nodes"), cannot be considered as instances of the VNode class ("Value nodes"), as well as attribute nodes cannot be considered as comment or text, despite the fact that they both are instances of VNode in the class hierarchy. The class xxl:NS captures instances used to describe namespaces through their prefix and URN (# 12a,b).

Note that the class NSNode plays a particular role: it is intended to capture nodes that may have a particular XML namespace, be they member of CNode (e.g. elements) or VNode (e.g. attributes). In some sense, this is a transverse class. Of course, the same constraints could be captured through many different equivalent RDF/OWL schemas.

2.3 Properties
The following table enumerates the properties used to model trees and defines their typing characteristics:

xxl:node rdfs:subPropertyOf *rdfs:Label*   (20a)
xxl:node rdfs:domain xxl:XNode   (20b)
xxl:comment rdfs:subPropertyOf *rdfs:comment, rfds:value*   (21a)
xxl:comment rdfs:domain xxl:Comment   (21b)
xxl:element rdfs:subPropertyOf xxl:node   (22a)
xxl:element rdfs:domain xxl:Element   (22b)
xxl:attribute rdfs:subPropertyOf xxl:node   (23a)
xxl:attribute rdfs:domain xxl:Atttribute   (23b)
xxl:namespace rdfs:domain xxl:NSNode   (24a,b)
xxl:namespace rdfs:range xxl:NS   (24c)
xxl:value rdfs:subPropertyOf *rfds:value*   (25)
xxl:ns-definition rdfs:domain xxl:NS   (26)

Basically, *xxl:node* is a general property that relates *xxl:XNode* to their name expressed as a RDF literal value (20a,b). Two sub-properties refine this notion, namely, *xxl:element* which domain is *xxl:Element* (22b), and *xxl:attribute* which domain is *xxl:Attribute* (23b). The use of property refinement (22a, 23a) is a convenient way to convey accurate typing information. Indeed, one triple such as

$$\{ \_:1 \; xxl{:}element \; "body" \}$$

captures the fact that the node _:1 is an instance of the class xxl:Element, and also that the corresponding tag name is "body". An alternative solution would be

$$\{ \_:1 \; rdf{:}type \; xxl{:}Element \; . \; \_:1 \; rdfs{:}label \; "body"\}$$

which requires two triples. This principle is applied in a systematic way in our encoding proposal. Another guiding principle of the schema founding our proposal is to also offer generalizing properties such as xxl:node, itself being a refinement of rdfs:label (20a). Defining a triple like

$$\{ \_:1 \; xxl{:}node \; "body" \}$$

would convey less information, as one can only deduce from the standard RDFS inference scheme that the node _:1 is an instance of xxl:XNode (20b). However, this notion becomes interesting from the querying process point of view. Indeed, looking for structural information about the encoded document, one may use a query pattern like

$$\{?x \; xxl{:}node \; ?name\}$$

to find out all elements and attributes name indistinctly. Similarly, the query may use an even more generic property such as

$$\{?x \; rdfs{:}label \; ?name\}$$

to query indistinctly triples capturing the document instance tags and attribute names, as well as other kind of triples just having a label in different context, as for instance triples from Dublin Core Metadata Initiative that aims at modeling meta information about documents (see [9]), and that could me mixed with our lower level tag description triples.

The *xxl:comment* property is defined as a sub-property of the generic RDF property *rdfs:comment* (this deserves a better usability of the schema, building on the original semantics of comment in XML/HTML standard, as explained above with different words). Last, *xxl:namespace* allows specifying how a namespace is attached to a node (24a, b, c). The namespace itself is described by an instance of *xxl:NS* class (#24), and uses *xxl:value* (a sub-property of *rdf:value*) to specify the URI associated with the namespace (#56, 57). The latter is, by design, a sub-property of the standard *rdf:value* property, again to increase the usability of our schema (#55). The property *xxl:prefix* (sub-property of *rdfs:label*) is used to specify the prefix found in the original XML qualified name (#52,53,54).

2.4 Properties for Capturing Tree Topology

The fundamental relation is *xxl:child-of*, aimed at capturing parent-children relationship, but in a reverse order (that is, a child-to-parent relation). This choice is key to confer to our model streaming abilities: triples can be produced incrementally when parsing a document and emitting SAX events, or when performing a leftmost innermost tree traversal.

xxl:child-of rdf:type owl:AP, owl:FP, owl:IP[1]	(30a,b,c)
xxl:child-of rdfs:domain xxl:XNode	(31)
xxl:child-of rdfs:range xxl:CNode	(32)
xxl:parent-of owl:inverseOf xxl:child-of	(33)
xxl:descendant-of rdf:type *owl:TransitiveProperty*	(34)
xxl:child-of rdfs:subPropertyOf xxl:descendant-of	(35)
xxl:ancestor-of owl:inverseOf xxl:descendant-of	(36)
xxl:sibling-of owl:propertyChainAxiom xxl:child-of, xxl:parent-of	(37)
xxl:sibling-of rdf:type *owl:TransitiveProperty*	(38)
xxl:attribute-of rdfs:subPropertyOf xxl:child-of	(39a)
xxl:attribute-of rdfs:domain xxl:Attribute	(39b)
xxl:attribute-of rdfs:range xxl:Element	(39c)

The following captures ordering relations (if required by the application; see also [12] for in-depth investigation of ordering issues with OWL):

xxl:order rdfs:domain xxl:XNode	(40,41)
xxl:order rdfs:range xsd:positiveInteger	(42)
xxl:following-sibling-of rdfs:subPropertyOf xxl:sibling-of	(43)
xxl:following-sibling-of rdf:type owl:AP, owl:FP, owl:IP[2]	(44)
xxl:preceding-sibling-of owl:inverseOf xxl:following-sibling-of	
xxl:preceding-sibling-of owl:propertyDisjointWith :following-sibling-of	

2.5 Handling namespaces

NS information is captured by two properties ranging over rdfs:Literal: xxl:prefix (with domain xxl:NS) and xxl:value (with domain xxl:VNode; serve also to specify the literal value of text and attribute nodes).

3. The translation algorithm

The mapping from (XML) tagged document to RDF triples complying with the proposed schema is defined as a top down tree traversal, which increments monotonically a counter i to register the order of node in the tree (this is a standard tree ordering technique). This function operates on an abstract representation of trees suitable to capture the information of any hierarchical structure involved in the various existing document representation standards. The function returns the set of produced triples and the total number of scanned nodes.

At each visited node, the mapping produces triples as illustrated in the next table for the main items only (using turtle notation [10]), the parameter f being an URI with the value indicated in the right most column, and p the previous value of f.

entry	produces	f
root (x:URL)	f a xxl:Document; rdfs:isDefinedBy x	_:root
text (v :String)	f xxl:text v; xxl:child-of p; xxl:order i	
element (n:Name)	f xxl:element n; xxl:child-of p; xxl:order i	_:i
attr(n:Name,v:String)	f xxl:attribute n; xxl:value v; xxl:attribute-of p	

---

[1] Stands for *AsymmetricProperty, FunctionalProperty, IrreflexiveProperty*

[2] Same remark than above

The corresponding algorithm can be easily and efficiently implemented through a recursive descent function (works on in-memory trees) or through an automaton driven by SAX parsing events (works with streaming parsing models).

4. Properties of the translation

Our mapping offers several key features and properties: it
- *handles homogenously XML/SGML/HTML.*
- *captures significant Syntactic constraints.* The most relevant structural constraints are inherently captured by our taxonomy of nodes: terminal nodes cannot have descendants (text, attributes, comments and processing instructions), element nodes can only have descendants of type element or terminal.
- *provides Specialization support* (translation of many XML schemas constraints into RDF). Many constraints expressed in a DTD, RelaxNG or XSD schema can be translated in RDF checking rules.
- *offers Query Computability* (handles queries over document structure and content). Our translation enables using the inferential mechanism of RDF/OWL to query the tree structure and links information. Most common XPath expressions can be translated into SPARQL query suited to the model we propose.
- *offers Streaming capability* as triples can be produced through the event flow emitted by a SAX parser. Therefore, one can design an RDF based process to transform and/or to interpret very big (or conceptually infinite) documents, similar to more standard processors driven by SAX events (indeed, triples may be volatile, in the sense that one can conceive a computing model where they are not memorized, or through a FIFO data structure of limited depth).
- *offers Customization capability* (with or without element order, with or without comments, with or without NS prefixes…).
- *provides natural integration with meta-data* oriented formats such as dublin core, GRDDL, RDFa, eRDF); in the coming years, deep efforts will probably be conducted toward adding semantics to web documents by the mean of such annotation standards, and we believe that our proposal is a natural way to combine them in a common applicative framework, at lower development costs.

5. Previous Work

The literature focused so far on mapping the semantic of a document into an RDF graph[3] [5], [6], [8], [11] whereas we propose to map the tree document's syntax into an RDF graph. Our approach doesn't need to interpret a schema and therefore is considerably more general. In [7], there is an attempt to propose such a general data model for XML documents. However, our proposal goes significantly beyond this approach, first because built upon the inferential potential of RDFS/OWL for an increase applicative power and simplicity, second because compliant with RDF in such a way that most common operations are simplified and conducted through the "expected" way. It does not require any specific schema to capture the target document model, although it has the potential to take benefit from this additional information.

Going into more details, [7] and [11] both use the rdf:_n container membership property, which is quite unsuitable to dynamic

---

[3] EARMARK [13] is an universal document model built on RDF/OWL annotations going beyond many limitations related to linear markup based approaches (both from the semantic and document's topology standpoint).

manipulation of structures, as revealed by our very first experiments.

6. Future work and perspectives

We just start exploring the operational properties of the model (storage space and runtime performance) using a home-made SW integration environment based on a general purpose query engine built on top of Python. So far, memory consumption scales in the expected way, and query expressiveness seems OK at this stage, provided that semantic oriented application appear to access tree information in a quite different way than encountered in XSLT/XQuery-like applications. Interestingly, many subtree sharing schemes can be implemented on the basis of the present proposal (this feature was already described in [13]), when appropriate with respect to the document type. Our next stage will be to take benefit of the streaming capability of our model to handle transformation/data extraction over big XML documents.

7. REFERENCES

[1] World Wide Web Consortium, Document Object Model, http://www.w3.org/DOM/

[2] XML-DEV mailing list, Simple API for XML, http://www.saxproject.org/

[3] W3C Recommendation, RDF Vocabulary Description Language, http://www.w3.org/TR/rdf-schema/

[4] W3C Recommendation, OWL 2 Web Ontology Language Document Overview, http://www.w3.org/TR/owl2-overview/

[5] Thuy, P. and Lee, Y. and Lee,S. and Jeong, B. , Transforming Valid XML Documents into RDF via RDF Schema, International Conference on Next Generation Web Services Practices, IEEE, October 2007.

[6] Thuy, P. and Lee, Y. and Lee,S. and Jeong, B. , Exploiting XML Schema for Interpreting XML Documents as RDF, SCC'08, IEEE, Hawaii, July 2008

[7] Melnik, S., Bridging the Gap between RDF and XML, Dec 16, 1999. http://infolab.stanford.edu/~melnik/rdf/fusion.html

[8] Bohring, H. and Auer,S. Mapping XML to OWL Ontologies, Leipziger Informatik-Tage, vol. 72 of LNI, 2005. http://citeseerx.ist.psu.edu/viewdoc/summary?doi=10.1.1.59.8897

[9] The Dublin Core Metadata Initiative, DCMI Metadata Terms, http://dublincore.org/documents/2012/06/14/dcmi-terms/

[10] W3C Candidate Recommendation, Terse RDF triple Language (Turtle), Feb. 2013, http://www.w3.org/TR/turtle/

[11] Battle, S. Round-tripping between XML and RDF, in Intern. Semantic Web Conf, 2004

[12] Drummond, N., Rector, A. L., Stevens, R., Moulton, G., Horridge, M., Wang, H., & Seidenberg, J. Putting OWL in Order: Patterns for Sequences in OWL. In OWLED.

[13] Peroni, S. and Vitali, F. Annotations with EARMARK for arbitrary, overlapping and out-of order markup. Document Engineering 2009.

Reviewing the TEI ODD system

Sebastian Rahtz

IT Services, University of Oxford
sebastian.rahtz@it.ox.ac.uk

Lou Burnard

Lou Burnard Consulting
lou.burnard@retired.ox.ac.uk

ABSTRACT

For many years the Text Encoding Initiative (TEI) has maintained a specialised high-level XML vocabulary in the 'literate programming' paradigm to define its influential *Guidelines*, from which schemas or DTDs in other schema languages are derived. This paper reviews the development of this vocabulary, known as ODD (for 'One Document Does it all'). We discuss some problems with the language, and propose solutions to make it more complete and extensible.

Categories and Subject Descriptors

H.3.7 [**Information Systems**]: Information Storage and Retrieval, Digital Libraries

General Terms

Standardization

Keywords

TEI ODD

1. INTRODUCTION

The Text Encoding Initiative (TEI) began in the late 1980s as a project to provide a consistent and extensible encoding system for digital text of all kinds. By 1991, when the TEI's initial workgroups started to send in their proposals for textual features which they felt really had to be distinguished in any sensible encoding project, it had become clear that something more than a database would be needed to keep track of the tags they were busy inventing, and the meanings associated with them. At that time, it was envisaged that the recently standardized SGML markup system ([3] and [2]) would provide the metalanguage in which those proposals would be expressed (though it is worth noting that even at this stage the TEI considered SGML to be only one possible means for such expression). However, there was no system readily available which combined formal specifications and descriptive explanatory prose in a single document in the spirit of Donald Knuth's concept of 'literate programming'.[1]

DocEng'13, September 10–13, 2013, Florence, Italy.
Copyright is held by the owner/author(s). Publication rights licensed to ACM.
ACM 978-1-4503-1770-2/13/09 ...$15.00.
http://dx.doi.org/10.1145/2494266.2494321.

In 1991, the TEI editors (Michael Sperberg-McQueen and Lou Burnard) developed the idea of using a single DTD to support both the documentation of an encoding scheme and its expression as a formal language. Like that of other contemporary SGML documentation systems such as Majour, they anticipated a need for documentation about each element in the system, providing English language expressions about its intended function, its name, why it was so called, the other elements it was associated with, usage examples, and cross-references to places where it was discussed. This would however be combined with formal SGML declarations both for the element and for its attribute list. Relevant portions of these "tag documents" could then be extracted into the running text, and the whole could be reprocessed to provide reference documentation as well as to generate document type declarations for the use of an SGML parser. SGML declarations were embedded as CDATA marked sections, effectively isolating them from the rest of the document, and thus making it impossible to process them in any way other than by simple inclusion. This system was named ODD ('One Document Does it all'), and versions of it were used in the definition and production of the first four releases of the TEI Guidelines (1992, 1994, 1996, 2000).

At the fifth major revision however (P5, released in 2007 after several further years of development; [7]), the TEI switched to XML, and to using RELAX NG[4] as the primary means of declaring the content model for each element specification. Pure RELAX NG schemas and XML DTDs were directly generated from this source, while W3C schemas were generated from the RELAX NG output in a second pass, using James Clark's trang processor. Another major change at TEI P5 was the extensive use of model classes as a more expressive and more flexible mechanism for generalization than had been possible using SGML parameter entities.

If there remained a problem with the ODD language, it was the continued presence of another formal language (now RELAX NG rather than SGML) within it. It was noted by the overseeing committee on the TEI Consortium (its Technical Council), notably in a critique by David Durand, that this was a compromise solution: the system neither used the full power of RELAX NG (eg to offer an attribute or child element as alternatives), nor attempted to make the TEI independent of current schema languages. Clearly, there were two ways of addressing this situation. One would be to use pure RELAX NG for *all* parts of the schema definition, embedding TEI documentations and examples in their own namespace within a native RELAX NG document.[1] Alternatively, the system should deploy native TEI constructs with an equivalent expressivity to the subset of RELAX NG currently in use. We present below an im-

---

[1] This is the approach taken for example in Eric Van der Vlist's hybrid 'Exemplotron'; see further http://examplotron.org

plementation of the second approach, by which content models are described in pure TEI.

2. THE CURRENT ODD LANGUAGE

The TEI *Guidelines* define a language for describing, in a single XML document, everything needed to define and describe a schema, from which multiple outputs may be generated. This language (first described in [5], and subsequently refined somewhat for the final release of TEI P5) is not tied to the TEI and can be used to define schemas for any XML language.[2] The outputs may include:

1. formal reference documentation for elements, attributes, element classes, patterns, etc.

2. detailed descriptive documentation, embedding some parts of the formal reference documentation, such as summary lists of tags

3. declarative code for one or more XML schema languages, specifically RELAX NG or W3C Schema.

4. declarative code for fragments which can be assembled to make up an XML Document Type Declaration.

5. ad hoc generated code, such as lists of elements which cannot contain character data, for use by XML processing tools.

The input required to generate these outputs consists of running prose, and special-purpose elements documenting the components (elements, classes, etc.) which are to be declared in the chosen schema language. All of this input is encoded in TEI XML. The same language can also be used to describe a *subset* or customization of the TEI. To make life slightly easier for users, the 560 elements of the TEI are grouped into 22 high-level modules; a typical customization will specify the modules it needs by providing several `<moduleRef>` elements within a top-level `<schemaSpec>` element, whose @*start* attribute specifies the elements allowed as the root of a document.

```
<schemaSpec start="TEI" ident="test1">
 <moduleRef key="core"/>
 <moduleRef key="header"/>
 <moduleRef key="figures"/>
 <moduleRef key="textstructure" include="body div"/>
</schemaSpec>
```

In the example above, the optional @*include* attribute says precisely which elements from a module are needed (where the default is all members). We may also, however, make more granular changes:

```
<schemaSpec start="TEI" ident="test1">
 <moduleRef key="core"/>
 <moduleRef key="header"/>
 <moduleRef key="textstructure" include="body div"/>
 <elementSpec ident="dimensions" mode="change">
  <attList>
   <attDef ident="type" mode="delete"/>
  </attList>
 </elementSpec>
</schemaSpec>
```

In this case the `<dimensions>` element is changed (using the @*mode* attribute), by having an `<attDef>` deleted, again using @*mode* — this can take the values 'change', 'delete', 'add' and 'replace' at most points in the specification, giving a high degree of control. Of course, this also makes it possible to create a schema

which conflicts with the TEI. For that reason, TEI P5 included for the first time a detailed discussion of the notion of TEI conformance, which declares some constraints on the type of modifications which may be made. One important principle is that a TEI-conformant modification may not alter the semantics of existing TEI elements; another is that only schemas which are *more specific* than the original can be regarded as TEI-conformant.

Other facilities in the language allow the user to rename elements (eg to internationalize them, while keeping the link to the original name), to encode equivalences with other languages (eg mapping the meaning of TEI elements to ontologies like CIDOC CRM), and to define named groups of customization.

The success of the ODD language is that it enables developers to create rich and complex schemas with a minimum of notation, while encouraging and facilitating the production of high-quality documentation and examples which is also expressive of the specific needs of a project.

3. THE ODD TOOLS

An ODD processor needs to be able to assemble all the components referenced or directly provided, resolve multiple declarations, emit a schema in one or more formal languages, and create selected documentary components. The majority of this work may be accomplished by means of XSLT transforms. The TEI Consortium maintains an extensive open source library of XSLT stylesheets to manage all the necessary tasks.[3] The same stylesheet library underpins a number of transformation tools, for example those made available within the oXygen editor, and is also at the heart of Ox-Garage.[4]

For non-expert users, writing specifications in XML is not a simple task. Recognizing this, the TEI also provides a graphical interface to the creation of TEI customizations in a web-based editor.[5]

4. COMPLETING THE LANGUAGE

In the current ODD language, the detailed content model of an element is expressed in RELAX NG embedded inside TEI markup. Can we instead define a set of additional elements which would permit the ODD language to cut its ties with existing schema languages, and make it an integrated and independent whole? We describe below the additional features needed to achieve this goal.

ODD currently supports the *intersection* of what is possible using three different schema languages (DTD, W3C Schema, and RELAX NG). In practice, this reduces our modelling requirements quite significantly. It becomes necessary to treat DTD as a sort of poor relation, due to its inherent lack of support for namespaces, or proper data-typing; it also becomes necessary to renounce some of the many additional facilities provided by W3C Schema and RELAX NG for content validation, and to resist the attractions of SGML-specific optimisations such as the ampersand connector — (a & b) as a shortcut for ((a,b) | (b,a)). As currently conceived, the ODD language has to support specification of content models which have the following characteristics:

---

[2]It was used successfully for the first version of W3C ITS, [6].

[3]http://www.tei-c.org/Tools/Stylesheets/

[4]http://oxgarage.oucs.ox.ac.uk:8080/ege-webclient/ a generic document transformation system which uses TEI as a pivot format. This can manage conversion from (for example) Microsoft Word and Open Office formats to TEI, and from TEI XML to Word, Open Office, HTML, ePub, LaTeX, XSL FO, RDF, JSON etc.

[5]http://www.tei-c.org/Roma/

- alternation, repetition, and sequencing of individual elements, element classes, or sub-models (groups of elements) are supported;

- only one kind of mixed content model — the classic (#PCDATA | g | hi)* — is permitted;

- a parser or validator is not required to do look ahead and consequently the model must be deterministic, that is, when applying the model to a document instance, there must be only one possible matching label in the model for each point in the document.

The first item above is of course common to all target schema languages. We address it by the following small incremental changes to the ODD language:

1) *Specification.* We use three pointing elements (`<elementRef>`, `<classRef>` and `<macroRef>`) to refer to components. For example, the old

```
<rng:ref name="model.pLike"/>
```

becomes

```
<classRef key="model.pLike"/>
```

2) *Repeatability.* RELAX NG indicates this by using the grouping `<rng:oneOrMore>` and `<rng:zeroOrMore>` elements. We follow the notation (from W3C Schema datatypes) already used in the TEI scheme to express cardinality of attribute values, and replace these by the use of a pair of attributes, @*minOccurs* and @*maxOccurs*, on the elenents `<elementRef>`, `<classRef>` and `<macroRef>`, which give more delicate and consistent control over what is possible within the components of a content model.

3) *Sequence and alternation.* Sequencing and alternation are currently indicated by elements defined in the RELAX NG namespace (`<rng:choose>`, `<rng:group>`, etc.) We replace these by similar but more constrained TEI equivalents `<sequence>` which is like `<rng:group>` in that its children form a sequence within a content model, and `<alternate>` which operates like `<rng:choose>` to supply a number of alternatives.

For handling character data, we follow the W3C Schema approach and define an attribute @*mixed* for each container element.

The other two constraints above are not formally expressed in the current or proposed ODD languages. We consider later some implications of relaxing them in the proposed modification. First, we provide some examples, showing how content models expressed using RELAX NG compact syntax may be re-expressed.

The content for `<TEI>` is modelled as follows

```
(teiHeader, (model.resourceLike+, \text?) | \text)
```

in which we have a sequence of a mandatory `<teiHeader>`, followed by a choice between some members of the 'model.resourceLike' class followed by an optional `<text>`, or just a mandatory `<text>`. This is expressed as follows:

```
<sequence>
 <elementRef key="teiHeader"/>
 <alternate>
  <sequence>
   <classRef
     key="model.resourceLike"
     minOccurs="1"
     maxOccurs="unbounded"/>
   <elementRef key="text" minOccurs="0"/>
  </sequence>
  <elementRef key="text"/>
 </alternate>
</sequence>
```

Repetition can be applied at any level. In the content model for `<index>` ((term, index?)*) we have a repeated sequence in which the second item is optional. This is expressed as follows:

```
<sequence minOccurs="0" maxOccurs="unbounded">
 <elementRef key="term"/>
 <elementRef key="index" minOccurs="0"/>
</sequence>
```

The content model for `<p>` is mixed:

```
(text | model.gLike | model.phrase | model.inter |
model.global | lg)*
```

This is now expressed as follows:

```
<content mixed="true">
 <alternate minOccurs="0" maxOccurs="unbounded">
  <classRef key="model.gLike"/>
  <classRef key="model.phrase"/>
  <classRef key="model.inter"/>
  <classRef key="model.global"/>
  <elementRef key="lg"/>
 </alternate>
</content>
```

With these changes, the ODD language is at least as expressive as it was before, and presents a uniform look to the user. We have lost the ability to use other features of the RELAX NG language, but we regard this as a benefit of the changes. The fact, for instance, that in our old ODD, attributes could be defined using the facilities of ODD (`<attDef>` and its children) or directly in the RELAX NG content model of elements presented the possibility of considerable confusion.

5. IMPLEMENTATION

Initial implementations of the changes to TEI ODD discussed in this paper have been fairly easy to put in place, and automated conversion of the 500-plus TEI element specifications has been completed. Conversions back to RELAX NG, DTD and W3C Schema are in place, and produce schemas which pass all the previous tests.

The TEI Guidelines serve as a testbed for the ODD language and for the tools implementing it. They consist of a single ODD document managed as a set of over 800 source files in a Sourceforge Subversion repository.[6] Every new release or update of the TEI Guidelines is the result of an integrated workflow in which the whole ODD document is processed to generate schemas and documentation; the document itself, and all examples therein, are tested against the schemas that have just been generated;[7] subset schemas specified by various other ODD specifications are then used to validate a suite of existing test files and the documentation processed to generate readable HTML, PDF, and ePub in one or more languages. The whole process is managed using a pair of Jenkins Continuation Integration servers at different locations.

6. GOING LARGE

As noted above, our current policy is to ensure that the content models expressible in ODD use only the intersection of the features of currently available schema languages. Very few of the features offered by RELAX NG beyond content model definition are used in the TEI. Instead, other mechanisms are used: a `<datatype>` element is used to associate datatypes with attribute values, using a layer of datatype abstraction additional to that provided by e.g.

---

[6]https://sourceforge.net/p/tei/code/HEAD/tree/
[7]In some cases, the examples are marked as *feasibly valid* using the felicitous notion introduced by James Clark in Jing, http://jing-trang.googlecode.com/svn/trunk/doc/

W3C Schema; the `<valList>` element is used to enumerate legal values for attributes, attribute classes, or element content; and the `<constraintSpec>` feature expresses such niceties as the requirement that a `<list>` element whose @*type* attribute has the value 'gloss' must contain a sequence of `<label>` and `<item>` pairs, or that the @*target* attribute of a `<delSpan>` element must point to an element which follows the `<delSpan>` in document order. These constraints are expressed using the ISO Schematron language, though the specification allows for other possibilities. The goal remains to avoid dependence on any one schema language

This pragmatically-motivated and cautious restriction is not however the only possible policy. Removing the intimate dependence of the ODD language on any specific schema language makes it possible to envisage a more adventurous policy, in which we select amongst all the language features on offer to determine those of most relevance to our user community's needs.

For example, the RELAX NG language has a very useful feature called interleave, which constrains an element's content to be a sequence of single specified elements appearing in any order; that is to say, to define a content model such as (a,b,c,d) but with the added proviso that the child elements may appear in any order. In SGML, the ampersand operator allowed something like this but there is no equivalent feature in the W3C Schema or DTD languages. Suppose now that we add to the ODD language a new grouping element such as `<interleave>`, or add an attribute @*preserveOrder* taking values 'true' or 'false' to our existing proposed `<sequence>` element. Generating a RELAX NG schema from such an ODD would be simple; for the other two schema languages, a processor would choose amongst the following strategies, in addition to the normal processing. Firstly, itt can simply reject the construct as infeasible; secondly, it can over-generate; that is, produce code which validates everything that is valid according to the ODD, but also other constructs that are not so valid; or, lastly, it cab generate very lax constraints, but in addition produce Schematron code to catch 'false positives'.

As a second example, consider the need for contextual variation in a content model. For example, a `<name>` or `<persName>` appearing inside a 'data-centric' situation, such as a `<listPerson>` element is unlikely to contain elements such as `<del>` or `<corr>`, although these are entirely appropriate and useful when encoding names found on a transcribed inscription. Similarly, in a linguistic corpus, it is very likely that the child elements permitted for `<p>` elements within the corpus texts will be quite different from those permitted within the corpus header — the latter are rather unlikely to include any part of speech tagging for example.

At present ISO Schematron rules allow us to define such contextual rules, and something analogous to them is provided by the W3C Schema notion of base types. Suppose, however, that an XPath-valued @*context* attribute were available on any of the elements `<elementRef>`, `<macroRef>`, or `<classRef>` restricting its applicability. Thus, the content model for `<p>` might say something like

```
<elementRef
  key="s"
  context="ancestor::text"
  minOccurs="1"/>
<macroRef
  key="macro.limitedContent"
  context="ancestor::teiHeader"/>
```

to indicate that a `<p>` within a `<text>` element must contain one or more `<s>` elements only, whereas one within a TEI Header must use the existing macro definition limitedContent. Again, we could generate a fully-functional native schema in some languages (W3C Schema), and produce a laxer one enhanced by generated Schematron in others.

Comparisons, as Mrs Malaprop says, are odorous. Each of the three formal schema languages currently available (RELAX NG, W3C and DTD) has distinct adherents and associated software tools. Although it is easy enough to trace their evolution, and to speculate about the differing motivations of their language designers, the practical consequence of this multiplicity is that true interoperability of document grammars becomes more difficult. The fact that these three schema languages diverge so widely in their feature sets suggests that it is prudent to define TEI content models in a way that is fully independent of any of them. Whether that independent definition should take the cautious route of providing only the intersection of their facilities, or the more adventurous one of trying to define a new synthesis, selecting those features most appropriate to the needs of a given user community, is currently less clear. The TEI community, which has long provided a testing ground for advances in document grammars,[8] is perhaps well qualified to decide the question, particularly since (as we have seen) the TEI approach to datatyping already extends the expressive power of the ODD language beyond simple syntactic constraints.

The real challenge of the value of our approach will come in the next decades when, or if, a new formalism replaces XML as the language of choice for structured textual data, and we start work on mapping our TEI abstract language to that new formalism.

7. REFERENCES

[1] Donald E Knuth. Literate Programming. CSLI Lecture Notes 27, Center for the Study of Language and Information, Stanford, California, 1992.

[2] C. F. Goldfarb. *The SGML Handbook*. Oxford, Clarendon Press, 1990.

[3] ISO. *Standard Generalized Markup Language (ISO 8879:1986 SGML)*. International Organization for Standardization, Geneva, 1986.

[4] ISO. *ISO/IEC 19757-2:Amd1 Document Schema Definition Language (DSDL) – Part 2: Regular-grammar-based validation – RELAX NG – Amendment 1: Compact Syntax. ISO version of the RELAX NG Compact Syntax*. International Organization for Standardization, Geneva, 2003.

[5] Lou Burnard and Sebastian Rahtz. RelaxNG with Son of ODD. In *Proceedings of Extreme Markup Languages Conference*. Extreme Markup Languages, Montréal, Québec, 2004.

[6] F. Sasaki and C. Lieske. Internationalization Tag Set (ITS) Version 1.0. Recommendation, W3C, 2007. 2010-10-25.

[7] TEI Consortium. TEI P5: Guidelines for Electronic Text Encoding and Interchange. Technical report, TEI Consortium, 2010. 2010-10-25.

---

[8]It should not be forgotten that the TEI has been a major proponent in the development of what constitutes current orthodoxy in markup languages. The ideas now standardized as XPointer, for example, were first sketched out as TEI extended pointers in TEI P1. Many of the characteristics of the usable subset of SGML which eventually became XML were first explored in the process of defining a scheme adequate to the needs of the TEI community.

Assisted Editing in the Biomedical Domain: Motivation and Challenges

Fabio Rinaldi
Institute for Computational Linguistics
University of Zurich, Switzerland
fabio.rinaldi@uzh.ch

ABSTRACT

One of the characteristics of biomedical scientific literature is the high ambiguity of the domain-specific terminology which can be used to describe technical concepts and specific objects of the domain. This is partly due to the very broad scope of the domain of interest and partly to inherent properties of the terminology itself. There are simply very large numbers of genes, proteins, organs, cell lines, cellular phenomena, experimental methods, and so on. For example, UniProt, the most authoritative protein database, currently contains more than 33 million entries. Clearly, the names which are typically used to refer to proteins are polysemic and might refer to hundreds of different entries in a reference database.

Such a large and extensive terminology necessarily makes it difficult to derive from the literature a simplified representation of the entities and relationships described in the articles, despite considerable efforts by the text mining community. In this paper we propose to complement such efforts with editing tools that can assist the authors in efficiently adding to their publications a minimal semantic annotation so that much of the ambiguity is avoided.

Categories and Subject Descriptors

H.4 [**Information Systems Applications**]: Miscellaneous

Keywords

biomedical literature processing, text mining

1. INTRODUCTION

An emerging trend in information processing is based upon the usage of **text mining** tools for the extraction of tailored information from textual reports such as newspaper articles or scientific publications. The constantly growing amount of information needs to be properly managed in order to be a support in everybody's daily life rather than a burden. One area where this problem is particularly evident is

that of research in **molecular biology**. Text Mining tools aim at supporting the process of knowledge gaining from the literature, by supporting the search for relevant articles, the semi-automated extraction of relevant passages, and the transformation of the information from the textual format to some suitable semantic format.

There are multiple possible scenarios for the application of text mining tools in biology. The most basic scenario, and the one currently most frequently pursued, is the creation of tools for supporting the professional end-user (e.g. a researcher in molecular biology), who autonomously wishes to browse the existing literature in search of information relevant to a particular information need. Another possible usage is within the process of literature curation, which is the activity performed by professionals who are paid to read the literature in search of particular items of information (e.g. newly detected protein interactions), and store such information in public databases, which can in turn be accessed later by the biologists. One example is IntAct [4], a database of protein-protein interactions maintained at the European Bioinformatics Institute. A third even more advanced usage scenario would be within advanced authoring tools for the authors of scientific literature. Novel text mining tools can be used to suggest candidate *semantic annotations* to the author or curators, depending on the scenario of application. The semantic annotations (formal descriptions of the main entities and relationships discussed in the paper), manually confirmed (or modified) by the author or curator, can then be stored together with the electronic version of the article, using one of the standard formats developed by the semantic web community, allowing a much more efficient information retrieval and processing.

The Semantic Web movement aims at enriching web resources with semantic annotations which will allow remote agents to easily find and use them. However the problem of creating these annotations is seldom addressed. Manual creation of the annotations is not a feasible option, except in a few experimental cases. We believe that Natural Language Processing techniques are mature enough to help addresses this issue, at least for textual resources (which still constitute the vast majority of the material available on the web). Documents can be analized fully automatically and converted into a semantic annotation, which can then be stored together with the original documents. It is this annotation that constitutes the machine understandable resource that remote agents can query. A semi-automatic approach is also considered, in which the system suggests candidate annotations and the user simply has to approve or reject them.

The benefits of the semantic web should come for free to most of the users: semantic markup should be a by-product of normal computer use. There is a real need to lower the barrier of entry: the vast majority of the users cannot be expected to understand and use formal ontologies. In order to achieve interoperability between software agents, a lot of human understandability has been sacrificed: precise ontologies and formally defined semantics are foreign concepts to the average users.

One of the motivations behind the semantic web movement was that computers are not powerful enough to process (and understand) natural language. Therefore machine understandable information should be added to web resources. This is still true: it would be unfeasible to process the enormous amounts of textual resources that are added to the web every day (let alone process all the existing web content). However, it is technically possible (and practically conceivable) to have specialised editors that process (in a transparent fashion) textual resources as the users publish them on the web, and add semantic annotations automatically extracted from the documents. In other words, the idea is to move the problem from the consumer to the producer of the information.

The OntoGene team at the University of Zurich has developed advanced text mining applications based on a combination of deep-linguistic analysis and machine learning techniques [14, 2, 11]. In the rest of this position paper, after describing in Section 2 the overall architecture of our text mining system, we illustrate our integrated assisted editing environment (Section 3), and we provide a short discussion on previous evaluations of the system through participation in community-organized text mining tasks (Section 4).

2. THE ONTOGENE TEXT MINING SYSTEM

In this section we provide a brief description of the OntoGene text mining environment. The first step in order to process a collection of biomedical literature consists in the annotation of names of relevant domain entities in biomedical literature (we consider in particular proteins, genes, species, experimental methods, and cell lines) and grounding them to widely accepted identifiers (IDs) such as those assigned by the UniProt Knowledge Base or the Cell Line Knowledge Base (CLKB). The term annotation uses a large term list that is compiled on the basis of the entity names extracted from the mentioned knowledge bases. This resulting list covers the common expression of the terms. A term normalization step is used to match the terms with their actual representation in the text, taking into account a number of possible surface variations. Finally, a disambiguation step tries to resolve the possible ambiguity of the matched terms [11].

A marked-up term can be ambiguous for two reasons. First, the term can be assigned an ID from different term types, e.g. a UniProtKB ID and a PSI-MI Ontology ID. This situation does not occur often and usually happens with terms that are probably not veru interesting. We disambiguate such terms by removing all the UniProtKB IDs, similarly to what done in [17]. Second, the term can be assigned several IDs from a single type. This usually happens

with UniProtKB terms and is typically due to the fact that the same protein occurs in many different species. One way to disambiguate such protein names is to apply knowledge about the organisms that are most likely to be the focus of the experiments described in the articles. We have described in [5] an approach to create a ranked list of 'focus' organisms. We use such a list in the disambiguation process by removing all the IDs that do not correspond to an organism present in the list. Additionally, the scores provided for each organism can be used in ranking the candidate IDs for each entity. Such a ranking is useful in a semi-automated curation environment where the curator is expected to take the final decision. However, it can also be used in a fully automated environment as a factor in ranking any other derived information, such as interactions where the given entity participates.

Using the information concerning mentions of relevant domain entities, derived as described above, and their corresponding unique identifiers obtained by the process of disambiguation, it is possible to create candidate interactions. We use an approach based on a combination of syntactic parsing and machine learning [12, 2]. From the results of syntactic analysis we can derive a number of possible entity interactions, such as protein-protein interactions [15] or drug-gene-disease interactions [14]. These candidate interactions can then be manually validated by the target users, be they expert database curators or the original authors of the article.

The end result of processing by the OntoGene pipeline is a richly annotated version of the original document, where annotations are organized into three levels:

- **Structural Annotations**

- **Lexical Annotations**

- **Semantic Annotations**

Structural annotations are used to define the physical structure of the document, it's organization into head and body, into sections, paragraphs and sentences. Lexical annotations identify lexical units that have some relevance for the project. Semantic annotations are meant to represent the propositional content of the document (the "meaning"). While structural annotations apply to large text spans, lexical annotations apply to smaller text spans (sub-sentence) and semantic annotations are not directly associated to a specific text span, however, they are linked to text units by co-referential identifiers. All annotations are required to have an unique ID and thus will be individually addressable, this allows semantic annotations to point to the lexical annotations to which they correspond. Semantic Annotations themselves are given a unique ID, and therefore can be elements of more complex annotations.

The structure of the documents is marked using an intuitively appropriate scheme based on the TEI recomendations. Broadly speaking, structural annotations are concerned with the organization of documents into sub-units, such as section, title, paragraphs and sentences.

Lexical Annotations are used to mark any text unit (smaller than a sentence), which can be of interest in the application. They include (but are not limited to): Named Entities in the classical MUC sense, new domain-specific Named Entities, Terms, Temporal Expressions, Events.

The relations that exist between lexical entities are expressed through the semantic annotations. So lexically identified entities can be linked to other entities in case they are in some interesting relationship, such a protein-protein interaction or a drug-gene correlation.

3. ODIN

Despite the significant improvements in the last couple of years, most experts agree that, at least for the time being, it is unrealistic to expect fully automated text mining systems to perform at a level acceptable for tasks that require high accuracy. However, existing systems can already achieve results which are sufficiently good to be used in a semi-automated context, where a human expert validates the output of the system. One application where this support is badly needed is biomedical literature curation. Our ODIN system was originally developed starting in 2008 as a visualization interface for the OntoGene text mining system (see Figure 1). It was later modified to serve as a literature curation tool, and in this new role it was first presented in 2010 [9]. We now plan to extend the usage of ODIN to authors of scientific paper, who, even better than curators, can easily disambiguate ambiguous terms, since they are in possession of the primary knowledge that drove their editing decisions.

In the past couple of years a few similar tools have been described in the literature. REFLECT [6] can be used to annotated publications with gene, protein, or small molecules. It can be operated either through a browser plugin or remotely via web interface. DOMEO [1] is a more recent literature curation tools which supports several types of curation paradigms (e.g. highlighting, adding notes, adding semantic tags). It is also notable for its strong integration with ontology services such as those provided by the NCBO (National Center for Biomedical Ontology). However, DOMEO does not offer text mining capabilities on its own, relying instead on external services for this purpose.

ODIN is unique in that it integrates advanced text mining capabilities with a user friendly interface. In case of ambiguity, the curator or author is offered the opportunity to correct the choices made by the system, at any of the different levels of processing: entity identification and disambiguation, organism selection, interaction candidates. The user can access all the possible readings given by the system and select the most accurate. Candidate interactions are presented in a ranked order, according to the score assigned by the system. The user can, for each of them, confirm, reject, or leave undecided. The results of the curation process can be fed back into the system, thus allowing incremental learning.

The documents and the annotations are represented consistently within a single XML file, which also contains a record of the user interaction, thus allowing advanced logging support. The annotations are selectively presented, in a ergonomic way through CSS formatting, according to different view modalities, While the XML annotations are transparent to the annotator (who therefore does not need to have any specialized knowledge beyond his biological expertise), his/her verification activities result in changes at the DOM of the XML document through client-side JavaScript. The use of modern AJAX methodology allows for online integration of background information, e.g. information from different term and knowledge bases, or further integration of foreign text mining services.

The presence of the raw XML in the browser document gives the flexibility to compile dynamically tabular grid views of terms and relations including filtering, reordering, and editing the annotations in a spreadsheet-like way (this includes also chart visualizations). To keep the implementation effort feasible, the use of a dedicated JavaScript application framework is crucial. Among several available JavaScript frameworks, ExtJS, jQuery and Prototype were our main candidates. We then decided for ExtJS because of its compact and coherent architecture covering all kinds of GUI widgets. The advantage of a client-side presentation logic is the flexibility for the end user and the data transparency. For text mining applications, it is important to be able to link back curated metainformation to its textual evidence.

4. EVALUATION

As a way to verify the quality of the core text mining functionalities of the OntoGene system, we have participated in a number of text mining evaluations campaigns [8, 3, 12, 13]. Some of most interesting results include best results in the detection of protein-protein interactions in BioCreative 2009 [15], top-ranked results in several tasks of BioCreative 2010 [16], best results in the triage task of BioCreative 2012 [8].

The usage of ODIN as a curation tool has been tested in a few collaborations with curation groups, including PharmGKB [9], CTD [7], RegulonDB [10]. The next challenge is to test it in a suitable assisted editing scenario.

5. CONCLUSIONS

We have presented an advanced text mining architecture (OntoGene Text Miner), which is embedded within a user-friendly curation interface (ODIN). Currently ODIN is meant to support the activities of expert database curators, however we are planning to further develop it into a tool that will assist authors in creating semantic annotations to be added to papers at time of creation by the authors themselves.

6. ACKNOWLEDGMENTS

The OntoGene group is partially supported by the Swiss National Science Foundation (grants $100014 - 118396/1$ and $105315 - 130558/1$) and by NIBR/IT, Text Mining Services, Novartis Pharma AG, Basel, Switzerland. The author would like to thank the anonymous reviewers for their useful comments.

7. REFERENCES

[1] P. Ciccarese, M. Ocana, and T. Clark. Open semantic annotation of scientific publications using DOMEO. *J Biomed Semantics*, 3 Suppl 1:S1, 2012.

[2] S. Clematide and F. Rinaldi. Ranking relations between diseases, drugs and genes for a curation task. *Journal of Biomedical Semantics*, 3(Suppl 3):S5, 2012.

[3] S. Clematide, F. Rinaldi, and G. Schneider. Ontogene at calbc ii and some thoughts on the need of document-wide harmonization. In *Proceedings of the CALBC II workshop, EBI, Cambridge, UK, 16-18 March*, 2011.

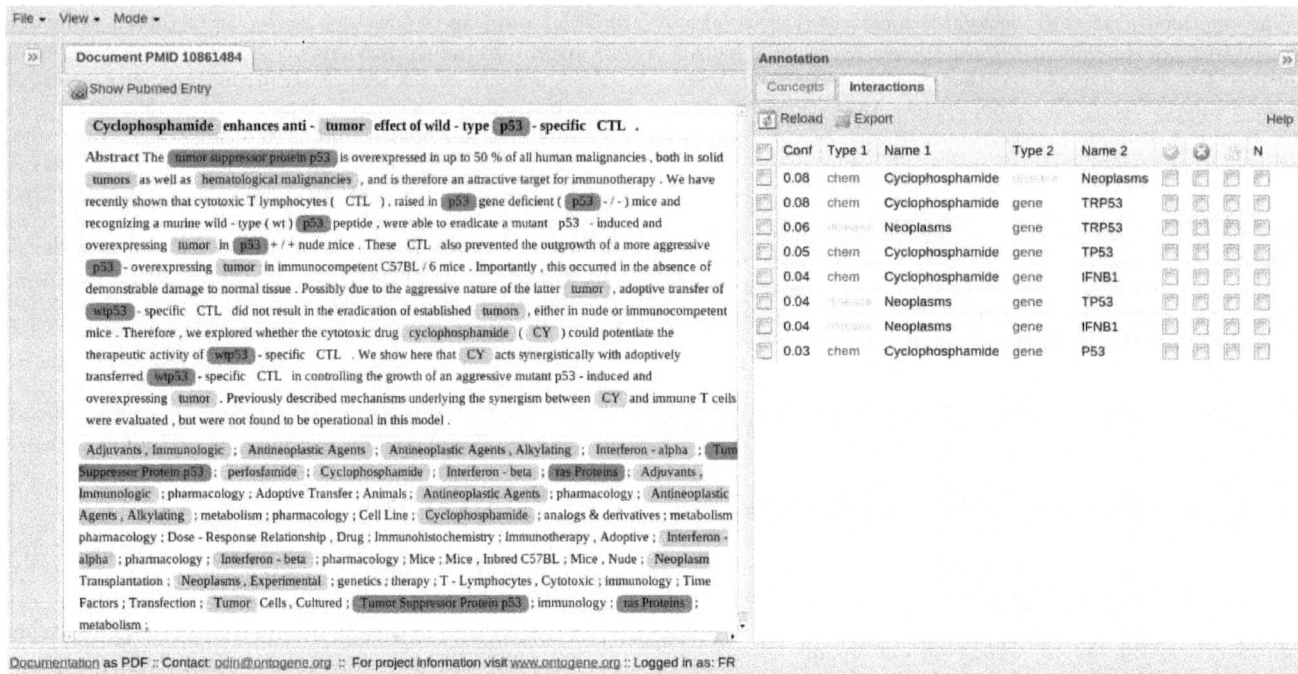

Figure 1: A screenshot showing the ODIN interface

[4] H. Hermjakob, L. Montecchi-Palazzi, C. Lewington, S. Mudali, S. Kerrien, S. Orchard, M. Vingron, B. Roechert, P. Roepstorff, A. Valencia, H. Margalit, J. Armstrong, A. Bairoch, G. Cesareni, D. Sherman, and R. Apweiler. IntAct: an open source molecular interaction database. *Nucl. Acids Res.*, 32(suppl 1):D452–455, 2004.

[5] T. Kappeler, K. Kaljurand, and F. Rinaldi. TX Task: Automatic Detection of Focus Organisms in Biomedical Publications. In *Proceedings of the BioNLP workshop, Boulder, Colorado*, pages 80–88, 2009.

[6] E. Pafilis, S. I. O'Donoghue, L. J. Jensen, H. Horn, M. Kuhn, N. P. Brown, and R. Schneider. Reflect: augmented browsing for the life scientist. *Nat. Biotechnol.*, 27(6):508–510, Jun 2009.

[7] F. Rinaldi, S. Clematide, Y. Garten, M. Whirl-Carrillo, L. Gong, J. M. Hebert, K. Sangkuhl, C. F. Thorn, T. E. Klein, and R. B. Altman. Using ODIN for a PharmGKB re-validation experiment. *Database: The Journal of Biological Databases and Curation*, 2012.

[8] F. Rinaldi, S. Clematide, S. Hafner, G. Schneider, G. Grigonyte, M. Romacker, and T. Vachon. Using the ontogene pipeline for the triage task of biocreative 2012. *The Journal of Biological Databases and Curation, Oxford Journals*, 2013.

[9] F. Rinaldi, S. Clematide, G. Schneider, M. Romacker, and T. Vachon. ODIN: An advanced interface for the curation of biomedical literature. In *Biocuration 2010, the Conference of the International Society for Biocuration and the 4th International Biocuration Conference.*, page 61, 2010. Available from Nature Precedings
http://dx.doi.org/10.1038/npre.2010.5169.1.

[10] F. Rinaldi, S. Gama-Castro, A. López-Fuentes, Y. Balderas-Martínez, and J. Collado-Vides. Digital curation experiments for regulondb. In *BioCuration 2013, April 10th, Cambridge, UK*, 2013.

[11] F. Rinaldi, K. Kaljurand, and R. Saetre. Terminological resources for text mining over biomedical scientific literature. *Journal of Artificial Intelligence in Medicine*, 52(2):107–114, June 2011.

[12] F. Rinaldi, T. Kappeler, K. Kaljurand, G. Schneider, M. Klenner, S. Clematide, M. Hess, J.-M. von Allmen, P. Parisot, M. Romacker, and T. Vachon. OntoGene in BioCreative II. *Genome Biology*, 9(Suppl 2):S13, 2008.

[13] F. Rinaldi, T. Kappeler, K. Kaljurand, G. Schneider, M. Klenner, M. Hess, J.-M. von Allmen, M. Romacker, and T. Vachon. OntoGene in Biocreative II. In *Proceedings of the II Biocreative Workshop*, 2007.

[14] F. Rinaldi, G. Schneider, and S. Clematide. Relation mining experiments in the pharmacogenomics domain. *Journal of Biomedical Informatics*, 45(5):851–861, 2012.

[15] F. Rinaldi, G. Schneider, K. Kaljurand, S. Clematide, T. Vachon, and M. Romacker. OntoGene in BioCreative II.5. *IEEE/ACM Transactions on Computational Biology and Bioinformatics*, 7(3):472–480, 2010.

[16] G. Schneider, S. Clematide, and F. Rinaldi. Detection of interaction articles and experimental methods in biomedical literature. *BMC Bioinformatics*, 12(Suppl 8):S13, 2011.

[17] L. Tanabe and W. Wilbur. Tagging gene and protein names in biomedical text. *bioinformatics*, 18(8):1124–32, 2002.

Managing Content, Metadata and User-Created Annotations in Web-Based Applications

Marián Šimko, Martin Franta, Martin Habdák, Petra Vrablecová
Institute of Informatics and Software Engineering
Slovak University of Technology in Bratislava
Ilkovičova, 842 16 Bratislava, Slovakia
{marian.simko, xfrantam, xhabdak, xvrablecovap}@stuba.sk

ABSTRACT

We introduce a tool aimed to facilitate the management of content, metadata and social annotations assigned to documents in semantic web-based applications. The COME^{2}T (COllaboration- and MEtadata-oriented COntent Management EnvironmenT) allows easy administration of lightweight semantics for the provided content and user-created annotations, which are often created as a result of implicit collaboration between users of a web-based application. We present the tool's most important features and briefly describe a pilot application of the tool when used to manage content for the adaptive learning portal ALEF.

Categories and Subject Descriptors

D.2.2 [**Software Engineering**]: Design Tools and Techniques; H.5.3 [**Information Interfaces and Presentation**]: User Interfaces

Keywords

Semantic Web, lightweight semantics, user-created content, social annotation, content management, adaptation

1. INTRODUCTION

With the emergence of the Semantic Web initiative [2] the need for semantic descriptions (metadata) necessary for machine-readable processing of the Web content or content provided by web-based applications has significantly increased. Semantics is required to enable advanced functionality (e.g., intelligent search or content adaptation). However, it is reported that there is still a lack of semantic data on the Web [3]. One of the possible reasons is the difficulty of manual metadata creation and maintenance.

Moreover, the recent emergence of Web 2.0 let a passive user change into an active author – a contributor – who tags, rates or assesses the content frequently. User-created annotations are becoming an intrinsic part of the Web content.

The content management as such faces new challenges related to metadata and collaborative aspects of the Web. It is important to design tools, which facilitate the management of content enriched with semantics and user-created annotations. Although there are many content authoring systems (e.g., in general-purpose web publishing), it is not unusual that content management in web-based applications is very tortuous, often performed on low-level (e.g., direct database access), not alleviating the content manager's work.

Fostered by the need to manage content for our adaptive learning portal ALEF [7], we have aimed to create a generic tool that will serve as:

1. a content authoring tool,
2. a tool for creating conceptual metadata about the content (lightweight semantics), and
3. a user-created annotations management system.

In this paper we introduce COME^{2}T (COllaboration- and MEtadata-oriented COntent Management EnvironmenT), a tool created to facilitate the management of content, metadata and social annotations assigned to documents used in semantic web-based applications. We describe the overview of the system including the most important features in section 2. We present a pilot application of the tool to manage content for the adaptive learning portal ALEF in section 3. We draw conclusions resulting from our work in section 4.

2. COME^{2}T: OVERVIEW

We designed COME^{2}T to support management of semantically enhanced and collaboratively created content. It is architecturally adapted for this purpose. COME^{2}T can be viewed as a service designed to be utilized by other systems for advanced management and maintenance of content they provide for their users. COME^{2}T is intended for content authors/managers who are responsible for managing content, metadata about the content and user-created annotations of the content. The core use case of the system can be described by the following scenario.

A content author/manager of a web application which provides content for its users – information consumers (e.g., educational system or enterprise knowledge base) – chooses COME^{2}T to manage the content of the web application externally. He creates and updates documents using the COME^{2}T and provides metadata for the documents. After he finishes, he synchronizes content in the COME^{2}T and the client application by sending the newest version of the content to the client application. From now on, the new content is available for users of the client applications. Later, the content author/manager discovers small mistakes in the content when checking user-created annotations. He uses COME²T to correct errors in the content and he modifies user-annotations accordingly. After that, he synchronizes content and user-created annotations with the client application again.

In such scenario – as well as in general – COME²T is a content management server offering services for various client applications which require managing content, metadata and user-created annotations (see Figure 1).

The server-client conception enables all changes by content manager to be made within the COME²T (once a CO-ME²T-client connection is established). The changes involve document changes, metadata changes and user-created annotation changes – the agenda that would be performed by a content author/manager in the client application. The changes in user-created annotations performed by users of the client application (which may or may not involve content authors) remains to be done in the client application. Obviously, the client application users (information consumers, not content managers) do not need to use COME²T at all.

COME²T's logical component model reflects main feature groups of the tool: (1) content management – including documents and repositories, (2) management of conceptual metadata about the content (i.e., conceptualization) – employing concepts of lightweight semantics in particular, and (3) management of user-created annotations. We describe the feature groups in more detail in the following sections.

2.1 Underlying Document Model

Document repositories represent storage for document collections. Each document belongs to exactly one repository.

COME²T currently supports XML documents. Users (content authors/managers) may provide document type definition to ensure validity of documents they want to manage. In addition, they can also supply XSL transformations changing XML into HTML in order to enable user-friendly preview of the documents. Each document can be assigned document-level metadata. COME²T currently supports predefined very basic and limited set of metadata sufficing for pivotal usage. Our next goal is to broaden the support to involve existing metadata standards (e.g., Dublin Core).

As intrinsic to hypertext environment, relationships between documents can be added. They can be defined either implicitly by referencing other documents from the collection within the text (e.g., citing other document, hypertext linking) or explicitly by defining own relationship type (e.g., document hierarchy).

Users (content authors/managers) can define various document types in COME²T to differentiate between documents according to their needs. The defined document types are repository-specific. By allowing to define document and

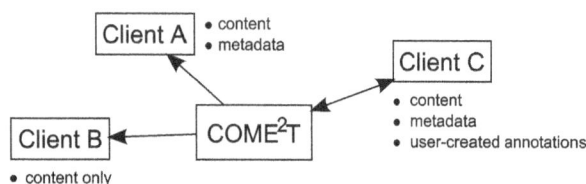

Figure 1: COME²T as a content management server offering services to various client applications.

relationship types on repository-level basis, various different-purpose repositories can be managed within COME²T.

Document creation and maintenance in COME²T is facilitated by various GUI components such as XML file editor, Document viewer and Fast document previewer (see Figure 2, last page).

2.2 Metadata: Lightweight Semantics

The second group of significant features of COME²T is support for content metadata management. We employ lightweight semantics as a form of conceptual metadata about the content. Lightweight semantic descriptions are typically restricted to concepts and relationships between concepts. They are less formal than their counterparts – formal, heavyweight ontologies [9]. We utilize the notion of *relevant domain terms* (RDT), which are elemental lightweight semantic descriptors of the domain area. For example, a document set about Florence can be described by relevant domain terms such as "Florence", "capital", "city", "central Italy", "Renaissance birthplace" or "art". Relevant domain terms can be interconnected by various types of relationships. For example, there can be created is-a relationship between "capital" and "city" or relatedness relationship between "Renaissance birthplace" and "art". Number of relationships to be defined is left to a user (content author/manager). Each relationship type can be defined by attributes such as label or weight. Users can define as many attributes as necessary.

A very important fact about lightweight semantics is that it forms a basis for advanced semantic structures. Hence, it can find application in ontology engineering. In COME²T, it is possible to export created metadata in a predefined XML format to use it in other ontology management systems.

Metadata are managed separately from the content in COME²T by using so called *metadata variants*. Metadata variant represents a view of subject domain's conceptualization. The advantage of separating metadata and content is that several metadata variants can be defined for a repository. This enables to manage different versions of metadata in time, different versions of metadata created by different authors or different-purpose metadata. Analogically to repositories' document types, RDT-RDT relationship types are defined on a metadata variant-level basis.

Each metadata variant is assigned to document repositories by document-RDT relationships. Similarly to conceptual-level relationships between RDTs and relationships between documents, various relationship types with arbitrary attributes can be defined by a user. Relationship types between documents and relevant domain terms can be defined uniquely for a repository-metadata variant pair.

Content metadata management is supported by various GUI components such as RDT table, RDT relationship table, RDT graph visualization (see Figure 2, last page).

2.3 User-Created Annotations

The third big group of COME²T's unique features is related to managing *user-created annotations* (e.g., tags, comments or highlights). We employ the annotation model that allows binding annotation to a particular document part. It has roots in a use case where users create annotations in client web-based systems by selecting a text part of the document and adding annotation content and properties by filling the showed form [6].

Various types of annotations can be defined by a user. Annotation types are repository-specific, i.e., they are not implicitly shared between different document repositories (but they can be easily copied between them).

COME^{2}T comprises various approaches to facilitate navigation and access within hundreds of annotations. It is inspired by approaches to annotation visualization in social web-based systems [8]. The following UI elements are provided in COME^{2}T to visualize annotations of a document:

- in-text presentation – annotations are visualized and can be accessed within displayed document's content.
- annotation sidebar – a sidebar is displayed along the document and it projects the document annotations into the one-dimensional "strip". Each annotation is visualized on the sidebar horizontally next to the place it is located as a mark.
- annotation list – all annotations assigned to the document are displayed in annotation list showing both the annotation's content sample and annotation context – a textual part of the document the annotation is assigned to, together with its textual neighborhood.

2.4 COME^{2}T-Client Communication

COME^{2}T is designed to be the content management environment – a server, which does not track information about its clients. COME^{2}T never requests information itself, it only responses to its clients' requests. Once the client-server connection is established (see Box 1), a client may request the following types of information:

- the managed repository's and metadata variant's actual version – to find out if a new version of documents or metadata is available in the server (COME^{2}T),
- the managed repository's and metadata variant's actual content – to update the content according to the newest version available in COME^{2}T. When requesting to update repository and/or metadata variant, all annotations from the client application are sent to the COME^{2}T (note the bi-directed line at Figure 1).
- invocation of COME^{2}T – to make changes in the document actually selected in the client application (facilitating content management from user perspective).

One of the results of the external content management is that the conflicts may arise between the content present in the client application and COME^{2}T server. This results from the nature of parallel content existence – one serving for presentation and the other serving for management. The

---

Communication establishment procedure:

1. The client asks a list of available repositories.
2. COME^{2}T responses with a list of available repositories together with metadata variants assigned to the repositories.
3. A user selects repository with a metadata variant (from the client application).
4. COME^{2}T generates API key for the client application to establish repository-level communication.

After the communication is established, the client application uses COME^{2}T to manage content, metadata and user-created annotations by using COME^{2}T's API.

Box 1: Interconnecting COME^{2}T and a client application.

cause are user-created annotations, which may be created by users (content consumers) in the client application while users (content managers) in COME^{2}T make changes to the content, e.g., by removing document parts with annotations assigned to it. COME^{2}T tracks information about different states of the content, metadata and annotations to deal with this issue. Particular actions on the managed content are enabled/disabled accordingly.

3. PILOT APPLICATION: CONTENT MANAGEMENT FOR LEARNING PORTAL

To pilot content management for an existing web-based application in praxis, we integrated COME^{2}T with adaptive learning portal ALEF [7].

ALEF is an adaptive interactive learning portal developed and currently employed at Faculty of Informatics and Information Technologies. It provides 4 educational courses related to programming learning and software engineering. It has already served for more than 700 students. It enables adaptive learning by personalizing learning experience via recommendation of educational documents (learning objects). ALEF allows students to interact with the educational content and implicitly collaborate with peers by using several types of annotation such as tags, comments, errors.

Since the main focus of ALEF developers was put on students from the beginning of ALEF, there existed no integrated content management support for educational text and conceptual metadata of educational courses. All data was created manually by creating XML documents and directly accessing the database.

By integrating COME^{2}T and ALEF, we provided convenient content management for 4 existing educational courses and their conceptual metadata (RDT-based lightweight semantics), which is utilized for learning object recommendation and summarization (see Figure 2 for an example). Table 1 provides a list how COME^{2}T and ALEF elements were interconnected. A comprehensive evaluation of the integration is the subject of our further research.

The particular advantage resulting from client-server architecture of the presented approach is that COME^{2}T supports multiple client applications. ALEF as a continuously evolving research project has various configurations such as production version and staging version. We found very useful that multiple ALEF instances have content managed separately by using COME^{2}T.

4. CONCLUSIONS

We introduced COME^{2}T, a tool for advanced management of semantically enhanced and collaboratively created content. COME^{2}T was designed as content management server providing services for various web-based client applications.

Table 1: COME^{2}T-ALEF interconnection mapping.

COME^{2}T	ALEF
Repositories	Educational Courses
Documents	Learning objects
Document types	Explanation, Exercise, Question
RDT relationship types	is-a, related-to, prerequisite-to
Annotation types	tag, comment, highlight, error

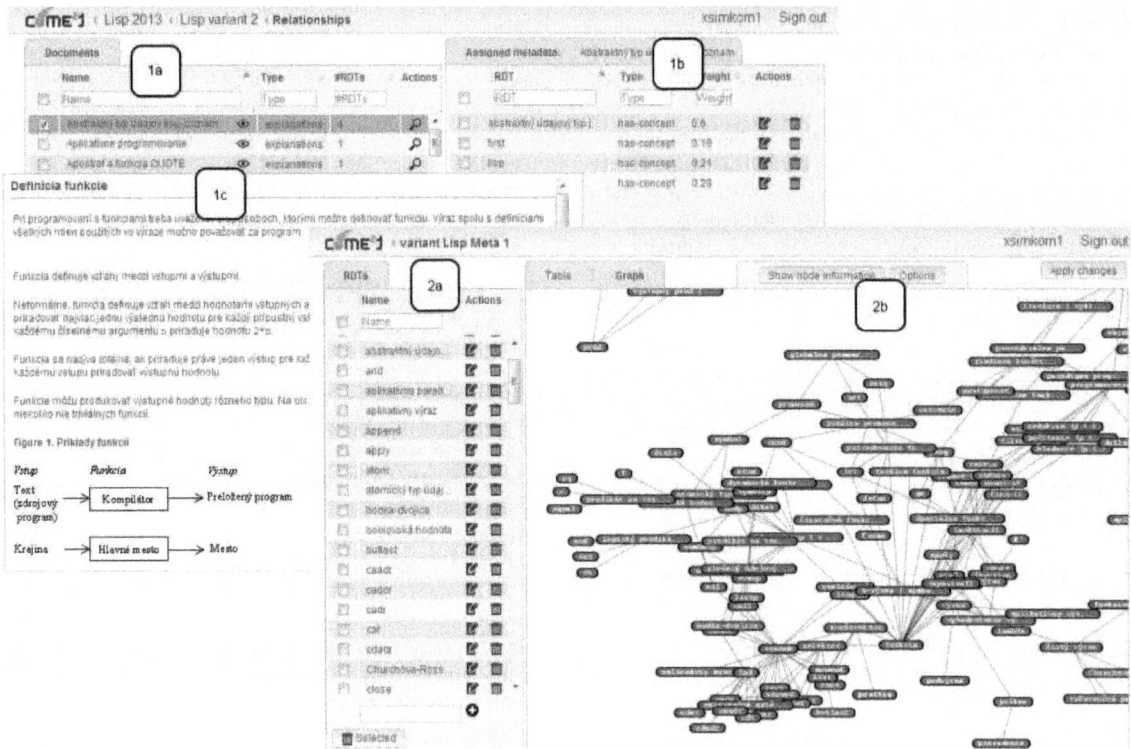

Figure 2: Screenshots of COME²T: 1. upper back – showing repository "Lisp 2013" and documents (learning objects) within (1a), and relevant domain terms assigned to the selected document (1b). Fast preview of the document "Function definition" is invoked after hovering on the eye icon (1c). 2. lower front – showing metadata variant "Lisp Meta 1": a list of relevant domain terms (2a) and graph-based visualization of relationships between relevant domain terms (2b). The presented content coming from ALEF is in Slovak.

Although still under development, core features can already facilitate content management in web-based applications.

We used the adaptive web-based learning portal ALEF [7] to pilot our solution. The content of this portal consists of documents referred to as learning objects and lightweight semantics based on relevant domain terms descriptions. An important distinguishing feature is the ability to assign various forms of annotations by students. In the case of ALEF, lightweight semantics is used by adaptation engine to perform recommendation and summarization of learning objects [5]. The rigid content management prevented to flexibly change and update learning content according to the teacher's needs. Many errors remained in the content and overall quality of the content was reduced. By introducing COME²T, the learning content is now conveniently managed separately from ALEF and allows sending change updates independently from other activity flows in ALEF.

In addition to providing graphical user interface to alleviate content manager's work by making user experience better, COME²T is designed to easily employ methods for semi-automatic metadata generation [1, 4], which can further reduce the burden of manual metadata creation in semantic web-based application.

Acknowledgement. This work was partially supported by the Scientific Grant Agency of Slovak Republic, grant No. VG1/0675/11 and the Slovak Research and Development Agency under the contract No. APVV-0208-10.

5. REFERENCES

[1] Barla, M., Bieliková, M.: On Deriving Tagsonomies: Keyword Relations coming from the Crowd. In Proc. of Int. Conf. on Computational Collective Intelligence, ICCCI 2009, LNAI 5796, Springer, pp. 309–320 (2009)

[2] Berners-Lee, T., Hendler, J., Lassila, O.: The Semantic Web. Scientific American Magazin, 284(5), pp. 34–43 (2001)

[3] Haas, K. et al.: Enhanced results for web search. In Proc. of the 34th Int. ACM SIGIR conf. on Research and development in Information. ACM, pp. 725–734 (2011)

[4] Harinek, J. Šimko, M. Improving term extraction by utilizing user annotations. In Proc. of the 2013 ACM symposium on Document engineering, DocEng 2013. Accepted.

[5] Móro, R., Bieliková. Personalized Text Summarization Based on Important Terms Identification. In Proc. of DEXA 2012 Workshops (TIR 2012), 23rd Int. Workshop on Database and Expert Systems Applications, IEEE, pp. 131–135 (2012)

[6] Rástočný, K., Bieliková, M.: Maintenance of human and machine metadata over the web content. In Proc. of the 12th int. conf. on Current Trends in Web Engineering, ICWE 2012. Springer, pp. 216–220 (2012)

[7] Šimko, M., Barla, M., Bieliková, M.: ALEF: A Framework for Adaptive Web-based Learning 2.0. In KCKS 2010, IFIP Advances in Information and Communication Technology, vol. 324. Springer, pp. 367–378 (2010)

[8] Šimko, M. et al.: Supporting Collaborative Web-Based Education via Annotations. In Proc. of World Conf. on Educational Multimedia, Hypermedia & Telecommunication, ED-MEDIA 2011. AACE, pp. 2576–2585 (2011)

[9] Wong, W., Liu, W., Bennamoun, M. Ontology learning from text: A look back and into the future. ACM Computing Surveys (CSUR), 44(4), Article 20 (2012)

Multimedia Authoring Based on Templates and Semi-automatic Generated Wizards

Roberto Gerson de Albuquerque Azevedo[1], Rodrigo Costa Mesquita Santos[2],
Eduardo Cruz Araújo[1], Luiz Fernando Gomes Soares[1], Carlos de Salles Soares Neto[2]

[1] Pontifical Catholic University of Rio de Janeiro
Rua Marquês de São Vicente, 225
22453-900 Rio de Janeiro, RJ, Brazil
+55 21 3527-1500 Ext: 3503

[2] Depto. de Informática – UFMA
Av. dos Portugueses, Bacanga
São Luís/MA – 65080-040 – Brasil
0055-98-3301-8224

razevedo@inf.puc-rio.br, rodrim.c@laws.deinf.ufma.br, {earaujo, lfgs}@inf.puc-rio.br,
csalles@deinf.ufma.br

ABSTRACT

Templates have been used to engage non-expert multimedia authors as content producers. In template-based authoring, templates with most of the relevant application logic and application constraints are developed by experts, who must also specify the template semantics, report which are the required gaps to be filled in, and how to do so. Filling template's gaps is the single task left to inexperienced users to produce the final applications. To do that, they usually must understand the padding instructions reported by template authors and learn some specific padding language. An alternative is using specific GUI components created specifically to each new developed template. This paper proposes a semi-automatic generation of GUI Wizards to guide end(-user) authors to create multimedia applications. The wizard can be tuned to improve the communication between the template author and the template end user, and also if the template specification is not complete. Many successful trial cases show that the generated wizards are usually simple enough to be used by non-experts. The contributions coming from this paper is not constrained to any specific template language or final-application format. Nevertheless, aiming at testing the proposal it was instantiated to work with TAL (Template Authoring Language) whose template processors can generate applications in different target languages.

Categories and Subject Descriptors

D.3.4 [**Programming Languages**]: Processors - *Code generation, Interpreters, Parsing.*

Keywords

Wizards, Template-based authoring, TAL, Multimedia, authoring.

1. INTRODUCTION

In recent years the proliferation of interactive multimedia applications is evident, both on the Web and on other environments such as digital TV. The increase of available network bandwidth and cheaper hardware are just some reasons that have caused this proliferation. Another important factor is certainly the evolution of processes, methods and techniques of end-user development (EUD) [1], allowing inexperienced users to author interactive multimedia applications.

Typically, templates have been used in authoring by less expert users. Templates define a family of documents that share the same specification for their compositional structure. They are incomplete specifications that have certain blanks that must be filled out in accordance with rules that constrain content and relationships that can be inserted. It is up to end authors to identify and fill the gaps to generate final application.

Frequently, current solutions force end authors to know the template language (to identify the gaps) as well as the padding language (to fill the gaps), which makes authoring by non-expert programmers very difficult. Obviously, it is possible to solve the first problem (to identify the gaps) through an outside documentation telling how to fill the gaps in. Ideally, this document tries to reduce the cognitive distance between the template author and the final application author. Although in some cases meta-languages for template semantic description are necessary, for simple scenarios an informal document can be sufficient.

As for the second problem (to fill the gaps) and for simple cases in which it is possible to use document-centered languages, a visual padding language following the WYSIWYG paradigm can be used. However, it is not that easy to have visual languages for interactive multimedia applications, mainly due to the difficulty to represent multiple (and possibly alternative) timelines and unpredictable events. In addition, languages that allow for specifying templates with constraints on their instantiation tend to make even more difficult the use of visual approaches to fill the gaps.

This paper proposes to use the Wizard pattern [2] to guide end authors in identifying both template's gaps to be filled and how to perform this task. Software Wizard is a graphic interface pattern that guides users through a sequence of well-defined steps to accomplish tasks. Wizards automate (and accelerate) repetitive activities and allow for non-expert users to perform complex tasks, dividing them into small subtasks. Wizards have been extensively used – from software targeting expert programmers (such as IDEs) to software targeting end users (such as word processors and software installers). The use of the Wizard pattern often brings the additional benefit of reducing extra documentation to guide users in producing applications [3].

However, to force template authors to create component interface (wizards) in addition to their basic tasks is not a good approach, since this may increase a lot the complexity of their work. Therefore, this paper proposes the semi-automatic generation of wizard components. Semi-automatic in the sense that the wizard can be tuned to improve the communication between the template author and the template end user, making the wizard questions easier to be understood; or tuned in the case that the template specification is not complete, as some template languages allow.

The next sections are structured as follows. Section 2 presents the template-based authoring background, identifying in which point wizard concept can be inserted. Section 3 discusses some related work. Section 4 introduces the wizard approach we propose and presents an instantiation of the wizard generator and wizard execution engine architecture. In Section 5 we describe an application example developed using the implementation previously presented. Finally, Section 6 is reserved for conclusions and future work.

2. TEMPLATE-BASED AUTHORING

Template-based authoring is discussed in [4] for hypermedia document generation. In this paper we will follow the same principles defined in that work.

Unlike usual design pattern definitions, some hypermedia template languages, like TAL (Template Authoring Language) [4], allow for defining not only common patterns but also a series of constraints on their uses. Thus a *template* for hypermedia applications can be generically described by means of a vocabulary of allowed child-object types (child elements), a set of allowed relations between those types, rules that constraint the instantiation of these child-object types and relations, and a set of fixed components (frozen spots) of the instantiated hypermedia applications.

A *padding document* can at least specify how to fill the blanks (hot spots) of a template. Nevertheless, to guarantee that the template will be strictly followed, the final desired application must be checked against the template specification. This is one of the main roles of a *template processor* that is in charge of processing the template together with the padding document to give rise to a new document in some specification language, called *target language*.

Of course, padding documents, as well as templates, can be generated using some visual language or textual language. Ideally, the padding document is written in any language understood by the template processor. Usually, a specific processor is required for each target language and for each padding document used. Figure 1 illustrates the process.

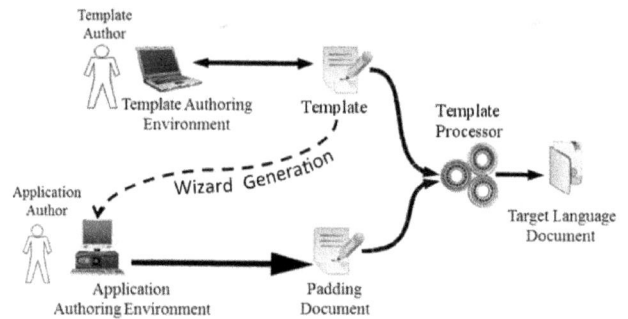

Figure 1.Hypermedia template-based authoring workflow.

The template processor generates the final document, but the process is completed only if the padding document does not deviate from the template specification. So, it is important that the Application Authoring Environment guides the end author to specify correct and complete padding documents.

Template-based authoring can considerably reduce the time for creating interactive multimedia applications. For example, when instantiating a template, authors do not have to worry about specifying complex relationships between objects that compound the application, but only to identify which are the objects that will be part of these relationships. Moreover, since complex applications are often generated from documents with multiple repetitive code chunks, the use of templates can eliminate (or at least noticeably reduce) the need for explicit code repetitions, thus, in addition, reducing the probability of semantic errors that are difficult to identify.

To illustrate the quantitative gain in employing the template approach, in [5] an application example with 10 interactive quizzes is discussed. The final application has 629 lines of target language code, while the padding document contains only 84 lines; almost 90% less than the final application document.

Despite of all advantages, there are still some challenges to be overcome to guarantee the success of template-based methodology when non-expert end-authors are the target. Two of them are focused on this paper: how to identify the hot spots (in a template definition) to be filled in; and how to fill them. Or placing the problem in other words: how to smoothly communicate to end authors which gaps they must fill, and how to help them to build the padding document.

We propose to use wizards in these two phases: wizards semi-automatically generated to assist template authors communicate the semantics and instructions about template fulfillments to end authors, in a language easy to understand; and wizards with a simple GUI to help end authors to fill template's gaps.

3. RELATED WORK

A lot of attention has been devoted to reduce efforts of template-authors in the scope of interactive multimedia applications. Template languages have being designed [4] [5] [6] and some visual tools implemented [7] [8] [9]. However, for multimedia templates with complex temporal/interactive semantics, the currently available visual tools are not much useful to guide end authors to identify and fill template gaps.

WYSIWYG user interfaces are commonly used to fill templates to document-centered languages, like HTML. The main commercial tools, like DreamWeaver, FrontPage, Microsoft Office, Power Point, etc. follow this approach. However, it is not that simple generating this kind of interfaces for languages with temporal semantics, like SMIL, NCL, SVG, etc.

Reference [9] proposes a general framework to non-XML end users. Based on XTiger [10] templates, it proposes a pseudo-WYSIWYG user interface in which a document-oriented editing metaphor or a form-oriented metaphor is provided, depending on the template type. The form-oriented metaphor is used for languages that are not document-centered (e.g. multimedia temporal languages). FORMS-XML [11] is another work that provides the form-oriented metaphor, but derived from XML Schema. The form-oriented metaphor is close to the wizard metaphor we are proposing, though we favored the division of complex tasks in some minor semantically related ones. Additionally, the two mentioned work are restricted to their respective template languages and limited by these languages expressiveness [12], while our proposal (detailed in Section 4) can be adapted and instantiated to work with different template and final document languages.

Like our proposal, other works also realized that a good way to fill in templates is through using the Wizard pattern. For instance, [5] proposes a way to select and fill templates defined in XTemplate 3.0 language using wizards with four fixed steps: the first two steps are related with the selection of templates in a repository; the third one shows the template description and its gaps; and the fourth step allows for users to fill the gaps. Different from our proposal, the questions presented to end users are not automatically generated (they must be created using RDF [13], without any tool support) and semantically related questions cannot be grouped. The solution relies completely on XTemplate 3.0 and, as in the previously mentioned works, does not define how it is possible to support other template languages.

There are a lot of efforts reported in the literature concerning the automatic generation of user interfaces. For brevity, we focus only on those related to the generation of wizards. In [14], Washizaki et al present an automatic approach to generate wizards for initializing software components. The target software components are those based on a framework for Java language modularization and reuse (namely JavaBean). In some perspectives, software components and multimedia templates are similar. However,

multimedia templates usually define complex time constraints that are not present in software components. In addition, accordingly to [15] there are two types of wizards: those that support the use of *software by end users*; and those that support the development of *software by developers*. Multimedia templates are mainly target to end users, while the work of Walshikazi *et al.* targets the automation of the programmer's job. This is an important distinction and it is one of the main reasons why we have included a review phase (characterizing our proposal as semi-automatic) in our wizard approach. To reach end authors, the text of wizard's questions cannot be too technical, making almost impossible its complete automatic generation.

4. TEMPLATES AND THE WIZARD PATTERN

In this section we detail our proposed approach for semi-automatic generation of wizards from multimedia templates (Section 4.1), and subsequently how this process has been implemented using TAL templates (Section 4.2).

4.1 Wizard Approach

The process starts with the template author specifying a template and submitting it to the Wizard Generator, as shown in Figure 2. From this input, the Wizard Generator is responsible for generating two documents: the Padding Document Prototype, and the Wizard Specification.

The role of the XML Padding Document Prototype is to serve as a common substrate for different template languages. The Wizard Generator (component that depends on the template language and on the padding language) must be able to extract from the template specification the hot spots to be fulfilled and to express them in this internal XML document that has the same syntax used by the padding language.

The Wizard Specification contains the step-by-step description of end-author actions to fill hot spots of the template. In an ideal automatic scenario, the Wizard Generator is able to get all necessary information from the template specification to generate the Wizard Specification, without any additional information.

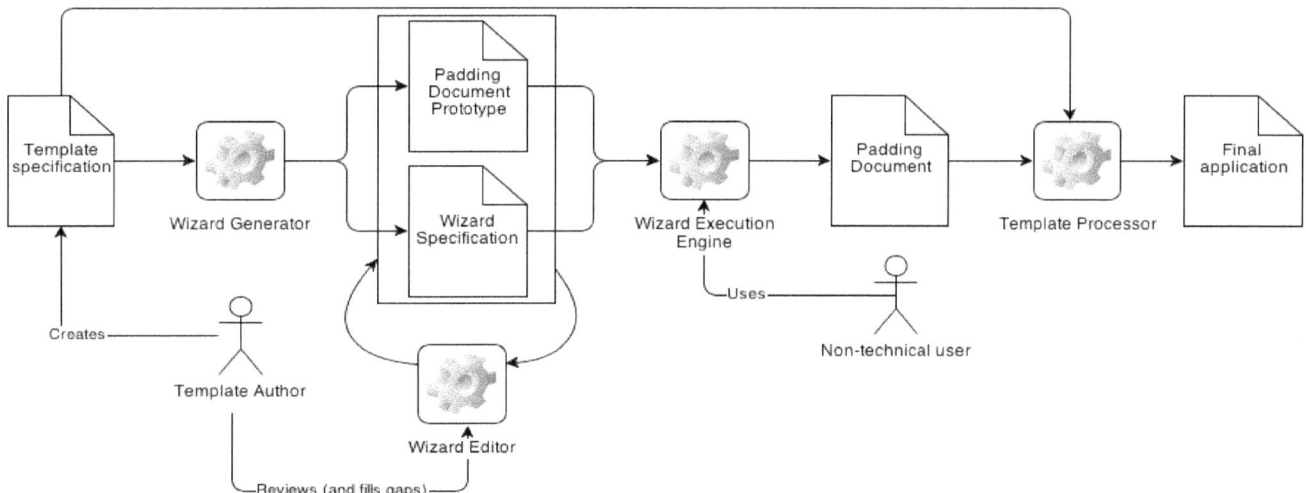

Figure 2. Semi-automatic generated wizard approach.

The generated guidelines for end authors must include all gaps to be filled and all constraints to be obeyed. However, aiming at refining the wizard communication with end authors, it can be tuned by the template author. Moreover, if the template language allows for the definition of families of documents without completely specifying the family members, the template author can also tune the Wizard Specification to restrict or to maintain such freedom.

As aforementioned, the Wizard Specification contains constraints to be obeyed extracted from the template definition. These constraints are compiled to an internal data structure of the Wizard Specification. This data structure will also be used by the Wizard Execution Engine, as discussed ahead in the paper. If some constraints cannot be compiled, the Wizard Specification must be tuned to informally add these constraints to questions to be posed to end authors.

Briefly, in the review phase, the Wizard Specification can be changed, by using the Wizard Editor component or any other external editor. The changes can range from the definition of questions to be asked to end authors until the redefinition of the order and grouping of these questions in steps.

It remains to be mentioned that the process of semi-automatic wizard generation makes sense only if revising the Wizard Specification is less laborious than the completely manual wizard development. The complexity of this review depends mainly on:

- the amount of information the Wizard Generator can extract from the source code of templates; and

- the heuristic adopted to group questions.

Obviously, when reviewing the wizard, template authors should also consider the best semantic flow to fill the template they have developed.

The Wizard Execution Engine guides end authors to answer the questions extracted from the Wizard Specification. With these answers, the Padding Document is built based on the Padding Document Prototype previously generated. Each answer coming from end authors is checked against the internal data structure of the Wizard Specification to which the template constraints were compiled, before filling the gaps specified by the template.

If all template constraints could be completely compiled into the internal data structure of the Wizard Specification, it remains to the Template Processor only to generate the final application from the generated Padding Document and the respective template. Otherwise, to guarantee that the template will be strictly followed, the final desired application must be checked against the template specification by the Template Processor.

We should stress that the Wizard Generator implementation depends on the template and the padding document languages. Moreover, the Template Processor implementation depends on the padding language and the target application language. However, the Wizard Execution Engine has no language dependency. It just transforms XML syntax (the one of the padding Document Prototype) to the same XML syntax (the one of the Padding Document).

We should also reemphasize that the Wizard Execution Engine can check all end-user actions if all template constraints can be compile by the Wizard Generator, making the Template Processor implementation easier.

4.2 Implementation

Moving back to Figure 1, a Template Processor for templates specified using TAL, and using NCL [16], both as padding document language and as target application language, had already been conceived, made publicly available, and discussed in [17]. We took profit of this previous solution in our instantiation of the Wizard approach to ease our current effort. As a consequence, our current implementation is specialized for templates defined in TAL and for padding documents specified in NCL.

4.2.1 From template to Wizard

Figure 3 presents the architecture of the Wizard Generator module, composed by three components.

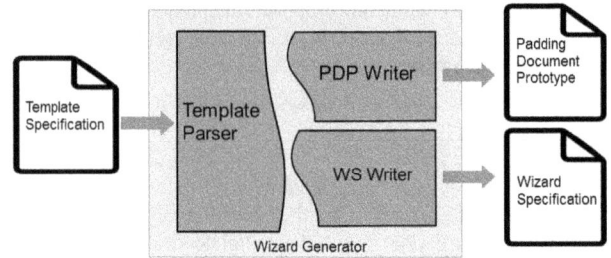

Figure 3. Wizard Generator Architecture.

Upon receiving the template specification document, the Template Parser component is responsible for parsing the TAL template to find hot-spots to be filled and the constraints to be obeyed. TAL vocabulary module [4] provides information about gaps to be filled through its <component>, <interface> and <relation> elements. TAL constraints module [4] provides information about constraints to be obeyed by using <assert>, <report> and <warning> elements. Constraint rules are specified similarly to Schematron [18].

Information removed by the Template Parser is passed to the PDP Writer component, one by one. This component is then responsible for generating the Padding Prototype Document, gradually.

TAL identifies the padding document element to fill a specific gap using CSS selectors [19], for example:

<component id="photo" selects= "media[class=photo]"/>

identifies a *<media class="photo"/>* element of the padding document that must be in agreement with the TAL <component> definition. Following this logic, each gap defined in the template vocabulary module is translated into elements of the Padding Document Prototype. It is a prototype since, depending on TAL constraints, each of its element can be removed or replicated, as discussed ahead.

We must stress the generality of the Wizard approach noting that changes in the Wizard Generator module to work with different template language only implies in changes on the Template Parser component. On the other hand, changes in the Wizard Generator module to work with different padding languages only implies in changes on the PDP Writer. All other components of the Wizard approach are independent from the template, padding and target application languages.

The Wizard Specification (Figure 2) is a document that defines a set of filling tasks or sub-tasks that are instantiated as a software wizard. The document can either be compiled to executable machine code, or interpreted. No matter if compiled or interpreted, the result to the end user (end author) must be a GUI that presents a sequence of steps to be followed by the end author to accomplish a task. In the current implementation the specification is interpreted.

A declarative XML language was defined for the Wizard Specification as an alternative to scripting languages, or other declarative languages like XUL [20] and XForms [21]), mainly to provide more flexibility in the review phase (discussed in Section 4.2.2). Table 1 resumes the most important language elements.

Element	Attributes	Content
wizard	id	step+, constraint*
step	id, title, next	elemInput+, step*
elemInput	id, selector	CDATA, attrInput*
attrInput	type, name, value	CDATA
constraints		assert*, report*, warning*
assert	test	CDATA
report	test	CDATA
warning	Test	CDATA

Table 1. XML elements of the Wizard Specification.

The <wizard> element contains a set of steps (<step> elements), each one representing a given filling task (or sub-task) to be accomplished by the end author. Each step consists of a set of questions (<elemInput> and <attrInput> elements) that the end author must answer.

Each <elemInput> refers to an element of the Padding Document Prototype, has a CDATA content (a question to be answered by end authors), and may have <attrInput> child elements.

The <attrInput> element refers to an attribute (identified by the *name* attribute) of the element referred by the <attrInput>'s parent element. The referred attribute can be completed in agreement with the *type* attribute value. If not completed, the default value defined by the *value* attribute is used. Like <elemInput> elements, <attrInput> elements have CDATA content (questions to be answered by end authors).

The CDATA content of the <elemInput> or the <attrInput> element is a question to be asked to end authors, but only if the constraints defined by the <constraints> element allow for.

Each question in the Wizard Specification document is related to at least one element in the Padding Document Prototype by using CSS selectors. Listing 2 illustrates the elements (questions) related with the <media> element of the Padding Document Prototype of Listing 1 (through class="classA" attribute), which describes a component (id="photo") of TAL.

Constraint rules are defined using <assert>, <report> and <warning> elements to validate end-author inputs. Rules are specified similarly to Schematron [18]. In all three elements the *test* attribute specifies the logical test to be evaluated on <elemInput> or <attrInput> elements, following the same syntax described in [4]. The error or warning message is defined in the content of these elements. The <assert> element requires the test

```
1.  <ncl ... >
2.  ...
3.     <body ...>
4.     ...
5.        <media id="photo" ... class="classA" attrX1="",
                    attrX2="value2", ... attrXn="valuen"/>
6.     ...
7.     ...</body>
8.  ...
9.  </ncl>
```

Listing 1. Example of a Padding Document Prototype.

```
1.  <step ... >
2.  ...
3.     <elemInput id="E1" selector="media[class=classA]">
4.        Do you want create a new "photo"? "
5.        <attrInput name="attrX1" type="string" value="">
6.           Please enter with the value for the attrX1
              attribute
7.        </attrInput>
8.        <attrInput name="attrX2" type="string" value="">
9.           Please enter a new value for the attrX2
              attribute, if you want to change the default
10.       </attrInput>
11.
12.    </elemInput>
13. ...
14. </step>
```

Listing 2. Example of Wizard Specification.

evaluation returns "true", otherwise its error message should be presented to the end author. The <report> element is similar but requires that the test be evaluated as false to not exhibit its error message to the end author. The <warning> element requires that the test be evaluated as false to exhibit its warning message.

Template information extracted by the Template Parser component is also passed to the WS Writer component, one by one. This component is then responsible for generating the Wizard Specification document, little by little.

The simplistic heuristic used in the current implementation creates a <step> element for each hot spot notified by the Template Parser. A <elemInput> element is then created as a child of the <step> element, containing <attrInput> child elements for each attribute required by the padding document for this type of element.

Since the Wizard Specification uses the same Schematron definitions for constraint specifications and the same syntax used by the TAL language, constraints notified by the Template Parser are merely copied to the Wizard Specification document, changing their references to <component>, <interface> and <relation> to references to respective <elemInput> elements.

4.2.2 Wizard Review

At the end of the wizard generation phase, the Wizard Specification document can be tuned using the Wizard Editor (see Figure 1), or using some text editor.

Through using the Wizard Editor, it is possible:

- to re-sort all questions to be asked, and to reorganize them in steps that may contain sub-steps, and so on;
- to rephrase questions to improve the communication between the template author and the template end user;
- to add new questions (introducing new <elemInput> or <attrInput> elements);
- to set new default values to attributes of padding document elements (setting values to *value* attributes of <attrInput>elements);
- to add new constraints (<assert>, <report>, and <warning> elements).

TAL allows for the definition of families of documents without completely specifying family members. Therefore, if desired, in the review phase the Wizard Specification can be tuned to restrict or to maintain such freedom, by editing questions, default attribute values, and constraints.

Moreover, although this is not the case of TAL, some template constraints may not be translated to constraints of the Wizard Specification without losing at least part of its semantics. In this case, tuning the Wizard Specification is imperative.

The Wizard Editor checks every entry against information extracted from the TAL template to only allow changes in compliance with the template specification. Note that the same cannot be guaranteed by editing the XML using a general purpose text editor. Figure 4 presents a screen of the Wizard Editor:

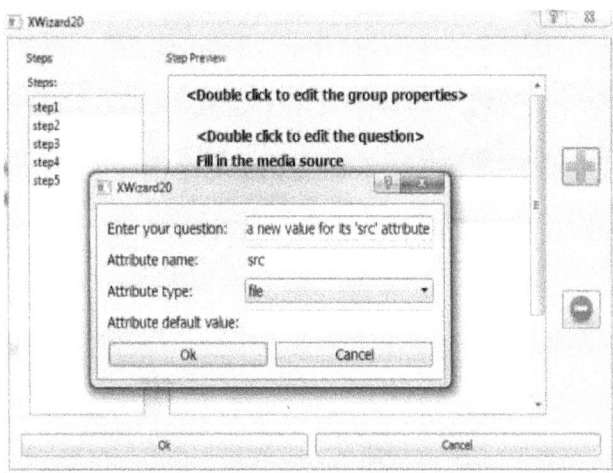

Figure 4. Wizard Editor.

4.2.3 From wizard to the padding document

The Wizard Execution Engine (Figure 1) presents a graphic interface to end authors to ask questions (and receive answers) defined in the Wizard Specification document.

In the current implementation, there is no translation, and questions are textually asked as they are in the Wizard Specification.

Every positive answer to create a new element based on an element of the Padding Document Prototype defines a new element in the padding document with the same structure of its prototype. Each new creation is checked against the Wizard Specification constraints before creating the padding document element.

To each created element, the Wizard Execution Engine asks for values to fill the element's attributes, as defined by the Wizard Specification.

At the end of this interactive process the padding document is completely created. Figure 5 shows a snapshot of the Wizard GUI.

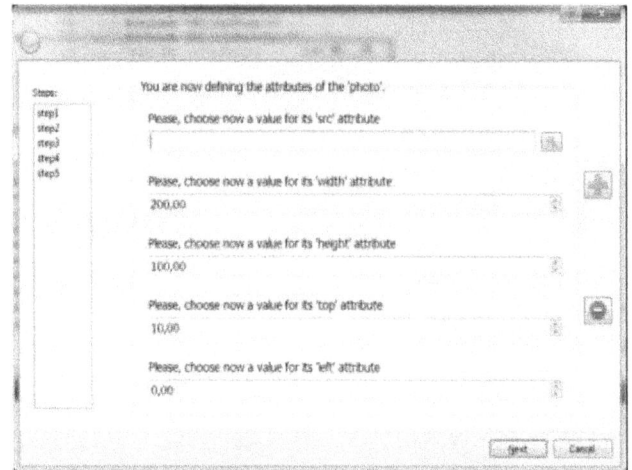

Figure 5. Wizard GUI.

4.2.4 From padding document to the final application

From the padding document and the template specification, the TAL Processor generates the final application. In [17] a complete description of the template processor used in our implementation can be found.

It should be noted that some template constraints cannot have translations to constraints allowed in Wizard Specifications, although it is not the case for TAL. If it is the case, the template processor has the responsibility to check these constraints during the final application generation.

5. USING THE WIZARD

We have tested the wizard approach in the development of many applications. For this section we have chosen one of them complex enough to demonstrate the tool facility but without impairing its prompt description.

We have chosen the family of documents specified in TAL called "Sightseeing of Today". It is an interactive TV show conceived to present a sightseeing tour of any city, in a non-linear and interactive audiovisual way. During the show, viewers are allowed to interact and choose the touristic point he/she wants to "visit" after the end of the current one being presented.

The template was conceived to be used during the FIFA World Cup of 2014 and the pilot instantiated family member is a touristic tour in Rio de Janeiro city (as shown in Figure 6).

Figure 6. "Sightseeing of Today" pilot running.

The family of applications begins with an initial video (template hot-spot: TAL <component> element). In a specific moment of the video presentation (template hot-spot: TAL <interface> element) a menu, composed of images (template hot-spot: TAL <component> element), is shown for a certain period (template hot-spot: TAL <interface> element) allowing viewers to choose the next video to be present. The number of images must be equal to the number of videos that may be chosen (template constraint: TAL <assert> element), and the number of videos has no limit (template constraint: TAL <assert> element). When the current video finishes, the flow continues presenting the video chosen by the interaction. During the next presentation, the selection pattern repeats until the presentation of the nth (template constraint: TAL <assert> element) video, when the video show ends.

TAL relationships (<link> elements) are not hot spots. Relationships are defined between elements of the template vocabulary (<component> and <interface> elements) specifying when each menu must appear and when the next video must start depending on viewer interactions.

For simplicity, let us develop an easy TAL template. Let us assume from now on that: we have a fixed number of videos, more precisely three videos, in the presentation sequence; every menu appear after the same fixed duration from the beginning of the corresponding video in presentation; every menu last for at most the same fixed duration. With these assumptions we have eliminated hot spots defined by TAL <interface> elements. The source code of Listing 3 partly describes this TAL template, badly structured but easy to be understood, in which <link> elements (TAL relationships) are omitted since they are not important to our discussion.

When the Wizard Generator receives the template of Listing 3 as input, it will output the Padding Prototype Document illustrated in Listing 4 and the Wizard Specification of Listing 5.

As can be noted, the Padding Document Prototype inherits the property-names defined in the TAL template translated to the syntax notation of the language used to specify the padding document prototype (NCL <property> elements). In the source code presented in Listing 4, the translated property-names are shown only for "videoA" component – see lines 6-8 of Listing 3 and compare with lines 4-8 of Listing 4. All default values are also inherited from TAL.

The required attributes of Padding Document Prototype elements (in NCL syntax *id* and *src* are required for <media> elements) are also included by default in the Padding Document Prototype. These attributes can be edited in the wizard review phase.

```
1.    <tal:tal id="template">
2.      <tal:template id="sightseen">
3.        <property name="next" value="0"/>
4.        <port id="pStart" component="videoA [1]"/>
5.        <!—Start Video  -->
6.        <tal:component id="videoA" ...
                              width="100%"
                              height="100%" ...
7.                            selects="media[class=videoA]"/>
8.
9.        <!—Second Videos and First Menu in the Sequence -->
10.       <tal:component id="videoB" ...
                              selects="media[class=videoB]"/>
11.       <tal:component id="imageB" ...
                              selects="media[class=imageB]"/>
12.       <!-- Third Videos and Second Menu -->
13.       <tal:component id="videoC" ...
                              selects="media[class=videoC]"/>
14.       <tal:component id="imageC" ...
                              selects="media[class=imageC]"/>
15.
16.       <!--Links are omitted because they are not important to
          our discussion -->
17.       ...
18.       <!-- Constraints -->
19.       <tal:assert test="#videoA== 1">
20.         There must be exactly one start video.
21.       </tal:assert>
22.       <tal:assert test="#videoB > 0">
23.         There must be at least one second video component.
24.         </tal:assert>
25.       <tal:assert test="#videoB == #imageB ">
26.         The number of second videos and the number of
            images to select these videos must be the same.
27.       </tal:assert>
28.       <tal:assert test="#videoC > 0">
            There must be at least one third video component.
29.       </tal:assert>
30.       <tal:assert test="#videoC == #imageC">
31.         The number of third videos and the number of
            images to select these videos must be the same.
32.       </tal:assert>
33.     </tal:template>
34.   </tal>
```

Listing 3. "Sightseeing of Today" TAL template.

```
1.   <ncl>
2.     <head/>
3.     <body>
4.       <media class="videoA" id="" src="">
5.         <property name="width" value="100%"/>
6.         <property name="height" value="100%"/>
7.         …
8.       </media >
9.       <media class="videoB" id="" src="">
10.        …
11.      </media >
12.      <media class="imageB" id="" src="">
13.        …
14.      </media >
15.      <media class="videoC" id="" src="">
16.        …
17.      </media >
18.      <media class="imageC" id=" " src="">
19.        …
20.      </media >
21.    </body>
22.  </ncl>
```

Listing 4. "Sightseeing of Today" NCL Padding Document Prototype.

For each component defined in Listing 3, an <elemInput> element with the same id is generated in Listing 5. For each required attribute (e.g., id and src) in the related element (<media> element) in the padding document prototype, an <attrInput> element is created.

6. CONCLUSIONS

The template-authoring method allows for inexperienced users to develop interactive multimedia applications, since the template semantic and how to fulfill the template's gaps are easily understood. The diversity of applications that have been developed using the semi-automatic wizard approach proposed in this paper allows us to believe that wizards are a good GUI solution for identifying and helping to fill template hot spots in general. From the experience gained upon developing some wizard examples, and after their use by end authors, it is possible to identify the advantages of the proposed approach:

(1) Assist in the communication between template author and template end-users;

(2) No need for additional outside documentation to help end-authors;

(3) Reduced difficulty in identifying template hot-spots (including in complex documents) since end authors are instructed to follow them gradually;

(4) Reduced difficulty in filling the gaps (even for complex documents) of multimedia templates by end authors, since they do not need to learn any padding language;

(5) Keeping authors (template author and template user) in their own abstraction level;

(6) Ensuring that padding documents contain all necessary information to instantiate templates;

(7) Ensuring that all template constraints are obeyed, by incrementally validating end-author inputs;

(8) Possibility of being adjusted to different template and padding languages.

```
1.   <wizard>
2.     <step id="step1">
3.       <elemInput id="videoA"
                         selector="media[class=videoA]">
4.       Please give a name for the identifier of the start video
5.         <attrInput name="src" type="URL">
6.         Please enter the value of the "start video" src
           attribute.
7.         </attrInput>
8.         <!--Here contains questions related to properties of the
           start video -->
9.       </elemInput>
10.    </step>
11.    <step id="step2">
12.      <!—Similar to the step1 -->
13.    </step>
14.    <step id="step3">
15.      <elemInput id="imageB"
                         selector="media[class=imageB]">
16.      Please enter the value of the "imageB" src
           attribute.
17.        <attrInput name="src" type="URL">
18.        Please enter the value of the "imageB" src attribute.
19.        </attrInput>
20.        <!--Here contains questions related to properties of the
           images -->
21.      </elemInput>
22.    </step>
23.    <step id="step4">
24.      <!—Similar to the step1 -->
25.    </step>
26.    <step id="step5">
27.      <!—Similar to the step3 -->
28.    </step>
29.    <constraints>
30.      <!--The constraints are exactly the same of the Listing
           3 -->
31.    </constraints>
32.  </wizard>
```

Listing 5. "Sightseeing of Today" Wizard Specification generated from Listing 3.

However, the approach has also some identified drawbacks:

(1) It is very difficult, if not impossible, to define a heuristic to generate a good Wizard for any document family domain automatically, i.e. without the template author intervention, even if the template comes with an outside metadata document specifying its semantics, hot-spots, and filling rules;

(2) If we can extract only little information from the template specification, the wizard review process can take more time than to write a natural language instructions to template users;

(3) Wizard interfaces are not close to the final result of multimedia presentations (i.e., they are not WYSIWYG);

(4) For particular document families, GUIs developed taking into account the specific concepts of these families can be simpler to be used by end authors;

(5) It can be very difficult, if not impossible, to compile constraints defined in some template language to constraints defined by the data structures of wizard specifications. As a consequence, wizards may not be able to guarantee that the

padding document is complete and correct. Therefore, template processors cannot be relieved of this checking task;

(6) The range of multimedia applications allowed by the instantiation of the process depends on the template language in use.

In special, the drawbacks (3) and (4) are inherited from using the Wizard pattern, mainly due to the data-centric approach of Wizards, which, unlike a document-centric approach, is usually more difficult to be mapped to the WYSYWYG abstraction.

As a data-centric approach, the Wizard pattern is very flexible. As a consequence, its real effectiveness, from the end-author's point of view, will severely depend on the quality of the generated Wizard. If the Wizard questions are easy enough to be understood and the Wizard is well organized in semantic related steps in agreement with the document family in question, it will be effective. On the other hand, if the questions are difficult to understand or the steps are not semantically related to semantics defined by the document family, the Wizard pattern will not be effective. As stated in the drawback (1) it is very difficult to define a general heuristic to create steps that will work on any document family. Thus the review phase is very important in the whole process effectiveness.

Additionally, as stated in drawback (6), the real range of multimedia presentations allowed by the proposed method will strictly dependent on the template language used.

During the wizard development we have devised several future improvements and work. The evolution of the wizard specification language (briefly presented in Table 1) is one of them. Constraint specifications were inherited from TAL that has inherited from Schematron. However, we cannot firmly argue in favor of the solution without trying the compilation of other language constraint definitions. The compilation process can affect the complexity of the Wizard Generator and the effective use of the approach, as exposed in the previous drawback list.

When Wizard Specification documents are reviewed and tuned by template authors, information coming from <attrInput>, <elemInput> and constraint elements can be used to annotate the template specifications. This reverse side effect of the proposed Wizard approach can also be explored as a tool to give some semantics to templates.

Instantiating the wizard approach to other template languages (e.g. XTiger) and other padding languages (e.g., HTML5) is also in our plans. It should be mentioned that TAL processors are also available to HTML padding documents (both targeting NCL and HTML final applications [12]). Having a solution targeting HTML5 using TAL templates is an interesting future work.

The integration of the Wizard implementation presented in Section 4.2 with the NCL Composer[1] authoring tool is another work in progress. NCL Composer will then be able to assist TAL template creation and its store in a Web Service based repository. Moreover, with NCL Composer it would be possible to look for a template in this Web repository and generate the padding document using the Wizard complemented with the views offered by NCL Composer. This can at least minimize the fact that the Wizard does not provide a WYSIWYG way to fill template's gaps.

The Wizards approach was recently integrated to a corporate digital TV solution. In this corporate broadcaster, the great majority of applications will be developed by journalists following specific templates. This will be an important field trial for which we have already started a qualitative research to get feedback from both template authors and end authors about the effectiveness of our Wizard approach.

7. ACKNOWLEDGMENTS

This work was partially supported by CNPq and CAPES, Brazilian funding agencies, and by the Brazilian Ministry of Science, Research and Innovation. We thank all TeleMidia and LAWS colleagues for their contributions to this work.

8. REFERENCES

[1] M BURNETT, "What is end-user software engineering and why does it matter?," *Proceedings of the 2nd International Symposium on End-User Development*, pp. 15–28, 2009.

[2] M. Welie, "The Wizard Pattern," in *CHI 2000 Workshop on Pattern Languages for Interaction Design: Building Momentum*, 2000.

[3] Lori Phelps, "Active documentation: wizards as a medium for meeting user needs," *Proceedings of the 15th annual international conference on Computer documentation (SIGDOC '97)*, pp. 207-210, 1997.

[4] C. S. Soares Neto, L. F. G. Soares, and C. S. de Souza, "TAL - Template Authoring Language," *Journal of the Brazilian Computer Society*, vol. 18, no. 3, pp. 185-199, September 2012.

[5] J. A. F. dos Santos and D. C. Muchaluat-Saade, "XTemplate 3.0: spatio-temporal semantics and structure reuse for hypermedia compositions," *Multimedia Tools and Applications*, vol. 61, pp. 645-673, December 2012.

[6] Stéphane Sire, Christine Vanoirbeek, Vincent Quint, and Cécile Roisin, "Authoring XML all the Time, Everywhere and by Everyone," in *XML Prague*, 2010.

[7] Romain Deltour and Cécile Roisin, "The limsee3 multimedia authoring model," in *2006 ACM symposium on Document engineering (DocEng '06)*, New York, NY, USA, 2006, pp. 173-175.

[8] J. Damasceno, J. dos Santos, and D. C. Muchaluat-Saade, "EDITEC: hypermedia composite template graphical editor for interactive tv authoring.," in *11th ACM symposium on Document engineering (DocEng '11).*, New York, NY, USA., 2011, pp. 77-80.

[9] C. Vanoirbeek, V. Quint, S. Sire, and C. Roisin, "A Lightweight Framework for Authoring XML Multimedia Content on the Web," *Multimedia Tools and Applications*, June 2012.

[10] St'ephane Sire. (2010, January) XTiger XML Language Specification. [Online]. http://media.epfl.ch/Templates/XTiger-XML-spec.html Accessed in 29/05/2013.

[11] Y. S. Kuo, N. C. Shih, Lendle Tseng, and Hsun-Cheng Hu, "Generating Form-Based User Interfaces for XML Vocabularies," in *DocENg*, Bristol, United Kingdom, 2005.

---

[1] http://composer.telemidia.puc-rio.br

[12] Francesc Campoy Flores, Vicent Quint, and Ir`ene Vatton ', "Templates, Microformats and Structured Editing ," in *ACM Symposium on Document Engineering*, Amsterdam, 2006.

[13] W3C. (2004) Resource description framework (rdf): Concepts and abstract syntax. [Online]. http://www.w3.org/TR/2004/REC-rdf-concepts-20040210/ Accessed in 29/05/2013.

[14] Hironori Washizaki, Shinichi Honiden, Rieko Yamamoto, Takao Adachi, and Yoshiaki Fukazawa, "Automatic Generation of Software Component Wizards based on the Wizard Pattern," in *Advances in Systems, Computing Sciences and Software Engineering*.: Springer Netherlands, 2006, pp. 61-68.

[15] Takao Adachi and Yoshiaki Fukazawa, "Generating Wizards for Initializing Software Components," in *7th IEEE International Conference on Computer and Information Technology, 2007. CIT 2007.*, Tokyo, 2007, pp. 873-878.

[16] L. F. G. Soares and R. F. Rodrigues, "Nested Context Language 3.0 Part 8 - NCL Digital TV Profiles," Informatics Department of PUC-Rio, Rio de Janeiro, MCC 35/06, 2006. [Online]. http://www.ncl.org.br/documentos/NCL3.0-DTV.pdf Accessed in 29/05/2013.

[17] C. S. Soares Neto, H. F. Pinto, and L. F. G. Soares, "TAL processor for hypermedia applications," in *2012 ACM symposium on Document engineering (DocEng '12).*, New York, NY, USA, 2012, pp. 69-78.

[18] Rick Jelliffe, "Schematron specification (ISO/IEC 19757-3)," 2006.

[19] W3C. (2009) Cascading style sheets level 2 revision 1 (CSS 2.1). [Online]. http://www.w3.org/TR/CSS2/ Accessed in 29/05/2013.

[20] XUL Wizard. [Online]. https://developer.mozilla.org/en-US/docs/XUL/wizard_Accessed in 29/05/2013

[21] W3C. (2012, August) XForms 2.0. W3C Working Draft 7 August 2012. [Online]. http://www.w3.org/TR/xforms20/ Accessed in 29/05/2013

Content-based Copy and Paste from Video Documents

Laurent Denoue
FX Palo Alto Laboratory
3174 Porter Dr.
Palo Alto, CA, 94304 USA
denoue@fxpal.com

Scott Carter
FX Palo Alto Laboratory
3174 Porter Dr.
Palo Alto, CA, 94304 USA
carter@fxpal.com

Matthew Cooper
FX Palo Alto Laboratory
3174 Porter Dr.
Palo Alto, CA, 94304 USA
cooper@fxpal.com

ABSTRACT
Unlike text, copying and pasting parts of video documents is challenging. Yet, the abundance of video documents now available including how-to tutorials requires simpler tools that allow users to easily copy and paste fragments of video materials into new documents. We describe new direct video manipulation techniques enabling users to quickly copy and paste content from video documents into a user's own multimedia document. While the video plays, users interact with the video canvas to select text regions, scrollable regions, slide sequences built up across many frames, or semantically meaningful regions such as dialog boxes. Instead of relying on the timeline to accurately select sub-parts of the video document, users navigate using familiar selection techniques such as mouse-wheel to scroll back and forward over a video shot in which the content scrolls, double-clicks over rectangular regions to select them, or clicks and drags over textual regions of the video canvas to select them. We describe the video processing techniques that run in real-time in modern web browsers using HTML5 and JavaScript; and show how they help users quickly copy and paste video fragments into new documents, allowing them to efficiently reuse video documents for authoring or note-taking.

Categories and Subject Descriptors
H.5.1 Multimedia Information Systems; I.7.5 [Document and Text Processing]: Document Capture - document analysis; H.5.2 [Information Interfaces and Presentation]: User Interfaces

Keywords
Video Document Structure and Analysis; User interaction for content reuse; Real-time Video Document Processing; Document Authoring Tools

1. INTRODUCTION
Every day, millions of users watch How-To video documents such as screencasts to educate themselves about programming, design, using new software or configuring computer systems, using a particular web site, listening to lectures, etc. Unlike text documents though, reusing content from video documents is hard. Few users would even take a simple screenshot of a video frame

because it involves too much work: users need to pause the video, take a screenshot, crop it, and paste the image into their favorite document editor.

Inspired by work on direct video manipulation such as [1] and [2], we developed a set of techniques where users directly interact with video content using familiar techniques such as dragging a selection box over an area to highlight text, mouse-wheel to scroll up and down, or double-click to identify rectangular areas of importance, and show how they can be extended to accommodate the temporal nature of video documents. We show how to adapt existing document processing techniques and create novel ones to make it easy for users to copy and paste parts of video documents.

2. MOTIVATIONAL SCENARIOS
To motivate this vision, we describe three scenarios based on our experience observing users manipulate video documents.

2.1 Copying text from a video
Many tutorial screencast videos primarily show the presenter typing computer code into a text editor. Ideally, the viewer would like to pause the video when the line is completely typed or the function finished in order to review the code. However, using the timeline to accurately position the video time can be challenging. Our goal is instead to allow the user to click and drag over the video canvas where the line is being typed; quickly drag her selection toward the right to reveal the next video frames and finally lift when the line appears complete. She can then paste that part of the video canvas into her personal notes document as an image, request that the image be converted to text via OCR, or paste the section as a sequence of frames encapsulated in an animated GIF showing how the text was originally entered.

2.2 Copying a scrolled region
Video screencasts depicting web site creation or use often involve the presenter scrolling up or down within a browser or text editor to reveal new content. To document this particular interaction a user needs to 1) carefully position the video when the page starts scrolling; 2) run her favorite screen recorder (possibly identifying what region to capture); 3) play the video until the scroll action is complete; 4) quickly stop the screen capture recorder, and 5) finally paste the video file into her favorite document editor (which may be a complicated process in and of itself). Our goal is to make this process easier by allowing the user to move the mouse-wheel up and down over the video canvas to indicate in a single action the beginning, end and region of interest. Our system can then automatically generate an animated GIF of that video segment and region, ready to be pasted into a document editor.

2.3 Copying a region of interest

Consider a user watching a tutorial explaining how to setup a project in XCode who wants to copy and paste a fragment of the video frame showing how to configure a particular dialog box. Currently the user would need to stop the video, capture a picture of the screen, paste it into a photo editor, select the region of interest, and then copy that to a document editor. Our goal is to allow her to directly double-click inside the dialog box and have the system automatically record and crop the frames while this dialog box is visible in the video stream, while again making content available for pasting into a document editor.

Below, we describe a system we implemented that exemplifies our vision. We first present the architecture that lets us process users' actions over a video canvas using HTML5 and JavaScript. We then describe how the system maps traditional mouse or touch-based interactions over the video canvas to selection actions, and present the accompanying document processing techniques used to find text, and identify scrolled and rectangular areas in the video. Finally we describe our multimedia document editor.

3. DETECTION AND SELECTION

The core of the system runs in a web browser. Video is embedded as an HTML5 video and JavaScript paints incoming frames in a CANVAS element. Pixel data is manipulated in JavaScript to perform real-time video and document processing such as binarization, frame differencing, line-detection, connected-components analysis and scroll detection across frames.

In order to process video frames from a VIDEO tag inside our web page, the original (currently YouTube hosted) video is served through a proxy server written in NodeJS. The proxy reads video content from YouTube and streams it back to the client's browser, thus solving the same-domain policy constraint.

A timer is used to continuously draw incoming frames onto a CANVAS element that the user sees. JavaScript event listeners are attached to this element and trigger the different actions: double-click triggers region detection, mouse-wheel triggers scroll-analysis, and click and drag triggers text detection. We now describe useful direct video manipulation techniques and how they are used to quickly copy and paste parts of video documents.

3.1 Detecting regions in the video document

Incoming frames are first binarized using a simplified edge detector that finds vertical and horizontal edges in the video frame: it reports 1 if the gray scale value of adjacent (horizontally or vertically) pixels is greater than 32 and 0 otherwise (see Figure 1). We then find edges by counting lines and columns where 1 is found more than 40 times in a row or column.

When the user double clicks on the canvas showing the video frames, the system finds the smallest encompassing rectangle using the horizontal and vertical lines found above. If a rectangle is found, the system draws a blue rectangle to show users their current "selection". Because there might be several candidate rectangles, subsequent double-clicks prompt the system to show the next rectangle outside the current one. When the last rectangle is shown, the cycle repeats.

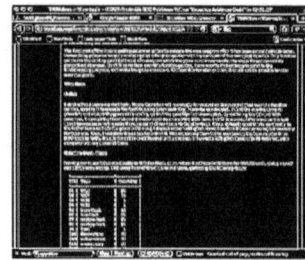

Figure 1. Video frames are binarized using a fast edge detector; vertical and horizontal lines are found by counting series of white pixels; when the user clicks, the system can find rectangular areas around the click position.

At this point, if the user initiates a Copy command using the keyboard or other means, the system automatically generates a PNG image out of the cropped area from the video canvas and copies it into the clipboard. If instead the user starts a left or right drag operation over the canvas, the system draws previous or next frames, depending on the drag direction. When the rectangular region is no longer detected at the same location, the system stops showing previous or next frames. At this point, if the user issues a Copy action, the system generates an animated GIF of all the frames found between the start and end time in the video sequence where that rectangular region was shown.

3.2 Detecting scrolling areas

In order to detect scrolled frame regions, we compute the difference between the binarized versions of the previous and current frames. Vertical and horizontal projection profiles are then computed to find the changed region. The best correlation is computed by finding the minimum difference of vertically shifted pairs of pixel columns, as shown on the bottom-right of Figure 2. If most columns agree on a similar vertical shift, we use the average of the votes as the scroll value, and store the frame in an array along with the current video playback time and scroll value. We currently do not compute horizontal scrolls because they are not common in screencasts, which typically depict computer content that scrolls vertically.

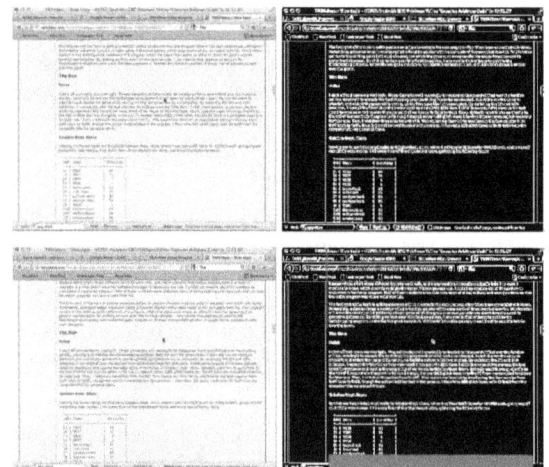

Figure 2. Left column shows 2 frames and their binary version on the right; Bottom-right: red overlay shows the amount of scroll found between the 2 binary images.

This computation is always performed, but frames and their scroll values are discarded after 5 seconds in order to minimize the memory footprint.

When the user initiates a mouse-wheel action over the video canvas when scrolled frames have been detected, the system overlays a scroll indicator to tell the user she is now driving the video using her mouse-wheel. At this point, mouse-wheel events indicate what frames to draw over the video canvas: mouse-wheel up shows previous frames and mouse-wheel down shows next frames. This method allows the user to quickly replay a passage of the video where content is scrolling vertically.

The system stops rewinding when the scroll value reaches 0 in either direction. Note that when the user started to mouse-wheel, the video kept playing in the background and frames were still being captured and processed to determine their scroll values. If the user's mouse-wheel event catches up with the real-time and frames are still being scrolled, the system keeps showing them to the user, and stops once no scrolling is found for at least 1 second.

When the user clicks over the canvas, the system records the time as either the beginning or end of the upcoming Copy action. Upon receipt of a Copy command, the system generates an animated GIF with the collection of frames between the start and end times. If the user has not clicked, the range is defined as the oldest and newest times reached by the user with mouse-wheel events.

3.3 Selecting text from video
When the user clicks over the video canvas, the system binarizes the current video frame, computes its connected components and their bounding boxes using [3] and defines the initial selection box rectangle (see Figure 3).

Figure 3. When the user starts a drag operation, the bounding boxes of connected components are computed

The system visually highlights the bounding boxes under this rectangle, mimicking what happens when a user selects text in a regular text-based widget. When the user initiates a drag to expand her selection box, the system updates the corresponding boxes underneath.

As before, the video is still playing in the background: the system accumulates incoming frames and performs connected components computations. Meanwhile, the user is shown the last frame corresponding to connected-components that match her selection box. This frame is updated whenever the selection changes and overlaps connected components in other frames. When found, the system draws that frame over the main canvas, giving the illusion that the video seeks to reveal more text (Figure 4). Similarly, if the user reduces the selection box to the left, the system finds previous frames that have connected components under the current selection but none to its right; again, this gives the illusion for the user that she navigates back into the video.

Figure 4. Text selection from video: as the user's selection extends to the right, the system displays future frames where boxes of connected-component are found under the user's selection box, allowing her to finely adjust the selection to copy into a new document.

When the user lifts the mouse pointer, the system copies the currently shown frame as an image and also generates an animated GIF of the frames accumulated from the left-most to the right-most selection points. When the user pastes this data, she can choose what flavor to keep.

3.4 Selecting text across many frames
In many conference or lecture-type video recordings, the presenter shows a deck of slides, either shown intermittently (presenter/slide/presenter/slide) or always in the background of the room. Based on previous work [4], video slides are automatically detected and indexed on the server. When a user initiates a text selection over a slide and extends her selection box, the system is able to seek the video past the non-slide frames and get frames of the new slide. This allows users to select text from slides that are built-up across longer spans of time. For example, the presenter shows a slide with one header, talks for 30 seconds, then shows the same slide with a new sub-header. Our user can select the first line when the slide is first shown, then extend her selection box below and automatically have the system "jump" to the time when the second slide is shown with the second line underneath. When the user lifts the mouse pointer, the system only generates an animation of the slides found in between.

4. MULTIMEDIA DOCUMENT EDITOR
In our system, content extracted from video documents is placed on the clipboard in multiple data formats to support graceful degradation across applications with different levels of multimedia support. For basic document editors, such as text and photo editors, we paste content in 'text/plain', 'image/jpeg', 'audio/mp3', etc. format as appropriate. For editors with slightly more support we paste content as 'text/html' to support more advanced interaction, such as links from the pasted content back to the source video. Finally, we also paste content onto the clipboard using a manually defined format that our HTML5-based multimedia document editing tool (Figures 5, 6, 7) can parse.

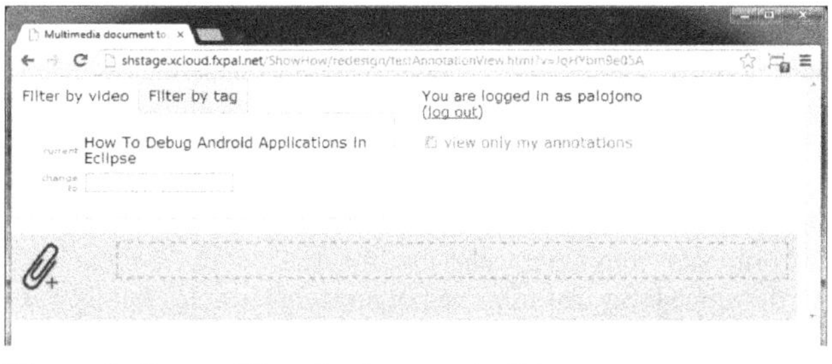

Figure 5. Our multimedia document editor.

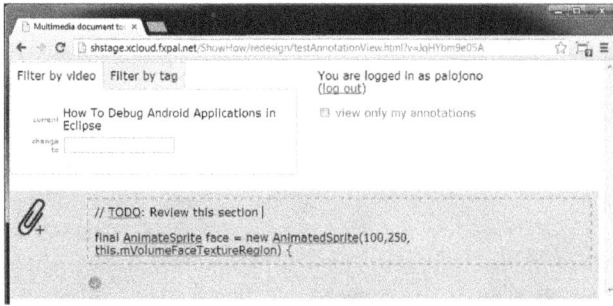

Figure 6. Users type or paste content into the yellow textboxes to begin creating a new annotation.

Figure 6 shows how users can create a new annotation within our multimedia document editor by pasting selected text that was copied from a video document. OCR tools are then used to convert the image (video frame) text to the pasted content. If the text conversion does not rise above a pre-set confidence threshold the content is instead pasted in as an image.

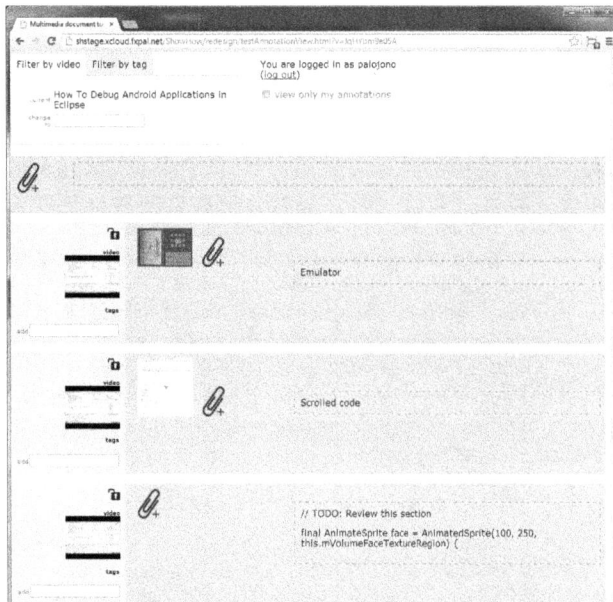

Figure 7. A view of the multimedia document from Figure 6 after using our tools to copy-and-paste a region from a video (top), a compilation of frames from a scrolled section of a video (middle), and the previously selected text (bottom) .

Figure 7 shows annotations extracted using the selection techniques described in Section 3 including a video region, a compilation of frames from a scrolled section of a video, and text. Each gray area is a separate, "annotation" containing any number of media attachments and text. The lighter gray area in the left portion of each annotation contains meta-data including the video with which the annotation is associated as well as tags and privacy settings. All annotation media are linked back to their source videos (if available). Users can drag-and-drop media onto the paperclip icons or use the keyboard to paste content. Media can originate from other webpages, the desktop, or from the tools we developed. So that users can organize their notes flexibly, all elements are immediately editable, and users can drag media between annotations as well as reorder the annotations.

5. FUTURE WORK

One can imagine interesting extensions to this work, such as tracking windows being moved over the video (perhaps using techniques presented in [2]) and navigating the video timeline accordingly, or listening to keyboard events such as backspace or cursor arrows to rewind or fast-forward the video to corresponding text elements.

Desktop widgets are another common type of content seen in screencasts, for example a series of drop down menus in a PhotoShop tutorial. It is conceivable that the user watching the video would want to click on the menu over the video canvas and have the system automatically skip to frames where sub-menus are showing, allowing the user to quickly copy and paste the entire sequence of actions into the new document.

Also, many recorded lectures feature the presenter's slides warped in a non-rectangular shape; we could extend our current rectangular region detection to accommodate for these geometries and let users paste a rectified rectangular portion of the slides.

6. CONCLUSION

With millions of people trying to learn every day from video documents, it is important to develop tools that allow them to quickly copy and paste fragments of these documents into new documents, like it is possible today with text-based documents.

We presented initial steps in that direction for certain kinds of video documents and proposed techniques to directly manipulate video content. Users can 1) easily scroll up and down over a video to automatically rewind or fast-forward the video, 2) easily select text content from video frames, including automatic skipping of frames until the desired text segment is shown, and 3) easily identify rectangular areas of the video canvas that correspond to commonly seen widgets such as windows and dialog boxes. We described an implementation of these techniques that runs in real-time inside a modern web browser using HTML5 video, CANVAS element and JavaScript.

7. ACKNOWLEDGMENTS

Our thanks to FXPAL management, especially Larry Rowe and Lynn Wilcox for supporting this research.

8. REFERENCES

[1] Dragicevic, P., Ramos, G., Bibliowitcz, J., Nowrouzezahrai, D., Balakrishnan, R., and Singh, K. 2008. Video Browsing by Direct Manipulation. In Proceedings of ACM CHI 2008. 237-246.

[2] Goldman , D.B, Gonterman, C., Curless, B., Salesin, D., Seitz, S.M. 2008. Video object annotation, navigation, and composition. In Proceedings of ACM UIST 2008. 3-12.

[3] Chang, F., Chen, C-J., and Lu, C-J. A linear-time component-labeling algorithm using contour tracing technique. Computer Vision and Image Understanding, 93(2). 2004. 206-220.

[4] Adcock, J., Cooper, M., Denoue, L., Pirsiavash, H., and Rowe, L.A. TalkMiner: A Lecture Webcast Search Engine. In Proceedings of ACM Multimedia 2010. 241-250.

MoViA: A Mobile Video Annotation Tool

Bruna C. R. Cunha, Olibário J. Machado Neto, Maria da Graça Pimentel
Universidade de São Paulo
São Carlos, SP - Brazil
{brunaru, olibario, mgp}@icmc.usp.br

ABSTRACT

The user interaction with mobile devices has dramatically improved over the last years. Increasingly we rely on smartphones and tablets for a wider range of tasks. Modern mobile devices enable users to access, manage and transmit multiple types of media in an easy, convenient and portable way. In this context, the playback of videos on mobile devices becomes a usual activity. Many works regarding video annotations have been made, but few are concerned with the mobile scenario. The ability to add annotations and to share them with others is a content enriching process which can improve activities from educational to entertainment purposes. In this paper, we present an intuitive tool that allows users to perform temporal video annotations on mobile devices. Using conventional tablets and smartphones equipped with the Android operating system, text, audio and digital ink annotations can be made on any video. It is possible to share text annotations with other users and play multiple annotations at the same time. The several display sizes and the possibility to switch between portrait and landscape mode have also been considered.

Categories and Subject Descriptors

H.5.2 [**Information Interfaces and Presentations**]: User Interfaces—*Input devices and strategies; Graphical user interfaces (GUI)*

General Terms

Design, Human Factors

Keywords

video annotation; mobile devices; authoring; user interfaces

1. INTRODUCTION

The flexibility and portability of mobile devices help people to do a series of tasks in different places and situations,

Permission to make digital or hard copies of all or part of this work for personal or classroom use is granted without fee provided that copies are not made or distributed for profit or commercial advantage and that copies bear this notice and the full citation on the first page. Copyrights for components of this work owned by others than ACM must be honored. Abstracting with credit is permitted. To copy otherwise, or republish, to post on servers or to redistribute to lists, requires prior specific permission and/or a fee. Request permissions from permissions@acm.org.
DocEng'13, September 10–13, 2013, Florence, Italy.
Copyright 2013 ACM 978-1-4503-1789-4/13/09 ...$15.00.
http://dx.doi.org/10.1145/2494266.2494267.

allowing them to take advantage of their idle time and perform urgent tasks. It has been observed that watching videos on mobile devices has become usual among users [7]. Users enjoy sharing media and performing comments and these practices can naturally enrich the original content. Annotations on video are useful in different contexts such as education, professional video analysis, choreography review and entertainment. Seeing the importance of annotations, many works have been conducted through the years. The tools developed by these works explore concepts of user experience, sharing, collaboration and multimodality. However, we observe that there is still a lack of tools that enable annotations using modern mobile devices. Observing this, we developed a tool that allows the creation and sharing of temporal annotations made by users while watching videos on their mobile devices. Our main goal is to enable the enrichment of the captured video and the sharing of comments with other users. Annotations are made on recorded videos because it requires less cognitive effort and their inclusion can be done whether the video is paused or not. The design considered the features of the current mobile devices, such as touch screen, multiple screen sizes, variable screen orientation and the input of data by a virtual keyboard.

2. RELATED WORK

We outlined works on video annotation that present tools with features of addition and synchronous playback of annotations. The Coreographer's Notebook [8] is a web annotation tool for dancers and choreographers that allows annotating recorded dance rehearsals. The system enables synchronous and asynchronous annotations using text, digital ink and even video. Another differential of the tool is the possibility to navigate by clicking on the respective annotation listed in a tab or by markings on the timeline. Its layout occupies a lot of space on the screen, which can be a disadvantage. Guimarães et al. [6] presented a web annotation tool that allows end-user time-based annotations on third party videos provided, for example, by YouTube. In their studies they observed that users find timed-based annotations very interesting when used for personal use or sharing with friends and family members, but not as subtitles. These works do not discuss the implementation or the possibility of use of the works on mobile devices.

Recent studies involving video annotations on mobile devices were also identified. El-Saban et al. [4] propose a system in which users can add tags to their videos while capturing. Tags are automatically returned by comparing in real-time of key frames with database images located on a centralized server. The annotations are performed in a semi-automatic way: suggested tags can be selected or rejected by the user. Bakopoulos et al. [2] present a mobile tool for annotation of short videos of emergency situations enriching them with predefined text and warning signs. The proposal seeks to facilitate immediate understanding in the treatment of emergencies through enhanced visual communication. The two systems are meant for individual use, i.e., the sharing of generated annotations is not enabled. In terms of collaborative annotation on video using mobile devices still there are few works in the area. The work of Huang and Fox [5] presents a collaborative annotation tool on Android-enabled devices in real-time data streams. It is possible to make synchronous annotations as text or digital ink and also communicate with a desktop version of the tool. The focus of the work is on the performance of their annotation framework and studies with users or usability tests of the tool were not reported.

3. MOVIA

The MoViA tool was developed as an Android application. This choice was made due to the better user experience and performance that the native application provides, in comparison with a web system. The design of the interface tried to solve and minimize some particular issues such as intuitive addition of annotations, virtual keyboard input, control of digital ink and audio annotations, display in different screen sizes, variable screen orientation, duration of display of textual annotations, video selection and multiple annotations displayed concurrently. The application can be executed regardless of the size of the screen and was tested with three real devices with very distinct sizes of screen: 4 inches, 7 inches and 10'1 inches. The next sections describe the features and the architecture of the tool. The open film Big Buck Bunny[1] was used for the screenshots shown by the figures.

3.1 Annotation

MoViA considers time-dependent annotations: when an user adds an annotation, it is linked to the respective instant of execution of the video. The system allows the addition of text, audio and digital ink. The first step to start the annotation process is to choose the authoring user, which is done by selecting a Google user account registered in the device. Thereafter, it is presented a screen with the names and thumbnails of the available videos. Next step is to choose the authors whose annotations the user wants to see concurrently during the playback: all annotations can be seen at the same time. Figure 1 displays the playback interface of the system. The vertical layout displays the video on the top screen with annotations controls (annotation mode). In the landscape setting the application shows only the video in full screen with annotations (view mode). Right below the video appears the textual annotation of the main author at the time it was added, if any. The duration of display is at least three seconds and increases with the number of characters of the text. The control of audio and digital ink annotation is accomplished via buttons that activate and deactivate these features. To avoid audio overlapping, when the user starts the recording of an audio annotation the video is automatically paused. The video playback is

also paused while the audio recording is played, but this can be skipped. The combo box for main author defines whose annotations will be shown immediately below the video and whose audio and ink annotations will be played. This option doesn't change the author, it only changes the displayed annotations. The bottom area is reserved to display annotations added by other users than the main author. In this way, textual annotations that occur at the same time or very closely can be shown concurrently. The main author can be changed at any time during the playback.

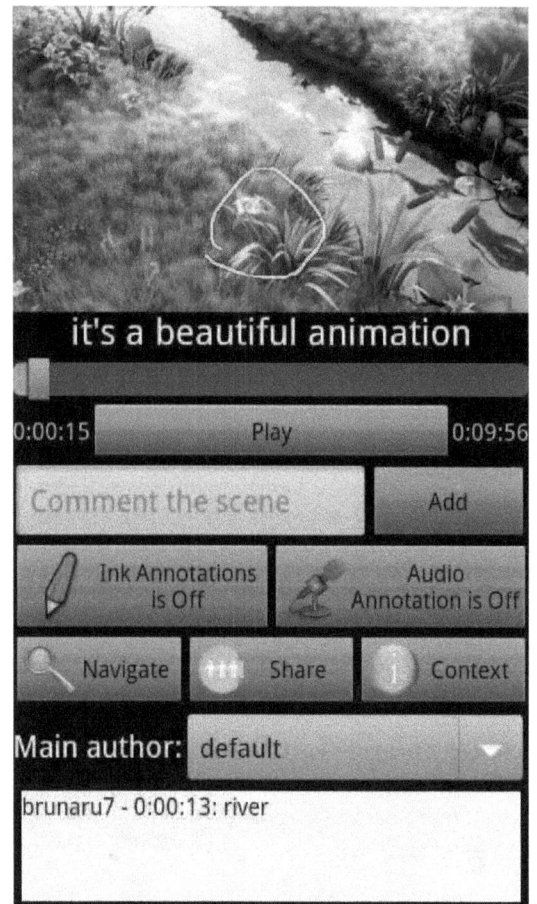

Figure 1: Playback and annotation screen.

3.2 Navigation

One simple strategy to navigate between points of interest is to draw marks on the video progress bar. This strategy is not efficient when we consider the current mobile devices' characteristics since there are limitations related to the screen size and sensitivity of the touch screen. Observing these limitations, we designed an alternative solution: a navigation screen shows a thumbnail captured from the video at the moment when the annotation is added with the respective time and the added text. When the thumbnail or text is touched the progress bar jumps to the corresponding annotation time, i.e. it jumps to the point of interest. This strategy seeks an easy way of finding the point of interest, which is in our case an annotation point, and selecting it with precision. Figure 2 shows an example of a navigation screen for text annotation. At the screen, there is an option

[1]http://www.bigbuckbunny.org/

220

to edit that permits changes on the text or even deleting it. The navigation screen for audio and digital ink follows the same model, but instead of the annotation text, the type of annotation is displayed (ink or audio). A limitation of this functionality is that the dynamic capturing of frames, i.e. the capture of the images used on the miniatures was not implemented on the application itself. The reason for that was the lack of infrastructure on the Android system's SDK (Software Development Kit). A desktop tool was created to automatically generate the miniatures that are copied along with their video to the device. The space used by the images is not representative, as they are just miniatures. Another solution would be using the Android's NDK (Native Development Kit) and a third-party video codec library to capture and decode frames.

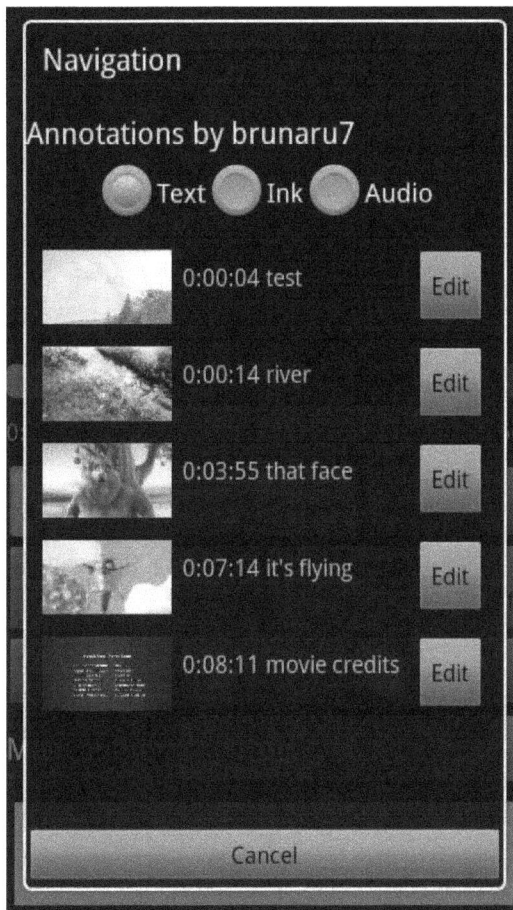

Figure 2: Text annotation navigation screen.

3.3 Collaboration

Currently the application permits the asynchronous sharing of the textual annotations. As shown by Figure 1 there is a button for annotation sharing. When the sharing button is pushed, file sharing options are made available: e-mail, Bluetooth, Dropbox, and others. The options exhibited depend on the systems available on user's device. Thus a user is able to share the annotations using the infrastructure from the applications he uses. By using the sharing option from the Dropbox service for example, it is possible to make the file public for any or specific users. The annotations are or-

ganized in an XML file which can be downloaded easily by other users. For the annotations to be recognized by the prototype they must be available in a specific directory on the system. To avoid the need for a manually performed copy, which can be a complicated task depending on the experience level of the user with Android systems, the tool contains an importing function on the initial screen. Our approach does not allow editing annotation files by any users besides the author. Instead, a transparency strategy is utilized. In a traditional scenario, a transparency paper with annotations made by an individual can be put over an original text to enrich it. Each individual has a transparency that can be put over the text adding more information without affecting others' transparencies. None will write on a transparency that they do not own. In this way, applying this idea to the tool, users have annotation files associated with their user names, only the owner can modify the annotations. However, files can be grouped together so users can view the whole set of annotations displayed with the video and, the most important, all at the same time.

3.4 Context Information

Context information is captured in a ubiquitous way, users do not have to manually provide any data to the system. Information is captured using the device features and stored data. The only situations that require user interaction is the selection of username and the confirmation of the event, which are made to verify the recovered information. The system captures context information during the annotation activity and exhibits it by clicking the context button. Captured information considers context dimensions defined by Truong et al. [9], on the following way:

- *Who*: storing of the user who did the interaction, a user name from Google account is stored. User from Google account was chosen because it's registry on the Android system device is in practice mandatory.

- *What*: type of annotation captured (text, ink or audio) and the performed activity by the user during the annotation activity. The information about the activities is taken from the scheduled event from the Google account registered on the device.

- *When*: moment from the first annotation added. It indicates the date of creation of the annotation file.

- *Where*: physical location (i.e., address) where the interaction took place.

- *How*: model of the capturing device and version of the Android system.

3.5 Generated Documents

Annotations performed by the users are stored in XML files. There is one file for each input type: text, digital ink and audio. Annotations are represented by classes that are directly mapped to the XML format. For each performed annotation the values stored are the text, the author, the current time of addition, the time when it occurs within the video and its duration interval. The set of annotations are represented as a list. Context information is also represented as a list. In our tool there will be only one possible user per file, since as explained in Section 3.3, users can edit only files created by them. However, the annotation model is flexible and permits to store multiple users and sets of context information. An audio annotation file is similar to the text annotation file, the differences are that an audio file path is stored instead of the text and duration interval is not necessary. For the digital ink annotation the path of the drawing is stored based on the x and y coordinates. The start position is the first point touched on the screen and every move from this position is captured. The end of each individual ink annotation is delimited by the release of contact. All the ink related actions are captured and stored until the functionality is turned off. The application uses its own document model to enhance efficiency, however the implementation was made to be easy to convert and there are plans to develop built-in converters for another models.

3.6 Architecture

The implementation relied mainly on APIs incorporated in the Android SDK. The only exception is the API Simple XML [1] used for the manipulation of the XML files. The Simple XML library performs the mapping of the XML schemes into Java classes, so the explicit processing of the XML files is not necessary. The Simple XML has high performance and requires low space which makes it adequate for Android applications development. The architecture of the tool was projected to enhance reuse and to facilitate extensions for different types of media. The organization consists in two main packages that are responsible for annotations and operators, a group of independent component and an integrated player that makes uses of the available functionalities and is responsible for user interface and interaction. The annotation package gathers the different types of input to centralize the access and enable the annotations to be read directly through the package. The operators' package has high-level operators that represents the system's main actions and is composed by three components: authoring operators, content operators and context operators. Authoring operators are responsible for writing, removal, updating and activation of annotation operations. Content operators are responsible for returning the occurrence of different types of annotations including their union. Context operators are responsible for providing the captured context information. The other independent components are: drawing area which is responsible for controlling the addition and exhibition of the electronic ink, audio recorder, navigation component which generates the navigation screens and the sharing component.

3.7 Evaluation

It is important to highlight that the development of the tool is embased by continuous evaluations. The tool went through an usability evaluation with users in a first phase and an heuristic evaluation by experts in a second one. Their analisys was used to enhance its interface and interaction. Results of the usability evaluation were detailed elsewhere [3].

4. CONCLUSIONS

We presented a video annotation tool for mobile devices that enables text, audio and digital ink annotation, allowing multiple data inputs. The MoViA tool also contains features of navigation, sharing and context information. The navigation is based on a screen that displays the time of addition and a thumbnail preview for each annotation and clicking

on these areas makes the video to be set at the moment of the selected annotation. The sharing of annotations can be done by using applications and services available on the dispositive and context information is pervasively captured during the authoring process. The architecture was designed to ease the reuse and the extension for other media types. Future works should implement the ability to perform synchronous collaboration, image annotation and the capture directly from the tool.

5. ACKNOWLEDGMENTS

We thank FAPESP (Fundação de Amparo à Pesquisa do Estado de São Paulo) and CNPq (Conselho Nacional de Desenvolvimento Científico e Tecnológico) for financial support.

6. REFERENCES

[1] Simple XML Serialization. http://simple.sourceforge.net/.

[2] M. Bakopoulos, S. Tsekeridou, E. Giannaka, Z.-H. Tan, and R. Prasad. Mobile video annotation for enhanced rich media communication during emergency handling. In *Proceedings of the 4th International Symposium on Applied Sciences in Biomedical and Communication Technologies*, pages 32:1–32:5. ACM, 2011.

[3] B. C. R. Cunha, D. Pedrosa, R. Goularte, and M. d. G. C. Pimentel. Video annotation and navigation on mobile devices. In *WebMedia '12: Proceedings of the 18th Brazilian Symposium on Multimedia and the Web*, pages 261–264. ACM, 2012.

[4] M. El-Saban, X.-J. Wang, N. Hasan, M. Bassiouny, and M. Refaat. Seamless annotation and enrichment of mobile captured video streams in real-time. In *Proceedings of the 2011 IEEE International Conference on Multimedia and Expo*, pages 1–4, Washington, DC, USA, 2011. IEEE Computer Society.

[5] T. Huang and G. Fox. Collaborative annotation of real time streams on Android-enabled devices. In *International Conference on Collaboration Technologies and Systems*, pages 39 –44, May 2012.

[6] R. Laiola Guimarães, P. Cesar, and D. C. Bulterman. Creating and sharing personalized time-based annotations of videos on the web. In *Proceedings of the 10th ACM Symposium on Document Engineering*, pages 27–36, New York, NY, USA, 2010. ACM.

[7] K. O'Hara, A. S. Mitchell, and A. Vorbau. Consuming video on mobile devices. In *Proceedings of the SIGCHI Conference on Human Factors in Computing Systems*, pages 857–866. ACM, 2007.

[8] V. Singh, C. Latulipe, E. Carroll, and D. Lottridge. The Choreographer's Notebook: a video annotation system for dancers and choreographers. In *Proceedings of the 8th ACM Conference on Creativity and Cognition*, pages 197–206. ACM, 2011.

[9] K. N. Truong, G. D. Abowd, and J. A. Brotherton. Who, what, when, where, how: Design issues of capture & access applications. In *Proceedings of the 3rd International Conference on Ubiquitous Computing*, pages 209–224. Springer-Verlag, 2001.

Enterprise Document System Cloud Deployment

Chris Wells
Hewlett-Packard
810 Bull Lea Run
Lexington, KY 40511
011-859-422-4776
chris.wells@hp.com

Joel Jirak
Hewlett-Packard
810 Bull Lea Run
Lexington, KY 40511
jirak@hp.com

Steve Pruitt
Hewlett-Packard
810 Bull Lea Run
Lexington, KY 40511
011-859-422-6257
steve.pruitt@hp.com

Anthony Wiley
Hewlett-Packard
810 Bull Lea Run
Lexington, KY 40511
011-859-422-6210
anthony.wiley@hp.com

ABSTRACT

The software used by enterprise businesses for creating variable-data customer documents must be highly reliable, and vendors are increasingly distributing such software via the cloud as an online service. This means that vendors now assume responsibility for the IT resources hosting and supporting the software as well as the customer documents and data. Vendors also assume responsibility for pushing updates to all customers simultaneously. To support the test and release of new versions, software vendors must deploy and configure the software at an unprecedented rate.

To reduce the time spent deploying and configuring software in the cloud, and to minimize the chance for human error, we present StackLauncher. By making it possible to automatically configure and launch software "stacks" with push-button simplicity, StackLauncher is a valuable addition to the software development lifecycle for cloud deployment of enterprise document software.

Categories and Subject Descriptors

B.4.5 [**Reliability and Testing**]: Built-in tests, Testability; C.4 [**Performance of Systems**]: Reliability, availability, and serviceability; D.2.9 [**Management**]: Lifecycle, Productivity, Programming teams, SQA; D.3.3 [**Language Constructs and Features**]: Frameworks

General Terms

Management, Measurement, Design, Economics, Legal Aspects, Reliability, Standardization, Verification

Keywords

Enterprise, Document Systems, Cloud-deployment, Tool

1. PROBLEM STATEMENT

Enterprise document software is a business-critical system that requires high reliability, but deploying this software as an online service poses challenges. One such service is HP Relate [1], a new document system provided as Software as a Service (SaaS). Like other cloud deployments, HP Relate supports multiple tenants, or business customers. Tenants use the same services, but services isolate the documents of each tenant from those of other tenants. All customers simultaneously receive upgrades to HP Relate, which magnifies any problems introduced in new versions. Mitigating these problems requires extensive testing and the ability to quickly provision customers back to a stable version.

DocEng'13, September 10–13, 2013, Florence, Italy.
ACM 978-1-4503-1789-4/13/09.
http://dx.doi.org/10.1145/2494266.2494292

SaaS solutions such as HP Relate compose IT and software elements into entities called *stacks*. A stack can contain virtual machines, load balancers, databases, initialization scripts, or a host of other resources. Configuring stacks and the relationships among them is complicated, prone to human error, and time consuming. In production, human error can translate into unavailability of services or data, exposure of a tenant's documents and data to other tenants, or even the deletion or corruption of customer data.

Throughout the product lifecycle, various teams—development, quality assurance, operations, support, professional services, and others—must reproduce each set of stacks. This process can become complex when developers make changes that affect the interaction of software services and IT resources. If the deployment process reflects this complexity—for example, by exposing it in a playbook of instructions—the possibility of human error grows.

2. OUR SOLUTION

StackLauncher is a utility that reduces the configuration and complexity of cloud deployments to push-button simplicity, and in so doing, reduces human labor and minimizes the possibility of human error. StackLauncher launches stacks from builds located in a staging repository and supports three basic types of entities: resource stacks, service stacks, and DNS [2] subdomains.

A **resource stack** is a collection of resources that persists across multiple versions of a deployment. A resource stack primarily contains storage and database resources, which in turn store customer documents, document metadata, and business audit logs.

A **service stack** is also a collection of resources, but it is replaced when deploying a new version of software—in our case, our web services. It is versioned and consists primarily of virtual machines and queues through which the virtual machines communicate. The service stack handles tasks such as authorization when accessing a document and processing a document during fulfillment.

Reserved **DNS subdomains** serve as unchanging endpoints through which users may access deployments. Remapping these endpoints enables operations to implement traditional **blue—green** [3] deployment by issuing a DNS cutover.

2.1 Staging Repository

A reproducible deployment strategy requires a well-known, centralized location for every item used in a deployment (software libraries, configuration scripts, utility programs, and so on). StackLauncher uses a staging repository to store this data. A build system automatically uploads its builds to the staging repository, which organizes builds in a simple hierarchy:

```
<branch>/<service>/<version>/<build number>
```

The build system determines the service name and version number according to the project it is building, and monotonically increases the build number. This organization allows the repository to support multiple services, branches, and versions. For a typical cloud deployment, a build in the repository contains the following subfolders:

- script—any bootstrap scripts for virtual machines
- template—template(s) for the cloud-hosted stack(s)
- war—the web archive artifact
- test—a test client program for the web artifact

2.2 Stack Actions

StackLauncher allows an operator to specify one or more actions in configuration. When run, StackLauncher builds a tree of stack actions and sorts them according to dependencies. For example, creating a stack depends on promoting the stack's build folder. After StackLauncher has built the action tree and prompted the user, it executes all actions in parallel. Actions that are dependent on the successful completion of other actions wait for the completion of those actions before beginning their own execution. StackLauncher can perform the following actions:

- **Promote**—Copy a build to a staging repository.
- **Create**—Create a stack according to a template.
- **Update**—Update an existing resource stack.
- **UpdateDNS**—Point a DNS mapping to a service stack.
- **Retire**—Delete all down-versions of a service stack.
- **Delete**—Delete a resource or service stack.
- **Upload**—Upload a build to a staging repository.
- **Publish**—Publish static content to a stack.
- **Test**—Run predefined tests against an existing stack.

2.3 Stack Naming Convention

StackLauncher groups related stacks and DNS subdomains into abstract entities called stages, which are represented by a human-readable prefix assigned to each entity in a stage. For example, our team uses stage names *dev*, *qa*, and *prod*, to ensure separation of our development stacks from our QA and production stacks. An operator can also specify a sub-stage name to prepend to service stack names and DNS subdomains. Sub-stage names allow developers and testers to launch sandbox stacks that access shared resources without disturbing shared deployments.

StackLauncher denotes a resource stack by prepending "resource" to its name, and denotes a service stack by appending its name with the stack's version and build numbers. A stack name assigned by StackLauncher has the following pattern:

[stagesubname-]stagename-[resource-]servicename[-version-build]

An operator may optionally specify a prefix to prepend to a DNS subdomain. This option allows operators to easily create temporary DNS subdomains for testing a preproduction stack.

When StackLauncher launches a service stack, it uses the stage name to query that stage's resource stacks. StackLauncher maps the outputs, or resource IDs, specified by the resource stacks to inputs specified in the service stack template. This coupling allows StackLauncher to automatically specify resource IDs to service stacks without relying on manual configuration.

2.4 Configuration

StackLauncher complements its actions and naming with a small set of configurable properties. For example, most actions use the StagingBucket property to locate the staging repository that contains the deployment build folder. The configurable properties allow operators to specify virtual machine characteristics, including availability zones, machine images, and machine types (CPU/memory). The configuration also includes properties specifying the DNS names that expose service stacks and URLs for external services.

Operators can filter StackLauncher's configurable properties using stage names, and also by using the cloud provider account id. Using configuration filtering, a single set of configuration properties can contain different DNS names for production, QA, and development. Filtering enables StackLauncher to contain default configuration values for a wide range of environments.

2.5 Monitoring

After operators launch a new stack, they can use StackLauncher to validate and monitor the stack. Each build folder in the staging repository contains a test application for its target service. When StackLauncher executes the Test action, it goes to the build folder in the staging repository, downloads the test application, and executes it. This allows an operator to quickly verify whether an existing stack is behaving as expected. The test application can be used in three roles: to test a stack during continuous integration; to validate a stack in preproduction prior to DNS cutover; and to monitor a production stack.

3. PROBLEMS SOLVED

Because StackLauncher performs all of the listed actions and deploys with a complete set of configuration properties, all teams who must manage stacks can do so by running StackLauncher. This makes deployment and monitoring of stacks easily reproducible, even in different environments.

HP Relate uses StackLauncher to manage stacks for integrated testing, providing rapid feedback for agile development. We also use StackLauncher for manual QA, pre-production testing, and production operations. HP Relate has used StackLauncher to launch hundreds of integrated testing and manual QA stacks, and dozens of production stacks used by customers.

4. PRIOR SOLUTIONS

Cloud deployment is a popular topic with many solutions. Some focus on configuration management, like Chef [4] and Puppet [5]. Some focus on apps written in a certain language's ecosystem, like Capistrano [6] for Ruby. Some are designed for a specific cloud environment, like the tooling that Heroku [7] provides.

StackLauncher's sweet spot, in contrast, is quickly deploying bundled Java applications to a cloud environment defined by a template, and providing test verification in that environment.

5. REFERENCES

[1] Steve Pruitt , Anthony Wiley, HP Relate – A Customer Communication System for the SMB Market, Proceedings of the 12th ACM symposium on Document Engineering, September 4-7, 2012, Paris, France

[2] http://tools.ietf.org/html/rfc1035

[3] http://martinfowler.com/bliki/BlueGreenDeployment.html.

[4] http://www.opscode.com/chef/

[5] https://puppetlabs.com/

[6] https://github.com/capistrano/capistrano/wiki

[7] https://www.heroku.com/

Bag of Subjects: Lecture Videos Multimodal Indexing

Nhu Van Nguyen
L3I, University of La Rochelle
La Rochelle, France
nhu-van.nguyen@univ-lr.fr

Jean-Marc Ogier
L3I, University of La Rochelle
La Rochelle, France
jean-marc.ogier@univ-lr.fr

Franck Charneau
@ctice, University of La Rochelle
La Rochelle, France
franck.charneau@univ-lr.fr

ABSTRACT

In this paper, we address multimodal indexing and retrieval for videos of lectures or seminars. This paper proposes a combination of technologies respectively issuing from image document analysis and text mining. Based on visual information and textual information extracted from slide images, we investigate a Bag of mixed Words (visual words and textual words) model to represent lecture slide's contents. Lecture videos are indexed and retrieved by using extended Bag of Words model. In this model, it is assumed that a video may contain multiple subjects; and this model discovers the visual representation of these subjects automatically and indexes the video accordingly. We discuss the mixed text/image query and proposed indexing approach for retrieval lecture videos and report a quantitative evaluation on lecture videos of our Lab.

Categories and Subject Descriptors

H.3 [**Information Storage and Retrieval**]: Content Analysis and Indexing, Information Search and Retrieval

Keywords

Multimodal indexing, lecture videos, bag of words

1. INTRODUCTION

In pedagogy, automatic analysis of recordings of courses (audiovisual streams) allows crossing information and automatically enriching contents by creating some linkages between various modalities. As the availability of digital copies of slides is not always realistic, we suppose that they are not included in lecture recordings, and that we cannot use this information for our indexing process. Actually, we have different modalities presented in lecture videos: "text," "speech," "graphics" in slides and white board. In our work, we concentrate on the multimodal indexing based on "graphics" and "text" which includes "printed text" detected in the images of slides (which are generrraly video-projected) and the

DocEng'13, September 10–13, 2013, Florence, Italy.

ACM 978-1-4503-1789-4/13/09.
http://dx.doi.org/10.1145/2494266.2494293.

transcription of speech. We focus our interests on multimodal lecture videos indexing and retrieval. For the speech an external partner is envisaged.

2. MULTIMODAL INDEXING

Lecture video indexing without digital sources (lecture slides) has been already studied in [1, 5] but there are still some remaining challenges. One of the main issue in existing systems is the lack of use of *multimodal analysis*. In the existing literature, several methods have been presented for fusion of multiple modalities for image and video modelling. In existing models, we have identified some remaining issues: 1) the existence of priori knowledge, often represented as annotations, is absolutely essential for the training phase; 2) None of the approaches are dealing with the problem of multiple modalities existing in same document i.e. lecture slides having text and image/graphics.

Another problem identified in the existing systems is the lack of use of semantic concept, such as "subjects" for retrieving multimodal documents such as lecture videos. Indeed, one important features of lecture videos is related to its semantic content, and the subjects it deals with. In our case, we can assume that each lecture video is composed of a number of subjects. Hence, the task of retrieval not only aims at retrieving the relevant videos but also the position (in terms time) of the relevant parts in each video, by using the "subject" notion. Subjects can be a slide or a set of slides.

In this paper, we assume the availability of document image segmentation method for text/graphics. We address the problem of multiple modalities existing in same document (text and graphics in lecture videos) which requires no special knowledge such as manual annotations or descriptions for document images like in other works. We present a multimodal lecture content indexing approach based on an extended Bag of Words model to retrieve video or parts of videos.

2.1 Indexing using Bag of Words model

Once printed text in slides is recognized by OCR tool, speech is transcribed and visual words are extracted from graphics, our lecture video is represented by a set of words (from text OCR'ed and text of transcription) and visual words (from graphic regions). Then the Bag of Words (BoW) model used in classical textual Information Retrieval methods [4] can be applied in order to compare our documents. Each document is represented by a bag of "words" describing the occurrence frequency of its words in a dictionary. In

Table 1: Video retrieval in our system

Indexation :	Bag of Subjects	Bag of mix Words	Printed-text	Graphics	Speech
Precision	95/141	86/141	78/141	30/141	65/141
	67.38%	60.99%	55.32%	21.28%	46.01%

our case, the TF-IDF (Term Frequency - Inverse Document Frequency) [4] is used to weigh each "word" depending on its frequency in the video on the one hand, and in all the database on the other hand.

In our system, BoW representation of a lecture video j is a weighted vector of words $V_j^{text} = (w_{j,1}, w_{j,2} \ldots w_{j,T})$ where $w_j = s_j + t_j$, in which s_j - the $TF * IDF$ weight of word j in the speech corpus of all videos, t_j - the $TF * IDF$ weight of word j in the text extracted corpus from all videos

With the same technique, BoVW (Bag of Visual Words) representation of a lecture video is a weighted vector of visual words $V_j^{graphic} = (vw_{j,1}, vw_{j,2} \ldots w_{j,V})$. Hence we have BoMW (Bag of Mix Words) representation for a lecture video: $V_j = \{V_j^{text}, V_j^{graphic}\}$. For the process of finding videos, video is recovered by calculating the similarity between the vector of frequencies of "mixed words" and those of other videos. Assuming that videos can contain several subjects, it is quite inefficient to use such "global description" to compare them. Indeed, a query can concern only a part of a lecture video, and renders a comparison between the query and the whole video unefficient. In order to get over this problem, we propose to extend the BoW model, presented in the next section.

2.2 Indexing using Bag of Subjects model

In order to consider the possibility to have a "partial" matching between a query and a video, we represent lecture videos by a Bag of Subjects (BoS) where each subjet corresponds to a set of similar slides, which in turn is represented by a BoMW. Two slides are similar if their content (text, speech, graphics) are similar. To discover subjects of lecture videos, we propose 2 different approaches which rely on multiple modalities presented in a video: the printed-text, graphics and text transcription of speech.

In the first approach, each subject j of a lecture video i is considered as a set of similar slides. This approach aims at grouping slides into different groups (the number is unknown) of similar slides by using a clustering algorithm. These groups are used to construct different subjects. The BoMW of s subject j of a lecture video i is the sum of BoMWs of slides in group j : $V_{i,j} = \sum s_{i,j}$.

The second approach is based on teacher's speech to identify subjects in a lecture video. In order to discover subjects from text transcription of teacher's speech, we make use of topic segmentation techniques in natural language processing which is studied for long time [2, 3]. After teacher's speech is segmented, we can group slides into multiple sets of slides by synchronysing the timestamp of topic segmented and slides.

3. EXPERIMENTATION

We analyzed 47 french lecture recordings of our Lab. The query set used in our experiment is images of slides detected from lecture videos. To construct this query set, we

randomly take 3 images of slides from each lecture video, contents of these slides (text, graphic speech) are not used in the indexation phrase of 47 videos. We insist that the query is a mix query of text/graphics. Each image slide query is segmented into text parts and graphic parts, then they are used to construct the BoMW representation for the query. Our system performance is evaluated by the average of $3 \times 47 = 141$ retrieval results.

Table 1 shows the precision of video retrieval. We compare 5 indexing schemas in our experimentation : multimodal indexing by Bag of Subjects, multimodal indexing by Bag of mix Words, indexing by text, indexing by speech and indexing by graphics. We obtain the best precision on multimodal indexing meanwhile the precision on unimodal indexing is lower. The use of multimodal indexing gives better results than that of unimodal indexing, while using Bag of Subjects indexing gives better result than using Bag of mix Words indexing. We can see that, we can retrieve correctly nine more videos with Bag of Subjects. In this case, these nine videos have subjects which are closest to queries but not the whole video.

4. CONCLUSION

We have presented our system of the automatic multimodal indexing of lecture recordings based on speech of teachers and lecture visual contents. By integrating multiple modalities, our system has given very promising performance for lecture video indexing. Using Bag of Subjects model for lecture videos, we obtain better result and we can retrieve not only videos but parts of videos which are relevant to the multimodal query.

5. ACKNOWLEDGMENTS

This project is supported in part by the Poitou Charentes Region and the European Union.

6. REFERENCES

[1] J. Adcock, M. Cooper, L. Denoue, H. Pirsiavash, and L. A. Rowe. Talkminer: a lecture webcast search engine. In *MM '10*, pages 241–250, NY, USA, 2010.

[2] F. Y. Y. Choi. Advances in domain independent linear text segmentation. In *NAACL 2000*, pages 26–33, Stroudsburg, PA, USA, 2000.

[3] M. A. Hearst. Texttiling: segmenting text into multi-paragraph subtopic passages. *Comput. Linguist.*, 23(1):33–64, Mar. 1997.

[4] K. S. Jones. Experiments in relevance weighting of search terms. *Information Processing & Management*, 15(3):133 – 144, 1979.

[5] M. Merler and J. R. Kender. Semantic keyword extraction via adaptive text binarization of unstructured unsourced video. In *ICIP 2010*, pages 261–264. IEEE, 2009.

tranScriptorium: A European Project on Handwritten Text Recognition

Joan Andreu Sánchez
Universitat Politècnica de València, ITI
46022 Camí de Vera s/n
València, Spain
jandreu@dsic.upv.es

Günter Mühlberger
Universitaet Innsbruck
6020 Innrain 52
Innsbruck, Austria
guenter.muehlberger@
uibk.ac.at

Basilis Gatos
National Center for Scientific Research "Demokritos"
15310 Patriarchou Gregoriou
Agia Paraskevi
Athens, Greece
bgat@iit.demokritos.gr

Philip Schofield
University College London
WC1E6BT Gower Street 1
London, UK
p.schofield@ucl.ac.uk

Katrien Depuydt
Instituut voor Nederlandse Lexicologie
2300RA Matthias de Vrieshof
2-3, 2311 BZ
Leiden, Netherlands
Katrien.Depuydt@inl.nl

Richard M. Davis
University of London
WC1E 7HU Malet Street
London, UK
r.davis@ulcc.ac.uk

ABSTRACT

The TRANSCRIPTORIUM project aims to develop innovative, efficient and cost-effective solutions for annotating handwritten historical documents using modern, holistic Handwritten Text Recognition (HTR) technology. Three actions are planned in TRANSCRIPTORIUM: i) improve basic image preprocessing and holistic HTR techniques; ii) develop novel indexing and keyword searching approaches; and iii) capitalize on new, user-friendly interactive-predictive HTR approaches for computer-assisted operation.

Categories and Subject Descriptors

H.3.7 [**Information Storage and Retrieval**]: Digital Libraries; I.5.4 [**Pattern Recognition**]: Applications—*Text Processing*; I.7.5 [**Document and Text Processing**]: Document Capture—*Document analysis*

Keywords

Interactive handwritten text recognition, digital libraries, document image analysis, crowd-sourcing

1. INTRODUCTION

TRANSCRIPTORIUM[1] is a three years project that started on January 2013 and it is funded by the European Union's Seventh Framework Programme. TRANSCRIPTORIUM project

---

[1] http://transcriptorium.eu

DocEng'13, September 1013, 2013, Florence, Italy.
ACM 978-1-4503-1789-4/13/09
http://dx.doi.org/10.1145/2494266.2494294.

aims to develop innovative, efficient and cost-effective solutions for the indexing, search and full transcription of historical handwritten document images, using modern, holistic Handwritten Text Recognition (HTR) technology.

The TRANSCRIPTORIUM consortium is composed by experts in HTR, Document Image Analysis (DIA), linguistic resources developers, content providers, crowd-sourcing experts and integration experts. The TRANSCRIPTORIUM partners are: Universitat Politècnica de València (UPVLC), Spain; University of Innsbruck (UIBK), Austria; National Center for Scientific Research "Demokritos" (NCSR), Greece; University College London (UCL), UK; Institute for Dutch Lexicology (INL), Netherlands; University of London Computer Centre (ULCC), UK.

TRANSCRIPTORIUM will address the following specific objectives: enhancing HTR technology for efficient transcription; bringing the HTR technology to users; and, integrating the HTR results in public web portals. For achieving these objectives, TRANSCRIPTORIUM will develop HTR tools that will be tested in two real-life scenarios: in the first scenario, the HTR technology will be made available through a content provider site for individual users; in the second scenario, the developed technology will be integrated in an existing crowd-sourcing platform.

2. HTR TECHNOLOGY

Current state-of-the-art transcription products rely on technology for isolated character recognition (OCR) developed in the last two decades. But character segmentation is just impossible in unconstrained handwritten text images like those encountered in most old documents of interest (see Figure 1) to the project. TRANSCRIPTORIUM will use the new segmentation-free *off-line* HTR technology [2] for such transcription tasks.

In contrast with OCR, this new HTR technology does not need the characters or even the words of a handwritten text image to be previously segmented or isolated. To some extent, the transcription of (old) handwritten text images is comparable with the task of recognising continuous speech in a (significantly degraded) audio file. And, in fact, recent technology for HTR borrows concepts and methods from the field of Automatic Speech Recognition, such as Hidden Markov Models (HMMs) and N-grams [1].

Currently available HTR technologies are far from offering satisfactory solutions. To obtain correct transcripts, heavy human-expert correction work is needed; but this "post-editing" process is inefficient and uncomfortable for the users and is not generally accepted by expert transcribers. As an alternative, computer assisted interactive predictive solutions [3] offer significant improvements in practical performance and user acceptance. In these approaches, the user and the system work interactively in tight mutual collaboration to obtain the perfect transcript of the given data [3].

To achieve good (plain or interactive) HTR accuracy, a combination of techniques is needed, such as layout analysis, text line extraction, preprocessing operations, lexical and language modelling, HMMs, etc. Although these technologies are already providing useful results in some cases, much remains to be developed, especially for historical documents, which suffer from typical degradations.

The models used in segmentation-free HTR are trained using already well known, powerful learning techniques, most of them based on the Expectation-Maximisation algorithm. TRANSCRIPTORIUM intends to make progress in automatic training techniques in order to achieve satisfactory accuracy.

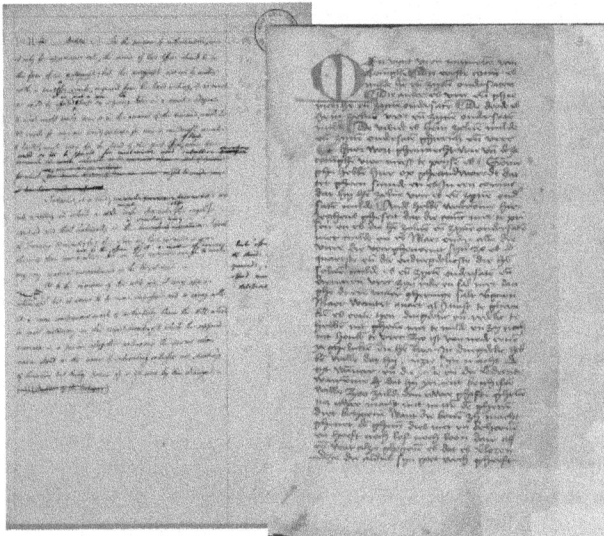

Figure 1: Document samples to be processed in TRANSCRIPTORIUM.

3. PROJECT OBJECTIVES

Despite recent significant improvements, currently available HTR technologies are still far from offering fully automated solutions for transcription. In this project, we will turn HTR into a mature technology by addressing the following objectives:

1. *Enhancing HTR technology for efficient transcription.*
   Departing from state-of-the-art HTR approaches, TRANSCRIPTORIUM will capitalise on interactive-predictive techniques for effective and user-friendly computer-assisted transcription [3].

2. *Bringing the HTR technology to users.*
   Expected users of the HTR technology belong mainly to two groups: a) individual researchers with experience in handwritten documents transcription interested in transcribing specific documents. For this kind of users, the HTR tools will be available through handwritten text image content provider portals. Archives and libraries will be also benefited from these users since they will be able to integretate the obtained transcripts in their collections; b) volunteers which collaborate in large transcription projects. For this kind of users, the HTR tools will be available through a specialised crowd-sourcing web portal which provides support for structured collaborative work.

3. *Integrating the HTR results in public web portals.*
   The HTR technology will become a support in the digitisation of the handwritten materials. Most digital libraries nowadays attach the output of modern OCR to the digitised pages of printed text documents. In a similar way, the outcomes of the TRANSCRIPTORIUM tools will be attached to the published handwritten document images. This includes not only full, correct transcriptions produced with the interactive HTR transcription techniques, but also partially correct transcriptions and other kinds of automatically produced metadata, useful for indexing and searching based on Key Word Spotting (KWS) techniques.

Within the TRANSCRIPTORIUM project span, it is intended to apply the developed HTR technology to historical documents in cursive handwriting, for which only HTR technology can offer appropriate solutions. TRANSCRIPTORIUM will focus on four languages: Spanish, German, English and Dutch.

4. ACKNOWLEDGMENTS

The research leading to these results has received funding from the European Union's Seventh Framework Programme (FP7/2007-2013) under grant agreement no. 600707 - tranScriptorium.

5. ADDITIONAL AUTHORS

Enrique Vidal, Universitat Politècnica de València, ITI, 46022 Camí de Vera s/n, València, Spain, email: evidal@iti.upv.es . Jesse de Does, Instituut voor Nederlandse Lexiicologie, 2300RA Matthias de Vrieshof 2-3, 2311 BZ, Leiden, Netherlands email: jesse.dedoes@inl.nl

6. REFERENCES

[1] F. Jelinek. *Statistical Methods for Speech Recognition.* MIT Press, 1998.

[2] A. H. Toselli, A. Juan, D. Keysers, J. González, I. Salvador, H. Ney, E. Vidal, and F. Casacuberta. Integrated Handwriting Recognition and Interpretation using Finite-State Models. *Int. Journal of PRAI,* 18(4):519–539, June 2004.

[3] A.H. Toselli, E. Vidal, and F. Casacuberta. *Multimodal Interactive Pattern Recognition and Applications.* Springer, 1st edition edition, 2011.

On the Performance of the Position() XPath Function

Luiz Augusto Matos da Silva
Federal University of Acre,
Brazil
luiz.matos@ufac.br

Luiz Laerte N. da Silva Jr.
Fluminense Federal
University, Brazil
luiznunes@id.uff.br

Marta Mattoso
Federal University of Rio de
Janeiro, Brazil
marta@cos.ufrj.br

Vanessa Braganholo
Fluminense Federal
University, Brazil
vanessa@ic.uff.br

ABSTRACT

In very large XML documents or collections, the query response times are not always satisfactory. To overcome this limitation, parallel processing can be applied. Data can be replicated in several processors and queries can be partitioned to run over different virtual data partitions on each processor, on an approach called virtual partitioning. PartiX-VP is a simple XML virtual partitioning approach that generates virtual data partitions by dividing the cardinality of the partitioning attribute by the number of allocated processors, resulting in intervals of equal size for each processor. In this approach, the XML query is rewritten and selection predicates are added to define the virtual partitions. These selection predicates use the position() XPath function that addresses a set of elements on a given position in the document. In this paper, we present an experimental evaluation of the position() XPath function in five XML native DBMS. We have identified differences in the processing time of the position() XPath function in large collections of XML documents. This may lead to load unbalancing in simple virtual partitioning approaches, thus this analysis opens space for improvements in virtual partitioning.

Categories and Subject Descriptors

H.2.4 [**Systems**]: Query processing.

Keywords

Scale and Performance; XML Query Processing.

1. INTRODUCTION

XML data is increasingly being used by academy and industry to represent semi-structured data [7]. In such setting, the query response times over large XML documents or collections are not always satisfactory. To overcome this limitation, parallel processing can be applied. Virtual data partitioning techniques [5, 8] apply parallel processing by replicating data in several processors and partitioning queries to run over different virtual data partitions on each processor. PartiX-VP [8] is a simple XML virtual partitioning approach that generates virtual data partitions by dividing the cardinality of the partitioning attribute by the number of allocated processors, resulting in intervals of equal size for each processor. In this approach, the XML query is rewritten and selection predicates are added to define the virtual partitions. These selection predicates use the position() XPath function [6] that addresses a set of elements on a given position interval in the document. Results in [8] show significant query processing time

DocEng'13, September 10–13, 2013, Florence, Italy.
ACM 978-1-4503-1789-4/13/09.
http://dx.doi.org/10.1145/2494266.2494295

gains when comparing virtual partitions with the sequential processing time for the whole document. However, the efficiency of this approach depends on the performance of the position() XPath function, since variations in the processing time of different partitions may lead to load unbalancing – if a processor $n2$ takes longer to process an interval from 10000 to 20000 than processor $n1$ takes for processing positions 1 to 9999, the total query processing time will be bounded by the slower processor $n2$. Although native XML databases claim they use smart index techniques to index XML elements, the success of the virtual partitioning technique depends on balanced access times. In this paper we present an experimental evaluation of the position() XPath function in five XML native DBMS (DBMSX). The goal is to study the behavior of this function when accessing different portions of large documents, so the efficiency of the virtual partitioning approach can be leveraged.

2. XML VIRTUAL PARTITIONING

Inspired by well established techniques for the relational model [1, 5], Rodrigues et al. [8] propose a simple virtual partitioning approach for XML documents. PartiX-VP works by replicating the database into several processors, and rewriting queries by adding selection predicates that use the position() XPath function. Each subquery then is executed under a specific subset of the data, and runs in parallel in each processor to accelerate total query processing time.

```
<results>
  {for $ctm in doc('insurance.xml')//customer[position() >= 1
  and position() < 40001]
    where $ctm/damaged_vehicle = "Yes"
    return
      < customer>{$ctm/name} {$ctm/age}</customer>
  }</results>
```

Figure 1. Example of subquery.

As an example, assume an XML document with 200000 customer elements of an insurance company. Assume also we have 5 processors to execute a query to retrieve names and ages of customers that had their car damaged. PartiX-VP would divide the cardinality of customers by the number of available processors, and rewrite the query to generate 5 subqueries, each of which processing an interval of 40000 customers. Figure 1 shows the first subquery generated by PartiX-VP. The selection predicate added by the approach is shown in bold in the Figure.

3. EXPERIMENTAL EVALUATION

To evaluate the performance of the position() XPath function in DBMSX, we measured the processing time of a query to the *article* element of the DBLP XML document [4]. The reason we chose this document is its large size. It has 1.2 GB, and thus does not fit in main memory (previous experiments with this dataset were unsuccessful in loading it to main memory, even using a file with half of the size we use here [2]). We selected five DBMSX to run our experiments. In this paper we refer to them as A, B, C, D and E due to copyright restrictions of one of them that prevents tests results to be published. Those DBMS were chosen because they offer stable standalone versions. They were installed in a computer with a 2.8 GHz quad core processor, 8 GB RAM and Linux Ubuntu OS. We evaluated XPath queries of the type */dblp/article[position() = p]*, where *p* assumes one of the tested positions. There are 999714 *article* elements in DBLP document. We generated 21 positions of equal distance from one another, resulting in intervals of size 49985. The corresponding 21 XPath queries were executed starting at position 1. Each query was executed 10 times. We discarded the processing time of the first execution and calculated the average of the remaining 9 executions. This hot cache approach simulates real applications running in DBMSX, since in such cases there will always be some data in cache to be used during query processing.

Figure 2 shows our experimental results. In this figure the horizontal axis represents the positions and the vertical axis represents the XPath query processing time in seconds, in a logarithmic scale. The continuous line represents the real query processing time for a given position. The dotted line represents the trend line that was obtained through a linear model given by the equation $y = x * a + b$, where y is the dependent variable (processing time), x is the independent variable (current position) and a and b are the regression coefficients, obtained with slope and intercept functions, respectively. We consider only positive values to the trend line representation.

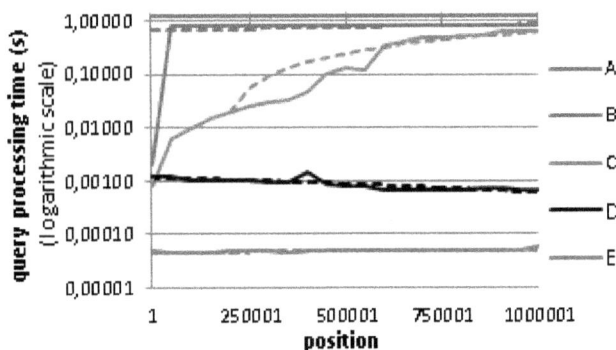

Figure 2. Performance on A, B, C, D and E DBMSX.

Figure 2 shows a linear increase of the processing time when the positions are incremented in C, showing that the greater the position the longer the processing time of the position() XPath function. A, B and E had nearly constant query processing time values after processing the first position. D was the only one that presented decrease of query processing time as we increased the positions being tested. However, its processing time variation was of 0.0012 to 0.0007 seconds, which is negligible considering the processing time obtained. The behavior of E was nearly constant (as A and B). However, its query processing time did not exceed 10^{-4} seconds. Its trend line has a slight inclination, but this is negligible considering the processing time obtained.

We noticed that except for DBMSX C, the processing time of the position() XPath function is not substantially affected by the element position being queried. However, the position() XPath function has different processing time among them. In C, there is an increase in query processing time. In D, there is a decrease. A, B and E presented nearly constant time and thus they are more adequate to be used in XML virtual partitioning approaches. With the heterogeneous behavior of system C, simple XML virtual partitioning may suffer from load imbalance when applied to large XML documents or collections.

Although the obtained processing times are small in a real scenario the queries are executed in many and different positions, resulting in overhead.

4. CONCLUSIONS

PartiX-VP is a virtual partitioning approach to efficiently process ad-hoc XML queries. It uses the elements position as selection predicates to define the virtual partitions. To obtain good performance, the query processing time must be independent of the position that is being accessed in a given virtual data partition.

In order to evaluate the performance of the position() XPath function, this paper presented an experimental evaluation using five XML DBMS. Our results have identified differences in the processing time of the position() XPath function in a large XML document. This may lead to load unbalancing in simple virtual partitioning approaches. Thus, the development of mechanisms that guarantee a constant response time, independently of the position of the accessed element, is a must.

PartiX-VP works with the abbreviated XPath syntax, and accepts both forward and reverse axes. However, in some cases (specially when the query involves reverse axes) our algorithm [8] may not find a proper place to insert the position() XPath function. In such cases, the query is executed in a single processor, mirroring a centralized environment. The ideas of [3] could be used to rewrite XPath expressions with reverse axes to equivalent forward-only expressions, thus minimizing this problem.

We are currently working on an adaptive virtual partitioning approach (inspired by [5]) to the XML query processing, based on the data distribution and on the tendency of the position() XPath function access time. The idea is to use a load balancing mechanism that applies linear regression for predicting the processing time using database statistics to define more adequate intervals for each virtual partition.

5. ACKNOWLEDGMENTS
We would like to thank FAPERJ and CNPq for partially supporting this work.

6. REFERENCES
[1] Akal, F. et al. OLAP Query Evaluation in a Database Cluster: A Performance Study on Intra-Query Parallelism. *Proc. of the East European Conference on Advances in Databases and Information Systems* (London, UK), pages 218-231, 2002.

[2] Ferraz, C.A. et al. ARAXA: Storing and Managing Active XML documents. *Web Semantics: Science, Services and Agents on the World Wide Web*. (8):209-224, 2010.

[3] Geneves, P. and Rose, K. Compiling XPath into a state-less forward-only subset. *Proc. of the International Workshop on High Performance XML Processing* (NY, USA), 2004.

[4] Ley, M. DBLP: Some Lessons Learned. *Proc. of the Int. Conference on Very Large Data Bases* (Lyon, FR), pages 1493-1500, 2009.

[5] Lima, A. et al. Adaptive virtual partitioning for OLAP query processing in a database cluster. *Journal of Information and Data Management*. 1(1):75-88, 2010.

[6] Malhotra, A. et al. *XQuery 1.0 and XPath 2.0 Functions and Operators*. 2005. Available at: <www.w3.org/TR/xpath-functions/>.

[7] Moro, M. M. et al. XML: Some Papers in a Haystack. *SIGMOD Record*. 38(2):29-34, 2009.

[8] Rodrigues, C. et al. Virtual partitioning ad-hoc queries over distributed XML databases. *Journal of Information and Data Management*. 2(3):495-510, 2011.

Incremental Hierarchical Text Clustering with Privileged Information*

Ricardo M. Marcacini
Federal University of Mato Grosso do Sul
Três Lagoas, MS, Brazil
ricardo.marcacini@ufms.br

Solange O. Rezende
Mathematical and Computer Sciences Institute
University of São Paulo, São Carlos, Brazil
solange@icmc.usp.br

ABSTRACT

In many text clustering tasks, there is some valuable knowledge about the problem domain, in addition to the original textual data involved in the clustering process. Traditional text clustering methods are unable to incorporate such additional (privileged) information into data clustering. Recently, a new paradigm called LUPI – Learning Using Privileged Information – was proposed by Vapnik to incorporate privileged information in classification tasks. In this paper, we extend the LUPI paradigm to deal with text clustering tasks. In particular, we show that the LUPI paradigm is potentially promising for incremental hierarchical text clustering, being very useful for organizing large textual databases. In our method, the privileged information about the text documents is applied to refine an initial clustering model by means of consensus clustering. The initial model is used for incremental clustering of the remaining text documents. We carried out an experimental evaluation on two benchmark text collections and the results showed that our method significantly improves the clustering accuracy when compared to a traditional hierarchical clustering method.

Categories and Subject Descriptors

H.3.3 [**Information Storage and Retrieval**]: Information Search and Retrieval—*Clustering*

Keywords

Incremental Hierarchical Clustering, Privileged Information.

1. INTRODUCTION

Hierarchical clustering methods are very useful for supporting exploratory data analysis in text collections [1]. In these methods, the knowledge extracted from text documents is organized into clusters and subclusters, where more

---

*The authors wish to thank FAPESP for financial support (process 2010/20564-8, and 2011/19850-9)

general knowledge is represented by clusters near the root, while more specific knowledge is detailed by subclusters in the lower levels. This hierarchical organization is important for many applications related to document engineering, since it provides the intuitive browsing and visualization of text collections at various levels of abstraction [2].

The vast majority of hierarchical clustering algorithms consider that the text documents are represented only by "technical information", i.e., words and phrases directly extracted from texts. On the other hand, in many text clustering tasks, there is an additional valuable knowledge about the problem domain that is not represented in the technical information. In general, this additional knowledge is composed of domain-specific features and are provided by human experts. Due to the high cost of obtaining this expert knowledge, the domain-specific features have often been named in the literature as "privileged information" [4]. Although the privileged information is available only for a small data sample, this additional knowledge is very useful for improving the knowledge extraction over the entire data set [4, 3].

Recently, a new paradigm called LUPI – Learning Using Privileged Information – was proposed by Vapnik to incorporate privileged information in classification tasks [4]. In the LUPI paradigm, the (small sample) data sub-set represented by both technical information and privileged information is used for learning a classifier model. During this step, an extension of the SVM method (the so called SVM+ method) is applied to use privileged information in a process of model refinement, thereby improving the decision space derived from technical information. Privileged information is usually not available to the remainder of the data set, then the obtained model is used to classify new objects represented only by the technical information. While the LUPI paradigm has been successfully used in some predictive tasks such as time series prediction and protein classification, the extension of the LUPI for unsupervised settings involving hierarchical text clustering is an aspect not addressed in the literature. To the best of our knowledge, the only study that investigates the LUPI for data clustering is reported in [3]. However, the authors focus on partitional data clustering, which is not suitable to the context of our work.

In this paper we introduce a LUPI-based Incremental Hierarchical Clustering (LIHC) to incorporate privileged information into text clustering tasks. In the LIHC method, several clusters are obtained from the subset of documents that have some kind of privileged information, by running various clustering algorithms. This procedure is repeated for the same subset of documents to also obtain clusters from the technical information. The clusters are combined into a single clustering solution using consensus clustering [2, 1], thereby obtaining an initial hierarchical clustering model. Thus, if a document is mistakenly allocated to a particular clustering solution from technical information, the same document will not necessarily be mistakenly allocated in clustering solutions from privileged information; and this error can be corrected in the final clustering solution obtained by consensus clustering. The initial model is used for incremental clustering of the remaining documents that are represented only by technical information. The new documents are inserted into hierarchical clustering according to the similarity between a new document and the cluster centroids. We carried out an experimental evaluation on Reuters and 20-NewsGroups text collections and the results show that the LIHC method achieves superior clustering accuracy when compared to a traditional hierarchical clustering method.

2. LUPI-BASED INCREMENTAL HIERARCHICAL CLUSTERING (LIHC)

For convenience, consider that a text collection is represented by two sets of features χ and χ^*, where χ are the technical information features (from the well-known bag-of-words model) and χ^* are privileged information features (domain-specific features). More formally, the text collection with n documents is defined by $X_{pri} = \{\mathbf{x}_1^*, ..., \mathbf{x}_m^*\}$ and $X_{tec} = \{\mathbf{x}_1, ..., \mathbf{x}_m, \mathbf{x}_{m+1}, ..., \mathbf{x}_n\}$, where $\mathbf{x}^* \in \chi^*$ and $\mathbf{x} \in \chi$. Note that the privileged information is available only for a sample of m documents, thereby forming a document subset $Y = \{(\mathbf{x}_1, \mathbf{x}_1^*), ..., (\mathbf{x}_m, \mathbf{x}_m^*)\}$.

The LIHC method uses the documents belonging to the subset Y to generate an initial hierarchical clustering model. For this purpose, we use consensus clustering to aggregate the technical information and privileged information into a single robust clustering solution. Initially, several clusters are generated from the Y documents by running various clustering algorithms or alternatively repeated runs of the same algorithm with different parameter values. The generated clusters are aggregated by means of a co-association matrix $M(i, j) = \frac{a_{ij}}{p}$, where a_{ij} is the number of times that documents i and j are in the same cluster and p is the number of clustering solutions. Thus, let M the co-association matrix from technical information data, and let M^* the co-association matrix obtained from privileged information data. We compute the consensual co-association matrix $M^C(i, j) = \alpha M(i, j) + (1 - \alpha)M^*(i, j)$ for all documents i and j, where α ($0 < \alpha < 1$) indicates the weight of each information (technical or privileged) for the consensus clustering. In fact, the co-association matrix M^C represents a new concept of proximity among documents. Thus, the initial model of the LIHC method is obtained by applying any hierarchical clustering algorithm from the matrix M^C.

The remaining text documents $\{\mathbf{x}_{m+1}, ..., \mathbf{x}_n\}$ are inserted incrementally into hierarchical clustering. The LIHC method uses a incremental clustering technique called "single-pass" to find the existing cluster centroid in the hierarchy that is more similar to a new document. This step continues until there are no more documents to be inserted, thereby obtaining an updated hierarchical clustering solution.

3. EXPERIMENTAL EVALUATION

We carried out an experimental evaluation using two benchmark text collections, Reuters and 20-NewsGroups, to com-

pare the performance of our LUPI-based Incremental Hierarchical Clustering (LIHC). About 10% of the number of documents of each collection contain privileged information, in particular, some domain-specific features. We selected these documents to generate the initial model (with $\alpha = 0.5$) and the remaining documents are used to perform the incremental clustering.

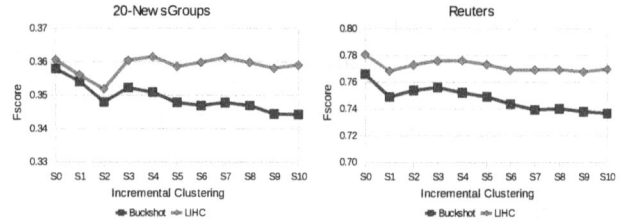

Figure 1: Incremental clustering accuracy of the LIHC and Buckshot methods

Figure 1 presents the incremental clustering accuracy (FScore index [2]) of the two methods: LIHC (our method) and Buckshot [1] (an traditional incremental clustering algorithm). It is important to observe that the step S_0 represents the clustering accuracy of the initial model, while the subsequent stages ($S_1, S_2, ..., S_{10}$) represent the incremental clustering. Statistical analysis (95% confidence level) from various runs of the clustering algorithms reveals that the LIHC method achieved superior results, thereby indicating that the privileged information was incorporated efficiently into hierarchical clustering. Furthermore, we observed that a better initial model also improves the quality of the incremental clustering (lower model degradation).

4. CONCLUDING REMARKS

We presented a LUPI-based incremental hierarchical clustering method for incorporating privileged information into clustering tasks. Our LIHC method is particularly interesting when there are domain-specific features for a small sample of the documents. This additional valuable information is used to obtain an initial hierarchical clustering model. As the vast majority of the documents are represented only by technical information, such as keywords and phrases, then the initial model is applied to cluster the remaining documents more effectively. Moreover, LIHC is based on incremental clustering, thereby allowing exploratory analysis of large text collections.

More details on the experimental results, as well as the text collections and our algorithms, are available online at http://sites.labic.icmc.usp.br/torch/doceng2013/.

5. REFERENCES

[1] C. C. Aggarwal and C. Zhai. A survey of text clustering algorithms. In *Mining Text Data*, pages 77–128. Springer-Verlag, 2012.

[2] D. C. Anastasiu, A. Tagarelli, and G. Karypis. Document Clustering: The Next Frontier. Technical Report. University of Minnesota, 2013.

[3] J. Feyereisl and U. Aickelin. Privileged information for data clustering. *Information Sciences*, 194:4–23, 2012.

[4] V. Vapnik and A. Vashist. A new learning paradigm: Learning using privileged information. *Neural Networks*, 22(5-6):544–557, 2009.

Beyond Term Clusters: Assigning Wikipedia Concepts to Scientific Documents

Ozge Yeloglu
Faculty of Computer Science
Dalhousie University
Halifax, Canada
yeloglu@cs.dal.ca

Evangelos Milios
Faculty of Computer Science
Dalhousie University
Halifax, Canada
eem@cs.dal.ca

A. Nur Zincir-Heywood
Faculty of Computer Science
Dalhousie University
Halifax, Canada
zincir@cs.dal.ca

ABSTRACT

We propose a model for assigning Wikipedia Concepts as scientific category labels to scientific documents where their terms are first grouped together using the well-known topic modelling method, Latent Dirichlet Allocation (LDA) and then assigned to Wikipedia Concepts by *wikification*. We *wikify* the terms of the topic model of a document to extract related concepts from Wikipedia. We experiment on two different datasets: the abstracts of the documents from the ACM Digital Library and the full papers of the UvT Collection. The ACM dataset includes Computer Science publications whereas UvT includes scientific publications from a range of topics[1]. Domain specific taxonomies are used for evaluation. Results show that our approach is able to assign Wikipedia Concepts to the scientific publications in an automated manner, removing any need for human supervision.

Categories and Subject Descriptors

H.3.3 [**Information Storage and Retrieval**]: Information Search and Retrieval; I.2.7 [**Artificial Intelligence**]: Natural Language Processing

Keywords

scientific corpora; topic labelling; categorizing term clusters

1. INTRODUCTION

Topic modelling has been a popular research problem due to its wide applicability. In general, topics are multinomial distributions over words or keyphrases generated in an unsupervised way to capture the meaning of huge volumes of text data. Although topic modelling is well studied in the literature, research on how to label the resulting topics meaningfully is still a major challenge.

---

[1] Faculties of UvT are: Center for Economic Research, Arts, Economics and Business Administration, Law, Philosophy, Social and Behavioral Sciences, and Business School.

DocEng'13, September 10–13, 2013, Florence, Italy.
ACM 978-1-4503-1789-4/13/09.
http://10.1145/2494266.2494297.

Candidate labels are selected from the topic models and ranked using a relevance score in [5]. Another way of automatic topic labelling is using readily available topic hierarchies or external sources. A set of similarity measures and topic labelling rules are defined in [3] to automatically label the topics according to a hierarchy. This hierarchy is obtained from the Google Directory service and expanded through the use of the OpenOffice English Thesaurus. A topic label candidate set is generated by sourcing topic label candidates from Wikipedia by querying with the top-N topic terms, identifying the top-ranked document titles and post-processing the document titles to extract sub-strings as label candidates to train a supervised method [2]. One can also argue for employing the well known lexical database WordNet as an external resource instead of Wikipedia. However, WordNet does not cover special domain vocabulary.

We propose to solve the topic labelling problem by automatically assigning Wikipedia concepts as higher level descriptions of a set of keyterms extracted from the document corpus.

1.1 Data Sets

ACM Collection, consists of abstracts and metadata of Computer Science publications from ACM Digital Library.

UvT Collection, is based on the Webwijs[2], a publicly accessible database of Tilburg University (UvT) employees (experts) who are involved in research or teaching.

1.2 Methods

Topic Modelling - LDA: Latent Dirichlet Allocation (LDA) [1] is a well known approach in the class of probabilistic topic models. We generated the topics (sets of words and terms) with the LDA implementation of the well-known MALLET toolkit [4].

Wikipedia Miner - *wikifier* function: We use the *wikify* function [6] of the Wikipedia Miner toolkit to map the set of topic keywords associated with each document by LDA to the related concepts from Wikipedia. As an example, the set of topic modelling keyterms (*active learning algorithm, adaptive mapping, bb dss algorithm, classification accuracy ...*) is mapped to (*Genetic Algorithms, Support Vector Machine, Evolutionary Computation ...*) by the *wikify* function.

2. EXPERIMENTAL RESULTS

We have conducted different topic labelling experiments on the ACM and UvT datasets.

---

[2] www.uvt.nl/webwijs/

Table 1: Mean Average Precision@3 Results of Topic Modelling approaches on the ACM Training Data

Number of Topics	Words	Terms	Words_Terms
100 Topics	0.68	0.67	0.76
50 Topics	0.71	0.77	0.80
20 Topics	0.88	0.84	0.90
10 Topics	0.97	0.92	0.95

Table 2: Number of matches between 115 gold-standard broad topics of UvT Collection and Log-Likelihood terms and Wikipedia Concepts.

Method Name	Top 5	Top 10	Top 20
Log-Likelihood	3 (2.6%)	5 (4.4%)	8 (7%)
Topic Modelling+*wikify*	18 (15.6%)	30 (26%)	38 (33%)

Table 3: Precision-Recall-F@3 Results on ACM Test-2006 Data.

Method	Input Data	Precision	Recall	F
100 Topics	Terms	0.34	0.62	0.42
100 Topics	Words_Terms	0.37	0.67	0.45
50 Topics	Terms	0.36	0.64	0.44
50 Topics	Words_Terms	0.36	0.65	0.45
10 Topics	Terms	0.38	0.68	0.46
10 Topics	Words_Terms	0.37	0.66	0.45

1) Mapping Term Sets to Wikipedia Concepts:
The LDA algorithm assigns to each document a set of words and/or terms. To label these sets and compare with the gold-standard data we follow these steps with the ACM dataset: 1) The ACM categories of the training document are associated with its set of terms. 2) Since a set of terms can be associated with more than one training document, ACM categories assigned to each set of terms are ranked depending on how many times a category is assigned as a label to that set. 3) Sets of terms are mapped to a set of Wikipedia concepts by the *wikify* function. 4) Concepts extracted from Wikipedia are then compared with the ACM categories and subcategories. Since Wikipedia concepts are not the same as the set of ACM categories, we *wikified* the ACM categories (including their subcategories) as well before the comparison.

Extracted Wikipedia concepts are able to represent **90%** of the ACM categories (**10 out of 11**). For the evaluation metric, we use Mean Average Precision (MAP) metric from Information Retrieval. MAP is the average of average precision values for a set of queries. That is, if the set of relevant documents for a query $q_j \in Q$ is $\{d_1,...,d_{mj}\}$ and R_{jk} is the set of ranked retrieval results from the top result until you get to document d_k, then

$$MAP(Q) = \frac{1}{|Q|} \sum_{j=1}^{|Q|} \frac{1}{m_j} \sum_{k=1}^{m_j} Precision(R_{jk})$$

In our case, LDA word/term set labels are ranked by their Wikipedia concept weights and the ground truth ACM categories are ranked by their frequency values. MAP values for 10, 20, 50, and 100 data points for the topic modelling method are shown in Table 1.

We have also employed UvT collection for mapping term sets to Wikipedia concepts. The gold-standard data in this experiment are the broad topics defined in the collection. Our task in this experiment is to automatically generate the broad topics of the collection using Wikipedia concepts.

We compare two methods on this dataset. The first method assigns the top ranking keyterms from the documents based on the Log-Likelihood ranking as topic labels. The second method assigns Wikipedia Concepts of the topic models determined by LDA as topic labels. 1149 keyterms extracted with CNC keyterm extraction method are clustered into 120 clusters using Weka's Expectation Maximization (EM) method and then the keyterms in each cluster are ranked with the popular Log-Likelihood method. Topic modelling is implemented using the MALLET toolkit and 120 topics are created. Keyterms, which are assigned by the LDA method to the topics, are then *wikified* to extract the corresponding Wikipedia concepts. Finally, we compute the overlap between the gold-standard broad topics and the resulting lists. Out of 115 broad topics, the baseline method matches the

least amount of term overlap with the gold-standard as seen in Table 2. LDA generates significantly better topic titles than the baseline method in every case.

2) Assigning Categories to Documents: In this experiment, we automatically assign Wikipedia concepts as labels to the training and test documents of ACM data set. For this purpose, sets of terms generated by the LDA model based on the training data are *wikified*. Each test document is assigned to a set of terms by LDA and then its corresponding Wikipedia concept. Then, these concepts are compared with the user-assigned ACM categories of each document.

Precision, Recall and F measures are calculated as the evaluation metrics for both training and test data. Test data is split into three. Test-2006 has 25,781 documents published in 2006. Test-2007 has 35,219 documents published in 2007. Finally, Test-2008 has 18310 documents published in 2008. Results of the Test-2006 are presented in Table 3. Results of Training, Test-2007 and Test-2008 are not included because of limited space and the similar F values.

3. REFERENCES

[1] D. M. Blei, A. Y. Ng, and M. I. Jordan. Latent dirichlet allocation. *Journal of Machine Learning Research*, 3:993–1022, 2003.

[2] J. H. Lau, K. Grieser, D. Newman, and T. Baldwin. Automatic Labelling of Topic Models. In *49th Annual Meeting of the Association of Computational Linguistics*, pages 1536–1545, 2011.

[3] D. Magatti, S. Calegari, D. Ciucci, and F. Stella. Automatic labeling of topics. In *Intelligent Systems Design and Applications*, pages 1227 –1232, 2009.

[4] A. K. McCallum. Mallet: A machine learning for language toolkit. http://mallet.cs.umass.edu, 2002.

[5] Q. Mei, X. Shen, and C. Zhai. Automatic labeling of multinomial topic models. *Proceedings of the 13th ACM SIGKDD International Conference on Knowledge Discovery and Data Mining*, 2007.

[6] D. Milne and I. H. Witten. Learning to link with wikipedia. In *Proceedings of the ACM Conference on Information and Knowledge Management*, 2008.

Cross Language Indexing and Retrieval of the Cypriot Digital Antiquities Repository

Dayu Yuan
Dept. of Computer Science and Engineering
The Pennsylvania State University
University Park, Pennsylvania, USA
duy113@psu.edu

Prasenjit Mitra
College of Information Sciences and Technology
The Pennsylvania State University
University Park, Pennsylvania, USA
pmitra@ist.psu.edu

ABSTRACT

We design and implement a cross-language retrieval system for the Cypriot Digital Antiquities Repository (cyDAR). Users can query either by English and Ancient Greek to search for documents written in Ancient Greek. Because of the lack of dictionary and parallel corpus, we use translation machine to translate the documents. We index both the original Ancient Greek text and translated English text to facilitated multi-language search.

Categories and Subject Descriptors

H.3 [**INFORMATION STORAGE AND RETRIEVAL**]: Information Search and Retrieval; I.2.7 [**Natural Language Processing**]: Machine translation

Keywords

Cross-language information retrieval; Digital Library

1. INTRODUCTION

cyDAR contains works describing scientific, philosophical, and social commentaries from antiquity to early Christian era. These works are written in Ancient Greek. It is important to design a cross-language retrieval system to support the search by both English and Ancient Greek. Users, represented by historians or archaeologists, may input a query in Ancient Greek describing what are found in a newly discovered document. They are interested in finding cyDAR documents that are similar to the query. Another type of users with information needs may formulate a query in English and search for related documents. The major goal of the cyDAR project is to help both types of users. In this paper, we design a cross-language retrieval platform to provide multi-lingual accesses to these priceless cyDAR documents.

A cross-language retrieval system can be designed with either *document translation* or *query translation*. For *document translation*, the cyDAR documents are first translated to

DocEng'13, September 10–13, 2013, Florence, Italy.

ACM 978-1-4503-1789-4/13/09.
http://dx.doi.org/10.1145/2494266.2494298.

English. And then, both the original corpus and the translated corpus are indexed separately for search. When an Ancient Greek query comes in, the system looks up the Ancient Greek index. When an English query comes in, the system looks up the English index. For a mixed query containing both the Ancient Greek and English terms, the system searches for both indexes and find the answer by combining results found on both indexes. The *query translation methods* only index the original documents (in Ancient Greek). When an English query or a mixed query comes, the system first translates the query into Ancient Greek and then searches for the documents related to the translated query. Although saves the off-line processing time, the query translation methods take more time on on-line query processing.

We adopt the document translation strategy based on users' requirements. Traditional users search on cross-language systems with no-English queries because they are incapable of formulating a query in English. Users of our system formulate a query in Ancient Greek because they want to find results related to the query in its original form (in Ancient Greek). To help users understand the search results, an English translation of the results are returned as well. Hence, translating the original corpus to English is inevitable and the document translation methods fit better than query translation methods. We further discuss the translation algorithms used for translation. Three candidates, i.e., machine-readable dictionary, statistical matching and machine translation are discussed in details. We choose to use machine translation for our system because of its good performance as shown in CLEF 09 'Ad-hoc track' [2].

2. DESIGN AND IMPLEMENTATION

Data Description: The cyDAR documents are written in Ancient Greek. They also have Modern Greek as translation. Ancient Greek is written in italics and Modern Greek is in normal font. This observation helps us distinguish the Modern Greek from Ancient Greek. The raw data is a collection of books, each of which contains multiple essays. Each essay is a work describing scientific, philosophical, or social commentary. We define each essay as a retrieval unit. It contains (may be partially) the original description in Ancient Greek, translated version in Modern Greek and commentary in Modern Greek. Other information, such as authors and sources, is also included.

System Architecture: Our system is implemented based on document translation. Figure 1 shows the overall design of our system. The system comprises three components: preprocessing, indexing and searching. In the preprocess-

(a)   (b)

Figure 2: Search Interface and Result

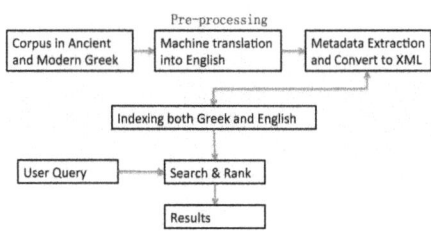

Figure 1: System Framework

ing step, the cyDAR documents are first segmented into retrieval units, and then translated into English by translation machines (will introduce later). Metadata is further extracted and each document is converted to a XML file. In the indexing step, those XML files are indexed by Solr (lucene.apache.org/solr/) with language-aware stemming. The indexing and matching steps are standard procedures as in monolingual retrieval system, we focus on the preprocessing step, especially the translation step.

2.1 Translation

Translation with machine-readable dictionary maps words (terms) from one language to another by looking up a dictionary. The assumption of this method is that words are independent to each other as in the bag-of-word model. Lexilogos(http://www.lexilogos.com/) can be used as a resource of dictionary. Lexilogos contains several dictionaries and it solves the translation problem to some extend, but not sufficient to address all issues. One challenge is the ambiguity and synonymy. That is, a word T may be translated to multiple words that may not be directly related to T given the context [1]. Another challenge is the out-of-word phenomena. The dictionary fails to map a word from one language to another language. In our system, given a word in Ancient Greek, the lexilogos dictionary may find no mapping words in English. There are many reasons for the out-of-word phenomena. One is because of the lack of coverage of the dictionary. Another is because of the morphemes of Ancient Greek. Hence, we dot not choose machine-readable dictionary methods. Statistical translation is an extension of the machine-readable dictionary. Statistical translation maps a word T to a set of words with different probability. The probability can be either context dependent or independent. However, in order to learn the probability, a large amount of parallel corpus are needed. Previous work has studied data collected from Wikipedia [3] or other sources for the learning task. There are very few parallel corpuses in both English and Ancient Greek. Hence, we rule out statistical translation methods. Machine translation is a third option

for the system implementation. Recent study on CLEF 09 'Ad-hoc track' [2] have shown that cross-language retrieval platform implemented with Google Translator can perform more than 90% as good as monolingual IR system, given popular languages. Although straightforward, it is hard to translate documents or queries in Ancient Greek directly to English by cutting-edge translation machines because Ancient Greek is not a popular language. However, we can use the translation machines to translate from Modern Greek to English, both of which are popular languages. In addition, in each retrieval unit, there is always a paragraph of Modern Greek as the translation of the original description in Ancient Greek. Thus, by the bridging of Modern Greek, we can use translation machine with a high precision.

2.2 Implementation and Demo

Figure 2 shows the query interface of the system. Four types of metadata can be searched together with the free text queries. These four types, i.e., author, book, fragment number and sources, are important on exploring the documents (retrieval units). Given an English query "Athenian War", the system searches the index and returns lists of results with order. Similarly, given an Ancient Greek query equivalent to Lucian, a list of documents containing this word are returned, as shown in Figure 2(b).

3. CONCLUSION AND FUTURE WORK

We introduce the design of a cross-language retrieval platform to support both English and Ancient Greek search. A document translation method is adopted. Metadata information is extracted to facilitate structural search. Our system has shortages as well. Given the two queries with the same meaning, but one in English and the other in Ancient Greek, the ranking of the results may be different. This is because we normalize the ranking score considering the length of documents. Since words in Ancient Greek and English are not mapped one-to-one, the length of a original document may be different from its translation. We plan to address this challenge in further study.

4. REFERENCES

[1] P. C. Carol Peters, Martin Braschler. *Multilingual Information Retrieval From Research To Practice.* Springer, 2012.

[2] N. Ferro and C. Peters. Clef 09 ad hoc track overview: Tel and persian tasks. In *CLEF (1)*, pages 13–35, 2009.

[3] M.-H. Li, V. Klyuev, and S.-H. Wu. Multilingual sentence alignment from wikipedia as multilingual comparable corpora. In *HC '10*, pages 167–171, 2010.

No Need to Justify Your Choice:
Pre-compiling Line Breaks to Improve eBook Readability

Alexander J. Pinkney
Document Engineering Lab.
School of Computer Science
University of Nottingham
Nottingham, NG8 1BB, UK
azp@cs.nott.ac.uk

Steven R. Bagley
Document Engineering Lab.
School of Computer Science
University of Nottingham
Nottingham, NG8 1BB, UK
srb@cs.nott.ac.uk

David F. Brailsford
Document Engineering Lab.
School of Computer Science
University of Nottingham
Nottingham, NG8 1BB, UK
dfb@cs.nott.ac.uk

ABSTRACT

Implementations of eBooks have existed in one form or another for at least the past 20 years, but it is only in the past 5 years that dedicated eBook hardware has become a mass-market item.

New screen technologies, such as e-paper, provide a reading experience similar to those of physical books, and even backlit LCD and OLED displays are beginning to have high enough pixel densities to render text crisply at small point sizes. Despite this, the major element of the physical book that has not yet made the transition to the eBook is high-quality typesetting.

The great advantage of eBooks is that the presentation of the page can adapt, at rendering time, to the physical screen size and to the reading preferences of the user. Until now, simple first-fit line-breaking algorithms have had to be used in order to give acceptable rendering speed whilst conserving battery life.

This paper describes a system for producing well-typeset, scalable document layouts for eBook readers, without the computational overhead normally associated with better-quality typesetting. We precompute many of the complex parts of the typesetting process, and perform the majority of the 'heavy lifting' at document compile-time, rather than at rendering time. Support is provided for floats (such as figures in an academic paper, or illustrations in a novel), for arbitrary screen sizes, and also for arbitrary point-size changes within the text.

Categories and Subject Descriptors

I.7.2 [**Document and Text Processing**]: Document Preparation—*format and notation, markup languages*; I.7.4 [**Document and Text Processing**]: Electronic Publishing

General Terms

Algorithms, Documentation, Experimentation

Keywords

eBooks, Document layout, Typesetting

DocEng'13, September 10–13, 2013, Florence, Italy.
Copyright is held by the owner/author(s). Publication rights licensed to ACM.
ACM 978-1-4503-1770-2/13/09 ...$15.00.
http://dx.doi.org/10.1145/2494266.2494310.

1. INTRODUCTION

Many studies [9, 5, 17, 13] have shown that good typography is the key to readability. In particular, Bill Hill in *The Magic of Reading* [9] emphasises that both the regularity of whitespace between words and the evenness of line lengths are of particular importance. Traditionally, good typography can be ensured as the document is being created — as is the case with documents stored as PDF — since the size and shape of the output medium is fixed. However, non-PDF eBook formats, such as EPUB and Amazon's Kindle format, do not have a fixed presentation associated with their textual content and therefore they rely on the eBook readers themselves to perform the typesetting and layout.

It would be hoped that eBook readers, being dedicated reading devices, would strive to typeset a book's content in the most readable form possible. Unfortunately, most eBook readers seem to rely on a simple first-fit line-breaking algorithm, which means that the whitespace between words can vary wildly between consecutive lines of text: extremely wide spacing on some lines, and extremely tight spacing on others. This can be avoided by using more complex line-breaking algorithms that can identify optimal breakpoints in the text, such as that detailed by Knuth and Plass in [12]. These algorithms are not currently used in eBook readers because they are computationally complex: the Knuth-Plass algorithm, for example, runs in $O(n^2)$ time, whereas first-fit runs in $O(n)$. (Both of these are per paragraph, where n is the number of possible breakpoints in the paragraph.) With some pruning, the effective complexity of the Knuth-Plass algorithm can be reduced to linear time [10, 7, 11], but large constant factors still make the algorithm slow in practice. In any case, the Knuth-Plass algorithm is certainly not the last word in line breaking algorithms. Mittelbach and Rowley [14] mention some limitations of the Knuth-Plass algorithm: as an example, it has no mechanism to avoid (nor indeed any knowledge of) vertical rivers of whitespace. Inevitably, adding support to avoid rivers, and for any of the other nuances used by hand compositors, would add further complexity. Portable eBook readers have both limited processing power and are powered by batteries; implementing a more computationally complex algorithm would not only make page turns and point-size changes noticeably slow, but it would also noticeably increase the drain on the battery.

In the absence of new battery technologies, one method to maximise battery life, and hence reading time, is to minimise the complexity of any algorithms that run on portable devices, and so letting their CPUs idle as much as possible. Given these constraints and desires (to maximise battery life and increase readability), we suggest a system whereby certain parts of the typesetting of the document are performed at "compile time" of the document, so that less processing power and battery power needs to be devoted at "view time" on the device.

In a previous paper [15], we described a simple system that enables documents to be partially pre-rendered, whilst retaining a reasonable degree of flowability. The paper outlined the concept of producing multiple partial renderings of a document, which effectively causes the system to 'compile out' the line-breaking algorithm. In this paper, we have reimplemented and extended this system, so that it can be tested on a wider range of devices, and can produce document layouts on the fly that previously would not have been possible. For convenience, in the remainder of this paper, we shall refer to the partially pre-compiled documents as *malleable documents*.

The rest of this paper details the implementation of our new system. Section 2 recaps the implementation of our previous system and also discusses related work in this area. Sections 3 and 4 describe how our malleable documents are generated and viewed respectively. Section 5 evaluates the performance of our system, while section 6 concludes by discussing future work.

2. RELATED WORK

Much work has been done in the field of automated document layout, though most systems are geared towards producing documents with one fixed presentation. Although these documents may have wonderful layout, they cannot easily be scaled to fit every one of the plethora of devices upon which the documents may be viewed.

A fairly comprehensive review of the literature around automatic document formatting was published in [11]. Since most (if not all) literature in this field is geared towards producing documents with static layouts, the computational complexity of the algorithms used has never been of huge concern. It seems that until now, not much thought has been given to the development of document formatting systems that run in real time, or on battery powered devices.

2.1 Our Previous Work

In our 2011 paper [15], we outlined the concept of pre-rendering a document's text multiple times, into multiple *galleys* of text. Each galley is effectively one long column, and each galley is rendered at a different width.

Once the text had been typeset into a galley, the resultant lines of text could be treated as atomic units. These units could then be placed onto the page individually; in particular, if the height of the page was altered, lines could be added to or removed from the bottom of the page, allowing the text to "flow" in a vertical direction.

The resultant document is composed of multiple galley renderings of the source document, each with a different width. At runtime, the renderer chooses the most appropriate width of galley to display, based upon the screen size of the device. If the screen size permits, the rendering algorithm may choose to display multiple columns, in order to best fill the available space. This system, very much a proof-of-concept prototype, provided no support for floats, and no support for any items (for example headers or footers) to span multiple columns.

The system was initially implemented within Component-Object Graphic (COG) PDF, a system developed at Nottingham that provides encapsulation for objects within PDF documents, and allows for their dynamic modification [16, 4, 3, 1]. This medium was chosen simply because the tools for creating these documents were readily available to us, and because PDF provides a reasonable guarantee that its contents will be rendered identically in any PDF viewer.

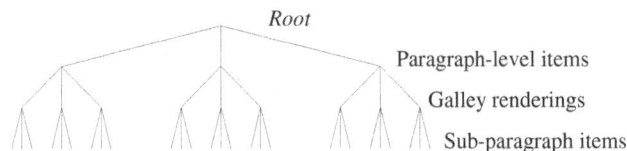

Figure 1: A simple document structure tree. The first level below the root represents all paragraph-level items: headings, paragraphs, figures etc. These items have one child for each galley rendering of the document. These in turn have one child for each sub-component of their content, for example the lines of a paragraph.

3. DOCUMENT GENERATION

Since the previous paper, the system has been reimplemented in HTML, JavaScript and CSS, as well as being extended to add support for floating items, and for items to span across multiple columns.

Previously, the generation of malleable documents involved a manual process built around a pre-existing solution developed at Nottingham. However, in order for the system to be usable, an automated process is required, through which a malleable document can be generated. The underlying principles of the system remain the same, for example the paragraph-tree structure described in [15], as shown in figure 1, is retained.

In our implementation, the source document is described in terms of separate logical blocks; a block is either designated as a 'float', or as a 'paragraph'. Floats are currently limited to referencing images only (with an optional size parameter). Paragraphs, on the other hand, are described by their desired textual content. This is deliberately simplistic, as an aid to testing. (We envisage that in a real system, the source document would have a richer language, perhaps marked up in a form similar to LATEX source, or in XML.)

Next, the source document is passed through a program to produce the output that becomes the malleable document itself. This program passes the text of each paragraph through an implementation of a line-breaking algorithm (we use Knuth-Plass, but this could be replaced by any other algorithm that performs line breaking and justification). Each paragraph is rendered multiple times, once for each galley width, in order to produce the document's multiple galley renderings. Each line of each rendering of every paragraph is converted into a list of its composite words. All of these words have an associated offset value, which is later used when drawing the text to ensure that each word is positioned on the line with the correct spacing.

The content of the floats is largely left unchanged. A reference to the image, along with its required dimensions, is simply passed through to the output. If dimensions were not explicitly specified in the source document, the pixel size of the image itself is used.

Finally, once the whole of the source document has been processed, the rendered content is output — in the form of the document structure tree shown in figure 1 — encoded in JSON. This becomes the data representing the source document, which, in conjunction with the viewer defined in the next section, becomes a *malleable document*.

4. THE VIEWER

In order to circumvent the browser's default text layout algorithm, and to ensure that our "high quality" pre-computed text layout is used, the viewer must be able to specify the absolute position of every word on each line, in a manner not dissimilar to the internals of a PDF file. The document generator described in the previous section ensures that all the information needed to lay out the text is contained within the generated JSON object representing the document structure tree.

When the viewer is launched, it decides which is the most appropriate galley rendering to display, based on some metric of which rendering will be most aesthetically pleasing. Since we feel it works well, we have not altered the metric defined in [15], which attempts to balance a penalty for excessive inter-column whitespace against a penalty for too many columns.

Although every galley is rendered in the same point size this can be scaled up or down, at view time, based on the preference of the user, to simulate point-size changes. The gaps between words are scaled proportionally, to allow the text to remain correctly justified.

4.1 Floats with a Queue

Our initial attempt at supporting floats took inspiration from TEX, which places floats into a queue until it finds somewhere it deems appropriate to place the first float. In order to emulate this, we define two queues: the *float queue*, and the *line queue*. ('Line queue' is perhaps a slight misnomer, but it is somewhat snappier than 'non-floating items queue'.)

If both queues are empty, as they will be at the start of the layout process, the document structure tree is traversed, and when the first paragraph-level item (see figure 1) is encountered, its subcomponents (of the chosen galley rendering) are added to the requisite queue: lines to the line queue, and floats to the float queue.

When at least one of the queues is not empty, document layout begins. If the float queue is nonempty, and the first float in the queue will fit below the last typeset item, it is placed on the page. If not, items from the line queue are placed one by one, until no more will fit in the current column. When this happens, a new column is started, and the first float in the float queue is output. Whenever the line queue is depleted, and no floats in the float queue will fit at the current point on the page, all subcomponents of the next paragraph-level item from the document structure tree are queued.

Pagination is reasonably simple with this queueing system: as soon as a page is full, the layout can be restarted at the origin of the page using the current status of both queues and the document structure tree. It is entirely possible that floats may appear on pages subsequent to their callout point in the text, but this effect should be no worse than in many current typesetting systems.

While this approach does produce reasonable layouts, and handles floats well without the need for backtracking, it is not particularly conducive to producing layouts with floats that span multiple columns. The queue-based layout described above is rather simplistic: it knows about the size of each component that it lays out but it does not remember the history of the positions of any of the components that are already laid out. This makes it difficult to have items that span more than one column, because there is no mechanism to mark space on the page as being reserved. In order to do this, we must take another approach.

4.2 A Grid-Based Layout

A simple method for allowing parts of a page to be reserved is to break it up into a grid. Grid-based layouts are useful in many situations [6]; one place of particular note is that of modern-day newspapers. We follow the example set by these newspapers, and define our grid's row height to be the same as the leading of the document's body text, and the grid's column width to be the measure of one text column plus the required gutter space.

Figure 2: An excerpt from our 2011 paper, typeset and rendered by our new system.

The viewer uses the dimensions of the float, as specified in the document structure tree (see section 3), to determine how many columns it should span. The float is scaled to span the integer multiple of column widths that most closely matches its 'natural' size, though for reasons that should hopefully be obvious, this number is limited to a minimum of 1, and a maximum of the number of columns on the page. Additionally, checks are made to ensure that the scaling will not cause the height of the figure to exceed that of the page.

An advantage of this grid-based approach is that it no longer requires the use of queues, either for lines, or for floats. The viewer simply traverses the document structure tree, placing each item in the first available place in the grid. In the case of floats, or other items larger than multiples of the main leading, spaces in the grid can be marked as reserved, to prevent other items from trampling over their reserved space. If a float will not fit directly below the previous item to be placed, the grid is walked over until a gap of sufficient size can be found. Figure 2 shows an example of a document laid out with this system.

Pagination becomes a little trickier when floats are allowed to span multiple columns. For example, if a float, whose natural size would lead it to span n columns, is encountered in the document structure tree when there are $(n-1)$ or fewer columns remaining to be typeset on the page, it must be decided how best to handle the situation. Three obvious options present themselves: alter the float to span fewer columns; delay the placement of the float until the start of the next page; or backtrack and check whether there is room to move the float back one or more columns, by shunting non-floatable text lines forwards.

The first option is clearly not desirable behaviour, given that shrinking a float may well reduce its legibility. Additionally, if this becomes a common problem, it it likely to be noticeable that floats spanning into the rightmost column of the page appear shrunken. The second option (delaying placement until the following page) is a reasonable compromise, though it will increase float-drift (whereby floats become separated from their callout points in the text), which is not ideal. The third option (backtracking and shunting) is likely to produce the most desirable output, although some computational overhead will be added. One approach is simply to check whether there is enough space immediately to the left (specifically a gap between other, already placed, floats) into which the current float can be placed, with the displaced lines being shunted forwards. This method will not produce layouts as optimal as methods that use full backtracking and check all possibilities, but it will run in much quicker time. A combination of all three of the above options is likely to work best in practice.

5. EVALUATION

Currently, our solution suffers from significantly bloated file-sizes: each rendering requires one full copy of the document's source text, in addition to positioning data for each word. Even after compression, this leads to filesizes that are an order of magnitude larger than the source text. We have not yet given great consideration to space efficiency: it is possible that by separating the text from the positioning data with the use of pointers (similar to the approach described in [2]) a more space-efficient encoding could be devised.

Another drawback of our system is that the choice of typeface must be set at document compile-time. There is no reason, in principle, why renderings in multiple typefaces could not be included within the file, though clearly it would be impractical to render the document in every typeface known to mankind. A carefully chosen selection of serif and sans-serif typefaces should hopefully cover most eventualities.

5.1 Computational Performance

The layout system described herein works in a similar manner to a first-fit line-breaking algorithm, in that it places elements on the page in order, in the first place they will fit. Items that are the same size as a single grid cell, such as lines of text set in the main point size, can simply be placed in the first empty slot in the current column, or the first empty slot in the next column, should there be no empty spaces. For the placement of items that are larger than a single grid cell, there is some overhead required to step through the grid until a suitable position can be found. Once a position has been found, each grid cell that it overlaps must be marked as being reserved.

Whilst this algorithm does have a greater-than-linear time complexity, the problem size is actually reduced in comparison to a first-fit text layout algorithm, since our system uses lines of text as its atomic units, rather than individual words. For this reason, we feel that our algorithm should still be efficient enough to merit use on portable eBook readers.

5.2 Aesthetic Performance

Aesthetically speaking, our system produces layouts that we feel most people would consider to be 'good'. The system can guarantee use of a high-quality line breaking algorithm, since it has effectively been compiled in, and so the only remaining concern is that the columns of text and floats are laid out in a pleasing manner.

Harrington et al. [8] identified nine aesthetic measures for automated document layout. A number of these measures (alignment, regularity, uniform separation, white-space free-flow, uniformity) are particularly well satisfied by our system, due to its use of a grid to provide regular layout.

We intend to run a user study to assess the more qualitative aspects of our system.

6. FUTURE WORK

The system as described in this paper has only very basic support for floats. A particular limitation is that unlike paragraphs, each float has only one rendering, which must be scaled up or down as required, to fit across multiples of columns. Whilst for image-based figures or illustrations, this is probably already the desired behaviour, other types of floats, such as tables or code listings, would almost certainly benefit from the inclusion of multiple width renderings, with the choice of which rendering to display to be made at view-time.

Since the malleable document and viewer are composed entirely from HTML, CSS, and JavaScript — the core technologies behind EPUB — modifying our system to produce self-contained EPUB files seems an obvious next step.

7. REFERENCES

[1] S. R. Bagley. COG extractor. In *Proceedings of the 2006 ACM Symposium on Document Engineering*, page 31. ACM Press, 2006.

[2] S. R. Bagley. Lessons from the dragon: Compiling PDF to machine code. In *Proceedings of the 2010 ACM Symposium on Document Engineering*, 2010.

[3] S. R. Bagley and D. F. Brailsford. Demo abstract: The COG scrapbook. In *Proceedings of the 2005 ACM Symposium on Document Engineering*, pages 233–234. ACM Press, 2005.

[4] S. R. Bagley, D. F. Brailsford, and M. R. B. Hardy. Creating reusable well-structured PDF as a sequence of component object graphic (COG) elements. In *Proceedings of the 2003 ACM Symposium on Document Engineering*, pages 58–67. ACM Press, 2003.

[5] R. Bringhurst. *The Elements of Typographic Style (v 3.2)*. Hartley & Marks, 2008.

[6] D. Collier. *Collier's Rules for Desktop Design and Typography*. Addison-Wesley, 1991.

[7] D. Eppstein and Z. Galil. Sparse dynamic programming II: Convex and concave cost functions. *J. ACM*, 39(3):546–567, 1992.

[8] S. J. Harrington, J. F. Naveda, R. P. Jones, P. Roetling, and N. Thakkar. Aesthetic measures for automated document layout. In *Proceedings of the 2004 ACM Symposium on Document Engineering*, pages 109–111. ACM Press, 2004.

[9] B. Hill. The magic of reading. Technical report, Microsoft, 1999.

[10] D. S. Hirschberg and L. L. Larmore. The least weight subsequence problem. *SIAM J. Comput.*, 16(4):628–638, 1987.

[11] N. Hurst, W. Li, and K. Marriott. Review of automatic document formatting. In *Proceedings of the 2009 ACM Symposium on Document Engineering*, 2009.

[12] D. E. Knuth and M. F. Plass. Breaking paragraphs into lines. *Software — Practice and Experience*, 11:1119–1184, 1981.

[13] G. E. Legge and C. A. Bigelow. Does print size matter for reading? A review of findings from vision science and typography. *Journal of Vision*, 11(5):8:1–22, 2011.

[14] F. Mittelbach and C. Rowley. The pursuit of quality — how can automated typesetting achieve the highest standards of craft typography? In *EP92 (Proceedings of Electronic Publishing)*, pages 261–273. Cambridge University Press, 1991.

[15] A. J. Pinkney, S. R. Bagley, and D. F. Brailsford. Reflowable documents composed from pre-rendered atomic components. In *Proceedings of the 11th ACM Symposium on Document Engineering*, DocEng '11, pages 163–166, New York, NY, USA, 2011. ACM.

[16] P. N. Smith and D. F. Brailsford. Towards structured, block-based PDF. *Electronic Publishing — Origination, Dissemination and Design*, 8(2 and 3):153–165, June/September 1995.

[17] G. Voorhees. Congeniality of reading on digital devices. Master's thesis, Rochester Institute of Technology, 2011.

Reflowing and Annotating Scientific Papers on eBook Readers

Simone Marinai
Dipartimento di Ingegneria dell'Informazione
Università di Firenze, Italy
simone.marinai@unifi.it

ABSTRACT

Working with scientific and technical papers on small screen devices, such as tablets and eBook readers, is difficult since these works are often typeset in multiple columns with a relatively small font size.

On tablets, pan and zoom operations allow users to visualize the text in the desired size, however, tracing the text in multiple columns can be uneasy and not appropriate for studying and working with the scientific works. Moreover, these operations are slow on most e-ink eBook readers that have limited computation resources. Document reflow is in this case one option, but it is difficult to provide a satisfactory visualization of scientific and technical papers.

In this paper, we describe one off-line tool for scientific document reflow that adopts document image processing techniques to generate one modified version of the original PDF organized as a single column text that can be easily visualized on eBook readers. Moreover, the tool allows the user to make free-form annotations on the modified paper using the tools of the eBook reader. These annotations are faithfully reproduced in the original two-column document.

Categories and Subject Descriptors

I.7.4 [**Document and Text Processing**]: Electronic Publishing; H.3.1 [**Content Analysis and Indexing**]: Indexing Methods

Keywords

eBook, ePub, SVG, Annotations

1. INTRODUCTION

While eBook readers are nowadays widely used to read novels and other text-only documents, their use with scientific and technical works is still challenging. There are two main problems: the low screen resolution, that is particularly critical to display two-column articles and the subsequent manipulation of free-form annotations.

DocEng'13, September 10–13, 2013, Florence, Italy.
Copyright 2013 ACM 978-1-4503-1789-4/13/09 ...$15.00.
http://dx.doi.org/10.1145/2494266.2494311 .

Most scientific and technical papers are printed on two-column formats. In this case, by resizing the page so that a single column is centered on the screen it is possible for users to easily read the text even on small screens. However, whenever the page to be read needs to be changed, a sequence of pan and zoom operations need to be done. These operations are quite simple if the sub-page is in the same column, but can be cumbersome when the reading order requires to continue on the next column or even the next page. Depending on the relationship between the column dimension and the eBook reader screen size, to read one page in the original document, six to eight operations would be required, each taking from few to several seconds.

Scientific works usually contain tables and illustrations that are referred in the text and are located in other places in the document. Even if the illustration is in the same page, but not in the same column, checking the illustration would require two operations (to visualize the illustration and to go back to the original text). All these context switches are particularly annoying when dealing with scientific papers either for study or for research.

The above problems, related to the small screen size, are well known and several approaches are considered to solve them.

One obvious solution is to distribute the scientific works in formats that are intrinsically reflowable, such as the ePub one. The direct production of digital works in ePub format is probably the best solution to this problem and has been addressed by IEEE for papers in Transactions and Magazines published since 2011 and downloaded by individual subscribers [1]. However, this initiative covers a few documents available only to some users.

Another solution is based on the conversion of the PDF document in reflowable formats. This conversion can be made on-line or off-line. In the on-line case the visualization software can dynamically extract the text in the PDF document and arrange it on the screen. Two examples of this approach are the Adobe$^{(c)}$ Reader Mobile software embedded in some devices (e.g. the SONY reader Touch Edition and the PocketBook Pro) and the Foxit PDF reader available as an Android App. In the offline case, appropriate tools are designed to extract the information from the PDF document and then convert it to ePub format, as has been done for books in human and social sciences in [6]

In both cases the reflow of PDF documents is usually satisfactory for text-intensive documents, but can be inadequate for scientific and technical documents. For example, in Fig-

with an interpolation with pages identified.

For each lp_i we identify one and only one $Entry_{k,j}$ ($j = 0, ..., m-1$) that corresponds to lp_k. This is the *actual title* ($Title_k$). When we identify the $Title_k$ we can link it with the *target title* adding a *bookmark* in the PDF file and including this information in the Epub ToC.

The search for $Title_k$ is made in two steps. First, we assign to each page one $score \in [0,1]$. Second, we check the pages with highest scores, and we find the *target title* position.

3.4.1 Page selection

We first search all the occurrences of the trigrams obtained from $Entry_{i,j}$. Let W_h ($h = 1, .., N$; N number of book pages) be the set of words in the page p_h with at least one trigram of $Entry_i$. We assign one score to each page p_h on the basis of a similarity measure of each word of $Entry_{i,j}$ with all the words in the list W_h. Let $Word_1$ and $Word_2$ be two words to be compared; let $TR(Word_i)$ be the set of trigrams that can be generated by the word $Word_i$. The similarity between the two words is computed as:

$$S(Word_1, Word_2) = \frac{\#(TR(Word_1) \bigcap TR(Word_2))}{Max(\#(TR(Word_1)), \#(TR(Word_2)))}$$

We can then assign a score to each word in $Entry_{i,j}$, by looking for the closest word in the page. Let $WordE_y$ be one word of $Entry_{i,j}$ and $Word_x$ be one word in W_h the score of $WordE_y$ is:

$$Sc(WordE_y) = \max S(WordE_y, Word_x)$$

The score of page p_h on the basis of $Entry_{i,j}$ is computed

trigrams that can be generated by the word $Word_i$. The

similarity between the two words is computed as:

$$S(Word_1, Word_2) =$$

$$\frac{\#(TR(Word_1) \bigcap TR(Word_2))}{Max(\#(TR(Word_1)), \#(TR(Word_2)))}$$

We can then assign a score to each word in $Entry_{i,j}$, by looking for the closest word in the page. Let $WordE_y$ be one word of $Entry_{i,j}$ and $Word_x$ be one word in W_h the score of $WordE_y$ is:

$$Sc(WordE_y) = \max S(WordE_y, Word_x) \qquad (1)$$

The score of page p_h on the basis of $Entry_{i,j}$ is computed by:

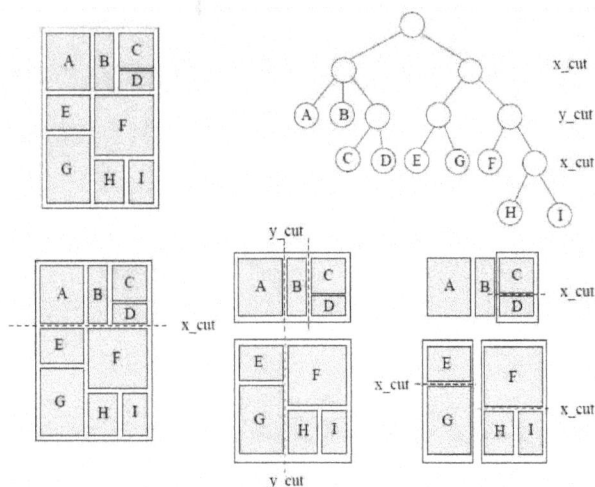

Figure 1: Left: part of a two-column paper reflowed by the proposed system. Right: the same document dynamically adapted on an eBook reader.

Figure 2: Example of XY tree. In the upper-left part of the image the original page is reported. The three images in the lower part describe the position of cuts at different levels of segmentation.

ure 1 we show, on the right, the dynamic resize of a scientific paper on the SONY reader Touch Edition.

Most eBook readers have a screen size of 6" and a resolution ranging from 800×600 to 1024×768. These values are appropriate to visualize each column of a two-column paper and usually there is no need to further zoom-in the document.

Starting from this observation we designed a prototype system, described in this paper, that identifies the page layout and arranges the document content in an equivalent single column document. During the document reconstruction it is essential to identify the actual reading order to minimize the page changes required when reading the document. This is achieved by using layout analysis techniques originally developed to process scanned documents. The final single-column document can be navigated with simple page-up and page-down actions that are intuitive and simple in most eBook readers.

One essential feature required when working with scientific and technical papers is the possibility of adding annotations on the document. Many eBook readers allow users to add handwritten notes over the PDF that is being visualized. Depending on the visualization software, annotations made on zoomed-in documents are not always preserved on the original document. On tablets, the annotations made on zoomed documents are preserved, but once again these annotations are made during a series of pan-and-zoom operations making the study of the scientific work rather complex.

In the proposed system the annotations are made on the reduced document and then repositioned in the appropriate position in the original document. Similar techniques have been considered for instance in [4] and [2] [8].

Some eBook readers store the free-form annotations as SVG files together with additional files that allow the device to retrieve and display the annotation. Starting from this information it is possible to locate the annotation in the modified document and subsequently reproduce it in the original document.

In the rest of this paper we describe the page segmentation and the document transformation, followed by annotations handling. Some preliminary experiments are analysed as well.

2. PAGE SEGMENTATION

The page segmentation [5] is based on the XY tree page decomposition. This segmentation can be performed either on scanned documents or on digital-born ones. In the first case the connected components are found in the image, while in the second case similar information can be computed from the PDF document. In particular, for each component we consider the coordinates of the bounding box of the component, the number of black pixels, and the Median value of Black horizontal Run lengths in the component (MBR). The latter value, together with the character height, is related to the font family and character attributes and allows us to merge together regions with uniform textual content.

In the next step the text lines are identified by grouping together adjacent components with similar height and MBR. When one text line is found, an estimated baseline for it is computed as well.

The text-lines can be grouped together in a top-down approach by using the MXY tree algorithm [3] one modified version of XY trees. The XY tree [7] is a widely used top-down method for page layout analysis. The basic method consists in using thresholded projection profiles to split the document into progressively smaller rectangular blocks. A projection profile is the histogram of the number of black pixels along parallel lines through the document. The blocks are split by alternately making horizontal and vertical "cuts" along white spaces that are found by using the thresholded projection profile. The result of such segmentation can be represented in a XY tree, where the root is for the whole page, the leaves are for blocks of the page, whereas each level alternatively represents the results of horizontal or vertical segmentation (Figure 2).

The various approaches differ in the way split regions are obtained. The extraction of regions is based on two processes: locating separators, and defining sub regions. In the algorithm used in this system, separators between different zones of text blocks are identified by looking for changes in the estimated font type.

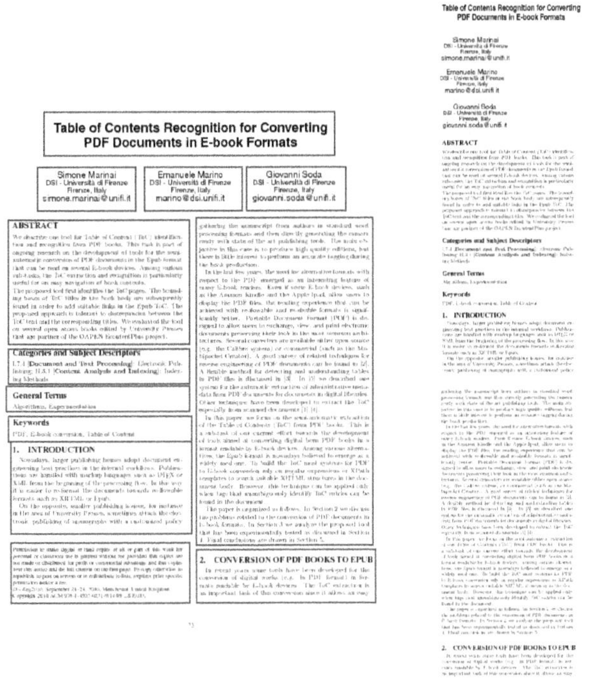

Figure 3: Left: page segmentation. Right: concatenation of regions in the output roll.

Cut spaces are found by evaluating a measure of font change that is computed for each horizontal white space. For each text line two features are computed: the Median value of Black horizontal Runs (MBR) and the Median value of Character Height (MCH). These values are computed from the features of the connected components. The Font Difference (FD) is computed for each horizontal white space as follows: let ΔMCH_i be the difference between the MCH of text lines i and $i + 1$ (and similarly for MBR). The FD_i for space S_i (between text lines i and $i + 1$) is computed as described in Eq. 1, where ΔMCH_i and ΔMBR_i are defined in Eq 2.

$$FD_i = \sqrt{3 \cdot \Delta MCH_i{}^2 + \Delta MBR_i{}^2} \qquad (1)$$

$$\begin{aligned} \Delta MCH_i &= MCH_i - MCH_{i+1} \\ \Delta MBR_i &= MBR_i - MBR_{i+1} \end{aligned} \qquad (2)$$

The multiplying factor before ΔMCH_i is considered to balance the contribution of ΔMCH_i and of ΔMBR_i. FD is used as a measure for identifying cutting spaces. When spaces are uniformly distributed cut positions are searched by computing the FD value for each space. At the end of the segmentation, each region is labelled on the basis of its content as Text (T) or Image (I).

3. DOCUMENT TRANSFORMATION

The segmentation step generates a sequence of regions in each page that can contain either text or graphical objects (e.g. illustrations or tables). The regions are then organized according to the expected reading order and scaled to the desired image width W_{out} (in the current implementation we

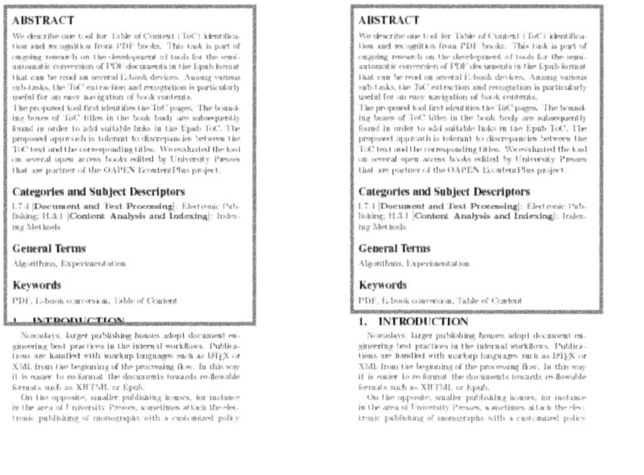

Figure 4: Left: wrong page cut, Right: cut adjustment.

consider $W_{out} = 600$ pixels). The images are concatenated in vertical obtaining a "roll" of the desired width (Figure 3).

In principle, it is possible to split the roll in locations that are multiple of the desired height ($H_{out} = 800$). However, in this way some text-lines could be split in the middle resulting in unreadable text. The algorithm therefore iteratively splits the roll in sub-pages by first hypothesizing a cut in a H_{out} height and then verifying whether white space exists in the corresponding position. If there is some text or graphics in the area, the cut position is moved back until a large enough white area is found.

For instance, in Figure 4 we show one wrong cut that would split one text–line and the adjusted cut. Since the cut location is identified by looking at the document image it is possible to avoid also breaks of illustrations and tables.

4. ANNOTATION REPOSITIONING

Different devices handle free-form annotations in different ways. In most cases, the annotations are saved as SVG files associated to the original PDF document. For instance, annotations are stored in the SONY Reader (PRS 650 Touch Edition) by the Adobe [c] Reader Mobile software in one folder for each annotated PDF that contains one SVG file describing the trace of the annotation. Multiple annotations made on the same page are stored in a unique SVG file. In addition to the SVG file one image of the corresponding page in the PDF is stored in the same folder.

This image can be used to identify the page in the resized document that contains the annotation. This is obtained by performing a simple comparison of the image with all the pages composing the resized document. This step is simple because there is no need to perform any image registration and, unlike scanned image, the images are in this case perfectly aligned.

Starting from the position of the bounding box of the note in the re-formatted page it is possible to identify the region of the original page that should contain the annotation. In some cases the free-form annotations could span multiple regions that can even belong to subsequent pages in the original document. If the note corresponds to more than one region it is split and the corresponding parts are assigned and copied to each region.

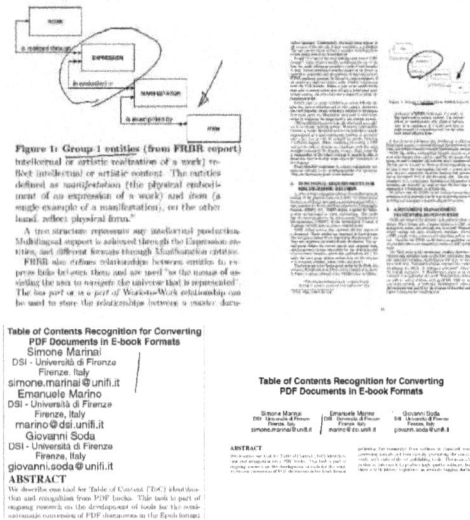

Figure 5: Examples of annotations. Left: annotations made on the resized documents. Right: annotations repositioned on the original page.

Categories & Subject Descriptors: H.3.7 [Digital Libraries]: Collection

General Terms: Management, Standardization,

Bio

The speaker is the Digitisation Programme Manager at the British Library, a post he took up in April 2003. He is responsible for the development and implementation of the policies, workflows and standards which govern digitisation of items from the Library's vast collections. He has been involved in many digitisation projects at the British Library including projects to digitise 25 million pages of 19th Century books, 4 million pages of pre-1900 newspapers and many manuscript

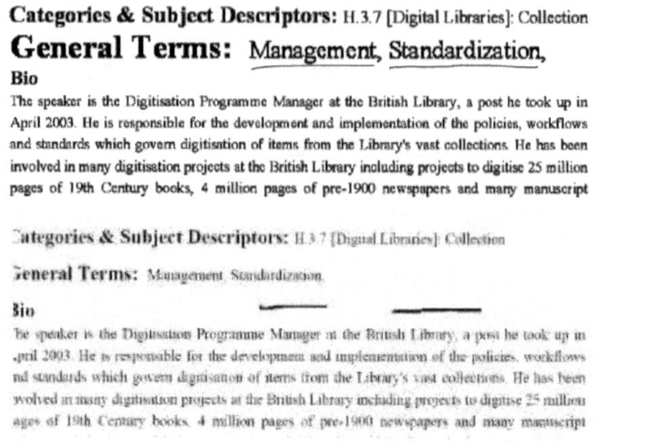

Figure 6: Annotation repositioned in the wrong place.

5. ANALYSIS

We tested the prototype with the papers published in the proceedings of the ACM Symposium on Document Engineering 2010.

Apart from one case, where one two-column page was not split in the two columns, in the remaining cases the columns were identified and the reading order identified. Other errors are due to excessive segmentation that considered text-lines with few characters as noise. To address this problem we are now modifying the segmentation algorithm to take into account the assumption that images, coming from digital-born documents, are intrinsically noise free. In other cases the images were split into multiple pages (because the illustrations contain white spaces inside the image).

To visually analyse the document transformation and the annotation repositioning we report two examples in Figure 5. In the top example some annotations in one illustration and one underlined text are accurately repositioned in the original two-column document. In the lower example some annotations made on two of the three authors of one article are repositioned on the original title page.

In total we made 28 annotations on different pages and checked the repositioned annotations. Of these, 25 have been accurately repositioned with one percentage of 89%. The errors are in this case due to annotations that are drawn in a different region with respect to the one containing the referenced text. One example is shown in Figure 6. It is important to notice that in the current implementation free-form annotations that span more than two patches are not considered.

6. CONCLUSIONS

The prototype system described in this paper demonstrates that state-of-the-art page segmentation algorithms can be used to transform scientific and technical papers printed on two columns. Free-form annotations can then be repositioned in the original document. Ongoing work is being performed to improve both the segmentation and the related document transformation. Future work includes user studies to asses the effectiveness of the proposed solution.

7. ACKNOWLEDGMENTS

We thank E. Marino, G. Cocchi, G. D'Avico, P. Gerini, and M. Massai for their contribution to this project.
This work has been partially supported by the PRIN project *Statistical Relational Learning: Algorithms and Applications*.

8. REFERENCES

[1] Ebooks of IEEE Computer Society Periodicals, may 2013. `http://www.computer.org/portal/web/publications/epub`

[2] D. Bargeron and T. Moscovich. Reflowing digital ink annotations. In G. Cockton and P. Korhonen, editors, *Proc. Conf. on Human Factors in Computing Systems*, pages 385–393. ACM, 2003.

[3] F. Cesarini, M. Gori, S. Marinai, and G. Soda. Structured document segmentation and representation by the modified X-Y tree. In *Proc. 5th ICDAR*, pages 563–566, 1999.

[4] G. Golovchinsky and L. Denoue. Moving markup: repositioning freeform annotations. In M. Beaudouin-Lafon, editor, *Proc. 15th Annual ACM Symposium on User Interface Software and Technology, Paris, France*, pages 21–30. ACM, 2002.

[5] S. Marinai, E. Marino, F. Cesarini, and G. Soda. A general system for the retrieval of document images from digital libraries. In *DIAL*, pages 150–173. IEEE Computer Society, 2004.

[6] S. Marinai, E. Marino, and G. Soda. Conversion of PDF books in epub format. *International Conference on Document Analysis and Recognition*, pages 478–482, 2011.

[7] G. Nagy and S. Seth. Hierarchical representation of optically scanned documents. In *Proc. 7th ICPR*, pages 347–349, 1984.

[8] M. Shilman and Z. Wei. Recognizing freeform digital ink annotations. In *Document Analysis Systems*, Lecture Notes in Computer Science, pages 322–331. Springer, 2004.

Automatic Generation of Limited-depth Hyper-documents from Clinical Guidelines

Mark Truran
School of Computing
Teesside University
United Kingdom
m.a.truran@tees.ac.uk

Jonathan Siddle
School of Computing
Teesside University
United Kingdom
j.siddle@tees.ac.uk

Gersende Georg
Haute Autorité de Santé
Saint-Denis La Plaine Cedex
France
g.georg@has-sante.fr

Marc Cavazza
School of Computing
Teesside University
United Kingdom
m.cavazza@tees.ac.uk

ABSTRACT

Research suggests that browsing clinical guidelines in a linear format is difficult for users. One national producer of clinical guidelines (HAS, the French National Authority for Health) has recently developed a new document format designed to improve accessibility. It is a limited-depth hypertext structurally constrained so that all information lies within two clicks of a central index ('reco2clics'). In the following paper, we introduce an authoring tool which converts full-length clinical guidelines to the 'reco2clics' format. Alongside routine editorial operations, this tool supports dynamic document restructuring, a complex operation using text segmentation algorithms and deontic analysis.

Categories and Subject Descriptors

I.7.2 [**Document and Text Processing**]: Document Preparation

Keywords

Clinical guidelines, document structure, hypertext

1. INTRODUCTION

Recent work has demonstrated that full-length clinical guidelines are not suitable for all of the anticipated users [10]. Many health professionals access guidelines online, extracting information in a piecemeal fashion rather than absorbing the document as a whole (as might be the case with offline, continuous medical education). The dense, linear format favoured by most guideline providers does not support this type of document access particularly well. This finding has led to a growing interest in hypertext clinical guidelines, which support non-linear use cases whilst being compatible with a variety of platforms (e.g., mobile phones, tablets).

Since October 2011, HAS have dual-published a number of their clinical guidelines. When this happens, the full-length guideline is accompanied by a *limited-depth* hypertext document. This hyper-document contains all of the substantive sections present in the full-length guideline, but nothing subsidiary (e.g., appendices, preambles, contact information etc.). This content is presented in a PDF file in which every document section is connected to a central index via internal hyperlinks. By definition, all information in a 'reco2clics' guideline must be reachable in two mouse clicks or less.

The 'reco2clics' format has proven extremely popular. An online survey hosted by HAS asked *Does 'reco2clics' improves information access?* 67% (of 720 respondents) answered 'Yes'. However, dual-publishing is proving to be time-consuming for the digital content teams. Once a full length clinical guideline has been developed, it must be carefully converted to the 'reco2clics' format. Most of the editorial tasks are routine (e.g. deleting appendices, inserting internal links), but some are decidedly non-trivial (e.g. document restructuring).

When an editor restructures a clinical guideline into the 'reco2clics' format, each section below the maximum depth is a 'problem' with two possible solutions. The 'problem' section can be *merged* with its hierarchical parent (e.g., the text of §2.1.1 would be added to the bottom of §2.1) or *promoted* to the next level of the structural hierarchical (e.g. §2.1.1 would become the new §2.2). On the face of it, merger seems the best option as it minimises disruption to the outline structure of the document.[1] However, while this is true in the majority of cases, there is an important exception. When a section is merged with its hierarchical parent, its title is removed. This can have a negative consequences for the user. Explicit document structure allows the reader to

---

[1] Assume we have two headings - '§2.1 Pulmonary Disease' and '§2.1.1 Bronchitis'. Concatenating all the text from §2.1.1 with §2.1 results in a single change to the outline structure (i.e. we lose one section heading). However, if we choose to promote §2.1.1 to §2.2, multiple changes may be required. For example, we may have to promote §2.1 *as well*, to retain the coherence of the hierarchical structure.

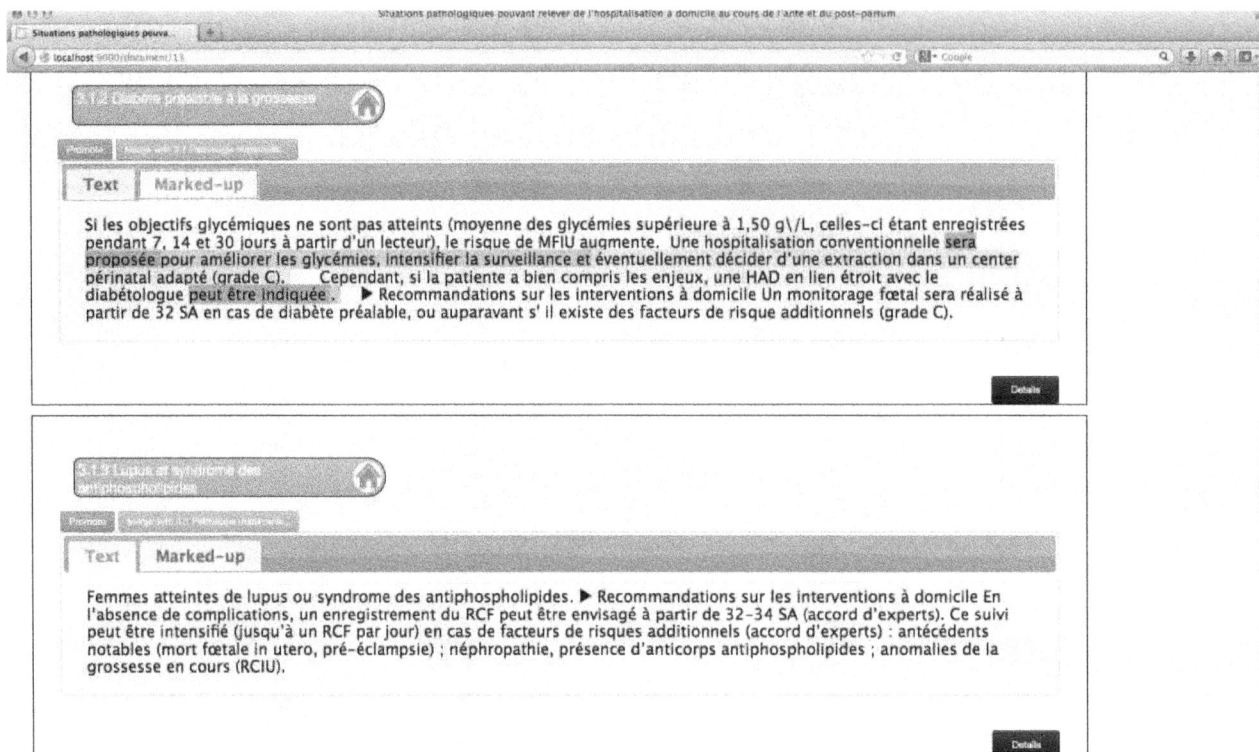

Figure 1: The tool makes suggestions for every 'problem' section (i.e., promote/merge). The user chooses a structuring option by clicking on the corresponding button. The option suggested by the system is green-lit.

interact with the guideline more effectively [3]. Section titles help users to locate relevant content efficiently. When the 'problem' section contains vital information, there is strong case for promotion because it preserves the content-specific title. Furthermore, research demonstrates that informative (i.e. specific) titles actually help readers to remember the accompanying text [2, 11].

Clearly, choosing the best solution for a 'problem' section is a complicated task. In the following sections, we describe an authoring tool that can simplify this task. It converts full-length clinical guidelines to the 'reco2clics' format, automating all routine editorial operations. It also supports semi-automatic, content-based document restructuring consistent with a 2-click heuristic.

Authoring tools capable of converting text to hypertext are, of course, fairly common [13]. The features which distinguish this work from previous work are as follows:

1. A technique for dynamically re-structuring documents which exploits the automatic recognition of deontic operators (see previous work in [5, 4, 12]).

2. A generalisable approach to section segmentation that exploits tables of contents.

2. RELATED WORK

2.1 Limited depth hypertext

The 'reco2clics' format is informed by research into the usability of hypertext navigation. Ignacio Madrid et al. [7] have previously demonstrated that path length (the number

of steps required to access information) is a major determinant of hypertext usability. Van Schaik and Ling [14] also analysed this relationship. Both studies provide support for the use of limited-depth hypertext guidelines.

2.2 Section segmentation

In our work, the process of section segmentation (i.e., parsing document sections from a clinical guideline) is complicated by two factors. The first factor is the *text extraction process*. Section segmentation requires plain text. The only universally available document format for HAS guidelines is PDF. The extraction of high quality text streams from PDF documents is highly problematic (see §6). The second factor is *corpus diversity*. There is significant diversity in the HAS guideline corpus in terms of logical structure and appearance. In this respect, our work is similar to research into hierarchy extraction from HTML [15, 9, 6].

3. SYSTEM OVERVIEW

Our system accepts a linear guideline as input and outputs a hypertext document in 'reco2clics' format. Note that this is *not* the finished product. Following previous work, our system implements a 'user in the loop' approach (see Figure 1). Our tool provides a *suggestion* for every 'problem' section. Suggestions are communicated to the user via buttons. If the tool suggests promotion, the 'promote' button will be green-lit. If the tool suggests merger, the 'merge' button will be green-lit. The user works through the various 'problem' sections, following or ignoring the suggestions as they see fit. Every time they make a decision (i.e., by clicking a button), the structure of the hypertext document is dynamically updated. When the user is satisfied with the re-structured guideline, it can be exported directly to PDF. This tool significantly shortens the time required to edit and publish a 'reco2clics' format guideline.

4. THE CONVERSION PROCESS

In this section, we describe the process of converting a guideline. First, we pre-process the guideline using a section segmentation algorithm. Second, we analyse the content of each 'problem' section. The latter step, which relies on the automatic recognition of deontic expressions, suggests the best option for each section (i.e., promotion or merger).

4.1 TOC-based section segmentation

In the first step of the conversion process, our tool extracts raw text from a full-length clinical guideline using Apache PDFBox.[2] Various routine editorial operations are performed (e.g., headers/footers are excised) and the table of contents (TOC) is analysed. The output of this analysis is a list of section titles. Our authoring tool uses this list to identify section boundaries in the guideline. This process requires *two* separate passes through the document. In the first pass, the tool looks for sentences that are identical to TOC entries. In the second pass, we use approximate string matching to catch multi-line section titles and entries corrupted by extraction noise (e.g. a multi-line title interrupted by a footnote).[3] When the section boundaries are confirmed, our authoring tool parses the sections.

4.2 Analysing the 'problem' sections

In the second step of the conversion process, each 'problem' section is analysed to determine if it should be promoted or merged. There is little substantive research to guide this activity. Therefore, we decided to develop an *experimental* heuristic which considers the presence of deontic structures. Deontic structures, which are recognised using shallow natural language processing (NLP), indicate the presence of clinical recommendations (i.e., statements conveying some degree of obligation) [5, 4, 12]. For example, 'En l'absence de facteur de risque additionnel, l'HAD n'est pas indiquée en antepartum pour les grossesses gémellaires', *trans:* 'In the absence of additional risk factors, homecare is not indicated for twin gestation/pregnancy'.

Given a 'problem' section, our algorithm will suggest promotion (rather than merger) if that section contains one or more clinical recommendations. This heuristic is supported by previous research into text comprehension and recall. As a general rule, the specificity of titles increases with section depth. A top level heading will announce the general theme (e.g., guideline 73 §3, 'Situations pathologiques pouvant relever d'une HAD en antepartum', *trans:* 'Pathologies compatible with outpatient or home care treatment before birth'), while sections lower in the hierarchy elaborate it (e.g., guideline 73, §3.3.1, 'Antécérdents d'hématome rétroplacentaire', *trans:* 'A history of placental abruption'). When a section is merged with its hierarchical parent, its title is excised. This removal can have negative consequences. Explicit document structure allows the reader to interact with the guideline more effectively [3]. Section titles help

users to locate relevant content quickly and efficiently. Furthermore, informative titles act as *advance notifiers*, helping readers to remember the accompanying text [2, 11]. Our heuristic tries to preserve content-specific titles, hopefully improving document accessibility and user recall.

5. EVALUATION

We carried out a two-stage evaluation designed to answer the following questions:

1. Was the TOC-based section segmentation algorithm accurate (i.e., did the algorithm parse sections from guideline correctly)?

2. Did the promote/merge algorithm function correctly (i.e., did it recognise clinical recommendations and recommend promotion when appropriate)?

5.1 Section segmentation algorithm

In the first stage of the evaluation, we measured the accuracy of our section segmentation algorithm using a set of full-length clinical guidelines randomly selected from the HAS corpus (5 guidelines comprising 127 sections, 201 pages). We processed each guideline using our conversion tool and compared the generated hypertext document to the original guideline. The accuracy of our algorithm was very good. 87% of the sections (i.e., 110/127) were correctly parsed (i.e., the text in the hypertext document was the same as the text in the guideline). The errors (17/127) were *all* related to footnotes (see further §6). These positive results validate the use of the TOC for section segmentation. Note that this is a transferable technique. It should be applicable to other semi-structured documents similar to clinical guidelines.

5.2 Promote/Merge algorithm

In the second stage of the evaluation, we created an artificial guideline which collected 50 'problem' sections. All of these sections were drawn from the HAS corpus. Half of the sections contained clinical recommendations. Half of the sections did not. We processed this guideline using our authoring tool and scored the output. 88% (22/25) of the sections containing deontic structures were processed correctly (i.e., the tool recommended promotion). 92% (23/25) of the sections without clinical recommendations were processed correctly (i.e., the tool recommended merger). The false negatives (3/25) and false positives (2/25) were attributed to the widespread use of 'pouvoir' (*trans:* be able to) in French, particularly in certain idiomatic expressions.

6. CONCLUSION AND FURTHER WORK

The creation of clinical guidelines is an expensive process, requiring considerable time and expertise. In this paper, we have presented an authoring tool that simplifies the process of converting a traditional clinical guideline into a hypertext document. It automates all routine editorial operations and provides dynamic support for the more complex. This tool has the potential to considerably reduce the overhead of creating 'reco2clics' guidelines for everyone involved in the process. It relieves digital publishing staff from multiple low-level formatting operations, and its document restructuring functions support the decisions taken by project managers.

In future work, we plan to improve our section segmentation algorithm. Text extraction from PDF source files often

---

[2]http://pdfbox.apache.org/
[3]We use *Levenshtein* distance for fuzzy string matching [8]

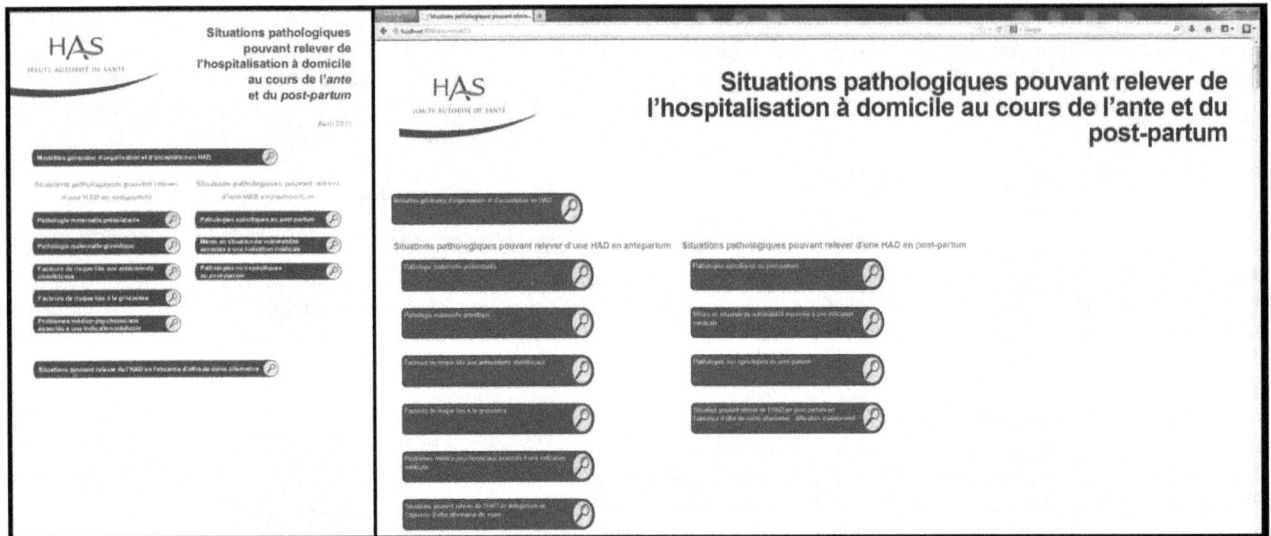

Figure 2: A manually generated 2011 HAS guideline in 'reco2clics' format (left), alongside sample output from our conversion tool (right). Minor differences are caused by the evolving house style for 'reco2clics'.

generates document noise, page layout artefacts that complicate textual analysis. Some of these artefacts are easy to remove from the raw text (e.g., page headers/footers). Others are more problematic. Footnotes are particularly troublesome. PDFBox usually folds footnotes into the last section on the page, contaminating the textual content of that section (see §5.1). We hope to use *positional data* to resolve this problem (i.e., we will identify footnotes by their page location, and pair them up with the correct references)[1].

7. ACKNOWLEDGEMENTS

This work was part funded by the European Commission through the FP7 Open FET MUSE Project (ICT-296703).

8. REFERENCES

[1] Ø. R. Berg, S. Oepen, and J. Read. Towards high-quality text stream extraction from pdf. In *Proceedings of the ACL-2012 Special Workshop on Rediscovering 50 Years of Discoveries*, pages 98–103. ACL, July 2012.

[2] J. Bransford and M. Johnson. Contextual prerequisites for understanding: Some investigations of comprehension and recall. *Journal of Verbal Learning and Verbal Behavior*, 11(6):717–726, 1972.

[3] D. K. Farkas. Explicit Structure in Print and On-Screen Documents. *Technical Communication Quarterly*, 14(1):9–30, 2005.

[4] G. Georg, H. Hernault, M. Cavazza, H. Prendinger, and M. Ishizuka. From rhetorical structures to document structure: shallow pragmatic analysis for document engineering. In *Proceedings of the 9th ACM symposium on Document engineering*, DocEng '09, pages 185–192, New York, NY, USA, 2009. ACM.

[5] G. Georg and M.-C. Jaulent. A document engineering environment for clinical guidelines. In *Proceedings of the 2007 ACM symposium on Document engineering*, DocEng '07, pages 69–78. ACM, 2007.

[6] S. Gupta, G. E. Kaiser, P. Grimm, M. F. Chiang, and J. Starren. Automating content extraction of html documents. *World Wide Web*, 8(2):179–224, June 2005.

[7] R. Ignacio Madrid, H. Van Oostendorp, and M. C. Puerta Melguizo. The effects of the number of links and navigation support on cognitive load and learning with hypertext: The mediating role of reading order. *Comput. Hum. Behav.*, 25(1):66–75, Jan. 2009.

[8] V. I. Levenshtein. Binary Codes Capable of Correcting Deletions, Insertions and Reversals. *Soviet Physics Doklady*, 10:707–710, Feb. 1966.

[9] F. Pembe and T. Gungor. Heading-based sectional hierarchy identification for html documents. In *Computer and information sciences, 2007. iscis 2007. 22nd international symposium on*, pages 1–6, 2007.

[10] A. H. Rø svik and H. P. Fosseng. Usability testing of clinical guidelines. Guidelines International Network Conference 2011, 2011.

[11] M. N. Schwarz and A. Flammer. Text structure and title - effects on comprehension and recall. *Journal of Verbal Learning and Verbal Behavior*, 20(1):61 – 66, 1981.

[12] M. Truran, G. Georg, M. Cavazza, and D. Zhou. Assessing the readability of clinical documents in a document engineering environment. In *Proceedings of the 10th ACM symposium on Document engineering*, DocEng '10, pages 125–134. ACM, 2010.

[13] M. Truran, J. Goulding, and H. Ashman. Autonomous authoring tools for hypertext. *ACM Comput. Surv.*, 39(3), Sept. 2007.

[14] P. van Schaik and J. Ling. A cognitive-experiential approach to modelling web navigation. *Int. J. Hum.-Comput. Stud.*, 70(9):630–651, 2012.

[15] Y. Xue, Y. Hu, G. Xin, R. Song, S. Shi, Y. Cao, C.-Y. Lin, and H. Li. Web page title extraction and its application. *Information Processing & Management*, 43(5):1332 – 1347, 2007.

Splitting Wide Tables Optimally

Mihai Bilauca
CSIS Department
University of Limerick
Limerick, Ireland
mihai@bilauca.net

Patrick Healy
CSIS Department
University of Limerick
Limerick, Ireland
patrick.healy@ul.ie

ABSTRACT

In this paper we discuss the problems that occur when splitting wide tables across multiple pages. We focus our attention on finding solutions that minimize the impact on the meaning of data when the objective is to reorder the columns such that the number of pages used is minimal. Reordering of columns in a table raises a number of complex optimization problems that we will study in this paper: minimizing page count and at the same time the number of column positions changes or the number of column groups split across pages. We show that by using integer programming solutions the number of pages used when splitting wide tables can be reduced by up to 25% and it can be achieved in short computational time.

Categories and Subject Descriptors

I.7.2 [**Document and Text Processing**]: Document Preparation—*Format and notation,Photocomposition/typesetting*; D.3.3 [**Programming Languages**]: Language Constructs and Features—*Constraints*

Keywords

table layout, constrained optimization, wide tables

1. INTRODUCTION

Presenting information using tables is a very efficient yet simple way to express complex relationships between data items in a limited physical space. Tables allow the reader to find precise answers to complex queries that could otherwise be difficult to answer. Thus, it is no surprise that tables are widely used and well supported in all modern document authoring tools. However, authoring tables is hard and the need to improve table layout tools has been highlighted on numerous occasions by the research community [1, 8, 2, 7].

Automatic table layout problems have been studied for many years in the context of constraint optimization due to the large scale and complex relationships that need to be described. So far, the problem of automatic optimal table layout – the problem of finding the minimum height layout of table which contains text for a given page width – has drawn particular attention [3, 5]. A recent review of table formatting methods can be found in a study presented recently by Hurst, Li and Marriott [6].

A problem in automatic tabular layout that we believe has not been given sufficient attention is splitting wide tables optimally; other researchers [1, 8] highlighted that the problems that occur when displaying large tables require further investigation.

As WYSIWYG tools have become increasingly popular they provide powerful features for authoring tables, yet they still suffer from a wide range of engineering issues [4, 2]. Authoring wide tables is another example where current WYSIWYG document authoring tools provide poor support.

When the author tries, for example, to present a wide table as a two-page broadside table there are cases when one or two columns require an additional page. This situation occurs in particular when the table consists of many wide columns. Therefore the author needs to implement a strategy to use the space available on each page more efficiently. The options available in this case are to narrow or reorder the columns so the space is used more efficiently but both alternatives have disadvantages. The author can reorder the columns with the condition that the meaning and readability of the table is not affected. By reordering the columns, the space on each page can be used more efficiently and, as a result, fewer pages become necessary. Using fewer pages to display a table is not only advantageous from an economical point of view but it also increases the readability of the table and it facilitates data editing.

Reordering of columns raises a number of problems that we will study in this paper. The problem of finding an arrangement of columns that minimizes the number of pages used is presented in Section 2. In Section 3 we suggest a solution to the problem of minimizing the number of pages and at the same time the number of changes in the column positions. A third problem that we discuss in Section 4 is the column reordering problem with the constraint that some columns should be kept together or "grouped" in as much as possible and at same time the number pages is minimized.

We conclude each of these sections with the performance evaluation of the proposed solutions using OPL, the Optimization Programming Language but other modelling languages can be used to implement these solutions. The results presented in all the evaluations have been obtained by using IBM ILOG OPL 6.3 with CPLEX engine 12.3 running on a

Listing 1: TSMin

```
1  dvar int+ pageSel[Pages] in 0..1;
2  dvar int+ X[Pages][Cols] in 0..1;
3  dexpr int pageCount = sum(p in Pages) pageSel[p];
4  minimize pageCount;
5  subject to {
6    ct1: forall(j in Cols)
7      sum(p in Pages) X[p][j] == 1;
8    ct2: forall(p in Pages)
9      sum(j in Cols)
10     colW[j] / pageW * X[p][j] <= pageSel[p]; }
```

Table 1: Run time for the Table Split model

Columns	10	20	30	40	50	60
PC	7	16	19	29	34	48
OPC	6	12	15	23	26	39
%Imp	14.28	25.00	21.05	20.68	23.52	18.75
Time	2.25	0.13	0.17	1.18	04:30	1.52

64-bit Linux laptop with an Intel i7-2640M CPU at 2.80GHz and 8Gb RAM. The full code of the listings is available upon request.

2. MINIMIZE PAGE COUNT

To minimize the number of pages used when a wide table is split across multiple pages we model the problem as a mixed integer programming model. This is a standard *bin packing* problem that can be simply modelled using OPL as in Listing 1.

The objective of this model is to determine values for the arrays of binary variables `pageSel[Pages]`, `X[Pages][Cols]` such that the number of pages used is minimized. The array `X[Pages][Cols]` will only contain the value 1 if column `j` in `Cols` is selected on page `p` in `Pages`. To improve the clarity of the code we defined the `Pages` range to be the same as the `Cols` range because there are maximum `NbCols` pages needed. The `colW[Cols]` stores the width values for each column.

Constraint `ct1` ensures that each column is only selected once while constraint `ct2` guarantees that the sum of column widths selected in a page `pageSel[p]` does not exceed the page width. It also ensures that `pageSel[p]` is set to 1 if any column `j` is displayed on page `p`. Thus, `pageCount`, the number of pages used, is introduced as the sum of all all values in `pageSel[p]`.

In Table 1 we show the running time and the optimum page count (OPC) for tables with up to 60 columns. We can see that by using this integer programming model the number of pages PC can be reduced by between 14.28% for a small table with 10 columns and 23.52% for a table with 50 columns. Also, we found that the difficulty of the problem is not directly linked to the problem size but to the data itself.

3. COLUMN POSITIONING

Using the method presented in the previous section we can determine the ordering of columns that will minimize the number of pages. As we will see, there may be several ways of ordering the columns that will allow the table to be displayed on this minimum number of pages. For example, a table with the following column widths will require 7 A4 pages to be displayed when the page width is set to 490

points and the columns presented in order:

$$colW : [210, 140, 210, 420, 280, 350, 70, 140, 140, 350]$$
$$pages : \{210, 140\}, \{210\}, \{420\}, \{280\}, \{350, 70\},$$
$$\{140, 140\}, \{350\}.$$

By reordering the columns with the positions shown in `colIdx` only 5 pages are required:

$$colIdx : [1, 7, 8, 5, 2, 9, 6, 10, 3, 4]$$
$$pages : \{210, 280\}, \{140, 350\}, \{420, 70\},$$
$$\{140, 210\}, \{350, 140\}.$$

It can easily be observed that the original order of columns is substantially changed. The second column is placed in position 7, the 3rd in position 8, the 4th in position 5 and the 5th column in position 2, etc. but the author is interested to find that ordering that has the least impact on the meaning of the data while still using the minimum amount of pages. An alternative ordering of columns that still requires only 5 pages to be used when splitting the table is presented below:

$$colIdx : [1, 2, 3, \underline{5}, \underline{4}, \underline{7}, \underline{6}, 8, 9, 10]$$
$$pages : \{210, 140\}, \{210, 280\}, \{420, 70\},$$
$$\{350, 140\}, \{140, 350\}.$$

This example shows that simply by swapping the positions of two sets of columns, i.e. column 4 with 5 and column 6 with 7 the number of pages can still be reduced to 5 but only with a few changes. Therefore the meaning of the data (as given by the original ordering) is less likely to be affected in this case compared with the previous ordering of columns.

To measure how many changes an ordering has compared to the original order of columns we introduce the `posDiff` variable, given by

$$posDiff = \sum_{j_1 < j_2}^{n} |posO(j_1, j_2) - posN(j_1, j_2)| \quad (1)$$

The $posO(j_1, j_2)$ function returns 1 if column j_1 is placed before j_2 and 0 otherwise. Because in the initial ordering of columns the position of column j is in fact j the function $posO$ returns 1 when $j_1 < j_2$ and 0 otherwise. $posO$ and $posN$ are given by:

$$posO(j_1, j_2) = \begin{cases} 1 & j_1 < j_2 \\ 0 & j_1 \geq j_2 \end{cases}, 1 \leq j_1 < j_2 \leq n \quad (2)$$

$$posN(j_1, j_2) = \begin{cases} 1 & P[j_1] < P[j_2] \\ 0 & P[j_1] \geq P[j_2] \end{cases}, 1 \leq j_1, j_2 \leq n \quad (3)$$

The $posN(j_1, j_2)$ function returns 1 if the new position of a column $P[j_1]$ is before the position of a second column $P[j_2]$, and 0 otherwise. Thus, `posDiff` counts how many times the new position $P[j]$ of any column j has changed in relation to any another column.

We model the problem of minimizing the number of pages used to split a wide table while minimizing relative column positioning changes as a multi-objective mixed integer programming model *TSMinCol* presented in Listing 2. We initialize `colP[Cols]` with the page index for each column. The initialisation code has been omitted for space reasons but the full code is available on request. The variables `a,b` and `obj1Val` are used for the multi-objective flow control of the optimization which we will describe later in this section.

Listing 2: TSMinCol

```
1   int colP[j in Cols];
2   dvar int+ pageSel[Pages] in 0..1;
3   dvar int+ colIdx[Cols] in Cols;
4   dvar int+ pageIdx[Cols] in Cols;
5   dexpr int posO[j1 in Cols,j2 in Cols] =
6                       j1 <= j2 − 1;
7   dexpr int posN[j1 in Cols,j2 in Cols] =
8                       (colIdx[j1] <= colIdx[j2] − 1);
9   dexpr float posDiff = sum(j1, j2 in Cols: j2 < j1)
10                      abs(posO[j1,j2] − posN[j1,j2]);
11  dexpr int pageCount = sum(i in Pages) pageSel[i];
12  minimize a * pageCount + b * posDiff;
13  subject to {
14   ct1: forall(p in Pages)
15     sum(j in Cols)
16       (colW[j]*(p==pageIdx[j])/pageW)<= pageSel[p];
17   ct2: forall(ordered j1,j2 in Cols)
18     (pageIdx[j1] <= pageIdx[j2]−1) −
19     (colIdx[j1] <= colIdx[j2]−1) == 0;
20   ct3: forall(ordered j1,j2 in Cols)
21     colIdx[j1] != colIdx[j2];
22   ct4: if (obj1Val >= 0) pageCount == obj1Val; }
```

The objective of this model is to determine values for the page selection variable `pageSel[Pages]`, new column index `colIdx[Cols]` which indicates the new position of columns and the new page index for each column `pageIdx[Cols]` such that the number of pages `pageCount` and the number of column changes `posDiff` is minimized. The decision expressions `posO[j1,j2]`, `posN[j1,j2]` and `posDiff` are expressed as in equations 1, 2 and 3.

The model has four constraints: `ct1` ensures that the total width of the columns assigned in a page does not exceed the page width. It also selects a page index `p` in the array of binary variables `pageSel[p]`; the `ct2` constraint ensures that if a column `j1` is selected on a previous page to column `j2` then its new index `colIdx[j1]` is less then the new index of column `j2`. Constraint `ct3` makes sure that unique values are assigned for each column index. The role of constraint `ct4` is to guarantee that the minimum number of pages found in a first pass of optimization is maintained in a second pass of the optimization flow which seeks to minimize the number of column position changes.

The flow of the optimization is controlled by using OPL script to call the optimization engine twice. As variable `a` is initialized with 1, `b` with 0 and `obj1Val` with -1 the first pass of the optimization will minimize the number of pages. The second objective, minimizing the number of column changes is then reached in a second pass by setting the `a` variable to 0, `b` to 1 and `obj1Val` with the minimum number of pages just found.

In our tests with column widths generated with random values between 20 and 450 and the page width set to 450 points we found that for a 10 column table that required 9 pages to be displayed it took 2.25 seconds to find an ordering of columns that minimized the number of pages to 8 and the number of column position changes to 4. By only optimizing the number of pages to 8 without minimizing column position changes the table would have had a `posDiff` of 33 changes so the advantage of this method can be easily observed. This has also been confirmed for a larger table with 20 columns that initially required 13 A4 pages when split. We determined an arrangement of columns that needed 11 pages with a `posDiff` of 194. Within 1m29.68s an arrange-

ment of columns was determined that had a `posDiff` of only 4 while the minimum page count was maintained at 11. The problem proved to be more difficult to solve as the number of columns increased but, as also found in the evaluation of the page count minimization, the difficulty of the problem depends on problem instance, and not solely on the problem size.

4. MINIMIZE GROUP SPLITTING

In this section we discuss the problem of minimizing page count when splitting tables across pages while minimizing the number of column groups splits. In practical cases, the user needs to specify which columns should *preferably* be kept together when a new ordering is determined. Here, the term *preferably* is essential because if columns *must* be kept together there are a number of simple solutions that can be used in this case (for example, a column group could be treated as one single wider column). If C is the set of columns we define a group C_g as a subset of C

$$C_g \subseteq C, \quad C_g \cap C_{g'} = \emptyset$$

and $\mathcal{G}$ is the set of column groups $\mathcal{G} = \{C_g\}$. When the user indicates which columns should *preferably* be kept together the problem is to find that ordering of columns that minimizes page count and at the same time it minimizes the number of groups that are split across pages. For the same example as in the previous section a possible reordering of the columns requires only 5 pages. When the user requires that columns 2,3 and 7 preferably be kept together the ordering presented in Section 3 is not satisfactory because column 7 is far from column 2 which is far from column 3. Therefore a better ordering is presented below:

$$colIdx : [2, 3, 7, 4, 9, 10, 6, 8, 1, 5]$$
$$pages : \{140, 210, 70\}, \{420\}, \{140, 350\},$$
$$\{350, 140\}, \{210, 280\}.$$

If, for a table we have $|\mathcal{G}|$ number of groups, for each column group g with $1 \leq g \leq |\mathcal{G}|$ we have C_g a set of column indices of the form $\{j \mid j \in C_g\}$ which records which columns j belong to the group index g. To count how many groups are split across pages we need to introduce an array $F[g]$ which specifies for each group index g the index j of the first column that belongs to that group. The problem is to determine for each column j the page index $P[j]$ that minimizes the number of pages. We will count in $S[g]$ how many columns j of C_g have a different page index $P[j]$ than the first column's page index $P[F[g]]$.

$$S[g] = \sum_{j \in C_g} \delta(g,j)$$

$$\delta(g,j) = \begin{cases} 1 & P[j] <> P[F[g]] \\ 0 & P[j] = P[F[g]] \end{cases} , \quad 1 \leq g \leq |\mathcal{G}|$$

If $\gamma(g)$ which takes the value 1 if a group g is split across multiple pages is defined as

$$\gamma(g) = \begin{cases} 1 & S[g] > 0 \\ 0 & S[g] = 0 \end{cases} , \quad 1 \leq g \leq |\mathcal{G}|$$

Listing 3: TSMinGroup - Table split with minimum page count and group splits

```
1   int colW[Cols] = ...;      // column widths
2   int colG[Cols] = ...;      // column groups
3   {int} groups = {colG[j] | j in Cols};
4   int gFirstCol[g in groups] =
5           first({j | j in Cols : colG[j] == g});
6   dvar int+ pageSel[Pages] in 0..1;
7   dvar int+ pageIdx[Cols] in Cols;
8   dexpr int gSplit[g in groups] =
9           sum(j in Cols: colG[j] == g )
10          (pageIdx[j] != pageIdx[gFirstCol[g]]);
11  dexpr int gSplitCount = sum(g in groups)
12          (gSplit[g] >= 1);
13  dexpr int pageCount = sum(p in Pages) pageSel[p];
14  minimize a * pageCount + b * gSplitCount;
15  subject to {
16   ct1:    // do not exceed page width
17    forall(p in Pages)
18     sum(j in Cols)
19      (colW[j] * (p == pageIdx[j]) / pageW) <=
20          pageSel[p];
21   ct2: if (obj1Val >= 0) pageCount == obj1Val; }
```

the number Γ of groups split across pages is defined as in equation 4

$$\Gamma = \sum_{g=1}^{|\mathcal{G}|} \gamma(g). \qquad (4)$$

We model this problem as a mixed integer programming problem *TSMinGroup* with two objectives as presented in Listing 3. We introduce a new array colG[Cols] which contains for each column j the group index. If the user does not specify any column groupings colG there is only one group with a 0 index. On line 13 we identify the set of groups and on line 16 we store in gFirstCol[g in groups] array the first column of each group g as given by the *first()* OPL function which returns the first element in a set. This optimization model finds values for an array of binary variables pageSel[Pages] and an array that stores the page index for each colum pageIdx[Cols] such that the page count pageCount and the number of groups split across pages gSplitCount are minimized.

The decision expression gSplit[g in groups] counts how many columns are on a different page than the group's first column and the expression gSplitCount counts how many groups are split across pages.

In our tests we identified cases where TSMinGroup found suitable solutions in a short time. For a table with 10 columns and 2 column groups where 7 pages were required TSMinGroup determined a solution in just 0.33 of a second where the number of pages is minimized and no groups are split. As the number of columns increases the time required to find suitable solutions for similar problems also increases. For a table with 20 columns which has 3 column groups a solution that keeps the columns together while minimizing page count to 9 pages instead of 12 was found in 1 minute. We also identified cases for table with 30 and 40 columns but the time required to find solutions increased from under 2 minutes to over 12 minutes in some larger instances. It is important to note that some column groupings can make the problem difficult to solve and therefore finding a solution may become time consuming. In practice, there may be cases where the table author could use the solution found to

a more relaxed problem (with fewer column groups) to adjust the ordering of columns in a shorter time than the time required to automatically find such a solution.

5. CONCLUSIONS AND FUTURE WORK

In this paper we discussed the problem of splitting wide tables across multiple pages. We defined the problems of minimizing the number of pages used and at the same time the number of relative column positions changes and the problem of minimizing page count while keeping together groups of columns as integer programming problems. We provided solutions based on combinatorial optimization methods. Based on the evaluation of these solutions we can draw the following conclusions:

- finding an optimal arrangement of columns such that the page count is minimized when splitting wide tables can be achieved in relatively short running time; for tables with 60 columns a solution has been found in less than 2s;

- if additional criteria are added, for example minimizing the number of relative column positions changes, the problems become harder as the number of columns increase; additional criteria can be easily modelled to resolve other preferred constraints;

- the difficulty of the problems not only depends on the problem size but on the complexity of the data;

A problem that would require further research is minimizing the overall page count when a large table containing text is displayed on fixed size pages and neither column widths or row heights are known in advance.

6. REFERENCES

[1] R. J. Beach. *Setting tables and illustrations with style*. PhD thesis, University of Waterloo, 1985.

[2] M. Bilauca. *Automatic table layout and formatting*. PhD thesis, University of Limerick, Ireland, 2012.

[3] M. Bilauca and P. Healy. A new model for automated table layout. In *Proceedings of the 10th ACM symposium on Document engineering*, DocEng '10, pages 169–176, New York, NY, USA, 2010. ACM.

[4] M. Bilauca and P. Healy. Table layout performance of document authoring tools. In *Proceedings of the 10th ACM symposium on Document engineering*, DocEng '10, pages 199–202, New York, NY, USA, 2010. ACM.

[5] G. Gange, K. Marriott, P. Moulder, and P. Stuckey. Optimal automatic table layout. In *Proceedings of the 11th ACM symposium on Document engineering*, DocEng '11, pages 23–32, New York, NY, USA, 2011. ACM.

[6] N. Hurst, W. Li, and K. Marriott. Review of automatic document formatting. In *DocEng '09: Proceedings of the 9th ACM symposium on Document engineering*, pages 99–108, New York, NY, USA, 2009. ACM.

[7] K. Marriott, P. Moulder, and N. Hurst. Html automatic table layout. *ACM Trans. Web*, 7(1):4:1–4:27, Mar. 2013.

[8] X. Wang. *Tabular abstraction, editing, and formatting*. PhD thesis, University of Waterloo, Waterloo, Ont., Canada, Canada, 1996. AAINN09397.

NCL4WEB - Translating NCL Applications to HTML5 Web Pages

Esdras Caleb O. Silva   Joel A. F. dos Santos   Débora C. Muchaluat-Saade

MídiaCom Lab
Computer Science Department
Universidade Federal Fluminense
R. Passo da Pátria, 156 - Bloco E - Sala 408 - Niterói, RJ - Brazil
(caleb, joel, debora)@midiacom.uff.br

ABSTRACT

Testing Digital TV applications is not a simple task. DTV applications either need to be transmitted by a TV broadcaster or someone with an equipment capable of generating a DTV signal with the application embedded. Alternatively, an interactive TV application developer may use a virtual execution environment, like a virtual set-top box installed in a computer, which implements the digital TV middleware standard. In both cases, the application usually does not reach a large number of final users, and developers may not be motivated to continue working with digital TV interactive content. On the other hand, HTML5 support for multimedia content will certainly attract multimedia authors to web development. Considering this scenario, this work proposes an alternative way of presenting a digital TV application developed in NCL for the Ginga declarative middleware, translating it into HTML5 web pages, so it can be presented using a common web browser. The translation tool is called NCL4WEB. Like HTML, NCL is XML-based, so NCL4WEB is based on XSLT stylesheets. It transforms NCL elements into HTML5 elements and a set of JavaScript functions that implement synchronization relationships among media objects, including user interaction. Using NCL4WEB, NCL developers are able to publish their interactive TV applications on the web. It is transparent for final users to access HTML5 or NCL content using a web browser.

Categories and Subject Descriptors

I.7.2 [**Document and Text Processing**]: Document Preparation—*Hypertext/hypermedia*; D.3.4 [**Programming Languages**]: Processors—*Translator writing systems and compiler generators*

Keywords

NCL, Multimedia Synchronization, HTML5, XSLT, IPTV, NCL4WEB

1. INTRODUCTION

Digital Television (DTV) changes the traditional audiovisual signal transmission. This represents not just a gain in image and audio quality, but also the possibility of transmitting interactive applications to the TV viewer. Interactive applications also allow the personalization of TV content.

NCL (Nested Context Language) [3] is an XML-based multimedia authoring language, which provides flexibility, reuse, multi-device support, application content and presentation adaptability, and mainly, easy definition of spatiotemporal synchronization among media assets, including user interaction. NCL was selected as part of Brazilian digital TV system [2] that was adopted not only in Brazil but in other countries in Latin America and Africa. In addition, Ginga-NCL is an ITU standard for IPTV services [12].

Such a scenario brings a fast growing in the market of interactive applications described with the NCL language. However, despite the growing digital TV market, such kind of applications still faces issues, like the need of authorization from TV broadcasters for deploying an application.

IPTV systems, on the other hand, make it easier for developers to deploy their applications, since just a server connected to an IP network is needed for streaming audiovisual content and applications.

Taking advantage of the characteristic of the Internet of enabling everyone to create its own service (e.g. a web page), one goal of this work is helping NCL developers publish and advertise their interactive applications, by allowing them to be deployed on the web with a simple tag addition to the NCL code. So, an interactive application developer can easily publish his work on the Internet, attracting attention to it and facilitating its deployment by TV broadcasters.

An advantage that comes with that goal is that NCL interactive applications are not limited to digital TV and IPTV anymore. Therefore, the same interactive application (e.g. an interactive advertisement) can be deployed in the broadcast terrestrial TV, IPTV and the Web.

This work presents a tool called NCL4WEB that enables NCL interactive applications to be presented in a web browser. NCL4WEB transforms an NCL [3] document into an HTML5 [23] + JavaScript [9] document using an XSLT stylesheet [22]. The same document presentation will be perceived by the final user when a given document is executed in a browser using NCL4WEB and in an NCL formatter (adherent to the NCL standard [3]). Therefore, a web browser that reads the NCL document making reference to the NCL4WEB stylesheet is able to open it as an HTML5 page. Besides making it easier for developers to publish an interactive TV application, NCL4WEB is also a tool for harmonization of IPTV and web applications.

The remaining of this paper is structured as follows. Section 2 presents related works, comparing each one to NCL4WEB. Section 3 gives a brief description of the NCL language. Section 4 discusses NCL4WEB project decisions and how XSLT and the JavaScript library are used. Section 5 shows the use of NCL4WEB with NCL documents created by the digital TV community. Section 6 discusses the tool limitations and Section 7 ends the paper with conclusions and future works.

2. RELATED WORK

SMIL State [13] is a tool that enables SMIL applications to use variables (global to the application) to personalize the application execution. SMIL State works on top of SMIL 2.1 [5] adding tools to read external data and interact with the user. A document authored with SMIL State can be exhibited with Ambulant [6], an open source tool, which was tested with the Safari browser as a plugin. In the paper, authors present SMIL State applications as the presentation of different advertisements depending on the user interaction. SMIL State was included in the SMIL standard in its last version [7].

SMIL State documents can be executed in a web browser using the Ambulant plugin, since no browser has native support to it. On the other hand, since NCL4WEB uses XSLT, a W3C standard supported by great part of available web browsers, it does not require any plugin. NCL4WEB was designed for presenting an NCL application alone as a full web page, but it can also be used embedded in a web page with an *iframe* element.

SmilingWeb [10] is a SMIL document player that works inside a web browser. It uses a JavaScript library to control the document presentation. The player works on top of HTML5 and has a scheduler, responsible for controlling the synchronization relationships between the beginning and end of a media presentation. The scheduler calculates the time those events will occur, searching all elements that are children of the media object and creating a table mapping each element begin and end. The player exhibition and scheduling capability were tested and all results were reasonable. The current version of the player does not support all SMIL tags.

NCL4WEB leaves the work of scheduling event occurrences to JavaScript functions. Each function is created from NCL links during the transformation and is activated by HTML5 events. The multimedia content exhibition capability of NCL4WEB is related to the browser being used.

Timesheet.js [8] allows a developer to use HTML5 and CSS3 [15] to create a multimedia presentation on the web. The presentation created with Timesheet is synchronized using SMIL Timing [21]. The work focuses on using HTML5 and CSS3 together with SMIL Timing and Timesheets for managing the temporization, synchronization and user interface. The engine works through the JavaScript framework *Timesheet.js* and a link for a SMIL document inside a web page.

NCL4WEB, as Timesheet, uses HTML5 functionalities to control events related to a document exhibition, allowing each element to treat its own presentation events. JavaScript is used for dealing with those event occurrences, perform-

ing the synchronization relationships among those elements. Timesheet does not translate the complete SMIL language. It just translates its timing functionalities, so they can be used on the web. This transformation uses XSLT, creating an HTML5 document that uses *Timesheet.js*. Our work, however, presents a solution for translating a complete document specified with the NCL language into an HTML5 document.

TAL [20] is an XML-based template language for creating NCL templates. Besides the language, the paper presents a processor that creates NCL or HTML5 documents. The HTML code created by the TAL processor is generated from an internal structure of the TAL processor, not from the NCL document created by using templates. In the translation, TAL uses HTML5 events to deal with the document presentation events. TAL attribution events, for example, are handled with the use of JavaScript.

The approach used by NCL4WEB is similar to the one used by TAL. NCL4WEB, however, is transparent to the NCL author, since it uses XSLT for translating the document. Another point to highlight is that the transformation done by TAL does not treat some NCL entities, like switches and rules, but NCL4WEB does.

WebNCL [14] is a JavaScript [9] framework capable of reading an NCL document and transforming it into HTML5 code. The paper presents a three-layer architecture: the first layer is responsible for reading the NCL file, the second layer manages event occurrences and the third layer is responsible for the document presentation. The first layer is composed of two components, one to read the file and another to structure it in an NCL object. The second layer is composed of five components, one responsible for controlling NCL contexts, an event manager, an interaction manager, an exhibition manager and a synchronization manager. The third layer is composed of four components, one for each type of media (audio, video, text and HTML). In the paper, the authors present the result of usability tests in multiple platforms indicating a reasonable performance.

The most important contribution of WebNCL is to enable the execution of NCL code on the web. WebNCL uses the Popcorn library [1]. NCL4WEB, on the other hand, does not use it, since the HTML5 events themselves are used for representing NCL events. The main contribution of NCL4WEB over WebNCL is that NCL4WEB uses XSLT to compile the document into HTML5 + JavaScript code, while WebNCL interprets the NCL code. An advantage of the compilation approach is that it reduces the amount of memory needed to execute the application (see Section 5). The JavaScript code generated by the transformation is used for controlling the synchronization among media objects. Another difference of both tools is that WebNCL uses a standard mapping of keyboard keys for simulating the TV remote control, or the exhibition of a virtual remote control to enable user interaction. NCL4WEB uses a different approach, enabling the user to configure the mapping of remote control keys to keyboard keys before the application is run. It is important to highlight that just the keys used in the application are configured. At last, another important contribution of NCL4WEB is the interpretation of NCL switches and rules, which are frequently used in NCL documents. This feature is not support by WebNCL.

---

[1]Popcorn.js - http://popcornjs.org/

As it can be seen, none of those approaches uses XSLT to do a full translation of the source NCL document as NCL4WEB does. In this aspect, this work brings a new approach for translating NCL documents into HTML5, which makes its use simple for NCL authors.

3. NESTED CONTEXT LANGUAGE

NCL is based on the Nested Context Model [19] and offers two types of nodes: content nodes and context nodes. A content node represents a media object, for example an audio, a video, a text or even a procedural application, such as a Lua script [11] or a Java Xlet [17]. A content node, however, does not contain the media object content, it only represents it inside the document, as media content elements in SMIL [5]. A context node represents a set of component nodes, which can be content nodes or nested context nodes, and a set of links that represent relationships among those component nodes.

An NCL document, as an HTML page, has two main parts: the document *head* and the document *body*. The *head* defines, or imports, regions, descriptors, rules, transitions and connectors. The *body* uses those definitions for specifying media objects and synchronization relationships among them.

NCL regions define areas on the screen where visible media objects will be presented. NCL descriptors are elements that describe how a media object will be presented. NCL transitions define an animation. Transitions are used by descriptors to indicate an animation to be performed when a note starts and/or stops its presentation. The descriptor may define, for example, the volume of an audio or video object, the transparency level of an image or even the duration of a media. The descriptor also defines the region where a media object, using this descriptor, will be presented.

Notice that the definition of regions, transitions and descriptors are independent of the media objects that will be presented. The definition of those elements is done in separate bases defined in the NCL document head, which are *regionBase*, *transitionBase* and *descriptorBase* elements.

Different from SMIL that provides temporal containers, NCL uses an event-based synchronization model providing connectors and links to specify relationships among nodes. NCL allows the definition of generic hypermedia relations, represented by connectors [16], which will be used in the definition of links, representing specific relationships among a set of nodes. An NCL connector represents a causal relation, where a condition, when satisfied, triggers an action. Connector conditions and actions are represented by roles. Connectors are defined in a *connectorBase* element, also contained in the document head.

One example of NCL connector is the *onBeginStart* connector. This connector defines two roles: *onBegin* and *start*. It specifies a relation that "the beginning of the presentation of a node, related to the *onBegin* role, causes the beginning of the presentation of another node, related to the *start* role". Notice that this connector does not specify which nodes will be attached to its roles, it just defines a relation type.

NCL rules define boolean expressions testing the value of document global variables. A rule is used inside a document in the definition of content control elements (*switch*). It is also used for defining alternative descriptors that a node can use (*descriptorSwitch*). In that case, the descriptor a node

will use is chosen at runtime, depending on the value of a global variable.

Region, descriptor, transition, rule and connector bases can be defined in the document head or imported from another NCL document.

NCL content nodes are defined by *media* elements. A content node, or media node, indicates the location of the media content, its type and the NCL descriptor that specifies its presentation characteristics. A media node may also define interface points, which can be anchors or properties. Anchors represent subsets of the media content, and properties represent node attributes. Listing 1 presents an NCL media node example.

Listing 1: Media node example

```
1  <media id="media1" src="videoclip.mpg"
        type="video/mpeg" descriptor="desc1">
2     <area id="track1" begin="2s" end="10s"/>
3  </media>
```

Listing 1 presents a media node that represents the video "videoclip.mpg". This media also defines an anchor (*area* element) that corresponds to the video content between two and ten seconds of the video.

Media elements can be reused across documents. When a media node is reused by another one, its attributes, properties and anchors are copied to the one referring to it. Once a media element reuses another, it defines the type of reuse. A media reuse with type *instSame* represents that both media elements will be the same instance during document exhibition, while with type *new*, it will represent another instance of that media during document exhibition.

As defined previously, a context node, or context, represents a set of nodes and links among them. Besides, a context has interface points, represented by ports, which map the context interface to one component node interface point. It is worth to notice that when a context presentation is started, if a context interface point is not defined, all its interface points will be started. As a consequence, all component nodes mapped by them are started, and all actions done in a context interface point are reflected to the mapped node.

A special type of context node is the *switch* element. It associates rules to component nodes. When a *switch* starts its presentation, it presents the first node whose associated rule is true. It is worth to notice that only one *switch* component node is presented at a time.

Contexts and switches can also be reused. When a context or *switch* is reused by another, the content of the reused context or *switch* and its inner elements are copied to the one referring to it.

NCL relationships are specified by links. Links are contained in context elements and can only connect component nodes directly contained in the same context. In order to create links among nodes contained in different contexts, specific context ports that map to those nodes must be used. A link uses a relation type defined by a connector and indicates the nodes that will play its roles. The participant nodes are defined by a set of binds, where each bind attaches a node interface point to a connector role. Listing 2 presents an example of NCL link.

Listing 2 presents an NCL link that uses the *onBeginStart* connector previously mentioned and indicates node *media1*, anchor *track1*, and node *media2* as the participants of this relationship. This means that when the presentation of *track1* is started, *media2* will be started.

Listing 2: NCL link example

```
1 <link xconnector="onBeginStart">
2   <bind component="media1" interface="track1"
        role="onBegin"/>
3   <bind component="media2" role="start"/>
4 </link>
```

Notice that the body of an NCL document is a context node, containing a set of ports, nodes and links.

4. NCL4WEB

NCL4WEB translates NCL documents into HTML5 web pages, using tools available as W3C standards. HTML5 brings new functionalities for the Web, allowing the exhibition of audio and video through specific elements and the possibility of using JavaScript to gather events triggered by those elements for synchronizing their presentation.

The translation of an NCL file to HTML5 is done using an XSLT stylesheet [22]. Since NCL is XML-based [4], XSLT can be used for transforming any NCL document into another XML-based format. In our case, the output format is HTML5. It is worth to notice that XSLT is supported by great part of available web browsers[2]. Although that support is limited to the 1.0 version of XSLT in most cases, it is enough for our transformation from NCL to HTML5.

NCL4WEB is composed by an XSLT stylesheet, that translates NCL elements into HTML5 elements and JavaScript functions. The resulting HTML5 page includes a JavaScript component named *ncl-complements.js*, which contains common functions (used by every translated NCL document) and manages user interaction. The choice for such an approach (i.e. XSLT + JavaScript), and for not using just JavaScript, took into account the facility of implementing the translator, once using just JavaScript would require an external page invoking the NCL code or hosting it in a web server, as WebNCL does [14]. Besides, using XSLT brings the possibility of performing the translation before deploying the application as a web page. Figure 1 shows how NCL4WEB works. All NCL documents use the same stylesheet (*ncl4web.xslt*) to make the transformation. Once the transformation is done, all HTML5 resulting pages call the same JavaScript module (*ncl-complements.js*) that contains common functions used by the resulting web page. CSS is also used for providing some exhibition features when a media node is active and hiding it when it has ended.

The choice for not implementing the translator using just XSLT allowed the separation between the code transformation and the event occurrence management, making the implementation more robust. Therefore, the JavaScript component can handle events generated by HTML, providing relationships that would not be possible without using JavaScript. For example, the interpretation of NCL properties is possible using XSLT, but managing those properties during exhibition is only possible using JavaScript.

That is why NCL4WEB uses both JavaScript and HTML5 with XSLT. The XSLT stylesheet translates the NCL document into an HTML5 web page and a JavaScript library to handle the exhibition of the created elements, functions

---

[2]Some Android browser implementations do not support it properly.

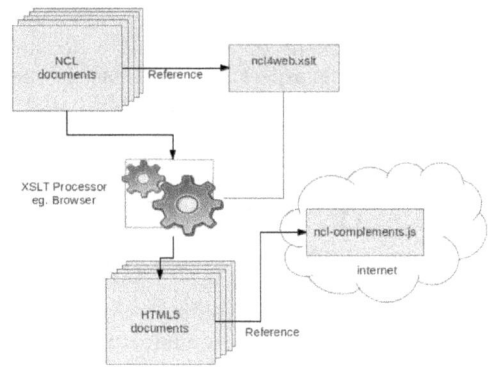

Figure 1: How NCL4WEB works

and events. To facilitate and make the development faster, JQuery [18] was used for handling HTML element manipulations and events. The general view of the NCL4WEB stylesheet is presented in Figure 2. There are six main templates that get elements inside the NCL document, and use the information inside the elements to build the resulting HTML5 document.

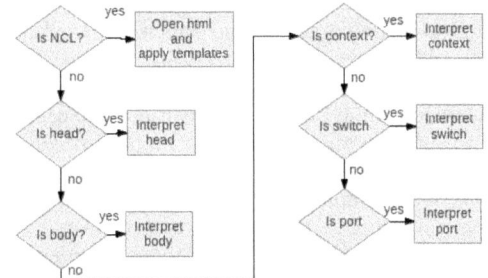

Figure 2: How the NCL4WEB stylesheet handles an NCL document

4.1 NCL to HTML5 translation

In order to present the transformation from NCL to HTML5, it is necessary to define how NCL elements will be represented as HTML5 tags. An NCL media object can be a video, an audio, a text, among other media types. All those types could be exhibited by HTML5 using the *embed* tag. However, that tag does not provide the functions necessary for controlling video presentation and also managing event occurrences related to it. Therefore, different HTML5 tags were used depending on the NCL element. Table 1 presents the NCL element and the translated HTML5 tag.

It is worth to notice that several different HTML structures were used to represent NCL entities. Although it would be possible to represent every NCL entity with (for example) the *div* tag, we have chosen to diversify the use of HTML tags in order to optimize the JavaScript processing while manipulating the HTML document. Moreover, the decision of which NCL entities would be translated to HTML5 elements and which would be translated to JavaScript code considered if the entity would be used for representing document content or document behavior, respectively.

In the transformation, NCL *links*, *rules* and *descriptor-Switches* are transformed in JavaScript functions. NCL *re-*

Table 1: NCL elements and translated HTML5 tags.

NCL element	Translated HTML5 tag
audio media	audio
video media	video
media of type settings	span (with class *settings*)
image media	img
text or html media	iframe
media using reference with type *instSame*	span (with class *instSame*)
context	*div*
region	*div* (parent of the elements that use the region)
descriptor	*div*
link + connector	JavaScript functions
switch	*ul* and *li* (invisible)
rule	JavaScript function that returns a boolean value
descriptorSwitch	JavaScript function triggered when a variable is changed
port	input/hidden with port class
property	input/hidden with property class
area	area

gions and *descriptors* defined in the document head become HTML *div* elements, where media content elements will be nested. NCL *ports* and *properties* become input elements with specific classes nested inside their parent elements. NCL *contexts* are also transformed into HTML *div* elements. This HTML structure will be manipulated by JavaScript functions created when NCL links are translated, making the document behave the same was as in an NCL formatter.

An NCL media element can be translated into different HTML5 tags, because each media type is handled differently in HTML5. Reused NCL media nodes with the same instance are translated in a different way. Only the original media is translated to a media content tag and the others are converted to an empty *span* tag that points to the original media tag.

An NCL region becomes a *div* element that has the same exhibition and position attributes as in the NCL document. An NCL *switch* becomes an invisible *ul* element that has the information of which media nodes that *switch* has. An NCL area element becomes an HTML5 *area* tag that is inside the correspondent media or, in case the HTML5 correspondent element cannot have child elements, it becomes an *area* tag referencing the media. The *area* tag is only a marker to the JavaScript code that will handle the anchor (in the current version, only temporal anchors are fully supported). The HTML5 *area* element was extended using JavaScript code, for representing a temporal interval of its parent audio or video element.

The CSS stylesheet used has three classes: one for handling media nodes inside regions that inherit their parent region's size and position, one for components that are not visible and one for handling active components. Other NCL presentation attributes (e.g. z-index and transparency) are handled by the style attribute of the correspondent HTML

media element, which is applied by JavaScript functions when it is started.

An NCL context becomes a *div* element that has ports, properties, switches and media tags. Media elements that are contained in an NCL context have an attribute that refers to that context.

First the main *html* element of the output page is created. After that, the HTML document head is created referring to the JavaScript components and containing functions to represent NCL rules, if they are found in the document. Then, it creates the document body where NCL contexts, switches, regions, descriptors, medias, properties, descriptorSwitches and links will be added. The specific steps for translating those elements will be described in the following paragraphs.

The translation is done by six XSLT *templates* with selection rules (translate ncl, head, body, context, switch and port) and seven *templates* called by them (translate region, rule, descriptor, descriptorSwitch, link, media and property). Other auxiliary templates are used for helping the translation.

The **head translation template** translates NCL *rules* and *transitions* defined in the document head. It also adds JavaScript components that manage event occurrences to the HTML document head.

The **body translation template** creates the HTML document body and calls the templates that translate ports, contexts, switches, medias, properties and links defined inside the NCL document body. It also calls the templates that translate regions, descriptors and descriptorSwitches defined inside the NCL document head, besides the ones that are imported from external documents.

Figure 3 details how the transformation happens. Notice that the descriptors that refer to a region are interpreted while the regions are interpreted, and media nodes that refer to a descriptor are interpreted while the descriptors are interpreted. These transformations will be detailed as follows.

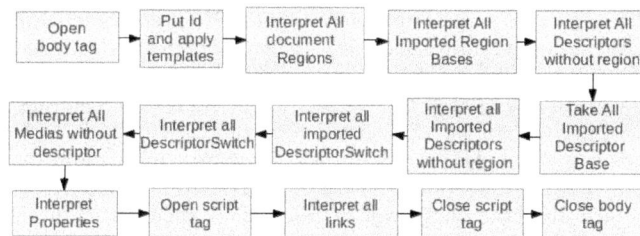

Figure 3: Details of how the transformation is done

The **rule translation template** creates JavaScript functions that get the value of the variable each rule tests and compares it to the defined value. The variable to be tested is an NCL *property* element defined inside a media element of type *application/x-ginga-settings*. Since rules can be imported from external documents, in such cases, the function that represents the rule is created with name *alias_id*, where *alias* is defined for identifying the imported document and *id* is the rule id. In case of NCL composite rules, the rule translation template creates functions for each child rule and returns the logical value of the resulting formula. Figure 4 summarizes the translation of NCL rules.

The **port translation template** creates *input* elements with type *hidden*, class *port* and attributes *id* equal to the

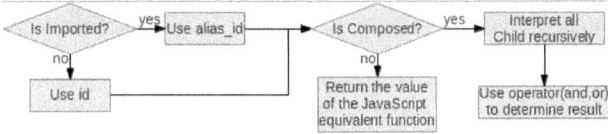

Figure 4: Translation of rules

port id and *value* equal to the port component attribute. In case the port has the *interface* attribute defined, the same attribute is added to the *input* element.

The **property translation template** creates *input* elements with type *hidden*, class *property* and attributes *id* equal to the property id and *value* equal to the property value attribute.

The **context translation template** creates a *div* for the context with class *context* and an attribute *context* that indicates its parent. Although the *div* elements representing the contexts are nested in HTML, that attribute helps JavaScript functions navigating in the document. Each *port*, *switch*, *context*, *media* and *property* nested in the context are translated using templates specific for each element.

The **switch translation template** creates a *ul* tag for the template and *li* tags inside it for each *bindRule* element inside an NCL switch. Each *li* will have the rule id (name of the JavaScript function) and the component to be activated when the rule is true, both coming from the related *bindRule* element. The NCL *switch defaultComponent* element is represented by an *li* element with attribute *default* containing the id of the component to be activated when no rule is true. NCL *switchPort* elements are transformed into *ul* elements inside an *li* element, and *li* elements with the id of the rule and the interface of the component to be executed.

The **region translation template** is used both for regions defined inside the document and regions imported from an external document. It has parameters: *region*, identifying the parent region, *alias*, with the alias used for importing the region (in case it is imported), *regionURI*, with the URI of the imported document and *originalDoc* with the document being translated. The template creates a *div* for the region with the same id of the element in the NCL document and with class *region*. The position attributes (*top*, *left*, *right* and *bottom*), the size attributes (*height* and *width*) and the *zIndex* attribute of the NCL region are used for defining the *style* attribute of the *div*. If the region *zIndex* attribute is not defined, an automatic value is chosen. In case the alias parameter is present, it means that the region is imported, so all descriptors referring to that region with the combination *alias#id* are translated as well. Figure 5 summarizes the translation of regions.

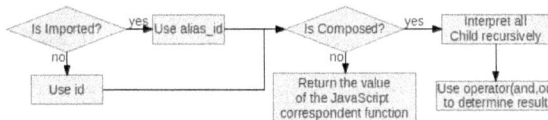

Figure 5: Translation of regions

Notice that NCL regions are not translated to CSS classes, but to *div* tags. The main reason for doing that is that NCL provides nested regions. A nested region defines its location on the screen relative to its parent. Besides, missing attributes are inherited from its parent. Although inheritance is possible in CSS classes, it overwrites the class attribute values, when it must sum them to behave like NCL. To define regions as classes in the HTML5 document head, it would require a complete knowledge of a region parent regions and the screen as a whole, which is not known in the translation stage.

The **descriptor translation template** is used both for descriptors inside the document and descriptors imported from an external document. It has the following parameters: *descriptor*, identifying the descriptor element, *alias*, with the alias used for importing the descriptor (in case it is imported) and *originalDoc* with the document being translated. The template creates a *div* with the same id of the descriptor and tests if it uses a region. If that is the case, the *div* owns a class indicating that it is inside the region, besides the one indicating that it is a descriptor. Then, the navigating attributes that control the navigation scheme *focusIndex*, *moveLeft*, *moveRight*, *moveUp* and *moveDown* are added to the *div*. Any *descriptorParam* inside the descriptor is translated into an *input* element with type *hidden*. In case the alias parameter is present, it means that the descriptor is imported, so all medias referring to that descriptor with the combination *alias#id* can be found. Figure 6 summarizes the translation of descriptors.

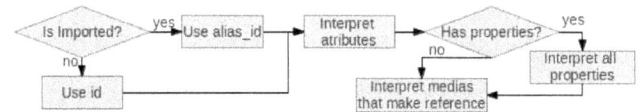

Figure 6: Translation of descriptors

The **media translation template** is called by other templates or by itself when the *refer* attribute is present. It has two parameters: the media being translated and an id of the media that refers to it (if that is the case). The template verifies if the media has the attribute *instance* equal to *instSame*. If so, it creates a *span* tag with class *instSame*, which is used for identifying that it is a reference to another media. If the media represents an image, it is translated into an *img* tag and its anchors are interpreted outside the element (some XSLT readers do not enable elements inside an *img* tag) with a *parent* attribute indicating that they are children of the media. If the media represents a web page, another NCL document or a text, it is translated into an *iframe* tag and its anchors are also interpreted outside the element. If the media represents a video or an audio, it is translated into a *video* or an *audio* tag, respectively. Besides, their anchors are interpreted inside those elements. If the media has the type *application/x-ginga-settings*, it is translated into a *span* tag with class *settings* identifying to the JavaScript component that it represents a global variable for the document. After a media is translated, the template searches for every media that refers to it and translates them. All visible medias receive a bind function to their click action, linking it to the select function, which selects the element, if it receives a mouse click. Figure 7 summarizes the translation of media elements.

The **descriptorSwitch translation template** uses the **descriptor translation template** to translate the *descriptor* elements inside the *descriptorSwitch*, transforming them into *div* tags. The template creates a *script* tag with a

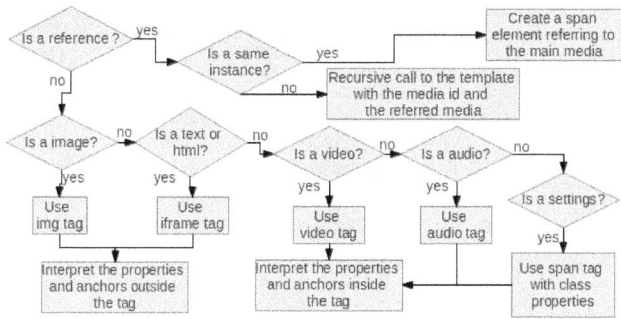

Figure 7: Translation of media elements

JavaScript function whose name is equal to the id of the *descriptorSwitch* or *alias_id*, if the *descriptorSwitch* is imported from another document. For each *bindRule* element inside the descriptorSwitch, the template creates a function that tests, during runtime, if the rule associated to that bindRule is true. In this case, it changes the *descriptor* of the media nodes that use the *descriptorSwitch* by the one identified in the *bindRule*.

The **link translation template** creates a set of JavaScript functions for each link in the document. The functions are created by this template in a *script* tag different from the one used for the *descriptorSwitch* functions. This is done to improve the readability of the created HTML5 document. Notice that the number of HTML lines of code produced by this template depends on the number of links an NCL document has. Figure 8 illustrates how this template works.

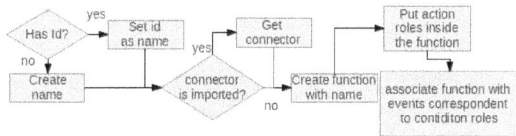

Figure 8: Details of how the link template works

At first, the template creates a unique name for the JavaScript function that represents the link. It uses the link id, if present, or creates a name from the concatenation of the following strings: the link condition and action role names and the condition and action target element ids, the connector used by the link. As an example, from a link that specifies that "when media1 ends, start media2" and that uses connector "connector1", the template would create the name "onEndmedia1startmedia2connector1".

The second step done by the template is to translate the connector used by the link. The function created in the previous step is filled with the actions described in the connector. If those actions are sequential, the functions for executing each action are called sequentially. If they are parallel, the functions for executing each action are related to an event, so they can be executed in parallel. It is worth to notice that the specification of whether a set of actions should be executed in sequence or in parallel (in any order) comes from the NCL connector definition. The link condition can be simple or compound. In the last case, the template creates an auxiliary function that tests if all conditions contained in it are true. Also, if a link condition tests a user interaction with a specific key, an auxiliary function

is also created to test if that key was pressed. When the selection is mapped to a specific key, two events are bound to the element, one with the key and one with the selection only, making it possible to select with a mouse click in devices that do not have a keyboard to map the keys (clicks activate the select function).

The following section details how the JavaScript library *ncl-complements.js* helps treating runtime events and describes its common functions.

4.2 NCL4WEB Execution

Using the documentLoad event to trigger a bootstrap function, *ncl-complements.js* makes an adaptation to the events returned by HTML5 elements making them trigger events with the same name of the NCL events (eg. ended from JavaScript triggers onEnd from NCL). *ncl-complements.js* also has common functions to access and handle media elements inside the HTML translated document.

At the beginning of a document execution, *ncl-complements.js* creates a configuration screen, in case the document uses remote control keys. To know if the document makes use of a remote control key, it searches for a variable responsible for indicating it, created at the translation stage. The configuration screen saves the user options, so that in the next execution, it is possible to avoid showing the configuration screen again. After the configuration screen is closed, the document is started by using the common use function "startContext", which searches for ports inside a context and starts all of them. In this case, the started context is the document body. That function can also be used to start only one of the context ports, when it is called together with an interface attribute.

The *ncl-complements* library also has a function to deal with user interaction. It checks the media currently in focus (it sets the focus to the media with the smallest NCL *focusIndex* attribute, if there is no media in focus) and the key pressed. If it is an arrow key, it changes the focus to the media with the same index defined in the NCL navigational attributes (*moveUp, moveDown, moveLeft, moveRight*). Every time the focus changes, the NCL global variable called "service.currentFocus" has its value changed to the focusIndex of the media on focus. If the key pressed is the *ENTER* key, it activates media selection. It also has functions to deal with elements that represent the same instance of other elements and changing the descriptor associated to a media object, either if the media uses a *descriptorSwitch* or if there is a link bind that defines a descriptor for that media. For every predefined connector condition role, NCL4WEB creates a custom event with the same name of the NCL condition role.

For every predefined NCL connector action role (*start, stop, set, pause, resume, abort*), NCL4WEB has a predefined JavaScript function. Figure 9 illustrates the general way those functions work.

Each element has a "state" attribute, which indicates the element current state. At first, the action role function reads this attribute to determine if the action can be performed over the element. Then, the role action function tests if the element is an instance of another element (it is indicated by an attribute created by the XSLT stylesheet). If this is the case, the action is executed over the referred element. In the case the action role function also receives an interface, it checks if the action is a start action, since its behavior

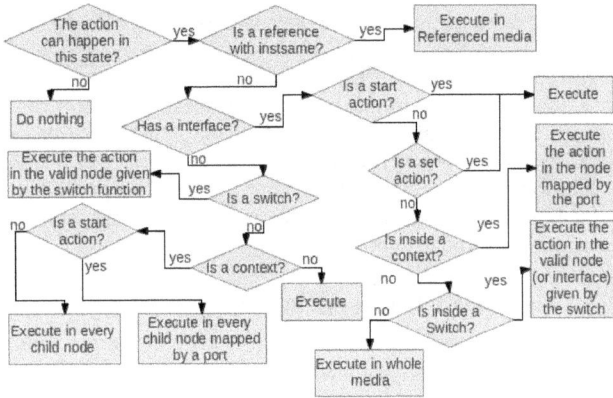

Figure 9: General way the action role functions work

is different from the other actions. It is also necessary to identify if the node where the action will be performed is a media node, a context or a switch, since the type of node also impacts in the way an action is performed. The following paragraphs detail such differences.

In a start action, when a media is presented inside a region, it receives the *zIndex* according to that region. If the media object uses a descriptor, it verifies if the focus is the smallest one, setting the focus to the media object, if that is the case. If the descriptor specifies a transition, the transition is executed and the media object presentation starts, once the transition finishes. The element then goes to the active state and tests the existent child anchors that should also be started. If the media object has an explicit duration, the object presentation will be presented until that duration is over. If the action target element is a context node, the start action is performed over all its ports, or the one identified by the interface attribute. In case it is a switch, the element to be executed is the one related to the rule whose value is true.

In a stop action, in case the target element is a media node, all its anchors are stopped as well. Any transition defined by the media descriptor to be executed when the presentation ends is executed. On the other hand, if the node is a context, the stop action is performed over all nodes inside the context or the node mapped by a port, in case the interface attribute is present. When the target element is a switch, the stop action is performed over every node inside it. The behavior of abort, pause and resume actions are similar to the stop action.

The **set** function is used for modifying the value of an element property. Like the other functions, it first verifies if the element makes reference to another one, so the property of the referred element will have its value changed. The attribution event is started both for the property and its parent element. In case the property is a child of a *settings* media and represents the "service.currentFocus" global variable, the descriptor with *focusIndex* equal to the new value will receive the focus.

The selection of an element can be done by clicking over the element or by pressing *ENTER* when the element is on focus. A function verifies if the element is a reference to another one representing the same instance, so the selection is considered to be done over the original element. Once an element is selected by clicking over it, the function needs to

verify if it is visible, then the value of the global variable "service.currentFocus" changes to the *focusIndex* of the selected element. Also if some element has an *onSelection* link with a key specified, and if this is the only *onSelection* link associated to it, it can be selected by the user click. If there are other *onSelection* links associated, they need the specific key to be activated. This facilitates the execution of NCL applications in devices that have a touch screen and enables it in a device that does not have a keyboard.

JQuery [18] is used for helping the manipulation of elements and events. All functions that control the document are created by NCL4WEB or they are already defined in *ncl-complements.js*. The idea of the JavaScript library named *ncl-complements* is to handle the initialization of the document and specify functions that will be used in all NCL documents. Besides functions to represent link action roles, there are also functions for handling other issues. There is a function for property interpretation, capable of searching properties in the element or in its descriptor. There is a function for handling switches, which receives the id and interface of a switch and returns the selected component and its interface (if there is a switchPort). There is a function for handling the trigger of events of every element that plays an action role, which verifies if the element is associated to a port or if it has elements with the same instance.

5. USING NCL4WEB

The use of NCL4WEB is quite simple. The NCL document developer only needs to insert an XML reference in the first line of the NCL document to link it to the XSLT stylesheet as presented below.

$$< ?xml-stylesheet type = ``text/xsl'' href = ``path/ncl4web.xsl''? >$$

It is possible to use NCL4WEB locally or in a web server. For local use, it is necessary to enable local file access in some browsers (like Google Chrome). For security reasons, the XSLT stylesheet needs to be hosted in the same server that hosts the NCL application, which means that the user needs to download the XSLT stylesheet to use it in an application. But all JavaScript modules used, *ncl-complements.js* and JQuery, are referred from remote servers and do not need to be downloaded by the user. It is also possible to translate the NCL code with NCL4WEB, using an XSLT parser and saving the result as an HTML5 page for future use. Therefore it is possible to avoid the translation of the NCL code every time the NCL document is executed. The choice of using this approach or leaving the translation to be done by the browser is up to the author.

NCL4WEB was tested with NCL interactive applications available from the NCL Club [1] that use just NCL code (Lua code [11] is not handled in the current version). The applications tested were: "Day Schedule", "Tic-tac-toe", "Live More", "First João" and "Photo frame". The application "Maranhão Tour" was translated correctly, but since it uses several video objects, it could not be exhibited in several web browsers since they restrict the number of videos that can be exhibited. The web browsers tested were Google Chrome, Internet Explorer, Mozilla Firefox and Safari.

From the tests, it was possible to observe that the main problem for exhibiting the applications is browser compatibility, since there is not a common video format for all of them (only Mozilla Firefox does not support MPEG, but there are plans for supporting it[3]). It was also possible to observe that the memory use was not high for exhibiting the applications. The applications were also exhibited in portable devices, like Ipads. One limitation faced was the fact that iOS can only execute one video at a time.

In Android devices, the default browser does not support XSLT transformation in smart phones[4], but it is possible to make the transformation with third-party browsers, like Opera-Mini or Chrome to Android. In mobile devices, as the virtual keyboard is not activated when a web page is loaded, it is difficult to map remote control keys to keyboard keys. This is partially overcome by the fact that selecting an image can activate the key selection event if it is the only selection event attached to the image.

In order to evaluate NCL4WEB performance, WebNCL [14] (a similar tool also used for running NCL code in web browsers) was used as benchmark. Two applications were used in the evaluation: "Live More" and "First João". Tests were done in the Google Chrome browser (version 22.0.1229.94) running over Windows 7. For the "Live More" application, NCL4WEB used 22KB of memory, while WebNCL used 40KB. For the "First João" application, NCL4WEB used 37KB of memory, while WebNCL used 50KB. Google Chrome uses GPU acceleration to handle video rendering, the difference of memory usage with GPU for NCL4WEB and WebNCL was not perceptible (less than one KB). The initial transformation made by the XSLT takes an additional time of less than 0.5 seconds for those examples. For larger documents (e.g. "Maranhão Guide"), the initial transformation took an additional time of 1 second. It is worth to highlight that the same document does not work with Web-NCL. We intend to conduct further tests for measuring the impact of the document size in the transformation time.

Figure 10 shows the screens of NCL4WEB (bottom) and WebNCL (top). NCL4WEB uses the same region definition as in the NCL document and uses all available screen space to show the application. WebNCL, on the other hand, uses part of screen space to show the virtual remote control. Notice that since the author defined a region with percentage values, images were scaled to the browser window size. Another point to highlight is that WebNCL requires an HTML web page that calls the NCL inside it. On the other hand, with NCL4WEB, an NCL document that calls the NCL4WEB stylesheet is directly loaded in the browser, making the transformation more transparent to the final user. This is the main difference of using NCL4WEB over WebNCL, the NCL code developer only needs to add one line in the top of the main NCL document, so it can be exhibited as an HTML5 page, not requiring any knowledge of HTML5 or JavaScript languages. On the other hand, WebNCL requires knowledge of HTML5 and JavaScript to include an NCL document inside an HTML page.

6. DISCUSSION AND LIMITATIONS

NCL4WEB was created to translate pure NCL applications (applications that do not use Lua script) to HTML5 web pages. NCL4WEB does not implement some NCL advanced features in the current version, like the possibility of using customized connector roles different from the default ones for creating action and condition roles. NCL4WEB

Figure 10: "Live More" application execution comparison WebNCL(top) NCL4WEB(bottom)

supports customized connector roles only for defining tests over media event states or other property values (NCL connector *assessmentStatement* element). It is worth to highlight that such features are not used in most NCL documents available (considering the NCL Club repository).

NCL provides several transition options. In NCL4WEB, this set was reduced to just *fadeIn* and *fadeOut*. The reason for this limitation is that the JQuery library only implements those two options. In the current version, independent of the transition defined in the NCL document, NCL4WEB will use *fadeIn* or *fadeOut*. Notice, however, that a transition is translated into a JavaScript object that implements it. Once a solution for implementing the other transition types is available, it is necessary to modify only that object code.

In order to avoid loading several videos not currently being presented, NCL4WEB uses the *preload* attribute of audios and videos as *none* by default. When the presentation of the media is started, the attribute value is changed to *auto*. This does not seem to interfere in the speed that a video is loaded in NCL applications (in all NCL club examples, none of them had a slow video start), but it can be possible to have problems, in case the video has a bigger size and the IP device connection speed is not fast enough to receive the video in real time.

One NCL4WEB limitation is that it cannot exhibit documents using Lua code [11]. A solution currently in use is to manually translate Lua scripts into JavaScript and add them to the HTML5 document. Although possible, this translation is not easy to be implemented.

NCL also provides the feature of importing a document as a whole in its head. This kind of reuse facility is not implemented in NCL4WEB in the current version. But it is possible to import individual bases like *regionBase, rule-*

---

[3]https://brendaneich.com/2012/10/html5-video-update/
[4]http://code.google.com/p/android/issues/detail?id=9312

Base, connectorBase, descriptorBase and *transitionBase* elements.

Another functionality of NCL is the support for multi-devices, where an NCL document can be executed across several devices. Multi-device support is possible in HTML with the use of JavaScript's user agent property in the global object "navigator". In the current version, NCL4WEB does not support the NCL facility for multiple devices.

These limitations will be overcome in a future version of NCL4WEB. The main propose of the current version was to implement more common used NCL features. In a future version, the full NCL specification will be supported.

7. CONCLUSION

This paper presented NCL4WEB, a tool that allows NCL application developers to exhibit their applications on the web. NCL4WEB enables the exhibition of applications following the Ginga-NCL standard and was tested with applications available in the NCL Club website. All tested NCL applications worked as expected.

NCL4WEB translates an NCL code into HTML5 + CSS + JavaScript code. The tool performance is slightly better than a similar tool called WebNCL, considering memory usage. Since NCL4WEB uses XSLT for translating the NCL document, the interactive application developer does not need to settle a web service for exhibiting the application and does not require any knowledge of HTML or JavaScript to be used. Besides, authors have the possibility of translating the NCL document to HTML5 prior to its deployment as a web page.

NCL4WEB is available under the license Creative Commons Attribution-NonCommercial 3.0 Unported License [5]. All tested NCL Club applications are also available in the NCL4WEB website.

A future work is to address the tool limitations, allowing documents to be imported as a whole, customized connector roles and being able to convert Lua scripts into JavaScript code.

8. REFERENCES

[1] Oficial site of ClubeNCL. http://clube.ncl.org.br.

[2] Oficial site of SBTVD. http://www.dtv.org.br, 2010.

[3] ABNT. 15606-2. Digital Terrestrial Television - Data Coding and Transmission Specification for Digital Broadcasting - Part 2: Ginga-NCL for fixed and mobile receivers - XML application language for application coding, 2011.

[4] T. Bray, J. Paoli, C. Sperberg-McQueen, E. Maler, and F. Yergeau. Extensible markup language (XML). *World Wide Web Journal*, 2(4):27–66, 1997.

[5] D. Bulterman, G. Grassel, J. Jansen, A. Koivisto, N. Layaïda, T. Michel, S. Mullender, and D. Zucker. Synchronized multimedia integration language (smil 2.1). *W3C Recommendation*, 13, 2005.

[6] D. Bulterman, J. Jansen, K. Kleanthous, K. Blom, and D. Benden. Ambulant: a fast, multi-platform open source SMIL player. In *ACM international conference on Multimedia*, volume 10, pages 492–495, 2004.

[7] D. Bulterman and L. Rutledge. *SMIL 3.0: Flexible Multimedia for Web, Mobile Devices and Daisy Talking Books*. Springer, 2008.

[8] F. Cazenave, V. Quint, and C. Roisin. Timesheets.js: Tools for web multimedia. In *ACM international conference on Multimedia*, pages 699–702, 2011.

[9] E. Ecma. 262: Ecmascript language specification. *ECMA (European Association for Standardizing Information and Communication Systems), pub-ECMA: adr,*, 1999.

[10] O. Gaggi and L. Danese. A SMIL player for any web browser. *DMS 2011*, pages 114–119, 2011.

[11] R. Ierusalimschy, L. De Figueiredo, and W. Filho. Lua-an extensible extension language. *Software Practice and Experience*, 26(6):635–652, 1996.

[12] ITU. Nested Context Language (NCL) and Ginga-NCL for IPTV services. http://www.itu.int/rec/T-REC-H.761-200904-S, 2009. ITU-T Recommendation H.761.

[13] J. Jansen and D. Bulterman. Enabling adaptive time-based web applications with SMIL state. In *ACM symposium on Document engineering*, pages 18–27, 2008.

[14] E. Melo, C. Viel, C. Teixeira, A. Rondon, D. Silva, D. Rodrigues, and E. Silva. Webncl: A web-based presentation machine for multimedia documents. In *Brazilian symposium on Multimedia and the web*, pages 403–410, 2012.

[15] E. Meyer and B. Bos. CSS3 Introduction. *W3C, Working Draft WD-css3-roadmap-20010523*, 2001.

[16] D. C. Muchaluat-Saade, R. F. Rodrigues, and L. F. G. Soares. Xconnector: extending xlink to provide multimedia synchronization. In *Proceedings of the 2002 ACM symposium on Document engineering*, pages 49–56. ACM, 2002.

[17] M. Pawlan. Introduction to Digital TV Applications Programming. *SDN article*, 2001.

[18] J. Resig et al. jquery: The write less, do more, javascript library. *Avaible at http://jquery. com/,*, 18(04):2009, 2009.

[19] L. F. G. Soares and R. F. Rodrigues. Nested Context Model 3.0 Part 1 - NCM Core. May 2005.

[20] C. Soares Neto, L. Soares, and C. de Souza. TAL - Template Authoring Language. *Journal of the Brazilian Computer Society*, pages 1–15, 2012.

[21] P. Vuorimaa, D. Bulterman, and P. Cesar. SMIL Timesheets 1.0. *W3C Working Draft*, 2008.

[22] W3C. XSL transformations (XSLT) version 1.0, 1999.

[23] W3C. HTML5: A vocabulary and associated APIs for HTML and XHTML. http://www.w3.org/TR/html5/, 2011. World-Wide Web Consortium Working Draft.

---

[5]NCL4WEB site www.midiacom.uff.br/~caleb/ncl4web

Go Beyond Boundaries of iTV Applications

Caio Cesar Viel[1], Erick Lazaro Melo[1], Maria da Graça Pimentel[2], Cesar A. C. Teixeira[1]
[1]Universidade Federal de São Carlos, Brazil — [2]Universidade de São Paulo, Brazil
{caio_viel|erick_melo|cesar}@dc.ufscar.br, mgp@icmc.usp.br,

ABSTRACT

The development of multimedia applications that require the manipulation and the synchronization of multiple media and the handling of different types of user interactions usually requires specialized knowledge in imperative languages. Declarative languages have been proposed in order to make this task easier, especially when applications are restricted to certain classes, as it is the case of Interactive TV applications in which user interactions are restricted to a few simple models. However, those simple models may be too simple when documents are reused in other platforms: for instance, when watching a video most web users expect an interactive timeline to be available — which is not the case in interactive TV videos. This paper presents a component-based approach to the enrichment of declarative languages for multimedia so that desirable user-media interactions are made possible at the same time that the original ease of authoring is maintained. We detail the components and present a corresponding proof-of-concept prototype. We also discuss design decisions associated with the development of the components, which should be useful in further extensions.

Categories and Subject Descriptors: H.5.1[**Multimedia Information Systems:**] *Video*. H.7.2[**Document Preparation**]*Hypertext/hypermedia, Index generation, Markup languages*.

Keywords: Time-based navigation, User Query, Spatial Composition, Annotation, Component-based development.

1. INTRODUCTION

The design of multimedia presentations or applications — for the web, desktop, mobile devices or interactive TV (iTV) — is an interdisciplinary activity which demands professionals from different fields such as communication, design, marketing and art. The development of multimedia applications, however, requires the work of professionals with good programming skills, usually in imperative languages.

Therefore, good communication and understanding among computer professionals and others involved in the creation of multimedia presentations is essential to produce applications faithful to the wishes of their authors.

The possibility of the same professionals that design multimedia presentations be also able to undertake part of its implementation, even in draft or prototype versions, can be productive, for instance to improve the communication among programmers in terms of improvements. Moreover, if the final implementation can be carried out by the creators of the presentation, economic gains can also be obtained. Furthermore, the easy authoring of multimedia presentations may result in an increase in the amount of presentations created.

Declarative languages for the specification of multimedia applications such as SMIL [5], for web applications, and NCL[1] [1, 27], for iTV applications, were proposed to facilitate the authoring of multimedia applications — when compared with authoring with imperative languages. However, given that these languages provide good options for synchronizing media but fewer options for user interaction, a limited class of multimedia applications is supported — at least as far as the ease of authoring is concerned. It is not trivial, for example, to create declarative applications that allow media annotations or, in the case of NCL, use a time-slider to allow usert to interact with continuous media — even though the latter is an operation which many Web users are used to.

The opportunity for authoring interactive multimedia documents automatically by combining information captured from live experiences has been extensively exploited — in particular considering the lecture environment. In this case, information captured in a classroom (video, audio, slides, electronic ink, etc.) is used in the composition of interactive web-based multimedia documents [2, 12, 15, 16].

Several platforms exist that allow, more or less automatically, combining captured information into web-based videos so that the result is a multimedia application usually encoded in HTML5 or Flash. Examples in the educational domain include Coursera[2], EDx[3] and EyA [6]. However, real world demands require that the generated multimedia documents be made available not only for the web and mobile platforms, in which HTML5 would suffice, but also for

---

[1]Declarative language adopted by the ISDB-Tb (International System for Digital Broadcast, Terrestrial, Brazilian version) and by the ITU-T for IPTV.
[2]www.coursera.org
[3]www.edx.org

the iTV environments. This lead us to investigate how to automatically generate interactive multimedia applications encoded in the NCL, since NCL interactive multimedia documents can be used both in compliant native iTV environments and in the web (using the WebNCL engine [34]).

A challenging requirement, given the many platforms available, is the production of multimedia documents that offer interaction facilities expected by users of all platforms — web users, for instance, are likely to be frustrated when facing a video without a time slider. Such requirement challenged us to build components that enable the necessary interactions at the same time that maintain the original declarative authoring approach. In this paper we present a component-based approach to the enrichment of declarative languages for multimedia so that desirable user-media interactions are made possible at the same time that the original ease of authoring is maintained. We also present a corresponding proof-of-concept prototype and discuss design decisions should be useful in future extensions.

This paper is organized as follows: in the next section we discuss related work, especially research related to simplicity in authoring of multimedia applications; in Section 3 we discuss both some interesting features for multimedia applications which have proven to be difficult to be implemented with declarative languages, and how these difficulties can be overcome; in Section 4 we present components that generate NCL + Lua code that implements these features; in Section 5 we illustrate the use of the components by means of the generation of a highly-interactive NCL Document. In Section 6 we present our final remarks.

2. RELATED WORK

Declarative languages for authoring hypermedia documents present some limitations that can usually be overcome with aid of imperative script languages. Efforts for reducing the dependence of script languages are reported by King et al. [14]: the authors add to SMIL some capabilities of functional languages, such as expression evaluation and value-based reactive events. Using a similar approach, Soares et al. [28] add to NCL the capability for store and retrieve values in variables. The authors also extended the NCL's causality relations to support variable-based conditions. Both works reduce the necessity for imperative code, but they achieve this by incorporating in declarative languages low-level features of non-declarative languages.

The development of modern multimedia application for the Web can be carried out using HTML5, CSS and JavaScript. Although the content, structure and style of applications can be defined using declarative languages, time (and complex spatial) synchronization must be done with aid of JavaScript. The work of Cazenave et al. [8] combine the flexibility of HTML5 and CSS with the SMIL Timing and Synchronization module in order to avoid using JavaScript code to perform synchronization in Web applications. The work represents an enhancement in the development of HTML-based applications, but does not offer an easier way for developing multimedia applications than the one offered by SMIL.

The work of Azevedo and Soares [3] extends NCL in order to add support for 3D scenes described in the declarative language X3D. The authors propose the use of X3D documents as NCL media nodes, mapping NCL anchors into equivalent elements of X3D documents. They also extended the NCL's causality relations to add some conditions related to

3D scenes, such as collisions. Although the combination of X3D and NCL allows the creation of complex and rich multimedia applications, composed by image, videos and 3D scene, it does not enhance the ease of authoring of multimedia applications.

One issue present in some declarative languages, especially in NCL, is the verbosity and recurrence of constructions. This lead to template-based generators such as XTemplate [25] and Template Authoring Language (TAL) [29]. These works specify languages for writing templates that can be imported into documents for further generation of multimedia applications in languages such as NCL or HTML. Although these works enhance the expressivity of the declarative languages by offering templates as high-level construction blocks, they lack in providing high-level interaction models such as timeline navigation.

Another common approach to ease the development of multimedia applications is the use of graphical tools such as SMIL builder [4], EDITEC [9] or FIND [24]. SMIL builder creates and validates SMIL documents using a visual representation of the SMIL timeline expressed in a specialized Petri Net. EDITEC allows the authoring of NCL documents using predefined constructions which are written in the XTemplate language. FIND proposes that authors add complementary content to video by means of annotations, and was inspired in the watch-and-comment approach [31] proposed to allow viewers to add annotations at the time of playback. FIND offers clues about moments in which annotations can be added, such as silence moments. Overall, these tools speed up the development of multimdia applications, but they may lead to a limited use of the expressivity of the declarative language.

Meixner and Kosch [18] propose a specific XML language to represent interactive non-linear video. The language maps the video reproduction into a flowchart at the same time that supports the synchronization of additional media with parts of the video. The SIVA Suite [20] is the authoring tool and player for non-linear video resulting provided by the authors, who also provide a player for android smartphones [19].

Tondorf et al. [32] propose a system for authoring and delivering multimedia problem-solving content. The authors noted the lack of some features in declarative language, such as indexed search for content, and implemented a specialized player with such features which is associated with a XML-based declarative language.

The work of Meixner and Kosch [18] and Tondorf et al. [32] are examples of results that ease the development of declarative language-based complex multimedia applications using for specific classes of applications.

The use of layered frameworks such as Django[4] or Grails[5] for speeding up the development of web applications is a common practice. Some researchers applied the same concept for the development of multimedia applications (e.g. [26] and [17]). However, while the first is more concerned with content adaptation among different devices than with easing the authoring task, the latter is based on an oriented-object approach rather than declarative languages.

---

[4]https://www.djangoproject.com/
[5]http://grails.org/

3. CHALLENGES IN THE DEVELOPMENT OF DECLARATIVE PRESENTATIONS

For interactive multimedia presentations specified in declarative languages such as NCL and SMIL, corresponding presentation machines machines exist which run on top of standard web technologies [11, 34]. As a result, the presentations can be deployed in any platform with a compatible browser including tablets, smartphone and Smart TVs.

However, declarative languages for hypermedia synchronization are usually designed to meet some common requirements and constrains of the platforms they are originally intended for. For instance, NCL 3.0 is design for iDTV and IPTV systems and the limitations imposed by these platforms may impact in the development of applications that might be reused in other platforms. Moreover, some applications that stand beyond the boundaries of the iDTV systems may be arduous to be implemented in NCL. One example of limitation is that in NCL the user's interaction is based on TV remote control, which is not appropriate for highly interactive applications [21].

In our experience with declarative languages for media synchronization [22, 30, 34], we identified some features common to multimedia presentations that are not trivial to be implemented in NCL because of its limitations. Other features are easy to be implemented, but demand a great effort in defining language entities [25].

By exploring NCL's expressivity, its integration with imperative Lua scripts and a bit of creativity, we were able to implement these non-trivial features. However, the complexity of the implementations is far from the expected for a declarative language. Next we detail the features we identified as hard or verbose to be implemented in NCL, along with the corresponding implementation solutions we offer.

3.1 Time-related Navigation

This functionality is common in multimedia presentations generated from the capture of human activities, such as recorded lectures or video conferences ([33], [10]). The presentations usually contain events such as *slide transition* or a *keyword spoken* and the users can navigate to the moment in which these events occur. For instance, one may navigate until the beginning of the previous slide transition or just after the next keyword.

The main difficulty in implementing this functionality using a declarative language lies in the necessity of keep tracking of which are the next and previous events for the current time in the presentation. This requires a complex control in which a variable registers what the current event is as the time advances during playback or the user interacts with the presentation. Since we are working with declarative languages, it is also necessary to consider all the possible values that the tracking variable can assume in order to perform the correct navigation for the next or previous event.

Time-related navigation can be implemented in NCL by mapping each of those events to temporal anchors in a media node. If it is necessary to synchronize different content by these events — such as different video camera streams that frame a classroom — all the related media nodes should also have temporal anchors.

In order to keep track of the events that correspond to the current time, the NCL variable capabilities can be used [28]. A virtual media node is (declared and) used to store the variable which tracks the current state. Moreover, a link

for each temporal anchor is also created to set the value of the tracking variable when the anchor begins (e.g. the associated event begins).

The actions that users can perform, such as *advance to the next slide transition*, can then be mapped into a button in the application's interface. When the user clicks or taps on this button, a NCL link, similar to the one presented in Listing 1, is triggered for each possible value that the tracking variable can assume. Upon checking the value of the tracking variable, only one of the links has its conditions met: this link then starts the media in the corresponding temporal anchor.

Listing 1: A "next slide" link

```
1   <link xconnector="...">
2     <bind role="onSelection"
3           component="btnNext"/>
4     <bind role="propertyType"
5           component="event_index"
6           interface="last_slide">
7       <bindParam name="testValue"
8                  value="slide_1"/>
9     </bind>
10    <bind role="abort" component="video"/>
11    <bind role="start" component="video"
12          interface="slide_2"/>
13  </link>
```

3.1.1 Multiple Navigation Indexes

Applications may allow users to navigate through different types of events. A user may opt at one time to navigate using type (or set) of events (e.g. *slide transition*), in another time a different set of events may be used (e.g. *annotations*), an in another time the union or intersection of the sets may be possible. In this work we refer to each set of events as a *Navigation Index*.

The control of navigation using different indexes is a complex task to be specified using a declarative language. Many possible situations should be considered, including the selection of the index an user may choose for navigation. This can be solved by mimicking a radio button. An image can represent the index for navigation. When clicking on the image, a variable is set to store the current active index. Moreover, the navigation links, such as the depicted in Listing 1, also need to check the active index variable.

3.2 Timeline Navigation

Timelines are common in applications presenting continuous media, as it is the case with YouTube and QuickTime. As a result, users expect to have a timeline in applications which manipulate video. In fact, when more than one video is availabe, users would also expect that a timeline synchronize the multiple continuous media streams as a single synchronous stream. For instance, it would be important to be able to control, with the same timeline, two video streams taken from different cameras that recorded the same scene but from different views.

The implementation of a timeline in NCL, a language that does not have native support for it, is complicated since: (i) some presentation machines do not allow to set the current time of a continuous media directly; (ii) representing the timeline interface with a composition of media would require a complex control; (iii) users are used to interact with the timeline using a mouse or touchscreen in Web and mobile environment. Such facilities are not common in interactive TV environments.

In order to solve (i), we opted to implement a discrete timeline, the same approach used by Vega-Oliveros, Martins and Pimentel [33]. Instead of allowing access to each instant of the continuous media, the media is split into several short segments (e.g. 1, 5, 10 or 20 seconds). A temporal anchor for each of these segments is added to the media node.

To solve (ii) we used a Lua script to draw the timeline (NCLua Canvas API). The Lua script must know the current time of the media, which can be implemented by using the events.time() function to count time. When the playback of continuous media starts, the Lua script starts to count time. If the playback of the continuous media is paused, the Lua script should stop counting time until the playback is resumed. The Lua script also has a property anchor named *current_time* which must be set when navigating in the media, in order to update the time information kept by the script. For instance, if the user navigates to the second 85, the *current_time* property is set to 85: the Lua scripts then starts counting time from the second 85.

Regarding (iii), we observed that the basic interaction with the timeline can be implemented using buttons such as *next* and *previous*, similar to the used for Time-related Navigation. Each segment of the discrete timeline can be handled as an event from the timeline index. The problem of this approach is that every time the next button is pressed, a number of links equal to the number of segments of the timeline would be triggered. For instance, in a presentation lasting 1 hour and split in 1-second segments, each time the *next* button is pressed, 3600 links would be triggered and checked for the value of the tracking variable so that one single link would be activated.

We avoided checking all possible (thousands of) conditions by using the Lua script as a proxy. The Lua node has "command" anchors for the next and previous buttons and one virtual temporal anchor for each segment. There is a link for each button that performs a start action over the related "command" anchor. Given that the Lua script knows the current time, it can easily compute which is the next/previous segment and, by using the NCLua events API, trigger a start event in its anchor related to that segment. Back to the NCL, there is a link which has the beginning of the Lua virtual temporal anchor as condition to be fired. It does the job of seeking the continuous media (Listing 2).

Listing 2: Timeline Link

```
1  <link xconnector="...">
2     <bind role="onBegin"
3            component="lua_timeline"
4            interface="t_segment_0"/>
5     <bind role="stop"
6            component="video"/>
7     <bind role="start"
8            component="video"
9            interface="v_segment_0"/>
10 </link>
```

Although this approach allows the user interaction with the timeline, it still does not solve (iii). Since we aim to make the multimedia presentations available in platforms such as the Web or mobile devices, the approach of using buttons to interact with the timeline is unfamiliar to users who are habituated with mouses or touchscreens. WebNCL [34] maps mouse and touchscreen interactions into common remote control events. When the mouse is over a media, that media receives the focus. If the left or right button is pressed, an OK button event is triggered. In touchscreen devices, tapping in a media without the focus is equivalent to change the focus to that media. A second tap (or double tap) on that media triggers an event equivalent to pressing the OK button.

In order to offer Web-like mouse interaction with the timeline, we added an invisible virtual media node above each segment of the timeline interface. When the user clicks on these virtual media nodes, a link performs a start action over the related Lua node's virtual temporal anchor. This action triggers the link of Listing 2 in charge of positioning the media in the desired segment.

3.2.1 Plotting indexes in the Timeline

It is possible to plot points on the timeline corresponding to events from a time index. Users may navigate to these events by clicking over the related points. In order to implement this feature we added a media for each event over the correct position on the timeline interface. It is also possible to show visual feedback about an event when the user moves the mouse over its media node on the timeline. For instance, in slide transition this visual feedback could be the new slide.

3.3 User Query

As an example of user query, an interactive video application that alerts the user about a scene which may contain inappropriate content offers user the option of watching or skipping the scene. As another example, at the end of a music video clip the user may choose which video clip is next.

In fact, asking the user to decide which media to play is a common requirement in many multimedia applications. It is not a complex functionality to implement, but it requires many different links to be implemented: (i) one to show the query, (ii) one to hide the query after a certain time, (iii) one for each possible alternative available.

3.4 Spatial Composition Changes

Spatial Composition Change is a common requirement of multi-video applications. For instance, in a camera system several streams may be presented in small windows which share the same screen. It may be possible to maximize one of the videos in order to verify something suspicious, choosing one of the video streams to be presented in a large (main) window while the other videos remain in small windows. Then, the user may select one video of the small windows to be swapped with the video presented in the main window. In a scenario in the educational domain, a multimedia presentation generated from a lecture may be composed of several video streams: one which captured the slides, another which captured the whiteboard or the instructor's computer, and others corresponding the different views of the instructor. The students may choose to focus their attention into one specific stream presented in one large (main) window while the other streams are presented in small windows – and may swap the video presented in the main window with any other. The change in spatial composition is also a requirement for

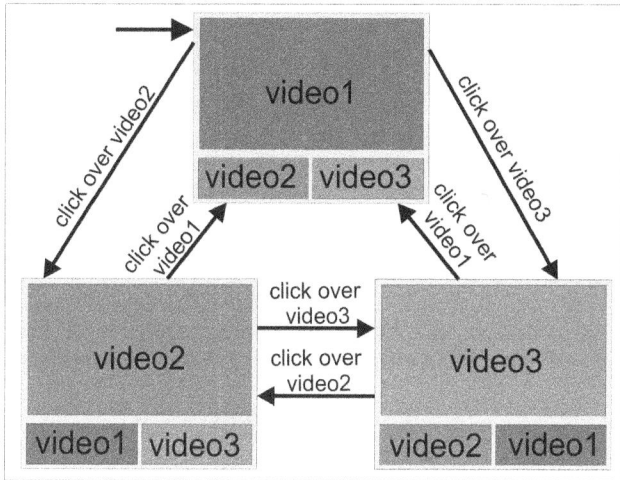

Figure 1: FSM for Spatial Composition

reactive applications that must change their layout in response to user interactions, such as when the orientation of the device changes or the display is resized.

The problem on implementing this functionality lies in keeping track the "window" in which each media is presented. Moreover, it may be necessary to declare links for the many possible combinations of media and positions in order to react properly to user's interactions. We implemented the changes in spatial composition using a finite-state machine (FSM). Each state in the FSM corresponds to a spatial composition the medias can assume. The user's interactions (or internal events) are the transitions in the FSM.

Figure 1 illustrates a FSM for a composition of 3 videos. There are 3 states, each one with one of the videos as the main (larger) video. When a user clicks on a video presented in a small screen, the corresponding a state transition is triggered and that stream is shown in the main video. We implemented this in NCL by using a variable to store the current state. When a interaction corresponding to a transition in the FSM is performed, a link for each transition related to that event is triggered. These links check the current state variable, if the current state has a transition that is triggered by that interaction, the corresponding link performs its actions, changing the video bounds and setting the current state variable to meet the new state configuration.

Note that in the configuration illustrated in Figure 1, if the current state is the one with the video2 as the main video and the user clicks over the video2 two links are triggered. However, since the current state does not have transitions related to this event, none of the links perform their actions.

3.5 Annotation

User annotation is an important requirement for multimedia applications. In our approach annotations are based on a timeline: the user marks some media segment as important, or adds some comment at a given instant of the media, etc.

One main concern about annotations in multimedia presentations is how to store and retrieve the annotations created by end users. A possible approach is to modify the multimedia presentation on-the-fly, adding new media and links to represent the annotations [7, 13, 22]. This could be implemented in NCL by using the Ginga-NCL live editing

API [23] and dumping the modified NCL document into a new XML file. A version control mechanism for these annotated NCL files would also be required.

We propose a different approach: a Web Service is used to store and retrieve the annotations. A Lua script accesses the Web Service and, using the data retrieved, draws the annotations over the timeline. In order to add a new annotation, the Lua script must know the current time of the media in which the annotation will be performed. This can be obtained from the Lua script that controls the Timeline Navigation.

The interface between the Lua script and the NCL document is implemented using some virtual anchors, as depicted in Listing 3.

Listing 3: myListing

```
1  <media id="timeline" src="timeline.lua">
2      <!-- ... -->
3      <area id="important" />
4  <area id="doubt" />
5  <area id="comment" />
6
7  <area id="next_annotation" />
8  <area id="previous_annotation" />
9
10  <area id="annotation1" />
11  <area id="annotation2" />
12  <!-- ... -->
13  <area id="annotation50" />
14
15  <property name="annotation1_bounds"
16          value="None" />
17  <property name="annotation2_bounds"
18          value="None" />
19  <!-- ... -->
20  <property name="annotation50_bounds"
21          value="None" />
22  </media>
```

We use images as buttons to allow users to create annotations while interacting with the presentation, as suggested by the watch-and-comment paradigm [7]. For instance, a button may be used to express that the segment is important and other to add that a textual comment. When these buttons are clicked, a link performs a start action over the correspondent virtual anchor of the Lua object (Listing 3, lines 3-5).

The Lua script uses the information about the current time to save the annotation in its internal structures (using the discrete segments of the timeline). It also saves the annotation in the web server. The annotations stored in the Lua internal structures are then drawn in the timeline.

It is possible to navigate among the annotations using the next and previous buttons. This is implemented using the Lua script as a proxy (similar to the timeline navigation). The buttons trigger links that perform start actions over the Lua object command anchors (Listing 3, lines 7-8) and the Lua script performs a start action over the appropriate Lua virtual temporal anchor.

In order to allow mouse navigation in the annotations, it is necessary to add virtual invisible nodes. Because at the time of the creation of the NCL document we do not know which annotations a continuous media will receive, it is necessary to add some media in advance for this purpose. However, we also do not know which segments will be annotated, which means that the positioning the invisible media in the timeline cannot be made when the NCL document is created.

The positioning of annotation media nodes are computed by a Lua script. The positions are sent to the NCL document when the Lua script performs a set action over one of the annotation bounds anchor properties (Listing 3, lines 15-21). The value the Lua script sets in these anchors are the positions in which the associated virtual nodes must be placed. Back to the NCL, a link that is triggered when a value is set to the annotation bounds anchor sets the bounds property of the associated virtual node. When the user clicks on these media nodes, a link performs a start action over corresponding virtual temporal anchors of the Lua object (Listing 3, lines 10-13). Finally, the Lua object performs a start action over the proper timeline segment anchor.

When a presentation begins, the Lua script retrieves all the previous annotations made by the user from the Web Service and set their positions in the timeline.

4. COMPONENTS

Despite the fact that the features discussed in the previous section can be found in many classes of multimedia presentations, the corresponding implementations in NCL are non-trivial. In order to ease the authoring, we designed and implemented components in Python that generate NCL + Lua code for these features. Figure 2 depicts a simplified UML class diagram of the components.

The components are grouped in a layered architecture inspired in the Model-View-Controller (MVC) design pattern. The bottom layer is the **Multimedia Layer**, wherein the media nodes used in the multimedia application are declared. In the case of a NCL document, they are the media and context nodes. The middle layer is the **Controller layer**, which holds the components that define the types of navigation and synchronization (both temporal and spatial) it is possible to perform with the media nodes. The top layer is the **View Layer**, which contains the components responsible for allowing users to interact with the applications.

In this layered architecture, which we refer to as *Multimedia-View-Controller* (MMVC) architecture, media nodes from the multimedia layer are manipulated by the components of the Controller Layer. The user, via components of the View Layer, may interact with the media. The view layer sends messages to the controller layer which performs the actions to manipulate the media.

Note that in Figure 2 the components **SpatialSlotManager** and **UserQuery** are above the line that separates the View and the Controller Layer. This is because the synchronizations defined in these components are intrinsically related to user interactions. For instance, the **SpatialSlotManager** component allows some media nodes to exchange the spatial position among themselves after a user selection. It would be possible to split it in two components the parts responsible for the interaction and responsible to define the behavior, each one in one layer, but these two components would, almost always, be used together.

The components **TimeIndex**, **AnnotataionBase** and **Timeline** implement the interface **NavigableIndex**. These components allow navigation operations such as *"go to the next point"* or *"move forward to the previous point"*.

The **TimeIndex** allows the creation of an array of time milestones for a media or a group of medias. For instance, Listing 4 depicts the creation of a time index for a media node. It is possible to bind media nodes via their unique ids in the NCL document (Listing 4, line 2) or via an instance of Media class (Listing 4, line 3-4). The milestones can be passed as a list of times in seconds or individually. A **NavigationBar** is a visual component that presents buttons like next and previous and allows user navigation by any type of **NavigableIndex** instance. Since it is a visual component, it is necessary to define the position in which the buttons must to be displayed. This is done by passing a NCL region to the component (Listing 4, line 7)

By combining the **TimeIndex** and the **NavigationBar** components, it is possible to implement the Time-related Navigation (Section 3.1).

Listing 4: TimeIndex

```
1  index=TimeIndex()
2  index.bind_media('video0')
3  index.bind_media(Media(id='video1',
4          src='video1.mp4'))
5  index.add_milestones([5, 48, 58.5])
6  index.add_milestone(78)
7  bar=NavigationBar('rNaviBar')
8  bar.add_index(index)
```

The **Timeline** component bounds a media or group of medias to a single timeline. It also enables the user to navigate in the media using a timeline. In order to do this, is necessary to bound it to a **TimeSlider** component. The **TimeSlider** is a visual component that draws a timeline and can be used to access any instant of a media or group of media. Together, these components implement the Timeline Navigation (Section 3.2).

Listing 5 depicts the instantiation of a **TimeLine** for a group of media nodes and show how to bind it to a **TimeSlider** visual component. The duration of the **TimeLine** and the length of the each discrete segment (in seconds) are informed in the constructor (Listing 5, line 1). It is possible to bind a media node and to define the time instant in which the timeline begins (for instance, the second 0 of the timeline corresponding to the second 80 from the media *video1* (Listing 4, line 3). It is necessary to define the NCL region of the **TimeSlider** component, as well the **TimeLine** instance it will draw and the means by which users can interact with the component (Listing 5, lines 4-6).

Listing 5: Timeline

```
1  tline=Timeline(duration=600, segment=1)
2  tline.bind_media('video0')
3  tline.bind_media('video1', begin=80)
4  ts=TimeSlider(mouse_interaction=True,
5          timeline=tline,
6          region='rTimeline')
```

Listing 6 illustrates the utilization of the components **AnnotationBase** and **AnnotatonBar**. The **AnnotationBase** allows to create and retrieve annotations made over a **TimeLine**. If, instead of a **TimeLine**, a continuous media is passed in the **AnnotationBase** constructor, a **TimeLine** will be automatically created and bounded with the media

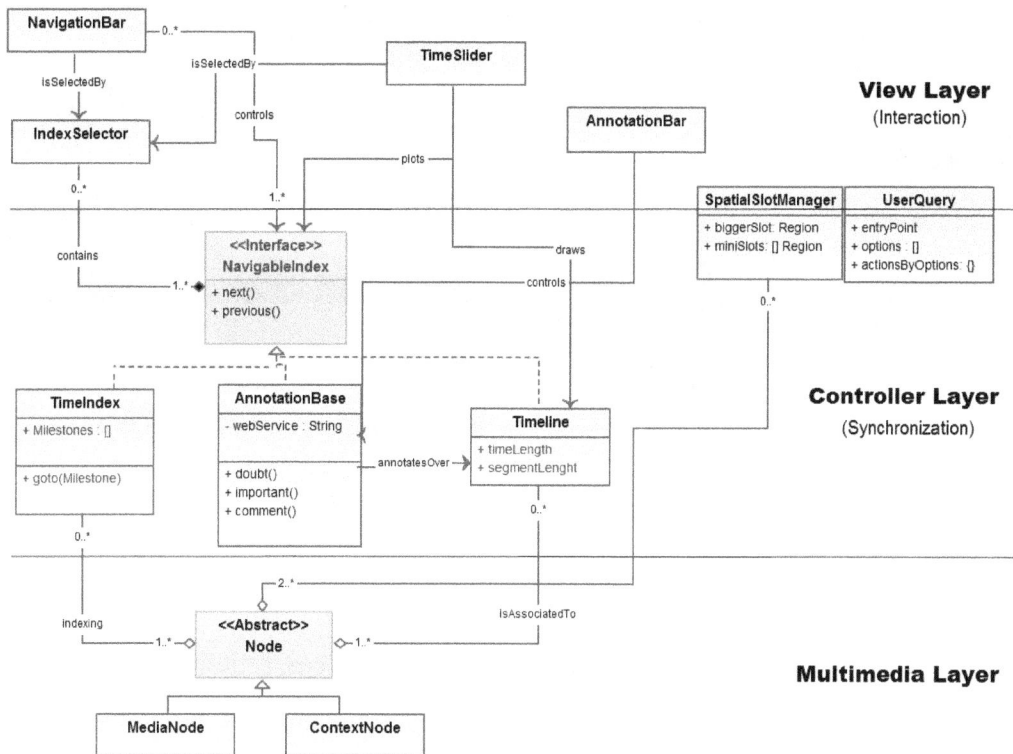

Figure 2: Class Diagram of the components

(Listing 6, lines 2). It is also necessary to pass the URL of the Web Service that will store the annotations (Listing 6, lines 3). Since **AnnotationBar** is a visual component, it is necessary to inform the NCL region in which it will be displayed (Listing 6, lines 4). These components implement the annotation functionality (Section 3.5).

Listing 6: Annotation

```
1  note_base=AnnotationBase(
2          timeline='video0',
3          url='localhost:8080/service')
4  note_bar=AnnotationBar(region='rBar',
5          base=note_base)
```

Both the **NavigationBar** and the **TimeSlider** can support more than one **NavigableIndex** instance. The **IndexSelector** component is necessary to allow the user chooses which of the possible index he or she wishes to use for navigation.

Listing 7 illustrates the use of a **SpatialSlotManager** component. This component displays a "maximized" media and a group of "minimized" in defined spatial slots. It is possible to maximize any of the minimized medias by clicking on them. The slots (both the bigger and smalls) are defined by a tuple with the slot spatial position (represented by a NCL region) and the media initially bounded to that slot. This component implements common cases of Spatial Composition Changes (Section 3.4).

The **UserQuery** can be used to take actions based on options queried to the user (Section 3.5). It is necessary to define an anchor that, when activated, will present the component to the user. The options are defined as a list

of text or images. After the user choice, among one of the options, the corresponding action is performed.

Listing 7: Annotation

```
1  sm=SpatialSlotManager()
2  sm.bigger_slot=('rMainSlot', 'video0')
3  sm.add_mini_slot(('rslot1', 'video1'))
4  sm.add_mini_slot(('rslot2', 'video12'))
```

5. VALIDATING THE COMPONENTS

We have used the components described in the previous section to build an application that generates NCL documents from captured lecture-style presentations. The result of the capture is a multi-video multimedia containing different views of the lecture, with video streams generated from capturing the slide presentation, the computers used by the instructor, various views of the classroom, etc. There is also an XML file which holds metadata from the captured lecture, such as the time instants in which slide transitions occur, or the lecturer used her computer or the (electronic or traditional) whiteboards. The orchestration of capture process and the metadata extraction is introduced [36] and detailed [35]elsewhere.

Figure 3 shows an example of an NCL document generated from the captured presentations. The NCL documents offer facilities that includes the synchronization of the captured video streams. The document in this example has two video streams captured from cameras (Figure 3(1) and Figure 3(3)), one stream capturing the slide presentation (Figure 3(2)) and the instructor's computer screen (Figure 3(4)).

Figure 3: Multi-video multimedia object captured from a lecture

(a) Empty

(b) Indexed

(c) Annotated

Figure 4: Timeline

They all have the same length and their synchronization is handled by a **Timeline** component.

Users may interact with the presentation and access any segment of the synchronized video streams via a **TimeSlider** component (Figure 3(6)). There are also temporal indexes implemented by instances of **TimeIndex** component. Indexes are provided for slide transition, lecturer's close and computer interactions. User may select an index for navigation using the **IndexSelector** component (Figure 3(7)), and the index-based navigation uses the **NavigationBar** component (Figure 3(5)).

Users can also annotate the document via the **AnnotationBar** component (Figure 3(8)). The annotations are stored in the **AnnotationBase** which saves the information in a Web-Service.

Similar to co-located lectures, wherein students may focus their attention to different contents (the lecturer, whiteboard, slide presentation, the textbook, etc.), the NCL document allows users to choose which video stream to see in detail in detail. One option is to show the video in the main window using the **SpatialSlotManager** component (Figure 3(1-4)); the other option is via the full-screen mode.

The **TimeSlider** component can be used to show annotations and marks or milestones (such as slides transitions) to the timeline interface. If none of the index are selected in the **IndexSelector** component, the timeline will bear no marks as in Figure 4(a). When a **TimeIndex** is selected, marks representing the milestones will be added to the timeline (Figure 4(b)). When an annotation index is selected, the annotations will be displayed in the timeline (Figure 4(c)).

5.1 Analysing the NCL Document

To illustrate the complexity of the NCL documents generated with the aid of the components, Table 1 summarizes the size the document generated automatically from a captured lecture lasting 1 hour and 18 minutes.

The NCL document uses 48 video clips: four of them can be played back simultaneously. Besides the videos, the document include 1197 other media items, mostly images. There are also 1898 links responsible for controlling all navigation alternatives (including timeline and index-based).

The NCL document itself has about 3.6 MB of size, not considering the videos, images and other media items. The

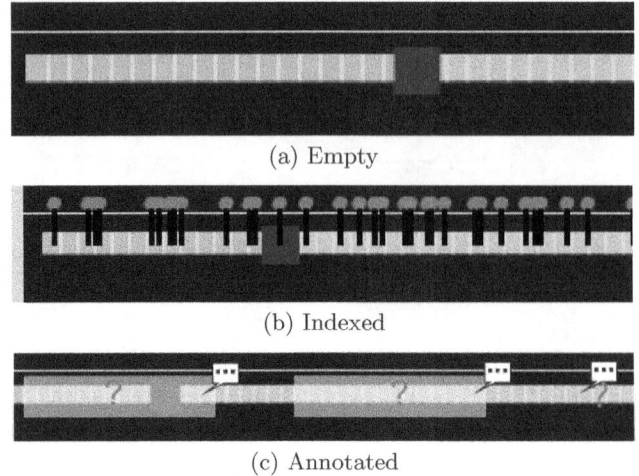

Table 1: NCL Document Numbers

Total Duration	78 minutes
NCL Document Size	3.6 MB
Lines of Code	65148
Links	1898
Media Node	1245
Videos	48

total size of the multimedia document, considering all media, is about 1GB [6]. All the media, anchors, links and the static elements of the NCL (regions, descriptors) add up to a total of 65148 lines of code.

We use the WebNCL presentation machine to render the interactive NCL Documents generated from captured lecture. Although the document sizes may suggest problems in its execution, the WebNCL has been able to reproduce the NCL Document smoothly.

Some improvements in the components may reduce the size of the generated NCL documents. The current version of the components generate a human readable code for debugging proposes, but renaming the NCL entities with concise names and removing white spaces can significantly reduce the document size. Other optimizations in the NCL code structure can also help reducing the document size.

6. FINAL REMARKS

Declarative languages for media synchronization were conceived to ease the development of multimedia presentations. However, declarative languages for hypermedia synchronization are usually designed to meet common requirements and constrains of the platforms they are originally intended for. The reuse of applications developed in declarative languages

---

[6] Each video has a version coded in H264 AVC and other coded in VP8, with resolution of 854x480 pixels and 24 frames per second. Note that some of the video streams, such as the on corresponding to the slide presentation, have many static segments which lead to small video size when codecs that remove temporal redundancy such as the H264 and VP8 are used.

in other platforms may be negatively impacted by these limitations.

In this work we elected NCL, a declarative language designed for DTV and IPTV systems, to develop applications that stand beyond the boundaries of such platforms. As result, we identified some features, common in general purpose multimedia applications, that are non-trivial to be implemented in NCL. Even though, we keep the choice to take advantage of several interesting features of such declarative language for multimedia synchronization. Although theoretically possible, implementing such features using only standard NCL resources would imply a complexity far from the expected for a declarative language.

In order to provide these features, keeping the ease of development, we implemented components organized in a Multimedia-View-Controller architecture that generate NCL + Lua code which implements the non-trivial functionality. We illustrate the use of the components generating a complex and highly-interactive multimedia presentation from a presentation generated with information captured from lectures.

Although the components presented here are not a comprehensive listing capable of implement many classes of multimedia applications, they are construction blocks that can be used in many common applications.

As a future work, we plan to use the components presented in this work as the base for a layered framework for authoring complex and platform-independent multimedia applications. It is important to note that the solutions proposed here, although implemented for NCL, are sufficiently generic to be exploited in similar situations found in other declarative languages for multimedia applications.

7. ACKNOWLEDGMENTS

We thank the Brazilian agencies CAPES, CNPq, FAPESP and FINEP for financial support.

8. REFERENCES

[1] ABNT. Associação Brasileira de Normas técnicas. 2007. Digital Terrestrial Television Standard 06: Data Codification and Transmission Specifications for Digital Broadcasting. Technical report, Part 2–GINGA-NCL: XML Application Language for Application Coding, year = 2007.

[2] G. D. Abowd, C. G. Atkeson, A. Feinstein, C. Hmelo, R. Kooper, S. Long, N. Sawhney, and M. Tani. Teaching and learning as multimedia authoring: the classroom 2000 project. In *Proc. ACM MULTIMEDIA'96*.

[3] R. G. Azevedo and L. F. G. Soares. Embedding 3d objects into ncl multimedia presentations. In *Proc. Int. Conf. on 3D Web Technology*, Web3D '12, pages 143–151. ACM, 2012.

[4] S. Bouyakoub and A. Belkhir. SMIL builder: An incremental authoring tool for smil documents. *ACM Trans. Multimedia Comput. Commun. Appl.*, 7(1):2:1–2:30, Feb. 2011.

[5] D. C. Bulterman and L. W. Rutledge. *SMIL 3.0: Flexible Multimedia for Web, Mobile Devices and Daisy Talking Books.* Springer Publishing Company, Incorporated, 2nd edition, 2008.

[6] E. Canessa, L. Tenze, C. Fonda, and M. Zennaro. Apps for synchronized photo-audio recordings to support students. In *Proc. LAK 2013 Workshop on Analytics on Video-based Learning*, pages 29–33, 2013.

[7] R. G. Cattelan, C. Teixeira, R. Goularte, and M. G. C. Pimentel. Watch-and-comment as a paradigm toward ubiquitous interactive video editing. *ACM Trans. Multimedia Comput. Commun. Appl.*, 4(4):28:1–28:24, Nov. 2008.

[8] F. Cazenave, V. Quint, and C. Roisin. Timesheets.js: when smil meets html5 and css3. In *Proc. DOCENG '11*, pages 43–52. ACM, 2011.

[9] J. Damasceno, J. dos Santos, and D. Muchaluat-Saade. EDITEC: hypermedia composite template graphical editor for interactive TV authoring. In *Proc. ACM DOCENG'2011*, pages 77–80. ACM, 2011.

[10] P. E. Dickson, D. I. Warshow, A. C. Goebel, C. C. Roache, and W. R. Adrion. Student reactions to classroom lecture capture. In *Proc. ITiCSE '12*, pages 144–149. ACM, 2012.

[11] O. Gaggi and L. Danese. A SMIL player for any web browser. In *Proc. Int. Conf. Distributed Multimedia Systems*, pages 114–119, Firenze, Italy, 2011.

[12] W. Hürst. Indexing, searching, and skimming of multimedia documents containing recorded lectures and live presentations. In *Proc. ACM MULTIMEDIA'03*, pages 450–451. ACM, 2003.

[13] J. Jansen, P. Cesar, and D. C. Bulterman. A model for editing operations on active temporal multimedia documents. In *Proc. ACM DOCENG'2010*, pages 87–96. ACM, 2010.

[14] P. King, P. Schmitz, and S. Thompson. Behavioral reactivity and real time programming in XML: functional programming meets SMIL animation. In *Proc. ACM DOCENG'2004*, pages 57–66. ACM, 2004.

[15] J. Lanir, K. S. Booth, and A. Tang. Multipresenter: a presentation system for (very) large display surfaces. In *Proc. ACM MULTIMEDIA'08*, pages 519–528. ACM, 2008.

[16] J. Lienhard and T. Lauer. Multi-layer recording as a new concept of combining lecture recording and students' handwritten notes. In *Proc. ACM MULTIMEDIA '02*, pages 335–338. ACM, 2002.

[17] J. Lin, J. Drake, H. Kim, and E. Song. A framework-based approach for interactive multimedia application development. In *Proc. ACM RECS'12*, pages 364–370. ACM, 2012.

[18] B. Meixner and H. Kosch. Interactive non-linear video: definition and XML structure. In *Proc. ACM DOCENG'2012*, pages 49–58. ACM, 2012.

[19] B. Meixner, J. Köstler, and H. Kosch. A mobile player for interactive non-linear video. In *Proc. ACM MULTIMEDIA '11*, pages 779–780. ACM, 2011.

[20] B. Meixner, B. Siegel, G. Hölbling, F. Lehner, and H. Kosch. Siva suite: authoring system and player for interactive non-linear videos. In *Proc. ACM MM '10*, pages 1563–1566. ACM, 2010.

[21] D. Pedrosa, J. A. C. Martins, Jr., E. L. Melo, and C. A. C. Teixeira. A multimodal interaction component for digital television. In *Proc. ACM SAC'11*, pages 1253–1258. ACM, 2011.

[22] M. G. Pimentel, R. G. Cattelan, E. L. Melo, A. F. Prado, and C. A. C. Teixeira. End-user live editing of iTV programmes. *International Journal of Advanced Media and Communication*, 4(1):78–103, 2010.

[23] R. M. Resende Costa, M. F. Moreno, R. F. Rodrigues, and L. F. G. Soares. Live editing of hypermedia documents. In *Proc. ACM DOCENG'2006*, pages 165–172. ACM, 2006.

[24] K. R. d. H. Rodrigues, S. d. S. Pereira, M. d. G. Pimentel, and C. A. C. Teixeira. FIND: facilitating the identification of intervals and moments for incorporation of additional content in continuous media. In *Proc. Brazilian WebMedia '12*, pages 265–268. ACM, 2012.

[25] J. A. Santos and D. C. Muchaluat-Saade. XTemplate 3.0: spatio-temporal semantics and structure reuse for hypermedia compositions. *Multimedia Tools Appl.*, 61(3):645–673, Dec. 2012.

[26] A. Scherp and S. Boll. *Managing Multimedia Semantics*, chapter MM4U: a framework for creating personalized multimedia content, pages 246–287. IRM Press, 2005.

[27] L. Soares, M. Moreno, and C. De Salles Soares Neto. Ginga-NCL: Declarative middleware for multimedia IPTV services. *Communications Magazine, IEEE*, 48(6):74–81, 2010.

[28] L. F. Soares, R. F. Rodrigues, R. Cerqueira, and S. D. Barbosa. Variable and state handling in NCL. *Multimedia Tools Appl.*, 50(3):465–489, Dec. 2010.

[29] C. S. Soares Neto, H. F. Pinto, and L. F. G. Soares. TAL processor for hypermedia applications. In *Proc. ACM DOCENG'2012*, pages 69–78. ACM, 2012.

[30] C. Teixeira, E. Melo, R. Cattelan, and M. Pimentel. Taking advantage of contextualized interactions while users watch TV. *Multimedia Tools and Applications*, 50(3):587–607, 2010.

[31] C. A. Teixeira, E. L. Melo, G. B. Freitas, C. A. Santos, and M. D. Pimentel. Discrimination of media moments and media intervals: sticker-based watch-and-comment annotation. *Multimedia Tools Appl.*, 61(3):675–696, Dec. 2012.

[32] K. Tonndorf, T. Knieper, B. Meixner, H. Kosch, and F. Lehner. Challenges in creating multimedia instructions for support systems and dynamic problem-solving. In *Proc. i-KNOW '12*, pages 33:1–33:4. ACM, 2012.

[33] D. A. Vega-Oliveros, D. S. Martins, and M. d. G. C. Pimentel. "this conversation will be recorded": automatically generating interactive documents from captured media. In *Proc. ACM DOCENG'2010*, pages 37–40. ACM, 2010.

[34] C. C. Viel, E. L. Melo, A. P. Godoy, D. R. C. Dias, L. C. Trevelin, and C. A. C. Teixeira. WebNCL: a web-based presentation machine for multimedia documents. In *Proc. Brazilian WebMedia '12*, pages 403–410. ACM, 2012.

[35] C. C. Viel, E. L. Melo, M. G. Pimentel, and C. A. C. Teixeira. Multimodal multi-device educational presentations preserved as interactive multi-video objects. In *Proc. Brazilian Webmedia'12 (to appear)*, page 8p, 2013.

[36] C. C. Viel, E. L. Melo, M. G. Pimentel, and C. A. C. Teixeira. Presentations preserved as interactive multi-video objects. In *Proc. Workshop on Analytics on Video-Based Learning*, pages 34–37, 2013.

Multimedia Document Synchronization in a Distributed Social Context

Jack Jansen, Pablo Cesar, Dick Bulterman

CWI: Centrum Wiskunde & Informatica
Science park 123
1098 XG Amsterdam, the Netherlands
+31 20 5924300

{Jack.Jansen, Pablo.Cesar, Dick.Bulterman}@cwi.nl

ABSTRACT

Watching digital content together and commenting on it is becoming a social habit between friends and family members living apart. It is also becoming an important value-added activity for business video conferencing. In both cases, the video sharing experience can easily be spoiled if synchronization problems arise, since the context of the conversation will not be consistent across locations. In the past, research has treated the distributed synchronization problem as a technical one, mainly focusing on timestamps, frame accuracy, and protocol-dependent control messages. That approach is based on a content agnostic approach which we feel does not adequately address the higher-level constraints of individual conversations.

In this paper we postulate that the technical issues are just part of the problem, so solutions need to take into account the media being shared and the social setting. Therefore, we propose a framework that allows researchers to experiment with different synchronization policies tailored to specific settings. The framework allows the evaluation of these policies through user testing, for finding the most appropriate policies and strategies.

Categories and Subject Descriptors

H.4.3 [**Information System Applications**]: Communication Applications - Computer conferencing, teleconferencing, and videoconferencing; I.7.2 [**Document and Text Processing**] Document Preparation - Languages and systems.

General Terms

Design, Experimentation, Human Factors.

Keywords

Video conferencing, Multimedia applications, Synchronization, User testing.

1. INTRODUCTION

The use of best-effort video conferencing for commercial and (especially) social purposes is becoming a commonplace activity. Sometimes, these video conversations are simple two-party connections using personal interfaces (such as Skype), other times

they may be best-effort group-based video (such as Google's Hangout), and in yet other instances, they may be speciality conferencing conversations using dedicated rooms, equipment and network support.

A common characteristic of all these systems is that support for the "quality" of the temporal connections is relegated to the networking layers of the document processing stack. Using conventional quality of service (QoS) and quality of experience (QoE) techniques, connections among users are established, video and audio data is transferred, and synchronization of content is either best-effort or based on one of the many "conventional" synchronization approaches [11]. These conventional techniques largely mimic the fetching, packaging and decoding of uni-directional video content (such as a YouTube video), but then across multiple connections.

In our experience of building interactive video applications, the content-agnostic approach taken by current video-based systems has exhibited fundamental limitations. By relegating synchronization support to the network layer, important semantic information is lost on the nature of the communication taking place, the relative priorities of the participants in the conversations, the purpose of the underlying social exchange that is manifested in the video communication and the needs of parties to maintain a content-based flow during the conferencing event.

Consider the social viewing activity illustrated in Figure 1. Here we see two parents discussing a video of their son singing a solo in a school concert. The concert video is shown at each location, along with a separate window showing conferencing participants.

The nature of the conversation between the two participants will largely determine the synchronization needs to the application.

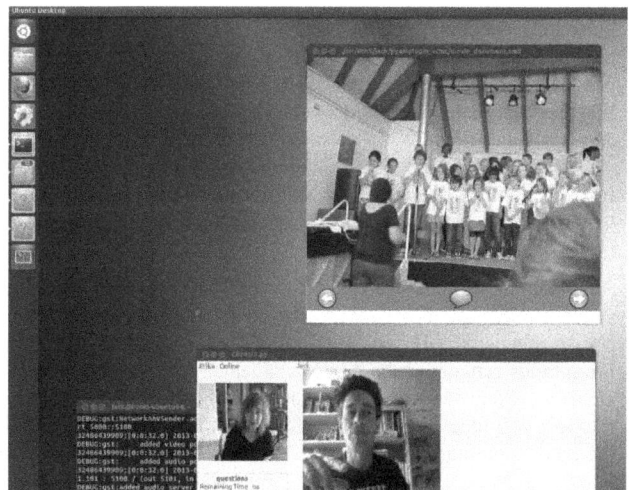

Figure 1 - Discussing a common video among video viewers

One user may want to point out a particularly interesting event in the common video using gesturing or voice annotation. At other times, one user (or the other, or both) may want to "scrub" back and forth in the video to find a particular moment of interest. It may be that any given conversation will extend across multiple sessions, in which case some form of memory of past roles and interactions may be necessary to assist in the future presentation of the content. All of these factors can be classified as *user-level content synchronization* issues.

There are multiple such synchronization needs in this example. This includes the video connections for each parent, but also the separate window containing the conversation's comment context. The video shown in the concert window needs to be synchronized with the 'annotation' provided by one of the two conference participants. Depending on the conversation flow, either one of the two parents may become the "synchronization master" of this discussion, pointing to concert events that should be display synchronously to all participants. This role is not fixed – depending on the family, it may change several times per spoken sentence!

Although there is wide agreement on basic cinematographic principles for capturing and analyzing content, there is no compelling taxonomy yet of user-level content synchronization principles that need to be supported by underlying communication systems. In order to develop these principles, experimental work is required that allows system and application designers to develop, test and evaluate new user-level content synchronization paradigms.

In this paper, we consider mechanisms for setting, controlling and evaluating multi-party content synchronization. In our work, we abstract essential communication parameters (such as delay or loss) into document-level settings that are used to guide presentation display. In particular, this paper discusses a user-level testbed environment in which communication designers can experiment with various algorithms and protocols to simulate communication events (latency, delay, loss) to help support more effective end-user communication based on the content of the underlying conversation.

In the following sections, we discuss related research and then define the contribution of our approach. We then discuss the design and implementation of our testbed approach and consider some initial results of our work.

2. RELATED WORK

Enabling watching media together, while apart, might be perceived as a solved problem, given the number of commercial products and research solutions. From enriched instant messaging services that allow for video sharing [8] to protocol-specific standards that provide the necessary types of RTCP packets [1]. The truth is that still many challenges exist for truly enabling inter-destination media synchronization [13], as previous solutions tend to be ad-hoc, implemented for specific use cases, protocols, and media types.

A plethora of use cases exist that require this type of synchronization [11]. For example, within the research field of social television [3], enabling conversation between different households remains to be a core challenge. Still the benefits are clear, as recent research show that social bonds between remote viewers of video programs are fostered when providing video-mediated communication [9]. According to this research, the

fidelity of the communication media influences the overall experience, so the provision of adequate synchronization becomes a key issue.

Typically, inter-destination media communication has been studied from the more technical perspective, leading to highly accurate solutions [4]. An overview of the work in this area can be found in [11]. In general, these solutions provide techniques and algorithms, aiming at precise synchronization, based on global clocks, media adjustment techniques, and timing information (timestamps or frame ids). They tend to provide the *enforcement mechanisms*, but not the *strategies*. Our view is that we have to first better understand the user requirements, so that adequate document-based models can be defined. This belief is based on more human-centered research aiming at identifying perceptual threshold for media synchronization [5] and the influence of different media communication formats [12].

3. CONTRIBUTION

In the introduction we have stated that our goal is studying distributed document synchronization techniques, and we have postulated that evaluating these techniques requires taking the document content and the social setting in which the document is shared into account.

We believe that there is no silver bullet to solve all distributed synchronization problems: if three people located on three continents are having a discussion, at the very least the speed of light is going to introduce different delays between them. This is already a problem in an audio-video conference without shared media (if one person tells a joke both the other participants think they themselves get it much quicker than the other person), but this is exacerbated if shared media are involved. As an example of this, consider three people watching a shared video and discussing it. If the video is of a football match it may be a good idea to enforce that audio from other participants is never ahead of the shared football video, to forestall early cheers and hisses from others ruining your experience. But if one person could be considered the narrator, for example because the video is his vacation movie and he is pointing out interesting sights to his friends, the best solution may well be to synchronize playout to the audio stream of the narrator. And sometimes it may be possible to dynamically assign the narrator, for example when people take turns annotating the document, the last annotator might be considered the narrator.

These ideas, and many more, need to be tested. Therefore, some form of user testing is going to play a prominent role in our future studies. Because of this, we need some way to allow users to participate in an audio-video teleconference with shared media, so that we can then either measure their performance for a given task, or ask their opinions through questionnaires or through some other means. Moreover, we must be able to easily implement new synchronization ideas for these tests, and we should have a way to alter the perceived network characteristics, such as bandwidth, packet loss, etc. This should allow us to test our ideas under different network conditions.

Our research question now becomes: can we design and build a system that allows experimenting with multimedia playback synchronization approaches, and presenting these to users in a realistic setting. This leads to a subsidiary question: what are the best possible synchronization and delays numbers this system gives us under ideal conditions, and are these good enough that the system itself does not influence the measurements overly.

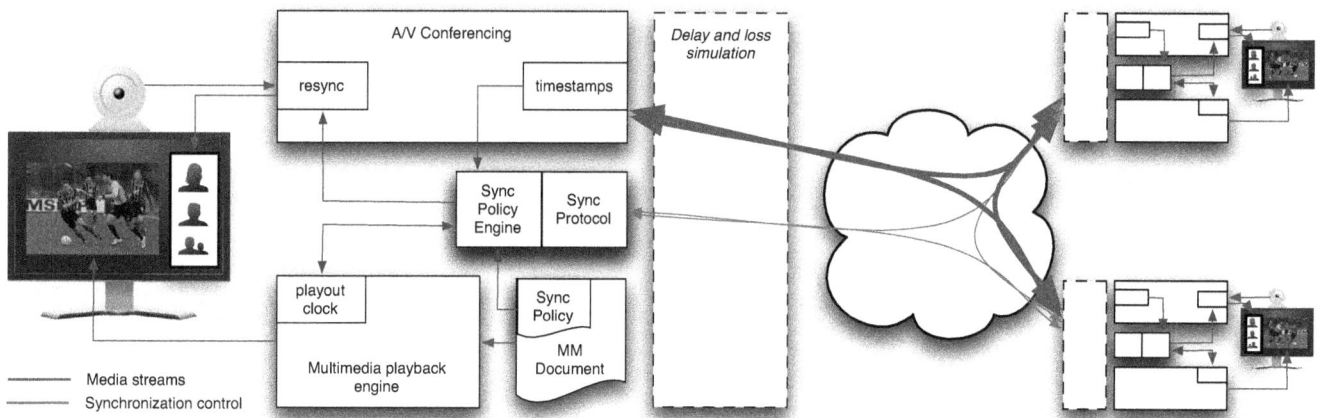

Figure 2 - Framework implementation

4. DESIGN AND IMPLEMENTATION

To answer our main research question we have set out to design and implement the testbed system. Our testbed system obviously needs a *conferencing component*, a *multimedia playback component* and a *synchronization policy and protocol component*, and all of these should be of sufficient quality in their own right that they do not negatively impact the user experience, otherwise we might interpret problems with playback as problems with synchronization. Because we envision doing many different synchronization experiments we need to have *full control over all time-related aspects* of the system: we may want to delay or catch up the playout of both the conferencing streams as well as the prerecorded multimedia document, and possibly transmission of the conferencing streams as well.

Moreover, we want to be able to *control synchronization policy on a fine-grained level*: per-user, per-role and possibly with varying assignment of roles during a conversation.

Finally, we want to be able to *model the network traffic* between participants, so we can simulate delays and packet loss and such, so we can run experiments in a single location while simulating wide-area conditions in a plausible manner.

We also have some non-goals, that lead to simplification:

- we can run our experiments in a single location (no worries about firewalls and such),
- we have technicians at hand (no worries about configuration and startup issues),
- we are only interested in synchronization (no worries about layout and integration as long as the system is plausible to the end users).

These goals and non-goals enabled us to reuse a conferencing tool and synchronized multimedia engine we had created previously, with minor modifications. This solved the "full timing control" requirement, and the non-goals meant that we could use loose coupling between the components.

Figure 2 shows the structure of the testbed system. The *A/V conferencing* component is VCMC, which is currently being used to do research into conversational patterns, and how those are influenced by the use of conferencing tools (as opposed to co-location of the participants) and real-life network conditions. A full description of VCMC will become available when that

research is published, here we will only state that it uses GStreamer[1] for media capture, encoding and transmission, with the control components written in Python. By design, VCMC already allows *delay and loss simulation*, and the toolkits used allow access to timestamps and control over playout time of individual media streams on both sending and receiving side.

The *multimedia playback engine* used is based on the Ambulant SMIL playback engine[2], with hooks for distributed playback. These hooks are described in [13] and, as for VCMC, allow access to current document clocks and control over those. In addition, all user interaction for document navigation and control (not only play/stop/pause but also link navigation and, in future, annotation) can be both intercepted and injected.

The *synchronization component* is the main new piece of software written for this work. It is written in Python, and runs as a plugin in Ambulant. When a specially prepared SMIL document is opened the plugin will register itself as the synchronization component for the playback engine. It will start VCMC and use Pyro4[3] to create a bidirectional control channel to it. From this point on, it has access to all required synchronization parameters, it can access the policy through Ambulant and it can use VCMC to communicate with its peers.

As an example of how the framework operates let us consider the "narrator" scenario from section 3, for which master/slave Receiver Scheme (MSRS) synchronization [6] is a plausible algorithm, with the audio from the narrator being the master clock for everything. After all participants have joined, the narrator would start playback of the SMIL document. This is intercepted by his policy engine, which has the master role. The policy engine periodically obtains the local conferencing transmitted audio timestamp and the document playback clock value and broadcasts these to all slave policy engines. These then obtain the local playout timestamp for the master audio stream, and combines this with the received timestamp and document clock to compute the desired document playout clock. The document engine is then speeded up or slowed down to synchronize playback.

---

[1] http://gstreamer.freedesktop.org
[2] http://www.ambulantplayer.org
[3] http://pythonhosted.org/Pyro4/

5. INITIAL RESULTS

We have shown that the testbed system works from a functional point of view, which leaves the question of performance to be answered (the subsidiary research question). For simplicity we have chosen to measure conferencing delay and distributed playback synchronization separately.

To measure conferencing delay we used the videoLat tool [7], which can measure glass-to-glass video delay, after an initial calibration phase. 250 measurements were taken, between two 4-core i7 Ubuntu systems on the same LAN. The measured delay (after correcting for videoLat delay and compensating for round-tripping) was 325ms (standard deviation 125ms). This is well below the 500ms suggested as a threshold in [12].

To measure distributed playback synchronization we used two instances of Ambulant running on a 2008 MacBookPro and a 2011 iMac, connected over a wifi network, synchronized with the software from [13]. The synchronization algorithm used was master-slave, with the master running on the faster computer. Both instances were playing a document consisting of a single video which had its timestamps encoded as QR codes. We then put the screens side-by-side, captured both with a third camera and analyzed the resulting video to compute the document playout time difference.

To ensure that our synchronizer actually works we ran the same experiment with the synchronizer turned off, and we saw a consistent drift between the two systems of a few milliseconds per second. Then we ran the measurement with the synchronizer. On average, the slave system was 96ms behind the master system, with a standard deviation of 143ms. While we know of no yardstick to compare this to (one of the reasons we are developing this software!) this number is far below the conferencing delay, and seems workable.

Taken together, these measurements show that our testbed components perform good enough to allow us to continue with our future goal: investigating document-based distributed synchronization policies from a user perspective.

6. ACKNOWLEDGEMENTS

The authors would like to thank their colleagues Marwin Schmitt and Simon Gunkel for giving us access to the VCMC tool.

This work was supported in part by funding from the European Community's Seventh Framework Programme (FP7/2007-2013) Vconect project, under grant agreement no. ICT-2011-287760.

7. REFERENCES

[1] F. Boronat, M. Montagud, H.M. Stokking, and O. Niamut. 2012. The need for inter-destination synchronization for emerging social interactive multimedia applications. In IEEE Communications Magazine, 50(11): 150-158. DOI= 10.1109/MCOM.2012.6353695

[2] Pablo Cesar, Dick C. A. Bulterman, Jack Jansen, David Geerts, Hendrik Knoche, and William Seager. 2009. Fragment, tag, enrich, and send: Enhancing social sharing of video. ACM Trans. Multimedia Comput. Commun. Appl. 5, 3, Article 19 (August 2009), 27 pages. DOI=10.1145/1556134.1556136

[3] Pablo Cesar and David Geerts. 2011. Past, present, and future of social TV: a categorization. In Proceedings of the Consumer Communications and Networking Conference (CCNC 2011), 347-351. DOI = 10.1109/CCNC.2011.5766487

[4] Cyril Concolato, Stéphane Thomas, Romain Bouqueau, and Jean Le Feuvre. 2012. Synchronized delivery of multimedia content over uncoordinated broadcast broadband networks. In Proceedings of the 3rd Multimedia Systems Conference (MMSys '12). ACM, New York, NY, USA, 227-232. DOI=10.1145/2155555.2155590

[5] David Geerts, Ishan Vaishnavi, Rufael Mekuria, Oskar van Deventer, and Pablo Cesar. 2011. Are we in sync?: synchronization requirements for watching online video together.. In Proceedings of the SIGCHI Conference on Human Factors in Computing Systems (CHI '11). ACM, New York, NY, USA, 311-314. DOI=10.1145/1978942.1978986

[6] Y Ishibashi and S Tasaka. 1997. A group synchronization mechanism for live media in multicast communications. In IEEE Global Telecommunications Conference. DOI=10.1109/GLOCOM.1997.638431

[7] Jack Jansen and Dick C. A. Bulterman. 2013. User-centric video delay measurements. In Proceeding of the 23rd ACM Workshop on Network and Operating Systems Support for Digital Audio and Video (NOSSDAV '13). ACM, New York, NY, USA, 37-42. DOI=10.1145/2460782.2460789

[8] Yiming Liu, Peter Shafton, David A. Shamma, and Jeannie Yang. 2007. Zync: the design of synchronized video sharing. In Proceedings of the 2007 conference on Designing for User eXperiences (DUX '07). ACM, New York, NY, USA, , Article 12 , 8 pages. DOI=10.1145/1389908.1389924

[9] Anna Macaranas, Gina Venolia, Kori Inkpen, and John Tang. 2013. Sharing Experiences over Video: watching video programs together at a distance. In Proceedings of INTERACT

[10] Rufael Mekuria, Pablo Cesar, and Dick Bulterman. 2012. Digital TV: the effect of delay when watching football. In Proceedings of the 10th European conference on Interactive tv and video (EuroiTV '12). ACM, New York, NY, USA, 71-74. DOI=10.1145/2325616.2325632

[11] M. Montagud, F. Boronat, H.M. Stokking, R. van Brandenburg. 2012. Inter-Destination multimedia synchronization: schemes, use cases and standardization. Multimedia Systems Journal, 18(6): 459-482. DOI=10.1007/s00530-012-0278-9

[12] Jennifer Tam, Elizabeth Carter, Sara Kiesler and Jessica Hodgins. 2012. Video increases the perception of naturalness during remote interactions with latency. In CHI EA (2012) pp. 2045-2050. ACM, New York, NY, USA. DOI= 10.1145/2212776.2223750

[13] Shahab Ud Din. 2012. An Architecture and Implementation for Evaluating Synchronization Support for Shared User Experiences. Masters thesis, Vrije Universiteit, Amsterdam, the Netherlands.

Interchanging and Preserving Presentation Recordings

Kai Michael Höver
Technische Universität Darmstadt
Dept. of Computer Science
64289 Darmstadt, Germany
hoever@acm.org

Max Mühlhäuser
Technische Universität Darmstadt
Dept. of Computer Science
64289 Darmstadt, Germany
Max.Muehlhaeuser@acm.org

ABSTRACT

The importance of presentation recordings is steadily increasing. This trend is indicated for example by the growing MOOCs market. Many systems for the production of such recordings exist. However, produced recordings are not exchangeable between systems due to different representation formats. In this paper, we present an ontology for the conceptual description of presentation recordings and describe the transformation process between different systems. Furthermore, we explain how this ontology can be used to preserve presentation recordings as ebooks.

Categories and Subject Descriptors

I.7 [**Document and Text Processing**]: Document Preparation; I.7 [**Document and Text Processing**]: Electronic Publishing

Keywords

Presentation Recordings, Ontology, Interoperability, Ebooks

1. INTRODUCTION

Presentations and presentation recordings are an important part of presenting and preserving information and knowledge in both business and education. The raise of massive open online courses (MOOCs) is a good indicator of this trend. However, several problems exist that restrict their reuse, mash-up, and preservation opportunities.

Problems: Due to different recording formats, users need to use different players for different recordings. Furthermore, presenters or lecturers cannot integrate recordings from other sources in their recordings for mashing-up new recordings by copying or even referencing recording elements.

Approach: A solution for these problems is writing converter programs that translate from one recording data format to another. This solution demands for $O(n^2)$ translators for n different data formats. Using an ontology reduces the

number of translators to only $O(n)$, hence "to assist interoperability, ontologies can be used to support translation between different languages and representations" [15]. Unlike data models, an ontology is independent of specific data model, it is "a representation of a world external to any particular system" [3], so that it "can be reused by different kinds of applications/tasks" [14]. Approaches like SMIL[1] and NCL[2] define the structure and synchronization of multimedia documents. However, they only define syntax but lack of semantics since they are based on XML Schema. In contrast, ontologies define a domain theory as a conceptual level on top of XML data.

In this paper, we present some representatives of presentation recording systems and analyze their characteristics. Using these analysis results, we present the presentation recording ontology. Subsequently, the transformation process from a presentation recording format to both another presentation format and an ebook is described.

2. CHARACTERISTICS OF PRESENTATION RECORDING SYSTEMS

In this section, we examined the characteristics of several prominent recording systems. This includes "Authoring on the Fly" (AOF) [11], *Camtasia*[3], eClass [2], *DLH/CLLS* [5], *MIT OpenCourseWare*[4], Opencast Matterhorn [7], Teleteaching Anywhere Solution Kit (tele-TASK) [12], and *virtPresenter* [10]. The following characteristics can be revealed:

Media: The review of recording systems revealed that presentation recordings consist of different elements and types of media. Table 1 provides an overview. We distinguish between the following media elements:

- Video/Audio: In its simplest form, a presentation recording is a video/audio recording. Usually, users can hear the presenter's voice, and see her, or the presented presentation contents.
- Extra content element (slide view): In addition to a lecture video or audio a separated content or slide window.is part of some presentation recording application. The slides view usually changes synchronously with the related playing audio or video.
- Navigation element: To support structure based navigation in a recording, slide thumbnails or text references of certain sections are provided.

DocEng'13, September 10–13, 2013, Florence, Italy.
Copyright 2013 ACM 978-1-4503-1789-4/13/09 ...$15.00.
http://dx.doi.org/10.1145/2494266.2494320.

---

[1] http://www.w3.org/AudioVideo/
[2] http://www.ncl.org.br/en
[3] http://www.techsmith.com
[4] http://ocw.mit.edu/

- Digital pen annotations: They are used to draw audience attention, or to add explanations. Digital pen annotations are both temporal and spatial.
- Text annotations: Some presentation recording systems support the annotation with text comments. They are temporal and often also spatial.
- Object representation of contents: Applications like AOF store slide contents as objects (text box, list item, rectangle etc.). Others like Camtasia allow annotating recordings with such geometrical objects afterwards.

Spatial and temporal arrangement: Presentation recordings have a time-based nature. In its simplest form, a recording consist of a single video or audio file. If there are additional elements like slides or pen annotations they have a time-based relation for synchronous replay. Some elements have also a 2D or 3D spatial position (x, y, and z-layer).

Metadata: Most systems use metadata to describe their content. Usually, this includes a title, a creator or presenter, and a creation timestamp. Systems like DLH/CLLS, Opencast Matterhorn, and tele-TASK [1] integrate elements of the Dublin Core Metadata Element Set[5] (DCMES).

3. TOWARDS AN ONTOLOGY FOR PRESENTATION RECORDINGS

The purpose of the ontology is to provide a consensual knowledge model of the presentation recording domain to be used in presentation recording applications, and for data exchange. For this purpose, we have analyzed the characteristics of presentation recording systems. In the first version of this ontology, we concentrate on the classic building blocks of presentation recordings.

Description of content structure: To support different content types, we need a concept taxonomy of content elements in our ontology. In particular, we need concepts for continuous and discrete data as well as object representations, e.g., for slide modeling and composition concepts. The ALOCoM ontology is a generic content model for defining learning content and its components [6]. In ALOCoM, *Content Fragments* are basic content units like audio, video, and images that cannot be further decomposed. A *Content Object* aggregates *Content Fragments* and/or other *Content Objects*. We integrate this ontology and add two concepts (*Presentation Recording* and *Slide*) as subclasses of a *Content Object*. The *hasPart* relation aggregates presentation recording elements.

Description of media: For the description of media resources we integrate the Media Resources vocabulary[6], which provides a core set of metadata properties. It allows us to set the file location of media resources as well as other metadata like *height* and *width* as well as *frame rate* and *duration* in case of video or audio resources.

Description of time: For the representation of time, we have developed an ontology called TOSM (Time Ontology for Synchronous Media) consisting of the two classes *TimeEntity* and *TimeUnit*. A *TimeEntity* is either an *TimeInstant* or *TimeInterval*. A *TimeInstant* describes a point of time, a *TimeInterval* an interval that has a beginning, and an end or a duration description. *Time Entities* can further have a relation to the synchronous media their time definition is relative to. Times can be defined in seconds.

The *TimeUnit* class defines concepts for converting between different time units, e.g., seconds to milliseconds. This simplifies the conversion if systems use different units of time.

Description of navigation: Users can often browse through presentation recordings via (slide) thumbnails and/or text titles. The *Structure Based Navigation* concept is defined as a set of one or more *Discrete Content Fragments* (graphics, image, text) and a time instant. This makes it possible to link a thumbnail image and/or text with a certain point in time temporally relative to synchronous media.

Description of metadata: Metadata augments information or data with additional properties that explain its creators, creation time, meaning, and other characteristics. DCMI Metadata Terms[7], which include DCMES, are integrated in the ontology for providing information about a presentation such as the author or the subject of, e.g., a slide or video. Elements of the IEEE Learning Object Metadata (LOM) [8] that are used by, e.g, MIT OpenCourseWare, can be mapped to this set although not fully reflected.

Rules: We use SWRL[8] (Semantic Web Rule Language) to define rules. One purpose of these rules is the conversion between units. This is especially useful if one application's data model uses seconds and another one uses milliseconds. Another set of rules infers the relations between events and intervals by determining transitive temporal relations like *after* and *before*. This allows to automatically determine if a slides precedes another one without explicitly defining this relation. Another benefit of using an ontology is to check if recording data is logically consistent. For instance, we can check if the time interval of two slides overlaps although they should be in sequence, or if a structural navigation element is assigned to more than one time instant.

Furthermore, rules can be defined to transform individuals of a presentation recording to a conceptual ebook representation (see subsection 4.3).

4. EXCHANGE AND PRESERVATION

The purpose of the presentation ontology is to serve as an inter-lingua between different systems so that it can be reused by different kinds of applications to exchange information. Therefore, it is also suitable for preservation of presentation recordings as it describes the concepts of a presentation in an application independent way. In the following, we describe the transformation process by example.

4.1 General transformation process

Figure 1 depicts the general transformation from one presentation recording document to another. For the translation between different presentation recording representations it is necessary to write a translator for each representation that translates from one specific application to the ontology and vice versa.

4.2 Transformation to presentation applications

As a proof of concept, we used the presentation recording ontology to convert Camtasia recordings to DLH/CLLS recordings, and vice versa. Camtasia recordings consist of a screen video recording and thumbnails for navigation. Recording metadata is stored as XML. Recordings that consist of videos only like MIT OpenCourseWare are also covered by

---

[5]http://dublincore.org/documents/dces/
[6]http://www.w3.org/TR/mediaont-10/

[7]http://purl.org/dc/terms/
[8]http://www.w3.org/Submission/SWRL/

Table 1: Characteristics of lecture recording systems

Characteristics	Systems							
	AOF/ Lecturnity	Cam- tasia	Classroom 2000/eClass	DLH/ CLLS	MIT Open- CourseWare	Opencast Matterhorn	tele- TASK	virtPre- senter
Video/Audio	x	x	x	x	x	x	x	x
Extra content element (slide view)	x	-	x	x	-	x	x	x
Navigation element	x	x	x	x	-	x	x	x
Digital pen annotations	x	-	x	x	-	-	-	-
Text annotations (spatial)	x(x)	-	-	x(-)	-	x(-)	-	-
Object representation of contents	x	x	-	-	-	-	x (head- lines)	x (SVG)

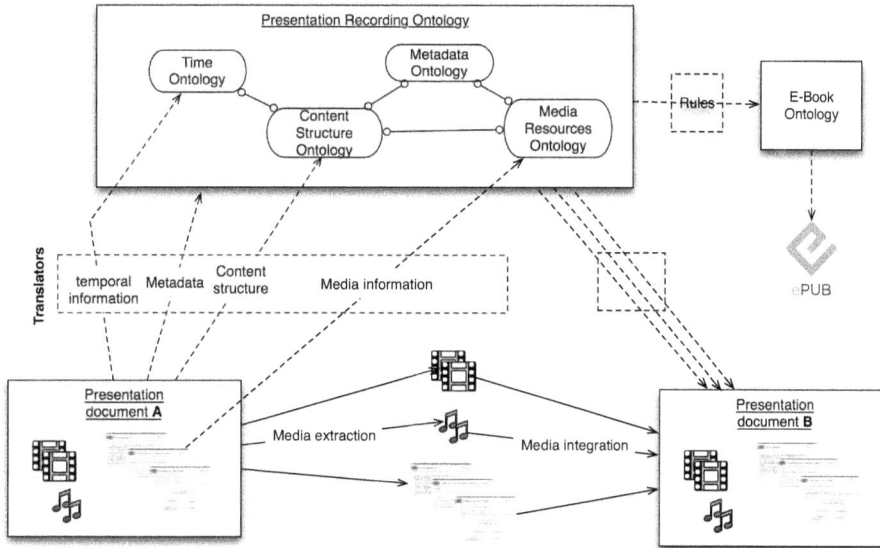

Figure 1: Transformation process from one presentation document to another

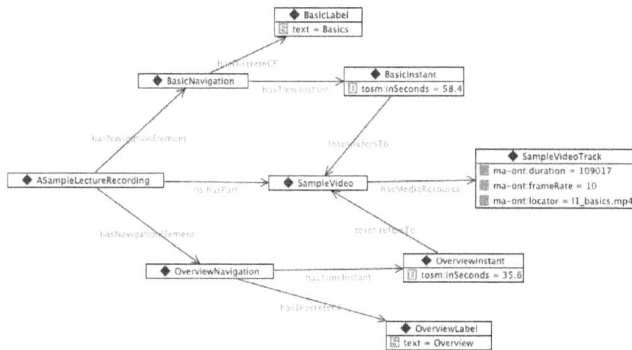

Figure 2: Ontology representation of a Camtasia recording

this test bed. As Camtasia only store start times for slides, but DLH/CLLS also end time, SWRL rules automatically compute the missing data. A representation of a Camtasia recording that consist of a video and textual navigation elements is shown diagrammatically in Figure 2.

4.3 Transformation to ebooks

Despite the increasing popularity of ebooks, their compiled format makes the suitable for preservation and thus getting more and more in focus of libraries. The EPUB 3.0 standard [4] describes such a compiled format. Contained documents are XHTML5 documents. CSS stylesheets define the layout of the content documents. The package document provides information about the content documents and their types, publication metadata (author, title, etc.), the default reading order (spine section). Another XHTML document describes the table of contents.

Next, we describe the translation process from the presentation recording ontology to EPUB3. To support this translation process we have created an ebook ontology. Figure 3 depicts its taxonomy. An ebook consists of a *table of contents* and one ore more *content documents*, which are pages in an ebook. A *table of contents* has several *items* that refer to the *content documents* of the ebook. A *content document* consist of several *body elements* like paragraphs, images, text sections, and audio/video elements. The translation steps from a presentation recording to an ebook are:

1. Translation from a presentation recording representation to an ontological representation. This includes the creation of instances of the presentation recording ontology and the relations between each other.
2. Automatic construction of instances of the ebook ontology from the presentation recording instances
3. Translation from the ebook ontology to EPUB3.

Subsequently, we describe the last two steps.

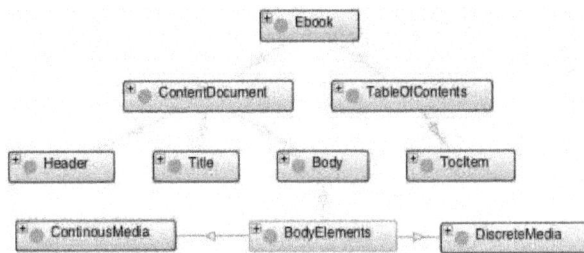
Figure 3: The core ebook taxonomy

4.3.1 Construction of ebook ontology instances

For the mapping between the presentation recording and the ebook ontology we use SPARQL construct queries [13]. In particular these queries create a *content document* (page) for each time interval. Each page consist of a header, an image, and a video/audio. An image refers to a slide image, a video to an video instance of the presentation ontology. The following example creates ebook pages with single slide images from slide images of the presentation ontology (without namespace declarations). In particular, the *construct* part creates a content document with an image inside a body for each slide, which are obtained in the *where* clause.

```
CONSTRUCT {
_:page a ebook:ContentDocument .
_:page ebook:hasPart _:part .
_:part a ebook:Body .
_:part ebook:hasPart _:image .
_:image a ebook:Image .
_:image ma:locator ?imagelocation . }
WHERE {
?slide a alocom:Slide .
?slide ns:hasPart ?slideimage .
?slideimage a ns:Image .
?slideimage pro:hasMediaResource ?imgresource .
?imgresource a ma:Image .
?imgresource ma:locator ?imagelocation . }
```

4.3.2 Creation of an EPUB3 document

For each ebook page an XHTML5 document is created. These documents are created from templates with placeholders for the title, the slide image, and the audio/video file(s). In case there is no single audio/video file for each slide but a single one, it can either be split in snippets for each page or W3C Media Fragments URI [9] can be used to tell the player which interval to replay.

5. SUMMARY AND FUTURE WORK

In this paper, we contribute an analysis and a resulting conceptualization of presentation recordings for the exchange of recording content between different representations. Furthermore, an ebook ontology including classes, properties, and rules, was created to translate presentation recordings into ebooks for content delivery and preservation.

Although the presented presentation recording ontology already covers most systems, not all aspects are covered yet. In our analysis, we did not consider SMIL for describing lecture recordings. This can be achieved by adding concepts for representing the layout or view. (Synchronous) annotations and augmentations are also not covered yet, but will be added in the next iteration version. We plan to add a 4-D coordinate systems $(x, y, layer, time)$ conceptualization for locating content entities both temporally and spatially. As data can be lost in the translation between LOM and

DCMES, ontology-based semantic mapping between metadata standards needs also further investigation.

6. REFERENCES

[1] H. S. Bert Baumann, A. Groß, and C. Meinel. Linking the tele-TASK Video Portal to the Semantic Web. In *Proceedings of the 9th International Conference on Innovative Internet Community Systems (I2CS 2009)*, volume 148, pages 205–216, Jena, Germany, 6 2009. GI LNI Press.

[2] J. A. Brotherton and G. D. Abowd. Lessons learned from eClass: Assessing automated capture and access in the classroom. *ACM Trans. Comput.-Hum. Interact.*, 11(2):121–155, 2004.

[3] R. M. Colomb. *Ontology and the Semantic Web*, volume 156 of *Frontiers in Artificial Intelligence and Applications*. IOS Press, 2007.

[4] EPUB Publication 3.0, Recommended Specification, 2011.

[5] K. M. Höver, G. von Bachhaus, M. Hartle, and M. Mühlhäuser. DLH/CLLS: An Open, Extensible System Design for Prosuming Lecture Recordings and Integrating Multimedia Learning Ecosystems. In *IEEE International Symposium on Multimedia (ISM) 2012*, pages 477–482, 12 2012.

[6] J. Jovanović, D. Gašević, K. Verbert, and E. Duval. Ontology of Learning Object Content Structure. In *Proceeding of the conference on Artificial Intelligence in Education*, pages 322–329, Amsterdam, The Netherlands, 2005. IOS Press.

[7] M. Ketterl, O. A. Schulte, and A. Hochman. Opencast Matterhorn: A Community-Driven Open Source Solution for Creation, Management and Distribution of Audio and Video in Academia. In *11th IEEE International Symposium on Multimedia (ISM)*, pages 687 –692, 12 2009.

[8] IEEE P1484.12.1-2002, Draft Standard for Learning Object Metadata, 2002.

[9] Media Fragments URI. W3C Recommendation. http://www.w3.org/TR/media-frags/, 9 2012.

[10] R. Mertens, M. Ketterl, and O. Vornberger. The virtPresenter lecture recording system: Automated production of web lectures with interactive content overviews. *Interactive Technology and Smart Education*, 4(1):55 – 65, 2007.

[11] R. Müller and T. Ottmann. The "Authoring on the Fly" system for automated recording and replay of (tele)presentations. *Multimedia Systems*, 8(3):158–176, 10 2000.

[12] V. Schillings and C. Meinel. tele-TASK: teleteaching anywhere solution kit. In *Proceedings of the 30th annual ACM SIGUCCS conference on User services*, SIGUCCS '02, pages 130–133, New York, NY, USA, 2002. ACM.

[13] SPARLQ 1.1, W3C Recommendation. http://www.w3.org/TR/sparql11-overview/, 3 2013.

[14] P. Spyns, R. Meersman, and M. Jarrar. Data modelling versus ontology engineering. *SIGMOD Record*, 31(4):12–17, 12 2002.

[15] M. Uschold and M. Gruninger. Ontologies: principles, methods and applications. *The Knowledge Engineering Review*, 11(02):93–136, 1996.

Document Changes: Modeling; Detection; Storing and Visualization (DChanges)

Gioele Barabucci
Department of Computer Science
Università di Bologna
Bologna, Italy
barabucc@cs.unibo.it

Angelo Di Iorio
Department of Computer Science
Università di Bologna
Bologna, Italy
diiorio@cs.unibo.it

Uwe M. Borghoff
Institute for Software Technology
Universität der Bundeswehr München
Neubiberg, Germany
uwe.borghoff@unibw.de

Sonja Maier
Institute for Software Technology
Universität der Bundeswehr München
Neubiberg, Germany
sonja.maier@unibw.de

ABSTRACT

Many people have approached the problem of investigating the evolution of documents and data from different perspectives, e.g. by tracking changes, versioning and diffing. The goal of this workshop is to share ideas, common issues and principles, and to foster research collaboration on these topics.

Categories and Subject Descriptors

I.7.1 [**Document and Text Processing**]: Document and Text Editing—*Version control; Document management*

General Terms

Algorithms; Management; Reliability; Theory

Keywords

applications; change analysis and interpretation; change detection; change tracking; merging changes

1. INTRODUCTION

The workshop is on diff models and algorithms, change tracking, document versioning and related subjects. One of the key aspects of the workshop is to look at these themes from different points of view and in different domains. For instance, there is a great overlap between the interests of the communities of document engineering and software engineering related to these issues. The workshop gives researchers the opportunity to discuss peculiarities of their domains and to distill common aspects that can be beneficial for other researchers.

DocEng'13, September 10–13, 2013, Florence, Italy.
Copyright 2013 ACM 978-1-4503-1789-4/13/09
http://dx.doi.org/10.1145/2494266.2494322

This is the first edition of the workshop. The idea is to start a series of events on these topics, considering their potential impact and relevance for the community. In fact, the main conference has routinely hosted presentations about these topics: delta models [5], domain-specific diff algorithms [3, 4, 2] and non-conventional diff algorithms [1]. The workshop aims at identifying open issues, possible solutions to existing problems and new research directions. One of the goals is also to identify more specific topics for a second edition of the workshop.

2. PROGRAM

The workshop opens with a keynote by Ethan Munson with the title "*Collaborative Authoring Requires Advanced Change Management*", followed by a session on peer-reviewed research papers and a round-table.

2.1 Invited Talk

Collaborative document authoring is a pervasive activity of modern life. It extends far beyond simple joint authorship to many forms of shared document work, including laws, patient charts, and the editing process. Software engineering is also a form of collaborative authoring, and in general, the software engineers have the best tools for managing collaborative changes, such as version control and build systems.

It is the thesis of this talk that collaborating authors of natural language documents need the same kinds of tools that software engineers take for granted. In fact, because of important domain differences, people collaborating on natural language documents need better tools than software engineers.

The document engineering research community has been working on this problem domain for a considerable time, particularly in the area of version control of XML documents, which is the primary representation for modern office documents. Key research results have included a variety of schemes for merging and patching XML document versions, advances in formalizing document deltas, a scheme for controlling author access to the various sections of a document, and demonstrations that authors can edit a document simultaneously over the Internet without locking mechanisms.

Ethan Munson will argue that document systems must adopt the full range of version management tools used by software engineers, including full branch-and-merge versioning, but then must extend those tools and simplify their use. Approaches are needed for sharing documents and merging their changes that are highly automated, that recognize the difference between formatting and content, that permit fine-grained access control, and that help users understand the provenance of changes so that responsibility is correctly assigned. He will show how his laboratory's work on Version-Aware Documents is addressing these issues and describe a longer term vision requiring further research. He will also suggest how the same techniques might impact other domains including medical informatics, eGovernment, and document analysis.

2.2 Research Papers Session

The core of the workshop is the session on research papers. We received 12 submissions from all around the world. They are still under review at this stage but their quality is very high and we are confident that the final program will be of great interest for the audience. The complete proceedings will be available at http://ceur-ws.org/Vol-1008/.

2.3 Round-Table Discussion

The workshop attendees will be split up into groups, each of them working on a different topic. After finishing their work, each group will present their findings.

The goal of this session is twofold: fostering research collaboration; eliciting topics for a second edition of the workshop.

3. TOPICS OF INTEREST

The workshop call for papers had identified five main areas of interest, though submissions were also accepted on other areas:

Change tracking models and algorithms for keeping track of modifications to documents and data. The interest is on different classes of documents (diagrams, models, ontologies, source code, etc.) and structures (plain text, tree-based, graphs, etc.);

Change detection models and algorithms to detect modifications between documents, with particular attention to the internal structure of deltas and their qualities;

Change analysis and interpretation solutions to better exploit and understand changes, by identifying editing patterns and domain-specific (semantic) descriptions of changes;

Merging changes techniques to merge different versions into a single one, handling conflicts and change propagation;

Applications tools and application domains for diffing and versioning techniques.

The received submissions cover over all these areas. Some of them focus on handling changes on documents, studying the relation between changes on these documents, their schemas and query languages. Some others focus on detecting changes on domain-specific documents, data models, UML diagrams and ontologies. Particular attention is also given to analyzing changes on source code.

The study of editing patterns is a common denominator of several works, together with the study of theoretical models and running infrastructures for collaborative editing and change-tracking.

4. PEOPLE

The workshop was organized by two people from Università di Bologna: Gioele Barabucci, who studied and implemented diff algorithms and delta models, and Angelo Di Iorio, who worked on various systems for document versioning and publishing, and collaborative editing. They were supported by two people from Universität der Bundeswehr München: Uwe M. Borghoff, who has a background in computer-supported cooperative work, and who published several papers on the management of changes in XML documents, and Sonja Maier, who focuses on tool creation and tool integration for (visual) domain-specific languages, and who is interested in tracking the evolution of text and diagrams.

The organizers have been helped by a committee of experts from all around the world. The quality of the submissions was very high. The hard work of the committee members has contributed to make it even higher. The workshop organizers would hereby like to thank all of them:

Serge Autexier (DFKI Bremen), Stéphane Ducasse (INRIA Lille Nord Europe research center), Boris Konev (University of Liverpool), John Lumley, Pascal Molli (Université de Nantes - LINA), Sebastian Rönnau, Wolfgang Stürzlinger (York University), Yannis Tzitzikas (University of Crete and FORTH-ICS), Fabio Vitali (Università di Bologna), and Jean-Yves Vion-Dury (Xerox Research Centre Europe).

5. REFERENCES

[1] LINDHOLM, T., KANGASHARJU, J., AND TARKOMA, S. Fast and simple XML tree differencing by sequence alignment. In *ACM Symposium on Document Engineering* (2006), D. C. A. Bulterman and D. F. Brailsford, Eds., ACM, pp. 75–84.

[2] MÜLLER, A., RÖNNAU, S., AND BORGHOFF, U. M. A file-type sensitive, auto-versioning file system. In *ACM Symposium on Document Engineering* (2010), A. Antonacopoulos, M. J. Gormish, and R. Ingold, Eds., ACM, pp. 271–274.

[3] RÖNNAU, S., PAULI, C., AND BORGHOFF, U. M. Merging changes in XML documents using reliable context fingerprints. In *ACM Symposium on Document Engineering* (2008), M. da Graça Campos Pimentel, D. C. A. Bulterman, and L. F. G. Soares, Eds., ACM, pp. 52–61.

[4] RÖNNAU, S., PHILIPP, G., AND BORGHOFF, U. M. Efficient change control of XML documents. In *ACM Symposium on Document Engineering* (2009), U. M. Borghoff and B. Chidlovskii, Eds., ACM, pp. 3–12.

[5] VION-DURY, J.-Y. A generic calculus of XML editing deltas. In *ACM Symposium on Document Engineering* (2011), M. R. B. Hardy and F. W. Tompa, Eds., ACM, pp. 113–120.

Collaborative Annotations in Shared Environments: Metadata, Vocabularies and Techniques in the Digital Humanities (DH-CASE 2013)

Francesca Tomasi
Dept. of Classical Philology and
Italian Studies
University of Bologna
via Zamboni 32
40126 - Bologna
+390512098539
francesca.tomasi@unibo.it

Fabio Vitali
Dept. of Computer Science and Engineering
University of Bologna
Mura Anteo Zamboni 7
40126 - Bologna
+390512094872
fabio@cs.unibo.it

ABSTRACT
We present here the workshop DH-CASE 2013, aimed at investigating the state of art in the field of collaboration in text annotation, by exploring methods, tools and techniques used in the domain of the Digital Humanities (DH).

Categories and Subject Descriptors
I.7 [**DOCUMENT AND TEXT PROCESSING**]: I.7.2 Document Preparation - *Markup languages*; H.3 [**INFORMATION STORAGE AND RETRIEVAL**]: H.3.1 Content Analysis and Indexing - *Thesauruses*; H.3.7 Digital Libraries - *Collection, dissemination, standards*.

Keywords
Digital Humanities, Metadata, Ontologies, Vocabularies, Annotation, Environment, Collaboration.

1. INTRODUCTION
In these last years, collections of digital text have strongly increased in number, especially in the field of humanities, also thanks to the TEI (*Text Encoding Initiative*) [16] role in defining an annotation model. Digital libraries of full-text documents, including digital editions of literary texts, are emerging as environments for the production, the management and the dissemination of complex annotated corpora.

The potential interpretative levels arising from the analysis of textual phenomena (including bibliographic, linguistic, thematic, structural, rhetorical and prosopographic aspects) converge to produce a stratification of annotations whose complex interactions may give light to new and unexpected potentials.

Yet, each community in the field of humanities (archives, libraries, museums, literary studies, etc.) have developed independent metadata models and annotation techniques for their corpora.

In a shared environment, the possibility to annotate different aspects of a text overlaps with metadata models and ontologies used for annotation, and related values vocabularies, but also with techniques for producing annotations, both with embedded or stand-off markup methods based on XML or other formal

DocEng'13, September 10–13, 2013, Florence, Italy.
ACM 978-1-4503-1789-4/13/09.
http://dx.doi.org/10.1145/2494266.2494323

languages, possibly even in a Linked Data perspective (see section 2).

The aim of the DH-CASE 2013 workshop is to explore the state of art in the field of collaboration in text annotation and to reflect on existing platforms for document sharing and management, methods and techniques for multi-level annotation, metadata and vocabularies for declaring interpretative instances.

"Collaboration within digital humanities is both a pertinent and a pressing topic" [2]. Some issues and questions have already been defined, and are clearly emerging from the accepted submissions (see section 3), aiming at understanding the complex levels of analysis of this challenging field.

Twenty-nine abstract have been submitted from worldwide and twenty-seven full papers have subsequently been submitted and evaluated by the Program Committee as well as by a list of additional selected reviewers (see section 4). Eighteen submissions, between research papers and demo/project presentation, were finally accepted.

These submissions showed interesting approaches coming from both the humanist and the computer science domain. The result of these interactions show the improvement of research results emerging from the collaboration in a Digital Humanities perspective.

2. RELATED WORKS
Related works are strongly connected with standards and models for documents description and data dissemination.

Metadata models have been defined for *literary texts* (TEI [16]), for the description of *archival documents* (EAD [6]), for the creation of *authority records* (EAC-CPF [5]), for *bibliographic data* (FRBR [10]) and for *information exposure* (DC [3]).

Likewise, several ontologies have been developed, for example, for *museums* (CIDOC-CRM [1]), *bibliographic records* (FRBR(OO) [8]), *lexical networks* (SKOS [13]), *cultural heritage* (EDM [7]) and other *general purposes* (DCTerms [4]).

Also, plenty of vocabularies are now available for the DH community, such as DDC, Geonames, LC, VIAF, Wordnet, Dbpedia (a comprehensive list can be found in [12]).

Procedures for annotating digital objects range from embedded markup to stand-off (a global reflection about these topics can be found in [15]), and the most used languages for annotations in the field of DH are OWL [17] and RDF [14]. In the same vein, Linked Data [9] is a new emerging method for metadata expression and dissemination.

A lot of environments and platforms have been proposed, such as ResearchSpace (http://www.researchspace.org/), TextGrid (http://www.textgrid.de/), DARIAH (http://www.dariah.eu/),

Interedition (http://www.interedition.eu/), or Clarin (http://www.clarin.eu/). Digital libraries are mostly studied towards the OAI [11] perspective.

3. TOPICS

The topics addressed by submissions that were selected are the following:

- Multi-level annotations in textual corpora. Problems of overlapping of annotation when different phenomena are of interest by different communities.
- Collaborative platforms. Infrastructure for digital text annotation and existent solutions.
- Dialogue and crosswalk between ontologies. Crosswalk in annotating digital textual resources. The dialogue between different ways to express meaning of annotation.
- Annotation and markup. Tools, technologies and techniques.
- Linked Data and the humanistic domain. Possibilities and perspectives in the interchange between digital/textual annotated objects.
- OAC (Open Annotation Collaboration) model. Utility and case studies in the DH domain. Is OAC a possible solution?
- Literary texts and digital editions. The DH role and approach to literature.

4. ACKNOWLEDGMENTS

Our thanks goes to AIUCD - *Associazione per l'Informatica Umanistica e la Cultura Digitale* for the sponsorship of the event. We also thank the Program Committee for the collaboration in the organization: Maristella Agosti, University of Padua, Italy; Gioele Barabucci, University of Bologna, Italy; John Bradley, King's College London, UK; Elisabeth Burr, University of Leipzig, Germany; Dino Buzzetti, University of Bologna, Italy; Paolo Ciccarese, Massachusetts General Hospital Biomedical Informatics Core, Boston MA, USA; Fabio Ciotti, University of Rome Tor Vergata, Italy; Julia Flanders, Brown University, Providence RI, USA; Claus Huitfeld, University of Bergen, Norway; Antoine Isaac, Vrije Universiteit Amsterdam, Netherlands; Jan Christoph Meister, Institut fu□r Germanistik II, Hamburg, Germany; Silvio Peroni, University of Bologna, Italy; Paul Spence, King's College London, UK; Melissa Terras, University College London, UK; Andreas Witt, Institut fu□r Deutsche Sprache, Mannheim, Germany.

We are finally grateful to our additional reviewers: Ilaria Bartolini, Federico Boschetti, Angelo Di Iorio, Nicola Ferro, Maurizio Lana, Damina Luzzi, Eliza Margaretha, Federico Meschini, Francesco Poggi, Roberto Rosselli Del Turco, Desmond Schmidt, Jacopo Zingoni.

5. REFERENCES

[1] Crofts, N., Doerr, M., Gill, T., Stead, S., Stiff, M. *Definition of the CIDOC Conceptual Reference Model*. Version 5.0.4 (November 2011). ICOM/CIDOC CRM Special Interest Group, http://www.cidoc-crm.org/docs/cidoc_crm_version_5.0.4.pdf

[2] Deegan M., McCarty W. (eds), *Collaborative Research in the Digital Humanities*, Ashgate 2012.

[3] Dublin Core Metadata Initiative. *Dublin Core Metadata Element Set*, Version 1.1. DCMI Recommendation (2010), http://dublincore.org/documents/dces/

[4] Dublin Core Metadata Initiative. *DCMI Metadata Terms. DCMI Recommendation* (2010), http://dublincore.org/documents/dcmi-terms/

[5] *Encoded Archival Context – Corporate bodies, Persons, and Families (EAC-CPF)*, http://eac.staatsbibliothek-berlin.de/

[6] *Encoded Archival Description (EAD)*, Version 2002, http://www.loc.gov/ead/

[7] Europeana. *Definition of the The Europeana Data Model (EDM) elements*, Version 5.2.3. Europeana v. 1.0 (24/02/2012), http://pro.europeana.eu/documents/900548/bb6b5 1df-ad11-4a78-8d8a-44cc41810f22

[8] *FRBR object-oriented definition and mapping to FRBR*, Version 0.9 draft. (January 2008), http://archive.ifla.org/VII/s13/wgfrbr/FRBRoo_V9.1_PR.pdf

[9] Heath, T., Bizer, C. *Linked Data: Evolving the Web into a Global Data Space*. Morgan & Claypool Publishers (2011). DOI: 10.2200/S00334ED1V01Y201102WBE001

[10] International Federation of Library Associations and Institutions. *Functional Requirements for Bibliographic Records Final Report* (2009), http://www.ifla.org/files/cataloguing/frbr/frbr_2008.pdf

[11] Lagoze, C., Van de Sompel, H., Johnston, P., Nelson, M., Sanderson, R., Warner, S. *Abstract Data Model. ORE Specification* (17 October 2008). Open Archives Initiative, http://www.openarchives.org/ore/1.0/datamodel

[12] *Library Linked Data Incubator Group: Datasets, Value Vocabularies, and Metadata Element Sets*. W3C Incubator Group Report (25 October 2011), http://www.w3.org/2005/Incubator/lld/XGR-lld-vocabdataset-20111025/

[13] Miles, A., Bechhofer, S. *SKOS Simple Knowledge Organization System Reference*. W3C Recommendation (18 August 2009), http://www.w3.org/TR/skos-reference/

[14] *Resource Description Framework* (RDF), http://www.w3.org/RDF/

[15] Schmidt D. *The inadequacy of embedded markup for cultural heritage texts*. Lit Linguist Computing (2010) 25 (3): 337-356. DOI: 10.1093/llc/fqq007.

[16] TEI Consortium, eds. *TEI P5: Guidelines for Electronic Text Encoding and Interchange*, http://www.tei-c.org/Guidelines/P5

[17] *Web Ontology Language* (OWL), http://www.w3.org/2004/OWL/

Reimagining Digital Publishing for Technical Documents

DocEng'13 Workshop Summary

Michael Wybrow
Caulfield School of Information Technology
Monash University, Caulfield 3145, Australia
Michael.Wybrow@monash.edu

ABSTRACT

This workshop asks how we might reimagine digital publishing for technical documents and proposes to investigate new adaptive approaches to document reading with flexible navigation and where contextual information—figures, references, definitions, etc—might be displayed dynamically at the point they are referred to. The workshop ultimately seeks to answer the question of what is needed for reading and annotation of technical documents on digital devices to become more comfortable and productive than on paper?

Categories and Subject Descriptors

I.7.4 [**Computing Methodologies**]: DOCUMENT AND TEXT PROCESSING—*Electronic Publishing*

Keywords

Digital reading environments, e-books, technical documents

1. BACKGROUND

As you well know, academics spend a lot of their time reading and annotating technical documents. These can be journal articles, conference papers, textbooks, student theses, and of course grant proposals. Academics frequently express a desire to do more of this reading and annotation digitally, rather than printing out reams of paper. Most have tried this and found the experience uncomfortable or inefficient for a variety of reasons. And so, almost 40 years after the term "paperless office" was coined, the offices of most academics are literally littered with stacks of paper.

Studies examining the use of existing e-book readers by academics in their everyday work, such as [7], find particular deficiencies in the responsiveness and navigation experience, leading to difficulties jumping around documents. Participants almost unanimously agree that text formatted as PDF results in a poor experience, leading to unnecessary repeated panning and zooming of text. They also specifically point out difficulties with jumping to other places in

DocEng'13, September 10–13, 2013, Florence, Italy.
ACM 978-1-4503-1789-4/13/09.
http://dx.doi.org/10.1145/2494266.2494324.

the document to check something—a reference, figure or previous chapter—while keeping their place. Most participants will persist with a trial but do not wish to continue using e-book readers for their subsequent daily work! These problems with document navigation, display formats and the constraints of the reading platform are consistently reaffirmed by similar studies, see for example [6, 3].

A fundamental problem is that most technical documents are formatted for print. As such, they don't take advantage of the capabilities of the devices on which they are displayed. Nor can they adapt to cater for the requirements of the reader. Additionally, people read in a non-linear fashion when reading technical documents, leading to difficulties using existing e-book readers [7]. That is, people spend a lot of time navigating documents to focus on different content of interest or to look at a piece of information that is referenced from elsewhere. This often becomes tedious for the person, who decides they can work faster on paper. Obviously, documents need fixed formats when they are printed in physical conference proceedings or as a bound textbook, but when reading online versions they should be optimised to the needs of the person as well as the reading medium.

There has been some prior work in the area of digital reading and adaptive display of technical documents. In [1] the authors explore the deficiencies with current digital document reading and present a novel document reader, Utopia Documents, that will display specially annotated PDFs and integrate additional rich, interactive information and visualisations throughout the document. This potentially makes the document a lot more useful, but still suffers from the static PDF layout of the original document. Prior work on document layout has focused on optimal techniques for digital display of print-style documents. For example, using complete search methods such as dynamic programming and $A^\star$ for figure placement in single- and multi-column documents [2, 4] and genetic algorithms for personalised document layout [5]. These approaches are not fast enough to be used interactively for dynamic layout, nor is truly optimal layout even necessarily required.

2. GOALS

Reimagine technical publishing for digital devices by designing and evaluating better layout approaches and interaction techniques for allowing people to read, annotate and edit these documents in adaptive, dynamic contexts.

It will be important to display documents dynamically, i.e., to reflow and relayout the text when viewing with different font sizes or on different devices. This could be done by displaying the main body text of the document as a continuous scroll, interrupted only by headings and other necessarily in-line content. Figures mights be shown on demand as the person views relevant information in the main text that refers to them. Contextual information about references, footnotes and other notations could be similarly displayed.

Technical documents are usually very deliberately structured and may have (multiple) suggested reading paths to best aid people in understanding particular concepts or topics. Such structural semantics are not well utilised in static documents and could be used to provide smart navigation.

Aim 1: Investigate novel ways to dynamically present technical documents in a digital context. This will inform the design of new dynamic reading environments for both desktop computers as well as portable touch-screen devices.

We need to explore what is known about the ergonomics of reading from the literature and various studies. Some fundamental questions are determining the best information to display at particular times, where to place it, and how it should change over time due to interaction. This is predominantly related to user interface and interaction design, but may also involve human cognition and perception research.

Aim 2: Investigate useful structural semantic information for documents. Explore how this could be specified by authors or automatically inferred from existing documents.

Providing better navigation and reading experience will require the use of structural semantics. There are two obvious approaches. Firstly, allowing authors to specify it themselves, effectively annotating their documents with these relationships. Alternatively, attempt to infer this information automatically from existing documents by examining their text and existing linking information within the document (such as figure/section references, footnotes, citations).

Aim 3: Investigate more effective interaction and layout techniques for the tasks of annotation and correction.

Extend the visualisation and interaction techniques to allow people to perform the common tasks of annotation and correction. The utilisation of dynamic layout could allow corrections and annotations to be shown in-place with better layout rather than simply superimposing them on the document as in many existing PDF reading software.

Aim 4: Verify the benefits of proposed new layout and interaction models for reading, annotation and correction.

Appropriate evaluations of proposed approaches to these problems are vital. This will require carefully designed user-based evaluations testing both efficiency and effectiveness—that is, looking at people's performance and satisfaction while reading, navigating, editing and annotating documents.

3. WORKSHOP

Planned discussion topics for the workshop include:

- How people currently read and work with paper-based technical documents? (For comprehension, skimming, or fact-finding. Measuring efficiency.)

- Issues with reading technical documents on current software/e-readers?

- How has the activity of "reading" been affected by increases in digital media? (When is use of videos, animations and visualizations no longer "reading?")

- How best to lay out the text and other information for optimum readability?

- Various approaches for document navigation? (Overview approaches, textual landmarks, possible tree or graph-like navigation?)

- Benefits and features afforded by semantically rich documents?

- How document semantics and metadata might better inform layout and navigation? (What aspects of structure and content impact the document's readability?)

- How best to produce or infer, and subsequently store semantic information?

- An optimal design for a new digital reading environment for technical documents? (Screen use, interaction, adaptation for different device and screen sizes.)

- Benefits and issues with showing non-textual content on demand where referenced? (Layout related issues. Can we show other contextually relevant material?)

- Necessary features and functionality for annotation and correction?

- Leveraging and integrating with upcoming systems for semantically rich documents? (Initiatives emerging from the "FORCE 11: Beyond the PDF" efforts.)

- Operating in the context of new academic/scientific publishing initiatives? (Supporting collaboration, various domain specific online databases, Wikipedia.)

- Possibility of supporting efficient authoring and editing within this new environment?

4. ACKNOWLEDGMENTS

Thanks to the organizing committee for the workshop: Paolo Ciccarese, Monica Landoni, Simone Marinai, Kim Marriott and Steve Pettifer. They provided valuable input and feedback on the proposed discussion topics.

5. REFERENCES

[1] T. Attwood, D. Kell, P. McDermott, J. Marsh, S. Pettifer, and D. Thorne. Calling International Rescue: knowledge lost in literature and data landslide! *Biochemical Journal*, 424:317–333, 2009.

[2] C. Jacobs, W. Li, E. Schrier, D. Bargeron, and D. Salesin. Adaptive grid-based document layout. *ACM Transactions on Graphics*, 22(3):838–847, 2003.

[3] G. Janssens and H. Martin. The feasibility of e-ink readers in distance learning: A field study. *International Journal of Mobile Learning*, 3(3):38–46, 2009.

[4] K. Marriott, P. Moulder, and N. Hurst. Automatic float placement in multi-column documents. In *Proc. of the 2007 ACM Symp. on Document Engineering*, pages 125–134. ACM Press, 2007.

[5] L. Purvis, S. Harrington, B. O'Sullivan, and E. Freuder. Creating personalized documents: An optimization approach. In *Proc. of the 2003 ACM Symp. on Document Engineering*, pages 68–77. ACM Press, 2003.

[6] J. Richardson Jr and K. Mahmood. eBook readers: user satisfaction and usability issues. *Library Hi Tech*, 30(1):170–185, 2012.

[7] H. van der Sluis. Exploring the usefulness of e-book readers for academic staff. Master's thesis.

Author Index

www.ingramcontent.com/pod-product-compliance
Lightning Source LLC
Chambersburg PA
CBHW061342210326
41598CB00035B/5857